SECURITY RIGHTS AND THE EUROPEAN INSOLVENCY REGULATION

SECURITY RIGHTS AND THE EUROPEAN INSOLVENCY REGULATION

Edited by
Gerard McCormack
Reinhard Bork

intersentia
Cambridge – Antwerp – Portland

Intersentia Ltd
Sheraton House | Castle Park
Cambridge | CB3 0AX | United Kingdom
Tel.: +44 1223 370 170 | Fax: +44 1223 370 169
Email: mail@intersentia.co.uk
www.intersentia.com | www.intersentia.co.uk

Distribution for the UK and Ireland:
NBN International
Airport Business Centre, 10 Thornbury Road
Plymouth, PL6 7 PP
United Kingdom
Tel.: +44 1752 202 301 | Fax: +44 1752 202 331
Email: orders@nbninternational.com

Distribution for Europe and all other countries:
Intersentia Publishing nv
Groenstraat 31
2640 Mortsel
Belgium
Tel.: +32 3 680 15 50 | Fax: +32 3 658 71 21
Email: mail@intersentia.be

Distribution for the USA and Canada:
International Specialized Book Services
920 NE 58th Ave. Suite 300
Portland, OR 97213
USA
Tel.: +1 800 944 6190 (toll free) | Fax: +1 503 280 8832
Email: info@isbs.com

ISBN 978-1-78068-317-1
D/2017/7849/4
NUR 820

GPRC
Guaranteed
Peer Reviewed
Content

British Library Cataloguing in Publication Data. A catalogue record for this book is available from the British Library.

DISCLAIMER

sreir
SECURITY RIGHTS & THE EUROPEAN INSOLVENCY REGULATION

Co-funded by the
Civil Justice Programme
of the European Union

Grant number is JUST/2013/JCIV/AG/4631.

This publication has been produced with the financial support of the Civil Justice Programme of the European Union. The contents of this publication are the sole responsibility of Gerard McCormack and Reinhard Bork/the authors and can in no way be taken to reflect the views of the European Commission.

PREFACE

This book arises out of a research project that was very generously funded by the European Commission under the Civil Justice Action programme – grant JUST/2013/JCIV/AG/4631. We thank the European Commission for their funding.

The events of 23 June 2016 may cast a long shadow but we hope that they do not dim unduly the prospects for further European scientific research and cooperation.

This book is very much a team effort led by Gerard McCormack at the University of Leeds in the UK and including Reinhard Bork at the University of Hamburg in Germany, Laura Carballo Piñeiro and Marta Carballo Fidalgo at the University of Santiago de Compostela in Galicia, Spain, Renato Mangano at the University of Palermo in Italy and last, but certainly not least, Tibor Tajti at the Central European University, Budapest, Hungary.

The book aims to analyse critically the provisions governing rights in rem (security rights) and transactional avoidance in the European Insolvency Regulation – now Regulation 2015/848 – and to address whether there is scope for reform of the law. Security rights are essentially rights over property intended to secure payment of a debt or other obligation. They are of fundamental importance to the granting of credit and are generally considered to increase the availability and lower the costs of credit with concomitant benefits for both debtors and the overall economy. But there are divergent views on the extent to which it should be possible to create and enforce security rights over assets.

The book also:

- assesses the extent of the protection given to security rights under the main EU legal traditions;
- evaluates the policy reasons behind protection;
- elaborates whether, and to what extent, this protection also applies in the context of insolvency proceedings affecting the debtor;
- assesses whether, and under what conditions, security rights created prior to the institution of insolvency proceedings can be set aside in those proceedings;

Moreover, it considers the need for further European harmonisation.

The first part of the book expounds common themes and ideas and suggests possible law reform measures. The project team as a whole has contributed to this part which considers the extent to which the relevant law in the EU countries under review measures up against international benchmarks such as the World Bank Doing Business 'getting credit' and 'resolving insolvency' indicators and the UNCITRAL Legislative Guides on Secured Transactions and Insolvency. It asks whether there is any pressing need for reform at the national or EU level in light of these international benchmarks and whether reform is a realistic and achievable goal. Finally, it considers what form any reform measures might take. The focus is very much on the business debtor and it does not consider possible measures of consumer protection that may be appropriate in particular instances.

The first part of the book is followed by a second part containing chapters that address Germanic legal systems, the Common Law, Roman legal systems and Central and Eastern European legal systems. It should be noted that the book is based on reports submitted to the European Commission on 1 May 2016, although in some cases it has been possible to take into account developments after that date, such as changes to Italian law.

In the course of the project and in the writing of the book we have incurred many debts, not least to members of our International Advisory board and to those who spoke at the three international conferences that we organised as part of the project – London (May 2015), Erice (Trapani) in Italy (November 2015), and Santiago de Compostela (April 2016).

Those to whom we are indebted – in no particular order – include Lina Aleknaite-van der Molen (Kazimieras Simonavicius University, Vilnius, Lithuania); Paul Beaumont (University of Aberdeen, UK); Maya Boureghda Chebeane (JURISMED, Tunis); Catherine Bridge (European Bank for Reconstruction and Development); Michael Bridge (University College London); John Briggs (South Square Chambers, London); Richard Calnan (Norton Rose Fulbright LLP); Reinhard Dammann (Clifford Chance, Paris); Eric Dirix (Leuven); Ian Fletcher (University College London); Francisco Garcimartín Alferez (UAM, Spain), Anna Gardella (European Banking Authority); Robert van Galen (INSOL Europe); Louise Gullifer (University of Oxford); Santiago Hurtado Iglesias (Deloitte Abogados); Krzysztof Kaźmierczyk (Dentons, Poland); Andrew Keay (University of Leeds); Lisa Linklater (Exchange Chambers); Karolina Lyczkowska (DLA Piper, Spain); Jennifer Marshall (Allen & Overy LLP); Irit Mevorach (University of Nottingham); Karim Mouttaki (Mouttaki and Partners, Casablanca); Federico Mucciarelli (SOAS University of London, and University of Modena e Reggio Emilia); Paul Omar (Nottingham Trent University, UK); Jacinto José Pérez Benitez (High Court Pontevedra, Spain); Françoise Pérochon (Université de Montpellier, France); Juana Pulgar Esquerra (UCM, Spain); Magda Raczynska (University College London); Wolf-Georg Ringe (Copenhagen Business School, Denmark); Teresa Rodríguez de las Heras Ballell (UC3M, Spain); Felix Steffek (University of Cambridge); Andrew

Steven (Scottish Law Commission); Heinz Vallender (Judge, Cologne); and Anna Veneziano (UNIDROIT). We apologise for any inadvertent omissions.

We would especially like to thank the overall project administrator, Alexandra Braithwaite, who is based at the University of Leeds, and her colleagues in the partner universities. We are also grateful for the tremendous support from our staff, especially Philipp Hartmann (University of Hamburg), who contributed significantly to the success of our project.

On a more personal note, Gerard McCormack would like to thank Presy, Amelia and Anthony. Reinhard Bork is grateful for the unlimited support from Nicole, Julius and Moritz. Laura Carballo Piñeiro is indebted to Manuel, Sara and Pepe for their care and patience. Marta Carballo Fidalgo sends her love to her sister Pili. Renato Mangano owes much to Giovanna for her encouragement. Tibor Tajti wants to thank for their support István Mándoki and Gergely Kovács (public notaries) and his doctoral students Catalin Stănescu, Virág Ilona Blazsek and Patricia Živković, as well as Éva Vas and the staff of the CEU library.

Gerard McCormack and Reinhard Bork
Leeds and Hamburg, July 2016

CONTENTS

QUESTIONNAIRE

A. Creation of Security Rights

D. Plurality of Security Rights

Question 22: Is it possible to have more than one set of security rights (security interest) over the same asset?

Question 23: What are the rules for determining priority between competing security interests in the same property?

Question 24: Are there special rules privileging the position of an acquisition financier, i.e. a secured party whose advance of funds funded the acquisition of a particular asset and who may be in a priority competition with an earlier general creditor whose security interest extends to all assets of the debtor whenever acquired?

E. Quasi-Security Agreements

Question 25: Does your legal system have any rules equating the treatment, in whole or in part, of security interest and 'quasi-security' agreements, i.e. agreements that in legal terms do not involve the creation of security interests but have many of the same economic consequences? Examples of quasi-security include the factoring or sale of receivables and finance leases, hire-purchase agreements and retention of title clauses in sale of goods contracts.

F. Transactional Avoidance

Question 26: Are there rules in your legal system that operate once the debtor enters insolvency proceedings and that provide for the invalidation of transactions entered into by the debtor prior to the commencement of the insolvency proceedings?

Question 27: Do these transactional avoidance rules catch security and quasi-security type transactions?

Question 28: If so, describe briefly these rules highlighting in particular (a) the rationale for the rules; (b) the conditions for the application of the rules; (c) the length of the 'suspect period'; (d) whether the rules apply to transactions with a cross-border element; (e) whether the rules operate more stringently in respect of transactions that favour parties who are connected to the debtor; and (f) any defences that may be availed of by a counterparty to the transaction, i.e. the defendant in an avoidance action.

TABLE OF CASES

References are to chapter (in bold) and paragraph number.

ECJ/CJEU CASES (ARRANGED BY CASE NAME)

ECJ/CJEU CASES (ARRANGED BY CASE NUMBER)

EFTA COURT CASES

NATIONAL CASES

AUSTRALIA

AUSTRIA

CHINA

FRANCE

GERMANY

HUNGARY

IRELAND

ITALY

MALAYSIA

NEW ZEALAND

POLAND

SPAIN

UNITED KINGDOM

UNITED STATES

TABLE OF ABBREVIATIONS

Abbreviation	Full text	Translation
AC	Law Reports, Appeal Cases (Third Series) (England)	–
AG	Advocate General (of the Court of Justice of the European Union)	–
AG	Amtsgericht (Germany)	lowest-instance court
AG	Aktiengesellschaft (Germany/Austria)	(public) company limited by shares
ABGB	Allgemeines Bürgerliches Gesetzbuch (Austria)	Civil Code
al.	et alii/et aliae/et alia	and others
ALR	Australian Law Review	–
All ER	All England Law Reports	–
a.M.	andere Meinung	disagreement, differing opinion
Anh.	Anhang	attachment, index, annex
AO	Ausgleichsordnung (Austria)	Act on the Composition with Creditors
App Cas	Law Reports Appeal Cases (Second Series) (England)	–
App.	Corte di appello (Italy)	Appeal Court
Art.	Article (of a statute)	–
Art. D.	Article d'un décret codifié (France)	Article of a Decree
Art. L.	Article d'une loi codifiée (France)	Article of a Law
Art. R.	Partie réglementaire d'un code (France)	Section of a Law Act
Az.	Aktenzeichen (Germany)	Reference Number
BAG	Bundesarbeitsgericht (Germany)	Federal Labour Court
BBTC	Banca, borsa e titoli di credito (journal, Italy)	Bank, stock exchange and credit instruments
BCC	British Company Law Cases	–

Abbreviation	Full text	Translation
BCCI	Bank of Credit and Commerce International	–
BCLC	Butterworths Company Law Cases (England)	–
Beschl.	Beschluss (Germany)	order
BGB	Bürgerliches Gesetzbuch (Germany)	Civil Code
BGH	Bundesgerichtshof (Germany)	Federal Supreme Court
BGHZ	Amtliche Sammlung der Entscheidungen des Bundesgerichtshofes in Zivilsachen (Germany)	official journal of decisions of the Federal Supreme Court
BH	Bírósági Határozatok (Hungary)	case law report of the Supreme Court
BOE	Boletín Oficial del Estado (Spain)	Official Bulletin
BPIR	Bankruptcy and Personal Insolvency Reports	–
BR	Bankruptcy Reporter (journal)	–
BV	Besloten Vennootschap met beperkte aansprakelijkheid (Netherlands)	limited company
C	I contratti (journal, Italy)	Contracts (journal, Italy)
CA	Companies Act (England)	–
Cass. civ.	Corte Suprema di Cassazione civile (Italy)	Supreme Court (Civil)
Cass. civ.	Cour de cassation – Chambre civile (France)	Supreme Court – Civil Division
Cass. comm.	Cour de cassation – Chambre commerciale, financière et économique (France)	Supreme Court – Division for Business and Financial Litigation
CB	Common Bench Reports (England)	–
CC	Code civil (French)	Civil Code
CC	Código civil (Spain)	Civil Code
CCCat	Codi civil de Catalunya (Spain)	Civil Code of Catalonia
CCMA	Code of Conduct on Mortgage Arrears (England)	–

Abbreviation	Full text	Translation
CCo	Código de comercio (Spain)	Commercial Code
CComm.	Code de commerce (France)	Commercial Code
CEE	Central and Eastern Europe Legal Systems	–
CEO	Chief Executive Officer	–
CEU	Central European University	–
cf.	conferre	compare
CG	Corriere Giuridico (journal, Italy)	Law Journal
ch	chapter	–
Ch	Chancery Division	–
Ch App	Law Reports, Chancery Appeal Cases (England)	
Ch D	Law Reports, Chancery Division (England)	–
CL	Colección Legislativa de España (Spain)	Legislative Collection
CLC	CCH Commercial Law Cases	
CLR	Commonwealth Law Review (Australia)	–
CM	Common Bench Reports	–
Cmnd 8558	Command Papers Cork Review Committee Report on Insolvency Law and Practice 1982	–
CMon and Fin	Code monétaire et financier (France)	Monetary and Financial Code
COM	Commission	–
Comm	Commission	–
Comm	Commercial Division	–
COM (2014)	Commission Recommendation from the European Commission 2014	–
COM (2012)	Commission Recommendation from the European Commission 2012	–
COM (1999)	Financial Services Action Plan	–
COMI	Centre of Main Interests	–
CRD	Capital Requirements Directive	–
CRO	Companies Registration Office	–

Abbreviation	Full text	Translation
CRR	Capital Requirements Regulation	–
CSOH	Court of Session Outer House (Scotland)	–
CTMs	Common Trade Marks	–
CVA	Company Voluntary Agreement	–
CFR	Common Frame of Reference	–
DB	database	–
DCFR	Draft academic European Common Frame of Reference	–
DF	Il diritto fallimentare e delle società commerciali (periodical, Italy)	The law of insolvency and of business companies
DGRN	Dirección General de los Registros y del Notariado (Spain)	General Directorate of Registries and Notaries
Dir	Directive	–
dir. priv.	Diritto privato (Italy)	Civil Law
d.l.	Decreto legge (Italy)	Law Decree
d.lgs.	Decreto legislativo (Italy)	Legislative Decree
d.m.	Decreto ministeriale (Italy)	Ministerial Decree
d.P.R.	Decreto del Presidente della Repubblica (Italy)	Presidential Decree
EBRD	European Bank for Reconstruction and Development	–
EC	European Commission	–
EC	European Community (prior name for the European Union)	–
ECGI	European Corporate Governance Institute	–
ECJ	European Court of Justice	–
ECR	European Court Reports	–
ed.	edited	–
ed.	edition	–
ed(s).	editor(s)	–
e.g.	*exempli gratia*	for example
EFTA	European Free Trade Association	–
ECLI	European Case Law Identifier	–

Abbreviation	Full text	Translation
EIR	(EU) Regulation 2015/848 of 20 May 2015 on Insolvency Proceedings	–
ENAC Civile	Ente Nazionale per l'Aviazione (Italy)	National Body for Civil Aviation
Entsch.	Entscheidung (Austria)	decision
EO	Erwerbsersatzordnung (Switzerland)	Regulation for Income Compensation
EPC	European Patent Convention	–
ER	English Reports	–
et al.	et alii	and others
etc.	et cetera	and so on
et seq.	et sequentia	and that which follows
EU	European Union	–
EULIS	European Land Information Service	–
EuLR	European Law Reports	–
EvBl	Evidenzblatt der Rechtsmittel-Entscheidungen (journal, Austria)	Journal on Appeal Cases
EWCA (Civ)	Court of Appeal of England and Wales, Civil Division	–
EWHC (Ch)	High Court of England and Wales, Chancery Division	–
Ex	Law Reports, Exchequer Division (England)	–
F	Il Fallimento (journal, Italy)	Bankruptcy
ff.	and the following	–
FI	Il Foro Italiano (journal, Italy)	–
fn.	footnote	–
FOGASA	Fondode Garantía Salarial (Spain)	wage guarantee fund
FP	Il Foro Padano (journal, Italy)	–
GBG	Grundbuchgesetz (Austria)	Land Registry Act
GI	Giurisprudenza italiana (journal, Italy)	Italian Law (Journal)
GBO	Grundbuchordnung (Germany)	Land Register Regulation

Abbreviation	Full text	Translation
GBV	Verordnung zur Durchführung der Grundbuchordnung (Germany)	Regulation on the Implementation of the Land Registry Code
GC	Giustizia civile (Italy)	Civil Law
GComm	Giurisprudenza commerciale (Italy)	Commercial Law
GDir	Guida al diritto (journal, Italy)	Guide to Law
Geo.	Geschäftsordnung für Gerichte I. und II. Instanz (Germany)	By-Laws for I. and II. level of jurisdiction
GmbH	Gesellschaft mit beschränkter Haftung	limited liability company
GmbHG	Gesetz betreffend die Gesellschaft mit beschränkter Haftung (Germany)	Limited Liability Companies Act
GmbHR	Die GmbH-Rundschau (journal, Germany)	The GmbH Review
GSZ	Großer Senat des Bundesgerichtshofs (Germany)	Grand Panel of the Federal Supreme Court
GUG	Grundbuchumstellungsgesetz (Austria)	Act concerning changes or transfers of Land Registers
HGB	Handelsgesetzbuch (Germany)	Commercial Code
HKLRD	Hong Kong Law Reports & Digest	–
HL Cas	Clark & Finnelly's House of Lords Reports New Series (England)	–
HR Rep	House Report	–
HUF	Hungary Forint	Hungarian currency
IBAN	international bank account number	–
ibid.	ibidem	in the same place
ICAO	International Civil Aviation Organisation	–
i.e	id est	that is to say
IEHC	High Court of Ireland	–
IESC	Supreme Court of Ireland	–
IILR	International Insolvency Law Review (journal)	–
ILRM	Irish Law Reports Monthly	–
inc	incorporated	–
InDret	InDret Revista para el Análisis del Derecho (journal, Spain)	InDret Journal of Legal Analysis

Abbreviation	Full text	Translation
IR	Irish Reports	–
in *Re*	in the matter of	–
InsO	Insolvenzordnung (Germany)	Insolvency Regulation
INSOL	International Association of Restructuring, Insolvency & Bankruptcy Professionals*	–
IP	insolvency practitioner	–
IO	Insolvenzordnung (Austria)	Insolvency Act
ITR	Ridgeway, Lapp & Schoales Irish Term Reports	–
J	Justice of Her Majesty's High Court (England)	–
JBl	Juristische Blätter (journal, Austria)	Law Papers
KB	Law Reports, King's Bench (England)	–
KO	Konkursordnung (Austria)	Former Insolvency Regulation
L.	Legislativo (Spain)	Law
L.	Legge (Italy)	Law
La. Civ.	Lousiana Civil Code	–
Law Com	The Law Comission (England)	–
LBF	Lehman Brothers Finance AG	–
LBIE	Lehman Brothers International (Europe)	–
LC	Ley Concursal (Spain)	Insolvency Act
LEC	Ley de Enjuiciamiento Civil (Spain)	Procedure Law
LEH	Ley de Enjuiciamiento Civil (Spain)	Civil Procedure Act
L.Fall.	Legge Fallimentare (Italy)	Insolvency Law
LH	Ley Hipoteracia (Spain)	Mortgage Law
LHMPSD	Ley de Hipoteca Mobiliaria y Prenda sin Desplazamiento (Spain)	Law on Chattel Mortgage and Non Possessory Pledge
LJ	Lord Justice of Appeal (England)	–
Lloyd's Rep Bank	Lloyd's Law Reports Banking (England)	–
Lloyd's Rep	Lloyd's Law Report (England)	–

* The European branch has a database of relevant European case law available on LexisLibrary.

Abbreviation	Full text	Translation
LLP	limited liability partnership	–
LMV	Ley del Mercado de Valores (Spain)	Law on Securities Markets
LNA	Ley de Navegación Aérea (Spain)	Aviation Law
LNM	Ley de Navegación Marítima (Spain)	Law on Shipping
LR	Law Reports (1st Series) (England)	–
L. Rev.	Law Review	–
Ltd	limited	–
LuftFzgG	Gesetz über Rechte an Luftfahrzeugen (Germany)	Act on Rights in Aircrafts
LVPBM	Ley de Venta a Plazos de Bienes Muebles (Spain)	Law on Hire Purchase Agreements
MAO	Mortgaging of Aircraft Order 1972 (England)	–
MCA	Master Custody Agreement	–
MCC	Maxwell Communication Corp plc	–
MDR	Monatszeitschrift für deutsches Recht (journal, Germany)	Monthly Journal for German Law
MER	Merivale's Chancery Reports (England)	–
MFI	Massimario del Foro Italiano (journal, Italy)	Law Report arranged by the journal 'Foro Italiano'
MFJ	Maxwell Finance Jersey	–
MGC	Massimario di Giustizia Civile (journal, Italy)	Law Report arranged by the journal 'Giustizia Civile'
MGl	Massimario di Giurisprudenza del Lavoro (journal, Italy)	Law Report on Labour Law
MittRhNotK	Mitteilungen der Rheinischen Notarkammer (journal, Germany)	Rhenish Notaries' Chamber Notifications
MLJ	Malayan Law Journal	–
N	Notariato (journal, Italy)	Public Notaries
NGOs	non-governmental organisations	–
NJW	Neue Juristische Wochenschrift (Germany)	New Jurists' Weekly Journal

Abbreviation	Full text	Translation
NJW-RR	Neue Juristische Wochenschrift Rechtsprechungs-Report (Germany)	New Jurists' Weekly Journal Case Law Report
No.	number	–
NO	Notariatsordnung (Austria)	Notarial Code
Nr.	Nummer (Germany)	number
NR	National Report	–
NZI	Neue Zeitschrift für Insolvenz- und Sanierungsrecht (Germany)	New Insolvency and Restructuring Law Journal
NZLR	New Zealand Law Reports	–
ÖBA	Zeitschrift für das gesamte Bank- und Börsenwesen (Austria)	Journal of Banking and Financial Research
OECD	Organisation for Economic Cooperation and Development	–
OGH	Oberster Gerichtshof (Austria)	Highest Court
OJ	Official Journal of the European Communities	–
ÖJZ	Österreichische Juristenzeitung (Austria)	Lawyers Journal
OLG	Oberlandesgericht (Germany)	Upper State Court*
OMC	Open Method of Coordination	–
Öster.	Österreichische	Austrian (referring to a decision)
OR	European Insolvency Regulation (Old Regulation)	–
OVPBM	Ordenanza de la Ley Venta a Agreements Plazos de Bienes Muebles (Spain)	Ordinance on the Law on Hire Purchase
Oy	Osakeyhtiö (Finland)	incorporated company
p.	page	–
para(s).	paragraph(s)	–
PatG	Patentgesetz (Austria)	Patent Act
PAYE	pay as you earn	–
PBl	Österreichisches Patenblatt (Austria)	Patent Law Papers

* Instance above Landgericht but below the Federal Supreme Court with mostly appellate but some original jurisdiction.

Abbreviation	Full text	Translation
P & CR	Planning and Compensation Reports (journal, England)	–
plc	public limited company (England)	–
PMSI	Purchase Money Security Interests	–
PRA	Publico Registro Automobilica (Italy)	Public Auromobile Register
PRIMA	place of the relevant intermediary approach	–
PPSAs	Personal Property Security Acts	
QB	Law Reports, Queen's Bench Division (England)	–
QBD	Law Reports, Queen's Bench Division (England)	–
RAN	Registro Aeronautico Nazionale (Italy)	National Aeronautical Register
RD	Real Decreto (Spain)	Royal Decree
r.d.	Regio decreto (Italy)	Royal Decree
RDGRN	Resolución de la Dirección General de los Registros y del Notariado (Spain)	Resolution of the General Directorate of Registries and Notaries
r.d.l.	Regio decreto legge (Italy)	Royal Decree
RdTW	Recht der Transportwirtschaft (journal, Germany)	Transport Business Law
Reg.	Regulation	–
RH	Reglamento Hipotecario (Spain)	Mortgage Regulation
RJ	Repertorio de Jurisprudencia (Spain)	Collection of Court Decisions
RN	Reglamento Notarial (Spain)	Notarial Code
RN	Rivista del Notariato (journal, Italy)	Journal on Notaries
ROT	retention of title	–
RRM	Reglamento del Registro Mercantil (Spain)	Regulation of the Business Registry
s.	section	–
SA	Société Anonyme (France)	(public) company limited by shares
Sch.	schedule	–

Abbreviation	Full text	Translation
SchiffRegO	Schiffsregisterordnung (Germany)	Ship Register Regulation
SchiffRG	Schiffsregistergesetz (Germany)	Maritime Register Act
SchiffRG	Schiffsregistergesetz (Austria)	Act on Rights over Registered Ships and Ships under Construction
Sez. Un.	Sezioni Unite (Italy)	United Chambers of the Italian Supreme Court of Cassation
SIP 16	Statement of Insolvency Practice 16	–
SJD	Scientiae Juridicae Doctor	Doctor of Laws
S.p.A.	Società per Azioni (Italy)	corporation
SREIR	Security Rights & European Insolvency Regulation	–
STS	Sentencia del Tribunal Supremo (Spain)	Supreme Court Decision
SSTS	Sentencia del Tribunal Supremo (Spain)	Supreme Court Decision
SWD	Commission Staff Working Document	–
SZ	Amtliche Sammlung Zivilrecht (Austria)	Official Journal of Civil Law Decisions
TLR	Times Law Reports (England)	–
TS	Tribunal Supremo de España (Spain)	Supreme Court
UAM	Universidad Autónoma de Madrid (Spain)	–
UCC	Uniform Commercial Code	–
UCM	Universidad Compultense de Madrid (Spain)	–
UC3M	Universidad Carlos III de Madrid (Spain)	–
UGB	Unternehmensgesetzbuch (Austria)	Companies Act
UHG	Urkundenhinterlegungsgesetz (Austria)	Act on the Deposit of Documents
UIBM	Ufficio Italiano Brevetti e Marchi (Italy)	Office of Patents and Trademark
UK	United Kingdom	–

Abbreviation	Full text	Translation
UKPC	United Kingdom Privy Council	–
UKSC	United Kingdom Supreme Court	–
UNCITRAL	United Nations Commission on International Trade Law	–
UrhG	Urheberrechtsgesetz (Germany)	Copyright Act
Urt.	Urteil (Germany)	judgment
US	United States (of America)	–
USAID	United States Agency for International Development	–
v	vom	of (referring to a date)
v	versus	against, in contrast to
VAT	Value Added Tax	–
V(-)C	Vice Chancellor High Court (England)	–
Ves	Vesey Junior's Chancery Reports (England)	–
Vol.	Volume	–
WM	Zeitschrift für Wirtschafts- und Bankrecht (journal, Germany)	Business and Banking Law
WN	Weekly Notes of Cases (England)	–
WLR	Weekly Law Reports (England)	–
WW	World War	–
ZB	Registerzeichen Beschwerden BGH (Germany)	Register
ZInsO	Zeitschrift für das gesamte Insolvenzrecht (Germany)	Journal for Insolvency Law
ZIP	Zeitschrift für Wirtschaftsrecht (Germany)	Journal for Business Law
ZPO	Zivilprozessordnung (Germany)	Code of Civil Procedure
ZVG	Gesetz über die Zwangsversteigerung und Zwangsverwaltung im Wege der Zwangsvollstreckung	Act on Forced Auctions

PART I

COMPARATIVE ANALYSIS

INTRODUCTION

1. This project is funded by the European Commission under the Civil Justice Action programme – grant JUST/2013/JCIV/AG/4631.

2. The intention is critically to analyse and evaluate the provisions governing rights in rem (security rights) and transactional avoidance in Regulation 1346/2000 and address whether there is scope for reform of the law. Security rights are essentially rights over property intended to secure payment of a debt or obligation. They are of fundamental importance to the granting of credit and are generally considered to increase the availability and lower the costs of credit with concomitant benefits for both debtors and the overall economy. However, there are divergent views on the extent to which it should be possible to create security rights over assets. Moreover, avoidance laws in many countries strike at advantage gaining by creditors in the period immediately before formal insolvency proceedings are instituted. This is seen as potentially unfair in that one creditor gets paid ahead of another, and because of transaction cost issues, or their own involuntary status, some creditors may not be in a position to bargain for security.

3. There is extensive academic and theoretical literature analysing security rights under the main European legal traditions as well as the advantages and disadvantages of recognising security rights from economic and distributional justice perspectives. There is a lack, however, of developed analyses that synthesise the legal protection of security rights under the different legal traditions as well as framing this analysis in the context of Articles 5 and 13 of Regulation 1346/2000. In particular, a Report on Harmonisation of Insolvency Law at EU Level presented by INSOL to the Directorate General for Internal Policies in 2010 in part acknowledges the gap.

4. The project aims to fill that gap and considers the need for further European harmonisation. The project:

- assesses the extent of the protection given to security rights under the main EU legal traditions;
- evaluates the policy reasons behind protection;
- examines whether, and to what extent, this protection also applies in the context of insolvency proceedings affecting the debtor;
- considers the strength of the case for divergence from general legal norms in insolvency;

- assesses the rationales for the invalidation of security rights in the interests of the general body of creditors; and
- assesses whether, and under what conditions, security rights created prior to the institution of insolvency proceedings can be set aside in those proceedings.

5. The project partners are experts in the law of security rights, insolvency, private international law and the harmonisation of law. They have produced separate reports that address the above objectives from the perspective of the Common Law, Germanic legal systems, Roman legal systems and Eastern European legal systems, though recognising that the concept of an Eastern European legal family may be problematic.

6. The project team then come together and produce a final report that synthesises the separate reports and also:

- evaluates the appropriateness of the description of rights in rem in Article 5 and whether this description is in conformity with the standard attributes of security rights under the main EU legal traditions;
- assesses the appropriateness of the protection given to rights under Article 5 of the European Insolvency Regulation (Article 8 of recast Regulation) in light of the Regulation's overriding objectives to facilitate the more effective administration of cross-border insolvency cases in Europe, to ensure the equitable treatment of creditors and to prevent the movement of assets from one jurisdiction to another so as to take advantage of a more favourable legal position (forum shopping);
- assesses the compatibility with Article 5 of particular provisions of national law that may (a) impose temporary stays on the enforcement of security rights during the course of insolvency proceedings or (b) permit the paying off or writing down of secured debt contrary to the wishes of the secured creditor;
- evaluates the reasons behind subjecting security rights over assets located in another EU State to the law of the State that opens the insolvency proceedings in respect of avoidance of pre-insolvency transactions;
- evaluates whether the safe harbour protection from the effects of avoidance law given to rights in rem under Article 13 (Article 16 of recast Regulation) is in conformity with the general philosophy of the Regulation and reflects policies that are common to the main EU legal traditions; and
- addresses whether reform of the law relating to security rights and the avoidance of transactions is appropriate and desirable.

7. This final synthesis report expounds common themes and ideas and suggests possible law reform measures. The focus is very much on the business debtor and it does not consider possible measures of debtor of consumer protection that may be appropriate in particular instances.

8. The final report is divided into four chapters as follows. The first chapter looks at the protection given to security rights in the Insolvency Regulation. The Regulation was 'recast' in 2015 as Regulation (EU) 2015/848 with most of the recast provisions coming into force on 26 June 2017. Nevertheless, the provisions governing security rights are largely the same in the recast Regulation as they are in the original Insolvency Regulation – Regulation 1346/2000 – with the exception of more detailed provisions on the 'localisation' of assets and extended recitals in the preamble to the Regulation. It considers how the relevant provisions might be reconsidered and reformed in future revisions of the Insolvency Regulation.

9. The second chapter looks the provisions governing transactional avoidance – the avoidance of transactions entered into the debtor in the period prior to the commencement of formal insolvency proceedings – in Regulation 1346/2000 (Articles 4 and 13) and in the recast (Articles 7 and 16). These provisions are essentially the same. It considers how these provisions might be reshaped in any future versions of the Insolvency Regulation.

10. The third chapter highlights the fact that the law on security rights differs significantly in the EU Member States that form the subject matter of this project and that these divergences may cause creditors to assess credit risk differently. The main body of the chapter summarises the national reports on the state of the law relating to security rights in the EU Member States. It draws attention to differences and similarities between these laws particularly in the context of the European Bank for Reconstruction and Development (EBRD) Core Principles for a modern secured transactions law. The chapter also considers how the law in the Member States measures up against other international indicators such as the United Nations Commission on International Trade Law (UNCITRAL) Legislative Guide on Secured Transactions and, in particular, the 'getting credit' indicators in the World Bank Doing Business reports and rankings. The chapter attempts to explain why EU Member States perform relatively poorly on the 'getting credit' indicator of the World Bank survey and asks how the positon of EU States might be improved in terms of the World Bank rankings. This leads on to possible reform measures and the question of convergence between the laws of Member States. It takes as a starting point the international indicators as well as the provisions on provisions on proprietary securities in the Draft academic European Common Frame of Reference (DCFR) on European private law.

11. Chapter 4 considers in detail and from a comparative perspective the substantive law on transactional avoidance in insolvency proceedings in the countries that form the subject matter of this study. The chapter highlights similarities and dissimilarities between these laws and sets out situations where the laws may be expressed in different ways but where the outcomes are substantially similar.

12. The second part of this chapter considers the extent to which the transactional avoidance law in the EU countries under review measures up against international benchmarks such as the World Bank Doing Business 'resolving insolvency' indicators and the UNCITRAL Legislative Guide on Insolvency. It asks whether there is any pressing need for reform at the national or EU level in light of these international benchmarks and whether reform is a realistic and achievable goal. Finally, it considers what form any reform measures might take.

A note on terminology

13. In this project we adopt a working definition of 'security' or 'security rights' or 'security interest/interests' as a right over property to ensure the payment of money or the performance of some other obligation.

14. The property over which the security right is taken is referred to as the secured property, or the collateral. The security right itself is also referred to as collateral.

15. Creating security over an asset we sometimes refer to as 'pledging' or creating a pledge over the assets irrespective of whether the security interest is possessory or non-possessory, i.e. whether the debtor or security has possession of the secured assets. This reflects common usage, though strictly speaking under English law the expression 'pledge' is generally used to refer to a possessory security right.

16. Reflecting common usage, the word 'lien' is also used occasionally to refer generally to possessory and non-possessory security rights though the expression has a narrower technical meaning.

17. The law in this area is referred to as the law of security rights, security law or the law of secured transactions.

CHAPTER 1

SECURITY RIGHTS UNDER ARTICLE 5 OF THE INSOLVENCY REGULATION AND ARTICLE 8 OF THE 'RECAST'

1. INTRODUCTION

18. This chapter critically evaluates the protection given to secured creditors by the Insolvency Regulation (EIR) – both in its 'original' and 'recast' versions – Regulation 1346/2000 and Regulation (EU) 2015/848.[1] It will assess the validity of the criticism that the protection is over-broad and also look at possible ways forward in any future revision of the Regulation by the European Commission.[2]

19. The Regulation establishes a detailed framework for the management of cross-border insolvency cases within Europe. It also goes some way towards harmonising conflicts-of-law rules. It does not, however, harmonise substantive insolvency law or the law relating to security rights. Its centralising mission stops short in this regard. The Regulation puts the law of the State where the debtor has its centre of main interests (COMI) at the heart of the insolvency administration process.[3] The COMI State is centre stage when it comes to collection and administration of the debtor's assets, surveying the debtor's legal affairs and the effect of the insolvency on other parties. Security rights, or 'rights in rem' as they are referred to in the Regulation,[4] are however at least partially

---

1 Regulation 1346/2000.

2 See *Report from the Commission on the application of Council Regulation (EC) No 1346/2000 of 29 May 2000 on insolvency proceedings* COM (2012) 743 final and *Proposal for a Regulation of the European Parliament and of the Council amending Council Regulation (EC) No 1346/2000 on insolvency proceedings* COM (2012) 744 final. The proposals are intended to align with 'the EU's current political priorities to promote economic recovery and sustainable growth, a higher investment rate and the preservation of employment, as set out in the Europe 2020 strategy.' For a critical overview see H. Eidenmüller, (2013) 20 *Maastricht Journal* 133.

3 Articles 3 and 4 and Articles 3 and 7 of the recast Regulation.

4 See the comment by M. Balz: 'Suffice it to say that liens (judicial, statutory, and contractual), mortgages, pledges, and security interests within the meaning of Article 9 of the Uniform Commercial Code would all be considered to be rights *in rem*': (1996) 70 *American Bankruptcy Law Journal* 485 at 508 fn. 98.

immunised from the centralising effects of the COMI. The Regulation is said to establish a 'hard and fast' rule[5] in this respect.

20. In addition to the Introduction, this chapter consists of four main sections, though section 4 is considerably larger than the others. Section 2 will examine the philosophy of the European Insolvency Regulation. Section 3 looks at the nature of security rights and what they can do for you. Section 4 contains a detailed analysis of the protection of security rights in rem under Article 5 (Article 8 of recast). It is divided into five subsections as follows:

- what counts as a 'right in rem';
- encumbered assets;
- location of encumbered asset;
- Article 5 as a substantive rule restricting the effects of the insolvency proceedings;
- conclusions on the interpretation of Article 5.

21. Finally, section 5 addresses options for reform.

2. THE PHILOSOPHY OF THE EUROPEAN INSOLVENCY REGULATION

22. The philosophy of the European Insolvency Regulation ties in with the overall philosophy of the EU to promote market efficiency and European economic integration. The preamble to the Regulation asserts the need for legislative provision on cross-border insolvency proceedings in advancing the goals of efficiency and effectiveness in the European internal market.[6] It points out that business undertakings are increasingly carrying on business on a cross-border basis and, because the insolvency of such undertakings affects the proper functioning of the internal market, there is a corresponding need for coordination measures at the European level. The preamble also speaks of preventing the movement of assets or legal proceedings from one jurisdiction to another so as to take advantage of a more favourable legal position – so-called forum shopping.[7]

---

5 For use of this expression see A. Berends, [2010] *Netherlands International Law Review* 423 at 429 and for discussion of rival approaches see 430–434.

6 Recitals 2 and 3. See generally on the Regulation and the Convention, G. Moss, I. Fletcher and S. Isaacs, *The EC Regulation on Insolvency Proceedings*; I. Fletcher, *Insolvency in Private International Law*.

7 Recital 4 and see generally M. Szydlo, (2010) 11 *European Business Organization Law Review* 253; W. Ringe, (2008) 9 *European Business Organization Law Review* 579; G. McCormack, (2009) 68 *Cambridge Law Journal* 213. More generally see J. Pottow, (2007) 32 *Brooklyn*

23. The EU Regulation establishes uniform rules on jurisdiction and choice of law and gives the country where a debtor has its 'centre of main interests', or COMI, the exclusive authority to open main insolvency proceedings.[8] The decision to open such proceedings must be given immediate, full and unqualified recognition throughout the EU.[9] If a debtor has an 'establishment' within a particular EU State, that State may open secondary insolvency proceedings in respect of the debtor.[10] The effect of these secondary proceedings is however, limited to assets within the State. The general rule established by the Regulation is that the law of the 'opening' State governs the conduct and effect of the insolvency proceedings. Article 4 sets out a number of matters which are specifically referred to the law governing the opening of the proceedings. These matters cover both substantive and procedural issues and include the assets which form part of the estate; the powers of the liquidator; rules governing the lodging, verification and admission of claims; and the priority ranking of creditors. There are, however, a whole host of exceptions to the Article 4 general rule and these are enumerated in Articles 5–15.

24. The generally accepted view sees the European Insolvency Regulation as embracing a policy of 'modified' universalism.[11] The universalist approach suggests that there should be a single insolvency proceeding in respect of a debtor and this proceeding should apply to all the debtor's assets on a worldwide basis and affecting the totality of the debtor's legal relationships.[12] Insofar as the Regulation embodies a universalist approach, this is tempered by the fact that secondary insolvency proceedings may be opened in respect of a debtor. These secondary proceedings are not simply mechanisms for the more convenient

---

Journal of International Law 785. For a distinction drawn between 'good' and 'bad' forum shopping see the opinion of Advocate General Colomber in Case-1/04 *Staubitz-Schreiber* [2006] ECR I-701 at paras. 71, 72.

8 Article 3(1). On COMI see the decisions of the European Court in Case C-341/04 *Re Eurofood IFSC Ltd* [2006] ECR I-3813; and in Case C-396/09 *Interedil* ECLI:EU:C:2011:671; and Case C-191/10 *Mediasucre* OJ 2012 C39/3.

9 Articles 16, 17 and 25 and Articles 19, 20 and 32 of the recast Regulation.

10 Article 3(2). In the *Interedil* case (C-396/09) the European Court suggested that the term 'establishment' had to be interpreted 'as requiring the presence of a structure consisting of a minimum level of organisation and a degree of stability necessary for the purpose of pursuing an economic activity'. See also *Re Olympic Airlines Ltd* [2015] UKSC 27.

11 See generally on the concept of 'modified universalism' the decision of the UK Privy Council in *Cambridge Gas Transport Corporation v Official Committee of Unsecured Creditors (of Navigator Holdings Plc)* [2007] 1 AC 508 and the UK Supreme Court in *Re HIH Casualty and General Insurance Ltd* [2008] 1 WLR 852 and more generally G. McCormack, (2012) 32 *Oxford Journal of Legal Studies* 325.

12 As the US court remarked in *In re Board of Directors of Multicanal SA* (2004) 314 *BR* 486 at 521 the centralisation of insolvency proceedings 'will frequently provide the optimal result for a debtor and its creditors alike by preventing certain creditors from gaining an advantage over others by virtue of differing judicial systems. A single primary proceeding also minimizes the time, expense and administrative burdens of managing full cases in multiple jurisdictions.'

collection of assets and their remission to the liquidator in the principal proceedings. The secondary proceedings have their own law applying to them with independent distributional consequences.

25. The rival philosophy to 'universalism' is 'territorialism' and this suggest that separate insolvency proceedings may be opened wherever a debtor has assets and that in general 'local' assets should be earmarked for 'local' creditors.[13] While Article 4 of the Regulation can be characterised in a universalist light, the breadth of the exceptions reflected in Articles 5–15 detract from this light. This is so much the case that at least one commentator has called the EU Regulation a universalist scheme with territorial pretensions.[14] Nevertheless, Articles 5–15 are at the heart of the political compromises that contributed to the consummation of the European insolvency initiative.

26. In the recast Regulation, Articles 7–18 mirror, while not exactly replicating, Articles 4–15. Article 7 in the recast mirrors Article 4 in the original, Article 8 mirrors Article 5 and Article 16 corresponds to Article 13. The recasting of the Insolvency Regulation has to be seen in the context of the Europe 2020 strategy proclaimed by the European Union,[15] which refers to fostering economic recovery and sustainable growth. The objective is to create a situation where economic and social systems are adaptable, resilient and fair and where economic activity is sustainable. The President of the European Council has said: 'The new legislation, through the protection of creditors and the survival of business, will contribute to the preservation of employment in these challenging times'.[16]

27. The changes to the Insolvency Regulation are not however as far reaching as this language might imply[17] save for a new set of provisions on group co-ordination proceedings. The main changes entail measures designed to extend

---

[13] For a defence of provisions that ring-fence assets for the benefit of 'local' creditors see the paper by the Singapore Chief Justice S.K. Chan, (2011) 23 *Singapore Academy of Law Journal* 413 at 419.

[14] See F. Tung, (2001) 23 *Michigan Journal of International Law* 31 at 77.

[15] See *Europe 2020 – A European Strategy for Smart, Sustainable and Inclusive Growth* (2010).

[16] See Press Release, *New Rules to Promote Economic Recovery* (4 December 2014) <http://www.consilium.europa.eu/en/press/press-releases/2015/03/12-insolvency-proceedings-new-rules-to-promote-economic-recovery/> accessed 9 May 2016. For the original European Commission recommendations for reform of the Regulation, see *Proposal for a new Regulation* COM (2012) 744 and see also *Report from the Commission on the application of Council Regulation (EC) No 1346/2000* COM (2012) 743 and the Hess–Oberhammer–Pfeiffer external evaluation of the Regulation commissioned by the European Commission – see JUST/2011/JCIV/PR/0049/A4. This evaluation is often referred to as the Heidelberg–Luxembourg–Vienna report or the Heidelberg–Vienna report.

[17] The original Commission proposals for revision of the Insolvency Regulation have been described by leading commentators as 'very decent': G. Moss QC, [2013] *Insolvency Intelligence* 55, and as a 'modest attempt … to improve the status quo': H. Eidenmüller, (2013) 20 *Maastricht Journal* 133 at 150.

the scope of the Regulation by bringing in certain pre-insolvency proceedings; clarifying disputed areas of interpretation; achieving better integration between main and secondary insolvency proceedings; and improving information flows by various means including through the linking of national insolvency registers.

28. In terms of scope, the original Regulation was limited to collective insolvency proceedings involving the partial or total disinvestment of the debtor and the appointment of a liquidator (Article 1) while the language of the recast is much broader. Article 1 of the recast Regulation states that it applies to public collective proceedings, which are based on a law relating to insolvency, and in which for the purpose of rescue, adjustment of debt, reorganisation or liquidation (a) the debtor is totally or partially divested of its assets with an insolvency practitioner (IP) appointed or (b) the debtor's assets and affairs are subject to control or supervision by a court or (c) there is a stay of individual enforcement proceedings against the debtor. If proceedings are commenced where there is only a likelihood of insolvency, their purpose has to be to avoid the debtor's insolvency or the cessation of its business activities.

29. In the original Regulation, liquidation was considered to be the paradigmatic insolvency procedure. Secondary proceedings commenced after main insolvency proceedings had been opened, could only be liquidation proceedings and secondary proceedings initiated before main insolvency proceedings had been opened had to be converted into liquidation proceedings at the request of the liquidator in the main proceedings.[18] Now under the recast Regulation, there is no requirement that secondary proceedings should be liquidation proceedings. The original Regulation referred to the person who took control of a debtor's affairs after main insolvency proceedings had been opened as a liquidator even though that person might have the task of preparing a restructuring plan. On the other hand, the recast Regulation opts for more neutral terminology and uses the expression insolvency practitioner (IP) throughout rather than liquidator.[19]

30. There are no changes to the fundamental structure of the Regulation and the law applicable to the insolvency proceedings is, in general, the law of the State where the proceedings are opened irrespective of whether these insolvency proceedings are main or secondary proceedings.[20] The recast Regulation keeps

---

18 See Articles 3(3), 3(4) and 37 of Regulation 1346/2000.

19 Article 2(5) Regulation (EU) 2015/848 defines an 'insolvency practitioner' (IP) as meaning 'any person or body whose function … is to: (i) verify and admit claims submitted in insolvency proceedings; (ii) represent the collective interest of the creditors; (iii) administer, either in full or in part, assets of which the debtor has been divested; (iv) liquidate the assets referred to in point (iii); or (v) supervise the administration of the debtor's affairs.' These persons or bodies are listed in Annex B of the recast Regulation.

20 For an analysis of the recast Regulation see G. McCormack, (2016) 79 *Modern Law Review* 121; L. Carballo Pineiro, (2014) 2 *Nederland Internationaal Privaatrecht* 207.

the same basic framework effecting a number of changes by way of clarification, but retaining the original structure, though for some commentators this is a missed opportunity.[21]

31. One of the provisions that remains unaltered is Article 5 in the original and Article 8 in the recast, stating that the opening of insolvency proceedings shall not affect rights in rem of creditors over assets located in a State other than the State of the opening of proceedings. Before examining Articles 5 and 8 and related provisions in detail, it is appropriate to consider why security rights are given this level of protection.

3. IMPORTANCE OF SECURITY RIGHTS

32. According to the influential Virgós–Schmit Report that forms part of the backdrop to the original European Insolvency Regulation, rights in rem or security rights play a very important role 'with regard to credit and the mobilisation of wealth. They insulate their holders against the risk of insolvency of the debtor and the interference of third parties'.[22]

33. It is probably only a small exaggeration to say that security rights over property are at the heart of the global economy. Security rights are considered to increase the availability and reduce the cost of credit with concomitant benefits for both debtors and the overall economy.[23] In short, recognising and giving effect to security rights will lead to more credit and at lower cost, and this in turn will help to stimulate economic activity and lead to better economic conditions for all. This is important at the macro level – central banks including the European Central Bank will normally insist on good quality collateral before advancing funds to commercial banks[24] – and also at the level of individual businesses. There is empirical evidence to the effect that the ability to 'collateralise' or use assets as security is an important determinant of credit supplied in the economy.[25]

---

21 See M. Veder, (2011) 3 *International Insolvency Law Review* 289; J. Marshall, (2011) 3 *International Insolvency Law Review* 268.

22 M. Virgós and E. Schmit, *Report on the Convention on Insolvency Proceedings* at para. 97. The report is on the draft EU Convention on Insolvency Proceedings, which foreshadowed the Regulation. The Virgós–Schmit Report has no official status and was not agreed to by all the EU Member States, but it is of persuasive authority and has been relied upon in many decided cases. The report can be found, inter alia, at <http://www.aei.pitt.edu/952> accessed 9 May 2016.

23 For security in the context of insolvency and cross-border transactions see the series of articles in (2011) 46 *Texas International Law Journal* 437–622.

24 See the website of the European Central Bank <http://www.ecb.int/paym/coll/html/questions.en.html> accessed 9 May 2016, for information on collateralised lending by the European Central Bank.

25 See R. Haselmann and K. Pistor, (2009) 23 *Review of Financial Studies* 549.

It is argued that collateral rights tend to reduce information gaps between lenders and borrowers, to even the playing field between foreign and domestic lenders, and to open up the credit market to new participants. Moreover, where using assets as security is legally possible, all but the largest borrowers should get better terms on a secured rather than on an unsecured loan.

According to the World Bank:[26]

> 'economic analysis suggests that small and medium sized businesses in countries that have stronger secured transactions laws and registries have greater access to credit, better ratings of financial system stability, lower rates of non-performing loans, and a lower cost of credit.'

In the view of the United Nations Commission on International Trade Law (UNCITRAL):[27]

> 'The key to the effectiveness of secured credit is that it allows borrowers to use the value inherent in their assets as a means of reducing credit risk for the creditor. Risk is mitigated because loans secured by the property of a borrower give lenders recourse to the property in the event of non-payment. Studies have shown that as the risk of non-payment is reduced, the availability of credit increases and the cost of credit falls. Studies have also shown that in States where lenders perceive the risks associated with transactions to be high, the cost of credit increases as lenders require increased compensation to evaluate and assume the increased risk.'

The argument is that banks and other financial institutions will not engage in large-scale lending activities if their position as secured creditors in the liquidation of their borrowers is not sufficiently certain, or that sufficient means for the enforcement of security are not available. The incentives of creditors and borrowers are aligned and a credible commitment is added to the relationship.[28] Economists suggest that security plays a crucial role in lending decisions by addressing the problems of adverse selection, moral hazard and uninsurable risk.[29]

34. Adverse selection refers to the fact that some borrowers may turn out to be over-optimistic or unreliable. A lender cannot simply raise interest rates to screen out these borrowers because honest borrowers with sound projects will drop out of the picture as well. The potential pay-off from the project may not be enough to meet the borrowing costs. Where security is taken, however, adverse

---

26 See World Bank, *Secured Transactions Systems and Collateral Registries*, 8.

27 Draft legislative guide on secured transactions – Report of the Secretary General A/CN9/WG VI/WP 2 (2002) addendum 1 para. 4.

28 See generally O. Hart and J. Moore, (1998) 113 *Quarterly Journal of Economics* 1.

29 See generally J. Stiglitz and A. Weiss, (1981) 71 *American Economic Review* 393. See also G. Akerlof, (1970) 84 *Quarterly Journal of Economics* 488.

selection problems are addressed more directly in that the lender can back up its assessment of the borrower and the soundness of the business plan with information on the value of the collateral. The lender can look to the collateral for repayment as well as to the revenues generated from the project. Moral hazard refers to the possibility that a borrower may abscond with the loan, and the larger the loan, the greater the moral hazard. If however the borrower provides security, the lender has lower costs in monitoring moral hazard since the lender has been given a hostage against flight risk in the shape of the security. Security reduces certain risks, i.e. the borrower not being able to repay due to loss of key customers, or losses on foreign exchange, that may not be easily insurable, or insurable at all. In unsecured lending uninsurable risk is reduced through 'spreading', i.e. through making smallish loans to a large number of borrowers. Security allows more concentrated lending and reduces uninsurable risk since the security serves as an alternative repayment mechanism.[30]

35. On the other hand, security rights may be seen by some as instinctively unfair in that they involve queue-jumping – one creditor being paid ahead of other creditors[31] – but in response it could be argued that the secured creditor has bargained for property rights and priority in respect of the debtor's assets. In the normal course of events, a social market economy should respect property rights and freedom of contract and recognise the parties' contractual freedom. Security is seen as a fair exchange for the credit; the secured creditor has bargained for security and priority, whereas other creditors have not. Consequently, it does not seem unfair to privilege the secured creditor over other creditors who could equally have contracted for security but chose not to do so.

36. There may however be involuntary creditors, i.e. creditors not in a contractual relationship with the debtor, who are not in a position to bargain for security. There may also be other non-adjusting creditors, or poorly adjusting creditors, where it is unrealistic to suppose that they could bargain for security or where the transaction costs of doing so are too great. These creditors in a weak bargaining position are perhaps most likely to be the ones that will be hit hardest by the debtor's insolvency. The insolvency may impact disproportionately on them in that they are not very capable of sharing or passing on the costs of the loss. Large financial institutions which are most likely to take security are in a much better position to pass on losses.

37. Different Member States adopt different views on how best to protect such 'vulnerable' creditors including unpaid employees. It may be however that the financial position of employees is best protected at EU level by enhancing the

---

30 See G. McCormack, *Secured Credit and the Harmonisation of Law*, chapter 3.

31 In the US context Professors L. LoPucki and E. Warren comment that 'security is a contract between A and B that C take nothing': L. Lopucki and E. Warren, *Secured Credit: A Systems Approach*, xxxi.

protections available under employment law directives and in particular by strengthening national wage guarantee funds and other employee safeguarding measures.

4. DETAILED ANALYSIS OF ARTICLE 5 EIR – ARTICLE 8 OF RECAST

38. Article 5 EIR is indexed 'Third parties' right in rem'. It lays down:

> '1. The opening of insolvency proceedings shall not affect the rights in rem of creditors or third parties in respect of tangible or intangible, moveable or immoveable assets, both specific assets and collections of indefinite assets as a whole which change from time to time, belonging to the debtor which are situated within the territory of another Member State at the time of the opening of proceedings.
> 2. The rights referred to in paragraph 1 shall, in particular, mean:
>   (a) the right to dispose of assets or have them disposed of and to obtain satisfaction from the proceeds of or income from those assets, in particular by virtue of a lien or a mortgage;
>   (b) the exclusive right to have a claim met, in particular a right guaranteed by a lien in respect of the claim or by assignment of the claim by way of a guarantee;
>   (c) the right to demand assets from, and/or to require restitution by, anyone having possession or use of them contrary to the wishes of the party so entitled;
>   (d) a right in rem to the beneficial use of assets.
> 3. The right, recorded in a public register and enforceable against third parties, based on which a right in rem within the meaning of paragraph 1 may be obtained, shall be considered to be a right in rem.
> 4. Paragraph 1 shall not preclude actions for voidness, voidability or unenforceability as referred to in point (m) of Article 4(2).'

Article 8 of the recast EIR reproduces, with some formal changes, the contents of Article 5.

4.1. WHAT COUNTS AS A 'RIGHT IN REM' – REFERRAL TO THE LEX SITUS

39. There has been some consideration of Article 5 by the Court of Justice in *Lutz v Bäuerle*.[32] The Court held that the provision enables a creditor to assert

[32] Case C-557/13 at para. 40 of the judgment.

effectively, and even after the opening of insolvency proceedings, a right in rem that was established before the opening of those proceedings. Moreover, in order to enable the creditor to assert its right in rem effectively, in principle that creditor must be able to exercise the right under the lex causae after the opening of the insolvency proceedings. The particular conditions under the lex causae, i.e. the law of the State where the assets are located, would apply rather than the law of the State of the opening of proceedings.

40. This lack of a definition in Article 5 is the consequence of a deliberate policy choice. On this point, the Virgós–Schmit Report clarifies:

> 'Article 5 refers to "rights in rem" but does not define what these are. The Convention [now, the EIR] does not intend to impose its own definition of a right in rem, running the risk of describing as rights in rem legal positions which the law of the State where the assets are located does not consider to be rights in rem, or of not encompassing rights in rem which do not fulfil the conditions of that definition'.[33]

Accordingly, the report further specifies: 'For this the characterisation of a right as a right in rem must be sought in the national law which, according to the normal pre-insolvency conflict-of-law rules, governs rights in rem'.[34] This means that Article 5(1) refers to the law governing the substance of the case (the so-called lex causae), which in the case of a right concerning 'property' or 'possession' is the lex situs (lex loci rei sitae). For instance, this means that the lex rei sitae is relevant to determine whether a 'floating charge', a 'trust', a 'finance lease', a 'Vormerkung', a 'mandato irrevocabile all'incasso' could be considered as a security right in rem in accordance with Article 5.[35] Nevertheless, the legal framework, including the Virgós–Schmit Report, provides for some interpretative aids.[36] These aids consist of Articles 5–7 of the Regulation and paragraphs 100 and 102 of the Virgós–Schmit Report.

41. Article 5 EIR is the first article of a group of articles which encompasses 'Third parties' right in rem' (Article 5), 'Set-off' (Article 6), and 'Reservation

---

33 Virgós–Schmit Report (fn. 22) para. 100.

34 *Ibid.*

35 Virgós–Schmit Report (fn. 22) paras. 100–102. See I. Fletcher, *Insolvency in Private International Law*, para. 7.93; I. Fletcher, in G. Moss, I. Fletcher and S. Isaacs (eds.), *The EC Regulation on Insolvency Proceedings*, para. 4.17; B. Wessels, *International Insolvency Law*, para. 10642. Nevertheless, on this point M. Virgós and F. Garcimartín, *The European Insolvency Regulation: Law and Practice*, para. 153, maintain that '"*priorities*" and "*privileges*" do not count as rights *in rem* for the purposes of Article 5. A privilege is not an independent right, but a quality associated with a claim which gives it a better ranking of payment compared with other creditors; and there is no doubt whatsoever that the scheme of distribution and the priorities are subject to the *lex fori concursus*'.

36 See also Virgós–Schmit, Report (fn. 22) para. 95.3. and T. Ingelmann, 'Article 5 – Third parties' rights in rem', in K. Pannen (ed.), *European Insolvency Regulation*, 245–253, para. 1.

of title' (Article 7). These provisions are reproduced in Articles 8–10 of the recast. The policy choice according to which security rights in rem are distinguished from other legal devices, such as 'Set-off' and 'Reservation of title' which perform many of the same function as security rights, suggests that the Insolvency Regulation adopts the formal rather than the functional approach to security rights. The adoption of the formal approach to security rights certainly corresponds to the national systems across Europe. This does not imply, however, that the formal approach is necessarily the best one, or that a putative functional approach adopted by the Insolvency Regulation would have been incompatible with the formal approach adopted at national level.

42. Article 5(2) provides:

> 'The rights referred to in paragraph 1 shall, in particular, mean: (a) the right to dispose of assets or have them disposed of and to obtain satisfaction from the proceeds of or income from those assets, in particular by virtue of a lien or a mortgage; (b) the exclusive right to have a claim met, in particular a right guaranteed by a lien in respect of the claim or by assignment of the claim by way of a guarantee; (c) the right to demand assets from, and/or to require restitution by, anyone having possession or use of them contrary to the wishes of the party so entitled; (d) a right in rem to the beneficial use of assets.'

This list serves a twofold purpose. Firstly, it identifies certain rights such as mortgages and liens and even, to a certain extent, the assignment of claims as rights in rem. Secondly, it identifies certain attributes of a right in rem such as beneficial use, and a right of disposal in respect of the assets. Nevertheless, this list is not necessarily clear and, on one view, could dramatically enlarge the scope of rights in rem.[37] Article 5(2)(d) is especially problematic for it is not entirely clear what is meant by the beneficial use of assets. Nowadays, the most common and economically advantageous form of security is the non-possessory charge or lien where the debtor, rather than the secured creditor, has possession and use of the secured property.[38] In common parlance, one could say that the debtor, and not the creditor, has beneficial use of the assets unless, and until, the creditor takes enforcement proceedings. There are other indications in Article 5, however, that it was not intended to disqualify non-possessory security from counting as rights in rem. Article 5(1) refers to rights in rem of creditors or third parties in respect of 'both specific assets and collections of indefinite assets as a whole which change from time to time'. From the preliminary materials on

---

[37] B. Wessels, *International Insolvency Law*, para. 10643.

[38] Millett LJ in *Re Cosslett (Contractors) Ltd* [1998] Ch 495 at 508 referred to the different types of security interest known to English law – mortgages, charges, pledges and liens – and distinguished between these different types. See now Briggs J in the *Lehman Brothers* 'extended lien' case [2012] EWHC 2997 (Ch).

the Regulation, it is clear that this phraseology was intended to embrace the English style floating charge which is non-possessory security.[39] The essence of the floating charge is that the debtor has management autonomy over the assets that serve as security until some event – known as a crystallising event – occurs which brings this autonomy to an end or, to put it another way, the debtor has beneficial use of the assets until crystallisation.[40]

43. On the 'enlargement' point, the Virgós–Schmit Report is aware of the risk of an excessive and unreasonable enlargement of the class of rights in rem. Accordingly, it provides two additional interpretative aids. Firstly, it refers to 'the interest of each State in protecting its market's trade, in the form of respect of rights in rem acquired over assets of the debtor located in that country under the law that is applicable before the opening of the insolvency proceedings.'[41] Secondly, it states that 'the rationale of Article 5 imposes certain limits to the national qualification of a right in rem.' It draws attention to the fact that Article 5 represents an important exception to the universal effect of the main proceedings and the application of the law of the State that opens insolvency proceedings to those proceedings.[42]

4.2. ENCUMBERED ASSETS

44. Article 5(1) provides:

> 'The opening of insolvency proceedings shall not affect the rights in rem of creditors or third parties in respect of tangible or intangible, moveable or immoveable assets, both specific assets and collections of indefinite assets as a whole which change from time to time, belonging to the debtor which are situated within the territory of another Member State at the time of the opening of proceedings.'

It is generally accepted that where assets are located in a third State, rather than in an EU Member State, then Article 5 does not apply[43] and instead it is a case for the application of the lex concursus.[44] This means that the lex concursus, including its private international law prescriptions, determines the nature,

---

[39] See Virgós–Schmit Report (fn. 22) para. 104; M. Balz, (1996) 70 *American Bankruptcy Law Journal* 485 at 508 fn. 98 and G. Moss, I. Fletcher and S. Isaacs, *The EC Regulation on Insolvency Proceedings*, 13 fn. 39.

[40] The leading case is now *National Westminster Bank plc v Spectrum Plus Ltd* [2005] 2 AC 680. See also *Re Brumark Ltd* [2001] AC 710.

[41] Virgós–Schmit Report (fn. 22) para. 100.2.

[42] Virgós–Schmit Report (fn. 22) para. 102.

[43] Virgós–Schmit Report, stating that 'if the assets are located in a non-Contracting State, Article 5 does not govern the issue.'

[44] I. Fletcher, in G. Moss, I. Fletcher and S. Isaacs, *The EC Regulation on Insolvency Proceedings*, para. 7.91.

extent and validity of the third party rights in rem, and that the lex concursus again determines the location of these assets and regulates them.

45. Moreover, Article 5 does not apply if the encumbered assets are fraudulently relocated. The Virgós–Schmit Report on this point states that the Article 5 provision is based on non-fraudulent location of the assets.[45] Non-application of Article 5 does not imply that the secured creditors lose their security rights: it simply means that Article 4 applies, and that the rights in rem created over the assets fraudulently reallocated are subject to the lex concursus. If the relocation proves detrimental to the general body of creditors, the Insolvency practitioner (IP) is entitled to bring avoidance actions, according to the combination of Articles 4(2)(m) and 13. Article 18(2) should also be noted in this connection. It provides: 'The liquidator appointed by a court which has jurisdiction pursuant to Article 3(2) may in any other Member State claim through the courts or out of court that moveable property was removed from the territory of the State of the opening of proceedings to the territory of that other Member State after the opening of the insolvency proceedings. He may also bring any action to set aside which is in the interests of the creditors'.[46]

46. Article 5(1) requires one to consider the following questions: (a) Who is the individual or entity to whom the assets belong?; (b) Who is the individual or entity that is entitled to the rights in rem?; (c) What is the nature of the assets?; (d) Where are the assets located?

47. On the first question, Article 5(1) EIR requires that the relevant assets 'belong' to the debtor. Since the concepts of property, possession and security vary widely from jurisdiction to jurisdiction,[47] it is commonly understood that the concept of 'belonging' is intentionally neutral, and that it refers to the lex situs. This means that, according to Article 5(1), the law of the State where the assets are situated determines whether those assets 'belong' to the debtor.[48] This filter excludes from the scope of Article 5 those cases where a person or an entity provides some assets as security for the indebtedness of a third party. This happens where a legal entity – without any personal obligation – mortgages its property to secure an obligation owed by a debtor towards its creditor. This raises the question of the application of Article 5(1) to cases of cross-collateralisation, i.e. where companies belonging to the same group secure the indebtedness of each other. The phenomenon of cross-collateralisation is very common and in some insolvency law systems, cross-collateralisation under certain circumstances may be considered to be an undervalue transaction and rendered void.[49]

---

45 Virgós–Schmit Report (fn. 22) para. 105.

46 This provision is now Article 21(2) of the recast Regulation.

47 See National Reports.

48 B. Wessels, *International Insolvency Law*, para. 10644.

49 See, for instance, Art. 49 of the Italian d.lgs. No. 270/1999 referring to Art. 67 of the Italian L. No. 267/1942.

48. According to the Virgós–Schmit Report,[50] Article 5(1) requires that the condition of 'belonging to the debtor must exist at the time of the opening of proceedings. This means that Article 5 'only applies to the rights in rem created before the opening of proceedings' If, on the other hand, the security right was created after the opening of the insolvency proceedings, the general rule of Article 4(2)(b) and the lex concursus would apply.

49. On the second question, Article 5(1) requires that 'creditors or third parties' have to be entitled to the rights in rem. This provision includes both the case where the individual or entity entitled is a creditor of the debtor, and the case where the individual or entity entitled is a third party different both from the creditor and from the debtor. Since the concepts of property and possession and, more generally, those of security vary widely from jurisdiction to jurisdiction, it is commonly understood that the concept of entitlement to 'creditors or third parties' depends on the lex situs, to which Article 5 refers.[51] In particular, Article 5 refers to national laws concerning the effectiveness of security rights against parties other than the debtor, which also vary from jurisdiction to jurisdiction.[52] Article 5 does not explicitly require that the procedures of attachment and perfection of the collateral should be completed before the time of the opening of proceedings but this seems to be required by implication. The proposition that the concept of entitlement to 'creditors or third parties' depends on the lex situs implies that Article 5(1) also includes security rights created before the opening of proceedings over future property, if, and only if, the law of the State where the assets are situated considers these forms of grant as conferring a security interest on the creditor immediately, without the need for any new act of transfer. This is the case under the common law systems of *England* and *Ireland*.

50. On the third question, Article 5(1) requires that security rights in rem must be 'in respect of tangible or intangible, moveable or immoveable assets, both specific assets and collections of indefinite assets as a whole which change from time to time.' The Article adopts a large-mesh criterion which includes security rights in rem created both over tangible assets, i.e. over assets which have a physical form (such as machinery, buildings, land, inventories, etc.), and over intangible assets, i.e. over assets which are non-physical (such as patents, trademarks, copyrights, goodwill and brand recognition). While security rights in rem over tangible assets may be either possessory or non-possessory, security rights in rem over intangibles must, of course, be non-possessory.

---

50 Virgós–Schmit Report (fn. 22) para. 96.

51 M. Virgós and F. Garcimartín, *The European Insolvency Regulation: Law and Practice*, para. 145 ff.

52 *Ibid.* at para. 147 ff.

Article 5(1) includes security rights in rem created both over specific assets, where the collateral is attached to assets which are specifically determined (such as machinery), and security rights over a shifting fund of assets, or, to use the language of Article 5(1) EIR, over a collection 'of indefinite assets as a whole which change from time to time.' This certainly happens in the case of the so-called 'floating charge', which is typical of common law jurisdictions, and in some modern security instruments that are increasingly adopted in other legal system and are intended to reproduce some features of the floating charge.

51. On the fourth question, Article 5(1) requires that the assets must be 'situated within the territory of another Member State at the time of the opening of proceedings' and this point is considered in detail in the next section. Some authors maintain that Article 5(1) does not cover the security rights created over 'a European patent with unitary effect, a Community trade mark or any other similar right established by Union law'.[53] This proposition is based firstly, on a combined interpretation of Articles 5 and 12 of the Insolvency Regulation, with the latter providing: 'For the purposes of this Regulation, a European patent with unitary effect, a Community trade mark or any other similar right established by Union law may be included only in the proceedings referred to in Article 3(1)'; and secondly, on the idea that Article 12 also refers to security rights in respect of these assets.

52. In short, this implies that Article 12 restricts the scope of Article 5. If this interpretation is accepted, it would apply only to Community Trade Marks (CTMs), which are trademarks with unitary effects, registered in the European Union as a whole rather than on a national level within the EU. Article 12 could not yet restrict the scope of Article 5 concerning so-called 'unitary patents', since the procedure aiming at creating these unitary patents has not yet been completed and moreover; there is not yet any evidence of 'any other similar right established by Union law.'

4.3. LOCATION OF ENCUMBERED ASSETS – ARTICLE 2(G) AND ARTICLE 2(9) OF THE RECAST REGULATION

53. Article 5(1) requires that the asset or assets must be situated in the territory of another Member State at the time of the opening of proceedings. Those who drew up the Insolvency Regulation were aware that the interpreter could encounter some difficulty in identifying the location of assets affected by Article 5. Therefore, the Regulation provides some criteria for localisation of assets in

---

53 See, for instance, B. Wessels, *International Insolvency Law*, para. 10715.

Article 2(g) but the guidance is limited since Article 2(g) refers only to 'tangible property', 'property and rights, ownership of or entitlement to which is entered in a public register', and 'claims'. In the recast Regulation, new rules are laid down in Article 2(9) to assist in determining the location of assets and these changes introduce a welcome measure of clarification. Article 2(9) also takes into account the fact that nowadays security rights in rem increasingly encumber new and more sophisticated asset forms such as shares and bonds held through chains of intermediaries.

54. Article 2(g) contains three rules on the location of assets: (1) tangible property is deemed to be located in the Member State where the property is situated; (2) 'property and rights, ownership of or entitlement to which must be entered in a public register' are deemed to be located in 'the Member State under the authority of which the register is kept'; and (3) claims are deemed to be located in the Member State where the third party required to meet the claim has its centre of main interests. There are however, at least three difficulties with the provision.[54] Firstly, it is not clear whether Article 2(g) is intended to provide an exhaustive set of rules on the location of assets or whether it merely gives examples in a non-exhaustive way.[55] For instance, can intellectual property rights or shares in companies be regarded as claims within the third limb of Article 2(g) or do they fall entirely outside Article 2(g)? Assuming Article 2(g) is merely a list of examples, the question arises how gaps in the list are to be filled. Should one rely on conflicts of law rules outside the Regulation to fill the gaps and, if so, should these be the conflicts rules in the COMI State, or the law of the place where the assets are allegedly situated? In *Nortel Networks SA v Rogeau*[56] the Advocate General implied that the Article 2(g) rules were exhaustive but it is not clear whether the court subscribed to the same approach though it did say that the 'regulation does lay down uniform rules, excluding, to that extent, any recourse to national law'.

55. Secondly, it is not clear whether there is a hierarchy, or order of priority, established between the three limbs of Article 2(g).[57] An example is that of a ship

54 See generally P. Smart, (2006) 15 *International Insolvency Review* 17 at 27–29.

55 See the discussion in Financial Markets Law Committee Issue paper no. 30 (September 2012) 'European Insolvency Regulation' at p. 9 and the comment that 'Article 2(g) does not appear to cater for the full range of assets' – see <www.fmlc.org> accessed 9 May 2016.

56 Case C-649/13 ECLI:EU:C:2015:384. See para. 67 of the opinion of the Advocate General: 'Article 2(g) ... may be insufficient to cover every type of asset, especially in view of the complexity of some estates, that provision nevertheless demonstrates the intention of the Community legislature to make the determination of the location of a debtor's assets subject to uniform rules. That choice and the incomplete nature of the list provided by Article 2(g) no doubt demand a major effort of interpretation on the part of national courts, which have the task of identifying a rule applicable to each specific case on the basis of that provision.' For the Court's view see para. 50 of its judgment.

57 For a discussion see J. Marshall, (2011) 3 *International Insolvency Law Review* 268.

which might be considered as tangible property and therefore falling within the first limb of Article 2(g) but the ownership of that ship could also be recorded in a public register and this appears to attract the application of the second limb of Article 2(g).[58] This issue was considered briefly in Case C-649/13 *Nortel Networks SA v Rogeau*[59] where the European Court suggested that the Article 2(g) establishes a hierarchy of rules that must be applied.

56. Thirdly, the final limb of Article 2(g) generates particular issues. It is stated that a claim is situated in the State where the third party required to meet the claim has its centre of main interests. This suggests that, in the case of bank accounts, the asset, i.e. the deposit, is deemed to be located where the bank holding the account has its COMI, rather than the place of the branch where the deposit was made. One of the co-authors of the influential Virgós–Schmit Report has however taken a different view in academic writing, stating:[60]

> 'In the case of current accounts and deposits in banking institutions, for these purposes each branch must be considered as an autonomous entity (i.e. as if it were a distinct debtor) in accordance with the special structure of these institutions; consequently the claim will be considered situated in the State where the office serving the customer account is located.'

This proposition, is however, advanced in a rather conclusory way and there is no independent doctrine of European law that each bank branch has to be regarded as an autonomous entity for legal purposes.[61]

57. By way of contrast, Article 2(9) of the recast Regulation is far more comprehensive than Article 2(g). It provides:

> '"the Member State in which assets are situated" means, in the case of:
> (i) registered shares in companies other than those referred to in point (ii), the Member State within the territory of which the company having issued the shares has its registered office;

58 See J. Marshall, (2011) 3 *International Insolvency Law Review* 268 at para. 20.

59 See para. 54 of its judgment.

60 See M. Virgós and F. Garcimartín, *The European Insolvency Regulation: Law and Practice*, 168 and see also G. Moss, I. Fletcher and S. Isaacs, *The EC Regulation on Insolvency Proceedings*, para. 6.53. The Virgós–Schmit Report (fn. 22) para. 69 does not express a definite view on the point.

61 The Financial Markets Law Committee Issue paper no. 30 (September 2012) – <www.fmlc.org> accessed 9 May 2016 – 'European Insolvency Regulation' at p. 10 points out that assets held by corporates may, for example, be subject to conflicting rules in the Insolvency Regulation and the Directive on financial collateral. This paper also highlights other potential uncertainties such as whether the protection afforded by Article 5 extends to income generated by assets after the opening of insolvency proceedings, including where that income is generated in the insolvency forum.

(ii) financial instruments, the title to which is evidenced by entries in a register or account maintained by or on behalf of an intermediary ("book entry securities"), the Member State in which the register or account in which the entries are made is maintained;
(iii) cash held in accounts with a credit institution, the Member State indicated in the account's IBAN, or, for cash held in accounts with a credit institution which does not have an IBAN, the Member State in which the credit institution holding the account has its central administration or, where the account is held with a branch, agency or other establishment, the Member State in which the branch, agency or other establishment is located;
(iv) property and rights, ownership of or entitlement to which is entered in a public register other than those referred to in point (i), the Member State under the authority of which the register is kept;
(v) European patents, the Member State for which the European patent is granted;
(vi) copyright and related rights, the Member State within the territory of which the owner of such rights has its habitual residence or registered office;
(vii) tangible property, other than that referred to in points (i) to (iv), the Member State within the territory of which the property is situated;
(viii) claims against third parties, other than those relating to assets referred to in point (iii), the Member State within the territory of which the third party required to meet the claims has the centre of its main interests, as determined in accordance with Article 3(1).'

Article 2(9)(i) refers to registered shares in companies other than those referred to in point (ii) and the shares are deemed to be located in the Member State where the issuer of the shares has its registered office.

Article 2(9)(ii) refers to financial instruments, including shares in companies, the title to which is evidenced by entries in a register or account maintained by or on behalf of an intermediary, i.e. to the so-called 'book entry securities'. This group of assets is particularly large, because it refers: both to debt issues (such as bonds, notes, debentures and loan stock) and to equity shares (such as shares, stock, warrants); both to registered financial instruments and to bearer financial instruments; both to financial instruments which were originally issued as paper-based instruments which have been later dematerialised, and to financial instruments which were originally issued as paper-less instruments.

58. In particular, this provision captures the increasingly popular trend for investors to hold financial instruments, including shares, indirectly, i.e. by means of an intermediary who enters every operation performed on the investor's behalf in a book provided for this purpose (hence the expression 'book entry securities'). While this phenomenon can follow various patterns, it always implies that the legal relationship of investment involves at least three parties: the issuer, the investor and the intermediary, where the intermediary also performs the function of a depository. The intermediary administers the financial instruments in a centralised way and may engage a second intermediary, who in turn may engage a third intermediary, and so on.

59. From the economic point of view, this phenomenon is particularly convenient, because it reduces the administration costs in respect of the financial instruments. This further implies that if an investor who participates in a depository intends to transfer its financial instruments to another investor, who is also participating in the same depository, it can perform this operation through a mere book entry. Moreover, if there is more than one intermediary, the introduction of every additional intermediary, with its own depository, enlarges the constituency of investors at the cost of increasing the number of parties who are actively involved by one unit only. Consequently, the longer the chain, the greater will be the possibility that investors can make their own operations through a mere book entry.

60. From the legal point of view, however, this phenomenon is problematic. Firstly, it is difficult to determine the rights of the investor and, in particular, whether the nature of the investor's 'entitlement' – to use the expression employed by Article 8 of the US Uniform Commercial Code[62] – varies according to whether the intermediary holds the financial instruments of a specific investor in an omnibus account without any designation of the specific investor or holds the financial instruments of a specific investor in an account expressly segregated for that investor. Secondly, the legal relationships extending from the issuer to the investor through one or many intermediaries according to the pattern 'issuer – intermediary1 – intermediary2 – intermediary3, etc. – investor' could have significant cross-border complications depending on whether the relevant parties are located in more than one country.

61. In relation to so-called 'book entry securities', Article 2(9)(ii) states that the financial instruments are deemed to be located in 'the Member State in which the register or account in which the entries are made is maintained.' This provision adopts the so-called 'place of the relevant intermediary approach' (PRIMA), which is also employed in other legal instruments relating to the same issue, e.g. the Settlement Finality Directive (Article 9(2)),[63] the Directive on Financial Collateral Arrangements (Article 9),[64] and the Hague Convention

---

62 See especially Art. 8-102(17) of the US Uniform Commercial Code, which states: '"Security entitlement" means the rights and property interest of an entitlement holder with respect to a financial asset …'

63 Directive 98/26/EC of the European Parliament and of the Council of 19 May 1998 on settlement finality in payment and securities settlement systems as amended.

64 Directive 2002/47/EC of the European Parliament and of the Council of 6 June 2002 on financial collateral arrangements as amended.

on Indirectly-held Securities.[65] But there may be difficulties in applying the provision in practice particularly where investments are held through a chain of intermediaries and these intermediaries are each located in different countries.

62. Article 2(9)(iii) refers to cash held in accounts and as the first instrument for determining location adopts the IBAN, which is an internationally agreed system of identifying bank accounts across national borders. Article 2(9)(iii) further provides that if cash is held in accounts with a credit institution which does not have an IBAN – which is still possible, even if increasingly rare – the encumbered assets are located in 'the Member State in which the credit institution holding the account has its central administration or, where the account is held with a branch, agency or other establishment, the Member State in which the branch, agency or other establishment is located.'

The wording of this particular provision is clear, but its application raises the question whether, in order to determine the place of 'central administration' and that of 'branch, agency or other establishment', the definitions of 'COMI' and 'establishment' laid down in the Insolvency Regulation itself are helpful and should be used. A positive answer would grant courts and IPs additional interpretative assistance help while a negative answer could take its cue from the idea that the concepts of 'COMI' and 'establishment' are distinctive and essentially aimed at combating fraudulent forum shopping.

63. Article 2(9)(iv) refers to 'property and rights, ownership of or entitlement to which is entered in a public register', and this locates the assets in 'the Member State under the authority of which the register is kept', along the lines of most private international rules. Registered shares within the meaning of Article 2(9)(i) are excluded from the operation of this location rule.[66]

64. Article 2(9)(v) refers to European patents which, according to the European Patent Convention (EPC), grant not a unitary right, but a group of essentially independent nationally enforceable and nationally revocable patents.[67] Article 2(9)(v) lays down that the encumbered assets is deemed to be located in 'the Member State for which the European patent is granted.' Article 2(9)(vi)

---

65 2006 Convention on 'The law applicable to certain rights in respect of securities held with an intermediary', where the Preamble states: 'Recognising that the "Place of the Relevant Intermediary Approach" (or PRIMA) as determined by account agreements with intermediaries provides the necessary legal certainty and predictability', while Art. 1(g) lays down: '"relevant intermediary" means the intermediary that maintains the securities account for the account holder'. The text of this Convention is available at <https://www.hcch.net/en/instruments/conventions/full-text/?cid=72> accessed 10 May 2016.

66 S. Riedemann, 'Article 2 – Definitions', in K. Pannen (ed.), *European Insolvency Regulation*, 49–66, para. 31.

67 The text of this Convention is available at <https://www.epo.org/law-practice/legal-texts/epc.html> accessed 10 May 2016.

refers to 'copyright and related rights.' Since most countries recognise copyright, without formal registration, Article 2(9)(vi) has localised it and the related rights in 'the Member State within the territory of which the owner of such rights has its habitual residence or registered office.'

65. Article 2(9)(vii) corresponds to a widely used private international law rule concerning movable and immovable tangible property. The principle is based on the consideration that, for immovable property, the property is under the control of the authorities of the country where the property is situated; and for movable property, on the fact that a person who acquires rights in goods should be able to rely on the local law in a particular State.[68]

66. Article 2(9)(viii) of the recast is another provision that is found in the current Regulation. It refers to claims against third parties and localises these assets in 'the Member State within the territory of which the third party required to meet the claims has the centre of its main interests, as determined in accordance with Article 3(1).' This criterion does not apply to claims relating to cash held in accounts, with regard to which Article 2(9)(iii) is relevant.

4.4. ARTICLE 5 AS A SUBSTANTIVE RULE RESTRICTING THE EFFECTS OF THE INSOLVENCY PROCEEDINGS

67. Article 5 lays down: 'The opening of insolvency proceedings shall not affect the rights in rem' and Article 8 of the recast is to same effect. The use of such a negative ('shall not') and vague ('affect') phrase makes the provision deceptive. Commentators argue that the expression 'shall not affect' could mean either (a) that the Regulation contains a substantive law rule restricting the effects of the opening of insolvency proceedings or (b) the Regulation contains a choice of law rule referring to the law of the State where the encumbered assets are located (i.e. to the so-called lex situs).

68. Most commentators maintain that Article 5 contains a substantive rule restricting the effects of the insolvency proceedings.[69] For the supporters of this thesis, the negative phrasing of Article 5 simply means that the opening of

---

68 S. Riedemann, 'Article 2 – Definitions', in K. Pannen (ed.), *European Insolvency Regulation*, para. 31.

69 T. Ingelmann, in K. Pannen (ed.), *European Insolvency Regulation*, paras. 10 and 16, referring the prevailing opinion; I. Fletcher, in G. Moss, I Fletcher and S. Isaacs (eds.), *The EC Regulation on Insolvency Proceedings*, para. 4.11; M. Virgós and F. Garcimartín, *The European Insolvency Regulation: Law and Practice*, para. 142 ff. and, especially para. 163 where both authors maintain that Art. 5 OR operates as a 'negative conflict rule'; M. Veder, (2011) 3 *International Insolvency Law Review* 289; J. Marshall, (2011) 3 *International Insolvency Law Review* 268. Similarly, R. Bork, in R. Bork and R. Mangano, *European Cross-Border Insolvency Law*, para. 4.67, with regard to Art. 8 of the recast Regulation.

insolvency proceedings does not produce any effects on the rights in rem, even in the form of putative referral to the law of the State where the encumbered assets are located. These commentators also place reliance on paragraph 99 of the Virgós–Schmit Report and recital 25 of the preamble to the Regulation (recital 68 of recast) which states: 'Where assets are subject to rights in rem under the lex situs in one Member State but the main insolvency proceedings are being carried out in another Member State, the liquidator in the main insolvency proceedings should be able to request the opening of secondary insolvency proceedings in the jurisdiction where the rights in rem arise if the debtor has an establishment there.' One commentator writes: 'If Article 5 (1) EIR was a choice of law rule, the opening of the main proceedings in Member State A would automatically have the effects on rights in rem for which the insolvency law of Member Stare B provides. Therefore, the original meaning of the provision in question is not to adapt the effects from the jurisdiction of the Member State A to the jurisdiction of the Member State B (choice of law rule), but instead to restrict these effects to assets situated in the territory of Member State A.'[70]

69. This view that Article 5 contains a substantive rule restricting the effects of the insolvency proceedings also derives some support from the decision of the European Court in the *German Graphics*, though this case actually deals with Article 7 of the Regulation on reservation of title. The Court ruled:

> 'The referring court has, however, doubts concerning the extent to which Article 7(1) of Regulation No 1346/2000 is liable to influence the classification of actions having a link with insolvency proceedings. That provision merely states that 'the opening of insolvency proceedings against the purchaser of an asset shall not affect the seller's rights based on a reservation of title where at the time of the opening of proceedings the asset is situated within the territory of a Member State other than the State of opening of proceedings'. In other words, that provision only constitutes a substantive rule intended to protect the seller with respect to assets which are situated outside the Member State of opening of insolvency proceedings.'[71]

While in this case the Court was asked for a preliminary ruling concerning Article 7, the position taken is certainly relevant for the interpretation of Article 5 because reservation of title is commonly considered as a regulatory device which performs the same function as a security right in rem and also because the regulatory strategy concerning the reservation of title is similar to that regarding rights in rem. According to the Heidelberg–Luxembourg–Vienna Report, the view that Article 5 contains a substantive rule restricting the effects of the insolvency reflects the dominant position in national courts. In particular,

[70] A. Piekenbrock, in B. Hess, P. Oberhammer and T. Pfeiffer (eds.), *European Insolvency Law. The Heidelberg–Luxembourg–Vienna Report*, para. 678.

[71] Case C-292/08 *German Graphics v van der Schee* ECLI:EU:C:2009:544, para. 35.

it is stated to be the prevailing opinion in 17 Member States, such as *Austria*, *Belgium*, *Cyprus*, *Finland*, *France*, *Germany Greece*, *Ireland*, *Latvia*, *Luxembourg* (with some complexity), the *Netherlands*, *Poland*, *Romania*, *Slovenia*, *Spain*, *Sweden* and the *UK*.[72]

70. Most supporters of the idea that Article 5 contains a substantive rule restricting the effects of the proceedings maintain, however, that the 'shall not affect' prescription has limited scope. For instance, if the lex concursus lays down that the IP has to inform all the creditors of the proceedings, including those who are secured by means of rights in rem, and if all the creditors, including those who are secured by means of rights in rem, have to lodge their claims in order to have them satisfied, these provisions are not deemed to affect the right in rem. This view derives support from Article 4(h) of the Regulation which provides that the lex concursus shall determine the rules governing the lodging, verification and admission of claims.[73] On this restricted interpretation of the 'shall not affect' formula, if the lex concursus allows an IP to realise the assets, there is no breach of the provision.[74] In effect, on this interpretation, Article 5 protects the value of rights in rem and not the encumbered assets.

71. While some commentators interpret the 'shall not affect' formula literally, others read this wording in the light of the Virgós–Schmit Report which, on this point, states that 'security rights in rem insulate their holders against the risk of insolvency of the debtor and the interference of third parties'; they allow credit to be obtained under conditions that would not be possible without this type of guarantee; and, therefore, the fundamental policy pursued by Article 5 is to 'protect the trade in the State where the assets are situated and legal certainty over the rights over them'.[75] According to a teleological interpretation, Article 5(1) means that the opening of insolvency proceedings shall not affect the rights in rem of creditors or third parties to the detriment of the holder of the right in rem.[76]

72. There are, nevertheless, disagreements about the proper construction of Article 5 with respect to: (a) powers to redeem assets; (b) powers to impose some general costs of the insolvency proceedings on the secured party; (c) moratoria; and (d) 'cram-down' rules and other effects of a rescue plan.

---

72 A. Piekenbrock, in B. Hess, P. Oberhammer and T. Pfeiffer (eds.), *European Insolvency Law. The Heidelberg-Luxembourg-Vienna Report*, para. 687 fn. 54.

73 B. Wessels, *International Insolvency Law*, para. 10658.

74 M. Virgós and F. Garcimartín, *The European Insolvency Regulation: Law and Practice*, para. 166(a), and B. Wessels, *International Insolvency Law*, para. 10658b.

75 Virgós–Schmit Report (fn. 22) para. 97, where the sentences appear in a different order.

76 B. Wessels, *International Insolvency Law*, para. 10657, stating that 'the text "shall not affect" ... may be interpreted to mean ... either "no effect whatsoever on the right in rem" or "not to be influenced to the detriment of the holder of the right in rem"'.

73. (a) In some countries, the IP is allowed to pay the secured creditors in order to redeem the encumbered assets. If the IP pays a secured creditor, this payment produces the extinction of the relevant security right. There is a difference of view between countries and between commentators. For some, it is not permissible for the IP to make a payment by way of redemption since this payment is designed to extinguish the security right and this extinction would conflict with the 'shall not affect' formula.[77] On the other hand, there is the alternative view that since the exercise of the right to redeem is not a consequence of the opening of insolvency proceedings – the 'shall not affect' formula does not protect the security right holder.[78]

This is certainly the view expressed in the Virgós–Schmit Report where it is stated that '[w]ithout affecting the economic value of the right or its immediate realizability' the IP is given the power 'to decide on the immediate payment of the claim guaranteed, and thus avoids the loss in value that certain assets could suffer when they are realized separately'.[79] The position is problematic, however, from the point of view of the secured creditor where it is under-secured and the IP merely offers the value of the collateral. In these circumstances, the secured creditor may prefer to hold on to the collateral in the hope, or expectation, that its value will increase leading to the debt being paid in full or in greater measure. In a common-sense understanding, the rights in rem of the secured creditor are affected if it is not allowed to do this. Comments, however, from those involved in the drafting process are somewhat ambiguous about whether this interpretation should be preferred. According to one of the drafters of the original Insolvency Regulation, Manfred Balz, 'the holder of a security interest in foreign situated collateral may proceed as if there were no insolvency of the debtor. The secured party may, for example, sell collateral or foreclose a mortgage under the conditions set out by the general law of the situs'.[80] Miguel Virgós, on the other hand, seems to suggest that not only the fully secured creditor but also the under-secured creditor can be paid off by the liquidator in this way.[81]

---

77 J. Marshall, (2011) 3 *International Insolvency Law Review* 268 who raises the issue.

78 B. Wessels, *International Insolvency Law,* para. 10656. On this point, see also also T. Ingelmann, in K. Pannen (ed.), *European Insolvency Regulation*, para. 28, who states: 'Logically the secured creditor should redeem his secured rights (or have them redeemed) before the court has a chance to make such an order that could lower the value of his security'; and P. Smart, (2006) 15 *International Insolvency Review* 17 at 26–27: 'The words "shall not affect" in Article 5 can reasonably be read as "shall not affect without the relevant creditor's consent"'.

79 Para. 99.

80 M. Balz, (1996) 70 *American Bankruptcy Law Journal* 485 at 509.

81 M. Virgós, (1998) 25 *Forum Internationale* 20. In M. Virgós and F. Garcimartín, *The European Insolvency Regulation: Law and Practice*, 107 it is stated that the secured creditor should not be prejudiced thereby but it is not clear what the authors understand by the concept of 'prejudice'. See generally the discussion in P. Smart, (2006) 15 *International Insolvency Review* 17 at 24–27.

74. (b) Some countries lay down that secured creditors have to pay some of the general costs of the insolvency proceedings. According to one view, if the lex concursus so provides, the creditor who is secured by a right in rem located in another Member State is exempted from paying these costs, since this conflicts with the wording of the 'shall not affect' formula: hence the IP may not enforce such payment.[82] There is, however, an alternative view that an obligation to contribute to the general costs of the insolvency proceedings does not conflict with the 'shall not affect' formula since it does not clash with the policy endorsed by the Insolvency Regulation.[83]

75. (c) Some countries provide a moratorium that, by operation of laws or following a court order, prevents the holder of a security right in rem from exercising its right for a restricted period of time without the IP's authorisation. For instance, this provision is laid down in certain circumstances under English, German and Dutch laws. The 'cooling-off' period allows the IP to have a breathing space to evaluate the best way to address the debtor's insolvency. If the encumbered assets are located in a Member State that is different from that of the opening of the proceedings, it is questionable whether Article 5, and its 'shall not affect' formula, prevails over the moratorium and prevents it from operating. While some commentators have interpreted the formula literally, and considered it to be incompatible with the moratorium,[84] other commentators have advocated a more flexible approach according to which Article 5 is not incompatible with moratoria, especially if they are designed to hamper the exercise of the security rights only temporarily.[85]

The recast Regulation, however, seems to solve any interpretative problems by supporting the more rigid approach according to which the 'shall not affect' formula would prevail over the moratorium and prevent it from operating on security rights in rem. It has a new recital, recital 69, relevant to this issue which does not have a counterpart in Regulation 1346/2000. Recital 69 states: 'This Regulation lays down several provisions for a court to order a stay of opening proceedings or a stay of enforcement proceedings. Any such stay should not affect the rights in rem of creditors or third parties.' Nevertheless, this argument does not allow anybody to take anything for granted, firstly because recitals are not binding, and secondly because the recast Regulation strongly endorses the 'rescue culture', i.e. the rescue of ailing businesses, which particularly favours moratoria.

76. (d) Some jurisdictions provide special rules aimed at facilitating the approval of a rescue plan, including 'cram-down' rules. Here again, while some authors

82 S. Kolmann, in P. Gottwald (ed.), *Insolvenz-Handbuch*, §132, para. 30.

83 B. Wessels, *International Insolvency Law*, para. 10658a.

84 J. Marshall, (2011) 3 *International Insolvency Law Review* 268.

85 B. Wessels, *International Insolvency Law*, para. 10657.

maintain that the 'shall not affect' formula prevents secured creditors from being impaired by a plan,[86] other commentators argue differently. They point to specific provisions in Article 4 (Article 7 of recast) which lay down that 'the law of the State of the opening of proceedings shall determine: (i) the rules governing the distribution of proceeds from the realisation of assets, the ranking of claims and the rights of creditors who have obtained partial satisfaction after the opening of insolvency proceedings by virtue of a right in rem or through a set-off; (j) the conditions for and the effects of closure of insolvency proceedings, in particular by composition; (k) creditors' rights after the closure of insolvency proceedings'. They maintain that this provision influences the interpretation of Article 5, thereby having the consequence that the lex concursus and any connected provisions impairing the holders of security rights in rem would prevail over the protective umbrella provided by the 'shall not affect' formula.[87]

77. Essentially the argument is that Article 5 protects only the security right itself and not the amount that may be recovered on foot of the security right from the collateral. In other words, measures that indirectly affect security through the forced reduction of claims in a restructuring plan are not caught by the Article 5 prohibition. Another way of putting it is to say that a distinction should be drawn between the right in rem itself and the underlying debt, and that while the in rem right may be sacrosanct, there is a possibility of striking at the underlying debt. For instance, the Heidelberg–Luxembourg–Vienna external evaluation of the Regulation commissioned by the European Commission suggests that it is questionable 'an adjustment, a reduction or even the discharge of the secured claim' affects the right in rem and is therefore prohibited by Article 5.[88] It seems more plausible however to suggest that if a restructuring plan could cut back the underlying debt owed to the secured creditor by say 10% or 20% or even 99.9%, 'this would strike at the very heart of the protection given by Article 5' to holders of in rem rights over collateral located in other Member States.[89] The argument that a secured claim can be discharged, at least partially, in this way would seem to contradict the policy of Article 5 and render impotent the security function

---

[86] J. Marshall, (2011) 3 *International Insolvency Law Review* 268 at 269; P. Smart, (2006) 15 *International Insolvency Review* 17 at 23–24; M. Veder, (2011) 3 *International Insolvency Law Review* 289 at 294.

[87] A. Flessner, 'Dingliche Sicherungsrechte nach dem Europäischen Insolvenz-Übereinkommen', in J. Basedow et al. (eds.), *Festschrift für U. Drobnig* 277; T. Ingelmann, in K. Pannen (ed.), *European Insolvency Regulation*, para. 28; B. Wessels, *International Insolvency Law*, para. 10658c; R. van Galen, [2002] *Tijdschrift voor Insolventierecht* 139 (quoted by M. Veder, (2011) 3 *International Insolvency Law Review* 289 fn. 19).

[88] JUST/2011/JCIV/PR/0049/A4, 260. The same point is made in the Report from the Commission on the application of the Insolvency Regulation – COM (2012) 743 final, 12. But for a different view see p. 283 of the *Heidelberg–Luxembourg–Vienna* evaluation.

[89] See G. Moss, I. Fletcher and S. Isaacs, *The EC Regulation on Insolvency Proceedings*, para. 6.56.

served by rights in rem.[90] It is also worth pointing out that one of the drafters of the Regulation has been very clear that the holders of collateral located abroad may not be impaired against their wishes by a restructuring plan.[91]

78. This debate illuminates the unsatisfactory nature of Article 5, the significance of the interests protected by its special regime and the fact that, while commentators agree that the relationship between Articles 4 and 5 has to be understood on a rule-exception basis, it is very difficult for them to determine case by case where the 'rule' finishes and where the 'exception' starts.

79. These difficulties are one factor leading some courts to rule that Article 5 contains a choice of law rule referring to the so-called lex situs.[92] Primarily, however, this interpretation takes its cue from the (almost) universally accepted idea that property is under the close control of the authorities of the country where the property is located. Indeed, this interpretation corresponds to the most common regulatory approach to cross-border property issues.[93] On cross-border property issues, not affected by insolvency proceedings, the application of the lex situs may also contain a reference back ('renvoi') to the choice of law rules of the country making the reference but the Insolvency Regulation is generally considered to exclude the doctrine of renvoi.[94]

80. The idea that Article 5 contains a choice of law rule referring to the lex situs gets some support from the comments of the Advocate General and the Court of Justice in the *ERSTE Bank Hungary* case. The case stemmed from the request for a preliminary ruling from the Supreme Court of *Hungary* and it concerned whether Article 5 was also applicable where the relevant asset of the debtor was situated within the territory of a state which became a Member State of the European Union after the insolvency proceedings had been opened. The Advocate General expressed the opinion that 'Article 5(1) of the Regulation, however, does not relate to the court's jurisdiction. That provision does not deal with the conflict between courts which is liable to arise as a result of the insolvency proceedings. The rule set out in Article 5(1) constitutes a conflict-of-laws rule in the form of an exception to the general principle, laid down in Article 4(1) of the Regulation, that the law of the Member State in which the insolvency proceedings were opened is to apply'.[95] The Court of Justice said: 'Article 5(1)

---

90 See P. Smart, (2006) 15 *International Insolvency Review* 17 at 33.

91 See M. Balz, (1996) 70 *American Bankruptcy Law Journal* 485 at 509 and see also M. Virgós and F. Garcimartín, *The European Insolvency Regulation: Law and Practice*, 104.

92 On this point, see A. Piekenbrock, in B. Hess, P. Oberhammer and T. Pfeiffer (eds.), *European Insolvency Law. The Heidelberg–Luxembourg–Vienna Report*, para. 687 fn. 54.

93 C. Clarkson and J. Hill, *The Conflict of Laws*, 472.

94 R. Mangano, in R. Bork and R. Mangano, *European Cross-Border Insolvency Law*, para. 1.56.

95 Case C-527/10 *ERSTE Bank ir Nyrt v Magyar Állam* ECLI:EU:C:2012:37, para. 36.

of the Regulation must be understood as a provision which, derogating from the rule of the law of the State of the opening of the proceedings, allows the law of the Member State on whose territory the asset concerned is situated to be applied to the right in rem of a creditor or a third party over certain assets belonging to the debtor'.[96]

81. In advancing the idea that Article 5 (and Article 8 of the recast) EIR contains a choice of law rule referring to the lex situs, one can also get some support from recital 68 of the recast in some of its linguistic versions. This includes the German version which uses the term '*Sonderanknüpfung*' while the French and the Italian versions of recital 68 employ the terms '*rattachement particulier*' and '*criteri speciali di collegamento*' respectively, which both bring to mind the concept of 'referral'.[97]

82. It should also be noted that during the gestation of the recast Insolvency Regulation, INSOL Europe expressly suggested reshaping the wording of Article 5 in the form of a choice of law rule as follows: 'The effects of insolvency proceedings on the rights in rem of creditors or third parties in respect of tangible or intangible, moveable or immoveable assets ... belonging to the debtor which are situated within the territory of another Member State at the time of the opening of proceedings shall be governed solely by the law of the Member State within which the assets are situated'.[98]

83. Nevertheless, the idea that Article 5 contains a choice of law rule referring to the so-called lex rei sitae is held by a minority. In fact, on this point the Heidelberg–Luxembourg–Vienna report states that only the Hungarian judiciary follow this line.[99]

4.5. CONCLUSIONS ON THE INTERPRETATIONS OF ARTICLE 5

84. Security rights are often seen to function as a risk reduction device that increases the availability, and lowers the cost, of credit. The minimisation of risk should encourage lenders to make loans and to reduce the risk premium they might otherwise input into the interest rate calculations.

---

96 *Ibid.* at para. 42.

97 A. Piekenbrock, in B. Hess, P. Oberhammer and T. Pfeiffer (eds.), *European Insolvency Law. The Heidelberg–Luxembourg–Vienna Report*, para. 678.

98 R. van Galen et al., *Revision of the European Insolvency Regulation. Proposals by INSOL Europe*, 10.

99 A. Piekenbrock, in B. Hess, P. Oberhammer and T. Pfeiffer (eds.), *European Insolvency Law. The Heidelberg–Luxembourg–Vienna Report*, para. 687, fn. 54.

85. On the other hand, the law of secured credit embodies cultural attitudes and public policy choices that vary greatly among States.[100] Many of the rules governing the enforcement of security rights reflect policy concerns interests that are external to the credit relationship itself such as the importance ascribed in a particular country to employment preservation and business continuity as distinct from security enforcement.[101] The debtor/creditor agreement cannot completely regulate the effect of the security right on third parties and the rules governing distribution of the debtor's assets may reflect local social goals such as 'carve-outs' for unsecured or involuntary creditors.

86. The balance between policy goals is struck differently in different countries and, as the EU Regulation recognises, attitudes towards security and the law relating to security interests vary widely across the EU.

87. The European Insolvency Regulation is explicitly designed to advance the goal of European market integration and, more prosaically, to improve the administration of cross-border insolvency cases within Europe. It introduces a general set of harmonised rules on jurisdiction and choice of law in insolvency cases based on the primacy of the law of the State where the debtor has its 'centre of main interests', or COMI. There are exceptions to this principle of primacy however, and opinions differ about the extent to which the centrality of the law of the COMI is carried through in practice. One of the more controversial aspects of the Regulation is Article 5 which mixes complexity and simplicity in a somewhat confusing brew. The typological definition, or rather description of rights in rem, is rather complex but then there is the apparent simplicity of the 'shall not affect' formula.

88. The general view reflected in the Virgós–Schmit Report[102] is that Article 5 embodies a 'hard and fast' or 'maximalist' rule, implying that the holder of the right in rem can exercise its rights without any exception or limitation stemming from collateral carve-outs for the benefit of unsecured creditors under the law of the COMI State. Under this interpretation, Article 5 constitutes an exception to Article 4(2(i) which states that the COMI State shall determine the rules

---

[100] See J. Garrido, (2011) 46 *Texas International Law Journal* 459 at 460–461, who states that: 'there are no two priority systems that are identical, and that harmonization or unification of the law in this area is extremely unlikely to happen. In fact, priority systems are but the expression of the hierarchy of values that permeate a given legal system. This means that graduation of creditors is primarily political, and that the influence of powerful groups of creditors, the inertia of legal tradition, or the conscious and deliberate choice to promote certain values, are the factors that explain the fundamental differences encountered in various jurisdictions around the world.'

[101] See generally S. Deakin and A. Koukiadaki, (2012) 33 *Comparative Labor Law and Policy Journal* 427; J. Armour and S. Deakin, (2003) 22 *International Review of Law and Economics* 443 and on different conceptions of corporate rescue see V. Finch, (2012) 32 *Legal Studies* 302, [2008] *Journal of Business Law* 75.

[102] Virgós–Schmit Report (fn. 22) para. 97.

'governing the distribution of proceeds from the realization of assets, the ranking of claims and the rights of creditors who have obtained partial satisfaction after the opening of insolvency proceedings by virtue of a right in rem or through a set-off'.[103]

89. Secured creditors are not affected by the opening of insolvency proceedings in another EU State but there are questions about what 'shall not affect' means in practice and in particular whether secured creditors are deemed to have been affected by certain actions taken in the course of the main proceedings such as moratoria, debt write-downs and redemption of loans.

90. There is considerable uncertainty about the proper interpretation of Article 5 and this led to calls for its reform, including by INSOL Europe. The section will now consider four options for reform:

- excluding security rights in rem from the scope of the Regulation;
- regulating security rights in rem by means of a referral to the lex situs;
- regulating security rights in rem by means of a double filter combining a referral to the lex fori concursus with a referral to the lex situs;
- regulating security rights in rem by means of a multilevel approach combining a top-down intervention with a bottom-up intervention, including the use of the 'Open Method of Coordination'.[104]

5. OPTIONS FOR REFORM

5.1. EXCLUDING SECURITY RIGHTS IN REM FROM THE SCOPE OF THE REGULATION

91. If security rights are not mentioned at all in the Insolvency Regulation this would leave a very large hole. Currently, Article 4(2(i) provides that the law of

---

103 The Financial Markets Law Committee Issue paper no. 30 (September 2012) 'European Insolvency Regulation' at p. 11 suggests however that there is some uncertainty on the point. See also Article 4(2)(l) on the role of the COMI State in determining who is to bear the costs and expenses incurred in the insolvency proceedings.

104 M. Virgós, (1998) 25 *Forum Internationale* 20 wrote that the Commission set up for the 1995 Convention had considered the following options: (i) cumulative application of the lex concursus and the lex rei sitae, (ii) application of the insolvency law of the situs, (iii) application of the insolvency law of the situs, but only with a 'veto' function in respect of infringements on the exercise of proprietary rights under the lex concursus that are not compatible with the protection of proprietary rights accorded by the law of the situs, and (iv) a distinction between the law applicable to the realisation of assets subject to security rights (to be governed by the lex concursus) on the one hand, and the (priority rules regarding the) distribution of the proceeds (to be governed by the lex rei sitae), on the other hand. By contrast, M. Virgós and F. Garcimartín, *The European Insolvency Regulation: Law and Practice*, para. 141, wrote that: 'In theory, *three general solutions* may be given', and that such solutions would consist in

the State that opens insolvency proceedings governs the rights of creditors who have obtained partial satisfaction by virtue of a right in rem and according to recital 25 of the preamble if secondary insolvency proceedings are not opened, then any surplus on the sale of an asset covered by rights in rem should be paid to the IP in the main insolvency proceedings.[105] Moreover, security rights are in principle subject to avoidance under the law of the State that opens the insolvency proceedings but subject to any possible defences under the law that applies to the transaction. Failure to address these matters in any European Insolvency Regulation would imperil the legal certainty that the Regulation is seeking to achieve. If insolvency proceedings are opened and a debtor has assets in another jurisdiction, then the Regulation has to address the matter, if only partially, of which law is applicable since security rights in rem are such a strong characteristic of the modern commercial credit-driven world.[106] A complete silence on the issue would seriously weaken the Insolvency Regulation as a European law harmonisation instrument.

5.2. REGULATING SECURITY RIGHTS IN REM BY MEANS OF A REFERRAL TO THE LEX SITUS

92. There appears to be considerable support for the proposition that security rights in rem should be regulated under the Insolvency Regulation by means of a referral to the lex situs.[107] As we have seen, this view has the backing of INSOL Europe.[108]

93. It has been argued that the current regime overprotects the secured creditor with foreign-located collateral giving a stronger level of protection against the debtor's insolvency than that demanded by the national law of the situs.[109] There is a so-called EU bonus – a bonus for secured creditors in European cross-border

adopting the lex fori concursus, in adopting the lex rei sitae, and in excluding rights in rem from the effects of the insolvency proceedings.

105 B. Wessels, *International Insolvency Law*, para. 10649.

106 On this point, see also M. Veder, (2011) 3 *International Insolvency Law Review* 289 at 293.

107 M. Veder, (2011) 3 *International Insolvency Law Review* 289 at 292, who also writes that 'Another option that could be considered is to assess the secured creditor's position in the debtor's insolvency in accordance with the insolvency rules of the law applicable to the security right, which does not necessarily coincide with the *lex rei sitae* (e.g. in respect of intangibles)'.

108 See the observations at para. 5.9 of the Insol Europe Report *Revision of the European Insolvency Regulation* (2012) 'INSOL Europe agrees with the objection that secured creditors are overprotected as a result of the hard and fast rule of the current text ... security rights in rem should not be affected to any larger extent than would be the case if local insolvency proceedings were opened'.

109 See para. 5.7 of the proposals prepared by INSOL Europe for *Revision of the European Insolvency Regulation* (2012).

insolvencies that is not available in domestic insolvencies.[110] Unless secondary insolvency proceedings are opened in a particular country, a secured creditor is allowed to enforce against collateral in that country even though the country's domestic law would not allow enforcement. The anomalies generated by this situation are demonstrated by the following example of creditor X with security rights against the assets located in the *UK* of two debtors A and B. Debtor A has its COMI in *France*. Main opening are opened in *France* and these proceedings are automatically recognised in the *UK* under the Insolvency Regulation but creditor X may still enforce against debtor A's assets in the *UK* unimpeded by any stay that arises under French insolvency law.

94. The position is different however in the case of debtor B who has his COMI in the *US* and in respect of whom main insolvency proceedings have been opened in the *US*. While the *US* proceedings are not automatically recognised in the *UK*, recognition may be granted under the UNCITRAL Model Law on Cross-Border Insolvency and the UK Cross-Border Insolvency Regulations. One of the consequences of recognition may be a stay on *UK* enforcement actions by creditor X.[111] While prima facie the stay imposed as a consequence of the recognition of foreign insolvency proceedings does not affect rights to enforce security, the foreign representative at the time of applying for recognition of the foreign proceedings may apply for a 'wider' stay.[112]

95. Debtor A's IP may want the benefit of a *UK* stay because it improves the prospects of a successful reorganisation of the debtor or its business. It is denied the benefits of a stay that is potentially available to a debtor with a COMI outside the EU and this seems highly anomalous. The IP does not have the ability to prevent secured creditors from seizing or disposing of assets that are useful or essential for the carrying on of the debtor's business. The present position does not do justice to the balance that national insolvency laws seek between secured creditors on the one hand and the bankruptcy estate and the unsecured creditors on the other. Under Article 5, secured creditors are given 'hold out' rights that can only be trumped by the opening of secondary proceedings, whenever possible, with all the disadvantages attendant on parallel proceedings such as increased costs and inconvenience.

---

110 See M. Virgós and F. Garcimartin, *The European Insolvency Regulation: Law and Practice*, 103–104: 'Article 5 functions more as a rule of substantive law than as a simple conflict rule and when, compared with the national laws concerned, it may afford a stronger level of protection against the insolvency of the debtor than that which these national laws demand'.

111 Art. 20. The discretion to lift or modify the moratorium/stay has been considered in cases like *Re Armada Shipping* [2011] EWHC 216, [2011] All ER 166 and *Re Pan Oceanic Maritime Inc* [2010] EWHC 1734.

112 The judicial discretion to order a wider stay was exercised in *Re Pan Oceanic Maritime Inc* [2010] EWHC 1734 where an 'administration stay' along the lines of para. 43 Sch. B1 Insolvency Act 1986 barring the enforcement of security was granted. See also *Re Transfield ER Cape Ltd* [2010] EWHC 2851.

96. If option (b) for reform were adopted and security rights were regulated by reference to the law of the place where the assets are located, then it would be up to the domestic law of the situs to give whatever effect it wishes to foreign insolvency proceedings over local assets. If, like the *UK*, it has adopted the UNCITRAL Model Law on Cross-Border Insolvency, it is likely to implement a foreign insolvency moratorium in respect of the collateral.

Against this option, however, one could argue that idea of regulating security rights in rem by means of a referral to the lex situs clashes dramatically with the approach of the EIR, which purports to be universalist. This approach is confirmed and reinforced in the recast Insolvency Regulation which tends to discourage the opening of territorial insolvency proceedings

5.3. REGULATING SECURITY RIGHTS IN REM BY MEANS OF A DOUBLE FILTER COMBINING A REFERRAL TO THE LEX FORI CONCURSUS WITH A REFERRAL TO THE LEX REI SITAE

97. The Heidelberg–Luxembourg–Vienna Report suggested the regulation of rights in rem through combining a referral to the lex fori concursus with a referral to the lex rei sitae.[113] In particular, it was proposed that the law of the State of the opening of insolvency proceedings should regulate 'the effects of insolvency proceedings on rights in rem of creditors or third parties … belonging to the debtor which are situated within the territory of another Member State at the time of the opening of proceedings' but that this provision should not be applicable 'insofar as a creditor or a third party provides proof that: (a) the secured assets have been situated within the territory of another Member State than the State of the opening of proceedings at the time of the opening of proceedings, and (b) the substantial effects of insolvency proceedings on rights in rem provided for under the law of the State of the opening of proceedings do not comply with the insolvency law of the Member State within the territory of which the assets were situated at the time of the opening of proceedings.'

98. The following example demonstrates how the proposal might operate. Debtor A has its COMI in *France*, while its creditor, B, has a mortgage encumbering the debtor's immovable property which is located in *Germany*. The main proceedings are opened in *France*. If one adopts the idea of regulating security rights in rem by means of a double filter combining a referral to the lex fori concursus with a referral to the lex rei sitae, the IP in the main proceedings may enforce this

---

113 A. Piekenbrock, in B. Hess, P. Oberhammer and T. Pfeiffer (eds.), *European Insolvency Law. The Heidelberg–Luxembourg–Vienna Report*, paras. 752–754.

security in accordance with French law. Creditor B may seek to prove, however, that French law on security rights does not comply with the German law on security rights and, because of this substantial difference, it may demand the application of German law.

99. This proposal mirrors the approach adopted in respect of avoidance rules under Articles 4(2)(m) and 13 of the Regulation and represents a compromise between the general universalist approach of the Insolvency Regulation and the need to protect trade and legal certainty. On the other hand, this approach seems complex and cumbersome and any provision would need to be carefully worded to prevent the complete non-application of the lex fori concursus.

5.4. REGULATING SECURITY RIGHTS IN REM THROUGH A MULTILEVEL APPROACH

100. The idea of regulating security rights in rem by means of a double filter combining a referral to the lex fori concursus with a referral to the lex situs is potentially complex but some of the complexity could be reduced if the EU decides to set in motion and support a process of harmonisation of national rules concerning security rights in rem. The idea of this kind of harmonisation is not a taboo given the appearance, both worldwide and at European level, of many initiatives varying in nature and adopting different techniques, which aim at promoting the harmonisation of security rights globally or regionally.[114]

101. At the wider European level, one can point to the European Bank for Reconstruction and Development (EBRD) Model Law on Secured Transactions and the associated Core Principles. The EBRD was established in 1991 to assist the former Socialist States in Central and Eastern Europe and the Soviet Union with the transition to a market economy. EBRD attempts to foster the transition to open market-oriented economies and to promote private and entrepreneurial initiative in its countries of operation.[115] EBRD has addressed reform of the law

---

114 See, for instance, the 2009 'Draft Common Frame of Reference (DCFR)' edited by C. von Bar, E. Clive and H. Schulte-Nölke, *Proprietary Security in Movable Assets*, Book IX <www.sgecc.net> accessed 10 May 2016; the 1998 UNIDROIT Convention on International Factoring; the 1988 UNIDROIT Convention on International Financial Leasing; and the 2001 UNIDROIT Cape Town Convention on International Interests in Mobile Equipment, and its associated Protocols.

115 See the Foreword by EBRD General Counsel E. Maurice in J.-H. Rover, *Secured Lending in Eastern Europe: Comparative Law of Secured Transactions and the EBRD Model Law*, v: 'EBRD has a special role amongst international financial institutions, because of the unique nature of its region, because of the emphasis placed on promoting the private sector, and because of widespread expectation that countries in the region should catch up rapidly with their western neighbours.'

of secured rights from its earliest days and this attention has continued to the present.[116]

102. Its 1994 Model Law of Secured Transactions resulted from a comparative survey of various laws on secured transactions, both in Europe and elsewhere in the world, and draws on both common law and civil law systems. The guiding principle was to produce a text that was compatible with the civil law concepts upon which many Central and Eastern European legal systems were based,[117] while simultaneously borrowing from common law systems which 'were said to have developed many useful solutions to accommodate modern financing techniques.'[118]

103. The Model Law is less comprehensive however, than some other international law instruments such as the UNCITRAL Legislative Guide on Secured Transactions and national law models such as Article 9 of the US Uniform Commercial Code. The EBRD Model Law, in its essence, implements five key elements for a modern secured transactions law that EBRD has later elaborated upon and refined. These are that:

- a security right should have the essential qualities of a property right;
- the law should provide for the granting of security in the widest possible range of circumstances;
- the existence of security over property must be effectively publicised;
- there should be a rapid and cost-effective means of recovering the debt from the secured asset;
- the cost of creating, maintaining and exercising the right should be kept at a reasonable level.

104. In Chapter 3 of this comparative analysis we look in more detail at international instruments providing for the harmonisation of the law of security rights including indicators drawn from the World Bank Doing Business reports.

105. In the EU, achieving the harmonisation goal in respect of security rights is likely to be very difficult at a practical level, even if it is desirable at a theoretical level. Securing the necessary level of political and technical agreement is likely to be problematic given the present divergences within Member States. Chapter 3 of this comparative analysis considers similarities and dissimilarities between substantive national laws on security rights. The study references the fact that the laws of Member States differ, sometimes quite significantly, at the present time on matters such as the degree of formality necessary to create a security interest;

---

116 See generally the EBRD website <*www.ebrd.com*> accessed 10 May 2016, and the 'secured transactions' section of the website.

117 Introduction, v.

118 *Ibid.*

the extent to which non-possessory security is recognised; the validation of all-assets or floating security; the availability of a single unitary security interest over the entirety of the debtor's assets; the extent to which security interests are subject to a publicity requirement whether by filing/registration or otherwise; and the possibility of out-of-court enforcement of security interests in the event of the debtor's default.

106. Secondly, it is unclear whether the EU has the necessary legal competence to introduce a Europe-wide harmonisation measure,[119] particularly since the introduction by the 1992 Treaty of Maastricht of the principle of subsidiarity which provides that the Union 'shall act only if and in so far as the objectives of the proposed action cannot be sufficiently achieved by the Member States, either at central level or at regional and local level, but can rather, by reason of the scale or effects of the proposed action, be better achieved at Union level'.[120]

107. Nevertheless, the subsidiarity principle does not necessarily mean a passive acceptance of the fragmentation of the legal framework nor regulatory competition between Member States.

108. States may learn from one another making use of the concepts of multilevel governance[121] and the Open Method of Coordination which have been applied generally to various aspects of EU decision-making.

109. The concept of multilevel governance provides for a new system of law-making across the EU which respects the principle of subsidiarity, but at the same time allows the EU and the Member States to cooperate with each other at different levels in order to achieve better laws and regulatory principles across Europe. The system has been conceived in order to allow interactions between governmental actors and non-State actors, such as NGOs, banks, etc., who nowadays play a crucial role in policy-making across the EU and in the development of national laws and best practices.[122] The concept of multilevel governance is based on the idea that the EU, alone, is not in charge of the whole of law-making, and that this activity results from a combination of different sources of law working at different levels: namely, at the level of the EU, at that of the Member States and at that of non-State actors. Law-making across the EU has also to involve Member States and non-State actors.

---

119 E. Ramaekers, (2015) 23 *European Review of Private Law* 437; J. Rutgers, 'Registered European Security Instrument in a Multilingual European Union', in S. van Erp, A. Salomons and B. Akkermans (eds.), *The Future of European Property Law*, 153–163; J. Rutgers, (2011) 7 *European Review of Contract Law* 350.

120 Art. 5(3) TEU.

121 L. Hooghe and G. Marks, *Multi-Level Governance and European Integration.*

122 See, for instance, H. Heinelt and M. Knodt (eds.), *Policies within the EU Multi-Level System.*

110. While there are possible variations in approach, generally the EU regulator is in charge of designing the regulatory architecture, including planning the balance between hard law and soft law; secondly, the role of the State is being transformed into that of an actor developing new strategies of coordination; and thirdly, decision-making at various territorial levels is characterised by the increased participation of non-State actors.[123]

111. One possible approach is for the EU to adopt a non-binding recommendation that Member States should observe certain guidelines in their national law-making. The Commission Recommendation of 12 March 2014 'on a new approach to business failure and insolvency' is a case in point.[124] Nevertheless, this policy instrument could prove to be unsuccessful in achieving the desired outcomes in a field which is as complex and variegated as that of security rights in rem. One must be wary of any top-down approach involving a one-way intervention which does not allow Member States to be in 'dialogue' with the EU and which does not necessarily involve non-State actors.

112. In 2000, the EU introduced the Open Method of Coordination (OMC), promising that a 'fully decentralised approach will be applied in line with the principle of subsidiarity in which the European union, the Member States, the regional and local levels, as well as the social partners and civil society, will be actively involved, using variable forms of partnership'.[125] The Open Method of Coordination has been successfully employed in the field of employment law. It has also been well received in other fields as a useful procedure aimed at achieving a kind of harmonisation of laws from the bottom up, thereby facilitating learning from diversity and cross-fertilisation between different cultures.[126]

113. But the use of the Open Method of Coordination is not a panacea.[127] It requires an intense dialogue between the Union, Member States and non-State

---

123 Regulatory interventions, even if different, are characterised by the fact that they are responsive or reflexive, i.e. they imply the involvement of addressees. See, for instance, the seminal book by I. Ayres and J. Braithwaite, *Responsive Regulation: Transcending the Deregulation Debate*.

124 C (2014) 1500 final and see also the Commission Communication, *A New European Approach to Business Failure and Insolvency* COM (2012) 742. For analysis of the Recommendation see, inter alia, S. Madaus, [2014] Insolvency Intelligence 81; K. van Zwieten, *Restructuring law – recommendations from the European Commission* <http://ebrd.com/downloads/research/law/lit114e.pdf> accessed 10 May 2016; H. Eidenmüller and K. van Zweiten, 'Restructuring the European Business Enterprise: The EU Commission Recommendation on a New Approach to Business Failure and Insolvency' (2015)16 *European Business Organization Law Review* 625.

125 Lisbon European Council, 23 and 24 March 2000, para. 38 <http://www.europarl.europa.eu/summits/lis1_en.htm> accessed 10 May 2016.

126 S. Deakin, (2007) 20 *Comparative Research in Law & Political Economy Research Paper* 1 ff.; S. Kröger, (2009) 13(1) *European Integration Online Papers*, Art. 5, p. 1 ff. <https://eiop.or.at/eiop/pdf/2009-005.pdf> accessed 23 May 2016.

127 See S. Kröger, (2009) 13(1) *European Integration online Papers*, Art. 5, p. 4 <https://eiop.or.at/eiop/pdf/2009-005.pdf> accessed 23 May 2016.

actors, the adoption of specific objectives, the establishment of benchmarks, periodic monitoring through the Commission and the Council, evaluation and peer review organised in the form of mutual learning processes. Nevertheless, in a field where harmonisation involves many conflicting interests of non-State actors, this approach has the advantage of providing an institutional umbrella of legitimacy to banks and other members of the financial industry, who are becoming increasingly European or even globalised. For this reason, they might prefer to replace a fragmented system of security rights in rem with a harmonised one, provided that the costs of achieving harmonisation (such as the implementation and testing of new rules, training personnel, etc.) are not greater than those in maintaining the status quo ante.

CHAPTER 2

TRANSACTIONAL AVOIDANCE AND THE INSOLVENCY REGULATION

114. This chapter will consider Articles 4(2)(m) and 13 of the Insolvency Regulation – Regulation 1346/2000 – and the equivalent provisions in the 'recast' Regulation, Regulation (EU) 2015/848. These provisions deal with transactional avoidance. Article 4 sets up the possibility for transactional avoidance while Article 13 provides a defence. After a brief section setting out the policy background, the main body of the chapter will consider the scope of application of Articles 4 and 13. The third section will consider options for reform of the relevant provisions.

1. INTRODUCTION

115. Transactional avoidance in insolvency situations is a feature of all the legal systems considered in this report. This is so for a number of different reasons, all of them related to the achievement of insolvency objectives, namely the enforcement of the system of priorities laid down by insolvency law; sanctioning the debtor's intention to defraud creditors; the protection of creditors against any actions detrimental to the insolvency estate; and finally assisting in the restructuring of the debtor's business. The Court of Justice has classified these actions as 'actions which derive directly from those proceedings and which are closely connected to them'.[128] By the same token, Article 4(2)(m) establishes that 'the rules relating to the voidness, voidability or unenforceability of legal acts detrimental to all the creditors' are subject to the law governing the insolvency proceedings, i.e. the lex fori concursus.

116. Nevertheless, and to safeguard the expectations of third parties and the certainty of transactions,[129] Article 13 lays down that 'Article 4(2)(m) shall

---

128 See Case C-339/07, *Seagon v Deko Marty Belgium*, paras. 21 and 28. This case law is now codified in Article 6(1) of the Regulation 2015/848, which specifically mentions avoidance actions though it does not define what these are.

129 See recital 24 EIR, recital 67 of Regulation 2015/848.

not apply where the person who benefited from an act detrimental to all the creditors provides proof that: the said act is subject to the law of a Member State other than that of the State of the opening of proceedings, and that law does not allow any means of challenging that act in the relevant case'. While transactional avoidance entails the impugning of apparently valid acts, this provision aims to protect legal certainty by making sure that the last word on the validity of an act or transaction is pronounced by the law governing it, i.e. the lex causae. Accordingly, if the lex causae deems the impugned transaction to be valid and this is established by the counterparty to the impugned transaction, the lex fori concursus is not enforced and there is no transactional avoidance.

117. In the framework of the SREIR Project, a questionnaire was distributed among practitioners and academics. One of the questions was whether Article 13 is to be understood as introducing a double avoidance rule. This was answered in the affirmative by a clear majority. The combination of Articles 4 and 13 means that a transaction detrimental to the general body of creditors can only be challenged in a cross-border insolvency proceeding where both the lex concursus and the lex causae deem it void, voidable or unenforceable; otherwise, that transaction is unchallengeable, either on the grounds of the lex concursus not allowing for avoidance or on account of the law governing the transaction act not providing for any means of challenge. Most answers to the questionnaire pointed out that no problems in applying Article 13 have been encountered in practice, although some suggested issues in determining the applicable law in respect of the impugned transaction as well as whether this law refers to both formal requirements and limitations periods. In the light of these difficulties, there were suggestions for modification of Article 13 in order to resolve the interpretative issues. There was majority, but not unanimous, support for the view that Article 13 is supported by a legitimate interest, i.e. that of protecting legal certainty. A clear majority was also in favour of harmonising avoidance rules.

118. The following sections address both Articles 4 and 13 in more detail by analysing their scope of application, the relevant connecting factors and how they operate, in particular in the light of the case law of the Court of Justice. This analysis is also relevant to Articles 7(2)(m) and 16 of the Regulation – Regulation (EU) 2015/848 – which applies to insolvency proceedings after 26th June 2017.[130] These provisions are the same as Articles 4(2)(m) and 13 of the original Regulation – Regulation 1346/2000.

[130] See Articles 84 and 92 of Regulation 2015/848.

2. HOW THE TRANSACTIONAL AVOIDANCE PROVISIONS IN THE REGULATION ARE TO BE INTERPRETED AND APPLIED

2.1. JURISDICTION OF THE COURT THAT OPENS INSOLVENCY PROCEEDINGS EXTENDS TO 'INSOLVENCY-RELATED ACTIONS' INCLUDING TRANSACTIONAL AVOIDANCE ACTIONS

119. According to recital 14 of the preamble to the Insolvency Regulation, the Regulation only applies where a debtor has its centre of main interests (COMI) in the European Union. Main insolvency proceedings with universal effects applying to all the debtor's assets may only be opened in the EU State where the debtor has its COMI but secondary proceedings limited in their effects to that particular State may be opened in any EU State where the debtor has an 'establishment'.

120. It seems clear from the case law of the Court of Justice that the jurisdiction to open insolvency proceedings in a particular State also includes the jurisdiction to hear 'insolvency-related' actions. In *Gourdain v Nadler*[131] and *Seagon v Deko*[132] it was held that insolvency-related actions are outside the Brussels I Regulation on Jurisdiction and Enforcement of Judgments in Civil and Commercial Matters[133] but are within the Insolvency Regulation. Therefore, in respect of an insolvency-related action, a defendant should be sued in the State that opens the insolvency proceedings rather than in his country of domicile.

121. Article 6 of the recast Regulation expressly extends the jurisdiction of the court that opened insolvency proceedings to insolvency-related actions. Essentially there is a codification of the decision in *Seagon v Deko*[134] and a clear statement that courts opening insolvency proceedings also have jurisdiction in respect of actions that derive directly from the insolvency proceedings and are closely linked with them.[135] There is, however, no guidance on what constitutes

131 Case 133/78 [1979] 3 CMLR 180.

132 Case C-339/07 [2009] ECR I-767.

133 Regulation 1215/2012/EU (Brussels 1 Regulation recast) replacing the original Brussels 1 Regulation – Council Regulation 44/2001 – which in turn replaced the earlier Brussels Convention on jurisdiction and the enforcement of judgments in civil and commercial matters (1968).

134 Case C-339/07 [2009] ECR I-767. See on the decision L. Carballo Pineiro, (2010) 3 *InDret* 1–23 and more generally A. Dutta, [2008] *Lloyds Maritime and Commercial Law Quarterly* 88 and G. McCormack, (2014) 15 *European Business Organization Law Review* 309.

135 The Regulation has been held to apply where the defendant in an insolvency-related action is resident outside the EU – see *Schmid v Hertel* (Case C-328/12 OJ 2014 C85/5); (2014) 1 WLR 633.

an insolvency linked action other than avoidance actions being highlighted as an example of the term.

122. It is clear from the case law, however, that the category of insolvency relations includes actions based on insolvency law that seek to fix liability on company officers. In the leading case of *Gourdain v Nadler* the Court of Justice held that an action is related to insolvency if it derives directly from the insolvency and is closely linked to proceedings for realising the assets or judicial supervision.[136] In this case, a French court had made an order requiring a German-based director of a French company that was the subject of French insolvency proceedings to contribute to the assets of the company. The order was made under provisions of French insolvency law that appeared to impose personal liability on directors if they failed to take sufficient care to ensure that company creditors had been paid in full. In essence, the Court of Justice held that the proceedings were insolvency-related proceedings since the basis of the action stemmed from provisions peculiar to insolvency law or from insolvency law adjustments of general legal norms. It was right therefore that the defendant should be sued in the State that opened the insolvency proceedings and not in his State of domicile.

123. *Gourdain v Nadler* seems to stand as authority for a general proposition that proceedings are insolvency related if they arose from provisions that are distinctive to insolvency law or from adjustments of general legal norms that are brought about by insolvency law.

124. The Court of Justice has also held in *H v HK*[137] that the concept of insolvency-related actions extends to actions brought by the liquidator against a company director for reimbursement of payments which were made after the company became insolvent. The court considered the relevant provisions of German law under which the director of a debtor company must reimburse payments that he made on behalf of the company after it became insolvent or after it was established that the company's liabilities exceeded its assets. The provision clearly derogated from the common rules of civil and commercial law because of the insolvency of the debtor company. It required the actual insolvency of the debtor and it did not matter for this purpose that insolvency proceedings had not formally been opened.

125. Actions based on insolvency law that seek to set aside pre-insolvency transactions entered into by the debtor have also been held to fall within the category of insolvency-related actions. Moreover, Article 6 of the recast Regulation specifically mentions avoidance actions as an example of

136 The English version of the court judgment at para. 4 actually uses the French terms '*liquidation des biens*' and '*règlement judiciaire*'.

137 Case C-295/13 ECLI:EU:C:2014:2410.

insolvency-linked actions. Therefore, the courts of the State where insolvency proceedings have been opened have jurisdiction in respect of these matters rather than the courts of the State where the defendant is domiciled.

126. This is clear from *Seagon v Deko*[138] where Court of Justice was asked whether the State of the opening of insolvency proceedings had jurisdiction in respect of an action to set aside a pre-insolvency transaction that was brought against a company with a registered office is in another EU state. The court essentially answered this question in the affirmative, noting that the avoidance action was intended to increase the assets of the insolvent company. In this case, a German company that was the subject of German insolvency proceedings had transferred funds before the insolvency proceedings were opened to a Belgian company that had its centre of main interests in *Belgium*. The German IP sought to have the transfer set aside and repayment of the amount transferred. The court noted that under German insolvency law it was only the IP who could bring such an action in the event of the debtor's insolvency. Moreover, the sole purpose of the avoidance action was to protect the interests of the general body of creditors.[139]

127. This decision, however, is to be contrasted with that of the Court in *F-Tex SIA*.[140] In this case a German registered company had, while insolvent, transferred money to a Lithuanian-based recipient. The payer later became the subject of insolvency proceedings in *Germany* and, under German law, the transfer could be set aside by the IP. The IP, however, assigned to a creditor all the debtor's claims against third parties including the claim for reversal of the transfer. The court held that the exercise by the assignee of the right acquired was not closely connected with the insolvency proceedings in that the assignee could freely decide whether to exercise the right; if it did so, it acted in its own interest and for its personal benefit; the proceeds of the action were owned by it personally and did not increase the assets of the insolvent debtor. The court said that the fact that the assignee was obliged to pay the IP a percentage of the proceeds did 'not alter that analysis, since it is merely a method of payment'. Moreover, under German law, the closure of the insolvency proceedings did not affect the assignee's claim.[141]

128. It may be that this is a decision that is very much confined to its own facts and does not provide much in the way of general guidance. On the other hand, the case may provide some support for the view that not all avoidance type proceedings are within the Insolvency Regulation rather than Brussels I. Relevant factors may include whether the proceedings are brought by the

---

138 Case C-339/07 [2009] ECR 1-767.

139 See para. 16.

140 Case C-213/10 *F-Tex SIA v Lietuvos-Anglijos UAB* ECLI:EU:C:2012:215.

141 *Ibid.* at paras. 42–46.

liquidator or a third party and whether all the recoveries accrue for the benefit of the debtor's estate.

129. In the English case *Re Baillies Ltd*,[142] for instance, it was suggested that proceedings under section 423 of the UK Insolvency Act 1986 seeking to set aside transactions that defraud creditors were not insolvency proceedings within the European Regulations. The judge pointed out that the provision was applicable irrespective of whether there was a liquidation or some other form of insolvency process and any victim could have brought the proceedings at any time.

130. Nevertheless, there is a body of case law from the Court of Justice, including *H v K*, that adjustment of general legal norms brought about by insolvency are 'insolvency-related'. Proceedings under section 423, however, are not strictly speaking based on the insolvency of the debtor although they are concerned with putting assets beyond the reach of creditors or otherwise prejudicing the claims of creditors.

2.2. APPLICABLE LAW IN RESPECT OF TRANSACTIONAL AVOIDANCE ACTIONS

131. The courts of a State with jurisdiction to open insolvency proceedings also have jurisdiction in respect of actions that are 'insolvency-related' including transactional avoidance actions. Moreover, the applicable law in respect of the proceedings is the law of the State that opens the proceedings – Article 4. Article 4(2) states that the law of the State of the opening of proceedings shall determine the conditions for the opening of those proceedings, their conduct and their closure[143] and then sets out a non-exhaustive list of matters that are specifically referred to the law governing the opening of the proceedings. These matters are both substantive and procedural in nature and include '(m) the rules relating to the voidness, voidability or unenforceability of legal acts detrimental to all the creditors'.

132. Article 4 has been considered by the Court of Justice in *Kornhaas v Dithmar*.[144] The Court referred to the fact that the lex fori concursus determines the 'conditions for the opening' of the insolvency proceedings. The Court held that in 'order to ensure the effectiveness of that provision, it must be interpreted as meaning that, first, the preconditions for the opening

[142] [2012] BCC 554 at para. [13]. See also the civil law *action pauliana*.

[143] The concept of closure of insolvency proceedings must be interpreted according to national law. There is no autonomous Community-wide interpretation – see Case C-116/11 *Bank Handlowy and Adamiak*, para. 52.

[144] Case C-594/14 ECLI:EU:C:2015:806.

of insolvency proceedings, second, the rules which designate the persons who are obliged to request the opening of those proceedings and, third, the consequences of an infringement of that obligation fall within its scope'. The case concerned a company incorporated under UK law but with its centre of main interests in *Germany* and in respect of which insolvency proceedings had been opened in *Germany*. The application of the relevant provisions of German law was held not to infringe the EU rules on freedom of establishment. The German law was not concerned with the formation of a company in a given Member State or its subsequent establishment in another Member State since the relevant law only applied after the company had been formed and after it had become insolvent.

133. Article 4(2)(m) makes it clear that legal acts detrimental to all the creditors may be challenged under the lex fori concursus. There are specific provisions in Articles 5, 6 and 7 of the Regulation clarifying that transactions involving third party security rights, set off and reservation of title may also be challenged on this basis under the provisions of the lex fori concursus. While these provisions mention only Article 4(2)(m), it is now generally accepted from the case law of the Court of Justice that the exception to the Article 4(2)(m) general rule represented by Article 13 must be applied.[145]

134. The regime brought about by the combination of Articles 4 and 13 does not apply however in the case of payments or transactions carried out in the context of payment systems and financial markets. Pursuant to Article 9(2), the law applicable in respect of transactional avoidance is the law that governs the relevant payment system or financial market. The policy reason behind this is to minimise the risk to these system and markets. Risk is minimised by submitting all operations arising out of them to only one law, that of the country where they are set up.[146] This conflict rule is in line with Directive 98/26/EC on settlement finality in payment and securities settlement systems.[147]

2.3. APPLYING ARTICLES 4 AND 13

135. In the light of Article 4, a transaction may be challenged in the framework of insolvency proceeding pursuant to the lex fori concursus. This law can be that

---

145 See Case C-557/13 *Lutz v Bäuerle* ECLI:EU:C:2015:227, para. 42.

146 The equivalent provision in the recast Regulation – Regulation 2015/848 – is Article 12(2). See also recitals of the original regulation and paras. 27 and 71 of the recast.

147 OJ 1998 L166/45. This Directive has been amended by Directive 2009/44/EC OJ 2009 L146/3 7 amending Directive 98/26/EC on settlement finality in payment and securities settlement systems and Directive 2002/47/EC on financial collateral arrangements as regards linked systems and credit claims.

governing main or secondary insolvency proceedings. In accordance with the Regulation, main insolvency proceedings may only be opened where the debtor has its 'centre of main interests' or COMI in an EU Member State and secondary proceedings may be opened where the debtor has an 'establishment' within an EU Member State. The possibility that proceedings may be started in two or more jurisdictions with differing laws means that conflicts between different transactional avoidance rules will inevitably arise. An attempt to minimise these problems is made by Article 27 (Article 34 in recast) through restricting the 'effects' of secondary proceedings to the 'assets of the debtor situated in the territory' of the Member State where the secondary insolvency proceedings are opened. There may be conflicts however concerning the situs of assets between the laws of different Member States, and so this provision will not eliminate all difficulties.

136. The lex fori concursus determines whether an act is subject to avoidance and its legal consequences, i.e. whether the act is void, voidable or unenforceable vis-à-vis the insolvency estate; the limitation periods; who has standing to challenge the act; and whether legal defences are available to the defendant in the avoidance action.

137. Where there is an attempt to impugn a transaction pursuant to the law governing the insolvency proceedings, the defendant in the avoidance action may argue that the act in question cannot be challenged pursuant to the lex causae. This is the Article 13 defence. Both Articles 4 and 13 only make reference to the law of a Member State. The application of Article 4 relies on a Member State having jurisdiction under the Regulation to open insolvency proceedings in respect of the relevant debtor. Article 13 gives an escape route from Article 4 where the person who benefited from an act detrimental to all the creditors provides proof that: (a) the act is subject to the law of a Member State other than that of the state of the opening of proceedings; and (b) that law does not allow any means of challenging that act in the relevant case. The wording suggests that the provision may not be applicable to the extent that the law governing the impugned transaction is that of a third State. Accordingly, where impugned transactions are governed by the law of a third State, it is up to the domestic law of each Member State to decide whether or not the transaction benefits from a rule similar to that enshrined in Article 13.

138. More generally, it is up to the counterparty to plead and rely upon the Article 13 defence. In other words, the defendant has to prove that the law governing the transaction is other than the lex fori concursus and that it does not allow any means of challenging the impugned transaction. The provision is an exception to the application of the lex fori concursus, i.e. to the general rule according to which transactional avoidance is submitted to the law governing the insolvency proceedings. As an exception, Article 13 is to be strictly interpreted and in accordance with its objective of protecting the legitimate expectations of the person benefitted by the challenged act.[148]

139. In the light of this strict interpretation, the defence can only be established where the transaction is concluded before the opening of the insolvency proceeding; otherwise, there would not be expectations to protect. The Court of Justice came to this conclusion in *Lutz v Bäuerle*.[149] The Court said that while the provision did not, in principle, apply to acts that take place after the opening of insolvency proceedings, the right being challenged in this particular case – a right to attach assets – had been established before the opening of the insolvency proceedings and therefore could benefit from special protection given by Article 13. The transaction was governed by Austrian law, which did not allow the transaction to be challenged and this was fatal to the liquidator's challenge under the law of the forum state, i.e. *Germany*.[150] The case confirms that the Article 13 defence also operates in respect of set off and reservation of title in spite of the fact that the relevant provisions in the Regulation provisions merely reference that they are subject to transactional avoidance as laid down by the lex fori concursus.

140. The Court of Justice in *Lutz v Bäuerle* also held that while the Article 13 defence is an exception that must be construed strictly, it applies in a broad range of situations and whenever either substantive or procedural rules (such as time limits or limitation periods) would prevent the bringing of the action. The Court said that if the Article 13 defence did not cover what were considered by the forum State to be procedural matters, that interpretation would lead to arbitrary discrimination according to the models of legal theory adopted in the different EU States and prevent a uniform application of Article 13.[151]

141. In *Nike European Operations Netherlands BV v Sportland Oy* the Court of Justice held that Article 13 'must be interpreted as meaning that its application is subject to the condition that, after taking account of all the circumstances of the case, the act at issue cannot be challenged on the basis of the law governing the act ("lex causae").'[152]

142. The terms of Article 13 are broader than those of Article 4(2)(m). While the latter refers to transactional avoidance in the sense of legal acts detrimental to all the creditors, Article 13 refers to 'any means of challenging that act in the relevant case', i.e. not only to the specifically insolvency rules on avoidance laid down by the lex causae, but also to any other rules dealing with voidness, voidability or

---

148 See Case C-557/13, para. 24; Case C-310/14 *Nike European Operations Netherlands BV v Sportland Oy, in liquidation*, para. 18.

149 Case C-557/13 ECLI:EU:C:2015:227.

150 *Ibid.* at para. 35.

151 *Ibid.* at paras. 47, 48.

152 Case C-310/14 ECLI:EU:C:2015:690, para. 22.

unenforceability of the act laid down in that legal system. Therefore, the person relying on Article 13 had to establish not only that the impugned transaction was not avoidable in accordance with the insolvency rules of the lex causae, but also under the general provisions and principles of that legal system that might permit a challenge.[153]

143. The Court said that it was for the defendant to provide proof, on the basis of the lex causae, that the act cannot be challenged. The defendant had to establish both the facts from which the conclusion can be drawn that the act is unchallengeable and the absence of any evidence that would militate against such a conclusion. The applicant was not required to claim or prove that the conditions were satisfied for the application of a provision of the lex causae which, in principle, would enable the act at issue to be challenged. On the other hand, while Article 13 expressly governed the burden of proof, it did not set out the ways in which evidence is to be elicited: what evidence is to be admissible before the appropriate national court, or the principles governing that court's assessment of the probative value of the evidence adduced before it. These were matters for each Member State but, in accordance with the principles of equivalence and effectiveness, these rules should be no less favourable than those governing similar domestic situations. These rules had to be sufficiently rigorous to prevent the shifting the burden of proof laid down in Article 13[154] but they should not make it excessively difficult or impossible in practice to exercise the right conferred by Article 13.

144. In the *Nike* case, insolvency proceedings had been opened in respect of a company in *Finland* and it was alleged that certain payments made by the company prior to the opening of the proceedings could be impugned under Finnish law. The counterparty was a Dutch registered entity and it asserted that the relevant transactions were governed by Dutch law which did not allow any means of challenging the transactions in the relevant case.

145. Article 30 of the Credit Institutions (Winding Up) Directive[155] is in similar terms to Article 13. Under the Directive, the law of the State that opens insolvency proceedings generally applies to those proceedings. This includes the 'rules relating to the voidness, voidability or unenforceability of legal acts detrimental to the creditors as a whole'. There is an exception however.

> 'where the beneficiary of these acts provides proof that:
> - the act detrimental to the creditors as a whole is subject to the law of a Member State other than the home Member State, and
> - that law does not allow any means of challenging that act in the case in point.'

153 See Case C-310/14, paras. 34 and 35.
154 *Ibid.* at paras. 25–29.
155 Directive 2001/24/EC on the reorganisation and winding up of credit institutions.

This provision was considered by the EFTA Court in *LBI v Merrill Lynch*[156] where certain transactions entered into by an insolvent Icelandic bank were challenged. The Icelandic bank had issued debt securities and shortly before it entered insolvency proceedings, it redeemed these securities. The IP sought the avoidance of the redemption transactions arguing that they were invalid under the relevant provisions of Icelandic law which, in certain circumstances, rendered invalid the repayment by an insolvent debtor of debts before these debts had matured. But the counterparty contended that the transaction constituted a purchase by the plaintiff of its own securities and not the repayment of a debt. In any event, it argued that, under Article 30 of the Directive, the measures in question could only be avoided if this were permissible under the law governing the debt securities which was English law and, in its view, rescission would not be possible under English law. The counterparty argued that the purpose of Article 30 was to ensure protection against retroactive actions by the debtor to invalidate a legal act where the creditor had legitimate expectations that the act would be binding on the debtor.

146. The EFTA Court held that the counterparty could avail of both procedural and substantive defences. There had to be a concrete assessment of the specific transaction and it was enough if the counterparty established that there was no possibility, or no longer any possibility, of challenging the transaction. Even if, in principle, the transaction could be challenged under the lex causae, it was sufficient if the beneficiary proved that the requirements for such a challenge were not fulfilled in the case at hand. Nevertheless, whether the counterparty had shown that the law governing the transaction did not allow any means of challenging it, this had to be assessed according to the rules of the forum State for determining the substance of foreign law.[157]

147. By way of conclusion, the case law on Article 13 (and the equivalent provision in the Credit Institutions Directive) as a whole seems to support the following propositions:

(a) In principle the Article 13 defence is to be strictly interpreted.
(b) Nevertheless, it potentially applies where transactions involving security rights, set off and reservation of title are sought to be impugned on the basis of Article 4(2)(m).

[156] Case E-28/13 <http://www.eftacourt.int/press-publications/detail/article/judgment-in-case-e-28 13-lbi-hf-v-merrill-lynch-int-ltd/> accessed 10 May 2016. See generally A. Keay, [2016] *European Law Review* 72 at 82 who suggests that the Court of Justice in *Lutz v Bäuerle* took the same approach as the EFTA Court in *LBI v Merrill Lynch*.

[157] Paragraphs [78]–[81] of the judgment.

(c) The Article 13 defence covers both substantive and procedural matters including limitation periods for the bringing of avoidance actions.[158]
(d) The person relying on the Article 13 defence cannot simply assert that the latter is unchallengeable pursuant to its governing law, but also has to provide evidence that the specific transaction is subject to a law other than the lex fori concursus; and moreover, that that law does not allow any means to challenge the transaction in the light of the concrete circumstances of the case.[159]
(e) In principle, the defendant has to show that the transaction is not avoidable under both the insolvency rules of the lex causae and also in accordance with the general rules and principles of that legal system.
(f) National rules of procedure cannot be applied that would make reliance on Article 13 impossible or excessively difficult, especially in connection with proof of the negative, namely that certain circumstances did not exist.
(g) On the other hand, the national rules of evidence must be sufficiently robust to mitigate the risk of any shifting of the burden of proof laid down in Article 13.[160]
(h) The defendant bears the burden of proof in respect of adducing evidence of foreign law but, in principle, it is for the national procedural rules to determine how the content of foreign law is to be established.

3. REFORM CONSIDERATIONS

148. Articles 4(2)(m) and 13 of the original Insolvency Regulation have been preserved in the same terms in the recast. The European Commission report on the application of the Insolvency Regulation[161] points out that despite the significance of transactional avoidance in the framework of insolvency proceedings, international cases are rare.

149. The fact that dysfunctions have not been found in practice has been advanced as a ground to maintain the status quo and there are also some further arguments to support the status quo. One argument is that the characterisation of transactional avoidance as an insolvency matter justifies the submission of this matter to the lex fori concursus. This approach is in line with the objectives of insolvency law and in keeping with the approach adopted in respect of matters such as the rules on directors' liability in the context of insolvency and

[158] See Case C-557/13, paras. 47, 48 and 53.
[159] See Case C-310/14.
[160] See Case C-310/14, para. 29.
[161] COM (2012) 733 final, 14.

restructuring plans. Nevertheless, the protection of legitimate expectations and the certainty of transactions is considered a legitimate interest by many stakeholders who speak against the uncertainty of having the transaction dependent on a non-predictable law; namely, the law governing the insolvency proceedings. The lex causae is more or less fixed at the time of the transaction but insolvency proceedings may be opened in different States depending on where the debtor's COMI or establishment may be at a particular point in time.

150. In favour of change, however, one could argue that the lack of cases may speak more of the difficulties in avoiding a cross-border transaction because of the combined application of two different laws. In this vein, the European Parliament suggested that the Insolvency Regulation should be amended to the extent that Article 13 'does not encourage cross-border avoidance actions but helps to prevent avoidance actions from succeeding by means of choice-of-law clauses'.[162]

151. The policy reflected in the Article 13 rule may be criticised on four inter-related grounds. The first is that the rule compromises the primacy of the forum state and partly undermines the goal of universality of insolvency proceedings that the Regulation is supposed to embody. Recital 12 of the preamble to the Regulation (recital 23 of recast)[163] refers to main insolvency proceedings in the debtor's COMI having universal scope and aiming to encompass all the debtor's assets. Article 13 is an exception eating away at the universalist principle and so much so that a US commentator has criticised the Regulation as 'essentially a territorial system with universalist pretensions'.[164]

152. Secondly, a transaction will escape avoidance unless it is avoidable under the laws of both the forum State and the State whose laws otherwise govern the transaction.[165] Such a rule with double avoidance requirements narrows greatly the potential application of avoidance provisions and weakens greatly implementation of the policies underlying such provisions such as fairness and maintaining priority entitlements.[166]

153. Thirdly, there is a mismatch between the mandatory goals of the forum State as reflected in its insolvency avoidance laws and the transactional integrity rationale of the Article 13 defence. Avoidance laws are concerned with

---

162 European Parliament resolution of 15 November 2011 with recommendations to the Commission on insolvency proceedings in the context of EU company law (2011/2006(INI)), Annex, para. 2(5).

163 But see also recital 14 of recast.

164 See F. Tung, (2001) 23 *Michigan Journal of International Law* 31 at 77 and see also J. Pottow, (2006) 104 *Michigan Law Review* 1899; (2005) 45 *Virginia Journal of International Law* 936.

165 See Virgós–Schmit Report (fn. 22) paras. 35–39.

166 J. Westbrook, (1991) 17 *Brooklyn Journal of International Law* 499 at 518 and for an empirical study see G. van Dijck, (2008) 17 *International Insolvency Review* 123.

vindicating the mandatory policies and principles of the forum State and setting aside transactions between the parties to give effect to these wider goals. But the Article 13 defence runs in the opposite direction by trumping these wider goals in the interests of party autonomy. The parties also have a very wide autonomy to structure their transaction in such a way that it is effectively immune from challenge.

154. The fourth criticism centres on the fact that the actual language used in Article 13 lacks complete clarity, though many of these interpretative difficulties have been resolved by the recent case law of the Court of Justice.

155. In considering possibilities for reform, there are essentially four options, though the fourth option is decidedly modest.[167] The first is to apply exclusively the law of the forum state. In other words, if insolvency proceedings are opened in a particular jurisdiction, that jurisdiction should apply its own substantive avoidance law in respect of transactions that involve the debtor, no matter how strong the foreign factors may be in a particular case. It could be argued that characterisation of transactional avoidance as an insolvency matter makes the lex fori concursus more suitable than any other law, or combination of laws, to govern the issue. On the other hand, one is faced with the issues of certainty of transactions and protecting legitimate expectations. In this connection, however, it should be noted that the provisions of the 'recast' Insolvency Regulation contain some measures to combat 'abusive' forum shopping. The importance of the debtor's centre of main interests is reinforced as a connecting factor,[168] and the opening of secondary insolvency proceedings is made more exceptional.[169] Against this background, it is difficult not to acknowledge that creditors are in general aware of their debtor's centre of main interests and thus of the law governing the main insolvency proceedings, including transactional avoidance.

156. INSOL Europe in their proposals for revision of the Insolvency Regulation have suggested that it was undesirable that a transaction could be rendered 'avoidance proof' by a choice of law clause in the transaction.[170] On the other hand, they were also conscious of the fact that COMI relocation might be detrimental to a counterparty if avoidance proceedings were easier to institute

---

167 See J. Westbrook, (1991) 17 *Brooklyn Journal of International Law* 499 at 525.

168 While the debtor's centre of main interests is now defined in Article 3(1) and recital 28 of Regulation 2015/848, Article 3(2) and recitals 29 to 31 provide for presumptions of where that centre is located making it clear that they are strong presumptions in line with *Eurofood* and *Interedil*. Anyway, the insolvency court is obliged to examine this issue *ex officio* and bound to explain its decision (see Article 4), which can always be challenged by creditors (see Article 5).

169 See Chapter III of Regulation 2015/848 and, in particular, Article 36 dealing with the conclusion of undertakings with a view to avoiding the opening of secondary insolvency proceedings.

170 R. van Galen et al., *Revision of the European Insolvency Regulation. Proposals by INSOL Europe* 11.

under the new COMI. It therefore suggested the following amendment: 'Article 4 (2) (m) shall not apply if the law of the Member State where the centre of main interests of the debtor was situated at the time of the legal act does not allow any means of challenging that legal act in the relevant case'.

157. Moreover, and depending on the extent of harmonisation, the issues of certainty and legitimate expectations are much less of a problem if substantive transactional avoidance law is at least partially harmonised across Europe. We consider divergences between transactional avoidance law across Europe and the harmonisation of this branch of insolvency law in Chapter 4.

158. The second reform possibility is to apply the law of the foreign jurisdiction – the lex causae – assuming that the act or transaction in question is subject to the law of that foreign jurisdiction. This might enhance the certainty of transactions but it also might increase costs for the IP and make its task more difficult. Essentially, the IP would have the task of ascertaining the content of potentially multiple foreign transactional avoidance laws and deciding whether to pursue an avoidance action under these laws would be worthwhile.

159. A third possibility is to allow avoidance if the law of either the home jurisdiction or the foreign jurisdiction permits avoidance. This means that an IP who is seeking to challenge a transaction entered into by the debtor can choose its battlefield by applying the avoidance law of whatever jurisdiction is most favourable to it. This possibility would greatly increase the chances of a transactional avoidance claim succeeding but would do so at the cost of upsetting the expectations of third parties and, for this reason, seems a non-starter.

160. The fourth approach is to limit the scope of the party autonomy granted by Article 13 by laying down that the law chosen by the parties to govern the impugned transaction must have some reasonable connection with the transaction. As a limitation on party autonomy it may not be very effective in practice for it would be a bold approach for the courts in a forum State to strike down as 'unreasonable' the choice by the parties of a governing law.

CHAPTER 3

SECURITY RIGHTS, NATIONAL LAWS AND POSSIBLE REFORMS

161. The previous chapters have highlighted the fact that security rights are considered to be vitally important and also the relatively privileged position of secured creditors in the context of the Insolvency Regulation and in particular Article 5 of the original and Article 8 of the recast Regulation. This chapter highlights the fact, however, that the law on security rights differs significantly between different Member States. These divergences may cause creditors to assess credit risk differently. Moreover, as a general proposition, EU Member States, including the States that form the subject matter of our study, do not score extremely well on the 'getting credit' indicator of the World Bank Doing Business survey. The chapter also considers how EU Member States fare in terms of other international indicators and asks how the relative positon of EU States might be improved in terms of the World Bank rankings. This leads on to possible reform measures and the question of convergence between the laws of Member States.

162. The chapter consists of three substantive sections. The first brief section sets the scene. It sharpens our consideration of the policy background and introduces the World Bank Doing Business project and the relatively poor position of EU countries on the World Bank rankings. The second section is far more extensive. It summarises the national reports on the state of the law on security rights in the EU Member States that form the subject matter of our study highlighting differences and similarities between these laws. It is divided into subsections as follows:

- terminology, legal families and EBRD's Core Principles and reform efforts in Central and Eastern Europe;
- basic features of credit and security laws;
- general features for the creation of security interests;
- enforcement of security interests;
- comparisons between countries.

163. The third section considers how the law in Member States measures up against international indicators such as the United Nations Commission on International Trade Law (UNCITRAL) Legislative Guide on Secured Transactions, the European Bank for Reconstruction and Development (EBRD) Model Law on Secured Transactions and the World Bank indicators. The third section also considers possible convergence between the laws of Member States and takes as a starting point the international indicators as well as the provisions on proprietary securities in the Draft academic European Common Frame of Reference (DCFR) on European private law.[171]

1. BACKGROUND AND POLICY

1.1. DIVERGENCES IN THE LAW, CREDIT RANKINGS AND THE WORLD BANK DOING BUSINESS PROJECT

164. Recital 11 of the preamble to the Insolvency Regulation (recital 22 in recast) suggests that 'as a result of widely differing substantive laws it is not practical to introduce insolvency proceedings with universal scope throughout the Union'. It cites in this connection the 'widely differing' national laws on security interests to be found in the Member States. Our study confirms the statement in the preamble that there are divergent views within Europe on the permissible limits of using assets as security.[172] Whether because of policy factors, legal inertia or political pressure group activity, some countries limit the priority of security rights or impose restrictions on the enforcement of security.[173] These differences between Member States may cause creditors to assess credit risk by reference to individual countries rather than on a Europe-wide basis, though undoubtedly a number of other factors enter into the assessment of credit risk and not just the law on security rights in a particular country.

165. Nevertheless, divergences in national law leading to divergent assessments of credit risk is one of the factors referenced by the European Commission in its September 2015 Action Plan on Building a Capital Markets Union.[174] The Action Plan is designed to strengthen Europe's economy and stimulate investment with a view to creating jobs. The Action Plan stresses the fundamental importance

---

171 For details see the website <www.sgecc.net> accessed 10 May 2016.

172 Recital 25 of the preamble to the Insolvency Regulation (recital 68 in recast) recognises, however, that security rights 'are of considerable importance for the granting of credit'.

173 See the statement by one of drafters of the European Insolvency Regulation, M. Balz, (1996) 70 *American Bankruptcy Law Journal* 485 at 509. For arguments in favour of the 'full' priority of secured claims see J. Armour, (2008) 5 *European Company and Financial Law Review* 3 and J. Armour, 'Should We Redistribute in Insolvency?', in J. Getzler and J. Payne (eds.), *Company Charges: Spectrum and Beyond*.

174 COM (2015) 468. For discussion of the Capital Markets Union see the symposium in (2015) 9 *Law and Financial Markets Review* 187–209 and see also G. Ringe, (2015) 9 *Law and Financial Markets Review* 5.

of stronger capital markets in providing new sources of funding for business, helping to increase options for savers and building up economic resilience. It highlights the fundamental role of law and legal structures, including insolvency and credit law more generally, in this process.

166. The Action Plan refers to the fact that the free flow of capital is one of the core foundation stones on which the European Union is built, but that Europe's capital markets are still relatively underdeveloped and fragmented. The Action Plan suggests that more integrated capital markets will lead to efficiency gains and support the EU's ability to fund growth.

167. The Action Plan and the accompanying staff working document[175] refers, inter alia, to difficulties for investors in assessing credit risk, particularly in respect of cross-border investments, given the fact that there are 28 divergent insolvency regimes in the EU. In this connection, the Action Plan references the World Bank *Doing Business* reports and rankings.[176]

168. The Doing Business reports and rankings have been issued annually since 2004 and they purport to measure a number of matters including 'getting credit' and 'resolving insolvency'. In general, EU countries perform well on the 'resolving insolvency' indicator and not so well on the 'getting credit' indicator.[177] On the 'resolving insolvency' report for 2016, *Finland* ranks 1st with *Germany* 3rd and *Portugal, Denmark, Belgium*, and the *Netherlands* ranked between 8th and 11th respectively. The *UK* follows at 13th and *Cyprus, Austria* and *Sweden* come 17th to 19th respectively. *Slovenia* is the first of the former 'Eastern bloc' countries and comes in 12th followed by *Czech Republic* at 22nd. Generally on the indicator Nordic and Western European countries score much better than Eastern European ones though in fact *Malta* is the lowest ranking EU Member State at 83rd.

169. In relation to the 'getting credit' indicator, *New Zealand* is 1st with the *US, Colombia* and *Rwanda* as joint 2nd, and *Australia* and *Mexico* as joint 5th. The highest ranked EU countries are *Romania* at joint 7th and then *Poland*, the *UK, Latvia* and *Hungary* at joint 19th. *Germany, Ireland, Denmark, Estonia, Czech Republic, Lithuania* and *Bulgaria* are all bunched together and follow at equal 28th. But some other EU countries fare much poorer. For instance, *France*,

---

175 See SWD (2015) 183 final and SWD (2015) 184 final. See in particular pp. 24–25 of the Action Plan and pp. 73–78 of the staff working document.

176 See the statement at p. 25 of the Action Plan – COM (2015) 468: 'The 2015 World Bank *Doing Business Report* ranks countries on the strength of their insolvency frameworks on a scale of 0–16. The EU simple average is 11.6, which is 5% below the OECD average for high income countries (12.2). Some Member States score below 8.' For suggestions of caution in the use of the report and rankings see generally G. McCormack, [2015] *Insolvency Intelligence* 119.

177 The reasons for the relatively poor performance on the 'getting credit' indicator are explored in Chapter 3.

the *Netherlands* and *Greece* are ranked equal 79th. Some of the results on the 'getting credit' indicator seem counter-intuitive. For example, despite the recent history of violence and political instability in these countries, *Colombia* and *Rwanda* score equal 2nd.[178]

170. It should be noted that the Doing Business methodology and the underlying legal origins literature on which it is based has been criticised for a supposedly US-centric methodology.[179] Essentially, the Doing Business reports use a creditor-centred approach with the highest grading given to countries that emphasise private contractual solutions rather than court-based ones. It may be that this approach is too one-dimensional. Certainly it has been criticised for a preference for free market solutions and deregulation over other values.[180] As a World Bank Independent Review Panel points out, the 'Doing Business project has, rightly or wrongly, been associated with a broad deregulation agenda.'[181]

171. The Independent Review Panel, commissioned by the World Bank, reported in 2013. Among other points, the Panel suggested that:

- the Doing Business report had the potential to be misinterpreted;
- it relied on a narrow information source;
- it only measured regulations applicable to categories of business that could be captured through its methodology;
- its data-collection methodology could be improved;
- it was not designed to help countries respond appropriately;
- the use of aggregate rankings was problematic.

The Review Panel was particularly concerned about rankings because they involve a process of aggregation across topics and this involved a value judgment about what was 'better' for doing business and how much better it was.

---

178 See generally on differences in outcomes when one measures 'law on the books' as distinct from its application in practice see M. Hallward-Driemeier and L. Pritchett, (2015) 29 *Journal of Economic Perspectives* 121.

179 See generally R. Michaels, (2009) 57 *American Journal of Comparative Law* 765 and the literature referred to therein.

180 See generally G. Sarfaty, (2009) 103 *American Journal of International Law* 647.

181 Page 11 of the *Independent Panel Review of the World Bank Doing Business Report* (World Bank, 2013). The Panel was chaired by Trevor Manuel, the former South African Minister of Finance. The Doing Business reports appear to have made some adjustments in response to the Independent Panel report but the fundamentals of the project remain unaltered – see p. vii of the foreword to the 2015 Doing Business report: 'Our attention has been drawn to many critiques by the Independent Panel on Doing Business, chaired by Trevor Manuel, which submitted its report in 2013. Following this report a decision was made to set a 2-year target to improve the methodology of Doing Business without damaging the overall integrity of this valuable publication.'

172. These criticisms apply with particular force to the 'getting credit' and 'resolving insolvency' indicators which are based on a more sophisticated version of the 'legal origins' or 'law matters' thesis developed by four economists – La Porta, Lopez de Silanes, Shleifer and Vishny.[182] They also draw to a certain extent upon the international standards in the field of secured credit law and insolvency law that have been developed by UNCITRAL and the World Bank itself. The Review Panel pointed out[183] that the 'getting credit' indicator does not measure directly what the indicator claimed to address. In reality, it measures whether a country has a secured transactions legal regime that allows entrepreneurs access to credit using movable property and a credit bureau system that has collected and distributed fundamental information about credit.

173. The first aspect purports to ascertain the extent to which certain elements are contained within the secured credit (collateral) and corporate insolvency (bankruptcy) laws of a particular country. The incorporation of these features in a country's laws will result in a positive score and the corollary also holds good. In other words, if some or all of the features are absent the country will get a poor grade.

174. The second aspect addresses the coverage, scope and accessibility of credit information that is available through credit reporting service providers such as credit bureaus or credit registries. 60% of the overall proportion of the ranking is made up of the 'legal rights' element and the remaining 40% is attributed to the 'sharing of credit information' element.

175. The relevant data is gathered through questionnaire responses by local lawyers and insolvency practitioners (IPs) and then verified through a study of laws and regulations as well as publicly available information on insolvency systems.[184] There is no attempt made to assess the actual availability of credit in a particular economy. The assessment is based on the 'law on the books' rather than its actual application in practice.[185]

176. It seems that unless one has laws on secured transactions that are modelled on the relevant US provisions – Article 9 of the US Uniform Commercial

---

182 See R. La Porta, F. Lopez de Silanes, A. Shleifer and R. Vishny, (1997) 52 *Journal of Finance* 1131; (1998) 106 *Journal of Political Economy* 113; R. La Porta, F. Lopez de Silanes and A. Shleifer refine the 'legal origins' thesis and defend it against criticisms in (2008) 46 *Journal of Economic Literature* 285.

183 *Independent Panel Review of the World Bank Doing Business Report*, 15.

184 For some explanation of the methodology on 'getting credit and 'resolving insolvency', see the World Bank 2016 Doing Business Report, 137–39 and 155–159.

185 See the 2016 Doing Business Report, v: 'the report does not attempt to capture a number of dimensions of macroeconomic stability, the prevalence of corruption, antitrust policies or the skills of the workforce, important as all these factors are for establishing a foundation for sustainable economic development. Even within the relatively small set of indicators included in *Doing Business* the focus is deliberately narrow'.

Code – then one will not do very well in the World Bank survey. *New Zealand*, *Australia* and *Canada* have all laws that are directly modelled on Article 9 and, along with the US, rank in the top 10 in the survey.[186] Article 9 has often been held out as 'state of the art' by secured credit reformers worldwide. Certainly, it has proved durable for the largest economy in the world and it has been tried and tested in mercantile practice and judicial interpretation. Its basic philosophy facilitates access to credit in terms of easy-to-comply-with rules for the creation of security interests and making those rules effective against third parties. Moreover, almost all kinds of assets may be collateralised. It has however to be viewed against the backdrop of US insolvency law, which restricts the enforcement of security during bankruptcy and restructuring proceedings.

177. Article 9, in its ideas and substance, is also reflected in the contents of Model Laws and Guiding Principles from international organisations including UNCITRAL and the World Bank in its Doing Business survey. For example the Doing Business project hails recent reforms in *Colombia* stating:[187] 'Colombia improved access to credit by adopting a new secured transactions law that establishes a functional secured transactions system and a centralized, notice-based collateral registry. The law broadens the range of assets that can be used as collateral, allows a general description of assets granted as collateral, establishes clear priority rules inside bankruptcy for secured creditors, sets out grounds for relief from a stay of enforcement actions by secured creditors during reorganization procedures and allows out-of-court enforcement of collateral'.

178. On the other hand, few if any EU countries, with the partial exception of the accession countries in Central and Eastern Europe, have laws that are modelled on Article 9. This partly explains the poor ranking of the countries under consideration in this study in the World Bank Doing Business rankings. In the third and final question of this chapter we will return to the Doing project and ask whether it can provide any inspiration for convergence efforts in respect of secured transactions law in the EU Member States.

179. The next section of this chapter now focuses on the countries in the study and considers the main features of their laws in respect of secured transactions/ secured credit.

186 It appears that Colombian and Rwandan law has also been remodelled along US lines – see <http://www.doingbusiness.org/reforms/overview/economy/colombia> and <http://www.doingbusiness.org/reforms/overview/economy/rwanda> both accessed 10 May 2016.

187 <http://www.doingbusiness.org/reforms/overview/economy/colombia/> accessed 10 May 2016 and see also World Bank 2016 Doing Business Report, 16.

2. NATIONAL LAWS ON SECURITY RIGHTS – SYNTHESISING THE NATIONAL REPORTS

2.1. TERMINOLOGY, LEGAL FAMILIES AND EBRD'S CORE PRINCIPLES AND REFORM EFFORTS IN CENTRAL AND EASTERN EUROPE

2.1.1. Terminology

180. In this Report, the term 'security right' (or 'security rights') denote security devices having *in rem effects*, known also as 'proprietary rights' especially in Anglo-Saxon legal systems. Each of the countries covered by this Report recognises such a class of security devices.

181. Even though some of the countries covered by this Report do not have a statutory or a universally recognised definition, the meaning of *security right* is very similar, if not identical. Hence, the definition borrowed from the National Report on Common Law Systems may be taken as appropriate for all the jurisdictions. According to this definition, a security right is 'a right over property to ensure the payment of money or the performance of some other obligation'[188] and the security right is enforceable against third parties and not just inter partes, i.e. between debtor and creditor.

182. Security rights in the above sense should be distinguished from *personal security devices*, likewise known by all countries covered by this Report (e.g. suretyship or bank guarantee). These do not grant a right over property to ensure the payment of money or the performance of some other obligation and hence will not be covered by this Report.

183. Transactions with economically identical or similar effects yet which, according to some or all jurisdictions covered in this Report, represent distinct legal categories from security rights, are referred to as '*quasi-securities*.' The variants of 'leasing' contracts or contracts containing retained title (ownership) are the most common examples of such transactions. As functional equivalents of security rights, these transactions are covered in the report.

2.1.2. Usefulness of classifications based on legal families

184. This project set out by recognising that while producing separate reports for the Common Law, Germanic and Roman legal systems is largely self-explanatory, recognising the concept of Eastern European legal family may be

---

[188] Common Law NR, para. 2.

problematic. Indeed, on a purely theoretical plane the teachings on legal families readily dictate such a conclusion given that the Central and Eastern European (CEE) legal systems bear the traits either of Germanic or Roman legal systems, or a mixture thereof.

185. The same conclusions can also be reached in relation to insolvency law. The countries of the region have generally passed new insolvency laws taking the laws in one of the major Western European legal systems as the benchmark. These systems have also followed the same practice in relation to restructuring and reorganisation law but also had regard to Chapter 11 of the US Bankruptcy Code.

186. If one relied exclusively however on the teachings on legal families, this would lead to mistaken conclusions especially with respect to the law on security rights. While the German law of in rem securities – one of the traditional models for CEE countries – has remained intact during the last few decades, essentially all the CEE jurisdictions have reformed their systems and mainly followed common law models. This, in particular, meant the introduction in the 1990s of new registries for registration of security interests on movables and intangibles. As a result, the creation of security rights in these systems is today invariably registrable. This is in stark contrast with German and other Germanic laws which is characterised by recognition of latent security rights. In short, it would be an error to presume that the findings of the Germanic national report are applicable also to those CEE systems that used to follow German law in the past. The same applies to *Romania*, a traditional follower of French law, where the secured transaction system was reformed largely on the lines of Article 9 of the US Uniform Commercial Code.[189]

187. Moreover, it may be said that the Roman legal systems addressed in this Report have been influenced by the concept of quasi-security interests originating in common law countries.

2.1.3. EBRD Core Principles and reform efforts in Central and Eastern Europe

188. As an internationally recognised benchmark to assess the quality of national security rights systems, one may refer to the Core Principles for a Secured Transactions Law formulated by the European Bank for Reconstruction

[189] See e.g. V. Padurari and A. Burtoiu, 'Taking Stock of Romanian Secured Transactions after 15 Years of Reform: A mapping of past, present and future milestones', in F. Dahan (ed.), *Research Handbook on Secured Financing in Commercial Transactions*; N. de la Peña and H. Fleisig, (2014) 29 *Review of Central and East European Law* 133 at 164; as well as I. Smeureanu and F. Giurgea, 'Enforcement of Contracts in Romania', in S. Messmann and T. Tajti (eds.), *Case Law of Central and Eastern Europe – Enforcement of Contracts*, 726.

and Development (EBRD).[190] As explained in Chapter 1, this organisation was established in the early 1990s to help the transition from a planned (socialist) economy to a market economy in Central and Eastern Europe at the beginning of the 1990s. Having recognised that access to credit and rudimentary secured transaction laws are major obstacles, EBRD at an early stage commenced its secured transactions law reform project. This project has produced not only a Secured Transactions Model Law (1994)[191] but also developed ten core principles. EBRD has proclaimed that '[t]he principles are drawn on the assumption that the role of a secured transactions law is economic. It is not needed as part of the essential legal infrastructure of a country: its only use is to provide the legal framework which enables a market for secured credit to operate.'[192]

189. These principles require that:

- The law should enable the quick, cheap and simple creation of a proprietary security right without depriving the person giving the security of the use of his assets.
- If the secured debt is not paid the holder of security should be able to have the charged assets realised and to have the proceeds applied towards satisfaction of his claim prior to other creditors.
- Enforcement procedures should enable prompt realisation at market value of the assets given as security.
- The security right should continue to be effective and enforceable after the bankruptcy or insolvency of the person who has given it subject to the possibility of a short-term moratorium during insolvency proceedings.
- The costs of taking, maintaining and enforcing security should be low.
- Security should be available (a) over all types of assets, (b) to secure all types of debts and (c) between all types of person.
- There should be an effective means of publicising the existence of security rights.
- The law should establish rules governing competing rights of persons holding security and other persons claiming rights in the assets given as security.
- As far as possible the parties should be able to adapt security to the needs of their particular transaction.

190. In general, according to the National Reports submitted as part of the Project, the various national laws are said to satisfy the requirements of the EBRD Core Principles though subject to certain qualifications.

---

190 See generally <http://www.ebrd.com/what-we-do/legal-reform/access-to-finance/transactions.html> accessed 10 May 2016.

191 See <http://www.ebrd.com/what-we-do/legal-reform/access-to-finance/transactions.html> accessed 10 May 2016. For analysis see, for example, G. McCormack, *Secured Credit and the Harmonisation of Law: The UNCITRAL Experience*, 105 et seq.

192 The Principles are available for download at the EBRD website.

191. In relation to *German* law, the most contentious issue is the lack of publicity as far as the main contract-based security devices are concerned (security transfer, retained title and security assignment). The Germanic National Report however stresses that the lack of provision of public notice about the existence of a security right does not 'negatively affect the German credit market;' in fact it is 'attractive for many borrowers.'[193]

192. As far as *English* law is concerned, although it 'scores quite well'[194] against the EBRD benchmark principles, it suffers from three main weaknesses. Firstly, the various security devices are scattered around various, often distinct, branches of law and as a result 'there is no single reference point for determining priorities between competing security interests in the same property.'[195] Secondly, there is a tension between security rights law and the policy goals of corporate rescue and rehabilitation. Thirdly, 'the relatively formalistic preoccupations of the law coupled with the fact that the law is not contained in a single source but in a mixture of common law and statute, and for this reason is not easily saleable internationally.'[196]

193. While the Roman systems (*France*, *Italy* and *Spain*) are also said to satisfy the EBRD Core Principles, they are somewhat rigid and have been described as 'debtor-oriented'.[197] Perhaps the most important caveat is that 'most security rights on movable assets are possessory with the result that their creation deprives the debtor of the use of his assets.'[198] Additionally, use of after-acquired property as collateral is also quite restricted (i.e. the movable to be used as collateral must be owned either by the debtor or by a third party at the time of the conclusion of the security agreement).

194. The post-socialist systems of Central and Eastern Europe that are the focus of the CEE National Report (*Hungary*, *Lithuania* and *Poland*) are in a peculiar position as far as their compatibility with the EBRD Core Principles is concerned. They have reformed their security rights law, directly or indirectly, either with the assistance of the EBRD, or at least taking into account the standards set by EBRD's Secured Transactions Law Reform team. As a result, all three countries now have a new specifically established registry system for the registration of security rights on movables, thereby providing public notice of such securities in a similar fashion to *England* and in contrast to *Austria* or *Germany*.[199] Nor are

---

193 See Germanic NR, para. 6.
194 Common Law NR, para. 12.
195 *Ibid.*
196 *Ibid.*
197 Roman NR, para. 25.
198 *Ibid.*
199 CEE NR, Question 6, para. 104 et seq.

there continuing obstacles for the creation of security rights over future assets in these countries.

195. Perhaps the most problematic issue for the CEE countries is in relation to the efficient enforcement of security rights, given that these systems still look at out-of-court remedies with a great deal of suspicion. This is the case notwithstanding changes aiming at increasing the efficiency of enforcement such as the privatisation of bailiffs systems, the appearance of private debt collection companies, and opening the doors to limited forms of self-help repossession.

2.2. BASIC FEATURES OF CREDIT AND SECURITY LAWS

196. In setting the scene for a comparative overview, one may ask whether the various national laws on secured credit have been significantly amended (or reformed) in the recent past and whether such reforms are contemplated by policy-makers. Secured transactions or personal property security law (in the common law vernacular) has clearly been the focus of reform efforts with the rules governing security over immovable property (mortgage law) changing comparatively little.

From this perspective, the systems could be classified as follows.

197. *Hungary*, *Poland* and *Lithuania* – like for most of the post-socialist Central and Eastern European (CEE) jurisdictions – ought to be classified as *reformed systems*. Essentially all of them has embarked on a major upgrading of their security laws in the post-1990 period typically following an international model (e.g. EBRD Secured Transactions Model Law). As a result of the sweeping overhaul of these laws, they have had a *comprehensive reform* of their laws with a significant infiltration of elements from the common law.[200]

198. *France* has also began the revamping of its law in the 21st century in a series of gradual steps and in a less comprehensive manner. Before that, it introduced a version of the enterprise (floating) charge and a system of registration for the leasing of motor vehicles. In both these respects, there have been some resemblances with English law and the laws of the common-law inspired CEE reform systems.

199. Nevertheless, the 2016 World Bank Doing Business Reports show that, as far as the 'getting credit' criterion is concerned, *France* still ranks very low at

---

200 See, e.g., T. Tajti, 'Post-1990 Secured Transaction Law Reforms in Central and Eastern Europe' in *Bulletin of the Chamber of Public Notaries of Szeged*, also available at <http://www.SSRN.com> accessed 10 May 2016.

79th place, behind not just the UK (19th place), *Germany* (28th), *Spain* (59th) but also the reformed CEE systems (*Hungary* – sharing 19th place with the *UK*).[201]

200. The other Roman legal systems, *Italy* and *Spain*, have so far failed to embark on the comprehensive reform of their security laws. A number of novel features have entered these jurisdictions, however, through organic growth, transplantation or other forms of cross-border movement of law. For example, each of the three systems have imported some transactions that qualify as quasi-securities, notably from common law jurisdictions.[202] The versions of leasing might be the best examples, be it the financial leasing known to Italian law[203] or the sale and lease back of Spanish law.[204]

201. *German* law, as a mature and developed European system serving as a source of inspiration to other countries, is an interesting case study as far as security law is concerned. Despite the traditionally strict adherence of German law to systems thinking and, in particular, the basic principle of property law known as the numerus clausus, in the 19th century it started to allow for a breach of these principles to satisfy business needs. This occurred through the practices followed by legal practitioners in drafting security contracts and in the acceptance of these practices and innovations by German courts. In other words, irrespective of the fact that there was no formal reform of security laws, the reality was that the system became very business-friendly through the invention of new security devices. Moreover, these practices and devices spread to neighbouring countries as a result of the expansion of German banks and businesses. *Germany* is thus an example of a country where reforms have come about through organic growth.

202. Another model and approach to security law is represented by *English* law, which traditionally has been regarded as a creditor-friendly system but rests on the simple proposition that 'if not broken, don't mend it.' As a result, no comprehensive reform of security laws has yet been initiated. This does not mean, however, that laws touching upon security laws have not been changed in the meantime. The 2002 Enterprise Act, for example, has brought about changes that make the well-known English security device – the floating charge – less powerful in an insolvency situation. Reform efforts have been successfully blocked by leading financial lawyers notwithstanding the continued insistence of some scholars on the need of reform following the US model in Article 9 of the Uniform Commercial Code.[205]

---

201 The country rankings are downloadable from <http://www.doingbusiness.org/rankings> accessed 10 May 2016.

202 See Roman NR, para. 1.

203 *Ibid.* at para. 518.

204 *Ibid.* at para. 519.

205 The Secured Transactions Law Reform project is today at the helm of the movement – see <http://securedtransactionslawreformproject.org> accessed 10 May 2016. See also the City of

203. While the reformed CEE systems have by and large managed to keep the law on security rights located in one or a small number of primary sources of law, the relevant laws in other countries are scattered over a number of different sources.[206] This is why it is justified to speak of the latter as compartmentalised systems with various forms of security instrument located at distant places of the legal system and also being subject to different, often conflicting legal regimes.

204. This has the additional consequence that the law is non-transparent and often difficult to find. This state of affairs may militate against the predictability that is so important for commercial law. The following comment in relation to English law may also be applied to the other compartmentalised systems to varying degree, i.e. there is a lack of 'a single reference point for determining priorities between competing security interests in the same property'.[207]

205. All of the systems, including the reformed or organically improving systems, appear to have some problematic feature in their security law. When considering a possible common European law on security rights, these matters require proper attention and treatment. The following are the most telling illustrations of the dimensions of the problems but are far from being exhaustive.

206. Firstly, although almost complete consensus exists in the *UK* that the 19th century Bills of Sale Acts governing security granted by individuals are outdated, no meaningful action has been taken so far to remedy the situation. It is not easy to comply with the requirements of the Acts in practice, notwithstanding the fact that non-compliance makes the security granted void. The Bills of Sale legislation was intended, among other matters, to protect consumer debtors by requiring the registration of non-possessory chattel mortgages[208] and also requiring the use of a certain prescribed form. Given, however, the 'obscure and archaic statutory provisions,'[209] consumer finance on secured basis is today predominantly done through quasi-security arrangements of hire-purchase or conditional sales.[210]

207. Secondly, in *Hungary*, the use of motor vehicles as collateral is problematic because of the unresolved status of the certificates of title of motor vehicles.

London Law Society Financial Law Committee User Guide for Secured Transactions Code and the Secured Transactions Code – Discussion Draft, available at <http://citysolicitors.org.uk/index.php?option=com_content&view=category&id=129&Itemid=469> accessed 10 May 2016.

206 For example, the Roman NR in para. 119 points out that '[t]he Spanish legal system for security rights in rem is spread over several laws.'

207 See Common Law NR, para. 12.

208 See, for example, G. McCormack, *Secured Credit and the Harmonisation of Law – the UNCITRAL Experience*, 95.

209 Common Law NR, para. 47.

210 *Ibid.*

This is anomalous given the fact that motor vehicles represent one of the most important types of movables that can be used as collateral. As a result of the secured transactions law reforms staring with the first amendment of the Civil Code provisions on security rights in 1996, registration of security interests on movables (chattel mortgages) has been introduced together with a new register that is maintained by the National Association of Public Notaries. In principle, security interests on motor vehicles could also be registered in this register. The law however is not fully clear about the relationship between entries in this register and entries on the face of the certificate of title. Certificates of title to motor vehicle are issued by other governmental bodies but transfers of title to motor vehicles can be achieved even if a no such certificate exists. This is often the case especially with older used cars.

2.2.1. Use of all types of assets as collateral

208. Generally, in principle, it is the case that all goods in commerce can be used as collateral.[211] But there are exceptions to this principle in all the legal systems. For example, the *Hungarian* Insolvency Act lists a number of asset types that may not be freely transferable and thus their pledging is either completely excluded or is subject to some specific restrictions. These include: national parks, historic buildings, public waters, land separated for restitution, former church estates separated for restitution, trade union membership fees, and unpaid taxes that have been deducted from an employee's wages before the opening of insolvency proceedings (against the employer) but have not been transferred to tax authorities.[212]

209. Furthermore, every system has provision for non-assignable claims and rights which cannot serve as collateral. Assignment may be excluded either by contract or by statutory law. For example, under *German* law a certain proportion of wages and other claims originating from an employment relationship (providing for a minimum social standard) is non-assignable.[213] Moreover, under German law, easements (e.g. land access rights) are not assignable either because they are deemed to be components of the beneficial real estate.[214] Neither is copyright assignable because of what is perceived to be its personal nature.[215]

210. Under *Spanish* law, the collateral provider must be the owner of the asset and have the right of disposal. This means, for example, that if naked ownership

---

211 For example, for Spain, see para. 164 of the Roman NR.
212 CEE NR, para. 84.
213 Germanic NR, para. 44.
214 *Ibid.* at para. 45.
215 *Ibid.* at para. 48.

(nuda proprietas) and usufruct[216] are held by different persons, both holders must agree on the use of such asset as collateral; otherwise, the transaction would not have effects towards third parties.[217] Spanish law is distinctive because the use of claims as collateral is not addressed by private law and neither does the law recognise the fiduciary transfer of claims. Notwithstanding this, the pledging of claims is commonly accepted and is of significant importance in business practice.[218]

2.2.2. Recognition of global securities covering all assets of the debtor

211. An important difference among the systems relates to the so-called global security, i.e. covering all assets of the debtor. In this respect, the floating charge of *English* law is the device with the longest history and as it has been exported virtually to all former UK colonies. It is also the most well-known such global security. It is, however, available solely in the case of corporate debtors and excluded in case of individuals.[219] In practice it normally operates together with its kin, the fixed charge, and is generally limited to circulating (shifting) assets of a corporate debtor[220] – fixed assets are encumbered by a fixed charge and the shifting assets by a floating charge.[221] Similarly to the German security devices on movables, the floating charge also springs from the practice of lawyers and judges and was designed to satisfy the 'needs of the commercial and industrial entrepreneurs of the time.'[222] There are only some specific aspects of the floating charge that have become the subject of statutory regulation (like the registration of floating charges) and there is no statutory definition of a floating charge. Therefore, one must resort to case law to determine its principal characteristics. The main feature seems to be that the security giver has 'control' over the charged assets and this entails a greater liberty to dispose of the assets in the ordinary course of business.[223] It should be pointed out, however, that the fixed charge has generally a higher priority ranking than the floating charge.[224]

212. *French* law also contains a similar comprehensive device as well as the pledge over a business.[225] In such a case, 'the subject of the security right is

216 *Black's Law Dictionary* defines usufruct – a term foreign to the common law – as follows: 'A right to use another's property for a time without damaging or diminishing it, although the property might naturally deteriorate over time. … In modern civil law, the owner of the usufruct is similar to a life tenant, and the owner of the thing burdened is the naked owner.'

217 Roman NR, para. 164.

218 *Ibid.* at para. 169.

219 Common Law NR, para. 45 et seq.

220 *Ibid.* at para. 50.

221 *Ibid.* at para. 53.

222 *Ibid.* at para. 51.

223 *Ibid.* at para. 54.

224 *Ibid.* at para. 56.

225 Roman NR, para. 202 et seq., in particular para. 205.

the totality of movable assets that make up a single entity at the service of the business activity, namely different tangible and intangible elements such as clients, merchandise, [raw] material, equipment, leases and industrial property rights.'[226] Enforcement of the security interest over the business is only possible by sale of the business as a whole. The assets making up the business cannot be sold separately.[227]

213. *Poland* and *Lithuania* have also introduced such wide-reaching security devices.

Lithuanian law recognises two versions of such a comprehensive security device: a narrower and a broader one. In the first version, asset groups made of shifting elements like equipment or receivables may be pledged. The latter is over all the assets of a company. The law requires in such cases the filing of a digital copy of the company's inventory with the Mortgage Registry.[228]

Similar to Lithuanian law, a full and a limited version of global security can also be created under Polish law. This possibility was introduced with the lex specialis Registered Pledge Act (1996). What makes the system somewhat unique is that, for example, mortgage of immovables or maritime mortgages cannot be covered by such global registered pledges. If they are also intended to be the subject of security, the security rights on them should be registered separately.[229]

214. *Hungary* had introduced initially with its first secured transactions law reform in 1996 such a global security device named the 'property encumbering charge', but the concept was discarded as unnecessary in the new 2013 Civil Code. With this new position Hungarian law has, in this respect, come close to the philosophy of German law according to which the same result can be achieved by combining different security interests.

215. Global security in *German* law would be contrary to the venerable 'specialty principle' requiring specification of specific individual assets used as collateral.[230] The rationale of this principle is to ensure that the system is clear and transparent so that it can always be clearly determined which asset is encumbered and which is not. Nevertheless, it is possible under German law to create security interests over whole generic classes of current and future assets without specifying every single item in the security agreement. In cases where a comprehensive security ownership agreement is combined with an equally comprehensive security assignment, the result may come close to that of a

---

226 *Ibid.* at para. 205.
227 *Ibid.*
228 CEE NR, para. 102.
229 *Ibid.* at para. 103.
230 Germanic NR, para. 139 et seq.

floating charge under English law.[231] This is possible because German case law has relaxed the specialty principle in the cases of security ownership and security assignments with a view to serving the needs of the economy; though certain restrictions apply also in such cases. A provision however, securing 'all claims arising from business operations [of debtor A]' would meet the requirements of German case law.[232]

216. In principle, *Italian* law does not recognise such global security devices though there is a debate about the so-called omnibus clauses that have been used by banks.[233] *Spanish* law makes provision for a business chattel mortgage, which is subject to registration in the Personal Property Registry in a specified manner.[234] Such business chattel mortgage automatically extends to after-acquired property. In order to be enforceable against third parties, however, the assets making up the property – the 'business' – must be specified and clearly identified in the underlying security agreement and in the registry.[235]

2.2.3. Creation of security interests over assets not yet owned by the debtor or not yet in existence

217. Generally speaking, the pledging of assets not yet owned and assets not in existence is possible in every system within the purview of this Report. The systems differ, however, in two main respects.

218. Some jurisdictions have specific rules for some asset types. For example, *French* law provides as a general principle that the pledging of other's property is invalid,[236] yet it does recognise the creation of encumbrances over all assets (present and future) of a company through specific explicit rules. *Spanish* law has a similar rule according to which apartments and business premises under construction (i.e. not yet in existence) may be mortgaged. This is a possibility because the building plans can be registered with the Land Registry.[237]

219. Systems differ also in respect of their regulatory technique. While under *English* or *Hungarian* law, pledging of after-acquired property is today possible as a general rule, French law comes close to this outcome via exceptions to the general rule.[238]

---

231 *Ibid.* at para. 139.

232 *Ibid.* at para. 143.

233 In Italy, it is also the principle of specificity that prevents the utilisation of such global securities. However, banking practice does recognise the so-called '*pegno omnibus*' (roughly: all-asset pledge) notwithstanding that the validity of such clauses is debated. As per the prevailing opinion, such clauses are valid only inter partes. Roman NR, para. 210.

234 Roman NR, para. 167.

235 *Ibid.*

236 *Ibid.* at para. 173.

237 *Ibid.* at para. 197.

238 *Ibid.* at para. 189.

220. *German* law also allows for pledging of both yet-to-be-acquired and yet-to-be-created assets. The two most important devices are the transfer of title by way of security ('*Sicherungsübereignung*')[239] and the 'assignment by way of security' ('*Sicherungsabtretung*').[240] Both devices can be called a security transfer as they entail the transfer of ownership rights for security purposes.

Both kinds of security transfer can take the form of an anticipated transfer of ownership by way of security ('*antizipierte Sicherungsübereignung/ Sicherungsabtretung*').[241] This is possible because the Civil Code (BGB) requires neither contemporaneous transfer of ownership and possession nor present ownership and possession as a prerequisite for the validity of a security agreement.[242] As a consequence, if this type of anticipated security agreement was made in respect of a movable that is not yet owned by the debtor at the time of the conclusion of the contract, 'the creditor acquires security ownership almost automatically at the moment title is transferred to the debtor by a third party.'[243]

221. A similar anticipated agreement can be made also when the buyer acquired an assets covered by a retained title (transfer of the expectant right to acquire title). Such expectant right – amounting to less than full right of ownership – has under German law quasi-in rem effects. This also means that it may be subject to transfer of title by way of security.[244]

222. *Italian* law validates agreements to pledge assets belonging to others but only with inter partes effect (i.e. not valid against third parties).[245]

223. *Hungarian* law explicitly states in its new 2013 Civil Code that a security interest may be registered also if 'the asset to be used as collateral does not exist, or the debtor does not own it, at the time of the registration of the security interest.'[246] Pledging of assets not currently owned by the debtor nor currently existing is also possible under *Lithuanian* law.

224. The *Polish* Civil Code does not have a general rule that would allow for security interests over assets that are not yet owned by the debtor or not yet in existence. Instead, it has specific rules by which the same general effects may be achieved. These were all introduced with the 1996 Registered Pledge Act

239 Germanic NR, para. 9.
240 *Ibid.* at para. 17 et seq.
241 *Ibid.* at para. 65 et seq.
242 *Ibid.* at para. 66.
243 *Ibid.* at para. 69.
244 *Ibid.* at para. 71.
245 Roman NR, para. 180.
246 New Hungarian Civil Code of 2013 §5:93(4).

that aimed to modernise Polish secured transactions law. These, in particular, include:

(a) automatic extension of security interests to products and proceeds of collateral and
(b) possibility to 'pledge' after-acquired (future) property, as well as the possibility to encumber not just the entirety of an enterprise but also some specific categories of assets of the enterprise.[247]

2.2.4. Relationship between the nature of the collateral and the applicable rules

225. The nature of assets used as collateral may significantly affect the legal rules. Although the primary distinction stems from the division of property (assets) into immovables or movables (including intangibles), other important divisions exist as well, as illustrated below.[248]

226. It is a common features of all systems that some specific types of property are subject to specific treatment. These commonly include: (a) ships and aircraft; (b) some intellectual property rights, and sometimes also (c) shares in limited liability companies.[249] Typically, these are subject to special statutes and the security interests in respect of them are registrable in distinct registries.[250]

227. As far as mortgage of immovables is concerned, it is common to all systems that these contracts have to be in writing or in some special form with registration of the security right in a public register also required. These systems reach broadly the same conclusion though in somewhat different ways. In the case of *Germany*, for example, mortgage agreements are usually concluded before a public notary because that is the easiest way to ensure that the agreements will be immediately binding notwithstanding that as a principle – similar to the encumbering of movables – no strict formal requirements apply as far as

---

247 CEE NR, para. 95.

248 It is to be stressed that the basic classification of assets differs from system to system. While the differences among civil law systems tend to be negligible, there are significant differences between common laws and civilian systems. The common law thinks in terms of real (realty) versus personal property (personality) and personal property is *everything* that is not real property, including rights and claims (intangibles). The category of common law 'personal property' is not identical with the civilian category of 'movables' as strictly speaking the English term of 'movable' is limited only to tangible assets. International scholarship has resolved this discrepancy by presuming that the term 'movable' automatically includes also intangibles with the civilian concept of 'movable' equated with the common law concept of 'personal property. The same general approach is employed in this report and where the term 'intangibles' is used, this is to emphasise that a particular rule applies also to this type of asset.

249 CEE NR, para. 144 on Hungary.

250 See e.g. Germanic NR, paras. 15 and 153; Common Law NR, para. 81 and 82; Roman NR, para. 249 for Italy.

the underlying mortgage agreement is concerned.[251] In any event, for creation (perfection) of a valid mortgage on immovables, entry into the Land Register is a requirement.[252]

228. Under the *UK* Law of Property (Miscellaneous Provisions) Act 1989 section 2, a contract for sale or creation of a security interest over land must be made in writing and thus oral security interests in respect of land are impermissible.[253] The new 2013 *Hungarian* Civil Code introduced the writing requirement for all types of security agreements[254] and it also requires registration for perfection purposes (i.e. erga omnes effect or validity against third parties).[255] In the case of *Poland*, a notarised deed (writing) and registration is needed, save in the case of banking contracts.[256] Similar rules also apply in *France*.[257]

229. In *Hungary* a specific device, the security-bailment (similar to the possessory pledges in other legal systems and perfection by control under UCC Article 9 and under the EU Financial Collateral Directive), can be created solely on certain specific types of assets (cash, investment property and payment accounts).[258]

230. Under *Polish* law, a registered pledge cannot be created on assets that may either be mortgaged or subject to a maritime mortgage.[259] This rule aims to streamline and make clear that different regimes apply depending on the types of assets involved.

2.3. GENERAL FORMALITIES FOR THE CREATION OF SECURITY INTERESTS – CONVERGENCE AND DIVERGENCE

231. As a general rule, all the legal systems considered as part of this study require a security agreement for the creation of encumbrances over assets. On this point, *German* and *Austrian* law require the most significant qualification because actually these laws require two agreements: a property law agreement

---

251 Germanic NR, para. 157.

252 *Ibid.* at para. 87.

253 Common Law NR, para. 77.

254 Hungarian Civil Code §5:89(6). The linked comment stresses that while it is not the Civil Code that determines what exact formal requirements are required to enter a mortgage into the registers, the aim of the new Code's drafters was to simplify the rules. See L. Vékás (ed.), *Complex Commentary*, 430.

255 Hungarian Civil Code §5:88(a).

256 CEE NR, para. 151 and the related footnotes on Polish law.

257 Roman NR, para. 221.

258 CEE NR, para. 83.

259 *Ibid.* at para. 89.

and another agreement that forms part of the law of obligations. In practice often security agreements are separated into two parts, 'the part under the law of obligations law and the part under property law.'[260] This is a consequence of the application of the so-called separation principle (*'Trennungsprinzip'*) under these laws.

232. Although some systems recognise oral security agreements, in most cases, written or some specific form is either required by the law or – even if not required specifically by the law – is used for evidentiary or other practical reasons. In a sense therefore, the following statement of English law is applicable more generally as well: '[Although] [b]oth charges and pledges may be created orally … invariably there will be a written security agreement which may be … long and detailed.'[261]

233. It is a common denominator of *most* systems – both common and civil laws – that the creation (or perfection) of the security interest requires the provision of public notice in some recognised form.[262] This is a precondition to make it valid in all circumstances against third parties (erga omnes effect). The systems, however, differ as far as the exact perfection requirements are concerned. *German* law is the exception, however, to the general rule in respect of non-possessory securities on movables but the German law requirements with respect to the encumbering of immovables and transfer of possession to create a possessory pledge are in line with the other European systems.

234. It seems to be common to civilian legal systems that they require specific description (identification) of the secured claim and the collateral; otherwise, the transaction may be invalid.[263] While it is hard to 'measure', one may conclude that legal systems, to respond to business needs, have relaxed the principle of speciality and some countries are more 'liberal' in this respect than others.

235. Since however the formalities imposed for creating security over immovables and movables (including intangibles) differ significantly, it makes sense to consider them separately.

2.3.1. Formalities for the creation of security interests over immovables

236. In general, it may be stated that the creation of security over immovables typically requires the most formal requirements. Besides a written form, registration in a public register is generally also required. Moreover, typically

---

260 Germanic NR, para. 147.

261 Common Law NR, para. 75.

262 For Italian law see para. 228; for Spanish law see para. 235 of the Roman NR.

263 Spanish law allows for the provision of security to cover unspecified present and future obligations. This is possible as long as a maximum liability is set. See Roman NR, para. 214.

a special written form contract is needed. For instance, *Spanish* law requires a notarised document plus registration in the Land Registry.[264]

237. In *England* since 2003 the only way of creating a legal mortgage over registered land is by a charge by deed expressed to be by way of legal mortgage. The shorthand for this is a legal charge and the deed simply states that the property in question has been charged with the debt by way of legal mortgage. An equitable mortgage over land can arise in two situations. The first is where the 'owner' has merely an equitable rather than a legal interest in the property. In this circumstance, any mortgage is necessarily equitable in character. The second situation is where there is a contract to create a legal mortgage. Equity regards as done what ought to have been done and an equitable mortgage is deemed to come into existence as soon as there is a specifically enforceable contract for the creation of a legal mortgage.[265]

238. In some countries, certain practices have become established. In *Germany*, for example, banks usually conclude mortgage agreements before a public notary. This ensures immediate validity of contractual agreements on transferring or granting rights over real property and allows for immediate levy of execution if necessary.[266] In other words, 'the notarial deed … constitutes a legally enforceable document [and if] enforcement proceedings become necessary, the creditor (bank) does not have to file court proceedings in order to obtain an enforceable judgment but can commence the enforcement proceedings immediately.'[267] More generally, parties usually need public notaries, and the form of a notarial deed, in real estate transactions in order to ensure that the whole registration process runs smoothly.

2.3.2. *Formalities in respect of the creation of security interests over movables (including intangibles)*

239. As far as the pledging of movables is concerned, we may conveniently divide the discussion into possessory and non-possessory securities.

240. Although one may be tempted to think that the rules on possessory pledges are equal in all systems, in fact that is not so. One may distinguish between two groups of systems: first, systems which presume that transfer of possession is sufficient to provide public notice of the creation of the security interest, and second those that require something in addition to that – but not registration in a public register. As an example of the latter, *Polish* law requires a written

264 Roman NR, para. 235.
265 Common Law NR, para. 79.
266 Germanic NR, para. 157.
267 *Ibid.*

document with a certified date;[268] similar to *French* law (Article 2336 of the French Civil Code). *German*,[269] *Austrian*,[270] *Italian*[271] and *Spanish* law[272] may be examples of the former in that they presume that transfer of possession is the appropriate way to inform third parties of the security interest.

241. *Hungary*'s distinct nominated security devices – the security-bailment – represents another variant as it can be perfected in some cases by transfer of possession and in other situations by control. While a security-bailment on cash and certificated securities has to be perfected by transfer of possession, that on bank accounts is perfected by control,[273] though exceptionally perfection by registration in the charge register is also possible.[274] The Civil Code does not restrict the use of this particular type of security only to banks. At one time, cash was the traditional subject of the security-bailment but today bank accounts and investment property (certificated and dematerialised securities) seem to dominate.

2.3.3. Non-possessory securities

242. As far as some specific types of movables are concerned, all systems have special registers for the registration of security rights on such assets. Typical examples are ships, aircraft, some intellectual property rights and some types of securities (investment property). For example in the *UK*, legal mortgages of ships must not only be executed in a special prescribed form as laid down by the Merchant Shipping Act 1995 and the Merchant Shipping (Registration of Ships) Regulations 1993 but also registered in a special register.[275] In *Germany*, a pledge on aircraft must be registered in the applicable register at the Local Court in Braunschweig.[276] Provision for this is made in a special statute. In *Hungary*, pledging of shares in limited liability companies is subject to registration in the company registry.[277]

243. In *France*, while the Ministry of Civil Aviation registers security interests on aircraft, the Customs Office is responsible for the registration of maritime

---

268 See CEE NR, para. 152. See also the section on idiosyncratic solutions below.
269 See Germanic NR, para. 154.
270 *Ibid.* at paras. 159, 160.
271 Roman NR, para. 230.
272 *Ibid.* at para. 238.
273 CEE NR, para. 129.
274 *Ibid.* at para. 130.
275 Common Law NR, para. 81.
276 Y. Strothmann, 'Chapter on Germany', in W. Moojen and S. Truiden (eds.), *Bank Securities and Other Credit Enhancement Methods*, 158.
277 See CEE NR, para. 144.

mortgage.[278] In *Spain*, ship mortgages are to be registered with the Personal Property Registry.[279]

244. In *Italy*, however, in order to create a security interest on motor vehicles, there must be a written form document and entry in the Public Automobile Register (P.R.A.) maintained by the Italian Automobile Club, as well as annotation on the certificate of title (ownership).[280]

245. As far as other (general) movables are concerned, save for *Austrian, German* and *Italian* law,[281] the other civil law systems in the purview of this project have registries for registration of security rights on movables (and some also on rights and claims). The distinguishing feature of *German* law, for example, is that the system rests on latent (secret) security interests on movables, rights and claims.[282]

246. Other systems also recognise to a certain extent latent securities but compared to *German* law they are the exceptions rather than the rule. This qualification applies especially to *France* and *Spain*. In the case of the former, one could mention the *fiducie-garantie* that escapes registration.[283]

247. *Spain* has an integrated Personal Property Register, which was created in large part from the former Chattel Mortgage and Non-Possessory Pledge Registry as well as the Hire Purchase Contracts Registry.[284]

248. In *France*, a national registry for transfer of ownership by way of security was created in 2010 (*Registre National des Fiducies*). The formalities for the creation of the transfer of ownership by way of security are also distinctive. The agreement must be in writing and include the following information:

- specification of the assets, transferred rights and security rights;
- duration of the security transfer of ownership (which cannot be for more than 90 years);
- identification of the debtor, secured creditor and beneficiaries or, alternatively, a statement of the of basis on which they can be appointed;
- scope of the administrative powers and the powers to dispose with the assets;
- secured claim and the appraised value of the asset or right that has been transferred.

---

278 Roman NR, paras. 60–61.
279 *Ibid.* at para. 235.
280 *Ibid.* at para. 250.
281 For Italian law see *ibid.* at paras. 243–251.
282 In Austria, the Supreme Court has held that in respect of movable tangibles the rules for the possessory pledge must also be applied to the transfer of title by way of security.
283 Roman NR, para. 458.
284 *Ibid.* at para. 235.

249. With a view to combating tax evasion, the contractual transfer of ownership as a security has to be registered with the tax authorities in the place of the secured creditor's residence within one month. If the transfer also involves immovables, the contract must be registered also with the Land Registry within two months.[285]

250. The reforms in Central and Eastern European countries have all introduced special registries for registration of security interests on movables though some of these reforms have distinctive features.

251. *Poland*, for example, established a new Register of Pledges where the 'registered pledges' introduced by the 1996 Act could be entered. This is in fact a chattel mortgage register where enterprise charges should also be entered. It has two features though which make it different from the Hungarian sister register. The first is that security interests on motor vehicles are subject to registration in this register notwithstanding that the security interest is annotated also on the certificate of title. In this sense, it is somewhat similar to the Italian solution. The second peculiarity is that security interests on civil aircraft and industrial property rights are subject to registration in the personal property register even though separate registers exist also for these types of assets. The Registered Pledge Act however contains provisions ensuring exchange of data among the various registers.[286]

252. Pledging of claims (receivables) is typically subject to a distinct regime. For example, *Lithuanian* law contains provisions on factoring which regulates the 'pledging' of claims though there is not much detail. The rules on factoring, however, do not require registration but rather notification of the account debtor; in other words, perfection is not by way of registration but by way of notification.[287]

253. *French* law requires a written form specifying the claims encumbered, identification of the debtor (in case of future claims), and notification of the account debtor (alternatively the account debtor must be present at the conclusion of the contract). The pledge is effective between the parties to the agreement and third parties from the date of creation.[288]

254. In *Spain*, pledging of claims is recognised yet not regulated by the Spanish Civil Code. Creation (perfection) requires recording the agreement in a public document and notification of the account debtor.[289]

---

285 *Ibid.* at para. 225.
286 CEE NR, para. 154.
287 *Ibid.* at para. 149.
288 Roman NR, para. 220.
289 *Ibid.* at para. 135.

255. As far as using of claims as collateral is concerned, *Italian* law requires notification of the pledge agreement to the debtor. The notification must be made in writing having a certain date in order to enjoy the right of preferential satisfaction. In fact, case law looks upon notification as a sine qua non for the very existence of the security interest, i.e. notification has a constitutive force.[290]

256. As a result of the infiltration of concepts that find an inspiration in Article 9 of the US Uniform Commercial Code, new discrepancies have also appeared in Europe. Partly, these are based around one of the central ideas in Article 9, that of notice filing. Filing under Article 9 merely provides notice that a security interest may exist. It does not conclusively prove that a security interest actually exists. Filing may take place either before or after the creation of a security interest and a filing may relate to a transaction that was at one stage contemplated but never actually materialised. Another Article 9 feature that has leaked to Europe is the extension of registration requirements to security interests over receivables and the assignments of receivables.

257. Traditionally, the registration of a mortgage on immovables in civil law systems had a constitutive effect, i.e. the mortgage becomes a full-scale in rem right enforceable against third parties with registration in a public register designated for that purpose. This also means that it is presumed that a mortgage exists if it has been entered into such a register. In most cases, and following the same logic, the same constitutive effect was attributed to registration of security rights on movables (naturally this does not apply to *Austria* and *Germany* as in these countries securities on movables are not subject to registration in a public register).

258. In *Hungary*, however, with the enactment of the new 2013 Civil Code and inspired by the American model, the effect of registration of security interests on movables was 'reduced' to a mere notice filing. In essence, from now on the entry in the register (maintained by the National Association of Public Notaries) is no more than a notice of the possible existence of a security interest, a minimal set of information on the debtor, secured creditor and the collateral. Based on this, inquirers may conduct further research.[291]

259. Moreover, under the 2013 Hungarian Civil Code, the creation (perfection) of security interests on rights and claims (receivables) which are not subject to registration in a specific register (e.g. patents) is also subject to registration in the public register of security interests on movables. The earlier law required notification of the account debtor only, but now – besides notification – registration, or rather filing, is a requirement.[292]

---

290 *Ibid.* at para. 245.

291 CEE NR, para. 136.

292 *Ibid.* at para. 139.

2.3.4. *Possible common principles on security rights*

260. As far as the creation of security interests is concerned, all civil law systems are familiar with the principle of specialty.[293] The exact meaning and reach of the principle differs, and the tendency is for the principle to become weakened. The civil law systems are now consequently much closer to the standards of the common law than a few decades earlier. The best examples of this tendency towards greater flexibility are the various examples of floating (global) securities or their kin that allow for the pledging of both existing and future assets of a debtor. As a result, in the CEE countries it is generally possible to create floating securities notwithstanding that the principle of specialty has – at least formally – been kept.[294]

261. Civilian systems also assert that security interests are of an accessory nature (the *accessority principle*).[295] This basically means that the existence (coming into being and cessation of existence) and the contents of the security interest depend on the claim it secures. As it is stated related to German law: 'the pledge strictly follows the secured claim.'[296] While the common laws do not assert the principle of accessority, they reach similar results through concrete statutory provisions or concrete rules. The similarities are especially evident if the relevant civil law system allows for the pledging of all present and future assets.[297]

262. Civilian systems share the *numerus clausus principle* of proprietary rights,[298] a principle that prohibits also recognition of new types of security rights. *Spain* may be the notable exception as it operates on the principle of numerus apertus, i.e. the number of recognised in rem rights is not limited.[299] Although still valid as a general proposition, in order to satisfy market needs the principle was either

---

293 Germanic NR, para. 68 for German law and para. 96 for Austria; Roman NR, para. 6 on the principle as being common to France, Italy and Spain. The Hungarian Civil Code is a good example of the tendency to loosen the confines of the principle. While it proclaims that 'for the creation of the security agreement the identification of the collateral and the secured claim is required [Code §5:89(3)]', it also adds that identification can be done by specifying the type (class) and quantity or by any other appropriate identification method (§5:89(4)).

294 In Hungary however, in 2013 the floating security was discarded.

295 See para. 5 of the Roman NR (the principle is common to France, Italy and Spain) and para. 9 of the Germanic NR for Germany and para. 31 for Austria. For Hungary see L. Vékás (ed.), *Complex Commentary,* 421.

296 See Germanic NR, para. 9.

297 See more on this topic in T. Tajti, (2014) 35 *Adelaide Law Review* 169. Under German and Austrian law, some of the inflexibilities of the accessority principle have been overcome by the security devices developed through legal practice.

298 See Germanic NR, para. 6 or Roman NR, para. 97 related to Italian law. For Hungary see the prefatory comments to the 2013 Civil Code, which declares the numerus clausus principle and the prohibition of divided ownership – L. Vékás (ed.), *Complex Commentary*, 363–365.

299 Roman NR, para. 123.

bypassed or reconceptualised to allow for the emergence of new types of security devices.[300] The best examples are the German court-approved security devices developed by legal practice – security transfers consisting of the transfer of title by way of security and the assignment by way of security, or the reformed laws in the CEE countries that embraced some version of floating (global) security.

263. Civilian systems, however, are far from being identical when it comes to general principles for the creation and recognition of security interests. The *German* and *Austrian* law's *separation principle* ('*Trennungsprinzip*') stands out in this respect. The essence of this principle is that 'the contractual agreement on the change of ownership as a matter of property law must be firmly distinguished from the underlying security agreement as a matter of the law of obligations.'[301] So every security transaction involves two contracts although one may be silently implied in the other. With the so-called *abstraction principle* ('*Abstraktionsprinzip*') German law takes the separation principle even one step further, which can be seen if one contrasts German and Austrian law in respect of an otherwise identical security device – the transfer of title by way of security – that is known to both legal systems. Under Austrian law, the contract creating the obligation to transfer ownership for security purposes from the debtor to the creditor (obligational contract) must be valid in order to transfer title irrespective of the validity of the agreement by which the title is actually transferred (property law contract). By way of contrast, under German law, however, the transfer of title (ownership) may be valid even if the underlying obligation turns out to be invalid but the security provider then is entitled to claim the retransfer of the collateral on the grounds of unjustified enrichment.

2.4. ENFORCEMENT OF SECURITY INTERESTS

264. As a general rule, it may be stated that enforcement of security rights via courts is the rule in civilian systems.[302] This stance has begun to change to a certain extent in various civil law jurisdictions covered by this project. One such change was introduced for financial collateral based on EU law.[303] Another example is *Poland*'s introduction of private receivership for enforcement of security interests on floating security, where the court 'gets involved only if the

---

300 See e.g. Germanic NR, para. 6 on German law.

301 *Ibid.* at para. 12.

302 See para. 174 of the Germanic NR for Germany, according to which the following steps need to be taken: (1) the secured creditor must obtain an enforceable judgment or equivalent (other enforceable document), then (2) he has to apply to local courts (*Amtsgerichte*) for enforcement, which is (3) to issue an attachment order stipulating also the method by which the security right is to be enforced (normally a public auction).

303 See e.g. for Spain, Roman NR, para. 184.

pledgor files a claim for an injunction to prevent enforcement.'[304] In *Spain*, the example is the foreclosure supervised by a public notary; a possibility available for all security rights save antichresis.[305]

265. As opposed to that, for *English* law '[t]he enforcement of security has been seen largely as a self-help remedy to be exercised by the secured creditor in accordance with the provisions of the security agreement.'[306] But enforcement through courts is possible in the UK as well.

A good illustration of the divide is the existence of receiverships in English law as a distinct private security enforcement method.[307] While enforcement of security rights in civilian systems is either via courts, or quasi-judicial bodies,[308] the receiver is a genuine private enforcement method because the receiver, while nominally the agent of the debtor has a 'primary duty ... to realise the assets in the interest of the charge holder [i.e. secured creditor, a floating charge] and its powers of management are really ancillary to that duty.'

The Enterprise Act 2002 introduced reforms that aimed at reducing the role of privately appointed receivers but there are still a considerable number of cases where they may still be appointed (e.g. in the context of project finance).[309]

266. It is a common feature of all European systems that typically debtor protection rules exist relating to the enforcement of all kinds of security rights. The highest level of protection applies in the case of security rights over dwelling houses. Although significant differences exist from country to country, the protection may include discretion given to the judge to suspend or postpone evictions[310] or lex specialis that exclude evictions in the winter period.

267. It is also a common denominator of all the legal systems that the enforcement of various security devices differs depending on the nature of the security devices and on the assets used as collateral.

2.4.1. *Enforcement of possessory pledges*

268. If there is a security device, the enforcement of which does not require court intervention in most systems, then that is the possessory pledge and its

---

304 CEE NR, para. 186.

305 Roman NR, para. 267.

306 Common Law NR, para. 83.

307 *Ibid.* at paras. 94–102.

308 In Hungary, enforcement is entrusted to private – so-called independent – bailiffs that were introduced by Act No. 53 of year 1994. The 'independent' means that the bailiffs are not the employees of courts anymore. They have a National Association with regulatory powers as well – see <http://www.mbvk.hu> accessed 10 May 2016.

309 Common Law NR, paras. 100, 101.

310 *Ibid.* at para. 92.

functional equivalents.[311] The rule in such cases is that if the pledgor (debtor) defaults, the pledgee (secured creditor) has authority to sell the goods pledged and to apply the moneys received to discharge the debt.[312]

269. In *Spain*, however, such sale can be undertaken solely under the supervision of either of a court or a public notary. At public auctions, the debtor must be notified in advance so that he could place bids. The secured creditor may in such cases acquire the asset only if a second attempted auction has proved to be unsuccessful yet without the right to sue for the deficiency.[313]

270. Notwithstanding the general rule stated above, however, significant differences exist as far as the procedural steps that need to be taken when enforcing a possessory pledge.

(a) While *English* law requires debtor default, it does not generally require anything more such as the debtor being warned as to the consequences of a failure to fulfil its obligations[314] whereas the civilian systems do provide for such rules. Under *German* law, the justification for such a requirement is to provide the debtor with a last chance to fulfil his obligations amicably.[315] In case of *Italy*, the notification of the intended sale is to be made by the bailiff.[316] According to *Spanish* law, it is the public notary that asks the debtor for payment.[317]
(b) The method of sale is not uniform either. For example, while *German* law requires sale via public auction,[318] *Hungarian* law allows both sale at public auction or at a private sale.[319] But the latter, in case of the so-called bailment securities (i.e. when cash, accounts or traded investment property are pledged), speeds up the enforcement process and allows the secured creditor simply to declare in a unilateral document that it enforces the security interest by acquiring title (ownership).

---

311 By functional equivalent we mean, for example, warehoused goods and the Hungarian specialty, the security bailment on which see paras. 126–132 of the CEE NR.

312 See para. 84 of the Common Law NR, para. 169 of the Germanic NR related to German law, para. 263 of the Roman NR related to Italian law and para. 269 related to Spanish law. See §5:138 of the Hungarian Civil Code on enforcement of security bailments.

313 Roman NR, para. 269.

314 See para. 93 of the Common Law NR.

315 See Germanic NR, para. 170 for German law, para. 263 of the Roman NR for Italy and para. 269 for Spain. As per §5:131(1) of the Hungarian Civil Code, the pledgor must notify the debtor, his personal guarantors and sureties, other secured creditors and all others who have registered in rem rights of his intention to sell the collateral.

316 Roman NR, para. 263.

317 *Ibid.* at para. 268.

318 Germanic NR, para. 170 referring to §1235(1) of the German Civil Code (BGB).

319 See §5:134(2)(b) of the Hungarian Civil Code.

(c) Typically special rules (derogations) apply in cases where investment property (securities like shares and bonds) traded on exchanges or goods that have a quoted market price have been pledged.[320]
(d) Often special rules apply in case of security agreements with consumers[321] or pawnshop transactions.[322]

2.4.2. Enforcement of mortgages on immovables

271. *English* law stands out here as well due to its benevolence towards self-help. Here, the focus is on allowing the secured creditor take first to control of the collateral in order to be able to sell it in practice.[323] As opposed to that, civilian systems do not necessarily aim at facilitating the secured creditor taking control or possession since sale via courts is the paradigm enforcement procedure.[324]

272. *Hungarian* law has a mixed solution as it gives the secured creditor the right to ask for transfer of possession of the immovable-collateral and it does not exclude the sale of immovables that remain in the possession of the debtor.[325] It imposes however a standstill period between the communication of the request to transfer possession and the effectuation of sale, which in respect of immovables is a minimum of 20 days (at least three months for dwelling houses).[326]

273. Some civilian systems have designed methods to make enforcement more efficient. In *German* law, the mortgagee-bank may either have a notarial document entitling it immediately to levy execution against the real estate, and in the absence of this it must obtain an enforceable court order.[327] It is important to note, however, that the notarial document only makes the enforcement speedier but it does not allow for bypassing of public auctions conducted by a court officer (save in the less common cases of court appointed receivers).[328]

---

320 For German law see para. 170 of the Germanic NR and para. 270 of the Roman NR for Spain. See §5:138(3) of the Hungarian Civil Code.

321 For example, §5:128 of the Hungarian Civil Code foresees that in case of security agreements concluded with consumers, (a) the collateral may be disposed of solely via public auction (unless – after default has occurred – the parties agree on private sale), and (b) acquisition of title (ownership) by the secured creditor is not possible.

322 Under English law, the pawnbroker has the right to take the pawned assets in satisfaction of the debt – even if their value is higher than the debt – if the collateral has not been redeemed for a period of at least six months and the amount of the credit is less than £75. See para. 85 of the Common Law NR.

323 Common Law NR, para. 89.

324 For Italy see para. 264 of the Roman NR.

325 See §5:132(1) and (4) of the Hungarian Civil Code.

326 See §5:132(2) of the Hungarian Civil Code.

327 Germanic NR, para. 177.

328 *Ibid.* at para. 178.

Spanish law, on the other hand, has a public notary-supervised enforcement procedure that applies to all security devices save for antichresis.[329]

2.4.3. Out-of-court repossession of movable collateral

274. Perhaps the most important divide among the countries relates to whether out-of-court enforcement of security (self-help) is possible. At one end of the spectrum are the common law jurisdictions that look upon self-help – including self-help repossession – as an important, integral part of commercial law.

275. In the civil law jurisdictions, the basic approach is different but there are significant variations between countries and the nomenclature is also different. In general, however, for civil laws countries, repossession presumes a demand to the debtor and voluntary surrender of the collateral. If the debtor is unwilling to cooperate, then resort to court is a requirement. Repossession is in principle possible only with the consent of the debtor.[330] If possession has been regained based on voluntary surrender by the debtor, the secured creditor then may dispose of the collateral without a court order either via public auction or through a private sale agreement.[331]

276. If the debtor fails to surrender the property, the secured creditor may either dispose of the collateral without repossessing it, which is theoretically possible but unlikely in practice since a buyer may not be found, or must resort to the court.

277. While, for instance, *Italian* law recognises the out-of-court enforcement of pledges, such bypassing of courts presumes resort to bailiffs, notification to the debtor and sale at a public auction after the notification period has expired.[332]

278. Interestingly, while neither English nor civil laws look favourably at enforcement of security rights by automatic acquisition of ownership upon default, ownership (title) of the collateral can be acquired in quite a number of civil law systems under some specific conditions – pactum commissorium. In this respect, English law is more conservative than some of the European civil law systems.

279. Under *English* law, the so-called foreclosure actions presume court sanction. Moreover, courts would today primarily opt for property sale in lieu of authorising acquisition of ownership by the secured creditor of the collateral.

---

329 See para. 267 of the Roman NR on Spanish law.

330 For German law see para. 167 in the Germanic NR. For Hungarian law see §5:132 of the Civil Code.

331 See para. 167 on German law in the Germanic NR.

332 See para. 263 on Italian law in the Roman NR.

In *Palk v Mortgage Services*[333] it was said: 'foreclosure actions are almost unheard of today and have been so for many years. Mortgagees prefer to exercise other remedies. They usually appoint a receiver or exercise their powers of sale.'

A device similar in effects to foreclosure was, however, introduced into English law when implementing the EU Financial Collateral Directive.[334] The new remedy is called 'appropriation,' which can be exercised under two preconditions: first, the parties must have agreed on it in their security financial collateral arrangement, and second, the parties have agreed also on the valuation of the financial instruments.[335] Only cash, financial instruments (investment property) and credit claims may be used as collateral under the Directive. In the UK, the collateral taker (secured creditor) may appropriate in accordance with the security financial collateral agreement and without any foreclosure order from the courts. While the collateral taker must account for any surplus, the debtor remains liable for any deficiency.[336] The central aim of the Directive is to ease the cross-border use of financial collateral in the EU, among others, by making the process of the creation or enforcement of collateral arrangements less onerous.[337]

280. There are somewhat similar provisions in *Spain* due to the transposition of the Directive by Royal Decree 5/2005.[338]

281. Generally in the civil law systems, contractual provisions that anticipate the secured creditor acquiring full ownership (title) of the collateral upon default are in broad terms prohibited. The relevant parties, however, may agree that the secured creditor should acquire ownership of the collateral in exchange for the discharge of the debt *after* the default has occurred.[339] This seems to be the rule under *Austrian*, *German*,[340] *Hungarian*[341] and also *Spanish* law.[342] *Hungarian* law, for evidentiary reasons, however requires in addition that the secured creditor may express to the debtor after default that he is willing to accept ownership on the collateral in lieu of full or partial payment (satisfaction) of the debt. This must be expressed in writing communicated to the debtor.[343]

---

333 See para. 104 in the Common Law NR.

334 Directive 2002/47/EC on financial collateral arrangements (OJ 2002 L168).

335 See para. 108 of the Common Law NR.

336 *Ibid.*

337 See para. 107 of the Common Law NR and recital 17 of the Directive.

338 Roman NR, para. 135.

339 This may be an enforcement method in the case of the German security transfer. See on that para. 167 of the Germanic NR.

340 For German law, see para. 167 of the Germanic NR. For a similar rule under Austrian law, see para. 181 of the Germanic NR.

341 For Hungarian law see paras. 177–181 in the CEE NR. For the similar Polish rules see para. 185 of the CEE NR.

342 For Spanish law, see para. 272 of the Roman NR.

343 See §5:137(1) of the Hungarian Civil Code.

282. According to *French* law, for example, the pactum commissorium is not permitted in the cases of pledge of stocks (shares) and mortgages of dwelling houses (immovable). It is specifically permitted in cases of:

- common possessory pledge;
- pledges over motor vehicles;
- pledge of claims;
- pledge of intangibles other than claims;
- mortgages (save in respect of dwelling houses).[344]

2.5. COMPARISONS BETWEEN COUNTRIES

283. First and foremost, all systems recognise the division of security devices into those having in rem (proprietary) effects versus those having in personam (personal) effects.[345]

284. Secondly, all the legal systems considered in the project recognise some form(s) of right of retention (possessory retention, legal liens,[346] or in the *UK* common law lien),[347] according to which a creditor who has performed a service on an asset of the debtor and remained unpaid has the right to keep the asset of the debtor in its hands until paid. The designations as well as the preconditions for the exercise of these rights differ from system to system. For example, *Hungarian* law refers to these as statutory security rights and requires for their constitution either the retention of possession over assets of the debtor or registration in a public register (if retained assets are not at stake).[348]

285. *Spanish* law recognises two types of such devices – the fixed asset claims (*'creditor refaccionarios'*) that are available in respect of the construction, reconstruction, repair or improvements of certain fixed assets and which are looked upon as in rem security rights (special privileges).[349] Moreover, although not considered as a security right by the Spanish Civil Code, the right of possessory retention (*'derecho de retencion'*) is used in practice. Notification of the debtor through a public notary is needed to create it and the debtor may challenge it legally only within two months of the notification.[350]

---

344 See para. 253 for French law in the Roman NR.

345 See para. 8 of the Germanic NR, para. 96 of the Roman NR related to Italy, or para. 69 of the CEE NR related to Hungary.

346 See Germanic NR, para. 16 relating to German law (the lessor's automatic legal lien on all assets brought into the rented flat by the tenant to secure outstanding rent payments).

347 Common Law NR, para. 40.

348 See L. Vékás (ed.), *Complex Commentary*, 430.

349 Roman NR, para. 144.

350 *Ibid.* at para. 128.

French law also recognises such a device and this may be used by four types of creditors as set out in the Civil Code.[351]

286. Thirdly, all the countries under consideration also distinguish between possessory and non-possessory security devices. It is a common denominator in all the countries that possessory securities have lost much of their economic utility and today non-possessory securities play the dominant role.

2.5.1. Possessory securities – comparison between countries

287. The countries under consideration have fairly similar laws relating to *possessory securities* (i.e. possessory pledge). It is also common to all systems that the utility of this security device has been radically reduced in modern business.

288. Pawnshops – which depend on possessory security – are of importance in the post-crisis Europe,[352] while warehousing finance and more generally the pledging of certificated investment property are of importance in certain countries.

289. Pledging of warehouse receipts is a form of possessory security where the creation of a security interest depends on the transfer of possession of a certificated warehouse receipt. In some European countries (e.g. *Hungary*), the utility of this specific form of pledging has increased as warehousing companies began offering these services not only in relation to goods that are warehoused in public warehouses but also in so-called artificial (or field) warehouses established on the premises of the debtor itself.[353] The activity of this new generation of warehouses is regulated in *Hungary* by statute. In *Austria*, on the other hand, the interpretations of the Supreme Court have established the parameters of the security. It is clear from Supreme Court interpretations that to create a valid security interest, conspicuous signs must be posted in the warehouse and an independent collateral agent must be appointed to control the warehoused goods.[354]

290. In some of the countries, the possessory pledge may be constituted in a relatively straightforward fashion, i.e. transferring possession of the collateral to the secured creditor (or its agent).[355] Other countries however have introduced

---

351 *Ibid.* at paras. 91–94.

352 See e.g. Common Law NR, para. 86 relating to the UK where the old Pawnbrokers Acts were replaced by the Consumer Credit Act 1974.

353 See para. 114 of the CEE Report on Hungarian artificial (or field) warehouses. See also T. Tajti, (2014) 55 *Acta Juridica Hungarica* 185.

354 See para. 96 of the Germanic Reports (applicable to Austria).

355 This rule applies, for example, in Italy (see Roman NR, para. 229), Germany (Germanic NR, para. 154, first sentence), English law (see Common Law NR, para. 36), or Spanish law (Roman NR, para. 238).

changes. Perhaps the most interesting is the *Polish* rule according to which such transfer of possession plus the pledge agreement – which may be oral – validates the contract only as between the debtor and the secured creditor. In order to generate erga omnes effect (validity against third parties), a written contract with a certified date is required. These requirements were introduced in 2009 (in force from February 2011) to prevent abuse and to facilitate establishing the existence of the pledge and the date when it was created.[356] A similar rule also applies in *Lithuania*[357] and *Spain*.[358]

2.5.2. *Non-possessory securities – comparison between countries*

291. As opposed to possessory security, the laws on non-possessory securities differ fairly radically. The differences, in particular, relate to:

(a) existence of legal versus equitable security interests (common law only);
(b) recognition of latent (secret) security devices;
(c) existence of idiosyncratic security devices and idiosyncratic rules;
(d) quasi-securities.

2.5.2.1. Legal versus equitable security interests

292. This peculiar dualism of security rights originates in the historical distinction between the separate systems of common law and equity and the difference has some practical consequences that relate, in particular, to priorities. In brief terms, while legal interests are good against the world (or as civilian lawyers would say have erga omnes effects), the equitable ones 'are said to bind all, save for a bona fide purchaser or a legal interest in the same property for value without notice of the prior equitable interest.'[359] Civil laws do not know a similar concept of legal and equitable security interests, but priority conflicts between different types of security interest arise in different civil law systems and are resolved in different ways.

2.5.2.2. Recognition of latent (secret) security interests

293. *German* law is the prime example in this respect[360] though *some* of the systems that have modelled themselves after German law also recognise some versions of latent security interests on movables and intangibles.

---

356 See CEE NR, para. 118 on Polish law.
357 See CEE NR, para. 115 on Lithuanian law.
358 See Roman NR, para. 238 related to Spain.
359 See Common Law NR, para. 26 related to English law.
360 See Germanic NR, in particular paras. 6, 15 and 153.

294. In *Germany*, the most popular security devices on movables and intangibles are all of this nature. This includes security transfers (transfer of title by way of security/assignment by way of security) and retained ownership ('*Eigentumsvorbehalt*') as well as the expanded and extended versions of these instruments. Neither business nor German scholarship looks at these as problematic and thus there are no significant initiatives to introduce registration requirements. Professor Ulrich Drobnig has however admitted in a paper from 2010 that 'it is true to say that the rate of litigation in cases of the buyers' bankruptcies is very high and as a result at least some of the initial saving of cost and time due to non-registration is later lost in litigating with the insolvency administrator.'[361]

295. Security transfers are actually identical to mortgages or charges known to common law, or the 'registered pledges' of Polish law, save for the fact that they are not subject to any kind of registration. They are secret security devices as nothing more is required for their constitution than inclusion into a valid security agreement (which in the case of security ownership also provides for the required constructive possession).

296. Except for retained ownership which is expressly recognised by statute these security devices exist outside the Civil and Commercial Codes and have become part of German law due to the willingness of German courts to recognise these products of ingenious contract drafting by lawyers in the relevant industry sector. This is why one may legitimately refer to them as well as contract based security devices ('*kautelarische Sicherheiten*'). These are very flexible security devices capable of '[fulfilling] the market needs in every specific situation.'[362]

297. Besides recognising the basic versions (called also simple retained title) of these contracts-based security devices, German courts have also legitimised their extension. The enlargement of these devices went in two directions: on one hand to automatic inclusion of future advances (subsequent credit tranches extended by the very same creditor to the debtor), and on the other expansion of the security to include after-acquired property (i.e. assets that will become part of the debtor's property after the conclusion of the security agreement). One of the leading authorities in the field, Rolf Serick, has referred in English to these broader security devices as extended and expanded security transfers or retained titles.[363]

---

361 U. Drobnig, 'Basic Issues of European Rules on Security in Movables', in J. de Lacy (ed.), *The Reform of UK Personal Property Security Law*, 448.

362 See Germanic NR, para. 6.

363 R. Serick, *Securities in Movables in German Law: An Outline.*

2.5.2.3. Idiosyncratic security devices

Most of the legal systems under consideration contain some idiosyncratic security devices apart from the equitable securities and floating security under English law.

298. *German* real estate property law should be mentioned because of the existence of two encumbrances (one may also say: two types of mortgages) on immovables: the '*Hypothek*' and the '*Grundschuld*.' For the sake of convenience, we will refer to the first as 'mortgage' and the second as 'land charge'. The key difference between the two is that the land charge is non-accessory. This in practical terms means that it is easier to secure several claims, to change the secured claim or to 'recharge' the land charge with a new claim secured by it after the original secured claim has been discharged. In the case of the land charge none of these operations require re-registration in the land register but re-registration would be required if a *Hypothek* was used in the transaction.[364] Because of this flexibility and lower transaction costs as a result, the land charge has almost completely replaced the *Hypothek* in practice. Interestingly however, Austrian law does not recognise the non-accessory land charge.[365]

299. The German contract-based security devices are distinctive in many respects. Firstly, as they are not referred to by the German Civil Code, the contractual provisions and the related case law (if any) govern them. For example, the enforcement of these security transfers is governed by the contractual provisions and the analogous application of the law on pledges provided by statute is not possible (save in very exceptional situations).[366]

300. Secondly, these are not subject to registration or any other kind of provision of public notice. In other words, they are latent (secret) security devices.

301. German law also contains system-specific institutions of security law developed through the case law of the German Federal Supreme Court (Bundesgerichtshof). These were developed based on §138 of the Civil Code (BGB) proclaiming that immoral transactions are invalid.[367] The three inter-linked security law institutions are aimed essentially at protecting the debtor and involve prohibitions of each of the following: (a) over-collateralisation, (b) incitement to breach the contract and (c) locked-in contracts. German law contains these rules against immoral contracts as a means of forcing the secured creditor to take account of the position of the debtor.

---

364 See Germanic NR, para. 21 on German law.

365 *Ibid.* at para. 35 on Austrian law.

366 *Ibid.* at para. 166.

367 *Ibid.* at para. 28.

302. Over-collateralisation exists if, at the time that the security interest is created, it is already certain that the realisable value of the collateral is disproportionately above the value of the debt. According to the literature, a 200% or higher collateral–debt ratio would be caught by the prohibition.[368] If a disproportion between the value of the collateral and the secured claim materialises only afterwards in the course of the credit relationship, then according to the case law a release claim to be implied into the contract whereby if the value of the collateral exceeds the debt by a certain percentage, the secured creditor (or supplier in case of retained title) will take steps to release the excess security. As a reaction to the case law, parties typically add express release clauses to their security agreements.

303. Incitement to breach a contract may arise where a party to a security agreement is forced not to reveal to a new financier that a security has already been created.[369] Admittedly, this rule may look strange from the perspective of other laws. The rule was created by case law because German security devices are not publicised (no public notice is provided by any perfection method save possessory pledge and forms of mortgage on immovables) and even though one might assume that, for example, goods are supplied under a retained title (ownership),[370] a party might be pressed not to reveal the security in order to get new financing on the strength of the collateral.[371]

304. Locked-in contracts exist in cases where the economic freedom of one of the parties is excessively restricted. This may happen also in the context of security agreements which are deemed to be immoral.[372]

305. *Hungarian* law deserves mention because of its particular security device – the *security-bailments* ('*óvadék*'). As one of the Commentaries of the new 2013 Civil Code says, the existence of this device – similar to possessory pledge – is due to peculiar historic reasons.[373] The security-bailment may cover the category of financial collateral referred to in the EU Financial Collateral Directive. The security-bailment is broader however, in that while only cash, financial instruments and credit claims can serve as financial collateral under the

---

368 *Ibid.* at para. 28 referring to R. Sack and P. Fischinger, in J. Staudinger, *BGB*, §138, para. 308.

369 Germanic NR, para. 28.

370 As U. Drobnig put it: 'Merchants are expected to know that nowadays most items of major equipment are bought on credit and that the purchase items serve as security.' In 'Basic Issues of European Rules on Security in Movable', in J. de Lacy (ed), *The Reform of UK Personal Property Security Law*, 448.

371 Germanic NR, para. 28.

372 *Ibid.* See also case 26 BGHZ 185 (1958) in which the debtor asserted that anticipatory assignment of a set of claims was invalid because they were not sufficiently determinable and because they 'unfairly restricted the economic freedom of the assignor [i.e. debtor].'

373 L. Vékás (ed.), *Complex Commentary*, 432.

Directive, it may possibly extend also to other similar assets, which however are to be defined by lex specialis.[374] Moreover, the secured creditor for the benefit of whom a security-bailment was constituted has the right of direct enforcement. The secured creditor may declare in a unilateral declaration addressed to the debtor that he has become the owner of the asset.[375] This is similar to 'the right of appropriation' under the EU Directive. The security-bailment device is perfected either by transfer of possession or control to the secured party.

306. *Italian* law should also be mentioned in this connection because of the so-called *privileges* that resemble security rights in certain limited respects. They exist under certain statutes which take the view that certain claims should be protected more than others.[376] Such privileges cannot be created consensually; therefore only statutes may grant (create) a privilege.[377]

307. Privileges, however, may confer one of two types of rights. *General privileges* confer the right of preferential satisfaction in priority to general unsecured creditors and only upon opening of insolvency proceedings or attachment. They operate, however, only if movable assets exist at the time of opening the insolvency proceedings or at the time of the attachment.[378] As opposed to that, a *special* privilege may apply to both movable and immovable assets and entitles the holder to trace the assets into the hands of third parties.[379]

308. Although both *French*[380] and *Spanish*[381] law recognise 'privileges', their legal status and treatment is significantly different from the Italian ones.

309. The Roman systems have also a particular security device – the antichresis defined as a 'security right in rem over immovables by which the secured creditor gains possession over the immovable asset and is entitled to acquire its fruits under the obligation of allocating them to paying the secured claim.'[382] This device is, however, rarely used in modern times. Moreover, while in some systems it is deemed to be an in rem device (e.g. *France*[383] and *Spain*),[384] in *Italy* it is not.[385]

---

374 See §5:95(1)(d) of the Hungarian Civil Code.
375 See §5:138 of the Hungarian Civil Code.
376 Roman NR, para. 107.
377 *Ibid.* at para. 110.
378 *Ibid.* at para. 108.
379 *Ibid.* at para. 109.
380 *Ibid.* at para. 33.
381 *Ibid.* at para. 118.
382 *Ibid.* at para. 3.
383 *Ibid.* at para. 27.
384 *Ibid.* at para. 127.
385 *Ibid.* Italy regulates antichresis in Arts. 1960–1964 of Civil Code.

2.5.2.4. Quasi securities

310. Generally, it can be stated that each of the legal systems considered recognise some kinds of quasi securities. The best known examples of these are leasing,[386] factoring and sales with a retention of title/ownership clause.

311. In some systems, however, leasing and factoring are not looked upon as a security device but rather as a distinct type of contract or transaction (e.g. *Lithuania*).

312. Security devices created via trust law are, however, known only to some European systems. Common law systems, subject to variation as to the frequency of use and thus economic importance, recognise two devices where trusts have a 'security type function':[387] the trust receipt and the Quistclose[388] (or conditional purpose) trusts. The latter is regarded as constituting a security interest because it is intended that the 'payer is to be protected from the claims of other creditors of the payee [on the latter's insolvency].'[389]

313. Although *German* law has its own version of trust (*'Treuhand'*), the Germanic National Report specifically mentions the so-called double trusts (*'Doppeltreuhand'*), which however are not own security devices but special variations of security ownership or security assignment used in several kinds of tripartite situations.[390] Accordingly they grant the trustee a right to separate satisfaction upon insolvency in favour of the beneficiary.[391] In the context of insolvency, they are mostly applied by provisional insolvency practitioners in order to raise liquidity in preliminary proceedings. They may also be used by employers to isolate the employees' pension claims from the creditors of the employer-company by transferring such assets to the trustee.

314. Although *Hungary* introduced the concept of trust into its legal system in 2013, it was not conceptualised as a security device but rather only as a distinct type of nominated contract to which the rules on mandate apply unless there is express regulation to the contrary in the Civil Code.[392] Hence, at this point in time it is not clear whether it will be used at all as a security device.

315. Many other civil law systems, however, still do not have the concept of the trust and, moreover, civilian trusts may differ significantly from one another even in terms of basic concept.

---

386 Financial leasing and 'sale and lease back' arrangements seem to be common.

387 Common Law NR, para. 256.

388 The designation stems from *Barclays Bank Ltd v Quistclose Investments Ltd* [1970] AC 567.

389 Common Law NR, para. 250.

390 Germanic NR, para. 347.

391 *Ibid.* at paras. 348, 349.

392 *See* §§6:310 through 6:330 of the 2013 Hungarian Civil Code.

2.5.3. *Conclusions on the diversity of national laws*

All the countries considered in this report have more or less developed versions of secured credit law. In none of them is there merely the rudimentary tandem of the possessory pledge and the mortgage of immovable. Instead, financiers have available to them a significant variety of security devices to secure payment and performance.

316. Nevertheless, significant divergences do exist between the various systems, though it may be that the same results are generally achieved via different legal techniques. For example, while German security devices on movables and intangibles are latent (secret), the common law and also the reformed Central and Eastern European systems require the provision of public notice.

317. It is the case, however, that the countries considered as part of this study do not score particularly well on the 'getting credit' indicator of the World Bank Doing Business rankings. This matter has been considered in the first section and will be explored further now in the third section. This section will also map the possible contours of any future EU harmonisation measures, though we do not consider the constitutional legitimacy of any EU action in this field.[393]

3. THE WORLD BANK, INTERNATIONAL BENCHMARKS AND POSSIBLE HARMONISATION MEASURES

318. The following table (Table 1) shows how the EU countries as a whole fare on the 'getting credit' indicator of the World Bank Doing Business. The rank in the table indicates how the particular country lies globally in relation to the particular indicator.

The relatively low ranking of the EU countries becomes comprehensible if one delves deeper into the methodology of how the rankings are constructed. As one can see, the 'getting credit' indicator includes both 'legal rights' and 'sharing of credit information' features. The first feature purports to ascertain the extent to which certain elements are contained within the secured credit (collateral) and corporate insolvency (bankruptcy) laws of a particular country. The second feature addresses the coverage, scope and accessibility of credit information that is available through credit reporting service providers such as credit bureaus or credit registries. 60% of the overall proportion of the ranking is made up of the

[393] For discussion on this see B. Akkermans and E. Ramaekers, (2013) 19 *European Law Journal* 237; M. di Luigi, [2008] *Journal of Business Law* 526; E. Ramaekers, (2015) 23 *European Review of Private Law* 437. See also more generally J. Armour, (2008) 5 *European Company and Financial Law Review* 3.

'legal rights' element and the remaining 40% is attributed to the 'sharing of credit information' element.

Table 1. EU countries ranked by the 'getting credit' indicator of the World Bank Doing Business report

Economy	Year	Rank	Strength of legal rights index (0–12)	Depth of credit information index (0–8)
Austria	DB2016	59	5	7
Belgium	DB2016	97	4	5
Bulgaria	DB2016	28	9	5
Croatia	DB2016	70	5	6
Cyprus	DB2016	42	7	6
Czech Republic	DB2016	28	7	7
Denmark	DB2016	28	8	6
Estonia	DB2016	28	7	7
Finland	DB2016	42	7	6
France	DB2016	79	4	6
Germany	DB2016	28	6	8
Greece	DB2016	79	3	7
Hungary	DB2016	19	10	5
Ireland	DB2016	28	7	7
Italy	DB2016	97	2	7
Latvia	DB2016	19	9	6
Lithuania	DB2016	28	6	8
Luxembourg	DB2016	167	3	0
Malta	DB2016	174	2	0
Netherlands	DB2016	79	3	7
Poland	DB2016	19	7	8
Portugal	DB2016	97	2	7
Romania	DB2016	7	10	7
Slovak Republic	DB2016	42	7	6
Slovenia	DB2016	126	3	4
Spain	DB2016	59f	5	7
Sweden	DB2016	70	6	5
United Kingdom	DB2016	19	7	8

319. Essentially the 'legal rights' component purports to measure the strength of secured creditor rights, particularly in insolvency proceedings, and builds on the 'legal origins' or 'law matters' thesis developed by four economists – La Porta,

Lopez de Silanes, Shleifer and Vishny.[394] The original creditor rights index constructed by La Porta et al. measured four powers of secured lenders in bankruptcy; (1) whether there are restrictions, such as creditor consent, when a debtor files for reorganisation; (2) whether secured creditors are able to seize collateral after the petition for reorganisation is approved, i.e. there is no stay imposed by the court; (3) secured creditors are paid first out of liquidation proceeds; and (4) whether an IP, and not management, is responsible for running the business during the reorganisation period. If a country's laws and regulations entrusted each of these powers to secured creditors, then a value of one was added to the creditor rights index. The scores were then aggregated and varied between 0 (poor creditor rights) and 4 (strong creditor rights).

320. The Doing Business reports and rankings, which have been issued annually since 2004 through the World Bank Group,[395] develop the legal origins literature and employ a more sophisticated version of the same methodology used by La Porta et al. The methodology section of the reports sets out how the reports are compiled and suggests how certain features of secured credit or secured transactions laws are considered desirable by the World Bank. If a particular country incorporates these features in its laws, it will get a positive score, whereas if some or all of the relevant features are absent, then the country will get poor marks.

321. The methodology was most recently revised in 2014 when two components were added on what type of collateral registry operates in a particular country and on how it operates. The scoring also now penalises countries for not having an automatic stay on enforcement during reorganisation procedures. The change is designed to ensure that a viable business can continue to operate. Furthermore, the index takes into account new elements relating to out-of-court enforcement procedures such as the types of auctions allowed.

322. The 'legal rights' index now purports to measure 10 features of collateral law and two aspects of bankruptcy law. The index assigns a score of 1 for each of the following aspects of the law in a country:

- The economy has an integrated or unified legal framework for secured transactions that extends to the creation, publicity and enforcement of four functional equivalents to security interests in movable assets: fiduciary transfer of title; financial leases; assignment or transfer of receivables; and sales with retention of title.

---

394 See R. La Porta, F. Lopez de Silanes, A. Shleifer and R. Vishny, (1997) 52 *Journal of Finance* 1131; (1998) 106 *Journal of Political Economy* 113. R. La Porta, F. Lopez de Silanes and A. Shleifer refine the 'legal origins' thesis and defend it against criticisms in (2008) 46 *Journal of Economic Literature* 285.

395 See <www.doingbusiness.org> accessed 10 May 2016.

- The law allows a business to grant a non-possessory security right in a single category of movable assets (such as machinery or inventory), without requiring a specific description of the collateral.
- The law allows a business to grant a non-possessory security right in substantially all its movable assets, without requiring a specific description of the collateral.
- A security right can be given over future or after-acquired assets and extends automatically to the products, proceeds or replacements of the original assets.
- A general description of debts and obligations is permitted in the collateral agreement and in registration documents, all types of debts and obligations can be secured between the parties, and the collateral agreement can include a maximum amount for which the assets are encumbered.
- A collateral registry or registration institution for security interests granted over movable property by incorporated and non-incorporated entities is in operation, unified geographically and with an electronic database indexed by debtors' names.
- The collateral registry is a notice-based registry – a registry that files only a notice of the existence of a security interest (not the underlying documents) and does not perform a legal review of the transaction. The registry also publicises functional equivalents to security interests.
- The collateral registry has modern features such as those that allow secured creditors (or their representatives) to register, search, amend or cancel security interests online.
- Secured creditors are paid first (for example, before tax claims and employee claims) when a debtor defaults outside an insolvency procedure.
- Secured creditors are paid first (for example, before tax claims and employee claims) when a business is liquidated.
- Secured creditors are subject to an automatic stay on enforcement procedures when a debtor enters a court-supervised reorganisation procedure, but the law protects secured creditors' rights by providing clear grounds for relief from the automatic stay (for example, if the movable property is in danger) or setting a time limit for it.
- The law allows parties to agree in the collateral agreement that the lender may enforce its security right out of court; the law allows public and private auctions and also permits the secured creditor to take the asset in satisfaction of the debt.

323. Scores are then aggregated, with the higher scores suggesting that the collateral and bankruptcy laws in a particular jurisdiction 'are better designed to expand access to credit'. The World Bank methodology essentially embodies a set of normative propositions on what a modern law of secured credit should ideally contain. These normative propositions draw to a certain extent upon international standards in the field of secured credit law that have been developed by

UNCITRAL in its Legislative Guide Secured Transactions and by the World Bank itself.

324. If EU countries in general, and the countries considered in this study in particular, wish to optimise their position in the World Bank rankings, then the obvious solution is to reform their secured credit and insolvency laws along the lines suggested by this set of normative propositions.[396] On this line of analysis, reforms are certainly needed in the insolvency sphere.[397] For instance, in some EU countries employee claims are treated as priority claims and may get paid first even ahead of secured creditors. *France* and to a certain extent *Italy* take this approach. But countries differ however on the extent to which employee claims are treated as priority claims and the monetary limits that may be applicable. Countries also differ on whether tax claims should have any preferential status in insolvency proceedings. *Germany* and the *UK* have removed the preferential status of tax claims – in *Germany's* case in 1982 and in the *UK* some 20 years later. Many other countries stick robustly to the line that since the revenue authorities are, to an extent, involuntary creditors their claims should have some element of priority in the insolvency of a taxpayer entity.

325. In terms of secured credit law, the UNCITRAL Secured Transactions Guide provides more detailed guidance on what a modern law should 'ideally' contain.[398]

3.1. UNCITRAL SECURED TRANSACTIONS GUIDE

326. The UNCITRAL guide is the product of reflection over many years by highly informed and interested parties. It reflects modern financing techniques and incorporates accumulated wisdom and practice as well as insights from highly developed and sophisticated economies at the cutting edge of global finance. It is a 'fuller', more contemporary and up-to-date product than the EBRD Model Law on Secured Transactions, as well as being more widely consulted and reflected upon. For these reasons it is bound to be referred to as a source of inspiration and guidance by EU States when seeking to update their law on secured transactions. UNCITRAL itself has asserted that 'the Guide is a valuable resource tool because it discusses all issues to be addressed in a secured transactions law, explains

---

396 For other suggestions on possible EU secured transactions law reforms see, for example, J. Rutgers, 'Registered European Security Instrument in a Multilingual European Union', in S. van Erp, A. Salomons and B. Akkermans (eds.), *The Future of European Property Law* 153–163; S. van Erp, 'Security Interests: A Secure Start for the Development of European Property Law', in M. Hinteregger and T. Boric (eds.) *Sicherungsrechte an Immobilien in Europa*, 3–39.

397 See also more generally S. Davydenko and J. Franks, (2008) 63 *Journal of Finance* 565.

398 The following sections draw heavily upon G. McCormack, *Secured Credit and the Harmonisation of Law* and in particular chapters 6 and 8.

all the workable approaches presenting their advantages and disadvantages and makes recommendations to the legislator'[399] and this is undoubtedly correct.

327. The EBRD Model Law and its Core Principles on Secured Transactions Laws[400] cover the same ground as the UNCITRAL Guide, and embody many of the same points, but they are on the whole much less detailed but also prescriptive – which may of course be a positive in a European context. For instance, the Core Principles do not track the content of Article 9 of the US Uniform Commercial Code to the same degree, i.e. while the Core Principles talk about having an effective means of publicising the existence of security rights, they differ from the UNCITRAL Guide in that they do not come down in favour of the US Article 9 system notice filing as distinct from transaction filing.

3.2. GENERAL PRINCIPLES OF THE UNCITRAL GUIDE

328. The Secured Transactions Guide is a detailed document and the details were increased in 2010 with the addition of a separate annex that applies to security over intellectual property rights.[401] Subject to certain limitations, the Guide is designed to be comprehensive in its reach, both in terms of the range of persons to whom it may apply and also in terms of the assets that may serve as security. Essentially the Guide is an exhortation to States to be as comprehensive as possible in the process of framing their secured credit law and not to leave inadvertent gaps in coverage.

329. The first recommendation in the Guide sets out this key objective stating that the law should be designed:

> '(a) To promote low-cost credit by enhancing the availability of secured credit; (b) To allow debtors to use the full value inherent in their assets to support credit; (c) To enable parties to obtain security rights in a simple and efficient manner; (d) To provide for equal treatment of diverse sources of credit and of diverse forms of secured transactions; (e) To validate non-possessory security rights in all types of asset; (f) To enhance certainty and transparency by providing for registration of a notice of a security right in a general security rights registry; (g) To establish clear and

---

399 See UN document A/CN.9/702/Add.1 – 'Possible future work on security interests' (2010) para. 51.

400 See generally F. Dahan and J. Simpson 'The European Bank for Reconstruction and Development's Secured Transactions Project: A Model Law and Ten Core Principles for a Modern Secured Transactions Law in Countries of Central and Eastern Europe (and Elsewhere!)', in E-M. Kieninger (ed.), *Security Rights in Movable Property in European Private Law*, 98.

401 See on the UNCITRAL website – <www.uncitral.org> accessed 10 May 2016 – 'Supplement on Security Rights in Intellectual Property'.

predictable priority rules; (h) To facilitate efficient enforcement of a secured creditor's rights; (i) To allow parties maximum flexibility to negotiate the terms of their security agreement; (j) To balance the interests of all persons affected by a secured transaction; and (k) To harmonise secured transactions laws, including conflict-of-laws rules relating to secured transactions.'

330. The Guide is broad and sweeping in its remit insofar as the kinds of assets that may be used as security. All types of movable property, both property presently owned by the debtor and property that may be acquired by the debtor in the future, can be 'collateralised'.[402] Moreover, a security right in assets extends to the proceeds, unless otherwise agreed.[403] An important aspect of the Secured Transactions Guide is to facilitate receivables financing and security may be created over future, fluctuating and conditional obligations owed to the debtor.[404] In addition, security rights may be created in bank accounts despite any contrary agreement between the grantor of the security interest and the depositary bank but, by virtue of the security agreement, no duties are thereby imposed on the depositary bank.

331. The Guide applies essentially to contractually created property rights. Security rights that arise by operation of law rather than from the agreement of the parties are outside its sphere of operation.[405] There is also a statement in the Guide to the effect that the law should apply equally to legal and natural persons, i.e. to both companies and individuals. The extension envisaged by the Guide to persons that do not necessarily transact business through the corporate form carries with it, however, the caveat that the scope of consumer protection legislation should not be affected.[406]

332. The Guide also does not apply to immovable property with the exception of chattels that are attached to land and become so-called 'fixtures'.[407] The reasons

---

402 See Recommendation 2(a) stating that the law should apply to 'Security rights in all types of movable asset, tangible or intangible, present or future, including inventory, equipment and other tangible assets, contractual and non-contractual receivables, contractual non-monetary claims, negotiable instruments, negotiable documents, rights to payment of funds credited to a bank account, rights to receive the proceeds under an independent undertaking and intellectual property'.

403 Recommendation 19.

404 See Recommendation 2(c).

405 See Recommendation 2 stating that the law should apply to 'all rights in movable assets created by agreement that secure payment or other performance of an obligation, regardless of the form of the transaction, the type of the movable asset, the status of the grantor or secured creditor or the nature of the secured obligation.'

406 Recommendation 2(b).

407 Recommendations 4 and 5. There are other exceptions in Recommendation 4.

for this exclusion appear pragmatic in that real property is often considered to be an area where sovereignty issues are particularly important. Article 9 applies only to personal property and against this backdrop it appeared logical to have a similar limitation on the sphere of application of the Guide. On the other hand, the European Bank for Reconstruction and Development (EBRD) Guide to Mortgage Law applicable to real estate is virtually identical in terms of substantive content to its Secured Transactions guidelines applicable to personal property.[408]

333. Under the Guide it is permissible to create 'all-assets security', i.e. the equivalent of a floating security or universal business security over the entirety of the business operations of an enterprise.[409] Reflecting the US Article 9, the validation of 'all-assets security' is one of the most significant features of the Guide.

3.3. CREATION AND THIRD PARTY EFFECTIVENESS OF SECURITY RIGHTS UNDER THE GUIDE

334. The Guide provides that a security right is created by an agreement concluded between the grantor and secured creditor. The relevant agreement may be oral if it is accompanied by dispossession of the grantor pursuant to the agreement.[410] Otherwise, however, it must be in writing or evidenced in writing. The Guide is nevertheless medium-neutral and the writing requirement can be met by something that serves as its electronic equivalent.[411] The security agreement must identify the parties and also reasonably describe both the secured obligation and the assets to be encumbered by the security interest.[412] The Guide cautions however against overly exact description requirements and suggests that a generic description of the secured obligation and the encumbered assets is sufficient. A security agreement may relate to property that is not yet in existence, or not yet owned by the grantor.[413] In those circumstances, the

---

408 See *Mortgages in Transition Economies – the Legal Framework for Mortgages and Mortgage Securities* (2010) <http://www.ebrd.com/news/publications/guides/mortgages-in-transition-economies.html> accessed 10 May 2016 and for discussion see J. Simpson and F. Dahan, 'Mortgages in transition economies', in F. Dahan and J. Simpson (eds.), *Secured Transactions Reform and Access to Credit*, 172.

409 Recommendation 17 providing that a security interest may encumber all assets of the debtor.

410 Recommendation 15.

411 See Recommendation 11 stating that where the law requires that a communication or a contract should be in writing, or provides consequences for the absence of writing, that requirement is met by an electronic communication if the information contained therein is accessible so as to be usable for subsequent reference.

412 Recommendation 14.

413 See Recommendation 17.

security right is deemed to have been created when the grantor acquires rights in the asset, or the power to encumber the asset.[414] It is also the case that a security right may be effective as between the grantor and the secured creditor even if it is not effective against third parties.[415]

335. As far as receivables financing is concerned, the Guide tracks the provisions of the United Nations Convention on the Assignment of Receivables in International Trade.[416] Bulk assignments, for example, are permissible and so too are the assignment of future receivables and parts of, and undivided interests in, receivables.[417] An assignment is declared to be effective despite a non-assignment clause in the contract creating the receivable.[418] With respect to the secured party, the Guide tries to limit liability for breach of a non-assignment clause. A third party who took an assignment notwithstanding the non-assignment clause is not liable, say, for inducing a breach of contract on the 'sole ground that it had knowledge of the agreement'.[419] It should be noted also that knowledge, in the context of the Guide, means 'actual knowledge' and not 'constructive knowledge', i.e. the knowledge that one would have acquired had one deigned to make reasonable inquiries.[420]

336. Under the Guide, third party effectiveness of security rights generally requires registration of the security in a general security rights register.[421] The Guide however also contains asset-specific recommendations along the lines of the US Article 9 that validate alternative methods of achieving third party effectiveness of security rights in relation to particular types of collateral.[422]

337. In terms of registration particulars, the Guide favours the US concept of notice filing rather than the concept of transaction filing found in English law,

---

414 Recommendation 13.

415 Recommendation 30.

416 See <https://www.uncitral.org/pdf/english/texts/payments/receivables/ctc-assignment-convention-e.pdf> accessed 11 May 2016.

417 Recommendation 23: 'The law should provide that: (a) An assignment of a contractual receivable that is not specifically identified, a future receivable or a part of or an undivided interest in a receivable is effective as between the assignor and the assignee and as against the debtor of the receivable as long as, at the time of the assignment or, in the case of a future receivable, at the time it arises, it can be identified to the assignment to which it relates; and (b) Unless otherwise agreed, an assignment of one or more future receivables is effective without a new act of transfer being required to assign each receivable.'

418 Recommendation 24. Certain common contracts where non-assignment clauses are often found are however excluded from the ban – see Recommendation 24(c).

419 Recommendation 24(b). Nothing in the recommendation affects any obligation or liability of the assignor for breach of the non-assignment agreement, but the other party to such agreement may not avoid the original contract or the assignment contract on the sole ground of that breach.

420 See Legislative Guide 'Terminology'.

421 See Recommendations 32–35.

422 Recommendations 48–53.

and also more familiar to other jurisdictions.[423] Under the notice filing regime, it is not the security agreement itself that is filed but a so-called 'financing statement' providing limited information.[424] The filed notice merely indicates that a person may have a security interest in the collateral concerned, and further inquiry by a searcher from the potential creditor and/or debtor will be necessary to ascertain the true state of affairs. Notice filing is party-specific rather than transaction-specific. The information filed is an invitation to further inquiry rather than being a summary of the transaction. The notice may be filed either before or after a particular transaction and a single filing is effective to cover multiple transactions.[425]

338. Advance registration allows a secured party to mark out its intentions in advance of the conclusion of the agreement and while negotiations between the parties are continuing. It is claimed that this is more convenient and flexible than 'after the event' transaction filing.[426] The parties are given more time to attend to registration rather than having to do it post-transaction when there may be a lot of other formalities to deal with. Moreover, the facility whereby a single filing covers multiple transactions renders more concrete the possibility of extending registration requirements to trade credit transactions where there may be a number of separate transactions between the same buyer and seller. If each one required individual registration, then cost and inconvenience would militate against registration being achieved in practice.

3.4. TREATMENT OF QUASI-SECURITIES

339. The Guide provides that the law should treat all devices that perform security functions as secured transactions, including the transfer of title to tangibles or the outright assignment of receivables for security purposes.[427] This

---

423 See Recommendations 54 and 57 of the Legislative Guide.

424 The first civil law jurisdictions to have introduced notice filing appear to have been the French province of Quebec and the US state of Louisiana – see generally T. Harrell, [1990] *Loyola Law Review* 711; M. Bridge, R. Macdonald, R. Simmonds and C. Walsh, (1999) 44 *McGill Law Journal* 567.

425 Recommendations 67 and 68.

426 The EBRD has been sceptical about the merits of allowing advance registration or pre-registration stating that 'the advantages of allowing a potential creditor to take priority during the negotiations are debatable' – see *Publicity of Security Rights: EBRD Guiding Principles for the Development of a Charges Registry* (December 2004) 14 <http://www.ebrd.com/downloads/legal/secured/pubsec.pdf> accessed 11 May 2016.

427 Recommendation 2(d), which states that the law should apply to 'all property rights created contractually to secure the payment or other performance of an obligation, including transfers of title to tangible assets for security purposes or assignments of receivables for security purposes, the various forms of retention-of-title agreements and financial leases'.

comprehensive approach would cover more or less all title transfer 'security' devices, i.e. rights of a proprietary kind that secure payment or the performance of obligations. The Guide enshrines the general principle that public notice of quasi-security interests must be given by means of filing in a register that is open to public inspection.[428]

340. Nevertheless, the Guide admits the possibility of a two different approaches when it comes to quasi-securities. The first option, the unitary approach, is essentially an Article 9-style regime with all its trappings. Under the second 'non-unitary' approach, the substantive treatment of functionally similar transactions would be the same as for security rights strictly so-called, but the legal characterisation would remain different.[429] In other words, States could still apply a different formal characterisation to quasi-security devices but they would effectively be obliged to apply the same legal rules to both security and quasi-security. Both types of transaction would be subject to filing or registration obligations for third party effectiveness.[430]

3.5. LESSONS FOR THE EUROPEAN LEGISLATOR

341. The UNCITRAL Secured Transactions Guide certainly adds to the toolbox for States wishing to reform their law on secured transactions. EU States and the European Commission itself could draw on it when proposing new legislative initiatives in this field. Nevertheless, while the World Bank 'getting credit' indicators mirror the principles in the UNCITRAL Guide, the policy choices embodied in these principles may be open to question. There are at least three areas where caution and further reflection is required by the European legislator particularly since the principles reflected in the Guide constitute a significant departure from general European norms. These are: firstly, legitimation of 'all-assets' security; secondly, application of a filing or publicity norm and indeed, a commitment to notice-filing rather than transaction filing; and thirdly, the treatment of quasi-securities.

342. On the first point, none of the countries covered in this report merely have a combination of the possessory pledge of movables coupled with the mortgage of immovable. Nevertheless, our study tends to bear out the results of an earlier

---

428 See Chapter IX of the Legislative Guide 'Acquisition Financing' with Option A Unitary Approach and Option B Non-Unitary Approach.

429 See generally Recommendation 192 of the Legislative Guide.

430 Recommendation 192. Both would also constitute an exception to the general first-to-file-has-priority principle underlying the Guide.

comparative study where it is suggested that[431] none of the EU Member States has developed a comprehensive, functional approach to security rights in movables. Instead, in each country there is a wide range of security devices, which differ from each other with respect to the character of the secured debt, the collateral that may be used, and the legal concept on which the security rights are based: title-based security rights such as retention of title, security transfer of ownership or leasing exist side by side with the possessory pledge and various devices that are based on the idea of the pledge such as non-possessory registered charges in individualised property or entities of assets.

343. In many cases there is sector-specific legislation that permits security in certain circumstances. This legislation may have been passed on the basis of lobbying by important political constituencies or pressure groups and it may be difficult to explain on more principled grounds. These constituencies who find their business needs satisfied have no particular need to urge the enactment of more universal security instruments.

344. In making provision for universal security rights, one might argue that the Guide merely legislates for the equivalent of an English-style floating charge, which has functional analogues in other countries.[432] These other countries however, including the *UK*, generally carve out a proportion of all-assets security for the benefit of unsecured creditors.[433] On the other hand, it may be that 'carve-outs' would be factored into the borrowing base with secured creditors extending less credit as a result. This might have a particularly adverse impact on marginal businesses resulting in further insolvencies.

345. On the second point, requiring public notice of the filing of security interests as a condition of general effectiveness is fairly controversial in *Austria* and *Germany*. The main forms of personal property security in *Germany* are outside any registration regime. Moreover, it does not seem that there is any major pressure for reform at the national level. Even the distinguished commentator Professor Ulrich Drobnig, who is generally favourably disposed to Article 9 type reforms, has downplayed the importance of the publicity principle in this connection, asking:

> 'is the complicated technical system really necessary if all the information it offers is a notice that there may exist a security interest, so that intending creditors are put on

---

431 See E.-M. Kieninger (ed.) *Security Rights in Movable Property in European Private Law*, 648. See also U. Drobnig, [2003] *European Review of Private Law* 623; C. Bourbon-Seclet, [2005] *Journal of International Banking Law and Regulation* 419; M. di Luigi, [2008] *Journal of Business Law* 526.

432 See P. Wood, *Law and Practice of International Finance*, 264, with a list of statutory general business charges of varying scope.

433 See what is now s. 176A Insolvency Act 1986 and the Insolvency Act 1986 (Prescribed Part) Order 2003 which fixes the proportion of collateral set aside. See generally G. McCormack, *Secured Credit under English and American Law*, 46–48 and 108–112.

notice but have to turn to the debtor in order to verify the true state of affairs. Is not nearly the same effect achieved in countries without a registration system where the courts proceed from a general presumption that business people must know that any major piece of equipment is bought on credit?'[434]

346. On the other hand, one might argue that a registrationless regime of personal property security only works well in a relatively closed credit market like *Germany* where there are a number of powerful players with a quasi-monopolistic control on credit.[435] In a closed credit market, leading banks have detailed information on the financial behaviour and credit needs of businesses. This is much less likely in a global credit market with financial institutions and bond traders operating across national frontiers. Potential lenders simply do not have the business background and information on potential borrowers. If one does not have information that is publicly available through a filing system, then financial institutions who are trying to enter the credit market are also effectively excluded. They do not have the fund of built-up knowledge and experience.

347. On notice filing rather than transaction filing, divorcing registration from particular individual transactions opens up the possibility that the register may become less reliable as a source of information. A searcher cannot be sure whether a particular entry on the register relates to an actual transaction between the parties or whether it relates to a transaction that was contemplated but never in fact materialised. The information that is publicly available is less than under a transaction filing system and, in the modern information age, this state of affairs hardly seems justifiable. The internet and modern methods of data capture should also allow easy registration of security instruments, and any loss of financial privacy associated with such a procedure could be alleviated by the hiving off of commercially sensitive information to a separate document.

348. Registration in advance of a transaction seems to provide relatively little advantages and, in any event, its benefits can largely be secured through a modification of a transaction-based filing system that allows registration in advance but under which the registration lapses if a confirmatory filing is not made within a particular period of time.

---

434 See U. Drobnig, [2003] *European Review of Private Law* 623 at 660.

435 For a somewhat sarcastic panegyric to the American system see J. White, (1995) 79 *Minnesota Law Review* 529 at 530: 'The filing system is an integral part of the most sophisticated secured lending system known to mankind. Only by an effective filing system can a secured lender know of other lenders and only by it can later secured lenders and unsecured lenders be encouraged to lend. Without such a system, lenders would grow wary, commerce would be hobbled, and the manifold commercial ends that are met by commercial lenders would be stunted, rendered more costly, or stymied altogether.'

349. On the third point, the Guide follows a broad Article 9 functional approach towards security with the treatment of title-retention devices assimilated to that of traditional security rights. Registration is required for third party effectiveness of the rights in question. The European approach is very different. By and large, European jurisdictions, both civil and common law, do not apply registration requirements to quasi-securities. The dividing line between security strictly so-called and 'quasi-securities' may be a thin one in particular cases, but it is a line that is generally respected. In the main, quasi-securities do not have to be publicised through registration as a condition of third party effectiveness, though the position is far from uniform and *Hungary* is a notable exception.

350. While subject to criticism in certain respects, the UNCITRAL Guide has influenced international law reform efforts in the secured transactions field. It has also influenced the rules on proprietary security in movable assets in the Draft European Common Frame of Reference (DCFR) in respect of European Private Law. The relevant rules are in Book IX of the DFCR and were prepared by a team headed up by Professor Ulrich Drobnig. We now turn to these provisions.

3.6. RULES ON PROPRIETARY SECURITIES IN BOOK IX OF THE DCFR

351. At the institutional level the genesis of the proposal for a Common Frame of Reference (CFR) comes from the 2001 European Commission Communication on Contract Law[436] and a 2003 Action Plan that suggested possible avenues of development including a CFR. The CFR was envisaged as having various functions. One would be to provide a set of model terms for contracting parties. Another would be to serve as a toolbox or source of inspiration for European institutions (or even national legislatures) contemplating further legislative initiatives. Another possibility saw the CFR standing as an optional instrument applying to cross-border contractual relationships and expressly or impliedly selected by the parties, whether on an 'opt-in' or 'opt-out' basis. It should be noted that in the whole process the European Commission took great care to avoid use of the word 'Code', but the task of producing the first draft of the CFR

[436] See the von Bar Study Group on the European Civil Code: <www.sgecc.net> accessed 11 May 2016 and the Acquis Group on European Private Law: <http://www.acquis-group.jura.uni-osnabrueck.de> accessed 11 May 2016, and see also the Joint Network on European Private Law: <www.copecl.org> accessed 11 May 2016 There is a vast academic literature, and for a taster see M. van Hoecke and F. Ost (eds.), *The Harmonisation of European Private Law*; H. Collins, *The European Civil Code*. See also M. Kenny, (2006) 12 *Columbia Journal of European Law* 775.

was given to an Academic Network led by a group called the Study Group on a European Civil Code.

352. The Study Group produced a comprehensive draft CFR covering broad areas of private law including secured transactions, or 'proprietary security' as it is called in the language of the CFR.[437] The standard reason given for the inclusion of proprietary securities in the CFR seems to be that they are part of private law, being generally the product of contract, and have often been included in national civil codes, though usually not in an exhaustive way.[438] In addition, it might be easier to find agreement on the content of such provisions than on, say, provisions of family law, where moral and ideological differences run deeper. There have been objections to the CFR proposal on constitutional, economic and cultural grounds and it may be that the case for a CFR is ultimately a political case, based on advancing the goal of European legal integration.

353. The proposals on proprietary securities in the DCFR undoubtedly have some similarities with the UNCITRAL guide. They take a flexible approach towards creation and permissible limits of security, appearing to permit the creation of security over all sorts of property for all types of credit provider, though this goal is less clearly articulated in the DCFR. This is, however, more a matter of inference in the DCFR than anything else. There is nothing equivalent to Recommendation 17 of the UNCITRAL Guide providing that a security right may encumber any type of asset, including parts of assets and undivided rights in assets.

354. The DCFR, in line with the Guide, distinguishes between the creation and third party effectiveness of security rights. It also provides for different methods of perfection depending on the nature of the secured property, though registration is available as a matter of securing third party effectiveness in all instances. Registration is clearly envisaged as the standard method of achieving third party effectiveness. Other methods, however, may be more effective in certain circumstances in the sense that a secured party who has registered its security rights may potentially lose out in a priority battle to another secured party who has gained third party effectiveness in a different way.

355. Again like the Guide, the DCFR adopts a recharacterisation approach, in essence treating retention of ownership devices as security interests by applying

---

437 A team headed by Professor U. Drobnig (Hamburg) has produced the part of the Academic Common Frame of Reference dealing with credit securities: see <www.sgecc.net> accessed 11 May 2016.

438 See generally J. Basedow, [2001] *Journal of Business Law* 569. See also U. Drobnig, 'A Subsidiary Plea: A European Contract Law for Intra-European Border-Crossing Contracts', in S. Grundmann and J. Stuyck (eds.), *An Academic Green Paper on European Contract Law*, 343.

registration requirements to the same.[439] Retention-of-ownership devices include reservation-of-title clauses in sale-of-goods contracts, hire-purchase contracts, consignment contracts and finance leases. The distinction between security rights strictly so-called and retention-of-ownership rights, however, is preserved in respect of default. On the realisation of the collateral, the holder of a security interest is not entitled to any 'surplus' over and above sums owing from the borrower. A 'retention-of-ownership' seller or lessee, on the other hand, is entitled to the surplus when the goods are repossessed and resold for more than the original purchase price.

356. The general line taken by the DCFR in respect of retention-of-ownership devices is the same as that in the Guide, though some of the details are different. The Guide makes express provision for a greater range of cases and also entertains the possibility of alternative provision in certain instances.

357. Both the DCFR and the Guide make provision for the general third party effectiveness of security rights through registration. The resemblances between the DCFR and the Guide are obvious in this respect but so too are the divergences. The DCFR is not as rigorously committed to the notion of notice filing and also disallows secured parties from relying on the benefits of the security in certain situations by making use of a concept akin to estoppel. Book IX – 3:305 of the DCFR echoes Recommendation 67 of the Guide, allowing entries to be made in the security rights register either before or after the contract for proprietary security has been concluded, but there is no provision that mirrors Recommendation 68 in stating that one notice is sufficient for multiple security rights arising from multiple agreements between the same parties.

358. The DCFR strikes out in a different direction from the Guide by imposing a duty on a registered security creditor to respond to requests by inquirers for information that concerns any security right covered by the entry so long as these requests are made with the security provider's approval.[440] This duty is owed both to the inquirer and to the security provider, and the secured creditor is liable in damages to both parties for any loss caused by breach of the duty.[441] But more significant than the liability in damages are the implications in terms of loss of priority if a secured party fails to handle information requests in the correct way. If the secured creditor incorrectly informs the inquirer that the assets concerned are not encumbered, the inquirer can within three months acquire a

---

439 See rr. 1.10 and 3.301 and also 3:303(1): 'For the purposes of the European register of proprietary security no distinction is made between retention of ownership devices and security.'

440 Rule 3.319.

441 Rule 3.319(4).

proprietary right in these assets in priority to the secured creditor despite the fact that there is an entry in the register covering the secured creditor's rights.[442]

359. Despite these differences it is probably fair to say that the similarities between the Guide and the DCFR outweigh the dissimilarities. The overall approach of the two instruments in significant respects is similar, although the general philosophy of the DCFR is not set out with the same clarity as the statement of key objectives in Recommendation 1 of the Guide. The DCFR, like the Guide, takes a facilitating and enabling approach towards the creation of security rights. Certain retention of ownership devices is deemed to create security rights. There is a general requirement of registration for third party effectiveness of security rights and also rules turning principally on the time of registration to determine priority between more than one security interest in the same collateral.

4. CONCLUSIONS ON CONVERGENCE AND REFORM

360. This study suggests that there is still wide divergence between the law in Member States in respect of security rights and the priority of secured creditor rights in insolvency proceedings. At the risk of over-generalisation, there appears to be a broad split between Germanic/Anglo-Saxon countries on the one hand, and 'Latin' countries on the other hand. The first camp assigns much greater priority to security interests in insolvency proceedings than the second camp. Eastern European countries have largely reformed their laws on secured interests and bankruptcy – in some cases under US influence – and tend to fall into the first camp.

361. While a variety of factors undoubtedly enter into the calculation of credit risk, the variations in respect of security rights and priority rights on insolvency may cause creditors to assess credit risk differently depending on the different EU country. This in turn may deter cross-border investments and hamper the growth of a single market in financial services across Europe. Measures to promote greater convergence in respect of Member States' laws may have the positive effect of stimulating cross-border investment and enhancing the single market.

362. EU Member States, on the whole, do not perform particularly well on the World Bank Doing Business indicators. This suggests that the laws in Member States are in need of 'modernisation' and reform to bring them up to international signifiers of best practice. Indeed in the past, the Doing Business reports have rebuked (albeit obliquely) German and Austrian law for not having

---

442 Rule 3.322.

a comprehensive system for the registration of security interests over personal property.[443] According to the reports, security rights need to be publicised through a reliable and affordable public registration system and in a system including several registries, the registries need to be integrated to the greatest extent possible so that that potential creditors can easily retrieve all notices of security interests that have been recorded.

363. By way of contrast the DCFR project on European private law has been commended with the World Bank stating that in in 'the European Union, as part of the efforts to harmonize private law, scholars from economies with different legal traditions have reached consensus on the importance of a single notion of security right – with pledges covered by the same rules and principles for creation, publicity and enforcement as assignments of claims, transfers of ownership, and sales and leaseback agreements.'[444]

364. There are however certain provisions in the DFCR recommendations that seem impractical given the present state of European integration. For instance, the CFR proposal makes provision for a Europe-wide register of security interests. In a Europe of nation States the idea of replacing separate national registers with a single, unified European register appears unrealistic, especially given the fact that in the US, notwithstanding political unity and despite Article 9 of the Uniform Commercial Code on security interests, there is not a uniform national register.

365. Moreover, the Doing Business 'getting credit' indicators are potentially misleading in that they measure the 'law on the books' rather than its actual implementation in practice. There may be a significant gap between the two. The nomenclature is also misleading because there is no attempt to measure the actual availability of credit in a particular country with the focus very much being on the 'formal' law.

366. Be that as it may, the 'getting credit' methodological criteria (together with the EBRD Model Law and Core Principles, the UNCITRAL Legislative guide and the DFCR recommendations) provide a resource tool for Member States (and the European Commission) in seeking to update their respective laws on secured credit and priority rights in insolvency. While reforms should be sensitive to local legal traditions and the history and traditions of Member States, history is not necessarily destiny and practical measures to bring about real improvements may be possible.

---

[443] See the World Bank Doing Business reports for 2005 and 2004, 47 and 68 respectively. The 2005 report suggests a simple solution to the problems afflicting personal property security law – the validation of universal charges and the creation of a unified registry of movable property charges indexed by the name of the debtor.

[444] World Bank 2015 Doing Business Report, 68.

CHAPTER 4
TRANSACTIONAL AVOIDANCE, NATIONAL LAWS AND POSSIBLE REFORMS

1. INTRODUCTION

367. In Chapter 2 it was explained that in cases with a cross-border EU element, Article 13 of the EIR (Article 16 of Recast) makes it difficult for an insolvency practitioner (IP) successfully to challenge transactions that have been entered into by the debtor prior to the commencement of formal insolvency proceedings and that are detrimental to the general body of creditors. The defendant in any avoidance action has a defence if it can show that the transaction was subject to the law of an EU Member State which does not allow avoidance in the particular case. Inevitably the IP's task is more difficult and it becomes a struggle to capture or recapture 'value' for the benefit of the insolvency estate. The effect of the Article 13 defence is greatly to narrow the potential application of avoidance provisions and therefore greatly to weaken implementation of the policies of fairness and priority that underlie such avoidance provisions. To take an example, the law of the forum State may have 7 avoidance preconditions in its insolvency law but only 2 of these are shared with the State to whose laws the transaction is subject. This State however, may have 5 additional requirements. Therefore, to challenge the transaction successfully the IP would need to overcome an effective double avoidance hurdle and establish that all 12 elements were present in the particular case once the defendant raised the lex causae as a defence. This is a tough burden for the IP on any reckoning.

368. The Article 13 defence is designed to safeguard the stability of transactions and to protect legitimate transactions. Chapter 2 discussed Article 13 in detail and explored various options for achieving a more appropriate balance in reconciling and accommodating the potentially conflicting goals of transactional avoidance and transactional stability. One of these options was to harmonise the substantive law on transactional avoidance in the EU Member States but this may not be a realistic and feasible option given the divergences between current national laws. The main part of this chapter considers in detail and from a comparative perspective, the substantive law on transactional avoidance in the countries that form the subject matter of this research project. It highlights similarities and dissimilarities between these laws and sets out situations where the laws may be expressed in different ways but the outcomes are substantially similar. The main part of this chapter is divided into nine sections as follows

- the scope of national avoidance rules;
- rationale of the avoidance rules;
- the conditions for the application of the rules and the length of the 'suspect period';
- general avoidance rules;
- distinctive avoidance rules in the legal systems;
- application of avoidance rules to transactions with a cross-border element;
- operation of the rules in respect of transactions that favour parties who are connected to the debtor;
- defences that may be availed of by the defendant in an avoidance action;
- conclusions on national transactional avoidance laws.

Some of these sections are further sub-divided.

369. The second part of this chapter considers the extent to which the transactional avoidance law in the EU countries under review measures up against international benchmarks such as the World Bank Doing Business 'resolving insolvency' indicators and the UNCITRAL Legislative Guide on Insolvency. It asks whether there is any pressing need for reform at the national or EU level in light of these international benchmarks. Finally, it considers what form any reform measures might take.

2. NATIONAL RULES ON TRANSACTIONAL AVOIDANCE

370. All the legal systems reviewed as part of this study contain rules that operate once a debtor enters insolvency proceedings and that provide for the invalidation of transactions entered into by the debtor prior the commencement of the insolvency proceedings. We now take a closer look at some general aspects connected to the avoidance of transactions in insolvency proceedings and subject them to a comparative overview.

2.1. THE SCOPE OF NATIONAL AVOIDANCE RULES

371. We focus on three parameters in determining whether the rules of transactional avoidance are applicable or not: (1) is the debtor a natural or a legal person?; (2) is the debtor running a business or is it a case of consumer/personal bankruptcy?; (3) what kind of insolvency proceedings are involved (i.e. liquidation or restructuring) proceedings)?

372. A majority of the legal systems reviewed provide for comprehensive avoidance regimes. In *Germany, Austria* and *Spain*, the transaction avoidance rules apply regardless of whether the debtor is a legal or natural person, whether she is running a business or not and whether the proceedings are liquidation proceedings or restructuring (plan/composition) proceedings except in the latter case if it otherwise provided for in the restructuring plan. Spanish law provides for certain pre-insolvency composition proceedings. Transactions carried out under a restructuring plan approved in such proceedings are, under certain circumstances, not subject to avoidance in later insolvency proceedings. This point is explained more fully later in this chapter.

373. *England* and *Poland* also have comprehensive transactional avoidance regimes. Although *English* law contains different avoidance provisions for corporate debtors and individual debtors, both sets of rules lay down mostly the same conditions under which a transaction is avoidable. Under English law there is also a provision only applying to natural persons engaged in business according to which unregistered general assignments of book debts may be subject to avoidance. This serves to a certain extent as the limited 'personal' equivalent of the registration of charge regime applying to companies. If a company creates a charge and this is not registered then the charge is invalid in the event of the company going into administration or liquidation.

374. *Polish* law, on the other hand, under the new Restructuring Act 2015 provides for specific avoidance rules as far as restructuring proceedings are concerned. These rules to a great extent mimic the rules of the Insolvency Act 2003 that are considered in the Polish national report and which remain relevant for liquidation proceedings over corporates and individuals as well as for consumer/private insolvency proceedings.

375. *Ireland* also provides for a relatively wide scope of avoidance rules. As under English law, a distinction is made between corporate and individual debtors but avoidance rules with a generally equivalent standard are provided for both. Nevertheless, the scope of avoidance under Irish law is limited compared to the other legal systems as avoidance rules in corporate insolvency proceedings apply in liquidation proceedings only whereas avoidance in administration proceedings (in Ireland: 'examinership') is not possible. This is the case because the proceedings are intended to be of relatively short duration and avoidance procedures would lengthen the process unduly.

376. *Hungarian* and *Lithuanian* law provide for insolvency proceedings in respect of individuals acting as entrepreneurs[445] and likewise there are no

[445] In Hungary the Act on Consolidation of Debts of Physical Persons providing for the first time insolvency proceedings in respect of individuals came into force on 1 September 2015.

limitations in the scope of avoidance provisions. Neither are there any limitations with respect to the nature of the insolvency proceedings (i.e. liquidation and administration).

377. Under *French* and *Italian* law, avoidance rules apply only if the debtor is engaged in business as an entrepreneur regardless of operating as a separate legal entity or as an individual and whether liquidation or restructuring proceedings are conducted. There is a distinctive rule in Italian law: all different insolvency proceedings under which avoidance rules apply (*fallimento* and *liquidazione coatta adminstrativa*, both aimed at liquidation, and *amministrazione straordinaria*, aimed at restructuring) are addressed only to 'medium-large' entrepreneurs.

378. Even where an avoidance regime does not distinguish between corporate and individual debtors, there may be specific rules that by nature only apply to debtors that are corporates or entrepreneurs (e.g. the invalidation of floating charges under *English* law, the avoidance of shareholder loans under *German* law, the avoidance of excessive remunerations for directors under *Polish* law).

2.1.1. Standing to bring avoidance actions legal consequences

379. The first question that arises is who is granted standing to start court proceedings? All the legal systems reviewed grant this right to the IP (insolvency practitioner, i.e. administrator, liquidator). This applies also where the law allows debtor in possession insolvency proceedings. Although in these debtor in possession proceedings the IP is generally granted a supervisory role, it is the IP (in German self-administration proceedings called 'custodian', in Austrian self-administration proceedings called 'restructuring administrator') who is entitled to standing. There are a few exceptions to this rule. The most important one is laid down in *Hungarian* law where the IP as well as the creditors are entitled to enforce not only the civil law-based actio pauliana (a remedy rooted in Roman civil law and still available under many legal systems which is aimed at reversing transactions made between the debtor and a creditor with the fraudulent intent to harm other creditors of the debtor) but also actions based on the avoidance rules provided by insolvency law, and regardless of whether the proceedings are liquidation or restructuring proceedings.

380. In *Spain* also, creditors may be entitled to file avoidance proceedings but only if they had requested the IP to do so and the IP had remained inactive for two months following the request. In *Austria*, where consumer/personal insolvency proceedings are usually conducted as debtor in possession proceedings and a restructuring administrator is not appointed, it is also up to the creditors in these proceedings to file court actions in connection to the avoidance of transactions. Other exceptions are provided for under *English* and *Irish* law.

English insolvency law contains a rule providing for the invalidation in certain circumstances of transactions putting assets beyond the reach of creditors. Although part of the Insolvency Act, the provision applies in and outside of insolvency proceedings. Therefore, alongside the liquidator or administrator, any affected person has standing to seek a court order under the rule. After the opening of formal insolvency proceedings, however, the leave of the court is necessary if the claimant is not the liquidator or administrator. Under *Irish* law, the provisions dealing with the avoidance of fraudulent transactions (there are two rules, one for corporate and one for individual debtors) grant standing to other creditors besides the IP. One last exception is provided for under *French* law. As well as the IP, the public prosecutor is granted standing on an equal footing.

381. In this context, it has to be mentioned that except for the *common law* and *German* law systems all the legal systems reviewed provide for the actio pauliana. However, in common law and the German law systems there are rules provided by insolvency law having a similar effect as the actio pauliana. For further details, see the discussion on the debtor's fraudulent intent as a reason for transactional avoidance and the explanations on the avoidance of fraudulent transactions under the national insolvency laws.

382. In the other legal systems reviewed, the actio pauliana is applicable in insolvency proceedings alongside the specific avoidance rules of insolvency law. Court proceedings based on the actio pauliana in insolvency proceedings can be brought not only by the IP but by every creditor who may be negatively affected by the transaction.

383. Another question is against whom the action must be brought? Under all the legal systems reviewed, the court action must be brought against the other party or parties to the impugned transaction who have received benefits out of the debtor's assets. The exception to this rule is *Spain* where the action must be brought against both the other party and the debtor.

384. As far as the consequences of avoidance are concerned, the *Spanish, Italian* and *Polish* national reports indicate that in consequence of a successful avoidance action the impugned transaction must be considered relatively ineffective only with respect to the insolvency estate but remains valid in all other aspects. *Austrian* law provides for the same consequence but also states that such a transaction must be declared ineffective with respect to insolvency creditors by the court making this declaration part of the court order. Similarly, the *French* national report indicates that successfully challenged transactions are declared null and void and the court does not restrict this conclusion to relative ineffectiveness. While French law itself declares certain transactions null and void if certain objective requirements are met (automatic transactional avoidance which is also provided under Italian law) a court order is still necessary since the court has to state the grounds of automatic avoidance. Under *German* law, the only consequence of avoidance is that the other party may not derive any rights from the transaction disadvantaging the insolvency estate but avoidance does not lead to any nullity of the impugned transaction.

385. However, the questions of absolute/relative ineffectiveness as a consequence of avoidance and whether the ineffectiveness must be established by a court order seem to be of relatively little significance. The economic result of avoidance actions is the same under all legal systems reviewed: the benefits that the other party received out of the debtor's assets as a result of the impugned transaction must be returned to the insolvency estate. If that is impossible, compensation consisting of the value of the performance received must be paid. The *German, Austrian, Hungarian* and *Spanish* national reports indicate that if the counterparty had provided the debtor with a consideration in respect of the avoided transaction, the other party is also entitled to claim the return of the consideration. Only the *English* law may provide for more flexible solutions leaving a certain degree of discretion to the court by stating that the court may make such order as it thinks fit for restoring the position to what would have been without the impugned transaction. Where the avoidance of extortionate credit transactions is at issue, the court may vary the contractual terms of the transaction.

2.1.2. Limitation periods

386. The limitation period in respect of claims arising from the avoidance of transactions for the benefit of the insolvency estate is of practical relevance especially since the Court of Justice has recently ruled that limitation periods are subject of the lex causae, regardless of whether the lex causae considers the limitation period rule as part of its substantive or procedural law.[446]

387. The shortest limitation periods are imposed by *Lithuanian* and *Hungarian* law. The *Lithuanian* national report indicates that the IP only has a time period of 6 months to examine the debtor's past transactions with a view to possible avoidance. Considering the general suspect period of three years under Lithuanian law this time period seems to be very short. Upon application however, the insolvency court is able to extend this limitation period for another six months. The limitation period does not start with the opening of insolvency proceedings but when the IP has received all relevant documents she needs for her examination. This appears to leave room for legal uncertainty. The *Hungarian* national report indicates that an avoidance action must be brought within 90 days after the IP

[446] C-557/13 *Lutz v Bäuerle* ECLI:EU:C:2015:227, para. 48 et seq.

has become aware of the possible avoidance of the transaction but not later than one year after the opening of insolvency proceedings.

388. Another rather short limitation period is imposed by *Austrian* law, where it is one year from the opening of insolvency proceedings.

389. Comparatively longer limitation periods are laid down in *Polish, German* and *Italian* law. In *Poland*, the limitation period for claims is two years from the beginning of insolvency proceedings. In *Germany*, it is three years beginning with the end of the year in which the insolvency proceedings have been opened. The *Italian* national report also indicates a limitation period of three years beginning with the opening of insolvency proceedings. But avoidance is not possible when the transaction in question dates back more than five years.

390. In *England* the limitation period under the Insolvency Act for bringing avoidance proceedings is 12 years but where the substance of the claim is to recover a sum of money the period is six years. The same general principles apply in *Ireland.*

391. Neither *French* law nor *Spanish* law impose any limitation periods on avoidance actions. So avoidance actions can be brought as long as insolvency proceedings continue and the responsible insolvency practitioners remain in their positions.

2.1.3. Application of the avoidance rules to security and quasi-security type transactions?

392. Generally it can be said that all the legal systems reviewed provide for avoidance rules that catch security rights in rem and quasi-security type transactions. There are three distinct approaches in respect of the application of avoidance rules to security rights.

393. The first one is to forego any particular provisions dealing with the granting of security rights but to use neutral formulations only in the statutory avoidance language such as 'transaction', 'preference', 'performance' and these expressions are to be interpreted widely to catch any kind of transaction including security and quasi-security right transactions. This approach applies under *English, Irish, Hungarian* and *Lithuanian* law.

394. A second approach is to use both particular provisions dealing expressly with avoiding the grant of security rights under certain circumstances and other neutrally formulated avoidance provisions which may also apply to the grant of security rights. Therefore the provisions that deal expressly with security rights are not of an exhaustive character. Especially in tripartite situations, the rules governing the avoidance of gratuitous or undervalue transactions may apply. This approach is found in *German, Austrian, French, Italian* and *Spanish* law.

395. The avoidance rules that deal particularly with security rights are designed only for the commonly known security rights in rem and in general do not apply to quasi-security rights such as the retention of title, leasing or factoring. One exception is provided under *German* and *Austrian* law. The provisions dealing with the grant of security or satisfaction of a claim (in Germany: 'coverage') are to be interpreted widely so the expression 'security' refers not only to security rights in rem. The creation of a set-off could also be a security under these laws. The transfer of claims under a factoring agreement as a matter of property law may be subject to these provisions regardless of whether this transfer is properly classified as the grant of a security or instead as the satisfaction of the claim to transfer the receivables under the factoring contract.

396. Furthermore, future claims assigned under an extended retention of title clause can be subject to the avoidance of security under *German* law. This, however, is not really an exception to the rule since such assignments, although referred to as a quasi-security right in this report, are fiduciary security assignments and therefore common security rights in rem under German law.

397. The third approach provides for a set of rules dealing expressly with the avoidance of security rights in an unquestionably exhaustive way. This approach is found in *Poland*. The relevant rules provide for the avoidance of security for immature claims. They also provide in tripartite situations for the avoidance of security for a third-party debt at no or extremely low consideration. In the latter case, under the other national avoidance regimes the rules for non-profit transactions, undervalue transactions or fraudulent transactions may apply. The rules are not however aimed at also catching quasi-security rights. The Polish national report further points out that it is not completely resolved whether fiduciary security rights (e.g. transfer of title by way of security) which are recognised under Polish law are caught by the provision. According to the Polish Supreme Court, this depends on whether, according to the contractual stipulations in each individual case, the fiduciary transfer serves a real collateral function or not.

398. Another point to mention is that according to the *Spanish* and the *Polish* national reports, financial collateral is generally not subject to avoidance under the national transactional avoidance laws. Other national laws contain similar, if possibly more limited exemptions, disallowing the application of certain limited types of avoidance laws to financial collateral following the translation of Directives 98/26/EC, 2002/47/EC and 2009/44/EC into national law.

399. According to Article 9(1) of Directive 98/26/EC (Directive on settlement finality in payment and securities settlement systems), security rights granted to national central banks, the European Central Bank, or any participant to a system as defined in Article 2(a) of the Directive, in connection to such system are generally not affected by the opening of insolvency proceedings over the estate of the security provider but may be realised in the insolvency proceedings in order to fulfil the secured claim. Further impacts on security rights imposed by national insolvency laws (including possible avoidance) are permitted according to Article 9(2) of the Directive only where securities are provided as collateral and the security right is legally recorded on a register located in a Member State. According to Article 8(1) of Directive 2002/47/EC (Directive on financial collateral arrangements) Member States are to ensure that, in the case of insolvency proceedings, the grant of financial collateral may not be declared void on the sole basis that the financial security has been provided on the day of the commencement of insolvency proceedings or other reorganisation measures but prior to the time of the actual commencement. Furthermore, where a financial collateral agreement contains an obligation to provide financial collateral, or additional financial collateral, in order to take account of changes in the value of the collateral or in the amount of the relevant financial obligations, Member States are to ensure that the provision of financial collateral etc. must not be treated as invalid, or declared void, on this sole basis or on the sole basis that the relevant financial obligations were incurred prior to the date of provision of the (additional) financial collateral or its replacement by other financial collateral. The last proviso is aimed at the avoidance of the grant of security rights for pre-existing claims which is common especially under Roman legal systems but certainly also influences the avoidance of general preferential transactions.

400. However, the effect of these rules in practice should be relatively small as financial collateral, in the understanding of the relevant European law, is mostly created in the interbank market (see the personal scope of Directive 2002/47/EC laid down in its Article 1(2)) or requires at least a specific contractual relationship based on certain financial instruments between a bank and its client (see the definition of a 'system' under Article 2(a) of Directive 98/26/EC). The typical creation of security rights over a borrower's fixed and current assets is not financial collateral in the understanding of the relevant European secondary law and the national rules implementing it.

401. The *Spanish* report also mentions that security rights in respect of certain claims arising from public law are not subject to avoidance.

2.2. RATIONALE OF THE AVOIDANCE RULES

402. There are four specific reasons for transactional avoidance suggested by the national reports: (1) avoidance rules as a remedy to enforce the pari passu principle in a period when formal insolvency proceedings are not yet opened; (2) avoidance rules as a sanction for the debtor's intention to defraud/disadvantage other creditors; (3) avoidance rules providing for a general protection of creditors against the depletion of the debtor's estate thereby ensuring the maximum possible satisfaction of creditor's claims in the insolvency proceedings; and (4) avoidance rules as a means to ensure the restructuring of the debtor's business by preventing creditors from withdrawing assets from a company's estate that are needed for its survival. Only the *Lithuanian* national report indicates that there has been less critical analysis of the underlying reasons for the avoidance provisions. It refers to a simple statement in the introduction of the Lithuanian Insolvency Act that the avoidance of certain transactions is a normal corollary of modern insolvency systems.

403. Most of the specific reasons are to a certain extent reflected by all the legal systems reviewed, although obviously not all these reasons are reflected in all the particular national avoidance rules.

2.2.1. Enforcement of the pari passu principle

404. The *English* law report and the *Italian* and the *German* national reports indicate expressly that the rationale for the avoidance rules is to extend the pari passu principle to a time when the debtor already is in a financial crisis although formal insolvency proceedings have not yet been opened. Bearing in mind that the collective nature of insolvency proceedings providing for the equal treatment of creditors is mainly justified by the fact that the debtor's assets are insufficient to satisfy all of its creditors, the displacement of individual satisfaction by the pari passu principle without the formal opening of insolvency proceedings can also be justified by the actual fact of insolvency, or at least a substantial financial crisis that would lead to insolvency in the near future. Accordingly, under *English* law the avoidance of undervalue transactions and the avoidance of preferences require the debtor to be unable to pay its debts at the time the transaction was made or to become unable to pay its debts as a consequence of the transaction. Under *Irish* law the avoidance of preferential transactions also requires that the debtor was unable to pay its debts at the time of the transaction which leads to the suggestion that the enforcement of the pari passu principle may also be regarded as one of the underlying reasons behind Irish transactional avoidance rules.

405. Under *Italian* law, all the provisions dealing with judicial transactional avoidance (in contrast to automatic transactional avoidance) require the debtor to be actually insolvent at the time of the transaction. Nevertheless, most influential Italian academic opinion considers that the revocatoria fallimentare constitutes a remedy designed not to enforce the pari passu principle, but to provide redress against the damages caused by an insolvent debtor to its creditors. Moreover, in Italy it is commonly accepted that this remedy is peculiar, that it has been cross-fertilised by other remedies (such as those concerning the avoidance of contracts), and there is no strict test of causation proving that the debtor has concretely damaged its creditors.

406. Moreover, under *German* and *Austrian* law, the avoidance of a 'coverage' (i.e. grant of a security or satisfaction of a claim) requires the debtor to be actually insolvent at the time of the transaction, or at least the debtor's imminent insolvency (in *Germany* one to two months before the request to open insolvency proceedings, in *Austria* 60 days before such a request) at the time of the transaction.

407. The pari passu principle seems to influence transactional avoidance under *Hungarian* law to a certain extent, and under *French* law, to an even larger extent. The Hungarian national report points out that, inter alia, the equal protection of creditors is provided for by the transactional avoidance provisions. The French national report states that a debtor in financial difficulties must be prevented from creating preferences in favour of specific creditors. Though none of the *Hungarian* avoidance rules requires the debtor to be actually insolvent at the time of the impugned transaction, preferential transactions are subject to avoidance only if they took place within 60–90 days before the request to open insolvency proceedings. This short suspect period applying only to the avoidance of preferences may justify the general assumption that a financial crisis on the part of the debtor had already occurred at the time that the relevant transaction was carried out, which in turn would justify application of a norm of equal treatment among creditors although insolvency proceedings have not yet been opened. Under *French* law, almost all avoidance provisions (automatic and judicial transactional avoidance) provided for in insolvency law (i.e. not the actio pauliana) require the cessation of payments on the part of the debtor at the time the relevant transaction was carried out which can be equated with the inability to pay one's debts or substantive insolvency.

408. The *Spanish* national report suggests a similar purpose for avoidance rules as it points out that the legal order of creditors shall be maintained before insolvency proceedings are opened. But since actual insolvency at the time of the relevant transaction is not required by any of the Spanish avoidance provisions and the general suspect period of two years seems to be too long generally to assume either imminent insolvency or indeed a financial crisis at the time of the impugned transaction, the pari passu principle seems hardly to be the predominant factor for the avoidance of transactions in Spain. Neither the *Polish* nor the *Lithuanian* national reports mention the enforcement of the pari passu principle as an underlying rationale for avoidance rules. Nevertheless, under *Polish* law the payment or grant of a security for an immature debt is avoidable only if, at the time of the transaction, the debtor was already insolvent and the other party was aware of the debtor's insolvency.

2.2.2. *Avoidance as a sanction for the debtor's intention to defraud other creditors*

409. Avoidance as a response to the debtor's fraudulent intention with respect to other creditors is expressly mentioned only in the *German, Austrian* and *Hungarian* national reports. Under *German* and *Austrian* law, there is one provision particularly based on this rationale. Under both legal systems, transactions are subject to avoidance if they were made by the debtor with the intention to disadvantage other creditors (avoidance of wilful disadvantage transactions). Under *Hungarian* law, there is a specific avoidance provision catching fraudulent transactions, which supposedly requires the intention to harm other debtors. *Hungary* also has the well-known civil law instrument aiming at redressing the damage caused to other creditors by fraudulent transactions – the actio pauliana.

410. The *Spanish* national report also mentions the debtor's fraudulent intent although, as under the other Roman legal systems reviewed, there are no specific provisions in insolvency law aiming at the avoidance of fraudulent transactions. This may be explained by the fact that in all these legal systems the civil law-based actio pauliana, which undoubtedly takes account of exactly this rationale, also applies in insolvency proceedings. Moreover, the actio pauliana is recognised under *Lithuanian* and *Polish* law as applying in insolvency proceedings. Under *Polish* law, however, the actio pauliana may be regarded as being of a subsidiary character in relation to the insolvency avoidance rules. It is only where the avoidance rules of insolvency law cannot provide any remedies for the general body of creditors that the actio pauliana is applicable. *Lithuanian* insolvency law also provides for the avoidance of transactions leading to a so-called 'fraudulent insolvency'. This expression implies the intention to bring about insolvency proceedings which normally would go hand in hand with the intention to disadvantage other creditors. Therefore, under Lithuanian law there are two avoidance provisions (although the actio pauliana is not originally part of insolvency law) that obviously take account of the debtor's fraudulent intention.

411. The *Common Law* Report does not mention the debtor's fraudulent intention either as a reason for the avoidance of transactions. Nevertheless, it suggests that a fraudulent intent on the part of the debtor also plays a role under avoidance law. *Irish* law, for instance, provides for the avoidance of fraudulent dispositions of company property in respect of corporate debtors and for the avoidance of fraudulent preferences with regard to individual debtors. Secondly, the avoidance of transactions putting assets beyond the reach of creditors under

English law requires that the relevant action was carried out by the debtor with the purpose to put these assets beyond the reach of creditors although it does not have to be the dominant purpose. Thirdly, the avoidance of preferential transactions under *English* and *Irish* law requires, besides the debtor's inability to pay its debts, the debtor's desire to put the other party in a better position in liquidation proceedings than it would have if the preference had not been given. The required desire brings the English and Irish provisions dealing with the avoidance of preferences closer to the actio pauliana and to other provisions that require a debtor's fraudulent intention.

2.2.3. Avoidance as a protection of creditors against any actions detrimental to the insolvency estate

412. This rationale is mentioned by all national reports except for the *Common Law* and the *Lithuanian* national report. The *Polish* national report suggests this rationale by stating that transactional avoidance provides for the satisfaction of creditors to the maximum extent which is a main goal of Polish insolvency law.

413. As part of this rationale, one might mention the rules providing for the avoidance of undervalue transactions or not-for-profit/gratuitous transactions. Such rules are contained in all legal systems reviewed except for *Lithuania* where a more generally worded rule provides for the avoidance of transactions contrary to the debtor's interests which should also catch such transactions. Secondly, most of the avoidance rules attacking preferential transactions which in different appearances are found in all the legal systems reviewed at least to a certain extent are based on this rationale but also balancing it with other factors.

2.2.4. Avoidance rules as a measure to assist in the successful restructuring of the debtor's business

414. The *English* report with regard to the avoidance of preferential transactions and the *Polish* national report in general mention that one purpose of avoidance rules is to prevent creditors from withdrawing assets from the debtor's business in the run-up to formal insolvency proceedings – assets that are needed for the debtor's business to survive. The *English* provision dealing with the avoidance of preferences operates comprehensively catching even the satisfaction of mature claims legally owed. On the other hand, its operation requires that factual insolvency on the part of the debtor has already occurred whereas one would assume that an avoidance rule aimed at enabling restructuring would start to operate at an earlier point of time helping to prevent such an occurrence. Moreover, the provision's mental requirement of a 'desire to prefer' on the part of the debtor does not seem to be fully in accordance with the goal of a strict maintenance of the debtor's business. The English report itself mentions that it is questionable whether the avoidance of preferences provision is able to fulfil its proclaimed purposes.

415. The *Polish* law on the other hand seems to focus strictly on preventing persons with insights on the debtor's financial status from withdrawing assets and liquidity from the debtor's business in the run-up to insolvency. Non-gratuitous transactions are only avoidable if they were made in favour of persons closely connected to the debtor. Additionally, excessive remuneration paid to directors of the debtor's business are avoidable. This is a rule which stands out among all the legal systems reviewed. In respect of other creditors, there are, however, no distinctive features that would lead to the assumption that Polish avoidance rules take restructurings more into account than other laws. It remains questionable whether the Polish law really provides better protection of the debtor's business compared with the other legal systems.

2.3. THE CONDITIONS FOR THE APPLICATION OF THE RULES AND THE LENGTH OF THE 'SUSPECT PERIOD'

416. Most of the avoidance regimes reviewed have the same systematic structure. They provide for different provisions laying down different situations under which a transaction can be avoided. Under some of the legal systems reviewed there are some general provisions worded in very broad terms (undervalue transactions, preferences, fraudulent transactions) as is the case with *English, Irish, Hungarian* and *Lithuanian* law. In *England* and *Ireland*, however, these general rules are accompanied by some specific provisions not having equivalents in other legal systems (the avoidance of floating charges under English and Irish law and the avoidance of extortionate credit transactions under English law).

417. In general, the *German* and the *Austrian* avoidance regimes are structured the same way. These laws do not provide a general rule for the avoidance of preferences but for rules governing the avoidance of granting a satisfaction or a security (in *Germany* collectively referred to as 'coverage'). The terms 'satisfaction' and 'security' are used as general expressions which should be understood comprehensively as aiming at situations that under these legal systems would constitute a preference (e.g. satisfaction not only includes payments but performance of services as well as the creation of a set-off, etc.).

418. Although using the expressions 'satisfaction' and 'security' in general terms, these rules are a little more detailed as they distinguish between whether the satisfaction or security was legally owed or not (German law refers to 'congruent' or 'incongruent coverage'). Furthermore, they provide for several variants depending on the financial status of the debtor at the time of the transaction and the other party's awareness of the debtor's financial circumstances. Additionally, German law contains a specific provision providing for the avoidance of shareholder loans. Moreover, both German and Austrian law require that the impugned transaction has caused a disadvantage to the other creditors.

419. *French* and *Italian* law also contain rules dealing with undervalue transactions and transactions made with a fraudulent intention (actio pauliana). French and Italian law contain a rather broad list of provisions describing with more or less specificity the different situations under which transactions are subject to avoidance. Within these broad avoidance categories they distinguish between situations which provide for the automatic avoidance of a transaction and situations which provide for a judicial avoidance of a transaction. The provisions governing automatic transactional avoidance invalidate the transaction automatically if certain exclusively objective requirements are met, whereas the provisions governing judicial transactional avoidance provide for relative invalidity only as a consequence of the successful avoidance action and require that the other party subjectively was aware of the debtor's financial crisis at the time of the transaction.

420. Under Italian law, there is a further sub-division in the category of transactions subject to judicial transactional avoidance into 'abnormal' and 'normal' transactions. In case of abnormal transactions, the avoidance is facilitated as there is a rebuttable presumption that the other party was aware of the debtor's actual insolvency at the time of the transaction. Moreover, under the rules providing for automatic transactional avoidance, it is not necessary that the transaction in question really caused a disadvantage to the debtor's estate. Such a disadvantage is objectively not required by the provisions.

421. Despite providing for comprehensive lists of specific avoidance situations, French and Italian law each contain a generally worded provision to fill possible gaps in the system. In French law, there is the general provision according to which payments and other onerous transactions are subject to judicial transactional avoidance. Under Italian law, there is a provision according to which all transactions made in the suspect period for valuable consideration may be subject to judicial transactional avoidance. The other party to the transaction is required to be aware of the debtor's financial position at the time of the transaction.

422. In a similar fashion to French and Italian law but not as comprehensive, *Polish* law also provides for a (rather short) list of specific avoidance provisions.

423. A different structure of avoidance rules is provided by *Spanish* insolvency law which contains only one general provision dealing with the avoidance of transactions. According to this provision, all transactions detrimental to the general body of creditors are subject to avoidance. Such detriment must be proved by the IP. However, this general rule is supplemented by some provisions stipulating that under specific circumstances there shall be a non-rebuttable or rebuttable presumption that the transaction caused the required detriment to the general body of creditors. The list of situations providing for such a presumption is to a great extent similar to the avoidance situations under French and Italian law. It is not as comprehensive, however, is probably due to the fact that French and Italian law do not provide for such an all-embracing general rule as Spanish law does.

2.3.1. Particularities of the Lithuanian avoidance regime

424. The *Lithuanian* avoidance provisions deserve special mention since they provide for avoidance situations which in their broad wording and content stand out among the other legal systems. Under Lithuanian law transactions are avoidable if (a) they were contrary to the debtor's interests, or (b) they would prevent a settlement with the debtor's creditors, or (c) they led to fraudulent insolvency.

425. The first provision seems to be problematic since without any mental requirements either on the debtor's or on the other party's side, and having regard to the general Lithuanian suspect period of 'at least' three years (the IP is obliged to examine transactions within the previous three years before the opening of insolvency proceedings but is free to examine earlier transactions within an indefinite reach back period), it seems questionable if the provision provides for legal certainty. Secondly the provision seems to be aimed at the debtor's interests and not the creditors' which is different from the other legal systems (e.g. the payment of a claim can be in the interest of the debtor but not in the interest of his other creditors when it comes to insolvency). Only undervalue transactions seem unquestionably to be caught by the provision.

426. The second rule seems to be reflected even less in the other legal systems reviewed. Its rationale is mentioned as questionable by the Lithuanian report as it apparently empowers creditors to influence the decision about what transactions should be challenged and apparently even enables the avoidance of transactions that were not performed under particularly suspicious circumstances (e.g. the satisfaction of a lawfully owed debt). Alongside the long suspect period, this may also cause a great uncertainty among business partners of the debtor. The third rule refers to the specific Lithuanian legal instrument of 'fraudulent insolvency' which sanctions the intended causation of insolvency by disposing of the debtor's assets accompanied by a fraudulent intention with respect to the general body of creditors.

2.3.2. Suspect periods

427. Most of the legal systems reviewed provide different suspect periods for the different avoidance situations.

428. In general, the longest suspect periods apply to those avoidance situations based on a fraudulent intent on the part of the debtor. In those legal systems providing for the actio pauliana it appears that there is an indefinite reach back period. Under *German* and *Austrian* law, transactions where the debtor has the intention to disadvantage other creditors are avoidable within a suspect period of 10 years before the request to open insolvency proceedings (Germany) or with a suspect period of 10 years before the onset of insolvency proceedings (Austria). Under *Hungarian* law, the suspect period for fraudulent transactions is 5 years before the request to open insolvency proceedings but Hungarian law also provides for the actio pauliana. A suspect period of three years for fraudulent transactions is referenced in the *Irish* report in respect of individual debtors.

429. Undervalue transactions are generally subject to a somewhat shorter avoidance period than 'fraudulent' transactions. In *Germany* the suspect period is four years before the request to open insolvency proceedings. In *England*, *Hungary* and *Austria* it is two years before the onset of insolvency proceedings. In *Poland* on the other hand, the suspect period is only one year before the request to open insolvency proceedings.

430. Preferential transactions, on the other hand, are avoidable only if they took place shortly before the opening of insolvency proceedings. In *England* and *Ireland*, the general suspect period is six months before the onset of insolvency proceedings. The same applies to *Poland*. In *Germany*, the grant of a security or satisfaction generally must have taken within three months before the request to open insolvency proceedings to be avoidable. *Austria* applies the same rule but under certain conditions the suspect period is extended to one year. *Hungarian* law also applies a suspect period of 90 days or sometimes only 60 days in case of a preferential performance.

431. Except for the avoidance of fraudulent transactions, the Roman legal systems do not provide such clear gradations in respect of the suspect period for the different avoidance situations. *Spanish* law provides for one suspect period of two years before the onset of insolvency and this applies to all avoidance situations. One general suspect period for all avoidance situations is provided under *French* law as well. The suspect period begins with the debtor's cessation of payments and runs until the opening of insolvency proceedings. In any case, however, it cannot be longer than 18 months. One particularity under French law is that the suspect period must be established by the insolvency court. This appears to be due to the fact that the cessation of payments is the trigger point instead of a fixed statutory time period reaching back from the time when insolvency proceedings were opened. In the case of not-for-profit transactions, the suspect period may be extended to six months before the debtor's cessation of payments.

432. *Italian* law distinguishes between normal and abnormal transactions, both forming part of the judicial avoidance regime, and transactions that are subject to automatic avoidance. In the first case, the suspect period is between six months (normal transactions) and one year (abnormal transactions). The suspect period in relation to automatic transactional avoidance is two years.

433. *Lithuanian* law provides for one general suspect period of three years which in relation to certain kinds of transactions might be disproportionally long leading to a high degree of legal uncertainty. This conclusion is reinforced by the fact the IP is legally obliged to examine all transaction within this time frame for potential avoidance but is free to examine and challenge transactions that date even longer. Therefore, the suspect period is to be understood as 'at least' three years.

2.4. GENERAL AVOIDANCE RULES

2.4.1. Fraudulent transactions/actio pauliana

434. The *Roman* legal systems as well as *Lithuanian* and *Polish* law do not provide for a special avoidance rule in insolvency law dealing with fraudulent transactions or any other transactions influenced by a dubious intention on the part of the debtor but each recognise the civil law-based actio pauliana and its potential application in insolvency proceedings. In its common understanding as described in the *Italian* national report, the actio pauliana requires the debtor's intention to disadvantage his other creditors and awareness, or unawareness due to negligence, of the counterparty that the transaction would cause a detriment to the general body of the debtor's creditors. The *French* national report indicates that the actio pauliana enables the IP and creditors to challenge even transactions that are outside the suspect period in respect of insolvency avoidance rules. The *Italian* national report points out that that in the case of an actio pauliana it must be established that the transaction caused damage to the other creditors whereas this is not required by the insolvency law-based avoidance rules. Under *Polish* law however, the actio pauliana is subsidiary to the insolvency law avoidance rules. This may be justified by the fact that, compared to insolvency avoidance rules, it is necessary to establish a detriment to the general body of creditors as well as mental requirements on both sides of the impugned transaction, which might be hard to prove. Therefore, insolvency practitioners would first try to challenge a transaction on the basis of the insolvency avoidance rules. However, some of the insolvency avoidance provisions (avoidance of gratuitous transactions and of transactions with persons connected to the debtor) under Polish law have evolved from legal presumptions established in the Polish civil code under the lex pauliana regime regarding detriment to creditors and knowledge of the parties.

435. The *Hungarian* national report indicates that fraudulent transfers (transactions) are subject to insolvency avoidance with a suspect period of five years before the request to open insolvency proceedings. The report further indicates that a fraudulent transfer requires the debtor's intention to defraud other creditors and the other party's awareness or negligent unawareness of the debtor's intention to defraud. Alongside this specific insolvency rule under Hungarian law, the actio pauliana also applies in insolvency proceedings and this has similar mental requirements. There does not appear to be any empirical data on whether avoidance actions are more often based on the insolvency avoidance rule or on the actio pauliana.

436. Both the *German* and the *Austrian* insolvency avoidance regimes contain rules providing for the avoidance of transactions wilfully disadvantaging other creditors. These provisions require the debtor's intention to disadvantage other creditors and the other party' awareness of the debtor's intention. So these rules are almost equivalent to the actio pauliana. The suspect period is 10 years before the request for the opening of insolvency proceedings. The *Austrian* national report indicates that the suspect period is reduced to two years if the other party was not aware of the debtor's intention but ought reasonably to have been aware of it.

437. The *Irish* law contains provisions in its insolvency law for the avoidance of fraudulent dispositions of property. The expression 'fraudulent' implies that, at least on the part of the debtor, the intention to disadvantage other creditors is required. There is a specific suspect period of three years before the opening of insolvency proceedings in respect of transactions involving individual debtors On the corporate side, the relevant provision does not state any suspect period but, in deciding whether it is just and equitable to make an order avoiding fraudulent dispositions of company property, the court is required to have regard to the rights of persons who have *bona fide* and for value acquired an interest in the property the subject of the application. Moreover, the relevant provision, in common with the actio pauliana under Roman and Eastern Europe legal systems, grants standing not only to the IP but also to other creditors.

438. In *Ireland*, the avoidance of preferential transactions may also be mentioned, in that the debtor, in carrying out the transaction, must have the 'dominant intention' to grant the other party a better position in a possible future winding up than the party would have without the transaction. This mental requirement at least shows elements of the intention to disadvantage other creditors as under the actio pauliana.

439. *English* law does not provides for the actio pauliana nor does it have specific insolvency avoidance rules dealing with fraudulent transactions. Nevertheless, it contains two provisions that require mental elements on the part of the debtor which indicate similarities with the actio pauliana. The avoidance of transactions that put the debtor's assets beyond the reach of creditors requires the debtor to act with exactly this purpose, although it does not have to be the dominant one.

This provision has other elements in common with the actio pauliana in that it grants standing not only to the IP but also to creditors, and it applies inside and outside insolvency proceedings. There is no specific suspect period connected to the rule. Secondly, comparable with Irish law, the avoidance of preferences, regardless of whether corporate or individual debtors are concerned, requires the debtor to be influenced mentally by the desire to put the other party in a better position in liquidation proceedings than it would have without the transaction. The rather short suspect period of six months before the opening of insolvency proceedings, however, shows however that this provision is based more on the pari passu principle than on the debtor's fraudulent intentions. The suspect period though is extended to two years in the case of transactions in favour of connected parties.

2.4.2. Undervalue transactions/not-for-profit acts

440. The legal systems reviewed, except for *Lithuania,* contain insolvency avoidance provisions dealing with undervalue transactions and/or not-for-profit acts.

441. The *English* report indicates that undervalue transactions are subject to avoidance both for corporates and for individual debtors, though under separate legislative provisions. The expression catches gifts or other transactions that do not provide for the debtor to receive any consideration at all as well as transactions resulting in a significant gap between the value of the performance and the value of the consideration received. The suspect period is two years before the onset of insolvency proceedings. Additionally, it is required that the debtor at the time of the transaction was unable to pay its debts.

442. *Irish* law, however, only contains provisions on the avoidance of undervalue transactions insofar as individuals are concerned with no such provisions applying to corporate debtors. The suspect period is three years. It is also required that the debtor was unable to pay its debts at the time of the transaction. The provision does not operate if the transaction was entered into bona fide and the other party had no notice of the debtor's financial circumstances. There is another provision operating only with respect to individual debtors and which provides for the invalidation of settlements of property not made in good faith and for valuable consideration. This rule does not require the debtor to be insolvent at the time of the transaction. If he was insolvent at that time, however, the suspect period is extended to five years.

443. The *Hungarian* and the *Polish* national report indicate that under their respective legal systems there is one avoidance provision catching both gratuitous and suspiciously (Hungary) or grossly (Poland) undervalue bilateral transactions. Under Hungarian law, the suspect period is two years before the opening of insolvency proceedings, whereas under Polish law it is one year before the request to open insolvency proceedings.

444. The situation is quite similar in the *French* and *Italian* legal systems. In *France*, there is one rule for not-for-profit transactions (gratuitous transactions) that result in the transfer of movable or immovable assets and another rule for significantly undervalue bilateral transactions. Both kinds of transactions are, however, subject to automatic avoidance with the opening of insolvency proceedings. It is necessary though that the relevant transaction was made during the suspect period. A third provision provides for the judicial avoidance (in contrast to the automatic avoidance) of not-for-profit transactions that were made within six months before the debtor's cessation of payments (beginning of the court established suspect period) if the other party at the time of the transaction knew of the debtor's financial crisis (which has to be proven by the IP). This is the only avoidance rule under French law that does not require actual insolvency (cessation of payments) at the time of the impugned transaction.

445. Under *Italian* law, there are separate provisions for not-for-profit transactions and for undervalue bilateral transactions. Not-for-profit transactions are subject to automatic transactional avoidance if they were made within two years before the opening of insolvency proceedings (suspect period). Undervalue bilateral transactions are subject to judicial transaction avoidance if the obligations of the debtor are more than 25% greater in value terms than the consideration received. The transaction must have been carried out within one year before the opening of insolvency proceedings; the debtor must have been insolvent at the time of the transaction and the other party must have been aware of this. This awareness, however, is rebuttably presumed since such undervalue transactions are categorised as abnormal transactions under Italian law.

446. Under *Spanish* law there is a specific provision in the case of not-for-profit transactions establishing a non-rebuttable presumption that the required detriment to the general body of creditors was caused by the transaction. Bilateral undervalue transactions remain subject to the general rule stipulating that transactions causing a detriment to the general body of creditors are subject to avoidance. The onus however is on the IP to prove such a detriment. The suspect period in each case is two years before the opening of insolvency proceedings.

447. The *German* and the *Austrian* legal systems contain rules according to which transactions granting the other party gratuitous benefits are subject to avoidance. Both provisions clearly catch transactions that do not provide for any consideration. In the case of mutual performance differing in their value one has to take the mental state of the parties into account. Under *German* law, there is no gratuitous (undervalue) transaction if, according to the subjective views of the parties, the consideration received by debtor is considered adequate although objectively not matching the value of the debtor's performance. However, the parties are granted only a certain degree of (economic) discretion to assess whether the consideration is adequate or not. In *Austria*, on the other hand, in the case of mutual performance objectively differing in value the operation of the rule depends on whether the debtor wanted to make a 'gift,' as it were, of part of its performance and whether the other party was aware of this intention. Under both laws it can be said that the more significantly the value of the consideration received is less than the value of the performance granted, the more likely it is that the transaction is avoidable. The suspect period in *Germany* extends back four years before the request to open insolvency proceedings whereas in *Austria* the suspect period is two years before the opening of insolvency proceedings.

448. Under *Lithuanian* law there are no specific provisions dealing with gratuitous transactions or undervalue transactions. There is, however, a general rule making transactions that were contrary to the debtor's interest subject to avoidance. Undervalue and gratuitous transactions are potentially caught by this provision. The suspect period is at least three years.

449. By way of conclusion, it can be said that most legal systems provide for rules facilitating the avoidance of undervalue or gratuitous transactions either by providing for a rather long suspect period or by establishing presumptions regarding mental requirements. Aside from *Lithuania*, only *Spain* seems to lag behind, since it does not have specific rules dealing with bilateral undervalue transactions. Nevertheless, under Spanish law such transactions can still be avoided if the IP proves that a detriment was caused to the general body of creditors which in the case of undervalue transactions should not be that difficult. Therefore, it is questionable whether the lack of a specific provision really leads to practical differences. This finding may also apply to *Lithuanian* law on the basis that gratuitous and undervalue transactions are caught by the provision declaring that all transactions against the debtor's interests are avoidable. Another matter to mention is that, except for the Germanic legal systems, most legal systems require a significant difference in values when it comes to the avoidance of bilateral transactions at an undervalue. The Germanic legal systems declare any undervalue (regardless of the size of the gap between performance and consideration) to be sufficient to trigger the operation of the avoidance rule but, on the other hand, there are stricter mental requirements to be satisfied.

450. Compared to the other legal systems, the *Polish* suspect period of one year in regard to gratuitous transactions seems rather short.

2.4.3. Preferences

451. The legal systems generally provide for the avoidance of preferences. Under *English* law, the relevant preferential act must have taken place within two years before the opening of insolvency proceedings. It is further required that the debtor at the time the transaction took place was not able to pay his debts and that the debtor was acting with the desire to grant the other party such preference. *Irish* law has a similar provision with respect to corporate debtors but the avoidance of preferences with respect to individual debtors is ostensibly restricted since only 'fraudulent' preferences are subject to avoidance though, in practice, the courts have interpreted the fraudulent preference provision as not requiring fraud in fact. The avoidance provision relating to corporate debtors further requires that the relevant transaction was made within six months before the company's winding up. As under English law, it is required that the debtor at the time of the transaction was not able to pay his debts and that the debtor was minded to give the other party such a preference over the other creditors.

452. *Hungarian* law declares the preferential treatment of creditors as subject to avoidance. The suspect period is 90 days before the request to open insolvency proceedings. There is, however, a specific suspect period of 60 days before the request to open insolvency proceedings if the preferential act constitutes the performance of a claim, which is expressly mentioned by law as a sub-type of the more general preferential treatment of creditors.

453. This distinction between a general preferential treatment and the performance of an obligation leads us to *German* and *Austrian* law. These laws provide for certain avoidance rules regarding two categories of transactions: the grant of a satisfaction and the grant of a security (in *Germany* referred to as granting a 'coverage'). A security is deemed to be every transaction which facilitates the enforcement of a claim. Examples are the creation of a set-off situation and also the standard security rights in rem. The enforcement of the set-off itself, on the other hand, would constitute a satisfaction. This shows that the expressions 'satisfaction' and 'security' may catch performances (payment, establishing a security right), the exercise of autonomous rights (set-off declaration) or even factual acts. These provisions, however, do not catch the conclusion of a contract as a matter of the law of obligations. The avoidance of obligational contracts is possible under the provisions governing fraudulent or undervalue transactions, as well as under other provisions providing for the general avoidance of transactions that disadvantage the general body of creditors.

454. Both *German* and *Austrian* law make a distinction between the grant of a satisfaction or security in the way it was lawfully owed and the grant of a satisfaction or security that was not owed at all or at least not owed at the time or in the way it was granted (in *Germany* referred to as 'congruent' or 'incongruent' coverage). In the latter case avoidance is facilitated since a creditor appears to be less worthy of protection if it was granted a performance or security it was not entitled to claim. Under *German* law, the grant of a satisfaction or security in the way it was lawfully owed is subject to avoidance if the transaction was made within the three months before the request to open insolvency proceedings, the debtor at the time of the transaction was actually insolvent and the other party was aware of the debtor's insolvency. Such a transaction is further subject to avoidance if it was made in the time between the request and the opening of insolvency proceedings, and the other party was aware either of the prior request to open insolvency proceedings or of the debtor's insolvency.

455. The grant of a satisfaction or security not in the way or at the time it was lawfully owed is, on the other hand, subject to avoidance if (1) the transaction took place within one month before the request to open insolvency proceedings (without any further requirements), or (2) the transaction was made within the second or third month before the request to open insolvency proceedings and the debtor at the time of the transaction was substantively insolvent, or (3) the transaction was made within the second or third month before the request to open insolvency proceedings and the other party was aware of the fact that the transaction would cause a disadvantage to the general body of creditors.

456. Under *Austrian* law, the grant of a satisfaction or security not in the way or at the time it was lawfully owed is generally avoidable if the transaction was made within 60 days before the request to open insolvency proceedings or within the 60 days before the debtor becomes actually insolvent. Avoidance is however excluded if the transaction dates back more than one year before the opening of insolvency proceedings. So the suspect period may be considerably longer than under German law. With the same suspect period, the grant of a satisfaction or security (regardless of whether the creditor was entitled to claim it in the way or at the time it was granted or not) is avoidable if the debtor acted with the intention to privilege the recipient compared to the other creditors and the recipient was aware of the debtor's intention. This required intention appears to be similar to the required desire to privilege the other party under English/Irish law. Furthermore, the grant of a satisfaction or security (regardless of whether the creditor was entitled to claim it the way or at the time it was granted or not) is avoidable if, at the time of the transaction, the debtor was already actually insolvent or there was a request to open insolvency proceedings and the other party was aware of the debtor's insolvency or the prior request to open insolvency proceedings. Avoidance is however excluded if the transaction dates back more than six months before the opening of insolvency proceedings.

457. It is questionable whether the concept of 'preferences' is interpreted in the same way in different laws. In *English* law, a preference is considered to be any act that puts a creditor in a better position in the event of the opening of insolvency proceedings than he would have without it. The *Hungarian* report mentions the modification of an existing contract for the benefit of a creditor or the granting of a security right for a creditor as examples which probably under all laws would be classified as a preference. Nevertheless, there may be differences, especially when it comes to the satisfaction of debts that were lawfully owed. Under *German* and *Austrian* law, payment of a debt lawfully owed may still be subject to avoidance but under stricter requirements than payments that were not lawfully owed. Under *English* law, the satisfaction of a debt lawfully owing by the debtor may be regarded as a preference as it makes a pari passu distribution among all creditors impossible (e.g. only one debt out of a few is paid). Under *English/Irish* preference avoidance law, there is a requirement that the debtor should be actually insolvent at the time of the transaction. The *Hungarian* national report, on the other hand, mentions as an example of a preferential performance the premature satisfaction of a debt, i.e. the satisfaction of a debt not lawfully owed at the time of the transaction. Conversely, it is at least questionable if the satisfaction of a claim lawfully owed would in any case constitute a preferential performance under Hungarian law.

458. This distinction between the satisfaction of claims lawfully owed and not lawfully owed can also be found in the other legal systems providing for a more detailed list of avoidance situations. When it comes to the payment of debts, these laws mostly distinguish between the payment of mature and immature debts.

459. The following is an overview of typical transactions which may, or may not, be regarded as preferential under the relevant national laws.

2.4.3.1. Payments of immature claims

460. Under all *Roman* legal systems reviewed there are provisions that deal with the avoidance of payments of immature debts. Under *French* law, the payment of immature debts within the suspect period reaching from the debtor's cessation of payments until the opening of insolvency proceedings but subject to an outer limit of 18 months is subject to automatic transactional avoidance. Under *Italian* law, on the other hand, the payment of immature claims is subject to automatic transactional avoidance with a suspect period of two years before the opening of insolvency proceedings, but only if the claim would not become due before the opening of the proceedings. Payments of immature claims that would have become due before that time are avoidable under the provision providing for the judicial transactional avoidance of payments of liquid and due debts by regular means of payments. The suspect period is six months before the opening of insolvency proceedings. As this provision is grouped within the provisions dealing with normal transactions, the IP is required to prove the other party's awareness of the debtor's insolvency at the time of the transaction.

461. Under *Spanish* law, there is a non-rebuttable presumption that the payment of a claim that would not have matured before the opening of insolvency proceedings causes a detriment to the general body of creditors and is therefore avoidable if the payment took place within two years before the opening of insolvency proceedings. If, on the other hand, the claim was secured by a security right in rem there is only a rebuttable presumption that the payment caused such a detriment. In all other cases, the general rule applies according to which any transaction can be subject to avoidance if it has caused a detriment to the general body of creditors and this is for the IP to prove.

462. *Polish* law also contains a specific provision according to which payments of immature claims are avoidable if the payment was made within six months before the opening of insolvency proceedings. It is further required that the debtor was insolvent at the time of the transaction and that the other party was aware of the debtor's insolvency but this awareness is rebuttably presumed.

463. Under *English* and *Irish* law, the payment of immature claims may constitute an avoidable preference. Since the satisfaction of lawfully owed debts may constitute a preference, the same applies a fortiori to the payment of immature claims. The payment of immature claims may also trigger a presumption that the debtor's desire is to privilege the creditor since payments of immature debts are not usual in business relationships.

464. The *Hungarian* report expressly mentions the payment of immature debts as a case of an avoidable preferential performance.

465. Under *German* and *Austrian* law, the payment of immature claims constitutes a satisfaction that was not owed at the time it was granted. The avoidance is therefore facilitated compared to payments of mature debts.

466. It seems that under *Lithuanian* law the payment of immature debts would be caught by the provision according to which all transactions contrary to the debtor's interests are avoidable, but this is not certain since it might depend on the individual circumstances of each case at hand. In the individual case, such a payment may also be avoidable if it would prevent a settlement with the debtor's creditors.

2.4.3.2. Grant of security rights in rem for pre-existing claims

467. All Roman legal systems reviewed contain specific avoidance provisions catching the creation of security rights in rem for pre-existing claims. Under

French law, such transactions are subject to automatic transactional avoidance and the French national report points out that this also applies if the creation of the security right is based on a pre-existing promise.

468. Under *Italian* law, such transactions are subject to judicial transactional avoidance. The Italian law, however, in regard to the suspect period distinguishes between securing pre-existing claims that, at the time the security was created, were immature and securing pre-existing claims that were due at the time the security was created. If the claim was not due at that time, the suspect period is one year before the opening of insolvency proceedings, irrespective of whether the claim would have matured before the opening of insolvency proceedings. If the claim was due, the suspect period is reduced to six months. It is further required that the debtor at the time of the transaction was insolvent and that the other party was aware of the debtor's insolvency. But since both variants of securing a pre-existing claim are categorised as abnormal transactions the required awareness of the other party is rebuttably presumed. Under *Spanish* law, there is the rebuttable presumption that granting a security right in rem for a pre-existing claim causes a detriment to the general body of creditors.

469. The *Polish* national report indicates that there is a specific avoidance provision according to which the grant of a security right in rem for immature claims is avoidable. The suspect period is six months before the request to open insolvency proceedings. It is further required that the debtor was insolvent at the time of the transaction and that the other party was aware of the debtor's insolvency. This awareness is rebuttably presumed. Although only referring to immature claims, the provision clearly catches the grant of security rights for pre-existing claims on condition that the claims have not yet matured at the time of the security transaction.

470. Under *English* and *Irish* law, the grant of a security for a pre-existing debt that was not previously secured before is avoidable as a preference under the previously described circumstances. The mere pre-existence of the claim might also trigger the presumption that the debtor's had a desire to privilege the creditor. The *Hungarian* national report as well points out that that the creation of a security right in the suspect period must be regarded as a preferential treatment.

471. Under *German* and *Austrian* law, avoidance of a security does not depend on whether the security right was granted for a pre-existing or for a concomitant claim. Nor does it depend on whether the claim has matured or not at the time of the security transaction. The decisive question is whether the creditor at the time of the security transaction was entitled to claim exactly this security right on the grounds of a prior or concomitant security agreement. If that is the case, the security can only be challenged according to the stricter provisions dealing with the avoidance of the grant of security lawfully owed. If the security right somehow deviates from the security agreement, avoidance is facilitated as the provision dealing with the avoidance of security rights not lawfully owed would operate. Moreover, the creation of a security for a pre-existing claim, even if pursuant to the security agreement, is avoidable as a security that was not lawfully owed if the security agreement was concluded in the suspect period provided for the avoidance of security rights that were not lawfully owed.

472. Under *Lithuanian* law, such transactions may be regarded as contrary to the debtor's interests depending on the relevant circumstances of each individual case. Such transactions might also be challenged under the provisions whereby transactions preventing a settlement with the debtor's creditors are subject to avoidance.

2.4.3.3. Satisfaction of due monetary debts not by means of money or other regular means of payment

473. *French* and *Italian* law contain avoidance provisions invalidating these kinds of transactions. The *French* national report indicates that payments of due debts by means that are unconventional in business relationships, e.g. giving an asset away by way of payment, are subject to automatic transactional avoidance. According to the *Italian* national report, transactions to pay off matured monetary debts that are not carried out through regular means of payment are subject to avoidance if they took place within one year before the opening of insolvency proceedings. As these transactions are regarded as abnormal transactions, the other party's awareness of the debtor's insolvency at the time of the transaction is presumed.

474. *Spanish* law, on the other hand, does not provide for any specific rules dealing with such kinds of transactions. It may therefore be assumed that the general rule applies according to which transactions made within two years prior to the opening of insolvency proceedings are avoidable if they caused a detriment to the general body of creditors.

475. Since under *English* and *Irish* law the satisfaction of lawfully owed debts may be regarded as a preference, a fortiori the satisfaction of debts by other means than originally agreed upon may also constitute a preference. Nevertheless, the necessary intention to prefer the creditor must still be established affirmatively.

476. It may be assumed that such kinds of transactions under *Hungarian* law would also constitute a preferential treatment of creditors.

477. Under *German* and *Austrian* law, the satisfaction of any debt (regardless of whether it is a monetary or other debt) by means that were not originally envisaged at the time of the transaction is regarded as a satisfaction not lawfully owed. The German report expressly mentions the granting of anything not originally owed on account of performance. Avoidance is therefore facilitated compared to a satisfaction that was granted in the way that it was owed.

478. *Polish* law does not contain any specific provisions for this kind of transactions. It seems as if such transactions are not subject to avoidance at all, as they do not constitute an undervalue transaction – this requires that the value for which the claim was satisfied exceeds significantly the amount of the claim.

479. Under *Lithuanian* law, there is no specific provision either, but it may be assumed that such transactions are contrary to the debtor's interest and are therefore avoidable on this basis. Such transactions might also be avoidable on the basis that they prevent a settlement with the debtor's creditors.

2.4.3.4. Lawfully owed payments of mature monetary debts

480. Under *French* and *Italian* law, the payment of mature debts may be avoided under certain circumstances but the requirements are stricter. Under *French* law, such payments may be caught by the generally worded gap-filling provision according to which payments and onerous acts undertaken during the suspect period (from the cessation of payments until the opening of insolvency proceedings but not longer than 18 months) are subject to avoidance if the creditor at the time of the transaction was aware of the debtor's cessation of payments. These transactions are subject to judicial rather than automatic avoidance. The awareness by the recipient of the payment of the debtor's insolvency must be established by the IP but it is not required that the transaction caused an actual detriment to the general body of creditors. *Italian* law contains a specific provision according to which payments of liquid and due debts performed by regular means of payment are subject to avoidance if they were made within six months before the opening of insolvency proceedings. The IP has to prove that the creditor was aware of the debtor's insolvency at the time the payment was made.

481. Under *Spanish* law, the general rule would apply according to which transactions detrimental to the general body of creditors are subject to avoidance. Nevertheless it is not clear whether under Spanish law the payment of a mature debt would cause a relevant detriment.

482. Under *Polish* law, there are no provisions for the avoidance of such transactions.

483. Under *English* law, the satisfaction of lawfully owed debts may constitute an avoidable preference if the further requirements (suspect period, mental requirements) are met. The *Hungarian* national report on the other hand suggests that the payment of lawfully owed mature debts is not regarded as preferential performance and is therefore not avoidable.

484. Under *German* and *Austrian* law, such payments may be avoided as the satisfaction of lawfully owed debts if the further requirements (suspect periods, mental requirements) are met.

485. Under *Lithuanian* law, it seems questionable whether the payment of due debts would constitute a transaction contrary to the debtor's interests. It seems possible, however, that the payment of due debts might constitute a transaction preventing a settlement with the debtor's creditors.

2.4.3.5. Avoidance of security rights created together with the secured claim

486. Only *Italian* law contains a special provision for such transactions which are subject to the possibility of judicial transactional avoidance. Such a transaction, however, like the payment of due debts by regular means, is considered a normal transaction so the suspect period is reduced to six months and the IP has the burden of proof regarding the other party's awareness of the debtor's insolvency at the time of the transaction. Under *French* law, the concomitant creation of security rights together with the secured claim may potentially be caught as an onerous act by the same general provision which may cover the payment of lawfully owed mature debts. It is required that the transaction takes place within the suspect period and the other party was aware of the debtor's cessation of payments.

487. Neither *Spanish* nor *Polish* law contain specific provisions for such transactions. It seems unlikely, according to *English*, *Irish* and *Hungarian* law, that such a transaction would constitute a preference. There is no specific exemption for such transactions but the conditions for the operation of the avoidance provisions are very unlikely to be met.

488. Under *German* and *Austrian* law, where the creation of a security right complies with the security agreement, the security right is avoidable only strict conditions. If it deviates from that agreement in any way, avoidance is facilitated as the security right then must be regarded as a security not lawfully owed.

2.4.3.6. Security rights acquired through enforcement proceedings

489. Only the *French, German* and *Austrian* national reports refer to the extent to which one can avoid preferential claims over debts that have been acquired in enforcement proceedings. Under the other legal systems, it seems very unlikely that avoidance is a possibility. The relevant *English* provision, for instance, refers to acts done by the debtor.

490. Under *French* law the acquisition of preventive judicial guarantees in enforcement proceedings during the suspect period are subject to automatic transactional avoidance. In France, there is another specific provision according to which the attachment of monetary claims, in particular bank accounts, during the suspect period is subject to judicial transactional avoidance rather than automatic transactional avoidance. This means that the creditor carrying out the seizure must be aware of the debtor's cessation of payments and this is for the IP to prove.

491. Under *German* and *Austrian* law, pledges and mortgages acquired as a mandatory consequence of enforcement proceedings are automatically void if they were established by seizure in the last month before the request to open insolvency proceedings or after such request (in *Austria* 60 days before the opening of insolvency proceedings). Furthermore, in *Germany* and *Austria* it is established by case law that such security rights must be regarded as security rights not lawfully owed. These security rights are avoidable under the avoidance provisions dealing with the granting of a satisfaction or security that was not lawfully owed. The rationale is to extend the application of the pari passu principle to a time when the debtor was already insolvent or at least in a serious financial crisis without insolvency proceedings being opened. Since the seizure in enforcement proceedings does not require any participation by the debtor but is carried out by the responsible authority, this result is also brought about by the wording of the provisions which generally declare that the grant of a satisfaction or security is avoidable regardless of whether the debtor or a third person granted it.

492. The *Italian* national report indicates that as far as the creation of security rights is concerned, the avoidance of the transaction does not require that it is the debtor who carried out the transaction. It may therefore be assumed that security rights acquired through execution against the debtor's assets are caught by the provisions dealing with the avoidance of security rights.

2.5. DISTINCTIVE AVOIDANCE RULES IN THE LEGAL SYSTEMS

493. There are some specific avoidance rules under the legal systems reviewed. These rules may fill gaps that in other legal systems are filled either by their general avoidance provisions or by rules contained in other fields of law such as general civil law or company law. The avoidance rules may also deal with legal instruments that are distinctive to the particular legal system. In this second category, are rules are providing for the avoidance of floating charges under *English* and *Irish* law. Under English and Irish law, floating charges are avoidable if they were created within one year before the opening of insolvency proceedings and the debtor at the time of the transaction was already unable to pay his debts (insolvent). Under *Irish* law, the rule applies only in case of a winding up and not in restructuring proceedings.

494. In the first category is the provision under *English* law according to which extortionate credit transactions are subject to avoidance. Under *German* and *Austrian* law, such an extortionate agreement would be legally classified as an immoral contract and therefore, according to general civil law rules, would be rendered void.

495. *German* law contains a specific provision according to which payments made by the insolvent company in order to satisfy loan recovery claims by its shareholders or the granting of a security for such claims, may be subject to avoidance. For payments, the suspect period is 10 years before the request to open insolvency proceedings or the time between such request and the court order to open insolvency proceedings. In the case of a security being granted, the suspect period is one year.

496. Under *Italian* law, claims for repayment of shareholder loans made at a time when a company was undercapitalised are, in certain circumstances, postponed to the satisfaction of other creditors. It is further provided that, if the loans were repaid during the year before the opening of insolvency proceedings, then the amount must be repaid to the IP. Although the relevant provision is contained in the Italian Civil Code it is considered to be part of insolvency law. This rule is extended to holding companies financing its subsidiaries.

497. In *Polish* insolvency law, excessive remuneration paid to the corporate debtor's directors/officers are subject to avoidance. The suspect period is six months before the request to open insolvency proceedings. Polish law also provides for the avoidance of payments that take the form of contractual penalties if the obligation secured by the penalty agreement was performed to a material extent or the penalty appears to be manifestly high. The suspect period is one year before the request to open insolvency proceedings.

2.6. APPLICATION OF AVOIDANCE RULES TO TRANSACTIONS WITH A CROSS-BORDER ELEMENT

498. Since all the countries whose legal systems are subject to this project are members of the European Union, cross-border insolvencies under the scope of the Insolvency Regulation and connected questions of the conflict of laws regarding avoidance are governed by Articles 4(2)(m) and 13 of the Regulation and the equivalent provisions in the recast Regulation. This means that the national avoidance rules apply to transactions with a cross-border element if the national insolvency law is the lex fori concursus. The rules may also be of importance if according to the lex fori concursus a transaction is avoidable and the defendant relies on the Article 13 defence, i.e. the transaction is not avoidable under the lex causae.

499. The question arises whether the rules could apply in cross-border cases, although the relevant case is caught neither by the Insolvency Regulation nor by the national rules implementing Directive 2001/17/EC (Directive on the reorganisation and winding up of insurance companies) and Directive 2001/24/EC (Directive on the reorganisation and winding up of credit institutions). In respect of transactional avoidance, these directives provide for conflict of laws rules similar to Articles 4(2)(m) and 13.

500. In relation to transactional avoidance there are certain situations where the national jurisdictional rules in respect of the opening of insolvency proceedings and national conflict of laws rules may apply such as where the debtor has its centre of main interests outside the European Union. The *French, German, Austrian* and *Polish* reports indicate that their avoidance rules apply to cross-border transactions if their national insolvency law applies as the lex fori concursus.

501. Based on the wording of the particular provision, the Article 13 defence to avoidance actions would not seem to apply if the relevant transaction was governed by the lex causae of a third country rather than another EU Member State or the asset given away by the debtor had been situated in a third country at the time the transaction was performed.

502. In *England*, once insolvency proceedings are opened, English transactional avoidance law will be applied in respect of any impugned transaction unless the transaction is deemed not to have a sufficient connection with England. The practical result is that the defendant in an avoidance action may have a defence similar to Article 13 even if the relevant transaction is not governed by the law of another EU Member State.

2.7. OPERATION OF THE RULES IN RESPECT OF TRANSACTIONS THAT FAVOUR PARTIES WHO ARE CONNECTED TO THE DEBTOR

503. Almost all of the legal systems reviewed make provision for a stricter operation of avoidance rules in respect of transactions between the debtor and parties closely connected to him. The exception to the rule is *Lithuanian* law, which does not contain any specific avoidance rules targeted on persons connected to the debtor.

504. In general, there appears to be two different ways of implementing such rules. The first is to provide for additional avoidance situations making certain kinds of transactions avoidable only if they are carried out between the debtor and a connected person. This approach can be found especially in *Polish* law. The second one is to supplement the existing avoidance provisions with variants applying only in relation to connected persons, e.g. by extending its suspect period or by providing legal presumptions regarding the required mental elements in respect of the parties.

505. *French* law appears to mix both elements at least to a certain extent. Under French law, the list of security rights that are subject to automatic avoidance extends to the specific French security right of the legal mortgage between spouses. French case law also makes it easier for the IP to prove the other party's awareness of the cessation of payments on the part of the debtor in case of judicial avoidance actions if the parties are relatives or there is a business relationship between them.

506. But the second approach seems to predominate across Europe. Under *Italian* law, the avoidance rules operate more strictly only with respect to the debtor's spouse. There is an indefinite reach back period and the spouse is always presumed to have known of the debtor's insolvency at the time of the transaction. The Italian national report also mentions the statutory obligation of shareholders of the debtor, and other companies within the debtor's group of companies, to subordinate claims for the repayment of loans made to the company at a time when the company was 'undercapitalised'.

507. *Spanish* law, on the other hand, is fairly comprehensive as far as the list of persons who are legally considered to be parties connected to the debtor, but contains a rather limited modification of the existing avoidance requirements. There is one rebuttable presumption that bilateral for-profit transactions have caused the required detriment to the general body of creditors if they were concluded between the debtor and a person closely connected to him. The avoidance of bilateral undervalue transactions should be facilitated by this provision. There are however no modifications of the suspect period.

508. For parties connected to the debtor, the *English* law contains modifications of the rules on the avoidance of undervalue transactions, preferential transactions and floating charges. The avoidance of undervalue transactions is facilitated as there is a reversal of the burden of proof, i.e. the onus is on the defendant to prove that the debtor was able to pay its debts at the relevant time. The avoidance of preferential transactions is supported as the suspect period is extended from six months to two years and the debtor is presumed to have been influenced by the desire to grant the preference. These same modifications regarding the avoidance of preferences are found in *Irish* law. The avoidance of floating charges in *England* is facilitated as the suspect period is extended from one year to two years and it is not necessary to establish that the debtor at the time of the transaction was unable to pay its debts. The same applies under *Irish* law.

509. The *Hungarian* avoidance rules for persons connected to the debtor refer strictly to entrepreneurial debtors. Persons connected to the debtor are business enterprises in which the debtor has a majority control, the members and chief officers of the debtor and business enterprises that are controlled by the same natural or legal person as the debtor. The debtor is presumed to have acted with a fraudulent intent if he entered into a gratuitous transaction or an undervalue transaction with a connected person. The result is that the suspect period applying to fraudulent transactions operates instead of the suspect period for undervalue transactions. The suspect period is therefore extended from two years to five years.

510. *German* and *Austrian* law provide for lists of persons who are considered to be connected to the debtor which in their comprehensiveness are comparable to Spanish law. The laws then apply presumptions insofar as the avoidance situations require mental elements to be established for one or other of the parties. Under *German* law, the avoidance of the grant of a satisfaction or security (regardless of whether lawfully owed or not) sometimes requires the other party's awareness of the debtor's insolvency at the time of the transaction or the awareness of the fact that the transaction would disadvantage other creditors. Such an awareness on the side of the other party is presumed if the other party is connected to the debtor thereby resulting in a reversal of the burden of proof. *Austrian* law applies the same presumption where either the awareness of the debtor's insolvency at the time of the transaction or the awareness of the debtor's intention to advantage the other party compared to other creditors is required. Under Austrian law, there is another reversal of the burden of proof in respect of transactions wilfully disadvantaging the other creditors. During a suspect period of two years before the opening of insolvency proceedings, the other party's awareness of the debtor's intent to disadvantage the other creditors or the other party's unawareness due to negligence is presumed.

511. *Polish* law, as far as the list of persons deemed to be connected to the debtor is concerned, also equals Spanish law as it provides for a very comprehensive list of persons who are legally considered to be connected to the debtor. It even goes beyond Spanish law as the list inter alia includes all partners or shareholders of the debtor and its subsidiaries. It further adds one specific provision to the avoidance regime according to which non-gratuitous bilateral transactions between the debtor and a connected person are subject to avoidance if they were made within six months before the opening of insolvency proceedings. The provision also catches the grant of security rights. As Polish law provides for the avoidance of grossly undervalue transactions within one year before the opening of insolvency proceedings, the provision can only be aimed at facilitating avoidance where it is hard to prove that that there was a difference in value between performance and consideration at all or one could argue about whether the difference justifies the assumption of a 'gross' undervalue.

512. The provision in its result resembles the situation under Spanish law, but may seem to be a little general as it declares all such transactions void regardless of their economic result and leaving no space for defences against avoidance. On the other hand, it provides a shorter suspect period than Spanish law. In the context of debtor-connected persons, the Polish national report also mentions the provision according to which payments of excessive remuneration paid to officers or directors are subject to avoidance. There is an assumption that persons with insights into the debtor's financial situation could be tempted to draw liquidity from the debtor under the cloak of remuneration, although it might be that it is the excessive character of the amount rather than the close connection that imposes a certain suspicion on such transactions justifying their avoidance.

2.8. DEFENCES THAT MAY BE AVAILED OF BY A COUNTERPARTY TO THE TRANSACTION, I.E. THE DEFENDANT IN AN AVOIDANCE ACTION

513. In providing a synthesis of the national report on the aspect of special defences that may be availed by the defendant in an avoidance action, two different aspects should be distinguished. Firstly, general civil procedural law should be considered. There may be special defences in the avoidance law that deviate from the general rules of procedural law, e.g. special rules regarding the burden of proof or special legal remedies against court rulings affirming the avoidance action. This does not however seem to be the case. Only the *Polish* national report indicates that there are deviations from general procedural law, as it states that court rulings affirming avoidance actions based on the grounds of avoidance of gratuitous/grossly undervalue transactions are not appealable. In other countries, the general national rules should also apply to avoidance actions, meaning that normally the IP has to prove that the requirements for the avoidance of a transaction are met unless the avoidance law provides for the reversal of proof regarding certain requirements. Moreover, the regular stages of appeal stipulated by procedural law also apply to avoidance actions.

514. The second aspect involves rules in the national avoidance regimes stating that a transaction that normally would be avoidable is exceptionally not subject to avoidance if certain requirements are met. According to the general rules, the defendant then would have to establish that these requirements were met.

515. The *English* report indicates that there are such rules concerning the avoidance of undervalue transactions and of floating charges. In the first case, a transaction remains valid if it is satisfied that the company entered into the transaction in good faith for the purpose of carrying on its business and that there were reasonable grounds for believing the transaction would benefit the company. The creation of a floating charge is avoidable only except to the extent that there was a consideration for establishing the floating charge and that this consideration consisted of 'new money'. 'New money' does not only include paid money but also goods or services supplied to the debtor or the reduction of debts. Another requirement for this exemption to operate is that the 'new money' has been provided at the same time or after the creation of the charge.

516. Under *German* law, there is a more general rule according to which the conclusion and performance of bilateral transactions may be caught only by the provision providing for the avoidance of fraudulent transactions (wilful disadvantage to the general body of creditors) if the consideration received equals the debtor's performance it its economic value. So transactions at an objective undervalue never benefit from this rule. There is a further requirement that performance and consideration were exchanged in a close time frame. Under *Austrian* law, there is a similar exception established by case law. According to this exception, avoidance of the grant of a satisfaction or security is not possible if performance and consideration are economically connected and take place more or less contemporaneously. The exception, however, seems to be not as comprehensive as under German law, as there are more other avoidance that still may apply. Under both *German* and *Austrian* law, there is another exemption of lesser importance regarding gratuitous performance. The rules that provide for the avoidance of gratuitous transactions are excluded if the transaction constitutes a usual social gift of minor value.

517. The *Italian* report suggests a few exceptions from avoidance and these can be grouped into three categories but all apply only to judicial transactional avoidance rules (i.e. not to automatic transactional avoidance): (1) transactions performed during the ordinary management of the insolvent firm; (2) transactions in connection with an attempted composition of a firm's debts; and (3) certain transactions deemed particularly worthy of protection from the point of view of the counterparty.

518. *Spanish* law provides for the protection of certain transactions in a manner comparable to the first two categories under Italian law. Article 71(5) LC states that ordinary acts of the debtor's business activity shall not be subject to avoidance rules. Secondly, all kinds of transactions are not avoidable if their conclusion and performance complied with the provisions laid down in a pre-insolvency restructuring agreement provided that the restructuring agreement meets certain requirements. Additionally, there is no presumption of a detriment to the general body of creditors in the case of not-for-profit transactions if the transaction was part of normal social interaction, e.g. comparable to the small gifts exemption under German and Austrian law.

519. Under *French* law, it is not possible to challenge a transaction that forms either part or the consequence of a pre-insolvency court-approved restructuring plan. In addition, transactions that took place before the approval of such an agreement are effectively protected from avoidance since the courts may not 'fix' the date of cessation of payments as being before the date of the conclusion of such an agreement.

2.9. CONCLUSION ON NATIONAL TRANSACTIONAL AVOIDANCE LAWS

520. A comparison of the national rules on transactional avoidance in insolvency proceedings reveals considerable similarities between the European legal families. This may derive from the fact that most of the underlying rationales for the avoidance of transactions are to a great extent similar. To a certain extent, however, these similarities are more of a general nature whereas divergences in details remain, especially with regard to the systematic structure of the avoidance regimes, limitation periods and certain additional prerequisites. There are also differences concerning the personal scope of national avoidance rules, as well as certain avoidance rules that are distinctive to a national legal regime. Moreover, the Lithuanian transactional avoidance regime in its general structure and approach is very different from the other legal regimes considered though the results reached in particular cases may be similar in practice. A comparison of the similarities and differences will therefore generally exclude Lithuania.

521. All the legal systems considered provide for rules to reverse three types of transaction. First are transactions where the debtor has the intention to disadvantage other creditors and the counterparty is aware or ought to be aware of this intention (this applies also to Lithuanian law). The relevant rules in this regard generally provide for the longest suspect periods and they normally do not require the debtor's insolvency at the time of the transaction (cf. the actio pauliana and the provisions of the German law systems). It is the debtor's mere intention to harm other creditors which justifies the invalidation of the transaction.

522. Secondly, all the legal systems considered provide for rules to avoid undervalue and gratuitous transactions. There is a view that giving assets away for no equal value without the intention to harm other creditors becomes questionable only at the moment when the debtor is unable to pay their debts or when a financial crisis is foreseeable. Therefore, under a few, but not all the legal systems, the avoidance of undervalue transactions requires the debtor to be insolvent at the time of the transaction (e.g. *England*, *France*, *Italy* only with respect to undervalue transactions in contrast to gratuitous transactions). Another issue that is treated differently in the different legal systems is how to determine whether there has been a relevant undervalue and the amount of this undervalue.

523. The third group of transactions are preferential transactions whereby one creditor is favoured by the transaction over the other creditors of the debtor. It seems accepted among the majority of the legal systems that the reason for the avoidance of such transactions is the command to treat all creditors equally which is deeply rooted in insolvency law – the principle of pari passu. Consequently, all the national provisions with partial exceptions under *Spanish* and *Italian* law either require insolvency on part of the debtor at the time of the transaction or at least operate with rather short suspect periods.

524. About half of the legal systems reviewed (*France*, *Italy*, *Germany*, *Austria*) make a further distinction between certain transactions regarded as 'abnormal' or obviously preferential and other transactions regarded as 'normal' (under German legal systems the criterion is whether a performance was owed by the debtor or whether it deviates in any way from what was originally owed). The avoidance of the latter type of transaction is made more difficult by the fact that suspect periods are shortened and/or the insolvency practitioner is required to prove either the counterparty's awareness of the debtor's insolvency or the debtor's intention to prefer. Examples par excellence of transactions that are regarded as obviously preferential are the payment of immature debts and the grant of security rights for pre-existing claims. These are regarded as unacceptable preferences in all the legal systems including those that contain only more generally worded avoidance provision aimed at preferences.

525. In making the separation between 'normal' and 'abnormal' transactions, certain legal systems also make clear that every kind of transaction is potentially avoidable even if it is not suspicious at first sight (like the payment of a due debt). Since, however, the avoidance of regular transactions may endanger the debtor's capacity to act in the run-up to insolvency, most of these legal systems which clearly admit the avoidance even of 'normal' transactions provide for a special defence, according to which ordinary acts of business activity or transactions which provide the debtor with a consideration equal to the value of its performance in a timely exchange are excluded from avoidance. In *England* (and *Ireland*), however, the avoidance of preferences requires, on the part of the debtor, a specific desire to prefer and this requirement may also serve to exclude regular business activity necessary to maintain the debtor's business from avoidance.

526. In *Poland* there is no general provision directed at the avoidance of preferences and, in this respect, the Polish regime seems somewhat limited compared with the other countries. There are however specific provisions dealing with the payment of premature claims and the granting of security rights for pre-existing claims.

527. The countries generally have some adjustments to the standard avoidance regime in respect of transactions between the debtor and 'connected' persons, however defined. A standard approach is to provide for a longer suspect period and/or to reverse the burden of proof in certain circumstances. There is however considerable variation in terms of detail. The differences range from *Hungarian* law providing essentially for a longer suspect period only for transactions at an undervalue, to *Spanish* and *Polish* law avoiding all kinds of transactions between a debtor and a party closely connected to him in the relevant suspect period.

528. All national avoidance rules would apply to transactions with a cross-border element. The question which national avoidance law applies, however, is a matter of cross-border insolvency law and, in most cases, will be answered by the rules provided under EU secondary law.

529. In terms of special defences against avoidance actions, some legal systems that provide for pre-insolvency restructuring proceedings have specifically exempted transactions made on the foot of such proceedings from the reach of avoidance provisions.

3. BROADER INTERNATIONAL INDICATORS

530. We saw in the previous chapter that EU countries perform not so well on the 'getting credit indicator of the World Bank Doing Business rankings. On the other hand, their performance is much better on the 'resolving insolvency' indicator. For instance, in the 'resolving insolvency' report for 2016, *Finland* ranks 1st with *Germany* 3rd and *Portugal*, *Denmark*, *Belgium*, and the *Netherlands* ranked between 8th and 11th respectively. The *UK* follows at 13th and *Cyprus*, *Austria* and *Sweden* come 17th to 19th respectively. *Slovenia* is the first of the former 'Eastern bloc' countries and comes in 12th followed by *Czech Republic* at 22nd. It is the case that on the indicator Nordic and Western European countries score much better than Eastern European ones though in fact *Malta* is the lowest ranking EU Member State at 83rd.

531. In determining the rankings, two factors are equally weighted, though the second factor which purports to measure the strength of the insolvency framework in a particular country was only introduced into the Doing Business methodology in 2015. The first factor is based on a calculation of the percentage recovery by secured creditors through restructuring, liquidation or debt enforcement proceedings and has been part of the 'resolving insolvency' rankings since their inception. The calculation takes into account whether the business emerges from the proceedings as a going concern or whether assets were sold piecemeal. Then the costs of the proceedings are deducted and, in line with international accounting practice, regard is also had to the value lost as a result of the money being tied up in insolvency proceedings for a particular period of time.

532. The recovery rate is calculated on the basis of outcome, time and cost of insolvency proceedings in respect of a particular kind of local company. But there is no attempt to assess whether this kind of company typifies the local economy or whether the outcomes and returns might be different in relation to different types of company. The measure also focuses exclusively on the return to secured creditors. In most countries, there will not be publicly available and accurate data on recovery rates by creditors and so an assessment of this rate will depend in large part on the subjective views of survey respondents on what are the returns to creditors in their particular countries. The respondents in the main are local IPs.[447]

533. The data for the second part of the rankings on the strength of the legal and insolvency framework also comes from local IPs but since this information is more law on the books, there is more scope for it be verified through a study of laws and regulations. The 2015 Doing Business report explains that this part of the rankings was developed in accordance with the World Bank's Principles for Effective Insolvency and Creditor/Debtor Regimes and the United Nations Commission on International Trade Law's Legislative Guide on Insolvency Law. The scale goes from 0 to 16, with the higher scores supposedly suggesting that the insolvency legislation more appropriately fits the goals of rehabilitating viable firms and liquidating nonviable ones.[448] This postulates a set of normative

---

447 See the 2016 World Bank Doing Business Report, 155–159. At p. 120 it is explained that the Doing Business methodology offers several advantages: 'It is transparent, using factual information about what laws and regulations say and allowing multiple interactions with local respondents to clarify potential misinterpretations of questions. Having representative samples of respondents is not an issue; Doing Business is not a statistical survey, and the texts of the relevant laws and regulations are collected and answers checked for accuracy. The methodology is inexpensive and easily replicable, so data can be collected in a large sample of economies. Because standard assumptions are used in the data collection, comparisons and benchmarks are valid across economies.'

448 See 2015 World Bank Doing Business Report, 27 et seq.

assumptions that some aspects of insolvency law are better or more desirable than others.

534. Essentially the index evaluates four aspects of insolvency law and practice:

- Firstly, the commencement of proceedings index judges whether debtors and creditors have the right to commence liquidation and/or restructuring proceedings and what standard is used to assess whether a debtor is insolvent.
- Secondly, the management of debtor's assets index determines the effect of insolvency proceedings on debtor contracts, whether preferential and undervalued transactions made by the debtor prior to the commencement of insolvency can be avoided; whether new financing is permitted; and the level of priority granted to creditors who provide new finance.
- Third, the reorganisation proceedings index records how restructuring plans are approved and what must be in the restructuring plan.
- Finally, the creditor participation index evaluates the extent to which creditors may participate collectively in insolvency proceedings and the rights of individual creditors to litigate and appeal decisions affecting their position.

A score of 4 is assigned for each of the four component indices and the sum of these four scores is then the overall score in the strength of insolvency framework index

535. One of the factors that is measured is whether undervalue pre-insolvency transactions are subject to the possibility of avoidance in the insolvency proceedings. But it could be argued however, that the assessment is relatively crude and misses out subtleties and nuances in the laws of a particular State. The measurement is done largely on a blunt all-or-nothing basis. There is no attempt made to consider whether avoidance proceedings are easy to accomplish in practice or whether there are circumstances or conditions in place, e.g. difficulties in obtaining litigation funding that render impracticable the possibility of success of an avoidance action in a particular case.

536. The table below is drawn from the World Bank Doing Business dataset for 2016 and looks at the performance of EU countries on the 'resolving insolvency' indicator.

Table 2. Performance of EU countries on the 'resolving insolvency' indicator

Economy	Year	Resolving Insolvency					Resolving Insolvency				
		Rank	Recovery rate (cents on the dollar)	Time (years)	Cost (% of estate)	Outcome (0 as piecemeal sale and 1 as going concern)	Strength of insolvency framework index (0–16)	Commencement of proceedings index (0–3)	Management of debtor's assets index (0–6)	Reorganisation proceedings index (0–3)	Creditor participation index (0–4)
Austria	DB2016	18	82.7	1.1	10	1	11	2.5	5.5	1	2
Belgium	DB2016	10	89.3	0.9	3.5	1	11.5	2.5	6	1	2
Bulgaria	DB2016	48	34	3.3	9	0	13	2.5	4	2.5	4
Cyprus	DB2016	17	71.4	1.5	14.5	1	13	3	4.5	2.5	3
Czech Republic	DB2016	22	66	2.1	17	1	13.5	3	5.5	3	2
Denmark	DB2016	9	87.8	1	4	1	12	3	6	1	2
Estonia	DB2016	40	40	3	9	0	14	2.5	5.5	2	4
Finland	DB2016	1	90.1	0.9	3.5	1	14.5	3	6	2.5	3
France	DB2016	24	77.5	1.9	9	1	11	3	6	1	1
Germany	DB2016	3	83.7	1.2	8	1	15	3	6	3	3
Greece	DB2016	54	34.9	3.5	9	0	12	2.5	5.5	3	1
Hungary	DB2016	65	41.7	2	14.5	0	9	2.5	5	0.5	1
Ireland	DB2016	20	87.7	0.4	9	1	10	3	4.5	1.5	1
Italy	DB2016	23	63.1	1.8	22	1	13.5	3	5.5	3	2
Latvia	DB2016	43	48.1	1.5	10	0	12	2.5	5	2.5	2
Lithuania	DB2016	70	42.8	2.3	10	0	8	2.5	4	0.5	1
Luxembourg	DB2016	80	43.8	2	14.5	0	7	2.5	3	0.5	1

(continued)

Table 2 *continued*

Economy	Year	Resolving Insolvency					Resolving Insolvency				
		Rank	Recovery rate (cents on the dollar)	Time (years)	Cost (% of estate)	Outcome (0 as piecemeal sale and 1 as going concern)	Strength of insolvency framework index (0–16)	Commencement of proceedings index (0–3)	Management of debtor's assets index (0–6)	Reorganisation proceedings index (0–3)	Creditor participation index (0–4)
Malta	DB2016	83	39.6	3	10	0	7.5	2.5	2	0	3
Netherlands	DB2016	11	88.9	1.1	3.5	1	11.5	2.5	6	1	2
Poland	DB2016	32	58.3	3	15	1	12.5	3	6	2.5	1
Portugal	DB2016	8	73.4	2	9	1	14.5	3	5.5	3	3
Romania	DB2016	46	32.7	3.3	10.5	0	13.5	3	6	2.5	2
Slovak Republic	DB2016	33	54.7	4	18	1	13	3	4	3	3
Slovenia	DB2016	12	88.2	0.8	4	1	11.5	2.5	6	2	1
Spain	DB2016	25	71.2	1.5	11	1	12	3	6	2	1
Sweden	DB2016	19	76.6	2	9	1	12	3	6	1	2
United Kingdom	DB2016	13	88.6	1	6	1	11	3	5	1	2

537. The 2016 Doing Business report argues that there a strong link between quality and efficiency with the 'resolving insolvency' indicator highlighted in this connection.[449] It is suggested that if there is a good legal framework for insolvency, then at the end of the insolvency process creditors will obtain a larger share of the amount due to them. *Finland* is given as an example: 'Resolving insolvency there takes 11 months on average and costs 4% of the debtor's estate, and the most likely outcome is that the company will be sold as a going concern. The average recovery rate for creditors is 90.1%. This high recovery rate is paired with a high score on the strength of insolvency framework index.'[450] The report suggests that Finnish insolvency law has a range of good practices including the fact that debtors are allowed to avoid preferential and undervalued transactions.

538. The 2015 Doing Business report in its review of the 'resolving insolvency' indicators also points to the link between efficiency and quality.[451] The recovery rate is said to be a measure of efficiency because it calculates the percentage recoveries by secured creditors in insolvency proceedings and time and cost are two important components of efficiency. On the other hand, the strength of insolvency framework index is said to serve as a proxy for quality in that it rates how insolvency laws accord with internationally recognised good practices. Few economies are said to have insolvency systems with a combination of high efficiency (recovery rate greater than 50%) and low quality (less than 8 of the possible 16 points on the strength of insolvency framework index).

539. There are however, counter-examples which do not bear out this proposition and also some anomalies and possible inconsistencies in the data. *Austria*, *France* and the *UK* get the relatively low mark of 11 on the insolvency framework but have recovery rates in excess of 70%. For *Austria* and the *UK*, the recovery rates are greater than 80%. There is an interesting contrast with *Bulgaria*, which scores 13 on the insolvency framework but with a recovery rate below 50%. Perhaps *Bulgaria* would be viewed by the Doing Business team as exemplifying 'an insolvency system with low efficiency and high quality. These are economies that have well-designed laws but face challenges in implementing them effectively.'[452] An alternative explanation suggests that the Doing Business data may not be robust and reliable in all instances.

540. Be that as it may, all the countries considered as part of our study have provisions in their laws that allow for the avoidance of certain pre-insolvency transactions once formal insolvency proceedings have commenced. To this extent, they pass muster on the Doing Business indicator.

---

449 *Ibid.* at 9.

450 *Ibid.*

451 *Ibid.* at 10.

452 *Ibid.*

3.1. INTERNATIONAL NORMS ON TRANSACTIONAL AVOIDANCE – UNCITRAL LEGISLATIVE GUIDE ON INSOLVENCY

541. The international norms in respect of transactional avoidance seem much less prescriptive than the norms in respect of secured credit if the Doing Business standards are anything to go by. This proposition is also borne out by a comparison between the UNCITRAL Legislative Guide on Insolvency and the UNCITRAL Legislative Guide on Secured Transactions. The previous chapter has pointed to the similarities between the secured transactions guide and Article 9 of the US Uniform Commercial Code. On the other hand, the provisions on transactional avoidance in the Insolvency Guide are less close to US norms.[453]

542. In the Insolvency Guide, Recommendation 87 states that the insolvency law should contain provisions that apply retroactively and are designed to overturn transactions, involving the debtor or assets of the estate, and that have the effect of either reducing the value of the estate or upsetting the principle of equitable treatment of creditors. This provision strikes at three kinds of transactions. The first are transactions that are intended to defeat, delay or hinder the ability of creditors to collect claims by putting assets beyond the reach of creditors, or potential creditors, or otherwise prejudicing the interests of creditors. The second are undervalue transactions, i.e. where an insolvent debtor in return for the transfer of property or the performance of an obligation, etc. has received inadequate value. The final type of transaction – preferential transactions – are where a creditor received more than its pro rata share of assets from an insolvent debtor. Transactions with persons that are connected to the debtor may have a longer avoidance period than transactions with persons not so connected, but there is no requirement that this should be the case. The Insolvency Guide allows latitude to States in this, and in other, aspects of avoidance proceedings. It does however provide that the costs of avoidance proceedings should generally be paid as part of the insolvency process but it allows for the possibility of alternative approaches that address the pursuit and funding of avoidance proceedings.

543. The Insolvency Guide is not prescriptive on time limits for the commencement of avoidance proceedings, on the elements that need to be established to avoid a particular transaction and on defences. It is provided, however, that the fact that the transaction was entered into in the ordinary course of business prior to commencement of insolvency proceedings may constitute a legitimate defence. The law may also set up presumptions and allow shifts

[453] For a UK/US comparison in this area see G. McCormack, (2006) 6 *Journal of Corporate Law Studies* 39.

in the burden of proof that are designed to facilitate the conduct of avoidance proceedings.

544. In the *US*, under section 547 of the US Bankruptcy Code there is an 'effects'-based test for invalidating allegedly preferential transactions.[454] The inquiry is whether the effect of the transaction gives the creditor more than it would have received in a liquidation case. Various defences are available in the case of an avoidance action, including whether the transaction or payment was in the ordinary course of business. The potential breadth of this defence has been subject to occasional criticism in the US. The argument is that any competent lawyer acting for a creditor in respect of an impugned transaction should be able to present an ordinary course of business defence that has at least a superficial air of plausibility. The prospect of large litigation costs in trying to counter such a defence may deter bankruptcy trustees from advancing many possibly meritorious preference avoidance actions and also influences them to settle other such cases on less advantageous terms.[455] The Insolvency Guide permits a number of different tests in respect of the avoidance of preferential transactions and indeed more generally in respect of transactional avoidance. Certainly it does not favour explicitly the US approach.

3.2. EUROPEAN HARMONISATION

545. Chapter 2 canvassed various approaches in relation to the reform of Article 13 of the Insolvency Regulation (Article 16 of recast). The most far-reaching approach was to seek to harmonise the avoidance rules across Europe. This approach has some support within INSOL Europe.[456] In 2010 a report from INSOL Europe concluded that avoidance rules were apt for harmonisation and that harmonisation in this field was desirable and achievable.[457] The report said that such an approach would contribute to transparency in that all parties know which law would apply. It should produce greater certainty and minimise or reduce forum shopping – the movement of assets or persons from one jurisdiction to another to take advantage of a more favourable legal position. There would be

[454] See generally on the US position V. Countryman, (1985) 38 *Vanderbilt Law Review* 713; R. Weisberg, (1986) 39 *Stanford Law Review* 3; M. Shanker, 'The American Bankruptcy Preference Law: Perceptions of the Past, the Transition to the Present, and Ideas for the Future', in J. Ziegel (ed.), *Current Developments in International and Comparative Corporate Insolvency Law*, 313.

[455] See C. Tabb, (1992) 43 *South Carolina Law Review* 981 at 1032.

[456] European Association of Insolvency Practitioners and Scholars.

[457] INSOL Europe, *Harmonisation of Insolvency Law at EU Level* (April 2010) 20 <http://www.europarl.europa.eu/meetdocs/2009_2014/documents/empl/dv/empl_study_insolvencyproceedings_/empl_study_insolvencyproceedings_en.pdf> accessed 11 May 2016.

a single set of avoidance rules applying to all insolvencies irrespective of where insolvency proceedings were opened, the location of assets and the applicable law under contracts and other transactions.

546. While the precedents and experiences in other countries, both inside and outside the EU, provide some lessons, there are however no widely agreed upon detailed international standards and benchmarks that may be drawn upon. The World Bank Doing Business indicator is notably lacking in detail and the UNCITRAL Insolvency Guide permits considerable flexibility and variety of approach in terms of transactional avoidance. The 2010 INSOL Europe report 'Harmonisation of Insolvency Law at EU Level' does however flesh out the details a bit more, though it does leave a number of issues still to be resolved.[458] The report suggests that an avoidance law should contain the following elements –

- a distinction between transactions in favour of parties connected with the debtor and parties not so connected;
- a minimum vulnerability period of, say, 90 days for detrimental acts with unconnected parties and one year for connected parties;
- a minimum list of transactions that are subject to possible avoidance;
- bad faith requirements with respect to the insolvent debtor and/or counterparty;
- provision as to where the burden of proof should lie in respect of establishing detriment and bad faith;
- provision for avoidance actions to be brought only by the IP on behalf of the insolvency estate.

547. The INSOL Europe report also sets out a minimum list of transactions that are subject to possible avoidance. These cover:

- all legal acts including the grant of security only entered into on the basis that the bankrupt has disposed of its assets gratuitously, or where the value of the bankrupt's performance significantly exceeds the value of the consideration received;
- the repayment of or the establishment of a debt that is not yet due, including a shareholder loan, effected by the bankrupt prior to the filing of the bankruptcy petition;
- any deposit and consignment of funds made in contravention of a judicial decision having res judicata status; and
- all legal acts concluded with parties who are connected either by personal or corporate ties.

---

458 See also R. de Weijs, (2011) 20 *International Insolvency Review* 219 and see generally G. van Dijck, (2008) 17 *International Insolvency Review* 123.

548. A 2011 report from the European Parliament suggests a somewhat different set of harmonised rules on transactional avoidance. The report was prepared by Klaus-Heiner Lehne who explains that, owing to his own background in the German legal system, the proposals contain some similarities with German insolvency law. The report provides:

- acts that can be the object of an avoidance action are transactions in a situation of imminent insolvency, the creation of security rights, transactions with connected parties and transactions carried out with the intention of defrauding creditors;
- the periods during which an act can be challenged by an avoidance action vary according to the nature of the act at issue; the periods start with the date of the request for the opening of proceedings; the periods could be between three and nine months for transactions carried out in a situation of imminent insolvency, between six and 12 months for the creation of security rights, between one and two years for transactions with connected parties, and between three and five years for transactions carried out with the intention of defrauding creditors;
- the onus of proof to show whether or not an act can be challenged lies in principle with the party who claims that the act can be challenged; for transactions with connected parties, the onus of proof lies with the connected person.

The report explains however that the proposals are not by way of conclusion or to pre-empt debate; they are intended merely to contribute to the agenda for further in-depth research and to assist in the preparation of legislative proposals by the European Commission.

549. Our study is a much wider comparative analysis and evaluation of the laws on transactional avoidance in important EU Member States. It adds significantly to the information and analysis available to the Commission in the consideration and possible elaboration of legislative proposals in this area. It may also facilitate individual Member States in enhancing their own domestic laws on transactional avoidance.

PART II

NATIONAL REPORTS

CHAPTER 5

SECURITY RIGHTS AND INSOLVENCY LAW IN THE GERMANIC LEGAL SYSTEM

Reinhard Bork

A. INTRODUCTION

1. The fact that German and Austrian law together with Swiss law and some other laws may be considered part of the Germanic Law System within the Continental Europe Law Family must not obscure the fact that these laws just like the laws of many other Continental European legal systems are greatly influenced by Roman law. This finding also applies to the security rights provided by German and Austrian law. The pledge (*pignus*) and even the disputed transfer of title by way of security (*fiducia cum creditore*) being common security rights in *Germany* and *Austria* have their roots in Roman law as well as the principle requiring the transfer of possession over tangible assets in order to establish security rights over them. There are, with some exclusions, no provisions for the registration of security rights over movable assets. As far as the transfer or establishment of security rights over real estate and certain types of movable assets is concerned this principle has been displaced by the introduction of specific registers which goes back to the introduction of certain court records during the Roman Imperium of the ancient German Nation.

2. Both German and Austrian law mostly meet the requirements of the core principles stipulated by the European Bank for Reconstruction and Development for an effective security rights law that fulfils the needs of the credit market. Despite the application of the principle of specialty (excluding a comprehensive security right such as the floating charge) generally all kinds of assets can be used as security to enable financing among all participants in legal transactions, legal entities as well as natural persons. Depending only on a contractual agreement and some publicity requirements, the contracting parties normally should be able to implement at any time security rights which can be created quickly and simply although this naturally may depend on the size of the transaction at hand. Where the longer process of registration in a public register is necessary to establish a valid security right, the law protects the acquirer of the security right in the period between the submission of the entry application to the authorities and its actual registration against the occurrence of circumstances detrimental to the establishment of the security right such as a statutory loss of power of disposal of the security provider or subsequent disposals over the same collateral.

3. Registration fees, as well as fees for public notaries who are normally instructed where the registration of a security right is required, are linked to the value of the specific transaction. Although this may lead to large fees in individual cases, a negative effect on the credit market has not been identified yet.

4. In the event of default both German and Austrian law enable the security holder to have the collateral realised quickly, either by private sale or by formal enforcement proceedings. Liquid market values surely will normally not be reached either way but market players react to this not legal but natural deficiency as well as to the predictable realisation costs by oversecuring creditors. German case law has approved this practice to an extent which ensures an effective credit market.

5. All types of contractual security rights entitle the creditor to prevent third parties from having the collateral seized in enforcement proceedings or at least to be satisfied out of the proceeds before the enforcing third party. Security holders are protected as well in insolvency over the debtor's assets as all security rights grant the right to separate satisfaction meaning that the holder of the security right is fully satisfied out of the proceeds and the unsecured creditors benefit from proceeds exceeding the secured claim only. These security rights are:

- the pledge (Pfandrecht) over tangible and/or intangible personal property;
- the transfer of title by way of security/security ownership (Sicherungseigentum) over tangible personal property;
- the assignment by way of security/security assignment over receivables and other intangible personal property;
- the mortgage (Hypothek) over real property similar in its dogmatic functioning to the pledge over personal property;
- only in *Germany* the non-assessory mortgage (Grundschuld – sometimes referred to as land charge in English texts) over real property similar in its dogmatic functioning to the transfer of transfer of title/assignment by way of security although it does not involve a transfer of ownership.

Also commonly referred to as a security right in *Germany* and *Austria* is the retention of title in sales contracts securing not a credit on money but a credit on goods. Nevertheless, its discussion under Question 25 (quasi-security rights) seems to be justified not only for reasons of uniformity. This is because, despite its undisputed security function, in its simplest form the retention of title is treated differently in legal terms when it comes to the insolvency of the buyer, as insolvency law treats the seller not as a secured creditor but as the true owner of the sold goods, granting him the even more effective right to separate the sold goods from the buyer's insolvency estate. The difference from the above-mentioned security rights is also reflected in the fact that the publicity rules governing the pledge and the security transfer/assignment under Austrian law do not apply. Besides these security rights, the finance industry has developed the means of financing other than secured loans, providing a secured in rem position for the creditor. These financing constructions are discussed under Question 25 as quasi-security rights. However, one has to bear in mind that the expression 'quasi-security right' in *Germany* and *Austria* is not an established legal expression as it is, for example, under English law. That is because except for the courts' application of specific rules (the right to separation from the insolvency estate or a mere right to separate satisfaction, the application of publicity rules) there has never been the general need to categorise rights under a functional approach as security rights (as was the case when Article 9 UCC was drafted which obviously had a significant impact on the understanding of security rights in all common law legal systems). Thus certain financing constructions are not commonly referred to as (quasi-)security devices in *Germany* and *Austria* although they may equal those regarded as quasi-security devices in other legal systems. Where several security rights over one asset are competing among each other or with other rights in rem, this conflict is regulated by priority rules that provide for a high degree of legal certainty.

6. Arguable, and still disputed in German literature, is the lack of publicity where the security ownership and the security assignment are concerned. The required transfer of possession is construed by granting the creditor constructive possession while the debtor stays in direct physical possession. The security assignment is considered a normal assignment for security purposes which under German law does not require any publicity such as notification of the third party debtor. On the other hand the lack of publicity makes these security rights attractive for money borrowers. It is not reported that this admitted lack of publicity would negatively affect the German credit market. Both security rights are dominant in practice. In *Austria* on the other hand, where the German manner of construing these security rights is considered an invalid violation of the principle requiring the transfer of possession, it is more difficult to use fixed and working assets for financing since the debtor is normally required to transfer the actual physical possession. This might have led to a growing importance of retention of title clauses and sale and lease back transactions which shows that although due to the numerus clausus of German and Austrian property law parties are tied to the legally predetermined types of security rights both laws have proved to be sufficiently flexible to fulfil the market's needs in every specific situation.

B. CREATION OF SECURITY RIGHTS

Question 1: In general terms, to what extent is it possible in your legal system to create security rights (rights in rem) over assets?

1. Germany

7. Generally under German law every type of asset of a debtor which has an economic value may be subject to a security right. German law distinguishes between two categories of assets: movables and immovables (real estate). Movables are sub-divided into tangibles and intangibles (rights). Rights can further be divided into different categories such as claims, land servitudes, trademarks, licences, shares, patents, etc.

8. German law distinguishes between personal and in rem securities. Examples of personal securities are guarantees and assumed joint liability. Where, in this report, I refer to security rights, that reference is always to security rights in rem.

1.1. Movables

1.1.1. Tangibles

9. As far as tangible objects are concerned, German law provides two types of security rights; namely the pledge, §§1204 et seq. BGB (German Civil Code),[1] and transfer of title by way of security/security ownership (Sicherungseigentum), §§929, 930 BGB. The pledge is characterised by being of an accessory nature and subject to specific formal publicity requirements. 'Being of an accessory nature' means that the pledge strictly follows the secured claim, §1210 BGB. While a pledge agreement may be concluded to secure a future claim, the pledge as a right in rem will not come into existence before the secured claim is created, even though all other requirements of establishing a pledge (pledge agreement and transfer of possession of the collateral) may have been fulfilled previously. The partial repayment of the secured claim automatically leads to the proportional reduction of the value of the pledge. The extinction of the claim entails the extinction of the pledge, §1252 BGB. Defences against the claim can also be brought against the pledge, §1211 BGB. And finally, the pledge can only be transferred together with the secured claim, §1250 BGB.

1 For an English translation of the German Civil Code see <http://www.gesetze-im-internet.de/englisch_bgb/index.html> accessed 24 May 2016.

1.1.1.1. Transfer of title by way of security

10. The transfer of title by way of security on the other hand is a non-accessory security right. The secured creditor holds title to the ownership of the asset in a fiduciary capacity. The only connection between the security right and the secured claim is the contractual security agreement.[2]

11. Transfer of title by way of security means the transfer of ownership for security purposes. Ownership for the purposes of security is not restricted, which means that full ownership as the most comprehensive right is transferred. Transfer of title by way of security therefore follows the legal rules provided for the transfer of ownership.

12. Transfer of ownership under German law requires, aside from the power of disposal (§185 BGB), a contractual agreement between the previous owner and the new owner on the transfer of ownership as well as the factual transfer of possession of the object concerned from the previous owner to the new owner, adhering to the 'Principle of Publicity' (Publizitätsprinzip) in German property law, §929 BGB. Because of the application of the 'separation principle' (Trennungsprinzip) under German law, the contractual agreement on the change of ownership as a matter of property law must be firmly distinguished from the underlying security agreement as a matter of the law of obligations.

13. §930 BGB was the tool by which German legal practice could develop the concept of transfer of title by way of security, given its advantage of enabling the creditor to remain in possession of the collateral. It stipulates that the fact that the legal transfer of ownership is subject to the transfer of possession does not necessarily require the new owner to exercise possession as actual physical control (unmittelbarer Besitz) over the object concerned. However, so-called constructive possession (Besitzkonstitut) suffices. If the previous owner continues exercising possession in terms of actual physical control, it is sufficient for the legally required transfer of possession that the new owner has the intention to possess the object concerned for himself and that the previous owner, despite having actual physical control, respects this intention and therefore exercises his actual physical control with the intention of possessing for the new owner rather than the intention of possessing for himself. Therefore the former owner keeps direct possession 'for someone else' (unmittelbarer Fremdbesitz) and is still able to use the object while the new owner acquires indirect possession 'for himself' (mittelbarer Eigenbesitz). The change of intention between these two types of possession is expressed by agreement to the underlying security agreement by the parties involved.

---

2 J. Oechsler in *Münchener Kommentar zum BGB*, Vol. 6, Anh. (Annex to) §§929–936, para. 10, 36.

14. §930 BGB does not apply in the law of pledges, which means that in the case of a pledge the required transfer of possession (§1205 BGB) cannot be replaced by a constructive possession agreement. The debtor therefore has to lose completely all physical control over the collateral.

15. Transfer of title by way of security therefore has a significant economic advantage over the pledge being given in that it does not require the transfer of possession of the asset to the creditor. The debtor is therefore able to keep using the asset to generate profits. Due to this disadvantage the pledge over tangibles is not very common in German legal practice. However, this does not apply where the transfer or establishment of pledges over tangibles does not require the transfer of possession but rather an entry in a specific register which, under German law, is the case with planes and ships of a certain size and power. Here the transfer of title by way of security would be cheaper where the valid transfer of ownership does not require its registration (as is the case with aircrafts, ocean vessels and inland waterway vessels up to a certain size) but on the other hand would cause considerable uncertainties for the parties. The creditor would be able to transfer ownership to third parties but also could lose his (security) ownership if a third party acquired ownership from the debtor in good faith. As far as ships are concerned the main problem of security ownership is that it can only be granted once over the same asset whereas the establishment of several mortgages in different ranks over the same collateral is possible. That is why security ownership in practice is not used at all as far as ocean vessels (Seeschiffe) are concerned. Because of the considerable values involved several lenders are usually involved in any financial transactions so security ownership would be unsuitable. Since many aircraft by their nature will at least from time to time be located abroad, the creditor would run the risk that the security ownership as a non-possessory pledge will not be recognised by the foreign law which might cause difficulties in regard to the security's enforcement. For these reasons security ownership in respect of ships and planes has not established itself in legal practice. It may occur occasionally in relation to small planes and inland waterway vessels (Binnenschiffe). Instead, the pledge (planes) and the mortgage (ships) are the common security rights in rem.[3] It can be said that the German property law in relation to ships and planes is similar to real estate property law. These provisions can be found in the German Maritime Register Act (Schiffsregistergesetz, SchiffRG) and in the German Act on Rights in Aircrafts (Gesetz über Rechte an Luftfahrzeugen, LuftFzgG).

---

[3] See for ships H.-H. Nöll in J. Staudinger, *BGB*, §8 SchiffsRG, para. 18; P. Dobberahn, [1998] *MittRhNotK* 146; see for planes H. Schölermann and K. Schmid-Burgk, [1990] *WM* 1137 at 1148; T. Grädler and J. Zintl, [2014] *RdTW* 261 at 261.

1.1.1.2. Pledge

16. Pledges over assets may be established by way of contract or as a mandatory consequence of enforcement proceedings against the immovable or movable assets of the debtor. The contractual agreement on creating the pledge as a matter of property law once again has to be firmly distinguished from the underlying security agreement as a matter of the law of obligations ('separation principle', cf. para. 12 and Question 6, para. 147). In relation to certain types of contracts, German law also stipulates legal liens for the benefit of one creditor (e.g. the lessor automatically acquires a legal lien on all objects brought into a flat by the tenant with outstanding rent obligations). To such liens the law of pledges applies as well, which is why they are referred to in *Germany* as statutory pledges in contrast to contractual pledges. Transfer of title by way of security on the other hand can only be established on a contractual basis.

1.1.2. Intangibles

17. As far as intangibles are concerned German law also provides for the pledge, §§1273 et seq. BGB, and the assignment by way of security, §§398, 413 BGB. The assignment by way of security is similar in its legal effect to the transfer of title by way of security. The creditor acquires ownership of the claim but is bound by the security agreement as a fiduciary.[4] Because of the application of the 'separation principle' (Trennungsprinzip) in German law, the contractual agreement on the assignment as a matter of property law must be firmly distinguished from the underlying security agreement as a matter of the law of obligations.

18. For the possible ways of establishing these rights reference should be made to the above (para. 16), the only difference being that legal liens on intangibles do not exist in German law.

19. In the case of claims the assignment by way of security is the common security right in rem in legal practice since it requires practically no acts of publicity whereas the pledge of a claim requires the notification of the debtor, §1280 BGB.

20. Under German law, it would also be possible to assign by way of security rights other than claims. However, this is not part of national legal practice since it presents no benefit for the concerned parties as compared with pledging the rights. The pledge of rights is established according to the provisions governing the transfer of the specific right itself. The publicity requirements would therefore be the same. Possession in relation to the rights is irrelevant. A further issue is

---

4 G. Roth in *Münchener Kommentar zum BGB*, Vol. 2, §398, para. 107 et seq.

that security ownership in many cases creates a lot of effort and risk for the creditor. Since he acquires full ownership of the right (subject only to fiduciary duties) he is responsible for meeting all obligations connected to the right (e.g. shareholder obligations). Therefore, as far as rights are concerned, creditors are generally not interested in security ownership. So the pledge is the common security right in these cases.

1.2. Immovables

21. German real estate property law provides for two different kinds of mortgages over real estate. The first one has the effect of a common pledge with its typical accessory[5] character, §§1113 et seq. BGB (Hypothek). The second one grants the same right to the creditor (satisfaction out of the proceeds of the forced sale or sequestration of the land) without having an accessory character, §§1191 et seq. BGB (Grundschuld). The "Grundschuld' is the common security right in German legal practice having replaced the 'Hypothek' entirely. It can secure different claims without the need to repeat its registration in the Land Register every time. The implementation of all-monies clauses is easier whereas such clauses in relation to accessory security rights are considered to be problematic. It is therefore more flexible and cheaper than the 'Hypothek'. Since the 'Grundschuld' is non-accessory, the connection to the secured claim is established by the fiduciary character of the security agreement.

22. A transfer of title by way of security in the field of real estate would be legally possible but would cause huge expense without having any advantages when compared with the 'Grundschuld'.

23. A 'Hypothek' may also be established as a mandatory consequence of enforcement proceedings against immovable assets of the debtor whereas the 'Grundschuld' can only be established contractually. Here also the contractual agreement on the creation of the security right as a matter of property law must be distinguished from the underlying contractual security agreement ('separation principle').

1.3. General provisions

24. The provider of collateral may be the debtor or (if e.g. the debtor has no assets or has already pledged all valuable assets to other creditors) a third party.

---

5 'Accessory' is understood in the same way as for pledges; cf. above para. 9.

25. The establishment of security rights over assets requires that the provider of collateral be entitled to dispose of the asset, see §185 BGB. Otherwise, it is possible for a creditor in good faith to acquire the security right where the law governing the transfer of ownership of the asset itself stipulates that an acquisition in good faith is valid if the specific legal requirements are met. This is true for security rights over immovables (§892 BGB) as well as for pledges (§1207 BGB) and transfer of title by way of security (§§932 et seq. BGB). However, it is not possible to rely on good faith in order to uphold the acquisition of a claim or a right of pledge over a claim, since the acquisition of a claim in good faith from a person who is not the creditor (owner) of the claim is not possible under German law.

26. One asset may be subject to several pledges/mortgages concurrently. In this case the satisfaction of the creditors out of the proceeds is based on the priority principle. Priority between competing security rights is usually determined by the chronological order of their establishment. So the creditor whose security interest was established first in time is satisfied out of the proceeds before the creditor whose security right was established second in time and so on (for further details regarding the priority principle see Question 23). In the case of the realisation of a right of pledge over an immovable asset, satisfaction of the creditors is based on the rank as listed in the Land Register (§879 BGB). However, the two principles most often result in the same outcome, since rank in the Land Register is generally determined according to the priority principle.

1.4. Restrictions

27. The main restriction on the possibility of establishing security rights over assets is contained in §1274 (2) BGB. This rule only applies to pledges on intangibles (rights). It states that a right cannot be pledged if it is not assignable to third parties (see Question 2, para. 43 et seq. for further details). This rule by implication applies also to assignments by way of security since in this case the assignment of the right itself would be required. The most relevant statutory bans on assignment can be found in German procedural law since §400 BGB stipulates that a claim/right is not assignable if it cannot legally be subject to attachment in enforcement proceedings (see Question 2, para. 43 et seq.).

28. Further restrictions are provided by the general part of civil law and other fields of law. Specific restrictions arise from §138 BGB which provides that immoral transactions are invalid. German Federal Supreme Court (Bundesgerichtshof) case law has developed a few categories in the field of security law which are deemed to fall within this provision, such as over-collateralisation,[6] incitement

[6] BGH Urt. v. 15.05.2003, Az.: IX ZR 218/02 = [2003] NJW-RR 1490, 1492.

to breach of contract[7] and locked-in contracts.[8] Over-collateralisation is assumed if at the time the security interest is created it is already certain that the realisable value of the collateral is disproportionately in excess of the amount of the claim ('"initial" over-collateralisation').[9] According to the literature this is the case where the realisable value exceeds 200% or more of the secured claim.[10] If on the other hand a disproportion between the value of the collateral and the secured claim occurs in the course of the credit-relationship due to a decrease in value of the secured claim or due to an increase in value of the collateral, §138 BGB does not apply. In this case the agreement between the parties to a release claim of the security provider in relation to the excess collateral shall be considered to be implied in the security agreement (if an express release claim is not contained in the agreement which will normally be the case in practice).[11] The threshold triggering the release claim is 110% of the collateral's realisable value or 150% of its book value but parties may agree to other values according to the specific circumstances at hand.[12] Due to the assumption of an implied release claim the application of §138 BGB is dispensable in case of the so called 'subsequent' over-collateralisation. It is established that the threshold triggering the release claim must not be equated with the threshold triggering the application of §138 BGB in case of 'initial' over-collateralisation (due to the much harsher consequence of the voidness of the whole security agreement).[13] An incitement to breach of contract is, for example, assumed where banks have future claims arising from future sales assigned to them by way of security from a debtor who, due to the nature of his economic activities, is typically supplied with goods under (extended) retention of title.[14] Since a following second assignment of the future claim to the supplier would not be valid according to the priority principle, the debtor relying on his supplies would have to conceal the prior security assignment from his suppliers insisting on having the affected claims assigned to them in order to secure payment of the delivered goods replacing the retained ownership as a security (for the extended retention of title see Question 25). Locked-in contracts are contracts which cause an excessive restriction on economic freedom of choice. In the case of security rights this normally goes hand in hand with the previously described groups of immoral contracts.

7 BGH Urt. v. 08.12.1998, Az.: Xi ZR 302/97 = [1999] NJW 940.
8 BGH Urt. v. 09.11.1955, Az.: IV ZR 196/54 = BGHZ 19, 12, 18.
9 BGH Urt. v. 15.05.2003, Az.: IX ZR 218/02 = [2003] NJW-RR 1490, 1492.
10 R. Sack and P. Fischinger in J. Staudinger, *BGB*, §138, para. 308.
11 BGH Beschl. v. 27.11.1997, Az.: GSZ 1/97 = BGHZ 137, 212, 218 et seq.
12 BGH Beschl. v. 27.11.1997, Az.: GSZ 1/97 = BGHZ 137, 212, 218 et seq.
13 BGH Urt. v. 12.03.1998, Az.: IX ZR 74–95 = [1998] NJW 2047.
14 See BGH Urt. v. 30.04.1959, Az.: VII ZR 19/58 = BGHZ 30, 149, 152.

29. A general restriction arises from §§1365, 1368 BGB which states that one spouse is unable to dispose of his patrimony (which may consist of just one asset) without the approval of the other.

2. Austria

30. Austrian law is in many respects similar to German law. The distinction between the different kinds of assets is the same, see §§285, 292 ABGB (Austrian Civil Code).[15] The 'separation principle' applies as well.

2.1. Movables

31. Austrian law, as well as German law, provides for the accessory pledge, §§447, 448 ABGB, and the transfer of title/assignment by way of security §§425, 426, 427, 452, 1392, 1393 ABGB.[16]

32. According to the interpretation of the law by the Austrian Supreme Court (Oberster Gerichtshof), the transfer of title/assignment by way of security must not lead to an evasion of the formal requirements which must be met in order to set up a right of pledge. So they are only valid if they fulfil the formal requirements that would have been necessary if the parties had agreed on establishing a right of pledge.[17] This especially means that the transfer of possession cannot be replaced by constructive possession as in German law (see Question 3, para. 95 et seq. for further details). As a consequence, while transfer of title/assignment by way of security are still the dominant security rights in Austrian legal practice, the pledge is not as irrelevant compared with *Germany*, at least as far as tangibles are concerned. This seems surprising since there is no real advantage to the transfer of title/assignment by way of security.[18]

33. As far as ships are concerned, Austrian law, like German law, provides for a mortgage (Schiffshypothek) as the relevant security right in rem. An entry into a specific register of ships is required. There is no register for rights over planes, so a pledge over a plane or the transfer of title over it is established in

---

15 A good overview of security rights under Austrian law is provided by G. Kodek, [2015] *IILR* 10 et seq.

16 G. Kodek, [2015] *IILR* 10 at 11 et seq.

17 Most of the court decisions cited in this report are available at: <https://www.ris.bka.gv.at/Jus/> accessed 24 May 2016; for transfer of title by way of security see OGH Urt. v. 23.10.1968, Az.: 3 Ob 112/68 = SZ 41/140; for assignment by way of security see OGH Urt. v. 01.03.1989, Az.: 1 Ob 697/88 = SZ 62/32.

18 H. Koziol and R. Welser, *Bürgerliches Recht*, Vol. I, p. 408.

accordance with the regular legal provisions. This means that planes are not common security assets since the transfer of their possession to the creditor would be required.

2.2. *Immovables*

34. Austrian law distinguishes between real estate registered in the Land Register and real estate not registered in the Land Register.

35. For registered land, Austrian law only provides for the accessory mortgage (Hypothek) as a security right in rem over real estate, §448 ABGB which requires its entry into the Land Register.[19] There is no 'Grundschuld' as in *Germany*.

36. For unregistered land, Austrian law provides for the pledge as a security right in rem, which requires the deposit of a notarised pledge agreement with the competent court, §§434, 451 ABGB. The rules governing the deposition are provided in the UHG (Austrian Act on the Deposit of Documents). Since unregistered land practically does not exist anymore, the provision of §434 ABGB is of little relevance in legal practice.[20]

2.3. *General provisions*

37. Reference should be made to the above description of German law.

2.4. *Restrictions*

38. Austrian law contains a restriction on the creation of pledges similar, but not identical, to German law, in §448 ABGB, which states that every asset which may be the subject of a civil transaction can be subject to a pledge. Since every immovable and tangible object may be the subject of such a transaction, this provision only restricts pledges in relation to intangibles. The decisive criterion is not whether the right can be assigned, as under German law, but whether the right has a value that can be realised.[21] Therefore personal rights and rights which are inseparably connected to an object (e.g. restricted personal servitudes over real property) or a person cannot be subject to a pledge.

39. Austrian procedural law also stipulates bans on the seizure of certain of the debtor's claims, and these also serve as bans on contractual rights of pledge.

---

19 G. Kodek, [2015] *IILR* 10 at 11.

20 H. Koziol and R. Welser, *Bürgerliches Recht*, Vol. I, p. 362.

21 M. Hinteregger in M. Schwimann (ed.), *Praxiskommentar ABGB*, Vol. 2, §448, para. 9; H. Koziol and R. Welser, *Bürgerliches Recht*, 374.

Other statutory bans on rights of pledge may be found in various fields of law, particularly in social security law. For further details see Question 2.

Question 2: Is it possible to create security rights over all assets of the debtor?

1. Germany

40. Not all of the debtor's assets can be subject to a pledge or assignment by way of security.

1.1. Movables

1.1.1. Tangibles

41. As far as movable tangibles are concerned there are no restrictions. Every asset may be subject to a security right. Although German procedural law declares certain objects (e.g. those needed for ensuring a certain life standard or enabling the debtor to continue his work) as excluded from being subject to attachment (§811 ZPO), this rule does not mean that the debtor is unable to dispose of these objects (as long as no insolvency proceedings are opened).

42. A contractual ban on disposal relating to specific objects has no legal effect in relation to third parties, §137 BGB. German law does not recognise contractual prohibitions on disposals. An exception is provided in §§399, 413 BGB for intangibles (para. 50).[22] However, attachment during enforcement procedures leads to the loss of power of disposal in relation to the attached object. In this case the establishment of a prior right of pledge or the unencumbered transfer of title by way of security depends on the good faith of the creditor in regards to the debtor's power of disposal, §§135 (2), 1208 BGB.

1.1.2. Intangibles

43. As mentioned under Question 1 (para. 27) only assignable rights can be subject to a contractual pledge agreement. Bans on assignment can result from contractual agreements or from statutory provisions.

1.1.2.1. Statutory bans on assignment/pledge

44. §§400, 413 BGB stipulate that a claim or other right which cannot legally be subject to attachment in enforcement proceedings is not assignable. Legally

[22] In German literature it is highly disputed whether §399 BGB constitutes a general exception to §137 BGB or whether a contractual ban on assignment becomes an integral part of the right and makes it by its very nature unassignable.

exempted from attachment are a certain proportion of wages and other claims resulting from an employment relationship, §§850, 850a, 850c ZPO. Other claims exempted from attachment are maintenance claims, claims on pensions for bodily injury or health issues, claims in relation to plans established for the maintenance of widows and orphans, claims in relation to aid and assistance plans, claims on health insurance funds, granted exclusively or predominantly for the purpose of providing maintenance, and claims under life insurance policies that have been taken out only against the risk of the insured party's dying, §850b ZPO.

45. There are various other legal bans of assignment outside of procedural law. Easements (e.g. land access rights) are legally considered components of the beneficial real estate (§96 BGB) and are therefore not assignable. Restricted personal servitudes and usufructs cannot be assigned although the exercise of a usufruct is assignable and can therefore be subject to a pledge, §§1059, 1092 BGB.

46. The legal principle behind these provisions is that the contractual establishment of such rights is normally based on a familiar or at least very personal relationship of trust, which makes a change of creditor unthinkable for the other party.

47. For the same reason the assignment of membership in a society or shares in partnerships is only permissible if assignment is permitted by the articles or is approved afterwards by all other partners, §§38, 717, 719 BGB, 705 HGB (German Commercial Code). On the other hand reimbursement claims by managing partners resulting from management operations are assignable, as are claims to distribution of profits or to the return of money placed in a non-segregated capital account. As far as corporations such as stock corporations or limited liability partnerships are concerned, shares are generally assignable and can therefore be subject to a pledge since personal ties are not considered to be relevant in these forms of partnership, §15 (1) GmbHG (German Act on Limited Liability Companies).

48. Copyright, as a highly personal right, is not assignable, §29 UrhG (German Copyright Act).

49. There are a few other statutory bans on assignment mostly regarding pension claims governed by public law. Generally, under German law assignments are banned in order to adhere to the constitutional 'Social State' principle or to protect a specific relationship of trust and confidence between a party and their contractual partners in relation to those partners' maintenance.

1.1.2.2. Contractual bans on assignment/pledge

50. According to §399 BGB a claim or other right is also not assignable and therefore not able to be subject to a contractual pledge or assignment by way of security where the parties involved have agreed a contractual ban on assignment of the claim or other right (e.g. ban of assignment of shares in the articles of the association). According to its interpretation by the German Federal Supreme Court (Bundesgerichtshof) and most of the legal literature, this provision gives contractual bans of assignment absolute effect in relation to potential third parties.[23] The rule is restricted by §354a HGB (German Commercial Code), which states that a contractual ban on assignment of a claim for money agreed between businessmen or corporate bodies does not have any effect against third parties: this makes those claims assignable. Furthermore, a contractual ban on assignment does not prevent the claim from being subject to attachment in enforcement proceedings if the object the claim is directed towards could legally be attached. So in most cases of contractual bans on assignment, only the contractual establishment of a pledge is not possible.

1.2. *Immovables*

51. There are no restrictions as far as real estate is concerned.

52. One exception to the lack of effect of contractual prohibitions on disposal in rem is the 'priority notice' (Vormerkung) in German real estate law, §883 BGB. If a creditor has a claim to be granted any right over a real estate he can, with the approval of the owner of the real estate, file for the entry of a 'priority notice' in the Land Register. Once the Land Registry (Grundbuchamt) as the competent authority (see Question 20, para. 297) has accepted the entry, all subsequent disposals (e.g. granting a mortgage) which are detrimental to realising the claim are ineffective against the creditor but not against other third parties.

2. Austria

53. In *Austria* as well, not every asset can be subject to a security right.

2.1. *Intangibles*

54. The legal situation is nearly the same as in *Germany*.

2.1.1. *Statutory bans on pledge*

55. Certain claims are legally banned from being subject to contractual pledges as well as to attachment under Austrian procedural law, §§293 (3), 290 et seq.

23 BGH Urt. v. 31.10.1990, Az.: IV ZR 24/90 = BGHZ 112, 387, 389; G. Roth in *Münchener Kommentar zum BGB*, Vol. 2, §399, para. 36 et seq.

EO (Austrian Enforcement Regulation). The claims concerned are, inter alia, claims to several forms of social aid, scholarships, and earned income up to a certain amount.

56. Furthermore, where the law provides for a legal ban on assignment of a right, it is mostly assumed that it is a highly personal right which cannot, therefore, be converted to a real right. Examples are the right of repurchase, the right of pre-emption and the right of resale, §§1070, 1071, 1074 ABGB. All these rights are therefore considered highly personal rights which cannot be subject to pledges.

57. Easements (e.g. land access rights) are not assignable and cannot be subject to pledges, since they are inseparably connected with a piece of land, §485 ABGB.

58. In relation to restricted personal servitudes and usufructs, a distinction must be made between the different kinds of servitudes. Restricted personal servitudes (e.g. the right to use, §504 ABGB, and the right of residence, §521 ABGB, must not be assigned by the beneficiary of those rights, §507 ABGB. They can neither be subject to pledge nor to attachment in enforcement proceedings. On the other hand the exercise of a usufruct, §509 ABGB, as in *Germany*, is considered assignable by Austrian Courts and legal literature and can therefore be pledged or attached although the right of usufruct itself is not assignable according to the general rule in §485 ABGB.[24]

59. As far as company shares are concerned Austrian law is exactly the same as German law. The wording of §124 UGB (Austrian Companies Act) is the same as in §719 BGB. Shares in stock corporations and limited liability partnerships can be pledged/attached.

60. Patents and other intellectual property rights can be subject to pledges. The one exception, as in *Germany*, is copyright, which is legally banned from assignment, §23 (3) UrhG (Austrian Copyright Act).

2.1.2. Contractual bans on pledge

61. Despite the lack of a provision such as §399 BGB in German law, the case law of the Austrian Supreme Court grants contractual bans on assignment absolute effect in relation to third parties.[25] Although in *Austria* the specific criterion deciding whether an asset can be subject to a pledge is not its assignability but whether it can be converted into a real right, this interpretation by the Austrian Supreme Court according to Austrian legal literature prevents claims

---

[24] OGH Urt. v. 02.09.1987, Az.: 3 Ob 87/87 = [1998] JBl 463, 464; M. Petrasch in P. Rummel, *ABGB*, §485, para. 1; D. Kiendl-Wendner in M. Schwimann (ed.), *Praxiskommentar zum ABGB*, §485, para. 2.

[25] OGH Urt. v. 16.01.1984, Az.: 5 Ob 609/81 = SZ 57/8.

or other rights which are subject to a contractual ban on assignment from being potentially subject to pledges.[26] The result is the same as in *Germany*. Such a contractual pledge does not prevent the claim concerned from being subject to attachment in enforcement proceedings.

2.2. Immovables/tangibles

62. Austrian law also contains the legal institution of the 'priority notice' with the same effects as in German law, §§35 et seq. GBG (Austrian Land Registry Act).

63. In contrast to German law, Austrian law provides for a contractual ban on disposal of real estate to have an in rem effect against third parties, §364c ABGB. Such a ban can only be concluded between persons with close personal relationships (between spouses, parent and child). It must also meet the formal requirement of registration in the Land Register. The only person bound by this agreement is the contracting party entitled to dispose of the land, and not their successors in title. The agreement may be limited to a ban on transfer or to a ban on encumbering the land. In such a case a contractual pledge would not be valid.

64. As far as movables are concerned, a contractual ban on assignment, as under German law, never has an absolute or in rem effect against third parties, §364c ABGB.

Question 3: Is it possible to create security rights over assets not yet owned by the debtor at the time of the creation of the security interest?

1. Germany

1.1. Movables

1.1.1. Tangibles

1.1.1.1. Transfer of title by way of security

1.1.1.1.1. Anticipated transfer of title by way of security, §§929, 930 BGB (antizipierte Sicherungsübereignung)[27]

65. For the legal construction of security ownership see Question 1, para. 11 et seq.

---

[26] M. Hinteregger in M. Schwimann (ed.), *Praxiskommentar zum ABGB*, Vol. 7, §448, para. 17.

[27] The legal construct of anticipated transfer of title by way of security is recognized by the German Federal Supreme Court, see for example BGH Urt. v. 20.12.1978, Az.: VIII ZR 288/77 = [1979] WM 300, 301.

66. §929 BGB does not state that the contractual agreement on the change of ownership and the transfer of possession have to coincide in time. The transfer of possession can follow the contractual agreement later on. Furthermore, §929 BGB does not require the disposing owner to have already acquired ownership and possession of the object concerned. The parties are able to agree on a change of ownership even though the disposing party does not yet own or possess the object concerned. This is called an anticipated agreement on the transfer of ownership. The transfer of possession from the disposing party (debtor) to the acquiring party (creditor) later on is still required in order to complete the change of ownership.

67. In the same way that §929 BGB enables an anticipated contractual agreement on the transfer of ownership, §930 BGB enables the parties to anticipate by way of agreement (the security agreement) the future statuses of direct or indirect possession that the parties will have (antizipiertes Besitzkonstitut). Since, however, the actual acquisition of possession by the disposing party (debtor) in favour of the new owner (creditor) is of a factual nature, it cannot be anticipated by the agreement.

68. Whether the subjects of the anticipated agreements under §§929, 930 BGB are assets which are not yet in existence (see Question 4) or assets which already exist but do not yet belong to the debtor is irrelevant.[28] Since groups of assets are often subject to anticipated security agreements, the 'principle of specialty' (Spezialtitätsgrundsatz) in German property law must be taken into account, which means that only one specific asset can be subject to a property law transaction. Nevertheless groups of assets can be subject to (anticipated) security ownership agreements without every single asset being listed in the agreement. Relevant in this context is, for example, the security ownership of goods in warehouses (with changing inventories). The German Federal Supreme Court ruled that the requirements of the 'principle of specialty' are met if everyone who is aware of the agreement is without any effort able to determine which assets are subject to the transfer of ownership and which are not (for further details see Question 5, para. 141 et seq.).[29]

69. If the parties have made anticipated arrangements according to §§929, 930 BGB concerning movable objects not yet owned by the debtor at the time the arrangements were made, the creditor acquires security ownership almost automatically at the moment title is transferred to the debtor by a third party. The debtor becomes the owner of the object for a split second, after which, according to the prior arrangements, the creditor becomes the new owner and

---

28 See for example BGH Urt. v. 01.04.1963, Az.: VIII ZR 211/61 = [1963] WM 504, 505.

29 BGH Urt. v. 03.12.1987, Az.: IX ZR 228/86 = [1998] WM 346, 347.

the debtor therefore exercises his physical control over the object concerned in favour of the creditor in order to complete the required transfer of possession (Durchgangserwerb/transferred acquisition).[30] In this moment, the right of ownership may be encumbered with the rights in rem of third parties, especially with legal liens (e.g. legal liens for lessors in the case of security ownership of goods in warehouses). This also means that the acquisition of security ownership according to §91 InsO (German Insolvency Regulation) is affected by insolvency proceedings that are opened in respect of the debtor's assets between the anticipated agreements and the acquisition of the asset by the debtor.[31] §91 InsO stipulates that after insolvency proceedings have been opened, the acquisition of rights from the debtor without the approval of the insolvency practitioner is no longer possible.

70. In summing up, it can be said that the parties are able to set up all necessary conditions for the future quasi-automatic establishment of security ownership of a movable object not yet owned by the debtor. But since the parties are neither able to anticipate the power of disposal over the object in question nor the required factual possession, the security ownership itself, as a right in rem, does not come into existence before the debtor has himself acquired ownership of the object, at least for that brief moment.[32]

1.1.1.1.2. Transfer of the expectant right to acquire title

71. If the debtor has bought a tangible object in which the seller has retained title, the debtor has an expectant right to acquire title. This occurs where the agreement on transferring ownership, according to §929 BGB, is subject to a condition precedent being met (in this case the full price being paid). Under German law, such an expectant right, which is less than the full right of ownership, is a secured legal position with a 'quasi' in rem effect.[33] It may therefore be subject to transfer of title by way of security in an analogous application of §§929, 930 BGB.[34] When the condition precedent is fulfilled, the expectant right owned at that time by the creditor is then elevated to a right of full ownership. The debtor as the provider of collateral does not in this situation acquire ownership for the moment of time referred to above (Direkterwerb/direct acquisition in contrast to transferred acquisition, see para. 69).[35] This may be an advantage

---

30 J. Oechsler in *Münchener Kommentar zum BGB*, Vol. 6, §930, para. 27; W. Wiegand in J. Staudinger, *BGB*, §930, para. 33.

31 H. Ganter in *Münchener Kommentar zur InsO*, Vol. 1, §51, para. 107.

32 W. Wiegand in J. Staudinger, *BGB*, §930, para. 33.

33 BGH Urt. v. 21.12.1960, Az.: VIII ZR 89/59 = BGHZ 34, 122,124; R. Beckmann in J. Staudinger, *BGB*, §449, para. 80.

34 H. Westermann in *Münchener Kommentar zum BGB*, Vol. 3, §449, para. 52 et seq.

35 BGH Urt. v. 22.02.1956, Az.: IV ZR 164/55 = BGHZ 20, 88, 98.

over the anticipated transfer of (security) ownership. Third party's rights cannot be established and in case of insolvency proceedings being opened over the debtor's assets between the transfer of the expectant right and the meeting of the condition precedent §91 InsO does not apply.[36]

1.1.1.1.3. Acquisition in good faith

72. Another way to create security ownership over tangibles not owned by the debtor would be an acquisition in good faith. However, since in the case of security ownership the transfer of possession is made according to §930 BGB, a good faith acquisition would be valid only at the time the creditor acquires direct possession of the collateral, §933 BGB. This is unlikely to happen in the case of security ownership which has the specific purpose of avoiding direct possession by the creditor.

1.1.1.1.4. Approval by the real owner

73. If the debtor disposes of, by way of security, ownership of collateral he does not own, then, regardless of the good faith of the creditor, the disposition is valid if the real owner has approved the disposition, either before or afterwards, §185 BGB.

1.1.1.2. Pledge

1.1.1.2.1. Anticipated pledge agreement, §§1204, 1205 BGB

74. A pledge, like the transfer of ownership, requires a contractual agreement as well as the transfer of possession as an act of publicity, §1205 BGB. §930 BGB does not apply, which means that the debtor needs to lose completely all physical control over the pledged collateral (cf. Question 1, para. 14, 15). While an anticipated contractual pledge agreement concerning collateral the debtor does not yet hold title to is possible,[37] the debtor will normally not be able to grant the creditor possession of the collateral until he himself becomes the owner of it. Since the validity of the pledge requires the transfer of possession from the collateral-providing party (debtor) to the creditor, the right of pledge as a security right does not come into existence until this transfer of possession is completed,[38] which means that normally the debtor will have to acquire ownership of the collateral before the pledge can be validly established.

---

36 W. Breuer in *Münchener Kommentar zur InsO*, Vol. 2, §91, para. 36.
37 W. Wiegand in J. Staudinger, *BGB*, §1204, para. 43.
38 *Ibid.*

1.1.1.2.2. Pledge over the expectant right to acquire title, §§1204, 1205 BGB

75. If the debtor is not the owner but already has an expectant right to acquire title to the collateral, this expectant right may be subject to a pledge agreement.[39] It is established in accordance with the provisions governing the establishment of a pledge over the full right of ownership, §§1204 et seq. BGB (transfer of possession is required). After the expectant right becomes the full right of ownership, the right of pledge then devolves to the full right of ownership. Its rank depends on the time when the pledge over the expectant right was established.

1.1.1.2.3. Good faith acquisition/approval of the real owner

76. If the debtor is able to grant possession to the creditor although he is neither the owner of the collateral nor owns an expectant right to acquire title to it, the creditor can only acquire a right of pledge if he acts in good faith regarding the debtor's ownership of the object, §§1207, 932, 934 BGB, or if the real owner has already approved the pledge or does so afterwards, §185 BGB.

1.1.2. Intangibles

1.1.2.1. Assignment by way of security

1.1.2.1.1. Anticipated assignment by way of security, §398 BGB

77. The assignment of a claim under German law requires, aside from the power of disposal, §185 BGB, merely a corresponding contractual agreement, §398. The principle of publicity in German property law in relation to the transfer of claims is not very strict. A notification of the third-party debtor or any other act of publicity is not required (for the protection of the third-party debtor who is unaware of the change of creditors see §§406 et seq. BGB). Nothing else applies to the security assignment since this is an assignment of a claim (§398 BGB) only in a fiduciary capacity for security purposes.

78. An anticipated assignment agreement over an already existing claim the disposing party is not yet entitled to is possible. However, the creditor at this time would not be entitled to dispose of the claim, §185 BGB. Therefore the creditor would not acquire the claim as a security right until the security provider (debtor) has acquired ownership of the claim, at least for the required

[39] BGH Urt. v. 10.04.1961, Az.: VIII ZR 68/60 = BGHZ 35, 85, 93; R. Beckmann in J. Staudinger, *BGB*, §449, para. 80.

moment, which leads to the application of §91 InsO in the case where insolvency proceedings are opened between the agreement and the acquisition of the claim by the debtor.

1.1.2.1.2. Assignment of the expectant right to acquire title

79. It may happen that the provider of collateral (debtor) is not yet the owner of the claim provided as collateral at the time the security assignment is concluded, but has already obtained an expectant right to acquire title (e.g. the claim has already been assigned to the debtor but the assignment is subject to a condition precedent being met).[40] If this is the case the expectant right can be subject to an assignment[41] and can therefore also be subject to an assignment by way of security. When the condition precedent is met, the assigned expectant right is elevated to full security ownership of the claim (similar to the situation with tangibles).

1.1.2.1.3. Good faith acquisition/approval of the real owner

80. An assignment (by way of security) of a claim not owned by the disposing party is valid if the real owner of the claim approves the assignment, §185 BGB. Acquisition of the claim merely by good faith of the creditor is not possible since German law does not provide for acquisition of claims merely by good faith.

1.1.2.2. Pledge

1.1.2.2.1. Anticipated pledge agreement over claims, §§1273, 1274, 1279 et seq. BGB

81. The validity of a pledge on a claim requires, in addition to the contractual agreement between the pledger (debtor) and the pledgee (creditor), notification to the debtor of the claim provided as collateral, as an act of publicity, §1280 BGB. This notification can only be carried out by the creditor of the claim which is provided as collateral.[42] As a consequence a valid pledge over a claim the pledgor or owner is not yet entitled to cannot be established unless the real owner/creditor approves the disposition (§185 BGB) and carries out the notification. An anticipated pledge agreement, followed by the notification to the debtor of the claim provided as collateral, carried out by the pledgor as soon as he has acquired the claim, seems possible. However, the pledge will not come

---

40 Intangibles can be subject to retention of title, see §§449, 453 BGB; B. Grunewald in W. Erman, *BGB*, §449, para. 8.

41 J. Busche in J. Staudinger, *BGB*, §398, para. 58.

42 D. Wiegand in J. Staudinger, *BGB*, §1280, para. 8.

into existence until the notification has been carried out, which requires the pledger to be the owner or creditor of the pledged claim.

82. Acquisition of a right of pledge by demonstrating good faith regarding the debtor's ownership is not possible. Pledges over intangibles are established in accordance with the legal provisions governing the transfer of ownership of the specific intangibles, §1274 (1) BGB. §§398 et seq. BGB do not provide for acquisition of a claim merely by demonstrating good faith.

83. As mentioned under Question 1 the pledge of claims is not part of German legal practice since the requirement of notification is considered a great disadvantage compared with the security assignment.

1.1.2.2.2. Anticipated pledge agreement over other rights, §§1273, 1274 BGB

84. Reference should be made to the aforesaid. The anticipated conclusion of a pledge agreement over existing rights not yet owned by the debtor is possible. However the right of pledge would not come into existence until the debtor has acquired ownership of the right. The situation is different where the debtor has already acquired an expectant right to acquire title and this expectant right is subject to the pledge agreement.[43] In this case the pledge devolves to the full right after it arises.

1.1.2.2.3. Good faith acquisition/approval of the real owner

85. Where the law provides for the acquisition of ownership of a specific right by demonstrating good faith, the acquisition of a pledge in good faith is possible, §1274 (1) BGB (e.g. GmbH shares, §16 (3) GmbHG; mortgages, §892 BGB).

86. §185 BGB applies in all cases.

1.2. Immovables

87. The valid establishment of a mortgage (it is irrelevant whether a 'Hypothek' or a 'Grundschuld' is in question) always requires entry in the Land Register, §873 (1) BGB. If the debtor as the provider of collateral is not registered as the owner of the real estate, the Land Registry according to §§19, 39 GBO (German Land Register Regulation) will refuse to make that entry (for further details about the Land Registry as the competent authority see Question 20, para. 297). These

43 For the practical relevance of a pledge of shares in a GmbH see J. Sieger and K. Hasselbach, [1999] *GmbHR* 633 at 635.

provisions stipulate that an entry in the land register must be made only if the person whose right over the land will be affected by the entry has approved the entry and that an entry shall only be made if the affected person is registered as the person entitled to dispose of the land. This means that as long as the debtor is not registered as the owner, a valid establishment of a mortgage without the approval of the registered owner is practically impossible.

88. On the other hand, if the debtor is registered as the owner, although he is not the owner, an establishment of a mortgage in favour of a creditor in good faith is possible, §892 BGB, if the creditor acts in good faith regarding the ownership of the debtor.

89. Approval of the establishment of a mortgage by the real owner is possible, §185 BGB.

90. If the debtor has already acquired an expectant right to acquire title,[44] this expectant right can be subject to a pledge agreement according to §§1273, 1274 BGB. When the expectant right becomes a full right of ownership the creditor automatically acquires a mortgage over the land even without registration, according to the analogous application of §1287 BGB.[45]

2. Austria

2.1. *Movables*

2.1.1. *Tangibles*

2.1.1.1. *Transfer of title by way of security*

2.1.1.1.1. *Anticipated transfer of title by way of security, §§425 et seq. ABGB (antizipierte Sicherungsübereignung)*

91. The validity of a transfer of ownership under Austrian law requires, aside from the power of disposal on the part of the provider of collateral (see §442 ABGB), a valid title (Titel) and procedure (Modus), §425 AGB. The title is provided by the underlying contract (e.g. purchase contract, see §1461 ABGB, in case of security rights this will be the security agreement) giving the causa for the transfer of ownership. A difference from German law is that the underlying obligational contract has to be valid in order for ownership to be transferred whereas under

[44] For its requirements see BGH Urt. v. 25.02.1966, Az.: V ZR 126/64 = BGHZ 45, 186, 188; BGH Urt. v. 30.04.1982, Az.: V ZR 104/81 = BGHZ 83, 395, 399.

[45] BGH Urt. v. 18.12.1967, Az.: V ZB 6/67 = BGHZ 49, 197, 205.

German law the underlying contract and the disposition of ownership as a matter of property law are completely independent from each other (under German law this is the so-called 'abstraction principle'/Abstraktionsprinzip).

92. The procedure (Modus) is determined by §§426 et seq. ABGB. Although not explicitly mentioned in these provisions, the procedure (Modus) requires, aside from the factual transfer of possession, a legal contractual agreement, which has to be distinguished from the contract providing the title (Titel) and giving the causa for the transfer of ownership (Trennungsprinzip).[46] However, according to the Austrian Supreme Court (Oberster Gerichtshof) and the prevailing opinion in legal literature, agreement on transferring ownership is normally included in the underlying contract.[47] It follows from this interpretation that the agreement on transferring ownership as a legal act and the transfer of possession as a factual act are different operations which do not have to coincide in time.[48]

93. §428 ABGB, as does §930 BGB under German law, provides for the possibility of replacing the transfer of possession by taking actual physical control with a constructive possession agreement (Besitzkonstitut).

94. According to the Austrian Supreme Court and the prevailing Austrian legal literature, Austrian law also recognises the anticipated constructive possession agreement (antizipiertes Besitzkonstitut).[49]

95. However, an anticipated transfer of title by way of security as provided by German law, under Austrian law involves a lot more effort, since the Austrian Supreme Court has ruled that the application of a constructive possession agreement in the case of security leads to an evasion of the publicity provisions in the law of pledge where – as under German law – the required transfer of possession cannot be replaced by a constructive possession agreement (see Question 1, para. 14).[50] Another act of granting possession to the creditor after the debtor has acquired possession is normally required.

96. For security ownership of warehouses with changing inventories, which is of practical relevance, the following applies: First, the agreement must adhere to the

---

46 H. Koziol and R. Welser, *Bürgerliches Recht*, Vol. I, p. 325.

47 OGH Urt. v. 23.11.1994, Az.: 7 Ob 39/94 = SZ 67/213; B. Eccher in H. Koziol, P. Bydlinski and R. Bollenberger (eds.), *ABGB*, §425, para. 1; M. Binder, *Sachenrecht*, para. 6/51.

48 Therefore by parts of Austrian legal literature the contractual agreement on transferrring ownership as the act of actual property law is not considered to be part of the procedure, see Question 6, para. 149.

49 OGH Urt. v. 11.07.2001, Az.: 3 Ob 57/01f = SZ 74/128; T. Klicka in M. Schwimann (ed.), *Praxiskommentar ABGB*, Vol. 2, §430, para. 6; H. Koziol and R. Welser, *Bürgerliches Recht*, Vol. II, p. 28.

50 See also G. Kodek, [2015] *IILR* 10 at 12.

'principle of specialty' which applies in *Austria* as well as in *Germany*.[51] Since a transfer of possession of the inventory of a whole warehouse is usually unfeasible §§452, 427 ABGB apply. These provisions state that if the transfer of possession, due to the nature of the pledged object (e.g. claims/other rights), is unfeasible, the parties must use signifiers which enable everyone to have easy notice of the transfer of ownership. In practice, signs displaying this information are fixed on, for example, the entrance gate of the warehouse. Although warehouses are expressly mentioned in §427 ABGB, the Austrian Supreme Court interprets the provision very strictly in order to protect the 'principle of publicity'. At least in the case of warehouses of a manageable size, the use of signifiers alone is not sufficient. The debtor has to lose physical control over the collateral completely. In order to meet this requirement and to enable operations to run smoothly, a collateral agent has to be appointed to whom the creditor transfers his power of disposal.[52] After that the creditor acquires security ownership of new goods coming into the warehouse quasi-automatically.

97. The transfer of ownership must be completed, which requires the transfer of possession (§427 ABGB) before insolvency proceedings are opened. Otherwise acquisition of ownership is not possible, §3 IO (Austrian Insolvency Regulation).[53] This means, in the case of a warehouse with a changing inventory, that new goods coming into the warehouse after insolvency proceedings are opened cannot be subject to valid security ownership.

2.1.1.1.2. Transfer of the expectant right to acquire title

98. Austrian law, like German law, recognises an expectant right to acquire title as a secured legal position with a 'quasi' in rem effect.[54] The owner of such a right can transfer it according to the provisions governing the transfer of the full right.[55] The right may be subject to a transfer of title by way of security.[56] If the debtor wants to transfer his expectant right by way of security this means, according to the ruling of the Austrian Supreme Court, that he has to grant

51 For the possibility of transferring ownership of groups of assets see Question 5, para. 145.

52 OGH Urt. v. 19.12.1984, Az.: 3 Ob 113/84 = JBl. 1985, 541, 542; OGH Urt. v. 27.04.1994, Az.: 3 Ob 45/94 = SZ 67/78, both rulings regarding security ownership of warehouses; OGH Urt. v. 14.12.1979, Az.:1 Ob 646/79 = [1980] JBl 435, regarding security ownership of livestock.

53 P. Apathy in P. Apathy, G. Iro and H. Koziol (eds.), *Österreichisches Bankvertragsrecht*, Vol. IX, Part 2, Ch. 4, para. 4/25; G. Kodek, [2015] *IILR* 10.

54 OGH Urt. v. 11.01.1938, Az.: 2 Ob 1151/37 = SZ 20/4; OGH Urt. v. 22.02.1972, Az.: 8 Ob 17/72 = SZ 45/18; M. Binder in M. Schwimann (ed.), *Praxiskommentar ABGB*, Vol. 5, §1063, para. 42.

55 H. Koziol and R. Welser, *Bürgerliches Recht*, Vol. I, p. 417.

56 P. Apathy in P. Apathy, G. Iro and H. Koziol (eds.), *Österreichisches Bankvertragsrecht*, Vol. IX, Part 2, Ch. 4, para. 4/4.

possession of the tangible object concerned to the creditor. For the effects, reference should be made to the discussion on German law. The debtor as the collateral provider as in *Germany* does not acquire title for a split second when the expectant right elevates to the full right of ownership (Direkterwerb/direct acquisition).[57]

2.1.1.1.3. Acquisition in good faith

99. The legal provision governing good faith acquisition of ownership of tangibles is §367 ABGB. According to Austrian legal literature, it is possible to acquire security ownership in good faith where the collateral provider (debtor) was not entitled to dispose of the collateral. As security ownership in *Austria* is regarded as similar to the right of pledge, acquisition by good faith is established according to the rules stated in §456 ABGB governing the good faith acquisition of a right of pledge.[58] This means that the real owner is granted the possibility of regaining ownership of the collateral if he satisfies the secured claim (Einlösungsrecht). It is necessary for the collateral to have been, at an earlier point, committed by the real owner to the provider of the collateral, §§456, 367 ABGB (for further details see the discussion on the good faith acquisition of a pledge below, para. 104).

2.1.1.1.4. Approval by the real owner

100. The transfer of security ownership carried out by a debtor who is not entitled to the collateral is valid if the real owner has approved the disposition or does so afterwards.[59]

2.1.1.2. Pledge

2.1.1.2.1. Anticipated pledge agreement, §§1368, 447, 1251 et seq. ABGB

101. The establishment of a pledge, like the transfer of ownership, requires a valid title (Titel) and procedure (Modus). The title can usually be seen in the security agreement in which the debtor undertakes to grant the creditor a

57 OGH Urt. v. 09.04.1968, Az.: 8 Ob 80/68 = SZ 41/37.

58 P. Apathy in P. Apathy, G. Iro and H. Koziol (eds.), *Österreichisches Bankvertragsrecht*, Vol. IX, Part 2, Ch. 4, para. 4/4; E. Karner, *Gutgläubiger Mobiliarerwerb*, p. 21; E. Bydlinski, [1988] *ÖBA* 958 at 971.

59 OGH Urt. v. 02.03.1988, Az.: 3 Ob 130/87 = SZ 61/51; T. Klicka in M. Schwimann (ed.), *Praxiskommentar ABGB*, §367, para. 20.

right of pledge (Pfandbestellungsvertrag).[60] The procedure requires the actual property law agreement to grant a pledge over the specific tangible object, §1368 ABGB (Pfandvertrag) and the transfer of possession as an act of publicity, §§451 ABGB et seq.

102. Already existing objects the provider of collateral does not yet own and is therefore not entitled to dispose of (see §442 ABGB) can only be subject to a security agreement (Pfandbestellungsvertrag). A valid pledge cannot be established over them.[61] Even if the security agreement were to include the pledge agreement (Pfandvertrag), the pledge would not come into existence until the provider of collateral had granted possession to the creditor.

2.1.1.2.2. Pledge over the expectant right to acquire title, §§1368, 447, 1251 et seq. ABGB

103. Under Austrian law, as with German law, the expectant right to acquire title can be subject to a pledge which is established in accordance with the provisions governing the establishment of a pledge over the full right of ownership.[62] Reference should be made to the discussion on German law.

2.1.1.2.3. Good faith acquisition/approval of the real owner

104. An acquisition of a pledge by a creditor acting in good faith regarding the ownership of the debtor is possible, §§456, 367 ABGB. Of the three different ways provided for in §367 ABGB, only the third variant applies: that the collateral had earlier on been committed to the debtor by the real owner.[63] A monetary consideration (see §367 ABGB) is not required.[64] A considerable difference with German law is that §456 ABGB grants the real owner the possibility of getting back the collateral if he fulfils the secured debt (Einlösungsrecht).

105. A pledge established between a debtor not entitled to dispose of the collateral and the creditor is valid if the real owner has approved it either before or afterwards.[65]

---

60 P. Mader in M. Schwimann (ed.), *Praxiskommentar ABGB*, Vol. 6, §§1368, 1369, para. 1.

61 M. Hinteregger in M. Schwimann (ed.), *Praxiskommentar ABGB*, Vol. 2, §448, para. 6.

62 M. Binder in M. Schwimann (ed.), *Praxiskommentar ABGB*, Vol. 4, §1063, para. 44.

63 B. Koch in H. Koziol, P. Bydlinski and R. Bollenberger (eds.), *ABGB*, §456, para. 1; K. Hofmann in P. Rummel, *ABGB*, Vol. 1, §456, para. 3.

64 H. Koziol and R. Welser, *Bürgerliches Recht*, Vol. I, p. 384; B. Koch in H. Koziol, P. Bydlinski and R. Bollenberger (eds.), *ABGB*, §456, para. 1.

65 OGH Urt. v. 02.03.1988, Az.: 3 Ob 130/87 = OGH SZ 61/51; M. Hinteregger in M. Schwimann (ed.), *Praxiskommentar ABGB*, Vol. 2, §456 para. 1.

2.1.2. Intangibles

2.1.2.1. Assignment by way of security

2.1.2.1.1. Anticipated assignment by way of security, §§1392, 452 ABGB

106. The assignment of claim requires a valid title (Titel) and a procedure (Modus). In case of security purposes the valid title is provided by the underlying security agreement.[66] The procedure on the other hand requires, as in *Germany*, only a contractual agreement on the transfer of the claim as the act of actual property law, §1392 ABGB. According to the Austrian Supreme Court this contractual agreement as the act of actual property law normally will be included already in the underlying security agreement.

107. An anticipated assignment agreement over an already existing claim the disposing party is not yet entitled to should be possible. However, since the debtor is not at this time able to dispose of the claim (see §442 ABGB), the creditor would not acquire the claim as a security right before the security provider (debtor) has acquired ownership of the claim for at least a split second.

108. Another problem would be the ruling of the Austrian Supreme Court which decided that assignment by way of security must not lead to an evasion of the publicity requirements in the law of pledge. Of great relevance is §452 ABGB which, according to the Austrian Supreme Court, applies to assignment by way of security as well. This provision states that if the transfer of possession, due to the nature of the pledged object (e.g. claims/other rights), is unfeasible, the parties must use signifiers which enable everyone to have easy notice of the pledge. The Austrian Supreme Court ruled that in case of the assignment/pledge of claims by way of security, there are two ways to meet this requirement. The first one is the notification of the debtor of the claim provided as collateral (in *Germany* §1280 BGB).[67] Where the provider of collateral (debtor) maintains an accounting system, the second way is for the debtor to make an entry in his accounting sheets, especially on the OP[68] list which reveals the date of the assignment and the claim subject to it.[69] The Austrian Supreme Court has ruled that for both the anticipated notification of the third-party debtor and the general entry note in the accountant

---

66 P. Apathy in P. Apathy, G. Iro and H. Koziol (eds.), *Österreichisches Bankvertragsrecht*, Vol. IX, Part 2, Ch. 4, para. 5/13.

67 OGH Urt. v. 07.09.1978, Az.: 6 Ob 662/78 = SZ 51/121.

68 Open Positions.

69 OGH Urt. v. 29.10.1997, Az.: 5 Ob 2155/96i = [1998] JBl 105, 108; OGH Urt. v. 26.06.2001, Az.: 1 Ob 290/00d = SZ 74/112.

sheets, the express inclusion of future claims is possible.[70] However, both these rulings concerned assignments of claims that did not yet exist. It is questionable, especially in the case of the notification of the third-party debtor, whether these rulings could be applied to already existing claims not yet owned by the debtor.

2.1.2.1.2. Assignment of the expectant right to acquire title

109. The main application of an expectant right to acquire title is in retention of title. The Austrian Supreme Court has ruled that the establishment of retention of title to intangibles cannot be recognised under Austrian law,[71] whereas parts of the legal literature consider such retention of title to be possible.[72] It remains unresolved whether the ruling can be seen as a general denial of the possibility of expectant rights to acquire title in relation to intangibles. If not, it remains further unresolved whether §452 ABGB applies. The lack of discussion in case law and the legal literature leads to the conclusion that expectant rights as far as intangibles are concerned are not seriously considered as security rights in legal practice.

2.1.2.1.3. Good faith acquisition/approval of the real owner

110. Reference should be made to the discussion on German law. A good faith acquisition of claims is not possible under Austrian law either (see §1394 ABGB).[73]

2.1.2.2. Pledge

2.1.2.2.1. Anticipated pledge agreement over claims, §§447, 448, 452 ABGB

111. An anticipated pledge agreement over a claim the debtor does not yet hold title to is possible. Regarding the difficulties arising from §452 ABGB reference should be made to the discussions about assignment by way of security under Austrian law. However, even if it were possible to meet the publicity requirements of §452 ABGB in advance of the debtor's acquisition of ownership of the claim provided as collateral, the pledge would not come into existence until this acquisition, since before this moment the debtor was lacking the necessary power of disposal.

---

70 OGH Urt. v. 29.09.1998, Az.: 1 Ob 406/97f = SZ 71/154; OGH Urt. v. 30.08.2000, Az: 6 Ob 174/00g = SZ 73/132.

71 OGH Urt. v. 30.04.1969, Az.: 5 Ob 14/69 = SZ 42/65.

72 J. Aicher in P. Rummel, *ABGB*, Vol. I, §1063, para. 34; M. Binder in M. Schwimann (ed.), *Praxiskommentar ABGB*, Vol. 4, §1063, para. 24.

73 H. Koziol and R. Welser, *Bürgerliches Recht*, Vol. I, p. 332.

112. According to §§456, 367, 1394 ABGB, the good faith acquisition of a pledge over a claim the provider of collateral (debtor) is not entitled to is not possible.

2.1.2.2.2. Anticipated pledge agreement over other rights, §§447, 448, 452 ABGB

113. Reference should be made to the aforesaid. Furthermore, in many fields (especially in intellectual property law), the validity of a pledge requires its entry into a register, which is not possible as long as the provider of the collateral is not entitled to the collateral.

2.1.2.2.3. Good faith acquisition

114. For the possibility of a good faith acquisition of a pledge over a right the provider of collateral (debtor) is not entitled to see para. 112.

2.2. Immovables

115. The valid establishment of a mortgage always requires entry in the Land Register, §§451 (1), 431 et seq. ABGB. Before the Land-Register Court (Grundbuchsgericht) as the competent authority (see for further details Question 20, para. 304) approves the entry it has to scrutinise the validity of the underlying transaction, especially the question of whether the disposing party was entitled to dispose of the land, §94 (1) Nr. 1 GBG. As long as the party providing collateral is not registered as the owner of the land, therefore, the establishment of a mortgage is not practically possible. The same applies for pledges over land which is not registered in the Land Register, §9 (1) Nr. 1 UHG.

116. If on the other hand the provider of collateral (debtor) is registered as the owner, the valid establishment of a mortgage in good faith according to the principle of reliance on the accuracy of the land register (see §§434, 1500 ABGB) is possible.[74] This principle does not apply to documents subject to deposit, §20 UHG. Nevertheless an acquisition of real estate not being registered in the land register in good faith according to parts of legal literature is possible by analogous application of §367 ABGB.[75]

---

[74] H. Koziol and R. Welser, *Bürgerliches Recht*, Vol. I, p. 364; for application of the principle see OGH Urt. v. 21.12.1989, Az.: 6 Ob 737/87 = SZ 62/219.

[75] T. Klicka in M. Schwimann (ed.), *Praxiskommentar ABGB*, Vol. 2, §367, para. 1; K. Spielbüchler in P. Rummel, *ABGB*, Vol. 1, §367, para. 2.

Question 4: Is it possible to create security rights over assets that are not yet in existence at the time of the execution of the security agreement?

1. Germany

1.1. *Movables*

1.1.1. *Tangibles*

1.1.1.1. *Anticipated transfer of title by way of security, §§929, 930 BGB (antizipierte Sicherungsübereignung)*

117. Reference should be made to the discussions in Question 3, para. 65 et seq. From a legal point of view it makes no difference whether the object of the anticipated agreement on the transfer of ownership and the anticipated constructive possession agreement is an existing asset the debtor is not yet entitled to or a not yet existing asset.

1.1.1.2. *Manufacturer's clauses*

118. Manufacturer's clauses are frequently used by suppliers of raw materials which are subject to retention of title. These clauses protect the suppliers against the statutory loss of ownership as a consequence of the buyer processing the raw materials into new goods, §950 BGB. Since these clauses are usually part of a retention of title clause, further details are discussed under Question 25, para. 340.

1.1.1.3. *Anticipated pledge agreement, §§1204, 1205 BGB*

119. Reference should be made to Question 3, para. 74. An anticipated pledge agreement is possible but the security right does not come into existence before the transfer of possession from the debtor to the creditor is completed.

1.1.2. *Intangibles*

1.1.2.1. *Anticipated assignment by way of security, §398 BGB*

120. The anticipated assignment of future claims is of great importance in German legal practice. Receivables from current or future business operations, future rental claims and future wage demands are frequently affected. The assignment of future claims is also often part of the so-called extended retention of title which is discussed under Question 25, para. 339.

121. With reference to Question 3, para. 78 an anticipated agreement on the assignment of future claims is possible. In this context the 'principle of specialty' (Spezialitätsgrundsatz) must be taken into account, although German courts do not apply strict criteria in the context of the assignment of future claims. The future claim does not have to be specified at the time of the assignment agreement. It only has to be ascertainable. Nor is it required that a legal basis for the assigned future claim(s) has already been created at the time the assignment agreement is concluded[76] or that the debtor of the future claim can already be defined.[77] It is sufficient if the creation of the claim in the future is considered likely by the parties[78] and that at the time the future claim comes into existence it can be determined (if necessary by interpretation of the assignment agreement) whether and to what extent the claim is subject to the assignment agreement.[79] The clause 'all existent and future trade receivables with the initial letters A–Z' meets the requirements of the 'principle of specialty'.[80]

122. The 'principle of specialty' must be considered carefully, especially in the case of blanket assignments (Globalzessionen) which often also include future claims (for the recognition of blanket assignments under German law see Question 5, para. 141, 143).

123. The more difficult question is determining the time at which the effects of the assignment come into force. The answer to this question determines the effects of the opening of insolvency proceedings between the conclusion of the assignment agreement and the creation of the future claim, since §91 InsO stipulates that after insolvency proceedings have been opened the acquisition of rights from the debtor without the approval of the insolvency practitioner is no longer possible.

124. It is established at least that although the assignment of a claim under German law requires nothing more than a contractual agreement (§398 BGB), the acquisition of the claim by the creditor as a right in rem is not completed before the (future) claim has come into existence.[81] Therefore the German Federal Supreme Court generally considers the assignment of future claims to be void if the (future) claims are created after the insolvency proceedings

---

76 BGH Urt. v. 22.09.1965, Az.: VIII ZR 265/63 = [1965] NJW 2197.

77 BGH Urt. v. 20.09.2012, Az.: IX ZR 208/11 = BGH [2013] NZI 42, para. 8.

78 G. Roth in *Münchener Kommentar zum BGB*, Vol. 2, §398, para. 79.

79 BGH Urt. v. 12.10.1999, Az.: XI ZR 24/99 = [2000] NJW 276 at 277.

80 BGH Urt. v. 29.11.2007, Az.: IX ZR 30/07 = BGHZ 174, 297, para. 27.

81 BGH Urt. v. 11.05.2006, Az.: IX ZR 247/03 = BGHZ 167, 363, para. 6; J. Busche in J. Staudinger, *BGB*, §398, para. 71.

have been opened, §91 InsO.[82] However, under certain conditions the German Federal Supreme Court recognises that such assignments may be unaffected by the opening of insolvency proceedings. The creditor is required to have already been granted a secured legal position before the insolvency proceedings are opened.[83] In the case of a (future) claim arising from a continuing obligation, this requirement shall be met if the claim at the time the assignment agreement is concluded already exists but is not yet due or enforceable (betagte Forderung).[84] This includes, for example, claims arising from a finance leasing agreement[85] but not claims arising from a rental agreement.[86] The distinction is justified by the contractually stipulated period and the limited termination rights in the case of finance leasing agreements. This justifies the assumption that all claims arising from a finance leasing agreement are determined by this agreement and therefore already come into existence with its conclusion. On the other hand, in the case of rental agreements, the creation of claims is subject to the condition precedent of leave to use in the specific periods of time. The same applies for wage demands which require the performance of services to be created.[87] For claims subject to a condition precedent, the German Federal Supreme Court has made clear that an assignment is not affected by the opening of insolvency proceedings only where the condition precedent has been met before insolvency proceedings are opened.[88] Using these principles, courts may avoid the application of §91 InsO where it seems appropriate. If the claims at the time of the conclusion of the assignment agreement already exist as claims, but are not due or enforceable, the acquisition of the claim(s) is completed with the conclusion of the assignment. The assignment of claims subject to a condition precedent on the other hand is completed when the condition precedent is met and therefor void if the condition were met after insolvency proceedings have been opened, §91 InsO. However, the distinction made by the German Federal Supreme Court between claims being already existent and merely not due or enforceable (secured legal position), and claims being subject to a condition precedent and therefore not in existence yet (not yet a secured legal position), may cause legal uncertainties. In any case, the minimum requirement for being unaffected by the opening of insolvency proceedings is an already existing legal basis at the time of the assignment.

---

82 BGH Urt. v. 11.05.2006, Az.: IX ZR 247/03 = BGHZ 167, 363, para. 6; BGH Urt. v. 10.11.2011, Az.: IX ZR 142/10 = BGHZ 191, 277, para. 9; BGH Urt. v. 25.04.2013, Az.: IX ZR 62/12 = [2013] NZI 586, para. 27.

83 BGH Urt. v. 11.05.2006, Az.: IX ZR 247/03 = BGHZ 167, 363, para. 6; BGH Urt. v. 10.11.2011, Az.: IX ZR 142/10 = BGHZ 191, 277, para. 12; BGH Urt. v. 21.02.2013, Az.: IX ZR 69/12 = [2013] NZI 42, para. 13.

84 BGH Urt. v. 11.05.2006, Az.: IX ZR 247/03 = BGHZ 167, 363, para. 6.

85 BGH Urt. v. 25.04.2013, Az.: IX ZR 62/12 = [2013] NZI 586, para. 29.

86 BGH Urt. v. 25.04.2013, Az.: IX ZR 62/12 = [2013] NZI 586, para. 28.

87 BGH Urt. v. 20.09.2012, Az.: IX ZR 208/11 = [2013] NZI 42, para. 14.

88 BGH Urt. v. 10.11.2011, Az.: IX ZR 142/10 = BGHZ 191, 277, paras. 12, 13.

125. In conclusion, it can be said that security assignments of claims are always possible as long as the requirements of the 'principle of specialty' are met. The security right does not come into existence before the creation of the claim. Another question is resistance to insolvency, which requires the creditor to have acquired a secured legal position before insolvency proceedings are opened.

1.1.2.2. Anticipated pledge agreement

1.1.2.2.1. Claims, §§1273, 1274, 1279 et seq. BGB

126. An anticipated pledge agreement between the debtor and the creditor over claims not yet in existence can be concluded. Regarding the 'principle of specialty' the same criteria apply as with the assignment of future claims.[89] The required notification of the (future) debtor of the claim provided as collateral (§1280 BGB) can also be carried out in advance of the creation of the claim if at the time of the notification the claim can be specified. Mere ascertainability is insufficient in this case.[90]

127. If the parties have set up all these conditions in advance the pledge right comes into existence with the creation of the claim, since a pledge right over a non-existing asset is not possible.[91] The effect of the opening of insolvency proceedings between the pledge agreement and the creation of the claim has to be answered according to the same criteria as with the assignment of future claims.[92]

1.1.2.2.2. Other rights, §§1273, 1274 BGB

128. Reference should be made to the discussion on pledges over future claims. If the transfer of the right requires a certain form (e.g. notarisation) the anticipated pledge agreement must be concluded according to this form as well, §1274 (1) BGB. The 'principle of specialty' must be taken into account as well.

1.2. Immovables

129. Since an as yet not existing real estate is by its nature not registered in the Land Register, at least the required registration of the mortgage is not possible as long as the real estate does not exist.

---

89 D. Wiegand in J. Staudinger, *BGB*, §1273, para. 15; J. Damrau in *Münchener Kommentar zum BGB*, Vol. 6, §1273, para. 4.

90 J. Damrau in *Münchener Kommentar zum BGB*, Vol. 6, §1273, para. 4.

91 OLG Köln Urt. v. 18.02.1987, Az.: 13 U 170/86 = NJW-RR 1988, 239; D. Wiegand in J. Staudinger, *BGB*, §1273, para. 16; J. Damrau in *Münchener Kommentar zum BGB*, Vol. 6, §1273, para. 4.

92 D. Wiegand in J. Staudinger, *BGB*, §1273, para. 16.

2. Austria

2.1. *Movables*

2.1.1. *Tangibles*

2.1.1.1. *Anticipated transfer of title by way of security, §§425 et seq. ABGB (antizipierte Sicherungsübereignung)*

130. Reference should be made to the discussion under Question 3, para. 91 et seq. A valid transfer of title by way of security can never be completed before the collateral has come into existence and the creditor has acquired direct possession over it (see for the application of §427 ABGB and its understanding in case of the practically relevant security ownership over warehouses with changing inventories para. 96).

2.1.1.2. *Anticipated pledge agreement, §§1368, 447, 1251 et seq. ABGB*

131. Reference should be made to Question 3, para. 101 et seq. Since the procedure (transfer of possession) cannot be completed as long as the collateral does not exist, a valid pledge requires the existence of the asset.[93]

2.1.2. *Intangibles*

2.1.2.1. *Anticipated assignment by way of security, §§1392, 452 ABGB*

132. Regarding the requirements of an assignment, reference should be made to Question 3, para. 106. As in *Germany*, claims that are not yet in existence can be subject to a security assignment agreement. Blanket security assignments which include future claims are possible under Austrian law as long as they adhere to the concurrently applicable 'principle of specialty' (see also Question 5, para. 145). The decisive criteria are the same as in *Germany*. At the time the claim comes into existence it must be possible to determine whether it is the assigned claim or not. It is sufficient to mention the legal basis the assigned future claim is likely to arise from in the assignment agreement.[94] Neither its amount nor the debtor of the future claim have to be defined in the assignment agreement as long as the claim is ascertainable.[95]

---

93 G. Kodek in M. Schwimann (ed.), *Taschenkommentar ABGB*, §448, para. 1.

94 OGH Urt. v. 25.02.1988, Az.: 7 Ob 723/87 = SZ 61/47.

95 A. Heidinger in Schwimann (ed.), *Praxiskommentar ABGB*, §1393, para. 39.

133. Under Austrian law it is established that the acquisition of the future claim for security purposes as a right in rem is not completed until the assigned claim comes into existence.[96]

134. It has already been mentioned (Question 3, para. 108) that, according to the Austrian Supreme Court, §452 ABGB applies to the security assignment as well. The ways of meeting the provision's requirements are discussed under Question 3, para. 108. As previously mentioned, the assignment of future claims remains possible, since the Austrian Supreme Court recognises the prior notification of the debtor of the claim provided as collateral before the claim comes into existence, at least in the case of claims against a defined business partner arising from an already established and defined business relationship,[97] as well as a general entry note of the assignment in the accounts expressing that future claims shall be included.[98]

135. As far as the effects of insolvency proceedings between the assignment agreement and the creation of the claim are concerned, the discussion does not go into that much detail as in *Germany*. It is generally assumed that the transfer of the claim has to be completed before insolvency proceedings are opened. The valid transfer requires not only the existence of the claim but also that the publicity requirements of §452 ABGB are met.[99] Otherwise, after the opening of insolvency proceedings, acquisition is not possible, §3 IO.[100]

2.1.2.2. Anticipated pledge agreement

2.1.2.2.1. Claims, §§447, 448, 452 ABGB

136. Reference should be made to the discussion on anticipated assignment by way of security, para. 132. According to the Austrian Supreme Court the pledge of claims and security assignment must be treated equally.

2.1.2.2.2. Other rights, §§447, 448, 452 ABGB

137. Future rights, aside from claims serving as subject to security rights in rem, are not discussed in Austrian literature. It is at least established that the pledge as a right in rem would not come into existence before the creation of the right. The application of §452 ABGB would be problematic. There are no rulings regarding

---

96 OGH Urt. v. 14.09.2004, Az.: 10 Ob 321/02g = [2005] ÖBA 1268/284, 285; P. Apathy in P. Apathy, G. Iro and H. Koziol (eds.), *Österreichisches Bankvertragsrecht*, Vol. IX, Part 2, Ch. 5, para. 5/6; D. Fuchs in M. Schwimann (ed.), *Taschenkommentar ABGB*, §1393, para. 2.

97 OGH Urt. v. 29.09.1998, Az.: 1 Ob 406/97f = SZ 71/154.

98 OGH Urt. v. 30.08.2000, Az.: 6 Ob 174/00g = SZ 73/132.

99 OGH Urt. v. 01.03.1989, Az.: 1 Ob 679/88 = OGH SZ 62/32; OGH Urt. v. 21.02.2002, Az. 8 Ob 194/01i = OGH SZ 2002/25.

100 P. Apathy in P. Apathy, G. Iro and H. Koziol (eds.), *Österreichisches Bankvertragsrecht*, Vol. IX, Part 2, Ch. 5, para. 5/40.

the meeting of publicity requirements in advance of the creation of rights other than claims.

2.2. *Immovables*

138. Reference should be made to the discussion on German law (para. 129).

Question 5: Is it possible to have a 'global security agreement', i.e. covering all assets of the debtor?

1. Germany

139. In German property law the 'specialty principle' (Spezialitäts-/ Bestimmtheitsgrundsatz) applies.[101] This principle stipulates that only specific individual assets can be subject to rights in rem (ownership, pledge, etc.). The principle is for the purpose of increasing the clarity and transparency of the law. The creation of a security right in rem over things in their entirety without specifying the individual assets would violate this principle. A global security agreement as an act of actual property law covering all assets of the debtor and establishing security rights in rem over them is therefore not possible.[102] On the level of the law of obligations, however, the debtor is able to undertake to grant security rights in rem over all of his assets to the creditor without specifying the individual assets. Such obligational contract, however, would not lead to an in rem encumbrance of the debtor's assets. The creditor would only be entitled to claim for the granting of in rem security rights over the assets. The actual security transaction providing for an in rem effect then again would have to adhere to the specialty principle in order to be valid.

140. The principle is breached where several single items, which individually do not have any economic value, are by general opinion considered to make up one larger item without being legally essential parts of it (legally essential parts of a whole item lose their legal identity and can therefore not be subject to rights in rem, §§93, 94 BGB). Examples would be a set of cards or one pound of coffee beans. In this case an agreement on establishing a right in rem over the whole item is possible and sufficient to create a right in rem over every individual item since individual items do not in this case lose their legal identity.

141. The 'specialty principle' in the fields of security ownership and security assignment is of practical relevance, since here usually more than one asset is

---

101 J. Baur and R. Stürner, *Sachenrecht*, §4, para. 17 et seq.; W. Wiegand in J. Staudinger, *BGB*, Anh. §§929–931, para. 95 et seq.

102 J. Baur and R. Stürner, *Sachenrecht*, §4, para. 19.

affected by the security agreement (law of obligations) as well as by the agreement on establishing the security right (property law) (e.g. security ownership of the inventory of warehouses, blanket assignments) and no act of publicity is required which would automatically cause a transparent individualisation of the assets concerned. German case law here has restricted the 'principle of speciality' for the benefit of the economy and recognises security ownership/ security assignment agreements over collective entities of assets as long as certain requirements are met.

142. As far as security ownership is concerned, the specific criterion for whether the agreement on the transfer of ownership is valid is whether third parties knowing of the contractual agreement between the debtor and the creditor can easily determine whether the specific asset is subject to the security ownership agreement.[103] For example the clause 'all current and future inventory of Room A shall be subject to security ownership' would meet the requirements of the 'specialty principle'. On the other hand the clause 'all bicycles belonging to the debtor shall be subject to security ownership' would not meet the requirements since, without looking into the account of the debtor or other further inquiries, it would be impossible for third parties to distinguish between bicycles the debtor really owns and bicycles that were maybe just leased or bicycles that are subject to retention of title.[104]

143. The security assignment of collective claims is also recognized under German law. For the requirements resulting from the 'principle of specialty', reference should be made to Question 4, para 121. The necessary ascertainability requires in any case that the legal basis of the assigned claim is made clear in the assignment agreement regardless of whether the legal basis already exists or not (e.g. in the case of future claims).[105] Even the clause 'all claims arising from business operations' would meet these requirements.

2. Austria

144. In Austrian property law the 'principle of specialty' applies as well.[106] For its meaning and consequences reference should be made to the discussion on German law.[107]

---

103 BGH Urt. v. 31.01.1979, Az.: VIII ZR 93/78 = BGHZ 73, 253, 254; BGH Urt. v. 03.12.1987, Az.: IX ZR 228/86 = [1988] WM 346, 347.

104 See BGH Urt. v. 20.03.1986, Az.: IX ZR 88/85 = [1986] NJW 1985, 1986; BGH Urt. v. 11.05.1995, Az.: IX ZR 170/94 = [1995] NJW 2348, 2350.

105 J. Busche in J. Staudinger, *BGB*, §389, para. 60.

106 G. Iro, *Sachenrecht*, para. 1/8; G. Kodek, [2015] *IILR* 10 at 11.

107 See G. Iro, *Sachenrecht*, para. 1/17, 10/5.

145. As far as security ownership and security assignment are concerned, Austrian courts also recognise the security transfer of collective entities of assets (see Question 3, para. 96; Question 4, para. 132). Although the wordings of the courts' judgments may differ slightly as far as the requirements of the 'principle of specialty' are concerned there should be no considerable difference with German law (see para. 142, 143).

Question 6: In general terms, what are the formalities in your legal system for the creation of a security interest over assets?

1. Germany

146. As a general rule it can be said that the establishing of security rights always follows the rules provided by the law governing the transfer of ownership of the specific kind of asset.

147. The valid contractual establishment of security rights in rem therefore requires in every case a contractual agreement as an act of actual property law by which the security right is created and usually another act of publicity due to the 'publicity principle' (Publizitätsprinzip) in German property law. The agreement on the creation of the security right must be distinguished from the underlying security agreement as an act of the law of obligations ('separation principle'/'Trennungsprinzip'). In practice, security agreements are often separated into two parts, namely the part under the law of obligations and the part under property law. If the security agreement, by express wording only, provides for the transfer or creation of the in rem security right as a matter of property law, the obligational security agreement entitling the creditor to be granted the security is normally considered to be implied in that agreement. Although under German law transactions in terms of property law (e.g. the creation of a security right) do not require the validity of the underlying obligational contract (this is referred to as the 'abstraction principle' which takes the 'separation principle' one step further) the result of the obligational security agreement being void for any reason or not existent at all would be that the security provider were entitled to claim the rescission of the creation of the security right (in the case of security ownership/assignment this would lead to the reverse transfer of ownership) on the ground of unjustified enrichment since the secured creditor would lack a valid title to the security right. A specific form (e.g. notarisation) of the agreement (as a matter of property law) according to the aforesaid is required where transfer of ownership of the specific asset would require such a specific form (for details see Question 7). Where this is not required, the agreement, like any other contract, can be concluded orally, although in business transactions the written form is normal.

2. Austria

148. In Austrian law the creation of a security right requires a valid title (Titel) and a procedure (Modus), see §§449, 451 ABGB. The title is usually provided by the underlying security agreement as an act of the law of obligations (Pfandbestellungsvertrag). The procedure consists of another contractual agreement on establishing the security right as an act of property law and an act of publicity. Thus the 'separation principle' (the principle of distinguishing between obligational contractual agreements and property law contractual agreements) and the 'publicity principle' apply as well. The difference with German law is that the voidness of the obligational contractual agreement providing for the title or causa for the security right affects the validity of the creation of the security as a matter of property law involving its voidness as well. In *Austria,* therefore, the further-going 'abstraction principle' does not apply.

149. As a result of the ruling of the Austrian Supreme Court that the security agreement providing the title/causa normally also includes the agreement on establishing the security right in rem,[108] some parts of Austrian legal literature consider the property law contractual agreement as not part of the procedure. According to this opinion, the procedure requires the factual act of publicity only.[109] However, as long as the 'Trennungsprinzip' itself is not challenged by this opinion this remains a question of mere terminology.

150. Unless more stringent requirements exist in law, contractual agreements can be concluded orally (for details see Question 7).

151. The general rule that the establishing of security rights always follows the rules provided by the law governing the transfer of ownership of the specific kind of asset is not applied as rigorously as in *Germany.*

Question 7: Do the rules for the creation of security rights vary depending on the nature of the asset in question?

1. Germany

152. As mentioned under Question 6, para. 146, the establishing of security rights generally follows the rules provided by the law governing the transfer of

108 OGH Urt. v. 23.11.1994, Az.: 7 Ob 39/94 = SZ 67/213; see also OGH Urt. v. 18.06.1986, Az.: 3 Ob 43/86 = [1987] 14 ÖBA 51, 52.

109 G. Iro, *Sachenrecht*, para. 10/2; G. Iro in P. Apathy, G. Iro and H. Koziol (eds.), *Österreichisches Bankvertragsrecht*, Vol. IX, Part. 2, Ch. 2, paras. 2/83, 2/88.

ownership of the specific kind of asset. Apparently this applies as well for the security ownership/assignment since these are 'normal' transfers of ownership of the asset, albeit in a fiduciary capacity. Since the legal rules on the contractual transfer of ownership of assets vary depending on the nature of the asset, the rules on the creation of security rights do so as well. The rules may vary in relation to the requirements set by the 'publicity principle' as well as the required form of the contractual agreement.

1.1. Publicity requirements

153. As far as the *security ownership/assignment* is concerned, an act of publicity is not required. In the case of security ownership, the necessary transfer of possession is construed by constructive possession, §930 BGB ('Besitzkonstitut', see Question 1, para. 13). The assignment of claims does not require any act of publicity, §§398 et seq. BGB. One exclusion is made for registered inland waterway vessels. Here the valid establishment of security ownership would require the creditor to be registered in the Ship Register as the new owner, §3 (1) SchiffRG. Inland waterway vessels of a certain size have to be registered, §10 (2) SchiffRegO (German Ship Register Regulation). The registration of smaller ones is voluntary.

154. As far as pledges are concerned, the necessary act of publicity required for the validity of the security right in the case of tangibles is the transfer of possession, §1204, 1205 BGB (exclusion: ships and airplanes where registration in a specific register is required). In the case of claims it is the notification of the debtor, §1280 BGB. As far as claims are concerned the 'publicity principle' is stricter with pledges than with the assignment, which does not require any notification. The pledge of rights other than claims, on the other hand, does not require any specific acts of publicity, since the assignment of rights also does not require any such act, §§398, 413 BGB. For some types of intellectual property rights, specific registers are provided in which, aside from ownership, pledge rights may also be registered (e.g. patents, utility patents, commercial designs). However, such registration would merely have a declaratory value and is not required for the valid creation of the pledge.[110]

155. As far as immovables are concerned, publicity is guaranteed by the validity requirement of the mortgage being registered in the Land Register, §873 BGB. The same applies for ships and planes, §§24 et seq. SchiffRG, §5 LuftFzgG.

110 For all types of intellectual property rights see J. Damrau in *Münchener Kommentar zum BGB*, Vol. 6, §1274, paras. 80 et seq.

1.2. *Form requirements of the contractual agreement*

156. As far as movables are concerned, there are generally no formal requirements. According to §1274 (1) BGB the pledge over rights follows the rules governing the transfer of the right, which leads to an important exclusion of the general rule. According to §15 (3) GmbHG the assignment of shares of a GmbH (Limited Liability Partnership) requires a notarised agreement (the underlying obligational security agreement requires the notarised form as well, §15 (4) GmbHG). According to §1274 (1) BGB the pledge over GmbH shares requires this form as well.[111] But as the form requirement of §15 (4) GmbHG only catches obligations to assign shares of a GmbHG and not to pledge such shares and §1274 (1) BGB governs only the agreement to create the pledge as a matter of property law, the underlying obligational security agreement would not require a notarised form. Nevertheless, since the parties would have to appear before the public notary anyway there is usually in practice one notarised contract containing (at least by implication) both the obligational security agreement and the agreement on the actual creation of the security right as a matter of property law.

157. As far as immovables are concerned, mortgage agreements do not require any stricter formal requirements either. However, in banking practice, mortgage agreements are usually concluded before a public notary (notarisation) for two reasons. First of all, §873 (2) BGB stipulates that contractual agreements on transferring or granting rights over real property become immediately binding only if they are notarised or if they are concluded before the Land Registry. Otherwise the agreement becomes binding at the moment it is submitted by the parties to the Land Registry (which requires a written form) or when the entitled party delivers its approval of the registration to the other party. The approval has to be officially certified, §§873 (2) BGB, 29 GBO. The second reason is that a notarial deed in which the debtor submits to immediate levy of execution constitutes a legally enforceable document, §794 (1) Nr. 5 ZPO. If enforcement proceedings become necessary, the creditor (bank) does not have to file court proceedings in order to obtain an enforceable judgment but can commence enforcement proceedings immediately.

2. Austria

158. In *Austria* as well, the rules for the creation of security rights vary in relation to the requirements of publicity and the required form of the contractual agreements depending on the nature of the asset in question.

---

[111] For the pledge of GmbH shares see D. Wiegand in J. Staudinger, *BGB*, §1274, para. 55.

2.1. Publicity requirements

159. As far as the security ownership is concerned, according to the Austrian Supreme Court the rules for the pledge over tangibles apply.[112] Transfer of possession is required, §451 (1) ABGB. If transfer of possession is not feasible because of the nature of the asset (the inventory of warehouses) the parties must use signifiers and appoint a collateral agent (for details see Question 3, para. 96), §§452, 427 ABGB. In the case of security assignments of claims §452 ABGB also applies. For its interpretation in this case by the Austrian Supreme Court see Question 3, para. 108 (notification of the debtor of the claim provided as collateral or entry into the accounts of the debtor).

160. As far as pledges over tangibles and claims are concerned, reference should be made to the aforesaid, since according to the Austrian Supreme Court, security ownership/assignment and the pledge must be treated equally.[113] One exclusion is the pledge (mortgage) over ships, which does not require the transfer of possession but registration in a specific register, §§24 et seq. SchiffRG (Austrian Act on Rights over Registered Ships and Ships under construction/Gesetz über Rechte an eingetragenen Schiffen und Schiffsbauwerken).

161. In the case of pledges over other rights, §452 ABGB also applies. Since a transfer of possession is not possible, the parties must use signifiers which enable everyone to easily have notice of the pledge. In the case of a pledge over shares of a partnership, the partnership must be notified.[114] The validity of a pledge over a trade mark requires its registration in the Trade Mark Register while other ways of meeting the requirements of §452 ABGB may also be possible.[115] For patents the specific provision of §43 PatG (Austrian Patent Act) stipulates that a valid pledge over a patent requires its registration in the Patent Register. The same applies for pledges over licenses to patents.

162. As far as immovables are concerned, the validity of a mortgage requires its registration in the land register, §§451, 431 ABGB.

---

[112] OGH Urt. v. 23.10.1968, Az.: 3 Ob 112/68 = SZ 41/140; OGH Urt. v. 09.01.1985, Az.: 3 Ob 116/85 = SZ 58/1.

[113] OGH Urt. v. 07.09.1978, Az.: 6 Ob 662/78 = SZ 51/121; OGH Urt. v. 01.03.1989, Az.: 1 Ob 697/88 = SZ 62/32.

[114] B. Koch in P. Apathy, G. Iro and H. Koziol (eds.), *Österreichisches Bankvertragsrecht*, Vol. IX, Part 2, Ch. 7, para. 7/58, 7/81.

[115] B. Koch in P. Apathy, G. Iro and H. Koziol (eds.), *Österreichisches Bankvertragsrecht*, Vol. IX, Part 2, Ch. 7, para. 7/94 et seq.

2.2. Form requirements of the contractual agreement

163. In the context of §452 ABGB regarding security assignments of claims, the Austrian Supreme Court has ruled that, aside from the requirements discussed under Question 3, para. 108, the assignment agreement has to be in written form, to enable third parties to easily have notice of the assignment.[116]

164. For the registration of a mortgage in the Land Register, the written security agreement providing the title for the acquisition must be submitted to the Land Registry, §26 GBO. It has to be a public document. If not, the signatures of the parties must be notarised, §31 GBG. If the requirements of §31 GBG are not met, the registration of a 'priority notice' (Vormerkung) may be possible, §35 GBG. The registration of a 'priority notice' would lead to a valid acquisition of a mortgage as well, §453 ABGB. But the registration of a 'priority notice' also requires a written document, §26 ABGB. Nevertheless, an oral security agreement would not be invalid, but it would require the security provider (debtor) to have all the preparations for registration completed in time.[117]

165. Since Austrian law also provides for a submission to immediate levy of execution in a notarial document to be legally enforceable, §§3, 3a NO (Austrian Notary Act), at least in banking practice, notarisation of the security agreement should be the standard.

C. ENFORCEMENT OF SECURITY RIGHTS

Question 8: To what extent is it possible for the secured party to enforce the security without having to use formal court procedures?

1. Germany

1.1. Movables

1.1.1. Tangibles

1.1.1.1. Transfer of title by way of security

166. Transfer of title by way of security is a security right which was not originally intended by the German legislator but which was invented in German

---

[116] OGH Urt. v. 21.01.1975, Az.: 5 Ob 322/74 = SZ 48/2; OGH Urt. v. 29.09.1998, Az.: 1 Ob 406/97f = SZ 71/154.

[117] G. Iro in P. Apathy in P. Apathy, G. Iro and H. Koziol (eds.), *Österreichisches Bankvertragsrecht*, Vol. IX, Part 2, Ch. 2, para. 2/77.

legal practice using the existing legal framework. Therefore there are no legal provisions governing the enforcement of this security right, meaning that its enforcement initially follows the contractual provisions laid down in the fiduciary security agreement. Even if the security agreement does not contain any provisions governing its enforcement, most questions can be solved by interpretation of the agreement. The analogous application of provisions on the law of pledges is therefore not generally possible except in particular situations.[118]

167. In the event of default (which will usually be the time when the secured payment becomes due), the debtor loses his right of possession regarding the collateral. The creditor is then entitled to demand that the debtor surrenders the collateral to him. After taking possession, the creditor, according to the security agreement, may realise the collateral without a court order. Realisation may be carried out either by public auction or a private purchase agreement. Another possibility under the contract is that the creditor is granted the opportunity to purchase the collateral himself for a reasonable price.[119] According to §1229 BGB, a provision in the law of pledges (for mortgages see the similar §1149 BGB), which applies analogously to security ownership,[120] clauses which stipulate that the creditor shall automatically acquire full non-security ownership at the time of default are banned. Such an agreement, according to §1229 BGB, is only valid if it is concluded after the time of default. The parties may also appoint a collateral agent to conduct the realisation. If there are no explicit provisions in the security agreement, interpretation of the agreement and the agreement's fiduciary nature require the creditor to take into account the interests of the collateral provider. The creditor is therefore obliged to conduct the realisation in the way which is most likely to lead to the best economic outcome. If he gives the collateral away for a price far below the market price he may be liable for damages.[121] The creditor is also always able to have the collateral attached in enforcement proceedings, given that he has previously acquired an enforceable document with regard to the secured claim (court order, submission to enforcement proceedings in the notarised security agreement). The fact that the creditor is the legal (security) owner of the collateral does not prevent the collateral from possibly being subject to attachment.[122] The following realisation

118 W. Wiegand in J. Staudinger, *BGB*, Anh. (annex to) §§929–931, para. 227.

119 BGH Urt. v. 23.11.1959, Az.: VII ZR 48/58 = [1960] WM 171; W. Wiegand in J. Staudinger, *BGB*, Anh. (annex to) §§929–931, para. 234.

120 Prevailing opinion, see J. Baur and R. Stürner, *Sachenrecht*, §57, para. 16; W. Wiegand in J. Staudinger, *BGB*, Anh. (annex to) §§929–932, para. 234; M. Henssler in H.-T. Soergel, *BGB*, Anh. (annex to) §930, para. 78, O. Jauernig in O. Jauernig, *BGB*, §930, para. 37.

121 LG Wiesbaden Urt. v. 06.04.1987, Az.: 1 S 413/86 = [1987] NJW-RR 1270.

122 J. Oechsler in *Münchener Kommentar zum BGB*, Vol. 6, Anh. (annex to) §§929–936, para. 50; J. Baur and R. Stürner, *Sachenrecht*, §57, para. 43.

is then conducted by the bailiff according to the provisions of procedural law, §§815 et seq. ZPO. If the proceeds of the realisation exceed the secured claim, the creditor is obliged to return the surplus to the debtor, even if this is not expressly mentioned in the security agreement, since this is a consequence of the security right's fiduciary character.

168. The creditor is only required to file court proceedings in order to gain an enforceable judgment to have the debtor surrender the collateral if the debtor does not honour its contractual obligation to grant the creditor possession of the collateral. The competent authority to enforce the surrender order would be the bailiff (cf. para. 174).

1.1.1.2. Pledge

169. Generally the German law of pledges also does not require the creditor to use court proceedings in order to enforce the security right.

170. §1228 BGB stipulates that a pledge right is enforced by a private sale of the collateral. The creditor is not entitled to realise the collateral before the secured payment is due, §1228 (2) BGB. In advance of the sale, the creditor has to warn the collateral provider (debtor) of the sale, §1234 BGB. The reason is to grant the collateral provider a last chance to prevent the enforcement by fulfilling the secured claim. The sale is to be conducted in a public auction, §1235 (1) BGB. Only where the collateral has a stock exchange price or a market price is a private purchase agreement also possible, §§1235 (2), 1221 BGB. §1235 BGB may be derogated from by agreement, but such agreements regarding the method of sale cannot be made before the creditor is entitled to realise the collateral (after the secured payment has become due), §1245 (2) BGB. The same applies to agreements which grant the creditor automatic acquisition of ownership of the collateral in case of default, §1229 BGB.

1.1.2. Intangibles

1.1.2.1. Assignment by way of security

171. Court proceedings are generally not necessary in order to enforce the security. Assignment by way of security is not specified by law. Provisions governing the pledge of claims are not applicable.[123] The security agreement determines the event triggering default, the method of realising the collateral (usually by collecting the claim, meaning that the creditor demands payment from the debtor of the claim provided as collateral) and the point of time at which

123 BGH Urt. v. 26.04.2005, Az.: XI ZR 289/04 = [2005] NJW-RR 1408 at 1409.

the collateral may be realised.[124] Where the disclosure of the assignment to the third party debtor, which is typically a natural consequence of its collection, would affect the debtor's economic survival, the security agreement must grant the debtor the chance to prevent the realisation of the collateral. The creditor therefore has to warn the debtor within a reasonable period before the intended realisation. If the security agreement is part of the general terms and conditions which do not contain such an obligation for the creditor, the assignment may not be valid.[125]

1.1.2.2. Pledge

1.1.2.2.1. Claims

172. §1282 BGB stipulates that after the secured payment has become due, the creditor is entitled to collect the claim. From this point on the debtor of the claim provided as collateral can only pay the creditor. Court proceedings are not necessary unless the debtor of the claim provided as collateral refuses to satisfy the claim. The provision is a specific rule for claims which deviates from the general rule in §1277 BGB applying to all types of rights (see the following paragraph).

1.1.2.2.2. Other rights

173. As far as pledges over rights are concerned, §1277 BGB stipulates that the enforcement of pledges over rights may be conducted only on the basis of an enforceable judgment (or other legally enforceable document) according to the provisions of German procedural law. The reason behind the provision is to protect the debtor from having his rights dissipated. Since the determination of the value of a right is often uncertain, allowing a private sale out of court seemed inappropriate to the legislator. If the creditor is not yet in possession of an enforceable document (especially a notarial deed in which the debtor is submitted to an immediate levy of execution, §794 (1) Nr. 5 ZPO against the collateral), he first has to obtain an enforceable court order against the debtor ordering compliance with enforcement proceedings in relation to the specific asset.

174. In German law, enforcement/execution proceedings are autonomous proceedings conducted by state authorities and not by the creditor himself. If a

---

124 J. Baur and R. Stürner, *Sachenrecht*, §58, para. 3; C. Herresthal in J. Staudinger, *BGB, Eckpfeiler des Zivilrechts*, para. 246.

125 BGH Urt. v. 26.04.2005, Az.: XI ZR 289/04 = [2005] NJW-RR 1408 at 1409, regarding the security assignment of wages.

creditor has obtained an enforceable judgment or other enforceable document he has to apply to the competent execution authority to carry out the enforcement. In the case of enforcement against rights which are the debtor's assets, the local courts (Amtsgerichte) are the competent enforcement authorities, §828 (1) ZPO. After the attachment order, the enforcement court makes an order stipulating the appropriate method by which the right should be realised (according to the general intention of the law, this should usually be a forced public auction), taking into account the arguments of the creditors, §857 ZPO.

175. However, §1277 BGB may be derogated from by agreement. The parties are able to make different arrangements in the agreement by which they have established the pledge. In legal practice, especially in the case of pledges over shares, parties usually agree on a private sale of the pledged shares. Since an agreement entitling the creditor to conclude a private purchase agreement can only be made after the secured payment has become due, §§1277, 1245 (2) BGB, the collateral, in legal practice, is usually realised through a public auction.[126] §1277 BGB also stipulates the application of §1229 BGB to intangible collateral (see para. 170).

1.2. Immovables

176. Reference should be made to para. 173, 174. Mortgages entitle the creditor to require the collateral provider (debtor) to comply with enforcement proceedings against the encumbered real estate, according to the provisions governing the enforcement/execution proceedings in German procedural law, §§1147, 1191 BGB.

177. If the creditor is a bank it will normally already have an enforceable notarial document, since the establishment of a mortgage in banking practice generally goes hand in hand with notarial submission to an immediate levy of execution against the real estate (see Question 7, para. 157). Otherwise, an enforceable court order must be granted first.

178. With the enforceable document the creditor may apply for enforcement proceedings to the competent authorities, which, in the case of enforcement proceedings against the real estate of the debtor, are the local courts in their role as enforcement courts, §1 ZVG (German Act on Forced Auctions and Sequestrations of Immovables). The legally permissible ways of realising the real estate are forced public auction and administrative receivership, which are ordered by the enforcement court.

126 D. Wiegand in J. Staudinger, *BGB*, §1277, para. 10 et seq.

179. According to §1149 BGB, agreements which derogate from §1147 BGB may be concluded only after the secured payment has become due. After that time, the creditor can be contractually entitled to an out-of-court sale. Since the collateral provider remains the owner of the collateral and the law does not provide for the right of realisation through a private sale (see §1228 BGB for pledges over tangibles) a power of attorney would be required. As far as such an agreement contains an obligation to have the collateral sold, both the agreement and the power of attorney, where it is expressly or factually irrevocable, require a notarised form, §311 b BGB.[127] Since the creditor does not have any right to claim the conclusion of an agreement on a private sale from the collateral provider, such agreements in practice would often be the result of pressure being applied to the debtor by the creditor, exploiting the debtor's financial distress, which may lead to the assumption that such an agreement is immoral and therefore invalid, §138 BGB.[128] The agreement would have to ensure that the creditor receives no financial advantage exceeding the amount of the secured claim. Rights of third parties to the collateral must not be affected or the agreement would also be invalid, §138 BGB.[129]

180. Such an agreement, according to §1149 BGB, would not have an in rem effect and could not be subject to an entry in the Land Register. §1149 BGB applies to the 'Hypothek' as well as to the 'Grundschuld'.[130] The lack of court decisions dealing with §1149 BGB leads to the conclusion that, in practice, creditors enforce their security rights by pursuing enforcement proceedings as provided for by the law, rather than using these contractual agreements.

2. Austria

2.1. Movables

2.1.1. Tangibles

2.1.1.1. Transfer of title by way of security

181. Reference should be made to German law, para. 166, 167. The parties are free to determine the method of realisation by the creditor, which is what

[127] H. Wolfsteiner in J. Staudinger, *BGB*, §1149, para. 16; see also OLG Brandenburg Urt. v. 14.03.2012, Az.: 4 U 60/10.

[128] For all legal risks connected to private sale agreements according to §1149 BGB see the circular of the Federal Association of Notaries (*Bundesnotarkammer*) from 07.03.2008 under the following link: <http://www.dnoti.de/DOC/2008/07_RS_2008.pdf> accessed 24 May 2016; H. Wolfsteiner in J. Staudinger, *BGB*, §1149, paras. 16 et seq.

[129] D. Eickmann in *Münchener Kommentar zum BGB*, Vol. 6, §1149, para. 11.

[130] H. Wolfsteiner in J. Staudinger, *BGB*, §1149, para. 23.

they mostly do in practice. A private sale can be agreed upon as long as mutual interests are taken care of and the requirements of §1371 ABGB, a provision relating to the law of pledges and which applies analogously, are met.[131] The provision bans clauses according to which the creditor automatically acquires full non-security ownership in case of default. Clauses according to which the creditor is able to acquire full non-security ownership of the collateral by paying a price determined in advance of the default are also banned (for further details regarding §1371 ABGB see para. 185).[132] If the parties have not made any agreement on the realisation of the collateral, out-of-court sale of the collateral by the creditor is possible by analogous application of §§466 a et seq. ABGB (for further details see para. 183).[133] The sale in this case must be conducted at a public auction, §466 b (2) ABGB. It has been further established by court ruling that the creditor in this case is free to initiate court proceedings with regard to the secured claim and have the collateral attached in enforcement proceedings,[134] which leads to a realisation of the collateral according to the rules of procedural law, either by private agreement or by forced public auction, depending on whether the collateral has a stock exchange price or not §§268, 270 EO. The sale has to be ordered by the court as the competent enforcement authority, which is also competent to make the decision whether the specific asset shall be attached or not, §264 EO.

2.1.1.2. Pledge

182. §461 ABGB has the same meaning as §1277 BGB (see para. 173), the only difference being that it applies not only to intangibles but also to pledges over all kinds of assets including the mortgage. In order to enforce pledges over all kinds of assets, the creditor has to obtain an enforceable court order first (if he has no other legally enforceable document), after which he can apply for its enforcement to the authorities.[135] For the possibility of contracting out of the provision see para. 185.

183. One exception to the general rule in §461 ABGB appears in §§466 a et seq. ABGB for tangible movables: the out-of court realisation of pledged collateral, which is equivalent to §§1228 et seq. BGB in German law. After the secured payment is due, the creditor is entitled to have the collateral sold at public auction, §466 b (1), (2) ABGB. A private purchase agreement is legally possible only if the collateral has a stock exchange price or a market price §466 b (4)

---

131 OGH Urt. v. 07.11.1951, Az.: 3 Ob 574/51 = SZ 24/303.

132 P. Apathy in P. Apathy, G. Iro and H. Koziol (eds.), *Österreichisches Bankvertragsrecht*, Vol. IX, Part 2, Ch. 4, para. 4/30.

133 P. Apathy in P. Apathy, G. Iro and H. Koziol (eds.), *Österreichisches Bankvertragsrecht*, Vol. IX, Part 2, Ch. 4, para. 4/31.

134 OGH Urt. v. 07.11.1951, Az.: 3 Ob 574/51 = SZ 24/303.

135 G. Kodek in M. Schwimann (ed.), *Taschenkommentar ABGB*, §461, Rn. 1.

ABGB, or if the parties have made a specific arrangement deviating from the general rule of public auction, which is possible under §466 a (3) ABGB. The collateral provider has to be warned of the intended sale at least one month before the sale, §466 b (1) ABGB. Contractual provisions which deviate from the statute must not violate §1371 ABGB (see para. 181, 185)

2.1.2. *Intangibles*

2.1.2.1. Assignment by way of security

184. General reference should be made to the discussion on German law, para. 171. The security right is enforced by the creditor collecting the assigned claim, meaning that he demands payment from the debtor of the claim provided as collateral. Court proceedings are not necessary. §1371 ABGB must be taken into account.[136]

2.1.2.2. Pledge

185. Reference should be made to para. 182. §461 ABGB applies, which means that the creditor has to file for court and enforcement proceedings. There is no exception for claims as there is in German law. However §461 ABGB may be derogated from by agreement. The parties can agree on other ways of realising the collateral as long as they take §1371 ABGB into account.[137] This provision generally bans clauses in pledge agreements which are contrary to the reasons and nature of a pledge right. The price of the collateral in a case where sale is agreed on by the creditor must not be determined in advance and it must be ensured that the interests of the collateral provider are taken care of by the creditor during realisation. The creditor has to warn the debtor of the intended sale and has to choose the type of sale which is most likely to promise the best economic result (it can generally be said that under the general clause of §1371 ABGB Austrian courts have developed requirements equivalent to the German written provisions of §§1229, 1234, 1245, 1149 BGB which provide protection for the debtor in case of pledges, as well as assumptions made by German courts resulting from the fiduciary character of security ownership/assignment). The restriction in §1371 ABGB applies only to contractual agreements on out-of-court realisations concluded before the secured payment is due, which is the same restriction as §§1229, 1245, 1149 BGB in German law.[138]

---

136 OGH Urt. v. 21.02.1973, Az.: 1 Ob 13/73 = OGH SZ 46/24.

137 M. Hinteregger in M. Schwimann (ed.), *Praxiskommentar ABGB*, §461, para. 6; in regard to pledges over shares B. Koch in P. Apathy, G. Iro and H. Koziol (eds.), *Österreichisches Bankvertragrecht*, Vol. IX, Part 2, Ch. 7, para. 7/65.

138 OGH Urt. v. 15.10.1998, Az.: 8 Ob 125/98k = [1999] ÖBA 805/568.

2.2. Immovables

186. §461 ABGB applies. Reference should be made to para. 182. The legal methods of realising real estate in *Austria* are the same as in Germany, namely forced public auction, §§133 et seq. EO, and administrative receivership, §§97 et seq. EO.

187. It is disputed whether §461 ABGB may be derogated from by agreement in regards to real estate. §1371 ABGB seems to lend support to the expansive interpretation, since it apparently allows contractual agreements which deviate from §461 ABGB and does not distinguish movable from immovable collateral. Therefore the Austrian Supreme Court and the prevailing opinion in legal literature recognise contractual agreements on the out-of-court realisation of real estate in connection to mortgage agreements, as long as they are concluded after the secured payment has become due.[139] Since the creditor is not the owner of the real estate, in the case of a private sale he has to act as a representative of the collateral provider. The power of attorney must be in written form (submission to the Land Registry is required) and meet the requirements of §31 (6) GBG. The legal situation should be the same as in Germany.

Question 9: Is the secured party affected by a 'stay' on the enforcement of security rights if the debtor enters insolvency proceedings?

1. Germany

1.1. General comments

188. A distinction must be drawn between the opening of insolvency proceedings proper and the opening of preliminary insolvency proceedings. When creditors or the debtor file for the opening of insolvency proceedings, the insolvency court usually orders the opening of preliminary insolvency proceedings and appoints a provisional insolvency practitioner (IP).[140] The court mandates the provisional IP to give an expert opinion on the question of whether the debtor is insolvent. If so, the court will then order the opening of insolvency proceedings and appoint the permanent IP (who in practice is the same person as the provisional IP), to

---

139 OGH v. 15.02.2002, Az.: 5 Ob 295/01w = SZ 2002/2; OGH Urt. v. 15.10.1998, Az.: 8 Ob 125/98k = [1999] ÖBA 803/568; G. Iro in P. Apathy, G. Iro and H. Koziol (eds.), *Österreichisches Bankvertragsrecht*, Vol. IX, Part 2, Ch. 2, para. 2/335; K. Hoffmann in P. Rummel, *ABGB*, §1371, para. 1.

140 German laws does not distinguish a liquidator from an administrator as the office holder is always an *Insolvenzverwalter*, who is responsible for both liquidation and administration in one unitary procedure. That is why the term 'insolvency practitioner' is used throughout the following text.

whom the power of administration and disposal will be transferred, §80 InsO. The debtor may, however, keep the power of administration and disposal if he has previously applied to conduct the insolvency proceedings as debtor in possession proceedings (self-administration, Eigenverwaltung), §§270 et seq. InsO, and the court has approved this application. In this case the court appoints a custodian (Sachwalter) to oversee the debtor's economic activities. In this situation the preliminary proceedings will still be conducted, but as preliminary debtor in possession proceedings with a provisional custodian instead of preliminary insolvency proceedings with a provisional IP.

189. All security rights discussed in this report in insolvency proceedings provide for a so-called right to separate satisfaction (Absonderungsrecht), §§49, 50, 51 Nr. 1 InsO. Firstly this means that the security right does not prevent the asset to which it is related from being legally part of the insolvency estate. Therefore the secured creditor is not entitled to claim its separation from the insolvency estate. Secondly the secured creditor is granted the right to demand preferential satisfaction up to the amount of this secured claim out of the proceeds of the specific asset's realisation. Only a realised surplus exceeding the amount of his secured claim belongs to the insolvency estate. Since in Germany insolvency proceedings are in principle aimed at liquidation, the collateral has to be realised sooner or later unless different arrangements have been made in an insolvency plan. Another question not prejudged by the classification as a right to separate satisfaction is whether the IP or the secured creditor is responsible for carrying out the realisation. The answer to this question depends on the kind of asset and the kind of security right in question as well as on whether the debtor (IP) or the secured creditor is in direct possession of the asset. If it is the IP who is responsible for the realisation, the secured creditor is no longer able to enforce his security right (see the following paragraphs for further details, para. 190 et seq.).

190. §89 InsO stipulates that insolvency creditors may not pursue enforcement proceedings against the insolvency estate or the debtor's other property during insolvency proceedings. On the other hand enforcement proceedings are generally possible in preliminary insolvency proceedings unless the court orders otherwise (§21 (2), (1) Nr. 3 InsO, cf. para. 199). However, this prohibition applies only to 'insolvency creditors' (§38 InsO), that is, creditors with obligational claims against the debtor at the time insolvency proceedings are opened. While secured creditors being insolvency creditors in regard to their secured claim are therefore no longer able to enforce their secured claims, it follows from §§49 et seq., 165 et seq. InsO that §89 InsO does not affect the enforcement of security rights which provide for a right to separate satisfaction, since these are not obligational rights but rights in rem. The enforcement of rights to separate satisfaction are governed by the specific provisions of §§165 et seq. InsO, which actually govern the realisation of the assets which are subject to those rights and not their enforcement. However, enforcement proceedings by secured creditors in relation to such assets are legally possible only to the extent to which these provisions enable the creditor to realise the value of their security.[141]

1.2. Movables

1.2.1. Tangibles

1.2.1.1. Transfer of title by way of security

191. §166 (1) InsO stipulates that after the opening of insolvency proceedings it is the task of the IP to realise collateral which is subject to rights to separate satisfaction. However, this is only true if he is in possession of the collateral, which as far as assets subject to security ownership are concerned will almost always be the case. The creditor on the other hand loses his right to realise the collateral. He therefore also loses his right to claim surrender of the collateral from the debtor and can no longer enforce this claim if the IP refuses to grant him possession of the collateral. The secured creditor can, however, come to a different agreement with the insolvency practitioner. The insolvency practitioner may by agreement entrust the secured creditor with the realisation, although the secured creditor would otherwise not be entitled to it. In debtor in possession proceedings the debtor is responsible for the realisation of the collateral after insolvency proceedings have been opened in coordination with the custodian, §282 InsO. If the IP does not realise the collateral immediately after the first creditors' assembly (§§157, 159 InsO), the creditor may claim interest on his secured claim from the insolvency estate, §169 InsO. Furthermore, if the IP uses the collateral for the debtor's enterprise before its realisation (as he is allowed to do, §172 InsO), and the use of the asset creates a loss in value that affects the security of the creditor, the creditor may claim for compensation from the insolvency estate.

192. According to §170 (1) InsO, the insolvency practitioner is to deduct the ascertainment and realisation costs from the proceeds of realisation which together are calculated at a fixed rate of 9%. The result is that these costs are borne by the secured creditor.

193. The ascertainment costs are paid by the secured creditor because the insolvency practitioner has to establish whether security rights exist over the asset in question at all, and if so in whose favour. The insolvency practitioner carries this out only for the benefit of the secured creditor; accordingly, the secured creditor alone shall bear the ascertainment costs instead of the other

141 W. Breuer in *Münchener Kommentar zur InsO*, Vol. 2, §89, para. 21; W. Uhlenbruck in W. Uhlenbruck, *InsO*, §89, para. 19.

creditors through the insolvency estate. Following §171 (1) InsO, these costs are calculated at a fixed rate of 4% of the proceeds of realisation. This amount does not go to the insolvency practitioner himself, but to the insolvency estate to be distributed amongst creditors.

194. The realisation costs (which must be distinguished from the ascertainment costs) are paid for by the secured creditor because the insolvency practitioner realises the asset in the secured creditor's interest; it is the secured creditor who receives the proceeds of realisation, §170 (1) (2) InsO. The insolvency practitioner is permitted, by §171 (2) (1) InsO, to calculate the costs at a fixed rate of 5%. He can, however, set a higher sum if the necessary costs actually incurred were considerably higher than 5%. Conversely, the secured creditor can demand to pay a lower sum if the costs were considerably lower than 5%.

195. In practice, IPs tend to request a higher contribution to the costs of up to 15% or even more. These contributions are paid to the insolvency estate.

196. In debtor in possession proceedings, ascertainment costs are not imposed at all, and only the costs of realisation actually incurred can be imposed, §282 (1) (2)/(3) InsO.

197. §166 InsO does not apply in preliminary proceedings. As long as insolvency proceedings are not opened, the creditor is generally free to realise the collateral and to enforce his claim to surrender of the collateral if necessary. However, according to §21 (1) InsO, the insolvency court has to take all measures which appear necessary to it in order to avoid any detriment to the financial status of the debtor until the court decides whether insolvency proceedings are to be opened or not. Since at the beginning of preliminary proceedings the court does not have any guidance to determine which measures may be necessary, in practice most of these measures at the preliminary stage are ordered on application by the provisional IP.

198. According to §21 (1) InsO, the insolvency court may, during the preliminary proceedings, prohibit the debtor from voluntarily surrendering the collateral to the creditor.[142]

199. In addition §21 (2) (1) Nr. 3 InsO stipulates that the court may, during the preliminary proceedings, order a 'stay' on all enforcement proceedings against the debtor's movable assets if the requirements stated in §21 (1) InsO are made out. Although the wording in §21 (2) Nr. 3 InsO is identical to the wording of §89 InsO, which relates to the actual insolvency proceedings, it is established that, in contrast to the situation in those proceedings, an order

142 H.-P. Kirchhof in *Heidelberger Kommentar zur InsO*, §21, para. 29.

issued in preliminary proceedings under §21 (2) (1) Nr. 3 InsO may also affect enforcement proceedings by secured creditors in relation to assets which are subject to security rights.[143]

200. Finally, the insolvency court may, during the preliminary proceedings, order that the collateral may not be realised by the creditor and that the debtor (or, respectively, the provisional IP) is allowed to use the collateral for the debtor's enterprise insofar as the collateral is of considerable significance to it, §21 (2) (1) Nr. 5 InsO. This order requires the continuation of the debtor's enterprise during the preliminary proceedings. In practice at least, the prohibition on realisation will only affect claims assigned by way of security, since tangibles which are subject to security ownership, at least those of considerable importance to the debtor's enterprise, will be in the possession of the debtor, which means that the creditor would not in any case be able to have them realised (unless the debtor were to surrender the collateral to him). If the use of the asset creates a loss in value that affects the security of the creditor, compensation has to be paid. A claim for such compensation becomes a claim against the insolvency estate if it is not satisfied before the opening of insolvency proceedings.[144] Furthermore, the secured creditor can claim interest for the time beginning three months after the court order, §169 InsO.

1.2.1.2. Pledge

201. Since in the case of pledges the creditor is normally in possession of the collateral, the opening of insolvency proceedings does not affect his right to realise the collateral according to the law or the security agreement, §§166 (1), 173 InsO. In this case, realisation costs are paid by the secured creditor anyway, so the insolvency practitioner does not have a claim for costs. §41 (1) InsO stipulates that claims against the debtor in insolvency proceedings are always to be considered as due even if they are not. So the creditor does not have to wait until his secured claim has become due according to the security agreement to be entitled to realise the asset.[145] If the creditor is responsible for the realisation, the IP can apply to the insolvency court in order to set a deadline by which the creditor must have the collateral realised. After the expiration of the deadline, the IP may claim for the surrender of the collateral in order to realise it himself, §173 (2) InsO.

---

143 H. Haarmeyer in *Münchener Kommentar zur InsO*, Vol. 1, §21, para. 72; H.-P. Kirchhof in *Heidelberger Kommentar zur InsO*, §21, para. 42; W. Uhlenbruck in W. Uhlenbruck, *InsO*, 4§282, para. 28.

144 H. Haarmeyer in *Münchener Kommentar zur InsO*, Vol. 1, §21, para. 101.

145 For the application of §41 (1) InsO to rights of separate satisfaction at least if the collateral provider is identical with the debtor of the secured claim see BGH Urt. v. 10.12.1959, Az.: VII ZR 210/59 = BGHZ 31, 337, 340 et seq.; G. Bitter in *Münchener Kommentar zur InsO*, Vol. 1, §41, paras. 13 et seq.

202. Since §21 (2) (1) Nr. 5 InsO refers to assets within the scope of §166 (1) InsO, an order as described in para. 200 is not possible.

1.2.2. Intangibles

1.2.2.1. Assignment by way of security

203. Similarly to §166 (1) InsO, §166 (2) InsO stipulates that after insolvency proceedings have been opened, the IP is responsible for the realisation of the receivable either by collecting the claim or by any other method. As a result of this provision the creditor loses his right to realise the assigned claim. In the case of debtor in possession proceedings, the debtor in coordination with the custodian is responsible for the realisation, §282 InsO.

204. §§170, 171 InsO apply, see para. 192 et seq.

205. §166 (2) InsO only applies to receivables subject to security assignments. Other rights that may be assigned by way of security fall under the scope of §173 InsO, meaning that notwithstanding the opening of insolvency proceedings, the creditor is free to realise the collateral himself according to the statute and contractual agreements.

206. In preliminary proceedings the insolvency court may issue an order prohibiting the creditor from realising the collateral, §21 (2) (1) Nr. 5 InsO. Reference should be made to para. 200.

1.2.2.2. Pledge

207. §166 InsO does not apply. That is true for both receivables and other rights. The creditor is free to realise the collateral, §173 InsO, and to pursue enforcement proceedings if necessary for realisation.

1.3. Immovables

208. §§49, 165 InsO stipulate a parallel power to realise the collateral. Both the IP and the secured creditor are able to apply to the enforcement court for a forced public auction or administrative sequestration (see Question 8, para. 178). If the creditor pursues enforcement proceedings, §30 d ZVG grants the IP the possibility to apply to the enforcement court for an order of a temporary 'stay' on the enforcement according to §30 d (1) Nr. 1–4 ZVG if:

- the first creditors' assembly under §§29 (1) Nr. 1, 156 InsO has not yet been held, or

- according to the result of the first creditors' assembly the real estate is still required either for the continuation of the debtor's enterprise or for the preparation of the intended sale of the debtor's undertaking or for the preparation of an intended sale of another group of the debtor's assets, or
- the sale of the real estate would impair the implementation of an insolvency plan which has already been submitted, or
- the sale of the real estate would in any other way make the appropriate realisation of the debtor's assets substantially more difficult.

209. As long as the stay endures, the creditor can claim interest on the secured payment, §30 e ZVG. The length of the stay depends on the time necessary for the requirements of the order of the stay to be met. It may last until the end of the insolvency proceedings.

210. Although not expressly stated in §30 d ZVG, in debtor in possession proceedings the debtor, in place of the IP, is able to apply for the prescribed court order.[146]

211. In the case of the realisation of immovables through enforcement proceedings according to procedural law (irrelevant if through forced auction or administrative sequestration) the costs incurred by the realisation proceedings also have to be paid first out of the proceeds, §§109, 155 ZVG. As far as ascertainment costs are concerned §10 (1) Nr. 1a ZVG stipulates that costs incurred due to determining whether movables have to be considered as accessories of the real estate or not (according to §1120 BGB mortgages extend to the accessories of the encumbered land) have to be paid out of the proceeds after the realisation costs but before the secured creditor may be satisfied (see for secured creditors §10 (1) Nr. 4 ZVG). These ascertainment costs fall on the insolvency estate. They are calculated at a fixed rate of 4% of the proceeds of realisation. Ascertainment costs are not imposed in debtor in possession proceedings since §10 (1) Nr. 1a ZVG requires the appointment of an IP.

212. Where the IP realises the real estate through private sale, no costs are legally imposed on the creditor at all. Therefore an IP will only be content to sell real estate privately if he was able to negotiate a voluntary financial contribution to the insolvency estate by the creditor or if the creditor at least agrees to indemnify him from any liability in relation to the sale.[147]

213. In preliminary proceedings the provisional IP/debtor can apply for an order for a temporary stay on the enforcement if he can provide prima facie evidence

146 C. Tetzlaff and A. Witting in *Münchener Kommentar zur InsO*, Vol. 3, §282, para. 18; W. Uhlenbruck in W. Uhlenbruck, *InsO*, §282, para. 2.

147 C. Tetzlaff in *Münchener Kommentar zur InsO*, §165, paras. 183 et seq.

to the effect that the stay is necessary in order to prevent a detrimental change in the debtor's financial situation, §30 d (4) ZVG.

2. Austria

2.1. General comments

214. As in German law all previously discussed types of security rights in insolvency proceedings are legally treated as rights to separate satisfaction, granting secured creditors the same right to demand a preferential satisfaction (preferential satisfaction stipulated expressly in §48 IO) as under German law while the collateral is still part of the insolvency estate (see para 189).[148] §49 (1) IO (Austrian Insolvency Code) stipulates that where the realisation of an asset is subject to a right to separate satisfaction, specific administration costs, realisation costs, and distribution costs (in a case where several creditors have security rights over the same asset) have to be paid first out of the proceeds before the secured creditors can be satisfied (for details see Question 15, para. 257).

215. As in German law, §10 (1) IO bans enforcement proceedings after the opening of insolvency proceedings insofar as they relate to the enforcement of obligational insolvency claims. This does not apply to security rights providing a right to separate satisfaction. According to the Austrian Supreme Court, it follows from §11 (1) IO, which stipulates that rights to separate satisfaction are not affected by the opening of insolvency proceedings, that owners of rights to separate satisfaction are free to file for court proceedings based on their security right and to pursue enforcement in relation to the specific collateral which is subject to the creditor's secured in rem position (see also §6 (2) IO).[149] This is different to German law, where holders of rights to separate satisfaction are only able to pursue enforcement proceedings if the law declares them responsible for realising the collateral.

216. In this context a statutory moratorium is provided in §11 (2), (3) IO applying to all rights to separate satisfaction. Neither the fulfilment of a claim based on a security right providing a right to separate satisfaction can be demanded nor can the right be enforced (where there is an enforceable order or document) within six months beginning with the opening of insolvency proceedings, if the fulfilment/enforcement would endanger the continuation of

---

[148] P. Apathy in R. Bartsch, R. Pollack and W. Buchegger (eds.), *Österreichisches Insolvenzrecht – Kommentar*, Vol. I, §11, para. 2; for the security ownership/assignment this follows already from the wording of §10 (3) IO.

[149] OGH Urt. v. 25.11.1992, Az.: 3 Ob 31, 1012/92 = [1993] ÖBA 401/665; G. Kodek, [2015] *IILR* 10 at 12 et seq.

the debtor's enterprise as a going concern. The moratorium does not apply if the creditor proves that the fulfilment of the claim or the enforcement would be necessary to prevent grave personal or economic disadvantage to himself and enforcement proceedings against other assets of the debtor (if possible) would be unlikely to lead to a full satisfaction of the creditor. If the creditor pursues court/enforcement proceedings it is up to the IP to prove the danger to the debtor's continued enterprise. Although not mentioned in the wording of the provision, according to parts of the legal literature, the affected holder of a right to separate satisfaction shall be entitled to demand payment of adequate compensation for the period of the stay out of the insolvency estate if he is not entitled to claim for a contractual consideration for the leave of possession anyway (this will be mostly the case with rights to claim separation from the insolvency estate to which §11 IO also applies as they are provided for example by leasing agreements, see Question 25).[150]

217. Under Austrian law preliminary insolvency proceedings are considered an exception to the rule that insolvency proceedings are opened immediately by the insolvency court. Only if the applicant has submitted incomplete documents or has not made the fact of insolvency clear enough to the court, the court is free to make temporary preservation orders of any type which seem appropriate until the question of insolvency status is resolved or other measures have been taken by the IP, §73 IO. After the opening of insolvency proceedings such orders may be renewed by the court. Although according to §11 (1) IO rights to separate satisfaction are not affected by the opening of insolvency proceedings, these orders may prevent the enforcement of the security rights at least as a matter of fact, see §78 (4) IO.[151]

2.2. *Movables*

2.2.1. *Tangibles*

218. According to §120 (2), (3) IO the creditor is responsible for the realisation of the collateral if he has custody of it.[152] Custody, at least on the part of the IP (see for this situation para. 219), means direct possession since only direct

150 E. Feil in E. Feil, *IO*, §11, para. 8; A. Riedler, [2011] *ÖJZ* 904 at 907 et seq. with reference to the legislative materials.

151 H. Schumacher in R. Bartsch, R. Pollak and W. Buchegger (eds.), *Österreichisches Insolvenzrecht*, Vol. II, §78, para. 61.

152 For the distinction as to whether the creditor or the IP is in custody see A. Burgstaller, *Das Pfandrecht in der Exekution*, 53, 155; R. Holzhammer, *Österreichisches Insolvenzrecht*, 67; G. Kodek in R. Bartsch, R. Pollak and W. Buchegger (eds.), *Österreichisches Insolvenzrecht*, Vol. IV, §120, para. 55.

possession enables the IP to have the asset sold.[153] Since both security ownership and pledge require the transfer of possession, it will generally be the creditor who has custody. In these cases the creditor is responsible for the realisation and may therefore pursue enforcement proceedings if necessary. The realisation has to be conducted in accordance with the security agreement or the statutory rules (see Question 8, para. 181 et seq.) which would normally lead to an out-of-court sale.[154] If the IP is not in possession of the collateral, §120 (1) IO grants the IP the right to fulfil the secured claim at any time, even before the secured claim has become due, in return for the surrender of the collateral (Einlösungsrecht).[155] This is a possibility if the proceeds are likely to exceed the amount of the secured claim, but it requires enough liquidity in the insolvency estate. As long as the secured claim is not yet due, the creditor is not entitled to the realisation and cannot be forced to realise by the IP. §14 IO which equals the provision of §41 (1) InsO under German law (see para. 201) does not apply to rights of separate satisfaction.[156] If the secured claim is due but the creditor still refuses the realisation, the IP can apply to the insolvency court in order to set a deadline by which the creditor must have the collateral realised. After the expiration of the deadline, the IP may claim for the surrender of the collateral in order to realise it himself, §120 (3) IO.

219. If the IP is in possession of the collateral (this is especially possible in the case of a legal lien of a lessor, since here the debtor stays in possession of the inventory, or where possession can be retained by using certain signifiers to demonstrate such retention, §452 ABGB) he is free to realise it, §§119, 120 (2) IO. He can have the asset sold by the enforcement court through forced public auction according to the rules provided by procedural law, if the insolvency court has approved of this form of sale, §119 IO, or he can realise the asset himself through a private sale out of court, see §120 (2) IO. In the latter case he needs to inform the secured creditor first, and the creditor has the right to oppose the sale within 14 days after the notification if he provides prima facie evidence to the effect that a sale by the enforcement court would be considerably more beneficial for him, §120 (2) IO. Even if the IP sells the asset privately, the distribution of the proceeds is carried out by the insolvency court according to procedural law, see §§209 (immovables), 285 (movables) EO.[157]

---

153 See G. Kodek in R. Bartsch, R. Pollak and W. Buchegger (eds.), *Österreichisches Insolvenzrecht*, Vol IV, §119, para. 5.

154 See G. Kodek, [2015] *IILR*, 10 at 13.

155 G. Kodek in R. Bartsch, R. Pollak and W. Buchegger (eds.), *Österreichisches Insolvenzrecht*, Vol. IV, §120, para. 10.

156 P. Apathy in R. Bartsch, R. Pollak and W. Buchegger (eds.), *Österreichisches Insolvenzrecht*, Vol. I, §11, para. 7.

157 OGH Beschl. v. 17.10.1996, Az.: 8 Ob 2114/96g = SZ 69/232 (immovables); OGH Beschl. v. 17.12.2007, Az.: 8 Ob 108/07a (movables).

220. There are different solutions to this issue in each of the debtor in possession proceedings. In restructuring proceedings (Sanierungsverfahren mit Eigenverwaltung, §§169 et seq. IO) the restructuring administrator (Sanierungsverwalter) supervising the debtor is responsible for the realisation, §172 (1) Nr. 5, 6 IO. In a judicial debt regulation procedure (private bankruptcy), §§181 et seq. IO, where the debtor being in possession is the normal situation according to the statute, §186 IO, the debtor always needs the approval of the insolvency court if he wants to dispose of assets subject to rights to separate satisfaction, §187 (1) Nr. 3 IO.[158]

2.2.2. Intangibles

2.2.2.1. Assignment by way of security

221. Regarding security assignment, the Austrian Supreme Court has ruled that in all cases the creditor is responsible for the realisation, by collection of the claim.[159] §120 (1), (3) IO apply, see para. 218.[160]

2.2.2.2. Pledge

222. The question seems unresolved as to who in the case of pledges over claims is responsible for realisation. Some authors aim to distinguish according to the different ways of meeting the publicity requirement of §452 ABGB. If the debtor of the claim provided as collateral was notified of the pledge, the creditor will be responsible for the realisation. If the pledge was made public by an entry into the accounts of the debtor, the IP will be responsible.[161] One could justify this distinction on the assumption that only a notification of the debtor that the claim had been pledged would lead to his loss of power of disposal over the claim, applying §455 ABGB by analogy.[162] However, this does not seem to be convincing. §120 (3) IO makes clear that the creditor is only entitled to realise the collateral if he has custody of it, which leads us to assume that the provision only applies to tangible assets.[163] The ruling of the Austrian Supreme Court regarding security assignments (see para. 221) can hardly be used in favour

158 E. Feil in E. Feil, *IO*, §187, paras. 5, 7.

159 OGH Urt. v. 11.06.2001, Az.: 8 Ob 313/00p = SZ 74/105.

160 P. Apathy in P. Apathy, G. Iro and H. Koziol (eds.), *Österreichisches Bankvertragsrecht*, Vol. IX, Part 2, Ch. 4, para. 5/41 making reference to OGH Urt. v. 10.06.1981, Az. 3 Ob 31, 32/81 = SZ 54/89.

161 A. Burgstaller, *Das Pfandrecht in der Exekution*, 144.; P. Apathy in P. Apathy, G. Iro and H. Koziol (eds.), *Österreichisches Bankvertragsrecht*, Vol. IX, Part 2, Ch. 4, para. 5/41.

162 A. Burgstaller, *Das Pfandrecht in der Exekution*, 134 et seq.

163 Apparently G. Kodek in R. Bartsch, R. Pollak and W. Buchegger (eds.), *Österreichisches Insolvenzrecht*, Vol. IV, §120, para. 60.

of any particular interpretation, since the Court ruled on the grounds that in the case of a security assignment, the creditor acquires full ownership of the claim (which is not the case with pledges). Where rights other than claims are concerned, there are no third-party debtors who could be notified, so in this case even the opposite opinion would probably assume that the IP is responsible for the realisation.

2.3. *Immovables*

223. As far as immovables are concerned, it is established that the IP is free to realise the asset according to §§119, 120 (2) IO.[164]

224. It is a particularly common occurrence with immovables that the secured creditor has acquired an enforceable document before the opening of insolvency proceedings and only begins or continues enforcement of that document, as he is entitled to do, after that opening.[165] This would lead to a realisation according to the provisions of procedural law. According to previous legislation, if the IP in this case considered private sale out of court to be economically more promising, he had only three options. Either the IP had to come to an agreement with the creditor, which was unlikely to happen if enforcement by the court would be likely to lead to the full satisfaction of the creditor, or the IP had to pay the creditor the value of the secured claim, §120 (1) IO, which would require liquidity. The third option was to have the asset sold before the creditor could finalise the enforcement proceedings, leading to a race to realise between the creditor and the IP.[166] Today in these cases §120a IO enables the IP to apply to the insolvency court for an order of a 'stay' on enforcement proceedings for 90 days beginning with the day on which the application to the court was submitted, if the IP intends to realise the asset by a private out-of-court sale, unless the continuation of enforcement proceedings is necessary for the creditor to avoid considerable economic disadvantage to himself. The creditor bears the burden of proving this.

225. By its wording §120a IO applies to all security rights providing a right to separate satisfaction. According to the Austrian Supreme Court every right to separate satisfaction grants the possibility of filing court proceedings and pursuing enforcement proceedings even after insolvency proceedings have

---

164 See G. Kodek in R. Bartsch, R. Pollak and W. Buchegger (eds.), *Österreichisches Insolvenzrecht*, Vol. IV, §120 a, para. 1.

165 OGH Urt. v. 23.06.1954, Az. 3 Ob 349, 350/54 = SZ 27/180; OGH Urt. v. 25.11.1992, Az.: 3 Ob 31, 1012/92 = ÖBA 1993, 401/665.

166 G. Kodek in R. Bartsch, R. Pollak and W. Buchegger (eds.), *Österreichisches Insolvenzrecht*, Vol. IV, §120 a, para. 1.

been opened.[167] However in literature §120a IO is only mentioned in relation to immovables.[168] It seems that in practice it is only in relation to immovables that enforcement procedures by the creditor have collided with the concurrent efforts of the IP to sell them.

226. If the IP on the other hand agrees with the realisation, according to procedural law, he can with the approval of the insolvency court join the debtor's enforcement proceedings, §119 (1), (4) IO.

Questions 10/11: Can the secured party apply to have any stay lifted? Under what circumstances can the stay be lifted?

1. Germany

1.1. Movables

227. As described in Question 9, para. 191 et seq., §§165 et seq. InsO provide for a statutory change of competence in relation to who may realise assets subject to certain security rights and not for a 'stay' on enforcement proceedings. As far as this change of competence leads to a ban on the pursuit of the enforcement of security rights by the creditor, there is no way for him to have this ban lifted by the court or to regain competence in relation to the realisation through a court order. However, the creditor is free to come to an alternative agreement with the IP entrusting him with the realisation although he would not otherwise be entitled to it, see §170 (2) InsO.

228. If the insolvency court in preliminary proceedings orders a 'stay' on enforcement proceedings or on the realisation of assets subject to security rights as a provisional measure in order to secure the current financial status of the debtor according to §21 InsO (see Question 9, para. 197 et seq.), there is no way for the creditor either to have the order lifted afterwards or to challenge the order with any specific remedy, see §21 (1).[169]

1.2. Immovables

229. If the enforcement court has ordered a 'stay' on enforcement proceedings according to §30 d (1) ZVG (see Question 9, para. 208), the creditor is free to

---

167 OGH Urt. v. 25.11.1992, Az.: 3 Ob 31, 1012/92 = ÖBA 1993, 401/665 (regarding a mortgage); OGH Urt. v. 09.04.1924, Az.: Ob II 202/24 = SZ 6/148 (regarding a legal lien of a lessor).

168 G. Kodek in R. Bartsch, R. Pollak and W. Buchegger (eds.), *Österreichisches Insolvenzrecht*, Vol. IV, §120 a, para. 1. et seq.; E. Feil in E. Feil, *IO*, §120 a, para. et seq.

169 H. Haarmeyer in *Münchener Kommentar zur InsO*, §21, para. 38 et seq.

apply to the court to have the stay lifted at any time. According to §30 f (1) ZVG the court has to approve this application if:

- the legal requirements for the order of the 'stay' (see Question 9, para. 208) have subsequently ceased to apply; or
- if the obligations ordered by the court according to §30 e ZVG (payment of interest and compensation for the loss of value incurred by the use of the real estate for the benefit of the insolvency estate) have not been met by the IP; or
- if the IP approves the application (if in case of a 'stay' under §30 d (1) Nr. 3 ZVG the insolvency plan was submitted by the debtor and not by the IP, it is the debtor who has to approve the application); or
- if insolvency proceedings are terminated.

230. If the 'stay' was ordered in preliminary proceedings under §30 d (4) ZVG (see Question 9, para 213) the creditor is also able to apply to the court to have the stay lifted, §30 f (2) ZVG. The court has to approve the application if:

- the application for the opening of insolvency proceedings has been denied by the insolvency court or has been withdrawn by the applicant; or
- under the same conditions as described in the preceding paragraph.

2. Austria

231. The moratorium of six months after the opening of insolvency proceedings (see Question 9, para. 216) during which claims or enforcement proceedings in relation to rights of separate satisfaction must not be pursued, according to §11 (2), (3) IO, is a statutory one and is not ordered by the court. It can therefore not be challenged using other remedies. Neither can it be lifted by the court.

232. The order of a 'stay' by the enforcement court according to §120 a I (1) IO requires the intention of the IP to have the asset sold privately (see Question 9, para. 224). In this case he has to inform the creditor about the intended private sale, §120 (2) IO. This notification is not valid if it fails to include the amount of the expected price.[170] After this notification the creditor can oppose the sale within 14 days with the argument that the continuation of enforcement proceedings is necessary in order to prevent considerable economic disadvantage on his part. If the creditor does so and the IP still wants to sell the asset privately, the

170 G. Kodek in R. Bartsch, R. Pollak and W. Buchegger (eds.), *Österreichisches Insolvenzrecht*, Vol. IV, §120, para. 23.

insolvency court has to decide whether the legal requirements for the opposition to the sale are met or not. This decision has to be taken into account by the enforcement court in relation to the order of a 'stay'. If the insolvency court rules in favour of the creditor that his opposition to the private sale is legitimate, the enforcement court, according to §120 a (2) IO, has to lift its previous order of a 'stay'. So a successful challenge to the private sale is the only way to have the 'stay' lifted before its legal expiration. The enforcement court has to lift the stay by law after a period of 90 days beginning with the day the IP submitted his application for a 'stay' to the enforcement court, §120 a (2) IO. After that the IP is no longer allowed to apply for an order of a further 'stay', §120 a (1) IO.

Question 12: In insolvency proceedings, can an insolvency practitioner (IP) 'enforce' the security, i.e. realise the secured assets, without the consent of the secured party?

1. Germany

233. Generally speaking, if the IP has the power to realise the secured assets he can do so without the consent of the secured party. However, there are some details to be mentioned.

1.1. Movables

234. If the IP intends to realise an asset, which, according to §166 InsO is his responsibility to do, he has to notify the creditor as the owner of a right to separate satisfaction at least one week before the planned realisation, §168 (1), (2) InsO. The notification must at least contain the method of realisation and the expected price for which the asset shall be sold.[171] The creditor than has a period of one week to identify another method of selling the asset which would be more beneficial to him. If the creditor has made use of his right to identify this method within a week or in good time before the intended sale, then, according to §168 (2) InsO, the IP has to use the method suggested by the creditor. Otherwise he has to compensate the creditor out of the insolvency estate as if he had used that method, §168 (2) InsO.

235. If the IP has not informed the creditor of the planned sale at all, he may be personally liable to pay damages. If on the other hand the IP notified the creditor in time and the creditor did not respond to that notification, the IP cannot be

[171] For further requirements see C. Tetzlaff in *Münchener Kommentar zur InsO*, §168, para. 17.

held liable to pay damages to the creditor if he is subsequently accused of having sold the asset for below market price.[172]

236. The more beneficial method of sale may consist of the creditor buying the asset himself for a higher price, §168 (3) InsO. The creditor will make use of this possibility if he is not able to find another buyer within a week but the expected price seems considerably too low for him. The creditor may then set-off his claim for payment of the proceeds against the claim of the insolvency estate for the payment of the purchase price.

1.2. *Immovables*

237. The IP does not need the consent of the creditor if he wants to realise the encumbered real estate by way of forced public auction or administrative sequestration. Creditors are free to join the enforcement proceedings, §27 ZVG.

238. If the IP wants to realise the real estate through a private sale out of court he depends, not legally but factually, on the consent of the creditor for whose benefit mortgages are registered in the Land Register. §168 InsO does not apply to immovables but potential buyers will not be willing to buy the land if security rights encumbering the land are not deleted from the Land Register before they make the purchase. In order to get the necessary consent to the cancellation of the mortgage entry from the secured creditor, the IP will have to come to an agreement with the secured creditor about the intended sale.[173]

239. Additionally an IP will only be willing to sell real estate privately if the creditor pays a voluntary contribution to the insolvency estate or indemnifies the insolvency estate from any liability in relation to the private sale (see Question 9, para. 212).

2. Austria

240. §120 (2) IO applies to all kinds of assets. The IP only has to inform the secured creditor if he wants to realise the asset subject to a security right by way of private sale. The law does not specifically provide an opportunity for the creditor to point out another method of selling the asset. Instead, it only gives him the right to oppose the sale if he prefers a sale through forced auction.

---

172 C. Tetzlaff in *Münchener Kommentar zur InsO*, §168, para. 17; W. Uhlenbruck in W. Uhlenbruck, *InsO*, §168, para. 15.

173 C. Tetzlaff in *Münchener Kommentar zur Insolvenzordnung*, §165, para. 179.

241. The same applies to immovables. The problem that, without the consent of the creditor, registered security rights cannot be deleted from the Land Register, leading to the situation that even if the creditor has not opposed the sale the IP is still prevented from selling privately (see for Germany para. 238), has been solved by the Austrian Supreme Court. It was always the policy of Austrian case law that even in private sales by the IP, the distribution of the proceeds was to be conducted by the insolvency court according to procedural law (see Question 9, para. 219, footnote 149). The court therefore has to conduct a meeting in which the distribution can be negotiated by all involved creditors and the IP (Verteilungstagssatzung), §212 EO. It then has to decide on the distribution (Verteilungsbeschluss), §214 EO. After this decision has become non-appealable the court may approve the deletion of registered mortgages from the Land Registry, §237 (3) EO without the consent of the creditor.[174]

Question 13: Are there any conditions that must be satisfied before an IP may 'enforce' the security?

1. Germany

242. According to the general clause §160 (1) InsO the IP needs the approval of the creditors' committee or, if such a committee has not been appointed, the approval of the creditors' assembly, if he wants to take any action being of particular importance to the insolvency proceedings. According to §160 (2) InsO this will always be the case where the sale of the debtor's whole enterprise or a part of it, the sale of a whole inventory of a warehouse, the private sale of real estate or the sale of shares in affiliated companies is in question. Next to these presumptive examples, the question whether actions of particular importance exist can only be answered by looking at the specific case at hand. The most important criteria to determine this question will usually be the expected effect of the intended action on the percentage share of the insolvency estate the insolvency creditors are likely to receive and the extent to which the planned action determines the further proceedings. However the relationship between the provisions of §160 InsO and §§165 et seq. InsO has not yet been satisfactorily explained. According to parts of legal literature a realisation of single assets which are encumbered with rights to separate satisfaction requires the approval of the creditor's assembly only if it imposes considerable liabilities on the insolvency estate either by the specific contractual conditions of the sale or by causing public charges.[175] According to other voices, an approval will never be

[174] OGH Beschl. v. 17.10.1996, Az.: 8 Ob 2114/96g = SZ 69/232; G. Kodek in R. Bartsch, R. Pollak and W. Buchegger (eds.), *Österreichisches Insolvenzrecht*, Vol. IV, §120, paras. 41 et seq.

[175] P. Esser in E. Braun, *InsO*, §160, para. 8.

required if the amount of the secured claim exceeds the value of the collateral since unsecured creditors in this case would not benefit from the proceeds.[176] Without distinguishing between collateral and unencumbered assets, the prevailing opinion in legal literature assumes that a realisation requires the approval of the creditor's assembly where it is not based on the prevailing market conditions, where it derogates from the provisions provided by the law or where it endangers the continuation of the debtor's enterprise respectively the implementation of an insolvency plan.[177] In summing up then, it can be viewed as established at least that an approval of the realisation seems to be necessary only if the realisation affects not only the interests of the secured creditor but also the interests of the body of creditors because of specific circumstances. If these interests are affected because the realisation would endanger the continuation of the debtor's enterprise, normally the specific provisions of §§157, 159 InsO will determine the IP's right to realise collateral (see the following para. 243). To ensure the requirements of §160 InsO are not violated, the IP should always seek the approval of the creditors if he is not sure about the particular importance of an intended action (for the similar situation in *Austria* see para. 245, 246).

243. Besides the requirements discussed under para. 242 and Question 12, specific legal conditions must at least be taken into account if the debtor is still running an enterprise as a going concern. §§22 (1), (2), 157 InsO provide the general principle that the (provisional) IP, if possible provided that the continuation of business operations does not lead to a further erosion of the debtor's liquidity, shall maintain a running enterprise at least until the first creditors' assembly (Berichtstermin). This meeting must be scheduled no later than three months after the opening of insolvency proceedings, §29 (1) InsO. In the creditors' assembly the creditors have to decide whether the enterprise shall be continued provisionally (in order to prepare an asset deal or to establish an insolvency plan which would enable the continuation of the debtor's enterprise on a permanent basis) or whether business operations should be closed down. Any realisation actions must not contradict the creditor's vote for continuation of the debtor's enterprise, §159 InsO, so the obligation to continue business operations may restrict the IP's right of realisation. If the IP wants to close down the enterprise before the creditors' assembly he needs the approval of the creditors' committee. If a creditors' committee has not been appointed he must inform the debtor who can challenge the IP's decision in court, §158 (2) InsO. In preliminary proceedings the closing down has to be approved by the court, §21 (1) InsO.

---

176 D. Decker in *Hamburger Kommentar zur InsO*, §160, para. 7, in relation to the realisation of immovables.

177 H. Görg and C. Janssen in *Münchener Kommentar zur InsO*, Vol. 2, paras. 8 et seq.; W. Uhlenbruck in W. Uhlenbruck, *InsO*, §160, para. 17; B. Wegener in *Frankfurter Kommentar zur InsO*, §160, para. 2.

244. The IP is generally prevented from realising assets which are required for the continuation of the debtor's enterprise as long as he is obliged to continue business operations. For this reason §§21 (2) (1) Nr. 5 InsO (applying only in preliminary proceedings), 30d ZVG provide the (provisional) IP with the possibility of applying for the order of a 'stay' on enforcement proceedings pursued by secured creditors if they would endanger the continuation of the enterprise (Question 9, para. 200, 208, 213). On the other hand, assets which are already in the possession of secured creditors are usually not required for the continuation of the debtor's enterprise. So any 'stay' on the realisation of such assets by the creditors is not considered necessary by the legislator. However, the secured creditor is protected against the delay of realisation by his right to claim interest and compensation payments (see Question 9, para. 191, 200, 209).

2. Austria

245. Generally, if the IP plans to take actions of importance to the proceedings to which none of the more specific provisions of §§116, 117 IO applies (see the following paragraph), he has to hear the creditors' committee first, §114 (1) IO. The provision expressively mentions the realisation of movable assets but is interpreted restrictively in that way as to apply only to movables which have a certain value.[178] It is disputed in literature how to handle the provision if a creditors' committee has not been appointed. One opinion wants to replace the hearing of the creditors' committee by a hearing of the insolvency court. According to another opinion in this case the planned action must even be approved by the insolvency court. A third opinion considers the provision not applicable in this case.[179]

246. Certain actions of the IP always require the approval of the creditors' committee and of the insolvency court. These include the sale of the debtor's enterprise as a whole, the sale of the debtor's shares in affiliated companies, the sale of all fixed and/or current assets or parts of it required for the continuation of the debtor's enterprise and (regardless of whether subject to the insolvency proceedings is a continued enterprise or not) the private sale of real estate, §117 (1) Nr. 1–3 IO.

247. If the IP wants to have assets realised by the court through a forced sale according to the procedural law he always needs the approval of the court, §119

[178] E. Lovrek in R. Bartsch, R. Pollak and W. Buchegger (eds.), *Österreichisches Insolvenzrecht*, Vol. IV, §114, para. 13.

[179] See with further evidence E. Lovrek in R. Bartsch, R. Pollak and W. Buchegger (eds.), *Österreichisches Insolvenzrecht*, §114, paras. 21 et seq.

(1) IO. The reason for this is to protect creditors and the debtor since normally a private sale generates greater proceeds than a forced sale.[180]

248. As in Germany there are some conditions that must be satisfied before an IP may enforce securities which are linked to the debtor running an enterprise as a going concern.

249. According to §114a (1) IO the IP has to maintain the debtor's enterprise at least until the creditors' assembly (Berichtstagssatzung, §91a IO), unless the continuation of the enterprise would obviously increase the default for the insolvency creditors. The provision also stipulates that before the report meeting the debtor's enterprise can only be sold as a whole which always (before and after the creditors' assembly) requires the approval of the creditors' committee and of the insolvency court, §117 (1) Nr. 1 IO. The closing down of the enterprise always (before and after the report meeting) requires the approval of the insolvency court, §§114 a (2), 115 (1) IO. In the creditors' assembly which has to be held within 90 days after the opening of insolvency proceedings, the creditors have to decide whether the enterprise is to be continued or closed down and whether an insolvency plan shall be established, §§91 a, 114 b IO. (In *Austria* the permanent continuation of the debtor's enterprise does not require the establishment of an insolvency plan.)[181] If the establishment of an insolvency plan seems possible and the debtor applies within two weeks after the report meeting to the court to be allowed to submit an insolvency plan, the realisation of the debtor's enterprise is statutorily banned for 90 days unless the continuation of the enterprise becomes impossible or the plan does not satisfy the economic interests of the creditors any more, §§114 b (2), 114 c IO. One example would be that the IP finds a potential buyer within this time willing to buy the enterprise for a price that promises a better return for the creditors than under the intended plan. If the plan is not approved by the creditors within these 90 days, the IP is free to realise the enterprise according to the general rules (see para. 245 et seq.) unless in view of the results of the existing procedure, especially the vote on a prior plan proposal, it seems likely that the plan will be approved later on, §114 c (2) IO. A ban according to §114 c IO only affects the IP and not the secured creditors since §11 (1) IO stipulates that rights to separate satisfaction are not affected by the opening of insolvency proceedings and bans on realisation in relation to the continuation of the debtor's enterprise are governed by the specific provision of §11 (2), (3) IO (see Question 9, para. 216). For the time after the opening of insolvency proceedings, the creditors can neither claim interest or compensation payments from the insolvency estate nor can these interest claims be asserted as

---

180 G. Kodek in R. Bartsch, R. Pollak and W. Buchegger (eds.), *Österreichisches Insolvenzrecht*, Vol. IV, §119, para. 1.

181 E. Feil in E. Feil, *IO*, §114 b, para. 1.

insolvency claims at all, §58 Nr. 1 IO. Only the collateral can be held liable for interest accruing after insolvency proceedings have been opened (§48 (1) IO). On the other hand, creditors do not have to fear a delay of realisation greater than six months (see §11 (2) IO) as under German law. After six months, they are in any case free to enforce their securities if the IP has not yet started the realisation, regardless of whether the creditors wish for the debtor's enterprise to be continued (for further details of the meaning of §11 IO for the role of secured creditors in insolvency proceedings see Question 17, para. 270).

Question 14: Do the rules or conditions differ depending on the nature of the insolvency proceedings in question?

1. Germany

250. Generally spoken, the rules are the same notwithstanding whether the debtor is a consumer or an entrepreneur. The differences between regular insolvency proceedings and debtor in possession proceedings with regard to responsibility for the realisation of assets and the application for 'stay' orders have already been discussed (Question 9, para. 191, 196, 203, 210).

251. One particularity in preliminary debtor in possession proceedings is provided in §270b (2) InsO. If the debtor had applied for the opening of insolvency on account of imminent insolvency or over-indebtedness and requested debtor in possession proceedings meeting the requirements of §270 b (1) InsO by proving that cash flow insolvency has not yet occurred and that an intended restructuring does not manifestly lack the prospect of success, the court has to order provisional measures according to §21 (2) (1) Nr. 3–5 InsO in preliminary proceedings if the debtor applies for them, §270b (2) InsO. Provisional orders then do no not depend on whether the legal requirements of §21 (1), (2) InsO are met or not.

2. Austria

252. All differences in regard to security rights between regular insolvency proceedings and debtor in possession proceedings (restructuring proceedings, see the following paragraph) have already been discussed (Question 9, para. 220).

253. If the debtor together with his petition for the opening of insolvency proceedings submits a restructuring plan (Sanierungsplan) to the court, insolvency proceedings are opened under the reference to restructuring proceedings (Sanierungsverfahren), §§167 et seq. IO. Besides the advantageous publicity effect of evading the expression 'insolvency' it provides the advantage for the debtor that the proceedings can be conducted as debtor in possession proceedings if the debtor fulfils the requirements of §169 IO. If insolvency proceedings under the name of restructuring proceedings have been opened, the realisation of the debtor's enterprise may only commence if the plan proposal submitted by the debtor has not been approved by the creditors within 90 days after the opening of proceedings. This is a difference from the general rule of §§114 et seq. IO (see Question 13, para. 245). If the requirements of establishing the plan are not met (any longer) or the plan has been denied by the creditors, the name of the proceedings must be changed from restructuring into insolvency proceedings, §167 (3) IO. Nevertheless restructuring proceedings are insolvency plan proceedings albeit under another label. Apart from the specific provisions of §§167 et seq. which mostly deal with the particularities of debtor in possession proceedings the general rules governing insolvency proceedings and the establishment of a restructuring plan (which is similar to an insolvency plan under German law) apply (see for the rules governing a restructuring plan Question 17, para. 269 et seq.)

Question 15: Is a secured party liable to pay the general costs, i.e. costs apart from those incurred in connection with the realisation of security, of insolvency proceedings affecting the debtor?

1. Germany

254. Holders of rights to separate satisfaction are not liable to pay the general costs of insolvency proceedings. Out of the proceeds of the realisation of assets subject to rights to separate satisfaction only the ascertainment costs and the costs of realisation have to be paid to the insolvency estate (for further details see Question 9, para. 192 et seq., 211, 212). Secured creditors are legally not charged further costs even if they were related to the specific asset such as administrative costs or maintenance costs. Such costs have to be borne by the insolvency estate. Only where such costs are necessary to enable a later realisation (e.g. feeding costs for livestock) a clear distinction between realisation costs and maintenance costs may cause uncertainties.[182] Such uncertainties in practice are usually solved by negotiation between the IP and the secured creditors.

255. Having said this, there are some specific administrative costs which have to be paid out of the proceeds before the secured creditor may be satisfied if immovables are realised by way of forced auction. These costs consist mostly of land taxes and other public charges (for details see §10 (1) Nr. 2, 3 ZVG).

[182] C. Tetzlaff in *Münchener Kommentar zur InsO*, Vol. 2, §170, para. 34.

256. However, creditors may protect themselves against a potential bad debt loss caused only by realisation and ascertainment costs by considering these potential costs while establishing their security interests. To have collateral furnished with values greater than the secured claim as a protection against these costs is legitimate as long as the boundary into over-collateralisation is not crossed.[183] If then the proceeds of the realisation exceed the amount of the secured claim, realisation and ascertainment costs have to be paid out of this surplus. The IP must not retain the surplus for the insolvency estate. Only a surplus remaining after the payment of realisation and ascertainment costs and after the satisfaction of the secured creditor belongs to the insolvency estate.

2. Austria

257. Holders of rights to separate satisfaction are not liable to pay the general costs of insolvency proceedings either. §49 IO stipulates that out of the services and the proceeds of the collateral must be paid the costs of specific administration, realisation and distribution before the secured creditors are satisfied. If the enforcement court is responsible for the distribution as a consequence of a realisation through forced sale, it has to apply the §§46 et seq. IO. In the case of disputes it has to apply to the insolvency court which is always competent for ruling over disputes arising from the application of these provisions, §47 (3) IO. Difficulties arise from the expression 'specific administration'. According to the Austrian Supreme Court, administration costs are only specific if they are caused by the mere existence of the asset independent of any use or consumption on the part of the debtor. The decisive question is whether the expenses for the insolvency estate would have been incurred even if the asset had not been part of the estate. If that is the case the administration costs are usually not to be considered as specific.[184] According to the court rulings dealing with this question such costs occur mainly in connection with immovables and include local public fees, insurance costs and even certain costs of repairs as long as the payment of these costs from an ex ante point of view could be considered as reasonable by the IP and likely to benefit the secured creditors in the end. On the other hand there is the advantage for creditors in *Austria* that the income from services (as long as the security right does not extend to these services) must be used to pay not only the specific administration costs but also the realisation costs and the distribution costs.

---

183 BGH Urt. v. 27.11.1997, Az.: GSZ 1, 2/97 = BGHZ 137, 212, 228; C. Tetzlaff in *Münchener Kommentar zur InsO*, Vol. 2, §170, paras. 35, 36.

184 OGH Beschl. v. 18.12.2006, Az.: 8 Ob 113/06k = SZ 2006/185; OGH Beschl. v. 18.02.2010, Az.: 8 Ob 105/09p = [2010] Ecolex 677.

258. Besides the specific administrative costs there are some other general costs that have to be paid out of the proceeds before the secured creditor may be satisfied if immovables are realised by forced auction. These costs consist mostly of land taxes and other public charges (for details see §216 (1) Nr. 2 EO).

Question 16: Is the secured party liable to 'set aside' any portion of the amount realised from the enforcement of security for the benefit of (a) preferential or (b) unsecured creditors of the debtor?

1. Germany

259. No, German insolvency law distinguishes between different ranks of creditors only as far as creditors of unsecured claims are concerned, §§38, 39, 53 InsO. Secured creditors on the other hand are granted a very safe position under German insolvency law. As a consequence of their in rem position their right to separate satisfaction devolves to the proceeds of the realisation of the collateral which therefor belong to the secured creditor exclusively up to the amount of the secured claim, cf. §170 (1) InsO. Legal restrictions are only made by the imposition of realisation and ascertainment costs (for further administration costs in connection to the realisation of immovables see §10 ZVG and Question 15, para. 255).

260. So considering secured creditors as one class of creditors, they do not have to contribute any payments for the benefit of other classes of creditors. Where of course an asset is subject to several security rights of different creditors, the distribution of the proceeds between the secured creditors depends on their rank which is generally determined by the priority principle.

2. Austria

261. There are no differences between German and Austrian law. Reference should therefore be made to the discussion on German law. The preferential satisfaction of secured creditors out of the proceeds is expressly stated in §48 IO.

Question 17: Can the secured party be bound against its wishes by a restructuring plan that negatively affects either the secured debt or the enforcement of the security interest?

1. Germany

262. It is possible that an insolvency plan (Insolvenzplan, §§217 et seq. InsO) negatively affects the rights of secured creditors either by affecting the secured claims or by affecting creditors' security rights or the enforcement of them, §§222 (1) Nr. 1, 223 InsO.

263. In insolvency plan proceedings groups of creditors have to be formed in which creditors with equal legal status and equal economic interests are set together, §222 InsO. If a plan is about to negatively affect the security rights (rights of separate satisfaction) of creditors in any way the secured creditors with rights to separate satisfaction have to be set together in their own group, §222 (1) Nr. 1 InsO. As a consequence of their double role in insolvency proceedings (see Question 18, para. 271) under-secured creditors may at the same time also be members of a group of unsecured insolvency creditors (it is disputed whether their votes within the group of unsecured insolvency creditors are weighted by the total amount of their secured claim or only by the amount of their expected default in the realisation of their collateral). If within the group of secured creditors members have different economic interests further sub-groups can be formed, §222 (2) InsO.

264. Generally a court may only approve of an insolvency plan if the plan has been accepted by each group of creditors, §§248, 244 InsO. A plan is considered as accepted by a group of creditors if the majority of its members taking part in the vote approve the plan and at the same time the sum of the claims held by the approving creditors makes up more than half of the total sum of claims held by all group members taking part in the vote, §244 InsO. This means that a secured creditor may be overruled only by the other secured creditors in his group (but see also para. 267).

265. Furthermore the cram-down rule of §245 InsO provides for a prohibition to obstruct. According to §245 (1) InsO even if a plan has been denied by a group of creditors this group shall be deemed to have consented if:

1. the members of such a group are likely not to be placed at a disadvantage by the insolvency plan compared with their situation without such plan;
2. the members of such a group participate to a reasonable extent in the economic value devolving on the parties under the plan; and
3. the majority of the voting groups have backed the plan with the necessary majorities.

266. According to §245 (2) InsO a reasonable participation of a group of creditors for the purpose of subsection (1) Nr. 2 shall exist if under the plan:

1. no other creditor will receive economic values exceeding the full amount of his claim;
2. neither a creditor with a lower-ranking claim to satisfaction without a plan, compared with the creditors forming his group, nor the debtor nor a person holding the debtor's shares receives an economic value; and

3. no creditor to be satisfied on an equal footing with the creditors forming his group without a plan receives an advantage with respect to such creditors.

267. As far as security rights are concerned it is important that according to existing case law and the prevailing opinion in legal literature §245 (2) Nr. 2 InsO does not apply to security rights. Creditors with rights to separate satisfaction do not stand in order of rank with other creditors. §245 (2) Nr. 2 InsO refers strictly to the insolvency creditors and the subordinated insolvency creditors according to §§38, 39 InsO but not to creditors with rights of separate satisfaction.[185] Secured creditors are sufficiently protected by §245 (1) Nr. 1 InsO. An insolvency plan may negatively affect security rights only if the secured creditor according to the plan receives compensation that offsets this affectation. Each secured creditor can oppose the plan in court if he considers himself likely to be placed at a disadvantage by the plan compared to his situation without the plan, §251 InsO. A creditor is able to do so even if he was overruled before in his own group of creditors.[186]

268. The establishment and execution of an insolvency plan is only possible in insolvency proceedings that have been opened. Outside of insolvency proceedings, German law does not provide for any possibility of negatively affecting any creditor's claims or rights against his wishes by a collective majority vote or contract (plan) concluded by other creditors.[187]

2. Austria

269. In *Austria* the situation is different. §149 (1) IO stipulates that claims of secured creditors are not affected by a restructuring plan (Sanierungsplan, §§140 et seq. IO). This is a consequence of the fact that under Austrian law in contrast to German law creditors with rights to separate satisfaction (not in their role as insolvency creditors) are not considered to be able to participate in insolvency proceedings but to stand outside of insolvency proceedings, although their rights are affected by certain provisions of insolvency law.[188] This stands in

[185] LG Traunstein Beschl. v. 27.08.1999, Az.: 4 T 2966/99 = [1999] NZI 461 at 464; W. Uhlenbruck in W. Uhlenbruck, *InsO*, §245, para. 24; C. Pleister in B. Kübler, H. Prütting and R. Bork, *Kommentar zur InsO*, Vol. III, §245, para. 23; A. Flessner in *Heidelberger Kommentar zur InsO*, §245, para. 22; T. Thies in *Hamburger Kommentar zur InsO*, §245, para. 12.

[186] R. Sinz in *Münchener Kommentar zur InsO*, Vol. 3, §251, para. 6.

[187] One exception is provided in the bond law for the restructuring of bonds which is not relevant in this context.

[188] See P. Apathy in R. Bartsch, R. Pollak and W. Buchegger (eds.), *Österreichisches Insolvenzrecht*, Vol. I, §11, paras. 7, 8; G. Kodek, [2015] *IILR* 10 at 13.

accordance with Austrian case law that permits secured creditors to pursue their security rights in enforcement proceedings although insolvency proceedings have been opened (see Question 9, para. 215, 225). The provision of §149 (1) IO further stipulates that after a restructuring plan has been approved by the court (§152 IO) the secured claims are considered limited to the amount of the value of the collateral. This means that a secured creditor must release the collateral if according to the plan he is paid at least the amount of the value of the collateral which may be important if the collateral is necessary for the continuation of the debtor's enterprise.[189]

270. If collateral of an under-secured creditor was realised before the establishment of the plan, the secured creditor participates in the plan proceedings as an insolvency creditor with the amount of the secured claim that could not be satisfied by the realisation, §149 (1) IO. If there has not yet been a realisation, the under-secured creditor participates in the plan proceedings as an insolvency creditor with the amount that will likely not be met by a subsequent realisation, §149 IO. So plan proceedings differ on this point from insolvency proceedings aiming only at realisation (§132 (1) IO, see Question 18, para. 273). This means that where the personal debtor and the collateral provider are identical, the under-secured creditor can only be made to release his collateral if he is granted his rights as a non-secured insolvency creditor on top of the payment of the value of his collateral.

Question 18: Can an under-secured creditor claim from the insolvency estate in respect of any deficiency arising as a result of the enforcement of the security?

1. Germany

271. The secured creditor under German law has a dual role in insolvency proceedings. As far as his security right is concerned he is a creditor with a right to separate satisfaction, §§49 et seq. InsO. As far as his secured claim is concerned he is considered an insolvency creditor, §38 InsO (given the fact that the personal debtor and the collateral provider are identical). These two roles are not mutually exclusive, §52 InsO. Therefore the creditor is free to report the full amount of his secured claim to the insolvency table even if he is pursuing his right to separate satisfaction during insolvency proceedings.

272. Nevertheless, the creditor takes part in the distribution of the proceeds of the realisation of the insolvency estate only with respect to the monetary amount

189 E. Feil in E. Feil, *IO*, §149, para. 1.

that has not been satisfied with the enforcement of his security. Therefore, if the creditor was responsible for the realisation of the asset subject to his security right, he has to inform the IP in time before the distribution about the amount to which his claim was not met by the separate satisfaction, §190 (1) InsO. In respect of the amount of the deficiency, the secured creditor will share pro rata with the general creditor. If the IP pursues an advanced distribution before the creditor has realised the collateral and the creditor wants to participate in this advanced distribution, he has to furnish prima facie evidence to the effect that the realisation process has already been initiated and the likely amount of the deficiency in the subsequent realisation, §190 (2) InsO. The IP than has to retain the creditor's corresponding share until the final distribution. If the secured creditor has not realised the collateral before the final distribution, his retained share will benefit the other creditors, §190 (2) InsO.

2. Austria

273. General reference should be made to the discussion on German law under para. 271. If in case of an advanced distribution the realisation of collateral has not yet taken place, the secured creditor according to §132 (1) IO, and in contrast to German law, is treated as an unsecured creditor meaning that he receives the pro rata share of the full amount of the secured claim. One reason for this is that due to a lack of maturity the creditor may be unable to realise the collateral (for the inapplicability of §14 IO to secured claims see Question 9, para. 218). The legislator did not want the secured creditor to suffer disadvantages from this legal situation.[190] If it turns out in a subsequent realisation of the collateral that the creditor had received more than he was entitled to claim on a pro rata basis for the amount of his claim that was not covered by the security right according to his actual default in its realisation, this surplus has to be paid back to the insolvency estate out of the proceeds of the realisation of the collateral, §132 (2) IO. If there had been a realisation of the collateral before a distribution (regardless whether an advanced or a final distribution is in question) it follows at least from the context of §132 (1), (2) IO that the under-secured creditor shall receive a pro rata distribution quota only on the amount of his claim that was not met by the realisation of the collateral.[191]

---

[190] G. Kodek in R. Bartsch, R. Pollak and W. Buchegger (eds.), *Österreichisches Insolvenzrecht*, Vol. IV, §132, para. 1.

[191] G. Kodek in R. Bartsch, R. Pollak and W. Buchegger (eds.), *Österreichisches Insolvenzrecht*, Vol. IV, §132, para. 4.

274. One exception to these principles is provided in §32 (4) IO for the security ownership, the security assignment and mortgages on real estate located abroad. Creditors holding these security rights take part in an advanced distribution only with respect to the amount of the likely deficiency in a subsequent realisation of their collateral. Their share then has to be retained until the final distribution, §133 (1) IO. If the creditors do not have their collateral realised until the final distribution their retained share, as in Germany, benefits the other creditors even if an earlier realisation was legally not possible.[192]

D. REGISTRATION OF SECURITY RIGHTS

Question 19: To what extent must security rights over assets be publicised by registration or filing to ensure the effectiveness of the security interest over parties other than the debtor and in the event of insolvency proceedings?

1. Germany

1.1. General comments

275. In *Germany* there is no general register for pledges or other security rights. A registration is only required in respect of certain security rights over certain assets, namely mortgages/pledges over ships, planes and real estate. Where the law requires security rights to be registered this registration requirement is conceived in a way that the validity of the security right depends (inter alia) on its registration regardless of which party is claiming the benefit of its existence. The question of validity or effectiveness of a security right can only be determined uniformly with respect to all possibly involved parties.

276. §91 (1) InsO stipulates that after the opening of insolvency proceedings the acquisition of rights from the debtor without the approval of the insolvency practitioner is no longer possible. Normally this would lead to the conclusion that a required registration must be carried out before insolvency proceedings are opened. Otherwise the acquisition of the security right would not be completed and according to §91 (1) InsO would no longer be possible. However, §91 (2) InsO provides for an exception to the general rule of §91 (1) InsO as far as the acquisition of (security) rights requires their registration in a specific register,

192 G. Kodek in R. Bartsch, R. Pollak and W. Buchegger (eds.), *Österreichisches Insolvenzrecht*, Vol. IV, §132, para. 13.

which is only the case with immovables, ships, and planes. The provision refers to §§878 BGB (immovables), 3 (3) SchiffRG (ships), 16, 17 LuftFzgG (planes) which all provide for the same legal rule: namely that a contractual declaration by the person entitled on granting another person a (security) right over the specific asset does not become ineffective as a result of the person entitled being restricted in their power of disposal after the declaration has a binding effect for the entitled person and the application for registration has been made to the competent registry authority (for the requirements of a contractual declaration as an act of property law becoming binding see Question 7, para. 157). The reason behind this rule is to protect parties who are granted rights over these specific assets from a change of circumstances that would prevent the valid establishment of the right in the period between the filing for registration and its actual execution. As soon as the parties have applied for the registration submitting all necessary documents, they have done everything they should to have the right registered. The parties lose any influence over the registration process or its acceleration and become defenceless against any delay of the registration caused by internal operations within the authority. That is why the legislator wanted to protect parties in this period. So if all other validity requirements for the establishment of the security right are met before the opening of insolvency proceedings except for its registration, and the parties have already filed for its registration before the opening of insolvency proceedings as well, the subsequent registration leads to the valid establishment of a security right providing for a right to separate satisfaction.

1.2. Movables

277. The mortgage over ships (Schiffshypothek) and the pledge over planes require registration respectively in the Ship Register (Schiffsregister) in the Register on Liens on Aircraft (Register für Pfandrechte an Luftfahrzeugen), §§8, 3, 24 SchiffRG, 5 (1), 24 LuftFzgG. Entry in the register must include the person of the creditor, the amount of the secured claim, where the claim bears interest, the interest rate, and if other supplementary payments are to be made, the amount of these payments, §§24 (1) SchiffRG, 24 (1) LuftFzgG.

278. §3 (1) SchiffRG stipulates that the transfer of ownership of registered inland waterway vessels (inland waterway vessels that reach a certain size have to be registered) requires the registration of the new owner which naturally applies to security ownership. Nevertheless this is not a particularity of its character as a security right but a consequence of the fact that the establishment of security ownership is a transfer of full ownership only in a fiduciary capacity. Therefore only the registration of the creditor as the new owner is required. Ownership of smaller inland waterway vessels and of planes is transferred outside of the specific register law according to the general rules of German property law, §§929 et seq.

BGB. The same applies to ocean vessels with the particularity that the transfer of ownership is governed by special provisions, §§929a BGB, 2 SchiffRG.

1.3. Immovables

279. The 'Hypothek' as well as the 'Grundschuld' require registration in the Land Register (Grundbuch), §873 (1) BGB. As a consequence of the accessory nature of the 'Hypothek' its registration includes the same information as under para. 277 including the amount of the secured claim, §1115 (1) BGB. On the other hand, registration of the 'Grundschuld' being of a non-accessory character does not require any reference to the secured claim but to the name of the creditor, the amount up to which the encumbered land shall be held liable, and if the 'Grundschuld' bears interest, details of the interest rate and other supplementary payments that may have to be made §§1191 (1), 1192 (1), (2) BGB.[193]

2. Austria

2.1. General comments

280. Reference should be made to the discussion on German law, para. 275. Registration is a legal requirement with respect to ships, patents and real estate. Besides where an appropriate register is provided for the entry of specific kinds of assets and their legal circumstances, registration may be necessary as it is the practically established way to meet the requirements of the general publicity rule of §452 ABGB (see Question 7, para. 161 for pledges over trade marks).

281. Austrian insolvency law provides §13 IO, a provision similar to §91 (2) InsO under German law. According to this provision registration in the Land Register can be made after the opening of Insolvency proceedings if the rank of the registration is determined by a point in time prior to the moment of the opening of insolvency proceedings. The provision refers to §29 GBG according to which the rank of a registration is determined by the point in time when the application of registration was submitted to the local court, which in *Austria* is the competent authority to manage the Land Register. So a registration after the opening of insolvency proceedings is possible if the petition for registration was submitted to the local court before the opening of insolvency proceedings was ordered.

282. According to its wording §13 IO applies only to registration of rights over immovables in the Land Register. However §43 (3) PatG (Austrian Act on Patents)

193 D. Eickmann in *Münchener Kommentar zum BGB*, Vol. 6, §1115, para. 44.

contains a provision equal to §29 GBG. In relation to the former provision §13 AO (Austrian Act on the Composition with Creditors),[194] whose wording was similar to the former §13 KO and the actual §13 IO, the Austrian Patent Office (Österreichisches Patentamt) ruled that the registration of a pledge over a patent in the Patent Register had to be carried out if the petition for registration was submitted to the Patent Office before the opening of composition proceedings was ordered by the court.[195] In a later decision dealing with the consequences of the opening of insolvency proceedings it ruled that according to §43 (3) PatG the relevant point in time for determining whether a petition is legitimate was the time of its submission to the Patent Office regardless of a subsequent loss of power of disposal by the petitioner due to the opening of insolvency proceedings.[196] So the result should be the same as with immovables.

283. The same goes for rights over ships. As in *Germany*, §3 (3) SchiffRG stipulates that a contractual declaration by the person entitled on granting another person a (security) right over the specific asset does not become ineffective as a result of the person entitled being restricted in their power of disposal after the declaration has a binding effect for them and the application for registration has been made to the competent registry authority.

2.1. *Movables*

284. As far as ships are concerned reference should be made to the discussion on German law (para. 277). The provisions in *Austria* are the same as in *Germany*.

285. As far as patents are concerned, §43 PatG stipulates that a valid pledge over a patent requires its registration in the Patent Register. There are no other provisions specifying this requirement, which leads to the conclusion that it was left up to the administrative practices to establish a way of registration and to determine which information has to be registered.

286. Other pledges over rights may also need to be registered as a consequence of §452 ABGB (see para. 280).

2.2. *Immovables*

287. Mortgages must be registered in the land register, §§451, 431 ABGB (Einverleibung). The registration includes the same information as in *Germany*

194 The composition proceedings were abolished during the last insolvency law reform in 2010.
195 Öster. Patentamt Entsch. v. 10.08.1957, Az.: B 58/57 = [1957] PBl 162.
196 Öster. Patentamt Entsch. v. 03.04.1975, Az.: B 67, 68/74 = [1976] PBl 8, 9.

(para. 279, 277), see §14 (1) GBG. The legal basis of the secured claim does not have to be specified. Therefore it has no effect on the validity of the mortgage if the legal basis in the Land Register has been entered incorrectly deviating from the document by which the entitled person approved the registration.[197] This document, which has to be submitted to the court before the registration can be carried out, must, inter alia, identify the title (causa) for the acquisition of the right, §26 GBG. So all information required for the registration is shown in that document.

Question 20: Can you describe briefly the nature of the filing or registration system and whether it is publicly accessible?

1. Germany

1.1. Movables

1.1.1. Ships

288. Ocean vessels operating under the German flag and inland waterway vessels of a certain size have to be registered in the Ship Register (for details see §10 SchiffRegO, German Shipping Register Code). There are two separate registers for ocean vessels and for inland waterway vessels. Registration includes, inter alia, the declaration of the ship's name, the type of vessel, the ship's home port and the name of her owner (for details see §§11, 12 SchiffRegO).

289. Each registered ship has her own folio (Registerblatt) within the register. The folio is divided into three sections. Mortgages are registered in the third section (the same principle applies to planes and immovables, cf. para. 296).

290. The Ship Register is kept at the register courts (Registergerichte) which are divisions of the local courts (Amtsgerichte). Each local court keeps the Ship Register only for those ships having their home port in its court district. Deviating from that German states are entitled to bundle competences in certain courts. In North Rhine-Westphalia, for example, there are only four local courts keeping the Ship Register.

291. The ship register itself is public. Each person is permitted to inspect the register, §8 (1) SchiffRegO. The inspection takes place in the rooms of the register court. The inspection of the files (Registerakten) belonging to the register (for example documents submitted by parties which were required for entries)

---

197 OGH Urt. v. 19.01.1960, Az.: 2 Ob 525/59 = [1960] JBl 383 at 384.

requires the appellant to establish prima facie evidence to the effect that they have a legitimate interest in the inspection, §8 (2) SchiffRegO (for more details about the expression 'legitimate interest' see para. 298).

292. According to §93 SchiffRegO which refers to §§126 et seq. GBO (see para. 301) German states are free to implement an electronic management of the Ship Register which would enable applicants to look at the register on the Internet. Until now no state has made use of this possibility so the register is still kept in written form only.

1.1.2. Planes

293. Pledges over planes registered in the Aircraft Register (Luftfahrzeugrolle) require their entry in the Register on Liens on Aircrafts (Register für Pfandrechte an Luftfahrzeugen), §5 (1) LuftFzgG. Thus in contrast to ships and immovable, there is one register only for the registration of pledges and priority notices connected with them. This register is kept at the local court in whose district the Federal Office for Civil Aeronautics (Luftfahrtbundesamt) is based, §78 LuftFzgG. This currently is the Local Court of Braunschweig.

294. As far as the content and the publicity of the register are concerned the rules are the same as for ships (§85 LuftFzgG) so reference should be made to para. 288, 291.

295. The register is still kept in written form although the implementation of electronic management would be legally possible.

1.2. Immovables

296. In *Germany* each plot of real estate is registered in the Land Register (Grundbuch). Each plot of real estate has its own folio (Grundbuchblatt) where all entries regarding the specific plot of real estate are made. Thus all information regarding a specific plot of real estate can be found in its folio. §873 BGB stipulates that the establishment of every right in rem (ownership, mortgage, usufructs, etc.) over real estate requires its registration in the Land Register. Mortgages are registered in the third section of the Land Register.

297. The Land Register is kept at the local courts (Amtsgerichte). Each local court keeps the Land Register only for those plots of real estate which are located in its court district. The competent authority to manage the Land Register (scrutinizing applications for entries, granting access and right of inspection, etc.) is the Land Registry (Grundbuchamt) which can be viewed as a department of the local courts. Decisions are generally not made by the judge but by judicial officers (Rechtspfleger). As it is part of the local (civil) courts, the Land Registry's decisions on entry applications are not administrative acts in the understanding of public law. The decision can be appealed similarly to a judge's ruling. In that case the decision is reviewed by a judge at the local court. The court of second instance is the Higher Regional Court (Oberlandesgericht).

298. Due to the constitutional right to informational self-determination, the public access to the Land Register is restricted by §12 GBO. According to this provision access to the Land Register shall be granted only to persons who have demonstrated a legitimate interest in its inspection. This includes, for example, potential lenders who want to gain information about the ability of the future debtor to grant them valuable securities. In this case proof of credit negotiations having started and of the intention to establish a mortgage may be necessary. So applying for access as a representative of the owner (potential debtor), submitting a power of attorney might be the easier way[198] since the demonstration of a legitimate interest is not required if owners of rights in rem over the specific real estate, public notaries, other state authorities, or publicly appointed surveyors apply for access to the Land Register, §43 (1), (2) GBV (German Regulation on the Implementation of the German Land Registry Code).

299. The granted right to access and inspection exists only to the extent required for satisfying the demonstrated legitimate interest. So access may be granted only to specific folios or parts of them.

300. After being granted access, the Land Register can be inspected in the rooms of the Land Registry at the specific local court. Access is free; only copies must be paid for.

301. Meanwhile in all states of *Germany* the Land Register is managed electronically, §§126 et seq. GBO. Unlimited online access to the Land Register may be granted to the privileged persons listed under para. 298 if they meet the requirements of §133 (2) GBO (which, in the case of notaries should always be the case). Since the restriction of §12 GBO must not be evaded, online access to owners of rights in rem can only be granted regarding the specific real estate over which they hold rights. Other persons may only, with the approval of the entitled person or if they intend to have the real estate attached in enforcement proceedings, apply for online access regarding certain single queries for the specific real estate in question, §133 (4) GBO. In any case (unlimited access as well as single queries) online access requires the approval of the competent authority. It is up to the German states to appoint their competent authority, §81 GBV. In most states the president of the higher regional court (Oberlandesgericht) appear to be competent.

---

198 E. Maaß in H.-J. Bauer and H. v. Oefele, *GBO*, §12, para. 41.

2. Austria

2.1. *Movables*

2.1.1. *Ships*

302. As far as ships are concerned reference should be made to the discussion on German law. The legal acts and the numbers of the provisions are mostly the same. The Ship Register is kept at the local courts and is publicly accessible with the previously described restrictions (para. 291) applying to files belonging to the Ship Register. The possibility of electronic management is not provided by law.

2.1.2. *Patents*

303. The Patent Register is kept and managed by the Austrian Patent Office in Vienna, §§57 (1), 58 (1), 80 (1) PatG. For all the information that has to be shown in the register see §80 (1) PatG. The Patent Register is publicly accessible, §80 (3) PatG.

2.2. *Immovables*

304. The Land Register is kept at the local courts (Bezirksgerichte). Each local court keeps the Land Register only for those plots of real estate located within the court's district.[199] Every application for a registration must be approved by the Land Register Court (Grundbuchsgericht), §75 GBG. The Land Register Court, like the Land Registry in *Germany*, is a department of the local courts. A judicial officer (Rechtspfleger) rather than a judge has authority to make decisions.[200] For its capacity as a part of a civil court (and not as an administrative agency in the sense of public law, at least as far as its decisions on applications for registrations are concerned) reference is made to the discussion on German law (para. 297)

305. The Land Register consists of the actual register (Hauptbuch) and the documents submitted by the parties to have their applications for registration approved (Urkundensammlung), §2 GBG. Mortgages are registered in the third section (C-Blatt) of the Land Register.[201]

306. The Land Register is publicly accessible, §7 GBG. Access must be granted to every person demanding it, §7 GBG. Since the Land Register is kept electronically, it can be accessed for the whole country in every local court not limited by its court's district, §5 (5) GUG (Grundbuchsumstellungsgesetz). For the access on the Internet see §§6, 7 GUG.

---

199 G. Kodek in G. Kodek (ed.), *Grundbuchsrecht*, GBG, §75, para. 6.

200 G. Kodek in G. Kodek (ed.), *Grundbuchsrecht*, GBG, §75, para. 23.

201 A. Höller in G. Kodek (ed.), *Grundbuchsrech*t, GBG, §1, para. 26.

Question 21: To what extent does 'possession' or control of the secured assets serve as an alternative method to registration or filing in ensuring third party effectiveness of the security interest?

1. Germany

307. Under German law there is no choice between having a security right registered and transferring possession of the collateral to the secured party. For certain types of assets and security rights the law requires the registration of security rights (mortgage over immovables and ships, pledge over planes); for others it requires the transfer of possession (pledge over other tangibles than ships and planes). As far as security ownership is concerned, the transfer of possession can be replaced by constructive possession. For details see Questions 7, 19.

2. Austria

308. General reference should be made to the discussion on German law. Registration is required for a mortgage over immovables and ships and for a pledge over patents. As far as other security rights over tangibles (security ownership and pledge) are concerned, generally transfer of possession is required unless the procedure is unfeasible. Where this is the case the parties have to use signifiers to adhere to the principle of publicity. This applies also to pledges and security assignments of intangibles where naturally the transfer of possession is not possible. The use of signifiers may consist of a registration in a register if an appropriate register is provided for (cf. Question 7, para. 161 for the pledge over a trade mark).

E. PLURALITY OF SECURITY RIGHTS

Question 22: Is it possible to have more than one set of security rights (security interests) over the same asset?

1. Germany

1.1. Movables

1.1.1. Tangibles

1.1.1.1. Transfer of title by way of security

309. Security ownership over the same asset can only be granted once. Since the entitled party loses ownership of the collateral as result of granting security ownership, they are no longer able to grant ownership (security) to another party but since the collateral providing party has a claim from the fiduciary security agreement for returning the ownership where the secured claim is satisfied, this claim can be subject to a security assignment to another creditor. The collateral providing party stays in possession of the collateral so another creditor would still be able to acquire security ownership of the asset in good faith but this is unlikely to happen because transfer of direct possession to the second creditor would be required, §933 BGB, which would contradict the purposes of security ownership (cf. Question 3, para. 72). However, even if an acquisition in good faith took place, the result would be that the creditor who was granted security ownership previously would then automatically lose his (security) ownership which means that in any case only one creditor would be the holder of security ownership.

1.1.1.2. Pledge

310. It is legally possible to establish multiple pledge rights over the same asset, cf. §1209 BGB. However, as pledges over tangibles require the transfer of possession this is unlikely to happen. After the first pledge the collateral providing party is normally no longer able to transfer possession of the pledged collateral to other creditors. To establish a second pledge over the same asset the debtor is therefore required to assign his release claim against the prior pledgee to the subsequent pledgee and to direct the prior pledgee to exercise his direct possession from now on for the subsequent pledgee. So the subsequent pledgee is granted indirect possession, which replaces the normally required transfer of direct possession if the pledger himself holds only indirect possession of the collateral at the time the pledge is established, §1205 (2) BGB. For ships and planes see para. 315.

1.1.1.3. Combinations

311. Combinations of different security rights are possible and may occur where the establishment of the first security right requires the transfer neither of ownership nor of possession, which is only the case with some legal liens and the mortgage/pledge over planes and ships. Since in these cases the debtor maintains ownership and possession, he is able to grant security ownership or further pledges to other creditors subsequently. The first set of security rights is not affected by the establishment of the second unless a good faith acquisition clearing previous encumbrances (gutgläubiger lastenfreier Erwerb) takes place, §936 BGB (see Question 24, para. 331)

1.1.2. Intangibles

1.1.2.1. Assignment by way of security

312. Reference should be made to para. 309. The secured creditor does not have to fear the loss of his security at all since an acquisition of claims in good faith is not possible under German law.

1.1.2.2. Pledge

313. It follows from §§1273, 1209 BGB that the establishment of multiple pledge rights over the same asset is possible. The creditor can establish them simply by contractual agreement with different creditors.

1.1.2.3. Combinations

314. Combinations of different security rights are also possible. After pledging a claim the collateral providing party is still able to assign the claim by way of security.

1.2. Immovables

315. It is possible to establish several mortgages over the same real estate, cf. §879 BGB. The mortgages are listed in the Land Register in the specific folio below one another in the section for mortgages. The same applies for ships and planes, cf. §§25 SchiffRG, 25 LuftFzgG.

2. Austria

2.1. Movables

2.1.1. Tangibles

2.1.1.1. Transfer of title by way of security

316. Reference should be made to the discussion on German law. The risk that a creditor may lose his security ownership through good faith acquisition of security ownership by a second creditor is very unlikely since the establishment of security ownership requires transfer of possession or the use of signifiers. So either the debtor would not be able to grant possession to the second creditor or the second creditor because of the signifiers would not be able to claim to have acted in good faith.

2.1.1.2. Pledge

317. Although not expressly mentioned by the law, the establishment of multiple pledge rights over the same asset is possible.[202] As far as tangibles are concerned this is unlikely to happen since the transfer of possession is required.[203] For ships see para. 322.

2.1.1.3. Combinations

318. As far as the combination of legal liens and security ownership is concerned, combinations are only possible where the security ownership does not require the transfer of possession to the creditor due to unfeasibility. This is because legal liens tend to lapse when the assets subject to the legal lien are moved out of the specific area in which located assets are subject to the legal lien (for the legal lien of tenants see §1101 (2) ABGB). Where the pledge does not require the transfer of possession, a combination with a later security ownership is also possible.

2.1.2. Intangibles

2.1.2.1. Assignment by way of security

319. Reference should be made to the discussion on German law (para. 312).

2.1.2.2. Pledge

320. The establishment of multiple pledge rights over the same asset is possible.[204] For the pledge over patents this follows from the wording of §43 (3) PatG.

2.1.2.3. Combinations

321. The combination of a pledge with a later security assignment should be possible.

---

202 M. Hinteregger in M. Schwimann (ed.), *Praxiskommentar ABGB*, Vol. 2, §447, para. 2, §464 paras. 3 et seq.; H. Koziol and R. Welser, *Bürgerliches Recht*, Vol. I, p. 393 et seq.

203 H. Koziol and R. Welser, *Bürgerliches Recht*, Vol. I, p. 393.

204 Cf. fn. 194 where the authors do not distinguish between tangibles and intangibles.

2.2. Immovables

322. It is possible to establish several mortgages over the same real estate, cf. §29 GBG. The mortgages are listed below one another in the Land Register in the section for mortgages. The same applies to ships, cf. §25 SchiffRG.

Question 23: What are the rules for determining priority between competing security interests in the same property?

1. Germany

1.1. Movables

323. The priority between competing security rights over the same asset is determined by the chronological order of their establishment. The security right which was established first in time has priority over the security right which was established second in time and so on. This derives from the legal principle that generally nobody shall be able to grant to anybody else more rights than he actually holds (*nemo plus iuris ad alium transferre potest quam ipse habet*). After granting a security right over an asset, the debtor is no longer able to grant to someone else unencumbered ownership of this asset or another security right with the same rank as the previously established security right. This rule applies regardless of whether contractual or statutory security rights are competing. If a debtor, for example, transfers contractual security ownership of a piece of his private inventory (for example a valuable painting) to a creditor, the creditor acquires the security ownership only encumbered with the legal lien of the lessor (given the fact that the lessor has open claims against the tenant/debtor from the rental agreement). The legal lien has priority over the security ownership since it was established before the security ownership automatically in the moment the debtor brought the collateral into his rental apartment. Although this principle applies to all rights in rem, not only to security rights, it is only expressed in the law of pledges, §1209 BGB.[205]

324. The rule also applies where anticipated security rights over future assets are competing. After a debtor has assigned a future claim by way of security he is not able to assign the claim a second time or to establish a pledge over it, even if the establishment of the second security interest has also been concluded before the future claim came into existence. Since the security assignment of a future claim is completed not before this claim comes into existence, one could argue that

[205] W. Wiegand in J. Staudinger, *BGB*, §1209, para. 2.

both the first and the second security interest are validly established at the same moment, namely when the future claim comes into existence. However, this is not the case. The determination of priority between anticipated security interests over future assets depends only on the chronological order of all requirements for establishing the security right being met except for the future collateral being part of the collateral provider's assets (for exceptions from this rule see Question 24, para. 330 et seq.). As a matter of priority in the sense of this question, the described principle may be relevant where pledges over future claims or other rights are in question whereas, in the prescribed example of several security assignments over the same receivable, the later concluded assignment would have to be held inoperative so there wouldn't be two existing sets of security interests competing with each other (see Question 22, para. 312, 309).

325. It may happen that two different sets of security rights come into existence at the same time. Of practical relevance at this point is especially the collision between the anticipated security ownership and the legal lien of a lessor. If a tenant brings new assets into a warehouse, the current and future inventory of which is subject to a security ownership agreement, the legal lien of the lessor of the warehouse and the security ownership of the finance creditor over the newly brought in assets come into existence at the same time. The German Federal Supreme Court decided the question of priority in this case in favour of the legal lien of the lessor which will have priority over the security ownership. To assume an equal rank would undermine the importance of the legal lien of the lessor in view of the fact that the amount of open claims of the finance creditor are usually many times greater than the open claims of the lessor from the rental agreement. That would contradict the intention of the legislator.[206]

1.2. *Immovables*

326. Priority between competing security rights over the same real estate is determined by the rank of their registration, 879 BGB. Entries in each section of the Land Register are continuously numbered depending on their chronological order. §17 GBO stipulates that the Land Registry shall process applications for entries in the Land Register in the chronological order in which they were submitted to the Land Registry. This is to ensure that a mortgage whose entry was applied for on 1 July 2014 is registered before a mortgage whose entry application was submitted to the Land Registry on the 2 July 2014. If, however, the Land Registry violates the provision of §17 GBO, the disadvantaged creditor cannot claim for correction of the Land Register since §17 GBO is a mere

206 BGH Urt. v. 12.02.1992, Az.: XII ZR 7/91 = BGHZ 117, 200, 207 et seq.

regulatory provision not being part of substantive law. In this case the affected creditor may only claim for damages against the state.[207]

2. Austria

2.1. Movables

327. Reference should be made to the discussion on German law (para. 323, 324).[208] It has to be taken into account that the security assignment and the pledge over receivables require an act of publicity by way of notification of the debtor of the claim provided as collateral or an entry into the accounts of the collateral provider. If two security assignments are competing, the creditor in whose favour the act of publicity was carried out first has priority.[209] This means that a later contractual security assignment may gain priority over a previously made security assignment if the previous security assignment has not yet become valid because the act of publicity has not yet been carried out. This applies also to competing anticipated security interests over future receivables.[210] In this context it should be kept in mind that both the notification of the third person debtor and the entry into the accounts of the collateral provider can be carried out in advance before the future claim comes into existence (see Question 4, para. 134; Question 3, para. 108). As under German law, the prescribed conflicts are a matter of priority in the sense of this question only when it comes to pledges over future receivables as the security assignment meeting the publicity requirements second in time must be held inoperative (Question 22, para. 319).

2.2. Immovables

328. The priority between competing security rights over the same real estate is determined by the rank of their registration. Although according to the wording of §29 GBG, the rank of competing rights is determined by the time the application for registration was submitted to the Court administering the Land Register, this provision has the same meaning as §17 GBO under German law (see para. 326).

---

207 J. Demharter in J. Demharter, *Grundbuchordnung*, §17, para. 17.

208 K. Hofmann in P. Rummel, *ABGB*, Vol. 1, §464, paras. 4 et seq.; M. Hinteregger in M. Schwimann (ed.), *Praxiskommentar ABGB*, Vol. 2, §464, para. 3; M. Binder in M. Schwimann (ed.), *Praxiskommentar ABGB*, Vol. 5, §1101, para. 11 with regard to the legal lien of the lessor.

209 W. Thöni in A. Fenyves, F. Kerschner and A. Vonkilch (eds.), H. Klang, *ABGB*, 1392, para. 87; G. Ertl in P. Rummel, *ABGB*, Vol. 2, §1392, para. 4.

210 W. Thöni in H. Klang, *ABGB*, 1393, para. 68.

So the substantive legal rank is determined not by the time of application but by the rank of the registration in the Land Register. Application documents are continuously numbered according to the time they were submitted and are processed according to these numbers. If, however, the court mixes up numbers or makes any other mistakes which would lead to a rank of the registration not in accordance with §29 GBG, the legal consequences seem to be not yet fully established. One opinion argues for granting the party disadvantaged by the registration the right to have the Land Register corrected which stands in accordance with the wording of §§450 (5) Geo (Geschäftsordnung für Gerichte erster und zweiter Instanz), 104 (2), (3) GBG.[211] Apparently the Austrian Supreme Court and another part of the legal literature argue for applying the provision of §104 GBG only if the actual registration differs from the court decision approving the registration.[212] If this is not the case, according to this opinion, there is no possibility of having the Land Register corrected.

Question 24: Are there special rules privileging the position of an acquisition financier, i.e. a secured party whose advance of funds funded the acquisition of a particular asset and who may be in a priority competition with an earlier general creditor whose security interest extends to all assets of the debtor whenever acquired?

1. Germany

329. There are no specific legal provisions privileging the position of an acquisition financier at the expense of earlier creditors. Nevertheless, privileges may arise from the application of the general rules of German property law which provide for two exceptions from the rule that priority is determined by the chronological order of the establishment of security rights.

330. The first exception concerns only the anticipated transfer of title by way of security over tangibles. It may happen that a debtor for the acquisition of a specific asset grants anticipated security ownership over this asset to the financing creditor although the asset would be subject to an earlier anticipated security ownership agreement covering this future asset only or as a part of an entity of future assets. By concluding this second anticipated security ownership agreement, the debtor expresses that he is no longer willing to recognise the constructive possession agreement with regard to the previous creditor but is

---

211 J. Rassi in A. Fenyves, F. Kerschner and A. Vonkilch (eds.), G. Kodek (ed.), *Grundbuchsrecht*, GBG, §29, para. 19.

212 Cf. OGH Urt. v. 12.02.1969, Az.: 5 Ob19/69 = [1969] EvBl 280; G. Kodek in G. Kodek (ed.), *Grundbuchsrecht*, GBG, §104, para. 14.

now willing to exercise his direct possession for the new financing creditor. Next to a contractual or legal relationship, constructive possession requires also the factual will to possess for the specific person. At the time the debtor acquires the financed asset this will no longer exists with regard to the earlier creditor but for the new financing creditor. So in this case the financing creditor would acquire security ownership after the debtor has acquired ownership at least for one brief moment (see for the anticipated security ownership Question 3, para. 69).[213] Such action might cause a breach of the earlier security agreement imposing a liability for damages on the debtor. On the level of property law, however, the security right would be validly established in favour of the new financing creditor as long as the new creditor has not incited the debtor to breach any former security agreement with other creditors. In the latter case the new security ownership would not be valid due to immorality, §138 BGB.

331. The other legal exception would be a good faith acquisition of the security right (clearing previous encumbrances), respectively the good faith acquisition of a prior rank (where pledges over movables would be competing, §1208 BGB) which is possible, if a creditor being granted a security right is, without acting in gross negligence, unaware of the existence of existing security rights over the asset. A good faith acquisition of security ownership clearing a previous pledge right is unlikely to happen because the transfer of direct possession to the financing creditor would be required, §936 (1) BGB. The same goes for a good faith acquisition of security ownership over an asset, which is already subject to a prior security ownership agreement. So the only realistic (but practically not relevant) possibility is to acquire a pledge over an asset in good faith, which is subject to a prior security ownership agreement. In case of intangibles, such good faith acquisitions are not possible due to the absence of grounds justifying the protection of good faith (in case of tangibles such grounds would always be the ability to grant direct possession), as far as immovables are concerned the registration of the previous mortgage in the Land Register would make acting in good faith impossible (so the same would apply for security rights competing with a previously registered pledge/mortgage over planes/ships).

332. In this context it should be mentioned that a previous set of security interests may be invalid as a consequence of its immorality, §138 BGB (see Question 1, para. 28). This may be the case if it restricts the debtor disproportionally in his economic freedom or forces him to conceal the previous security right from his suppliers committing breach of contract. However this is not really a question of priority since the earlier security right never would have been validly set up.

---

213 W. Wiegand in J. Staudinger, *BGB*, §930, para. 33.

2. Austria

333. Under Austrian law there are no specific legal provisions privileging the position of an acquisition financier at the expense of earlier creditors.

334. Each security right (especially the security ownership and the security assignment) requires an act of publicity. The security right is not established before this act has been carried out. If a debtor assigns a future claim by way of security which is subject to a former blanket security assignment, the second security assignment may become valid if the act of publicity is carried out in favour of the new creditor earlier than in favour of the party of the blanket security assignment. The same principle applies for the security ownership. If there are two colliding anticipated security agreements over future assets the question which of the creditors will acquire the security ownership depends on which of them is granted direct possession first or in favour of which of them a trustee is set up first to hold the collateral. So as far as the act of publicity has not been carried out (which is especially relevant in regard to anticipated security agreements over future assets) there would be a way for a financing creditor to 'overtake' earlier security agreements and acquire the security right over the financed asset.

335. The good faith acquisition of a security right respectively of a prior rank is possible as well, §456 (2) ABGB, but unlikely to happen due to the strict publicity requirements under Austrian security rights law.

F. QUASI-SECURITY AGREEMENTS

Question 25: Does your legal system have any rules equating the treatment, in whole or in part, of security interest and 'quasi-security' agreements, i.e. agreements that in legal terms do not involve the creation of security interests but have many of the same economic consequences? Examples of quasi-security include the factoring or sale of receivables and finance leases, hire-purchase agreements and retention of title clauses in sale of goods contracts.

1. Germany

336. The financing constructions explained hereinafter all have in common that they provide a financing function and a secured in rem position in insolvency and enforcement proceedings for the creditor without normally being referred to as security rights or quasi-security rights. One exception is the retention of title which is commonly referred to as a security right in German/Austrian literature. The expression 'quasi-security rights' and the thinking in categories such as security and quasi-security rights is not commonplace in *Germany* and *Austria*, cf. Introduction, para. 5. A deeper examination of the functional character of a finance instrument (whether it serves a security function or not) is namely important when it comes to the determination of whether the creditor must be granted a right of separate satisfaction as a (mere) secured creditor in insolvency proceedings over the debtor's estate or whether he must be granted the right to separation from the insolvency estate being the true owner of the collateral meaning not only for security purposes (in *Austria* this examination may also be important when it comes to publicity and priority issues, see para. 356 et seq.). In enforcement proceedings conducted by third parties the distinction is not as important since enforcement law does not distinguish between security rights in rem and other rights in rem held over objects being subject to enforcement proceedings.

1.1. Retention of title

337. Retention of title clauses ensure that in the case of a sale of goods the seller remains the owner of the goods until the buyer has paid the whole price for the goods. These clauses normally go hand in hand with an instalment payment agreement which makes up its financing function. Since no money but goods are 'advanced' the sale under retention of title is referred to as a credit on goods (Warenkredit).

338. The possibility of retention of title clauses is recognised by the law, cf. §449 BGB. Legally the retention of title is construed by making the agreement on the transfer of ownership as the act of property law subject to the condition precedent that the full purchase price is paid. The underlying obligational contract is a sales contract normally containing an instalment payment agreement.

339. Besides this simple form, there are two other forms of retention of title clauses, namely the extended retention of title (verlängerter Eigentumsvorbehalt) and the expanded retention of title (erweiterter Eigentumsvorbehalt), the latter often occurring in the form of current account clauses. The extended retention of title permits the buyer to resale the delivered goods in the ordinary course of business while the future claim arising from this resale is assigned by way of security to the seller replacing the retained ownership as a security for the delivery payment.[214] So it is rather a combination of a retention of title (simple or expanded) with a regular security assignment of future claims than a security device of its own (see for the resistance to insolvency of assignments of future debts, para. 124). Under an expanded title of ownership the seller remains owner of the goods not only until the claim arising from the particular sales contract

214 H. Westermann in *Münchener Kommentar zur InsO*, Vol. 3, §449, paras. 87 et seq.

is met but until all or certain open claims arising from the business relationship between the seller and the buyer are fulfilled.[215]

340. Where the sale of raw materials which are to be processed into new goods by the buyer is in question, a manufacturer's clause/processing clause must be added to the retention of title clause in order to prevent the retention of title clause from being useless. A mere retention of title clause would not prevent the seller from losing ownership of the supplied raw materials if they were processed into new goods by the seller. The binding provision of §950 BGB stipulates that a party who creates a new movable asset by processing or transformation of one or more substances (the manufacturer) acquires ownership of the new item. In manufacturer's clauses parties declare that the buyer shall process the supplied raw materials on behalf of the seller, transferring the capacity as manufacturer from the buyer to the seller. The result of these clauses, approved by the German Supreme Court's case law, is that the supplier acquires ownership of the new goods directly in the moment of their creation.[216] In the case of several suppliers using manufacturer's clauses, all suppliers acquire co-ownership of the newly created item proportionate to the value of their raw materials used in the processing.[217] According to the prevailing legal literature this interpretation leads to an evasion of the binding provision of §950 BGB. The determination of the capacity as manufacturer has to be made according to the specific objective criteria of each case and is not subject to contractual freedom. These clauses should therefore be interpreted as anticipated security ownership agreements.[218] This would lead to the conclusion that the buyer as the manufacturer would acquire ownership over the newly created goods for one brief moment before ownership is 'returned' as security from him to the seller.

341. In the event of insolvency of the buyer the seller, still being the owner, is protected by a claim for separation of the item subject to the sales contract from the insolvency estate if the IP refuses the performance of the contract, §47 InsO (for the refusal of performance cf. §103 InsO).[219] This treatment of the seller by insolvency law as the true owner and not merely as a secured creditor (secured creditors are granted a right to separate satisfaction, see Question 9, para. 189) has been questioned although the legal situation is clear.[220] Nevertheless, the prevailing opinion argues that retained ownership is not comparable to a

215 H. Westermann in *Münchener Kommentar zur InsO*, Vol. 3, §449, paras. 81 et seq.

216 BGH Urt. v. 03.03.1956, Az.: IV ZR 334/55 = BGHZ 20, 159, 163.

217 OLG Frankfurt a.M. Urt. v. 09.12.1958, Az.: 5 U 74/58 = [1959] MDR 578 at 579.

218 W. Wiegand in J. Staudinger, *BGB*, §950, para. 41.; H. Ganter in *Münchener Kommentar zur InsO*, Vol. 1, §47, para. 108; P. Bassenge in O. Palandt, *BGB*, §950, paras. 9, 11.

219 BGH Urt. v. 08.05.2014, Az.: IX ZR 128/12 =, para. 12 et seq.

220 P. Bülow, (2007) *WM* 429 at 432; L. Häsemeyer, *Insolvenzrecht*, para. 18.34 et seq.

pledge or to security ownership as it does not secure the claim for the purchase price but the claim to be retransferred the sold goods where the execution of the contract fails and does not provide a transfer of ownership.[221] This was the view of the legislator as well as it did not include retained ownership in the list of security rights providing only for a right to separate satisfaction in the rather new provision of §51 InsO.[222] Nevertheless, retained ownership in *Germany* is recognised as a security right explained as such in most legal textbooks on secured finance. Furthermore, where the retained ownership equals the function of security ownership/assignment the courts grant the seller only a right to separate satisfaction. At first, this is the case with the expanded retention of title if the original claim has already been met and the retained ownership is securing only other open claims from the business relationship.[223] Secondly, after the resale of sold goods under an extended retention of title clause the original seller only has a right to separate satisfaction over the assigned claims since the assignment is a regular assignment by way of security.[224]

1.2. *Finance leasing/sale and lease back*

342. Another type of contract having a finance and credit function is the leasing contract. Normally a finance leasing arrangement involves three parties namely the supplier of the item subject to the actual leasing agreement, the lessor who usually will be a bank and the lessee. The lessor buys the item from the supplier and lets it to the lessee on the terms of the leasing agreement which is concluded only between the lessor and the lessee. Characteristic of the finance leasing is that according to the monthly leasing rates and the expected period of the contract it is ensured that the lessor's expenses connected to the acquisition of the item will be fully compensated by the end of the contract (Amortisationsprinzip) in return for the leave of use which imparts a similar effect as a loan agreement. The lessor assigns his statutory warranty rights arising from the sales contract to the lessee, contractually excluding his own statutory liability for potential defects at the same time. Since the leasing contract is mainly aimed at the leave for use it is

---

221 H. Ganter in *Münchener Kommentar zur InsO*, Vol. 1, §47, para. 55 et seq.; W. Henckel in E. Jaeger, *InsO*, Vol. 1, §47, para. 43; D. Reinicke and K. Tiedke, *Kreditsicherung*, S. 245.

222 Cf. BGH Urt. v. 08.05.2014, Az.: IX ZR 128/12 = [2014] NJW 2358, para. 13.

223 BGH Urt. v. 08.05.2014, Az.: IX ZR 128/12 = [2014] NJW 2358, para. 14; BGH Urt. v. 09.07.1986, Az.: VIII ZR 232/85 = BGHZ 98, 160, 170; according to the prevailing legal literature this shall also be the case with goods created out of raw materials subject to a retention of title and manufacturer's clause, see H. Ganter in *Münchener Kommentar zur InsO*, Vol. 1, §47, para. 47; M. Brinkmann in W. Uhlenbruck, *InsO*, §47, para. 26; P. Gottwald and J. Adolphsen in P. Gottwald (ed.), *Insolvenzrechtshandbuch*, §43, para. 39.

224 Cf. BGH Urt. v. 08.05.2014, Az.: IX ZR 128/12 = [2014] NJW 2358, para. 13.

regarded by the German Federal Supreme Court as an atypical rental agreement, applying the legal provisions governing rental agreements (§§535 et seq. BGB) analogously, although its function as a financial accommodation is obvious.[225] Nevertheless, despite this being obvious, German case law regards the ownership of the lessor as full ownership and not merely as security ownership.[226]

343. In the case of a sale and lease back contract the lessor acquires ownership of the item subject to the leasing agreement not from a third party but from the lessee through a sales contract and leaves it to the lessee at the same time for use according to the terms of a leasing contract. Both contracts are normally concluded in one contractual document. The transfer of ownership is construed according to §930 BGB which means that the lessor at no point in time will be in direct possession of the item. Even without the typical tripartite nature, the sale and lease back contract is considered a type of finance leasing since it is also aimed at the full recovery of the lessor by the end of the contract.[227] The appropriateness of the exclusion of all statutory liabilities for defects of the leased item is justified by the fact that the lessee would be liable for initial defects himself from the sales contract and that the lessee was, in contrast to the lessor, always in direct possession of the item.

344. As the lessor is regarded the true owner, in the event of insolvency of the lessee he is able to claim for separation of the leased item from the insolvency estate if the IP refuses the performance of the contract, §47 InsO.[228] So, despite the fully secured in rem position of the lessor, finance leasing is commonly referred to as a finance instrument but not really in the context of financial security rights.

1.3. Factoring

345. Another common way to generate cash developed by the finance industry is the factoring commonly referred to as the purchase of receivables. German legal practice basically distinguishes between two forms of factoring, namely the non-recourse factoring (echtes factoring) and the recourse factoring (unechtes factoring). In case of the non-recourse factoring the creditor of a claim sells

225 BGH Urt. v. 23.02.1977, Az.: VIII ZR 124/75 = BGHZ 68, 118, 123.

226 BGH Urt. v. 27.02.1985, Az.: VIII ZR 328/83 = BGHZ 94, 44, 49; this is also the prevailing opinion in German legal literature, cf. the references in H. Ganter in *Münchener Kommentar zur InsO*, Vol. 2, §47, para. 223.

227 J. Koch in *Münchener Kommentar zum BGB*, Vol. 3, Finanzierungsleasing, para. 13; M. Stoffels in J. Staudinger *BGB*, Leasingrecht, para. 31.

228 H-G. Eckert in *Münchener Kommentar zur InsO*, Vol. 2, §108, para. 176; R. Sinz in W. Uhlenbruck, *InsO*, §108, para. 106; M. Stoffels in J. Staudinger, *BGB*, Leasingrecht, para. 31; see for the lease of immovables the specific provision of §108 (1) InsO.

and assigns it to the factor. In return he receives the purchase price which will be under the nominal value of the claim in order to ensure a profit for the factor. The factor normally will be responsible for collecting the claim. The characteristic of the non-recourse factoring is that the factor runs the risk of the transferred claim turning out to be valueless because the debtor is financially unable to pay his debt. This bestows on the non-recourse factoring the character of a real sale transaction rather than a credit transaction. Accordingly, after paying the purchase price and being assigned the claims subject to the factoring agreement the factor is regarded as the true owner of the claims as he is entitled to separate them from the assignor's insolvency estate if insolvency proceedings are opened, §47 InsO.[229] In the case of recourse factoring on the other hand the factor can take recourse against the provider of the claim if it turns out to be uncollectable. So the only real difference to a loan agreement is that the liability of the original creditor is not of a primary but of a secondary nature since the factor according to the factoring agreement has to pursue his satisfaction out of the transferred claim first before he may take recourse against its original owner. The assignment of the claim to the factor is made only on account of performance (erfüllungshalber), pursuing to a certain extent security purposes, to repay a granted credit amount which makes it an atypical loan agreement.[230] Therefore the recourse factoring is regarded by the German Federal Supreme Court as a real credit transaction.[231] Accordingly, in this case the factor is not entitled to separation of the assigned claims but only to separate satisfaction like a secured creditor, §51 Nr. 1 InsO.[232] Nevertheless in German legal literature non-recourse factoring is not really discussed as a financial security device although, based on a German understanding, this might be appropriate.

346. The distinction between the two forms of factoring is also of practical relevance when it comes to the collision of blanket assignments agreed upon in framework factoring agreements and security assignments for the benefit of suppliers of goods in connection with extended retention of title clauses. In the case of recourse factoring, a prior blanket assignment is considered invalid due to incitement to breach of contract if the original owner of the claim is forced to conceal the blanket assignment from his suppliers because otherwise they would cease their deliveries, §138 BGB (cf. Question 1, para. 28).[233] On the other

229 BGH Urt. v. 10.12.2009, Az.: IX ZR 1/09 = [2010] NZI 138, para. 13; H. Ganter in *Münchener Kommentar zur InsO*, Vol. 1, §47, Rn. 265.

230 Prevailing opinion, see BGH Urt. v. 03.05.1972, Az.: VIII ZR 170/71 = BGHZ 58, 364, 366; M. Martinek in H. Schimansky, H.-J. Bunte and H.-J. Lwowski, *Bankrechts-Handbuch*, §102, para. 46.

231 BGH Urt. v. 03.05.1972, Az.: VIII ZR 170/71 = BGHZ 58, 364, 366.

232 BGH Beschl. v. 20.12.2007, Az.: IX ZR 105/07, para. 19; H. Ganter in *Münchener Kommentar zur InsO*, Vol. 1, §47, Rn. 266.

233 BGH Urt. v. 14.10.1981, Az.: VIII ZR 149/80 = BGHZ 82, 50, 64 et seq.

hand this will not be the case if the blanket assignment was made under a non-recourse factoring agreement. Here suppliers would not suffer any disadvantages compared to the situation where the buyer resales the delivered goods in the ordinary course of business and collects the purchase price for the supplier, which he is entitled to according to retention of title clauses. The purchase price for the claim paid by the factor replaces the price the buyer would have received for the resold goods. Although the purchase price does not reach the nominal value of the claim, it will be sufficient to pay the supplier's open claim due to the potential profit margin the buyer would have generated.[234]

1.4. Double trusts (Doppeltreuhand)

347. Double trusts, serving a security function with an in rem effect, are established in secured finance transactions whenever a security is not granted to the creditor himself but to a trustee who holds the security for the creditor as it is often the case where more than one lender is involved (syndicated lending). The secured assets are held by the trustee in an administrative function for the benefit of the security provider and in a security function for the secured creditor(s). Used for security purposes double trusts generally consist of a regular security transfer to a trustee instead of the secured party. On the level of the law of obligations there is the additional trust agreement, that until default has occurred the trustee shall hold the collateral for the party providing the collateral. The obligational contract usually is of a tripartite character. It seems to be appropriate to describe double trusts set up for security purposes generally as a special variation of security ownership/assignment instead of an own secured finance device.

348. In connection to insolvency, however, there are two fields of application of double trusts which deserve being mentioned here:At first, double trusts may be used by a 'weak' provisional IP (that is when the power of administration and disposal during preliminary proceedings remains with the debtor, which is very common since a 'strong' preliminary IP would be exposed to the same strict liabilities as the IP in main proceedings) to obtain advanced services of all kinds (delivery of goods by suppliers, works by subcontractors, electricity by electricity suppliers, etc.) needed to maintain the debtor's business during preliminary insolvency proceedings. After the opening of preliminary proceedings the debtor's suppliers of goods or services will normally only be willing to contract with the debtor or to execute their owed performances against prepayment. This is to prevent themselves from a partial loss of their claims as being insolvency creditors after the main insolvency proceedings are opened. (If they would

[234] BGH Urt. v. 19.09.1977, Az.: VIII ZR 169/76 = BGHZ 69, 254, 258.

contract with a 'strong' provisional IP their claims in opened main insolvency proceedings would not be treated as regular insolvency claims but as claims against the insolvency estate which enjoy a prior rank so in this case suppliers would already be secured at least to a certain degree.) Such prepayment will usually be impossible to grant since at the start of preliminary proceedings a serious lack of liquidity will already have incurred on the part of the debtor. As the debtor's business depends on the continuing supply of goods and services this situation poses a serious threat to the maintenance of the debtor's business. Suppliers of goods may then protect themselves by using (extended) retention of title clauses but this does not apply to suppliers of services (and even the retention of title may bear uncertainties where the delivered goods are to be processed or used up). So in order to make suppliers execute advanced performances it must be ensured that their claims arising during preliminary proceedings will get paid even after the main insolvency proceedings have been opened. This result can be reached by establishing a double trust. The debtor and the preliminary IP enter into a trust agreement according to which the preliminary IP shall hold the returns generated by the debtor during preliminary proceedings as a trustee for certain suppliers up to the amounts of their open claims. Accordingly the debtor assigns these future claims by way of security to the preliminary IP as a trustee (who then enjoys a double function: IP and trustee). The preliminary IP opens a trust account (separated from the regular escrow account through which the debtor's normal transactions are handled during preliminary proceedings (if such an account has been opened) into which the assigned claims are collected. If there are funds that are not needed (unlikely to happen) these could also be transferred to the trust account immediately. The preliminary IP also enters into another trust agreement with the suppliers and/or even with certain consumers (in this case it could be a tripartite trust) of the debtor in regard to the assets held by him as a trustee.[235] As far as details are concerned such trust constructions may vary in their final legal form depending on the specific situation at hand. The result, however, is that the transfer of assets from the debtor to the trustee is regarded as a security transfer granting the trustee, being the legal owner of the assets, a right to separate satisfaction over the assets held by him.[236] The

235 It is not completely solved whether this trust agreement is a prerequisite for the resistance of the trust against insolvency or whether the trustee function in relation to the suppliers could be established merely by the trust agreement with the debtor as a contract to the benefit of third parties, see H. Ganter, [2012] *NZI* 433 at 434.

236 This should at least be the case where the profit margins generated by the debtor are also collected to the trust account as it will usually be the case since it is impracticable for the debtor as well as for consumers to split up their debts and transfer money to different accounts. Then the trust account at least from an economic point of view belongs to the insolvency estate, see BGH Urt. v. 12.10.1989, Az.: IX ZR 184/88 = BGHZ 109, 47, 53. Literature tends to assume a right to separate satisfaction generally instead of a right to claim the separation from the insolvency estate, see R. Bork, [2003] *ZIP* 1421, 1424; H. Ganter, [2012] *NZI* 433 at 436.

suppliers are entitled to claim for the proceeds against the trustee based on their trust agreement. The double trust as an insolvency resistant security for suppliers during preliminary proceedings is widely accepted in practice and in the legal literature.[237] The German Supreme Court has approved its resistance to insolvency.[238] But since the judgment was made under a former legislative situation and many legal details of such double trust agreements are not fully clarified,[239] there remain uncertainties.[240] Some insolvency courts have approved of double trusts only under specific conditions and on condition of a former court authorisation.[241] So in practice the (provisional) IP should obtain the (informal) the court's authorisation first before setting up a double trust.

349. Secondly, in order to protect employees' part-time retirement and pension claims from a potential employer's insolvency, companies may transfer assets (e.g. stocks) to a trustee. According to the trust agreement the trustee shall administer these assets for the benefit of the enterprise. In the case of default (insolvency of the company) the trustee shall pay open claims of the employees described above out of these administrated assets. The trustee becomes the legal owner of the transferred assets but since the company remains the owner of the assets from an economic point of view they belong to the insolvency estate in case of insolvency proceedings.[242] Therefore, and since the effect of the double trust is similar to the security ownership/assignment with the difference that the collateral is not held by the creditor himself, the trustee is granted a right to separate satisfaction in the case of the company's insolvency which according to the trust agreement he has to pursue for the benefit of the employees.[243]

2. Austria

2.1. Retention of title

350. As far as the simple and the extended retention of title are concerned, reference should be made to the discussion on German law. In *Austria* retention

---

237 See R. Bork, [2003] *ZIP* 1421 at 1423 et seq.; H. Ganter, [2012] *NZI* 433 at 434 et seq.; H. Haarmeyer in *Münchener Kommentar zur InsO*, Vol. 1, §22, para. 71; W. Gerhardt in E. Jaeger, *InsO*, Vol. 1, §22, para. 132; S-H. Undritz, [2003] *NZI* 136 at 141; U. Schmerbach in *Frankfurter Kommentar zur InsO*, §22, para. 104; H. Vallender in W. Uhlenbruck, *InsO*, §22, para. 242 et seq.

238 BGH Urt. v. 12.10.1989, Az.: IX ZR 184/88 =BGHZ 109, 47.

239 As for the possible legal consequences if the trustee is not identical with the provisional IP see W. Marotzke, [2005] *ZInsO* 561 at 566; for the application of §181 BGB see R. Bork, [2005] *NZI* 530 et seq.

240 Denying the possibility of double trusts at all P. Windel, [2009] *ZIP* 101 et seq.

241 AG Hamburg Beschl. v. 20.02.2006, Az.: 67g IN 513/05 = [2006] ZInsO 218 at 219.

242 BAG Urt. v. 18.07.2013, Az.: 6 AZR 47/12 = [2014] NZI 167, para. 18.

243 BAG Urt. v. 18.07.2013, Az.: 6 AZR 47/12 = [2014] NZI 167, paras. 18 et seq.

of title is also regarded as a security right securing a credit on goods. In addition to its particularities in insolvency law it shows another element distinguishing it from the other security rights explained in Questions 1 et seq.: the publicity rules regarding the pledge and the security ownership/assignment do not apply. Retention of title is construed by making the transfer of ownership as the act of actual property law subject to the condition precedent that the full purchase price is paid by the buyer.[244] In the case of insolvency of the buyer the seller generally has the right to claim for separation of the sold object from the insolvency estate in the case of payment default. This right is restricted by the provisions of §§11 (2), 25 a IO if the sold object is required for the continuation of the debtor's enterprise. In this case separation from the insolvency estate can only be claimed after a period of six months beginning with the opening of insolvency proceedings, regardless of whether the default of payment has already occurred before the opening of insolvency proceedings or is caused by the IP during insolvency proceedings, unless the creditor proves that the fulfilment of the claim or its enforcement would be necessary to prevent grave personal or economic disadvantage to himself, §11 (2) IO (for rights to separate satisfaction see Question 9, para. 216). So unlike German law, Austrian law imposes a 'stay' not only on the enforcement of rights to separate satisfaction but also on rights to separation. According to this, §25 a (1) Nr. 2, (2) Nr. 1 IO stipulates that if default of payment has occurred before the opening of insolvency proceedings but the seller had not withdrawn from the contract, he is not able to exercise his right of withdrawal after the opening of insolvency proceedings until after the first six months of the insolvency proceedings unless the creditor proves that the withdrawal would be necessary to prevent grave personal or economic disadvantage to himself. If, on the other hand, the default of payment occurs during opened insolvency proceedings, the seller shall be free to withdraw from the contract immediately but his right to claim separation from the insolvency estate shall still be bound by the restriction of §11 (2) IO.[245] §11 (2) IO shall also apply if the IP chooses to withdraw from the contract (see for the IP's right to withdrawal §21 IO).[246] Where the asset subject to an extended retention of title clause has been resold by the buyer, the seller holds a right to separate satisfaction over the claim from the resale, which previously had been assigned to him by way of security, regardless of whether the resale took place before or after the buyer's insolvency proceedings were opened.[247]

---

244 M. Binder and M. Spitzer in M. Schwimann (ed.), *Praxiskommentar ABGB*, Vol. 4, §1063, para. 18.

245 A. Riedler in P. Apathy, G. Iro and H. Koziol (eds.), *Österreichisches Bankvertragsrecht*, Vol. IX, Part 2, Ch. 3, para. 3/29; A. Riedler, [2011] *ÖJZ*, 904 at 912.

246 A. Riedler, [2011] *ÖJZ* 904 at 913 et seq.

247 OGH Urt. v. 30.03.1989, Az.: 8 Ob 48/88 = SZ 62/55.

351. Manufacturer's clauses supplementing extended retention of title clauses are not necessary under Austrian law. Austrian law does not provide for a statutory loss of ownership in the case of goods being processed into new things by someone else, §§414, 415 ABGB. If a buyer processes raw materials which are subject to retention of title into new goods, according to the Austrian Supreme Court the owner of the raw materials (supplier/seller) becomes co-owner of the new goods in proportion to the value added by him, which will be the value of his delivered raw materials. The seller remains the sole owner if the value created by the processing is not considerable in proportion to the value of the delivered goods/raw materials.[248]

352. Expanded retention of title clauses (see para. 339) are considered invalid according to the case law of the Austrian Supreme Court and by the prevailing legal literature. It is assumed that these clauses violate the publicity principle under Austrian property law.[249]

2.2. *Finance leasing/sale and lease back*

353. Reference should be made to the discussion on German law (para. 342 et seq.) The actual finance leasing contract between the lessor and the lessee under Austrian law is considered a legal transaction of a special kind which mostly contains elements of rental and sales contracts.[250]

354. In relation to sale and lease back agreements the Austrian Supreme Court ruled several times that the transfer of ownership from the lessee to the lessor in order to lease the transferred object back at the same time, using a constructive possession agreement, must not be regarded as a security ownership agreement. As a consequence §452 ABGB does not apply (analogously) and the transfer of possession as an act of publicity is not required (cf. Question 3, para. 95 et seq.; Question 1, para. 32).[251]

355. For the right of the IP as the lessee to terminate the leasing contract see §23 IO, which applies to leasing contracts as well.[252] In the case of termination the

---

248 OGH Urt. v. 15.11.1976, Az.: 4 Ob 525/76 = SZ 49/138.

249 OGH Beschl. v. 25.09.1997, Az.: 2 Ob 210/97i = SZ 70/188; M. Binder and M. Spitzer in M. Schwimann (ed.), *Praxiskommentar ABGB*, Vol. 4, §1063, para. 26; J. Aicher in P. Rummel, *ABGB*, Vol. 1, §1063, para. 108.

250 OGH Urt. v. 22.11.1984, Az.: 8 Ob 607/84 = SZ 57/186; See for further details M. Binder in M. Schwimann (ed.), *Praxiskommentar ABGB*, Vol. 5, §1090, paras. 71 et seq.

251 OGH Beschl. v. 26.07.2006, Az.: 3 Ob 48/05p = [2007] 1405/234, 237; OGH Urt. v. 22.03.1988, Az.: 6 Ob 575/86 = SZ 61/70; OGH Urt. v. 24.01.1989, Az.: 4 Ob 623/88.

252 E. Feil in E. Feil, *IO*, §23, para. 7; H. Gamerith in R. Bartsch, R. Pollack and W. Buchegger (eds.), *Österreichisches Insolvenzrecht*, Vol. I, §23, para. 4.

lessor has the right to claim for separation of the leased item from the insolvency estate, §44 (1) IO, with the restrictions of §11 (2) IO (see para. 350).

2.3. *Factoring*

356. General reference should be made to the discussion on German law. Austrian law also distinguishes between non-recourse factoring (echtes Factoring) and recourse factoring (unechtes Factoring) depending on whether the factor shall bear the risk of the claim turning out to be uncollectable or not.[253] As mentioned under para. 345, where a factoring agreement bears most of the characteristics of a credit transaction, the assignment of claims is made on account of performance and therefore pursues, at least to a certain extent, security purposes (to secure the return of the advanced money paid as a purchase price). Therefore the Austrian Supreme Court had to deal several times with the question whether blanket assignments in relation to factoring contracts had to be considered as security assignments, which therefore had to meet the publicity requirements of §452 ABGB. Only in one case the court held that the assignments had to be characterised as security assignments. In that case the factor advanced the assigned claims with 80% of their nominal value. According to the factoring framework contract, after collecting the claim the remaining 20% was not to be paid out to the entrepreneur but was to be kept by the factor for the offset of potentially uncollectable claims. That was the main reason the court saw a similarity to a secured current-account loan (credit line).[254] Shortly before this, the court had ruled that a factoring contract had to be considered as a sales contract although according to the contract the factor was able to declare the cancellation of the 'sale' of specific claims if they turned out to be uncollectable and the entrepreneur had to pay interest on the advanced money. Because of the characterisation as a sales contract the assignments were not considered security assignments.[255] In later decisions the court held that ruling 8 Ob 619/92 was not to be generalised and that the established factoring contracts in practice were to be considered sales contracts even if they had a credit function, so the assignments of claims did not have to meet the publicity requirements of §452 ABGB.[256] So the courts have a tendency not to apply §452 ABGB to assignments made in connection with factoring contracts even if the contracts were characterised as

---

253 W. Thöni in A. Fenyves, F. Kerschner and A. Vonkilch (eds.), H. Klang, *ABGB*, §1392, para. 115.

254 OGH Urt. v. 13.10. 1994, Az.: 8 Ob 619/92 = [1995] ÖBA 475, 217.

255 OGH Urt. v. 17.02.1994, Az.: 2 Ob 504/94 = OGH SZ 67/29.

256 OGH Urt. v. 22.10.1998, Az.: 8 Ob 271/98f = [1999] ÖBA 806, 649; OGH Urt. v. 20.05.1999, Az.: 2 Ob 114/99z = [2000] ÖBA 841, 77, 81.

recourse factoring contracts. This may be in contradiction to the stand of the Austrian Supreme Court that an assignment made on account of performance does not have to meet the publicity requirements of §452 ABGB only if its sole purpose is to constitute the fulfilment of the sales contract without any security purposes involved,[257] which, in the case of recourse factoring agreements would generally not be the case.[258]

357. The characterisation of the assignments made under a factoring agreement as security assignments or not is of practical relevance. At first the application of §452 ABGB depends on this question, which can determine the priority between competing assignment agreements. If the assignment is not a security assignment only the contractual assignment agreement is required. Later assignments, regardless of whether they are made for security purposes or not, must be held inoperative. In the case of a security assignment, on the other hand, later assignments can 'overtake' as long as the publicity requirements are not met. The second issue that turns on this characterisation is whether the assignment gives a right to claim separation from the insolvency estate or (merely) a right to separate satisfaction (see Question 9, para. 214).[259]

358. Under Austrian law, blanket assignments in connection with factoring contracts are not considered invalid due to immorality even if they include future sales claims, which likely will be subject to an extended retention of title. Suppliers are deemed to be able to inform themselves about possible assignments of future claims that have already been made and the factoring agreement provides the entrepreneur with cash so that he is able to pay purchase prices immediately and does not require credit in respect of the goods.[260] Besides that, it is assumed that the permission to resale the delivered goods in the ordinary course of business shall be contractually valid only if the supplier actually acquires the assigned future claim arising from the resale, which would not be the case if the claim was subject to an earlier blanket assignment.[261]

---

257 OGH Urt. v. 13.10. 1994, Az.: 8 Ob 619/92 = 1 1995/475, 217, 219; OGH Urt. v. 26.06.2001, Az.: 1 Ob 290/00d = SZ 74/112.

258 W. Thöni in A. Fenyves, F. Kerschner and A. Vonkilch (eds.), H. Klang, *ABGB*, §1392, para. 120.

259 *Ibid.* at para. 121.

260 *Ibid.* at para. 121; A. Heidinger in M. Schwimann (ed.), *Praxiskommentar ABGB*, Vol. 6, §1392, para. 71; G. Ertl in P. Rummel, *ABGB*, Vol. 2, §1392, para. 104.

261 A. Heidinger in M. Schwimann (ed.), *Praxiskommentar ABGB*, Vol. 6, §1392, para. 48, with reference to OGH Urt. v. 21.06.1988, Az.: 5 Ob 566/88 = SZ 61/142.

G. TRANSACTIONS AVOIDANCE

Question 26: Are there rules in your legal system that operate once the debtor enters insolvency proceedings and that provide for the invalidation of transactions entered into by the debtor prior to the commencement of the insolvency proceedings?

1. Germany

359. German insolvency law provides for such rules. First of all §88 InsO stipulates that securities (pledges) established as a mandatory consequence of enforcement/execution proceedings become legally invalid with the opening of insolvency proceedings if they have been established within the month preceding the application for insolvency proceedings or after such request. The avoidance of legal transactions and the legal consequences of avoidance are governed by the provisions of §§129–146 InsO. These rules entitle the IP to challenge certain transactions with the consequence that received performances (or their value if the performance itself cannot be returned) must be returned to the insolvency estate, §143 InsO. If the opponent of the challenged transaction in return for a received performance which is subject to avoidance had granted a consideration to the debtor, he may claim the return of this consideration or its value as well, §144 InsO. The limitation period of this claim for return is three years, §§146 I InsO, 195 BGB InsO. To avoid the objection of limitation the IP has to bring the claim to the courts (the different limitation periods and formal requirements of declaring the avoidance of a transaction under German and Austrian law and the question in how far Article 13 EIR addresses these points were subject to a recent ECJ judgment,[262] see also the following para. 358). The specific situations under which a transaction is subject to avoidance are laid down in §§130–136 InsO. The scope of the avoidance provisions is comprehensive as the rules are applicable regardless of whether the insolvency proceedings are conducted as liquidation or plan proceedings, whether plan proceedings are conducted as debtor in possession proceedings or whether it is a case of consumer/private bankruptcy.

2. Austria

360. The situation is nearly the same as under German law. According to §12 (1)–(3) IO pledges established as a mandatory consequence of enforcement/

262 C-557/13 *Lutz v Bäuerle*, ECLI:EU:C:2015:227, para. 44.

execution proceedings become legally invalid if they have been established within the 60 days before the opening of insolvency proceedings, and the enforcement proceedings have to be terminated. The security comes into effect again if the insolvency proceedings are terminated according to §123 a IO. The security does not become legally invalid according to this provision if the attachment was made for the benefit of an authority claiming payment of public fees or charges. But in this case the attachment may be subject to contestation by the IP as §12 IO does not, in general, exclude the applicability of the avoidance rules.[263] If the attached asset already has been realised the proceeds have to be paid out to the insolvency estate. The avoidance of legal transactions is governed by the provisions of §§27–43 IO. §27 IO stipulates that any legal transactions affecting the debtor's assets can be contested by the IP according to the following provisions and therefore is to be declared invalid with respect to the insolvency creditors. The specific situations of avoidance are prescribed in §§28–32 IO. The claims of the insolvency estate and the counterparty which arise from a successful contestation are governed by §§39, 41 IO. Performances received (or their value) generally have to be returned to the insolvency estate, §39 IO. As in *Germany* the challenge of a transaction can only be declared by means of court action, §43 I IO. This action must be brought to court within one year after the opening of insolvency proceedings, §43 II IIO (see above para. 357 for Geman law and the recent ECJ judgment regarding formal requirements and limitation periods in *Germany* and *Austria* under Article 13 EIR). In its comprehensiveness the scope of the provisions is comparable to the situation under German law. One difference is that in the case of consumer/private bankruptcy it is the creditors who are granted standing to file avoidance actions since an IP is usually not appointed.

Question 27: Do these transactional avoidance rules catch security and quasi-security type transactions?

1. Germany

361. Every legal transaction disadvantaging the entirety of creditors may be subject to avoidance, §129 InsO. Due to the separation principle the IP must consider whether he has to contest either or both the conclusion of an obligational contract or the transfer or establishment of (security) rights as a matter of property law.[264] The expression 'legal transaction' in §129 InsO is

[263] P. Apathy in R. Bartsch, R. Pollack and W. Buchegger (eds.), *Österreichisches Insolvenzrecht*, Vol. I, §12, para. 8; B. König, *Die Anfechtung nach der IO*, para. 13/27.

[264] See for the expression 'legal transaction' G. Kayser in *Münchener Kommentar zur InsO*, Vol. 2, §129, paras. 7 et seq.

interpreted widely. Thus it catches any act that entails legal consequences, not only the conclusion of a contract but also factual acts. The wording of §§130 (1), 131 (1), 135 (1) Nr. 1 InsO expressly mentions the granting of securities to be possible subject to avoidance.

362. According to §129 (2) InsO an omission shall be deemed equivalent to an active transaction and therefore may be subject to avoidance as well.

2. Austria

363. As in *Germany* the expression legal transaction is interpreted widely and also includes factual acts such as the execution of a work, conduct of service, transfer of possession.[265] §§30 (1), 31 (1) IO expressly mention the granting of securities to be possible subject to avoidance.

364. According to §36 IO an omission shall be deemed equivalent to an active transaction and therefore may be subject to avoidance as well.

Question 28: If so, describe briefly these rules highlighting in particular (a) the rationale for the rules; (b) the conditions for the application of the rules; (c) the length of the 'suspect period'; (d) whether the rules apply to transactions with a cross-border element; (e) whether the rules operate more stringently in respect of transactions that favour parties who are connected to the debtor; and (f) any defences that may be availed of by a counterparty to the transaction, i.e. the defendant in an avoidance action.

1. Germany

1.1. Rationale[266]

365. Under German insolvency law the principle of equality between creditors (pari passu rule) applies. All creditors shall be satisfied out of the debtor's assets proportionate to the amount of their claims (*par condicio creditorum*). In insolvency proceedings the principle of equality between creditors displaces the principle of priority which governs the individual creditor's enforcement by writ. The principle only applies statutorily in opened insolvency proceedings but in preliminary proceedings according to §21 InsO the insolvency court may

---

265 B. König, *Die Anfechtung nach der IO*, para. 3/2.

266 See R. Bork in B. Kübler, H. Prütting and R. Bork, *Kommentar zur InsO*, Vol. II, Vor §129, para. 1 et seq.; H.-P. Kirchhof in *Münchener Kommentar zur InsO*, Vol. 2, Vor §§129–147, para. 1 et seq.

order provisional measures (such as the transfer of the power of disposal to the provisional IP, 'stays' on enforcement proceedings, etc.) which on the whole may ensure the equal treatment of creditors with almost the same effect as if insolvency proceedings had already been opened.

366. However, under specific circumstances it may seem appropriate to extend the time of a strict application of the principle to a period before the opening of insolvency proceedings or even before the request to open insolvency proceedings. There may be two main reasons for this: the first reason is that a transaction disadvantaging the creditors was carried out at a time when the debtor's insolvency was imminent or had already occurred although insolvency proceedings had not formally been filed. Here an application of the principle of equality between creditors should not depend on the formal opening of insolvency proceedings. The second reason may be that the debtor has performed the transaction with the intention to harm other creditors. While the first reason requires limiting the application of the pari passu rule to a certain period before the formal opening of insolvency proceedings (the time when substantive insolvency already has occurred or is imminent), the second reason would generally justify the avoidance of transactions prior to the commencement of insolvency proceedings without time limits. In contrast to this stands the principle of legal certainty and the legitimate expectations of contract partners as to the validity of legal transactions made with the debtor. This must be taken into account with respect to the fact that the contractual freedom of the debtor formally still exists until the opening of insolvency proceedings or until it is restricted by provisional court measures. On the other hand the expectations of other parties seem to be less worthy of protection if they are aware of the debtor's financial situation or of his intention to disadvantage other creditors, but parties cannot generally be blamed for not being aware of the distressed financial situation of their contract partners as long as it has not been made public by the opening of (preliminary) insolvency proceedings. The provisions of §§130–134 InsO prescribe the situations under which legal transactions can be contested by the IP regarding combining and balancing all the aforementioned aspects.

367. So the rationale of avoidance law in *Germany* is mainly to ensure that the pari passu principle is applied and enforced even before insolvency proceedings are filed where this seems to be appropriate. A second reason for avoidance rules connected to the first reason is to protect insolvency creditors from the debtor dissipating his assets before the opening of insolvency proceedings and from successfully withholding his assets from the attachment entailed by the opening of insolvency proceedings. This reason is especially highlighted in §134 InsO (avoidance of gratuitous benefits from the debtor). Generally speaking, avoidance rules also serve to enhance the insolvency estate in terms of the insolvency creditors.

368. The provision of §§135 InsO must be explained historically in the context of the German Federal Supreme Court's case law dealing with the restitution of shareholder loans meaning loans which are granted by shareholders to the company in the company's financial crisis.

1.2. Conditions of application/suspect period

369. One general requirement applying to all avoidance rules is that the contested legal transaction has caused a disadvantage for the creditors, §129 (1) InsO. This is the case where the transaction has increased the debtor's liabilities or reduced the value of the debtor's assets thwarting, impeding, endangering or delaying their attachment by the opening of insolvency proceedings.[267] By highlighting the relevant point in time, namely the opening of insolvency proceedings, it becomes clear that even a financially balanced transaction may constitute a disadvantage for the other creditors due to the subsequent occurrence of specific circumstances (the opening of insolvency proceedings itself may be such a circumstance). A disadvantage can be made out whenever the amount of the existing assets of the debtor available for the satisfaction of the insolvency creditors at the time of the opening of insolvency proceedings would have been higher if the contested transaction had not been concluded or conducted so only a conditional link between the transaction and the disadvantage for creditors is required. Accordingly the relevant point in time to determine whether the transaction has caused such a disadvantage to the creditors is the last hearing of facts concerning the avoidance action.[268] If a disadvantage is caused immediately by the transaction the disadvantage is called a direct disadvantage. A simple example would be the debtor's sale of an item below the market price. If the disadvantage is caused not by the transaction but afterwards due to further circumstances, it is called an indirect disadvantage. This would be the case, for example, if the debtor sold the item for the market price but the received money is no longer available for the creditors at the time insolvency proceedings are opened because the debtor lost it in the meantime.[269] Here the transaction (sale) as it was financially balanced has not caused a disadvantage for the creditors directly. Nevertheless, if it had not been concluded, the value of the insolvency estate would be greater since the sold asset would be part of it and the originally

---

267 BGH Urt. v. 16.11.2007, Az.: IX ZR 194/04 = BGHZ 174, 228, para. 18.

268 BGH Urt. v. 12.11.1992, Az.: IX ZR 237/91 = [1993] NJW-RR 235 at 236.

269 See for the distinction between direct and indirect disadvantages U. Ehricke in B. Kübler, H. Prütting and R. Bork, *Kommentar zur InsO*, Vol. 2, 129, paras. 91 et seq.; G. Kayser in *Münchener Kommentar zur InsO*, Vol. 2, §129, paras. 111 et seq.; W. Uhlenbruck in W. Uhlenbruck, *InsO*, §129, paras. 124 et seq.

received consideration, having been lost in the meantime, cannot make up for it. For the payment of a mature debt to a creditor who in opened insolvency proceedings would be an insolvency creditor see para. 387. §132 (1) InsO expressly requires a direct disadvantage for insolvency creditors. In all other cases an indirect disadvantage is sufficient.[270]

370. Some avoidance provisions require the debtor to be substantively insolvent at the time the contested legal transaction was made (§§130 (1) Nr. 1, 131 (1) Nr. 2, §132 (1) Nr. 1 InsO). These provisions refer to insolvency as the legal reason for the opening of insolvency proceedings according to §17 InsO. They do not refer to other legal reasons for the opening of insolvency proceedings being imminent insolvency (§18 InsO) and over-indebtedness (§19 InsO)[271] since otherwise the suspect period of a possible avoidance would be inadequately extended. According to the German Federal Supreme Court insolvency under §17 InsO can generally be assumed in the case of a liquidity gap of 10% or more of the total amount of the mature liabilities unless it is expected with a probability bordering on certainty that this gap will be completely or almost completely closed in the near future. So generally speaking a company must be able to satisfy more than 90% of its mature liabilities. If the gap is less than 10% of all mature debts insolvency generally must be denied unless it is already foreseeable that the gap will increase to 10% or more in the near future. Regardless of how big a liquidity gap may be, a mere delay in payments (Zahlungsstockung) excluding insolvency must be assumed if the gap can be completely closed within the next three weeks.[272]

1.2.1. §130 InsO, congruent coverage

371. According to §130 (1) InsO a transaction granting or facilitating an insolvency creditor a security or satisfaction may be contested:

1. if it was made during the last three months prior to the request to open insolvency proceedings if the debtor was insolvent at the date of the transaction, and if the creditor was aware of the debtor's insolvency on this date, or
2. if it was made after the request to open insolvency proceedings and if the creditor was aware of the debtor's insolvency on the date of the transaction, or of the request to open insolvency proceedings.

---

270 See for example BGH Urt. v. 21.06.2007, Az.: IX ZR 231/04 = [2007] NJW-RR 1419, para. 44.

271 OLG Köln urt. v. 29.09.2004, Az.: 2 U 1/04, 2 U 01/04 = [2005] NZI 112 at 114; G. Kayser in *Münchener Kommentar zur InsO*, Vol. 2, §130, para. 28c; H. Schoppmeyer in B. Kübler, H. Prütting and R. Bork, *Kommentar zur InsO*, Vol. 2, §130, para. 92.

272 See for the determination of insolvency the key decision BGH Urt. v. 24.05.2005, Az.: IX ZR 123/04 = BGHZ 163, 143.

According to §130 (2) InsO awareness of circumstances pointing directly to insolvency or to a request to open insolvency proceedings shall be considered equivalent to awareness of insolvency or of the request to open insolvency proceedings.

372. §130 InsO deals with the congruent coverage – as opposed to §131 InsO dealing with the incongruent (i.e. not owed) coverage (cf. para. 376 et seq.). The expression 'coverage' used in these provisions' headlines as it can be seen by the wording of these provisions means the granting or facilitating of either a satisfaction of a claim or of a security for a claim. Such a satisfaction or security is congruent if the creditor at the time of the transaction was entitled to claim for being granted the satisfaction or security exactly the way it was actually granted to him. It is incongruent on the other hand, if at the time of the transaction he was not entitled to such satisfaction or security at all or he was either not entitled to the kind of satisfaction or security or the satisfaction or security was granted to him at a time when he was not entitled to it (see the wording of §131 I InsO, para. 376)

373. If the coverage is congruent, §130 InsO impedes the contestation by the IP considerably by requiring the substantive insolvency of the debtor and the awareness of the creditor of the insolvency status. The IP bears the burden of proof also in respect of the subjective requirement on the side of the creditor. Awareness of circumstances pointing directly to insolvency (subsection 2) in case of institutional creditors may be assumed if the creditor is aware of the debtor's current non-payment of loans and social security liabilities. On the other hand the German Federal Supreme Court ruled that an employee who had no insight into the account of the debtor was not aware of such circumstances although he knew that the majority of the employees had not received their wages for months and newspaper articles had been published describing the financial situation of his employer.[273] So the court's interpretation (at least where no institutional creditors are involved) is rather strict.

374. §130 InsO according to its wording does not require the contested transaction to be made by the debtor. So, for example, the termination of a contract by the creditor may be subject to avoidance according to §130 InsO (if it constitutes the facilitation of a satisfaction). On the other hand, the provision requires that the benefited party would be an insolvency creditor in opened insolvency proceedings.

375. The requirement of a 'security' is interpreted widely. It not only includes the common personal and in rem credit securities. Every legal position which facilitates the enforcement of the claim for which it was granted is deemed a

273 BGH Urt. v. 19.02.2009, Az.: IX ZR 62/08 = BGHZ 180, 63, 68 et seq.

security. The granting of cheques on account of performance or the creation of an off-setting situation may be securities under §§130, 131 InsO whereas the set-off declaration itself would lead to a satisfaction of the claim.[274]

1.2.2. §131 InsO, incongruent coverage

376. According to §131 (1) InsO a transaction granting or facilitating an insolvency creditor a security or satisfaction without his entitlement to such security or satisfaction, or the kind or date of such security or satisfaction, may be contested if such transaction was made:

1. during the last month prior to the request to open insolvency proceedings or after such request;
2. within the second or third month prior to the request to open insolvency proceedings, and the debtor was insolvent on the date of the transaction;
3. within the second or third month prior to the request to open insolvency proceedings, and the creditor was aware of the disadvantage to the insolvency creditors arising from such transaction on its date.

According to §131 (2) InsO for the application of §131 (1) Nr. 3 InsO the awareness of circumstances pointing directly to the disadvantage for the creditors is treated equally to the awareness of the disadvantage itself.

377. Compared to §130 InsO, the provision facilitates the contestation of transactions by the IP as it does not require mental elements on the side of the counterparty unless the debtor was not substantively insolvent at the time of the transaction, §131 (1) Nr. 3 InsO.

378. As far as satisfactions are concerned, incongruence is assumed, for example, if anything is granted to the creditor on account of performance,[275] if a time-barred or non-actionable claim is satisfied[276] or if debt is satisfied prior to its maturity.[277]

379. If the right to a security is provided in the same contract by which the secured claim is created, the subsequent granting of the security can never constitute an incongruent coverage as long as the security is established in accordance with the security agreement because in this case the creditor has

274 G. Kayser in *Münchener Kommentar zur InsO*, Vol. 2, §130, para. 8 et seq.
275 W. Uhlenbruck in W. Uhlenbruck, *InsO*, §131, Rn. 7.
276 G. Kayser in *Münchener Kommentar zur InsO*, Vol. 2, §131, para. 14a.
277 W. Uhlenbruck in W. Uhlenbruck, *InsO*, §131, Rn. 13.

always been entitled to demand the security.[278] If then the establishment of the security cannot be contested as a congruent coverage under §130 InsO the whole contract may be contested under §§132 et seq. InsO. So §131 InsO catches the subsequent establishment of securities after the secured claim was created where originally no security rights were agreed upon or where the establishment of the security somehow deviates from an earlier security agreement. If the right to be granted a security right is agreed on after the creation of the secured claim, this security agreement cannot prevent the actual establishment of the security from being incongruent if the security agreement itself was concluded in the suspect period of §131 (1) InsO and can therefore be challenged.[279]

380. A claim to being granted a security cannot prevent the establishment of the security right from being treated as an incongruent coverage either if the security is not specified in the obligational security agreement leaving the debtor a degree of discretion to decide which assets or which kind of security he wants to grant and when he wants to grant it. So the establishment of a mortgage for the benefit of a bank is incongruent if it is established as a performance of a security agreement included in the bank's general terms and conditions only entitling the bank to claim at any time of providing or increasing of securities.[280] The question of discretion on the side of the debtor also arose where the creation of claims which were subject to an earlier blanket security assignment of future claims by the debtor was challenged by an IP. At first the German Federal Supreme Court held that creating the future claim by concluding contracts with third parties and making the future claim solid and sustainable through acts of performance such as the transfer of the item of purchase to a buyer are to be considered independent legal acts which therefore may be challenged individually. The Court than denied a discretion on the part of the debtor in respect of creating the claims (choosing the third-party contract partner, the time when to create the claim by concluding a contract, the price, etc.) on the grounds that it was clear that future claims arising in the ordinary course of business were subject to the assignment and that the parties made the agreement assuming that the debtor would continue his business accordingly.[281] Besides, according to the Court, the parties were not able at the time of the security agreement to specify these future claims any further. The Court confirmed this ruling in relation to security

---

278 BGH Urt. v. 18.03.2010, Az.: IX ZR 57/09 = [2010] NZI 439, para. 16; BGH Urt. v. 11.03.2004, Az.: IX ZR 160/02 = BGH NJW-RR 2004, 1130, 1131; BGH Urt. v. 04.12.1997, Az.: IX ZR 47/97 = NJW 1998, 1561, 1563.

279 BGH Urt. v. 25.09.1972, Az.: VIII ZR 216/71 = BGHZ 59, 230, 235 et seq.; G. Kayser in *Münchener Kommentar zur InsO*, Vol. 2, §131, para. 19a.

280 BGH Urt. v. 15.11.1960, Az.: V ZR 35/59 = BGHZ 33, 389, 393.

281 BGH Urt. v. 29.11.2007, Az.: IX ZR 30/07 = BGHZ 174, 297, para. 14 et seq.

assignments under extended and expanded retention of title clauses.[282] So it is now clarified that creating future claims under a blanket security assignment and making them solid and sustainable constitutes a congruent and not an incongruent security and can therefore only be challenged under the stricter provision of §130 I InsO. As far as the avoidance of the creation of the assigned claim is concerned, in the aforementioned cases this can be equated with the avoidance of the in rem assignment agreement. This is because according to §140 InsO the challenged transaction is deemed to be made at the time it has legal effect which in relation to the assignment of future claims is the time when the claim is created (see Question 4, para. 125 et seq.).[283] The avoidance of the underlying obligational contracts must always be regarded separately.

381. As under §130 InsO it is not required that the debtor is a party to the contested transaction (cf. para 374). If, for example, a creditor holds a mortgage over the debtor's real estate securing all of his current and future claims and another creditor of the debtor assigns to the mortgagee his unsecured claims against the debtor which are now covered by the mortgage security, this assignment is a transaction granting the mortgagee an incongruent coverage that may be contested under §131 InsO as well.[284] According to the German Supreme Court every security or satisfaction acquired by way of enforcement measures is an incongruent coverage.[285] Since this provision extends the application of the pari passu principle to the time when formal insolvency proceedings have not yet been opened although substantive insolvency has already occurred including the payment of mature debts made by the debtor after he had been put under pressure by the creditor with a threat to commence enforcement proceedings or to file for insolvency proceedings, is considered to be an incongruent coverage.[286]

1.2.3. §133 InsO, wilful disadvantage

382. According to §133 (1) InsO a transaction made by the debtor during the last ten years prior to the request to open insolvency proceedings or subsequent to such request with the intention to disadvantage his creditors, may be contested if the other party was aware of the debtor's intention on the date of such

282 BGH Urt. v. 17.03.2011, Az.: IX ZR 63/10 = BGHZ 198, 1, para. 36 et seq. In this case as far as the assigned claim only covers the value of the sold item the entirety of creditors is not even disadvantaged because the assigned claim replaces merely the security of retained ownership (exchange of securities). So only the assignment of the amount covering the margin disadvantages the other creditors.

283 BGH Urt. v. 08.03.2007, Az.: IX ZR 127/05 = [2007] NZI 337, para. 17.

284 See BGH Urt. v. 25.09.1972, Az.: VIII ZR 216/71 = BGHZ 59, 230, 235 et seq.

285 BGH Urt. v. 09.09.1997, Az.: IX ZR 14/97 = BGHZ 136, 309, 311 et seq.; BGH Urt. v. 23.03.2006, Az.: IX ZR 116/03 = BGHZ 167, 11, para. 9.

286 BGH Urt. v. 11.04.2002, Az.: IX ZR 211/01 = [2002] NJW 2568 at 2569.

transaction. Such awareness shall be presumed if the other party knew of the debtor's imminent insolvency and of the transaction constituting a disadvantage for the creditors.

383. The provision does not relate to the substantive insolvency of the debtor as do the provisions of §§130–132 InsO but imposes sanctions against a certain form of behaviour by the debtor.[287]

384. It catches all types of legal transactions including the agreement on obligational contracts and contracts on the disposal of rights such as the granting of securities and satisfaction. §133 InsO is applicable in parallel with §§130, 131, 132 and 134 InsO. It requires the challenged transaction to be made by the debtor, so for example any enforcement measures against the debtor on behalf of a creditor cannot be contested under that provision.

385. Wilful behaviour requires only a conditional intent with respect to the disadvantage for creditors. It is not required that the disadvantage for creditors is the main purpose pursued by the debtor. It is sufficient that the debtor considers a disadvantage for his creditors caused by the transaction as possible but still conducts the transaction, willing to accept this disadvantage.[288]

386. Particularly high standards must be set for proving a wilful disadvantage where the debtor performs a due claim in the way it was owed (congruent coverage) since in this case the goal of the debtor normally aims at the discharge of his debt without taking into account a disadvantage for other creditors.[289] The sale of an asset for the regular market price by the debtor alone does not justify the assumption of a wilful disadvantage just because the debtor is aware of the fact that the asset would have been easier to be attached by creditors than the money received as consideration. Here it would be required to prove the original intention of the debtor to put the received money beyond the reach of creditors.[290] The granting of an incongruent coverage, on the other hand, is considered evidence of the debtor's intention to disadvantage other creditors and the other party's awareness.[291] An intention to disadvantage creditors may be denied if the transaction in question was part of a restructuring effort even if the attempted restructuring was unsuccessful. The defence on these grounds against an avoidance action requires the restructuring attempt to be put into practice at the time of the transaction and its underlying restructuring concept

287 BGH Urt. v. 10.02.2005, Az.: IX ZR 211/02 = BGHZ 162, 143, 149 et seq.

288 BGH Urt. v. 05.03.2009, Az.: IX ZR 85/07 = BGHZ 180, 98, para. 10.

289 BGH Urt. v. 20.12.2007, Az.: IX ZR 93/06 = [2008] NZI 231, para. 19.

290 G. Kayser in *Münchener Kommentar zur InsO*, Vol. 2, §133, para. 34.

291 BGH Urt. v. 18.03.2010, Az.: IX ZR 57/09 = [2010] NZI 439, para. 18.

to be conclusive.[292] Because of its consequences for the argumentation and evidential means with respect to the subjective requirements of §133 InsO the determination whether a transaction constitutes a congruent or incongruent coverage may be very important even if the transaction was conducted before the suspect period of §§130, 131 InsO.

387. In practice, the provision is frequently applied in cases of payments made before the shorter suspect period of §§130, 131 InsO with the intention to prevent creditors from starting enforcement proceedings after the creditor or the competent enforcement authorities on behalf of the creditor have threatened the debtor with enforcement proceedings (Druckzahlungen, cf. para. 381). These are not enforcement measures as the payments are acts of the debtor designed to prevent such enforcement measures. The fact that open mature debts are satisfied by these payments (financially balanced transaction) does not prevent a disadvantage to the creditors because otherwise the money would have been attached for the entirety of the creditors and the satisfied creditor as an insolvency creditor would have received only a percentage share (indirect disadvantage, cf. para. 369).[293] In these cases substantive insolvency often has already occurred or is about to occur. If the debtor is aware of his financial situation, a conditional intent to disadvantage other creditors is presumed by the courts since the debtor then knows that these monies can no longer be used to satisfy other creditors.[294] This applies even if the payment constitutes a congruent coverage.[295] The benefited creditor, on the other hand, in such a situation will often be aware of the debtor's (imminent) insolvency because of previous unsuccessful enforcement attempts: the fact that the debt has only been partly satisfied or the fact that debtor has sought more time to pay. If in such situation the satisfied creditor is further aware of the fact that he is not the only creditor with open claims, it is presumed that the satisfied creditor knew that his satisfaction would constitute a disadvantage for the other insolvency creditors.[296]

1.2.4. §134 InsO, transactions at an undervalue[297]

388. According to §134 (1) InsO a gratuitous benefit granted by the debtor may be contested unless it was made earlier than four years prior to the request to

[292] BGH Urt. v. 08.12.2011, Az.: IX ZR 156/09 = [2012] NZI 142, para. 11.

[293] BGH Urt. v. 27.05.2003, Az.: IX ZR 169/02 = BGHZ 155, 75, 81; G. Kayser in *Münchener Kommentar zur InsO*, Vol. 2, §129, para. 123.

[294] BGH Urt. v. 27.05.2003, Az.: IX ZR 169/02 = BGHZ 155, 75, 83 et seq.

[295] BGH Urt. v. 20.12.2007, Az.: IX ZR 93/06 = [2008] NZI 231, para. 19.

[296] BGH Urt. v. 27.05.2003, Az.: IX ZR 169/02 = BGHZ 155, 75, 83 et seq.

[297] Details at R. Bork, (2014) 14 *Journal of Corporate Law Studies* 453–477.

open insolvency proceedings. According to §134 (2) InsO such benefit may not be contested if it comprises a usual casual gift of minor value.

389. The expression 'granting a gratuitous benefit' is interpreted widely. It not only includes payments or dispositions of rights such as transferring ownership or assigning receivables. It also includes the undertaking to make donations and acts such as the performance of work[298] or services.[299]

390. The determination of gratuity according to the policy of the provision (that the receiver of a gratuitous performance is less worthy of protection) depends on whether the recipient has made a 'financial sacrifice' that can be considered an adequate consideration. If this is the case, a transaction is not gratuitous even if the beneficiary of the consideration is not the debtor but a third party if the debtor had agreed to this point (see also the following para. 391).[300] It is required that such a consideration must be linked conditionally to the performance of the debtor but this link does not have to be of a synallagmatic nature.[301] The question of adequacy must be based on an objective appraisal of the facts.[302] It is only where an objectively inadequate consideration is established that the subjective ideas of the parties must be taken into account. Gratuitousness must be denied where according to the ideas of the parties the consideration was held adequate unless the parties have crossed their margin of (economic) discretion.[303] This is why fire sales under the market price are generally not considered to be gratuitous benefits.[304] The satisfaction of own debts by the creditor is gratuitous if the satisfied claim was created gratuitously. Statutory claims (e.g. liabilities in tort) are not considered to be created gratuitously.[305] Where the claim was not created gratuitously the adequate consideration is the loss of the claim on the part of the creditor. The granting of a security for a debt is only gratuitous if the debt itself was created gratuitously.[306]

391. The satisfaction of a third-party debt is gratuitous in relation to the satisfied creditor only if the satisfied claim was economically valueless because otherwise the loss of the valuable claim would be the financial sacrifice constituting the

298 BGH Urt. v. 19.04.2007, Az.: IX ZR 79/05 = [2007] NZI 403, paras. 14 et seq.
299 H. Hirte in W. Uhlenbruck, *InsO*, §134, para. 26; H. Rogge and F. Leptien in *Hamburger Kommentar zur InsO*, §134, para. 3.
300 BGH Urt. v. 24.06.1993, Az.: IX ZR 96/92 = [1993] NJW 1379, 1381.
301 G. Kayser in *Münchener Kommentar zur InsO*, Vol. 2, §134, para. 17a.
302 BGH Urt. v. 05.06.2008, Az.: IX ZR 17/07 = [2008] NJW 2008, 2506, para. 11.
303 BGH Urt. v. 01.04.2004, Az.: IX ZR 305/00 = [2004] NZI 376 at 378; BGH Urt. v. 29.11.1990, Az.: IX ZR 29/90 = BGHZ 113, 98, 102.
304 G. Kayser in *Münchener Kommentar zur InsO*, Vol. 2, §134, para. 25.
305 BGH Urt. v. 18.03.2010, Az.: IX ZR 57/09 = [2010] NZI 439, para. 9.
306 BGH Urt. v. 12.07.1990, Az.: IX ZR 245/89 = BGHZ 112, 136, 137 et seq.

adequate consideration.[307] In relation to the discharged third-party debtor, the satisfaction of his liability is gratuitous unless the debtor has fulfilled an own non-gratuitous commitment towards the third-party debtor by paying his debt because in this case the debtor only would have satisfied an own non-gratuitous liability.[308] If however this commitment itself was created gratuitously, the discharge of the third-party debtor is gratuitous as well. Granting a creditor a security for a third-party debt after the secured claim had been created is generally gratuitous in relation to the creditor unless it constitutes the discharge of a non-gratuitous commitment to the creditor[309] or the creditor provides adequate consideration for the security.[310] The continuation of a loan that could have been terminated is not an adequate consideration.[311] If the security agreement on the other hand was concluded before or at the same time as the loan agreement, the security is not granted gratuitously as the granting of credit (to the third party debtor) constitutes adequate consideration.[312]

1.2.5. §135 InsO, shareholder loans

392. According to §135 (1) InsO a transaction may be contested which, in consideration of a shareholder's claim to recovery of his loan or in consideration of an equivalent claim:

1. provided a security if such transaction was made during the ten years prior to the request to open insolvency proceedings or subsequent to such request; or
2. provided satisfaction if such transaction was made during the year prior to the request to open insolvency proceedings or subsequent to such request.

According to §135 (2) InsO a transaction may be contested by means of which a company has provided satisfaction to a third party for a claim to recovery of a loan within the period quoted in subsection (1) Nr. 2 if a shareholder

307 BGH Urt. v. 03.03.2005, Az.: IX ZR 441/00 = BGHZ 162, 276, 277 et seq.; BGH Urt. v. 16.11.2006, Az.:IX ZR 194/04 = BGHZ 174, 228, para. 8.

308 BGH Urt. v. 15.04.1964, Az.: VIII ZR 232/62 = BGHZ 41, 298, 299 et seq.

309 BGH Urt. v. 01.06.2006, Az.: IX ZR 159/04 = [2006] NZI 524, para. 7.

310 See G. Kayser in *Münchener Kommentar zur InsO*, Vol. 2, §134, para. 33a.

311 BGH Urt. v. 07.05.2009, Az.: IX ZR 71/08 = [2009] NJW 2065, para. 12; BGH Urt. v. 20.12.2012, Az.: IX ZR 21/12 = [2013] NZI 258, para. 31.

312 G. Kayser in *Münchener Kommentar zur InsO*, Vol. 2, §134, para. 33a; H. Rogge and F. Leptien in *Hamburger Kommentar zur InsO*, §134, para. 27; see also BGH Urt. v. 20.12.2012, Az.: IX ZR 21/12 = NZI 2013, 258, para. 31.

has provided security for the claim or was liable as guarantor; this shall apply correspondingly to benefits which correspond in economic terms to a loan.

393. The provisions of §§39 (1) Nr. 5, (4), (5), 44 a, 135 InsO have transferred into the insolvency law the rules governing the recovery of loans made to companies by its shareholders so as to alleviate the company's financial difficulties (old versions of §§32 a, 32 b GmbHG). These rules go back to the case law of the German Federal Supreme Court according to which such loans had to be treated not as loans but as equity capital.[313] The reason behind this rule is that in the event of a company's financial difficulties, shareholders would try to protect themselves by granting loans instead of fresh equity capital. Since shareholders in insolvency proceedings are to be paid from the remaining equity capital only after all other creditors have been satisfied (§199 InsO (which means that they will usually be left empty-handed) the shareholder's claims for the recovery of a company loan had to be treated as a subordinated claim.

394. §135 (1) InsO corresponds to §39 (1) Nr. 5 InsO according to which claims for recovery of a loan or claims resulting from legal transactions corresponding in economic terms to such a loan are considered to be subordinated claims which are to be satisfied out of the insolvency estate only after the satisfaction of the insolvency creditors. Therefore legal transactions undermining this subordination are subject to avoidance.

395. §135 (2) InsO corresponds to §44 a InsO according to which in insolvency proceedings concerning the assets of a company, a creditor may only request proportionate satisfaction from the insolvency estate for a claim for recovery of a loan for which a shareholder has provided security or for which a shareholder is liable as guarantor insofar as he is no longer able to claim the shareholder's security or liability. This is because the granting of a security or a guarantee by a shareholder for a company loan is considered to be a replacement of the loan. So the shareholder's recourse claim against the company would be subordinated according to §39 (1) Nr. 5 InsO.[314] Therefore it must be ensured that that the creditor seeks satisfaction out of the securities provided by the shareholder first before he can request satisfaction from the insolvency estate.[315] The defendant in an action for avoidance under §135 (2) InsO is not the satisfied creditor but the shareholder who by the satisfaction of the creditor was released from his liability as a security provider. The shareholder than has to reimburse the amount by which the creditor was satisfied up to the value of the security or the amount of the guarantee, §143 (3) InsO.

---

313 BGH Urt. v. 14.12.1959, Az.: II ZR 187/57 = BGHZ 258, 268 et seq.

314 G. Bitter in *Münchener Kommentar zur InsO*, Vol. 1, §44 a, paras. 24 et seq.

315 M. Gehrlein in *Münchener Kommentar zur InsO*, Vol. 2, §135, para. 37.

1.3. Restrictions

396. The possibility of challenge is restricted by the provision of §142 InsO according to which performance on the part of the debtor in return for which his property benefited directly from an equitable consideration may only be challenged under the conditions of §133 (1) InsO (wilful disadvantage, paras. 384 et seq.).

397. The application of the provision requires three conditions to be met. At first an exchange of performance and consideration must have taken place. An exchange in the sense of the provision requires that performance and consideration are linked with each other by an agreement between the parties. This is never the case where the creditor is granted an incongruent coverage since an incongruent coverage always departs from the original agreement.[316]

398. Secondly the received consideration must be considered equivalent in the sense that the received consideration must be of an equal economic value to the performance of the debtor. Whether this is the case must be determined by the objective facts at the time the first contractual service is performed. This means that only transactions causing an indirect disadvantage to creditors may benefit from the provision since transactions causing a direct disadvantage would always lack an equitable consideration (see for the distinction between a direct and an indirect disadvantage, para. 369). As far as the furnishing of securities for being granted a loan is concerned, the value of the collateral may exceed the nominal value of the loan by up to 50% and it is still considered equitable.[317] An expanded retention of title clause excludes the assumption of an equitable consideration.[318] As far as recourse and non-recourse factoring contracts are concerned, the payment by the factor not matching the nominal value of the assigned claim is considered to be an equitable consideration as it allows for a reduction in the risk of insolvency and the fees for the factor.[319]

399. The third requirement is that the exchange of performance and consideration must be exercised in a short period of time. In the case of exchange agreements a maximum period of 30 days between the performance and the counter-performance may constitute a cash transaction.[320] A cash

---

[316] BGH Urt. v. 30.09.1993, Az.: IX ZR 227/92 = BGHZ 123, 320, 328 et seq.; BGH Urt. v. 10.05.2007, Az.:IX ZR 146/05 = NZI 2007, 456, para. 10.

[317] U. Ehricke in B. Kübler, H. Prütting and R. Bork, *Kommentar zur InsO*, Vol. II, §142, para. 8; H.-P. Kirchhof in *Münchener Kommentar zur InsO*, Vol. 2, §142, para. 13c with reference to BGH Urt. v. 27.11.1997, Az.: GSZ 1/97, GSZ 2/97 = BGHZ 137, 212.

[318] H.-P. Kirchhof in *Münchener Kommentar zur InsO*, Vol. 2, §142, para. 13d.

[319] H. Hirte in W. Uhlenbruck, *InsO*, §142, para. 11. H. Rogge and F. Leptien in *Hamburger Kommentar zur InsO*, §142, para. 24.

[320] BGH Urt. v. 10.7.2014, Az.: IX ZR 192/13 = [2014] NJW 2579, para. 33.

transaction was denied where a security was established six months after the loan was granted.[321]

400. The reason behind this rule is the following: since especially under §§130, 131 InsO an indirect disadvantage for creditors is sufficient for challenging a transactionit would be almost impossible for the debtor in the financially critical time to conclude legal transactions even if he were immediately to receive an equitable consideration (e.g. buying for cash, hence the somewhat misleading heading of the provision) since contract partners would fear the later avoidance of the transaction. So the provision enables the debtor, to a certain degree, to continue business although insolvency may have already occurred.

1.4. Avoidance of transactions with a cross-border element

401. There are no restrictions in the German law on avoidance as far as cross-border transactions are concerned. German international insolvency law contains of §339 InsO which stipulates the same as Articles 4 and 13 EIR. This should imply the application of German avoidance law in cross-border cases either as the lex fori concursus or as the lex causae where the transaction is governed by German law not being the lex fori concursus.

1.5. Persons with a close relationship to the debtor

402. German avoidance law in certain aspects operates more stringently in respect of transactions that favour parties having a close relationship to the debtor (*nahestehende Personen*). §138 InsO determines which persons are legally considered to have such a relationship to the debtor. If the debtor is a natural person, persons with a close relationship will be:

1. the debtor's spouse even if the marriage was contracted only after the transaction or was dissolved during the year prior to the transaction;
   1a. the debtor's civil partner, even if the civil partnership was contracted only after the transaction or was dissolved during the year prior to the transaction;
2. the ascendants or descendants of the debtor or of the spouse designated at no. 1, or the civil partner designated at no. 1a, the debtor's full and half-blood siblings, or the spouse designated at no. 1, or the civil partner designated at no. 1a, and the spouses of such persons;

[321] BGH Beschl. v. 08.05.2008, Az.: IX ZR 116/07 = [2009] *MittBayNot* 61, para. 5.

3. persons living in the debtor's household or having lived in the debtor's household during the year prior to the transaction, as well as persons who can provide information on the debtor's financial circumstances on the grounds of a relationship based on a contract of employment or service with the debtor;
4. a legal person or a company without legal personality if the debtor or one of the persons referred to at nos. 1 to 3 is a member of the body representing or supervising the debtor, a general partner or persons holding more than one quarter of the debtor's capital, or is able, on the basis of a comparable relationship under company law or a contract of employment or service, of providing information regarding the debtor's financial circumstances.

If the debtor is a legal person or a company without legal personality, the persons with a close relationship to the debtor shall be:

1. the members of the body representing or supervising the debtor, as well as his general partners and persons holding more than one quarter of the debtor's capital;
2. a person or a company having, on the basis of a comparable association with the debtor under company law or under a service contract, the opportunity to become aware of the debtor's financial circumstances;
3. a person having a personal relationship detailed at subsection (1) with a person named at no. 1 or 2; this shall not apply if the persons named at no. 1 or 2 are legally bound to secrecy regarding the debtor's affairs.

403. §130 (3) InsO states that a person with a close relationship to the debtor existing on the date of such transaction shall be presumed to have been aware of the debtor's insolvency or of the request to open insolvency proceedings. So the first tightening of the law is provided for in the field of congruent coverages (§130 InsO) in the form of a reversal of burden of proof as far as a subjective awareness of the insolvency status of the debtor on side of the insolvency creditor is required (§130 (1) Nr. 2 InsO). The closely connected insolvency creditor has to proof that he was not aware of the insolvency at the time of the transaction.

404. The same applies to incongruent coverages and transactions directly disadvantaging insolvency creditors, §§131, 132 InsO. According to §131 (3) InsO a person with a close relationship to the debtor on the date of the transaction shall be presumed to have been aware of the disadvantage to the insolvency creditors (see §131 (1) Nr. 3 InsO). §§130 (3), 131 (3) InsO apply to §132 InsO as well, §132 (3) InsO.

405. Finally according to §133 (2) InsO an onerous contract entered into by the debtor with a person with a close relationship with him (§138) directly constituting a disadvantage for the insolvency creditors may be contested. Such contestation shall be excluded if the contract was entered into earlier than two years prior to the request to open insolvency proceedings, or if the other party was not aware of the debtor's intention to disadvantage the creditors on the date of such contract.

1.6. Defences against avoidance actions

406. There are no special defences against such actions by the IP. The general rules of civil procedure law apply. The IP has to prove that the requirements for the specific avoidance situation his action is based on are met where he bears the burden of proof and the other party denies these requirements. If he is successful or where the meeting of the requirements is legally presumed the other party has to produce (counter-)evidence that the requirements are not met.

2. Austria

2.1. Rationale

407. Reference should be made to the discussion on German law.[322]

2.2. Conditions of application/suspect period

408. As in *Germany* a general requirement of every challenge is that the challenged transaction has caused a disadvantage to the other insolvency creditors. A distinction is also made between a direct and an indirect disadvantage (see §31 Nr. 2 IO in its second variant and para. 439). The interpretation is the same as under German law so reference should be made to para. 369.[323] Furthermore under Austrian law a distinction is made between the disadvantage to creditors and the likely improvement in the position of the insolvency creditors by the challenge (Befriedigungstauglichkeit) the latter also being a requirement of a successful challenge.[324] In the German legal literature and practice this aspect

322 See B. König, *Die Anfechtung nach der IO*, paras. 1/1 et seq.

323 For details see B. König, *Die Anfechtung nach der IO*, paras. 5/32 et seq., 11/68 et seq.

324 See OGH Beschl. v. 09.02.1995, Az.: 8 Ob 27/94 = SZ 68/29.

is part of the discussion on 'disadvantage for creditors'. An example would be the debtor's sale of real estate encumbered with mortgages far exceeding its market value. Under German law such a transaction would lack the required disadvantage for insolvency creditors since the proceeds only would have benefited the holders of rights to separate satisfaction. Under Austrian law a challenge would not be successful because it would not lead to an improvement in the position of insolvency creditors.

409. As under German law some provisions governing the avoidance of transactions require that the debtor was insolvent at the time the transaction was made or determine the suspect period with reference to the fact of insolvency (§§30 (1), 31 (1) IO). According to the Austrian Supreme Court, insolvency can generally be assumed if the debtor has a liquidity gap of more than 5% of the total amount of his mature liabilities. In this case the defendant has the burden of proof that the behaviour of the debtor represented merely a delay in payments but not insolvency. Such proof requires that it seemed likely from an ex ante point of view that the debtor, after a reasonable, not too long period of time, needed to acquire enough liquidity would be able once more to pay all of his debts punctually. The required period usually must not exceed three months. A longer period of up to five months may exclude insolvency only if the assumption of a continuous liquidity gap after that time can be ruled out with a probability bordering on certainty.[325]

2.2.1. §28 (a) IO, wilful disadvantage

410. According to §28 (a) Nr. 1 IO a transaction made by the debtor during the last ten years prior to the opening of insolvency proceedings with the intention to disadvantage his creditors may be challenged if the other party was aware of the debtor's intention.

According to §28 (a) Nr. 2 IO such a transaction made by the debtor during the last two years prior to the opening of insolvency proceedings may be contested if the other party was not aware but ought to have been aware of the debtor's intention.

411. §28 (a) Nr. 1 IO is comparable to §133 (1) InsO under German law. The interpretation of the elements required by this provision mostly equals the situation in *Germany* (see para. 382 et seq.). Every type of legal transaction can be subject to challenge according to §28 (a) IO. Since the provision requires the transaction to be made by the debtor, acts of enforcement authorities conducted

[325] See the key decision on insolvency OGH Urt. v. 19.01.2011, Az.: 3 Ob99/10w = SZ 2011/2.

in enforcement/execution proceedings are considered not to be caught by the provision.[326] As far as the intention to disadvantage other creditors is concerned, a conditional intent is sufficient (cf. para. 385).[327] The granting of a congruent satisfaction or security (although not using the expression 'coverage', Austrian law distinguishes between the granting of congruent and incongruent satisfactions and securities the same way as German law, cf. para. 424) may be subject to avoidance under §28 (a) IO.[328] If a congruent performance or security was granted at a time when substantive insolvency had already occurred and the debtor was aware of his insolvency status the intention to disadvantage other creditors shall be presumed.[329] If the debtor at that time was not substantively insolvent, further specific signs of evidence for the intention are required. These could be, for example, that the debtor satisfying one creditor was at the same time denying performance towards other creditors or was delaying or preventing recovery by them in any way.[330] The granting of an incongruent coverage may be substantial evidence of the intention to disadvantage other creditors.[331] These principles also apply where payments are made to prevent creditors from pursuing enforcement proceedings.[332]

412. §28 (a) Nr. 1 IO does not contain a legal presumption concerning the awareness of the intention to disadvantage creditors on side of the other party. Nevertheless if the other party is aware of all the facts (for example the substantive insolvency in case of congruent payments) that justify the presumption of wilful behaviour by the debtor, it shall also be presumed that the other party is aware of the intention to disadvantage other creditors.[333] The other party must be aware of the intention at the time the transaction was concluded.[334]

413. §28 (a) Nr. 2 IO does not require awareness of the wilful behaviour but lack of awareness due to negligence on the side of the other party. Sufficient is any form of negligence, not only gross negligence. Whether the other party acted with negligence must be determined according to the facts of each individual case. Forms of evidence may be the obviously unfavourable conditions of the transaction, the time of the transaction, the disparity between the financial

---

326 OGH Beschl. v. 12.04.2007, Az.: 2 Ob 177/06b = SZ 2007/55; H. Koziol and R. Bollenberger in R. Bartsch, R. Pollak and W. Buchegger (eds.), *Österreichisches Insolvenzrecht*, Vol. I, §28, para. 4; B. König, *Die Anfechtung nach der IO*, para. 7/11.

327 OGH Urt. v. 30.03.2000, Az.: 8 Ob 28/00a.

328 OGH Urt. v. 03.02.1994, Az.: 6 Ob 641/93 = SZ 67/20;

329 OGH Urt. v. 03.02.1994, Az.: 6 Ob 641/93 = SZ 67/20.

330 B. König, *Die Anfechtung nach der IO*, para. 7/17.

331 OGH Urt. v. 22.11.1995, Az.:1 Ob 521/95 = SZ 68/221.

332 B. König, *Die Anfechtung nach der IO*, para. 7/17.

333 *Ibid.* at paras. 7/40, 7/32.

334 H. Koziol and R. Bollenberger in R. Bartsch, R. Pollak and W. Buchegger (eds.), *Österreichisches Insolvenzrecht*, Vol. I, §28, para. 13.

amount of the transaction and the financial status of the debtor if the other party is aware of this status.[335]

414. §28 (a) Nr. 3 IO equals Nr. 2 as far as the suspect period is concerned (two years before the opening of insolvency proceedings) and contains the legal presumption that if the transaction was concluded with or for the benefit of a party with a close relationship to the debtor (§32 IO, see para. 446) the other party was aware or due to negligence unaware of the debtor's intention to disadvantage other creditors. So the other party bears the burden of proof to the contrary.

2.2.2. §28 (b) Nr. 4 IO, dissipation of assets

415. According to §28 (b) Nr. 4 IO the conclusion of a sales, exchange or supply contract during the last year before the opening of insolvency proceedings may be challenged if the other party was aware or ought to be aware of the fact that the transaction constituted a dissipation of assets.

416. According to a part of the legal literature, in contrast to the wording, the provision shall also include the avoidance of work contracts.[336] In any case it is required that the debtor is party to the contested contract.

417. A 'dissipation of assets' requires the objective element of a considerable disparity between performance and consideration and the subjective element of recklessness on side of the debtor. Due to the subjective element, contracts which still must be considered reasonable from an economic point of view even though they might include a disparity between performance and consideration such as discounts during sales periods, do not constitute a 'dissipation of assets.'[337]

418. The provision is of little practical relevance.[338] Firstly, a considerable disparity between performance and consideration normally will indicate the intention to disadvantage other creditors, §28 (a) IO. Secondly, it must be taken into account that the avoidance of individual sales transactions of movable items in the course of the debtor's business is restricted by §34 IO. According to this provision such a transaction can only be contested according to §28 (a) IO.

---

335 *Ibid.* at para. 17.

336 *Ibid.* at para. 26; B. König, *Die Anfechtung nach der IO*, para. 8/4.

337 H. Koziol and R. Bollenberger in R. Bartsch, R. Pollak and W. Buchegger (eds.), *Österreichisches Insolvenzrecht*, Vol. I, §28, para. 29.

338 B. König, *Die Anfechtung nach der IO*, para. 8/5.

2.2.3. *§29 IO, gratuitous disposals*

419. According to §29 Nr. 1 IO gratuitous disposals of the debtor made during the last two years before the opening of insolvency proceedings may be challenged unless the transaction constitutes the satisfaction of a statutory claim, comprises a usual gift or, as long as its value must be considered appropriate, was made for charitable purposes or corresponds to a moral obligation.

420. §29 Nr. 1 IO is comparable with §134 (1) InsO under German law as far as its legal requirements and the underlying idea of the provision are concerned. The expression 'disposals' is representative for the expression legal transactions.[339]

421. According to the Austrian Supreme Court the determination of gratuity includes a considerable subjective element. On side of the debtor Austrian case law requires the intention to act gratuitously (Schenkungsabsicht).[340] As far as the subjective requirements on the other party's side are concerned, a distinction is made between one-sided gratuitous benefits and mutual contracts that contain only a partly gratuitous performance by the debtor. In the first case, the Austrian Supreme Court requires that the debtor's intention to grant a gratuitous benefit was merely recognisable by the other party.[341] In the latter case, the Austrian Supreme Court requires the other party's awareness of the intended gratuity.[342] Objective facts such as a considerable disparity between performance and consideration may be evidentiary indicators of these subjective requirements being met.[343]

422. For further details reference should be made to the discussion on German law since the interpretation of the provision equals the interpretation of §134 (1) InsO (para. 389 et seq.).[344] A difference is made where the subsequent granting of securities for an own debt is concerned. Such a transaction may constitute a gratuitous benefit even if the secured claim had not been created gratuitously, if no additional consideration is received for the security and the subjective requirements are met.[345]

---

339 *Ibid.* at para. 8/5.

340 OGH Urt. v. 24.03.2010, Az.: 3 Ob 239/09g = SZ 2010/24.

341 OGH Urt. v. 24.03.2010, Az.: 3 Ob 239/09g = SZ 2010/24.

342 OGH Urt. v. 18.10.2001, 6Ob175/01f.

343 B. König, *Die Anfechtung nach der IO*, para. 9/15.

344 See *ibid.* at para. 9/15; for the avoidance of a satisfaction of an (economically valueless) third-party debt see OGH Urt. v. 29.06.1983, Az.: 1 Ob 616/83 = [1984] JBl 495.

345 OGH Urt. v. 02.05.1979, Az.: 1 Ob 583/79; B. König, *Die Anfechtung nach der IO*, para. 9/35.

2.2.4. §30 IO, preferences

423. According to §30 (1) IO a transaction granting a creditor a security or satisfaction of the creditor's debt made after the onset of insolvency, after the request to open insolvency proceedings, or within the previous 60 days, can be challenged if:

1. the transaction granted a creditor a security or satisfaction without his entitlement to such security or satisfaction, or the kind or date of such security or satisfaction unless he was not advantaged by the transaction compared to other creditors;
2. the security or satisfaction was granted for the benefit of a party with a close relationship to the debtor (§32 IO) unless the benefited party was neither aware nor ought to have been aware of the intention of the debtor to advantage them compared to other creditors;
3. the transaction benefited an unrelated party and this party was aware of the intention of the debtor to advantage them compared to other creditors.

According to §30 (2) IO the avoidance is excluded if the advantage was granted earlier than one year before the opening of insolvency proceedings.

424. The provision deals with the granting of a security or satisfaction. Austrian law does not summarise these cases under the expression 'coverage' as German law does (cf. para. 372). Nevertheless it reveals the same underlying system (the same system is shown in §31 (1) Nr. 1, 2 IO, see para. 437). §30 (1) Nr. 1 IO has almost the same wording as §131 InsO under German law requiring an incongruent satisfaction or security whereas §30 (1) Nr. 2, 3 catches both congruent as well as incongruent satisfactions and securities. For the meaning of 'insolvency' reference should be made to para. 409.

425. All situations described in this provision require the benefited party to be a creditor at the time the transaction was made. On the other hand he is not required to be an insolvency creditor. So holders of rights to separate satisfaction or to claim separation from the insolvency estate not being insolvency creditors at the same time may be affected as well. The requirement of being a creditor excludes performances up-front from avoidance according to these provisions if the capacity of being a creditor is created only afterwards.

426. It is important to know that any contemporaneous performances (Zug-um-Zug-Leistungen) are excluded from avoidance under the provisions dealing with the granting of a congruent or incongruent satisfaction or security (§§130, 131 Nr. 1 second variant, Nr. 2 second variant IO). Contemporaneous performance is not only assumed in case of an exchange between performance and consideration but also where the creditor is provided with an additional performance he was insisting on as a condition of concluding the contract. Examples would be the buying on credit from the creditor granting him a demanded security at the same time or satisfying or securing an old debt in order to be granted new credit.[346] This is accepted by the Austrian Supreme Court on the basis that the performance by the debtor constituting a satisfaction or security is roughly contemporaneous and bears an economic connection with the consideration of the creditor. In this case the granting of a satisfaction or security is generally excluded from avoidance under §§130, 131 Nr. 1 second variant, Nr. 2 second variant IO since the other party is not considered to be a creditor in the meaning of these provisions.[347] The making of lease payments in the specific periods in which they become due also constitutes contemporaneous performance.[348]

427. The exclusion of contemporaneous performance is similar to the exclusion of cash transactions from being subject to avoidance under German law, §142 InsO (see para. 396 et seq.). Nevertheless the restriction under Austrian law is not as comprehensive since contemporaneous performance can still be challenged according to §§28, 31 Nr. 1 variant 2, Nr. 2 variant 2, Nr. 3 IO (cf. para. 438).[349]

428. §30 (1) Nr. 1 IO further requires an incongruent satisfaction or security meaning that it was either not owed at all or not exactly granted the way as it was owed. Examples of an incongruent satisfaction are the payment of a non-actionable claim, an assignment of a claim in lieu of payment if the agreement entitling the debtor to this assignment was made in the suspect period of §30 IO as well,[350] the payment of the claim before its maturity. Not incongruent shall be part payments even if they were made under pressure to prevent a creditor from pursuing enforcement proceedings,[351] presenting a cheque instead of cash payment, and the payment made by a third person according to a previous payment order issued by the debtor since this shall be considered a common practice.[352]

---

346 B. König, *Die Anfechtung nach der IO*, para. 9/41; H. Koziol and R. Bollenberger in R. Bartsch, R. Pollak and W. Buchegger (eds.), *Österreichisches Insolvenzrecht*, Vol. I, §30, para. 14, §31, para. 12.

347 OGH Urt. v. 18.01.2012, Az.: 3 Ob 168/11v = [2012] JBl 316; OGH Urt. v. 26.04.1988, Az.: 4 Ob 514/88 = SZ 61/101.

348 OGH Urt. v. 25.03.2009, Az.: 3 Ob 232/08a = SZ 2009/36.

349 B. König, *Die Anfechtung nach der IO*, para. 10/8.

350 *Ibid.* at para. 10/89 with reference to OGH Urt. v. 05.12.1983, Az.: 6 Ob 770/82; OGH Urt. v. 14.08.1996, Az.: 6 Ob 665/95.

351 B. König, *Die Anfechtung nach der IO*, para. 10/88.

352 OGH Urt. v. 14.08.1996, Az.: 6 Ob 665/95.

429. The granting of a security shall be incongruent if the creditor was not entitled to claim it according to a security agreement concluded before the suspect period, or, where the secured claim was created within the suspect period, according to the agreement by which the secured claim was created the creditor was not entitled to claim the security in the way it was granted to him.[353] If the secured claim was created within the suspect period and at the same time the parties agreed on establishing a security, the subsequent granting of the security is congruent if it was established according to the agreement.[354]

430. As under German law (see para. 380) congruence requires that the kind of security and the assets constituting the collateral are specified in the security agreement.[355] The formula 'unconditional receivables resulting from delivery and performance according to the contract up to an amount of ...% of the credit drawn' in a blanket assignment was held to be sufficiently specified.[356]

431. §§30, 31 IO do not require the legal transaction under challenge to be carried out by the debtor. So a pledge established in enforcement proceedings as a consequence of the attachment of an asset is an incongruent security which can be contested according to §30 (1) Nr. 1 IO. Avoidance is only excluded if the creditor had already been substantively entitled to demand such a pledge being granted by the debtor. An enforceable court ruling alone (concerning a claim for payment) does not entitle the creditor to be granted a pledge.[357] The satisfaction out of the proceeds in the course of the realisation of an incongruent pledge established in enforcement proceedings, on the other hand, shall be a congruent satisfaction since the creditor receives money which he originally was entitled to claim.[358]

432. §30 (1) Nr. 1 IO also requires that the creditor is advantaged by the transaction compared to other creditors. The wording of the provision ('... unless he is not advantaged ...') imposes the burden of proof for not being advantaged on the creditor. According to the Austrian Supreme Court a creditor is not advantaged if he proves that he was granted exactly what he would have received and would have been entitled to claim in opened insolvency proceedings. However, this shall only be the case if he was secured by an unavoidable security granting a right to separate satisfaction, if the satisfaction concerned a claim granting a

353 OGH Urt. v. 17.05.1988, Az.:8 Ob 608/87 = SZ 61, 122.
354 B. König, *Die Anfechtung nach der IO*, para. 10/88.
355 OGH Urt. v. 08.05.1984, Az.: 4 Ob 559/83 = SZ 57/87.
356 OGH Urt. v. 23.08.2001, Az.: 6 Ob157/01h.
357 OGH Urt. v. 07.02.1972, Az.: 6 Ob 131/71 = SZ 45/12.
358 OGH Urt. v. 07.02.1972, Az.: 6 Ob 131/71 = SZ 45/12.

right to claim separation from the insolvency estate, or if the creditor would have enjoyed a prior rank in insolvency proceedings and his claim is likely to have been fulfilled.[359]

433. §30 (1) Nr. 2, 3 IO govern the avoidance of securities or payments made because of the awareness of the debtor's intention to privilege the other party compared to other creditors. A distinction between congruence and incongruence is not made. Since the provision refers to the debtor's intention, it is argued that in contrast to §30 (1) Nr. 1 IO it is necessary that the contested transaction should have been made by the creditor.[360]

434. The intention to advantage the other party does not necessarily include the intention to disadvantage other creditors (cf. §28 IO).[361] Nevertheless the criteria to determine this intention should be nearly the same as those proving the intention to disadvantage other creditors, so reference should be made to para. 411. A conditional intention is sufficient.[362] The only difference between §30 (1) Nr. 2 and 3 IO is the different allocation of the burden of proof. Persons with a close relationship to the debtor are presumed to be aware of his intention so they bear the burden of proving the contrary.

2.2.5. *§31 IO, awareness of the debtor's insolvency*

435. According to §31 (1) IO the following transactions made after insolvency has occurred or after the request to open insolvency may be challenged:

1. a transaction granting a security or satisfaction to a party with a close relationship to the debtor for his insolvency claim and all other transactions concluded between the debtor and such a party disadvantaging the creditors unless the other party at the time of the transaction was neither aware nor ought to have been aware of the debtor's insolvency or of the request to open insolvency proceedings and in case of another transaction the disadvantage for other creditors was objectively not predictable;
2. a transaction granting a security or satisfaction to another insolvency creditor and all other transactions concluded between the debtor and another party directly disadvantaging the other creditors if the other

---

359 OGH Urt. v. 07.02.1972, Az.: 6 Ob 131/71 = SZ 45/12; B. König, *Die Anfechtung nach der IO*, para. 10/127.

360 OGH Beschl. v. 12.12.1995, Az.: 10 Ob 512/95; H. Koziol and R. Bollenberger in R. Bartsch, R. Pollak and W. Buchegger (eds.), *Österreichisches Insolvenzrecht*, Vol. I, §30, para. 10.

361 B. König, *Die Anfechtung nach der IO*, para. 10/143.

362 For details see *ibid.* at paras. 10/132 et seq.

party was aware or ought to have been aware of the debtor's insolvency or of the request to open insolvency proceedings;

3. all transactions concluded between the debtor and another party disadvantaging the other creditors if the other party was aware or ought to have been aware of the debtor's insolvency or of the request to open insolvency proceedings and the disadvantage was objectively predictable. An objective predictability can especially be made out if a restructuring concept is obviously unsuitable.

According to §31 (2) IO avoidance is excluded if the challenged transaction was made earlier than six months before the opening of insolvency proceedings.

436. For the meaning of 'insolvency' reference should be made to para. 409.

437. §31 (1) Nr. 1 and 2 IO in their first variant deal with the grant of satisfaction or security (coverage). Here it is required that the other party is an insolvency creditor and it must be kept in mind that contemporaneous performances (Zug-um-Zug-Leistungen) are not subject to avoidance under the provisions governing the avoidance of a coverage (see for further details para. 426).[363] The provision does not distinguish between congruence and incongruence and also sanctifies the other party's ignorance of the debtor's financial situation caused by negligence. It is not required that the coverage was granted by the debtor, so acts of enforcement authorities establishing pledges by attachment may be subject to avoidance according to the provision.

438. §31 (1) Nr. 1 and 2 IO in their second variant together with Nr. 3 deal with other transactions disadvantaging the other creditors. Because of the slightly different German wording between variants one and two ('Rechtsgeschäfte' instead of 'Rechtshandlungen') it is assumed that only contracts between the debtor and another party are possible subjects of avoidance.[364] Especially contracts providing for a concurrent delivery of performances (contemporaneous performances) may be challenged according to this provision (cf. para. 426).[365]

439. §30 (1) Nr. 2 IO in its second variant requires that the challenged transaction caused a direct disadvantage to other creditors. The interpretation of this legal requirement equals its German interpretation so reference should be made to

---

363 H. Koziol and R. Bollenberger in R. Bartsch, R. Pollak and W. Buchegger (eds.), *Österreichisches Insolvenzrecht*, Vol. I, §31, para. 12.

364 B. König, *Die Anfechtung nach der IO*, para. 11/49; H. Koziol and R. Bollenberger in R. Bartsch, R. Pollak and W. Buchegger (eds.), *Österreichisches Insolvenzrecht*, Vol. I, §31, para. 17.

365 B. König, *Die Anfechtung nach der IO*, para. 11/51.

para. 369.[366] §30 (1) Nr 1 IO in its second variant and Nr. 3 require merely an indirect disadvantage.

440. Where only an indirect disadvantage is required, the provision demands additionally that this advantage was objectively predictable. In most cases of concurrent delivery with no disparity between the performance and the consideration this will not be the case even if the other party was aware of the debtor's financial crisis especially if the item delivered to the debtor is suddenly lost afterwards or if the debtor later fraudulently evades the attachment of the asset entailed by the opening of insolvency proceedings.[367]

441. All situations described in §31 IO require the awareness of the other party of the debtor's insolvency or of the request to open insolvency proceedings or where there is a lack of awareness, that this was caused by negligence. As far as negligence is concerned this requirement can only be determined in each individual case at hand balancing the sources of information that were available for the other party, if it was reasonable to draw on these sources and if the given information was properly assessed.[368] If there are grounds to assume a financial crisis, the other party may be subject to further investigation duties and not meeting them may justify the assumption of negligence.[369] If the other party is a bank, generally a stricter standard applies.[370]

442. The awareness or the negligent lack of awareness and the objective predictability of the disadvantage are presumed where the other party is a person with a close relationship to the debtor ('... unless ...'); otherwise the burden of proof is imposed on the contesting IP.

2.3. *Restrictions*

2.3.1. *Contemporaneous performances*

443. At first a restriction must be seen in the Austrian Supreme Court's case law excluding agreements providing for a concurrent delivery from being subject to avoidance of congruent or incongruent satisfaction or security, see para. 426.

---

366 For example a mutual contract with a considerable disparity in value between performance and consideration see OGH Urt. v. 25.03.2009, Az.: 3 Ob 232/08a = SZ 2009/36.

367 B. König, *Die Anfechtung nach der IO*, para. 11/83 et seq.

368 OGH Urt. v. 04.05.1982, Az.: 5 Ob 586/82 = SZ 55/65.

369 OGH Beschl. v. 14.03.2012, Az.: 3 Ob 33/12t = [2013] ÖBA 1895/146.

370 OGH Urt. v. 10.07.1986, Az.: 6 Ob 595/86.

2.3.2. *§34 IO, individual sales*

444. Performances of individual sales agreements made in the debtor's course of business can only be contested according to §28 a Nr. 1–3 IO, cf. para. 418.

2.4. *Avoidance of transactions with a cross-border element*

445. §§221, 229 IO equal Article 4, 13 EIR. Reference should be made to the discussion on German law, para. 401.

2.5. *Persons with a close relationship to the debtor*

446. The persons deemed to have a close relationship to the debtor are determined by §32 IO which in most parts equals §138 InsO, see para. 402. As far as the rules of avoidance are stricter with respect to these persons reference should be made to para. 414, 434, 402.

2.6. *Defences against avoidance actions*

447. Reference should be made to the discussion on German law, para. 406.

CHAPTER 6

SECURITY RIGHTS AND INSOLVENCY LAW IN THE COMMON LAW SYSTEM

Gerard McCormack

1. The following report is drafted from the perspective of the common law. It focuses on the law in *England* though incidental references are made to the law in the *Republic of Ireland* where the law is fundamentally the same though some statutory differences do exist. The report does not consider specifically the law in *Scotland* where there is a mixed Common Law/Civil Law heritage though the statutory provisions in respect of insolvency are largely the same as those in *England.*

A. INTRODUCTION

2. There is no universally recognised definition of security rights under the common law but 'security' in this context is generally taken as signifying a right over property to ensure the payment of money or the performance of some other obligation[1] and the property over which security is taken is referred to as 'secured' or 'collateralised'.

3. It is widely understood among the international lending community that a modern law of security rights or interests/secured transactions should conform to certain key elements. These key elements are reflected in the 'Core principles for a secured transactions law' drawn up by the European Bank for Reconstruction and Development (EBRD).[2] In summary these principles are as follows:

---

1 See N. Browne-Wilkinson VC in *Re Paramount Airways Ltd* [1990] BCC 130 at 149.

2 <http://www.ebrd.com/what-we-do/sectors/legal-reform/access-to-finance.html> accessed 17 May 2016. Important work has also been done in this area by the United Nations Commission on International Trade Law (UNCITRAL) with is Legislative Guide on Secured Transactions available at <www.uncitral.org> accessed 17 May 2016 and the World Bank Group <http://www.ifc.org/wps/wcm/connect/industry_ext_content/ifc_external_corporate_site/industries/financial+markets/publications/secured+transactions+and+collateral+registries/> accessed 17 May 2016, and see generally G. McCormack, *Secured Transactions and the Harmonisation of Law.*

- the security right should constitute a property right (right in rem) that is effective in the event of the debtor's insolvency;
- the law should provide for the granting of security in the widest possible range of circumstances;
- the existence of a security right over property must be effectively publicised;
- there should be a rapid and cost-effective means of recovering the debt from the secured asset;
- the cost of creating, maintaining and exercising the right should be kept at a reasonable level.[3]

4. In essence, the common law implements these principles.[4] Firstly, security rights under the common law are rights in rem. In other words, they are enforceable against third parties including the debtor's insolvency representative and not just inter partes, i.e. between debtor and creditor.

5. Secondly, the common law provides for the granting of security in the widest possible range of circumstances. Through the 'floating charge' it is possible to create security over the entirety of a company's business operations by simply 'charging' – creating a security over – what is referred to as the company's undertaking. It is also possible to create a fixed charge over almost any asset provided that the debtor (charge giver) is restricted in the manner that it can deal with the assets that form the subject matter of the security. For instance, the courts have acknowledged the possibility of creating a 'fixed charge' over receivables that may come into existence in the future provided that the charge giver pays the proceeds of the receivables into a special bank account under the control of the charge taker.[5]

6. It is in this area of extensiveness of possible security interests that the common law earns a reputation for being favourably disposed towards the secured creditor.[6] In the 19th century legal practitioners and the courts responded to the growing needs of commerce by recognising the validity of fixed forms of security on the debtor's after-acquired property[7] and also by recognising an all-encompassing form of security – the floating charge. A floating charge is essentially a charge on a class of assets, both present and future, which permits the company creating

---

3 See also the Preface to the *Model Law on Secured Transactions* published by the European Bank for Reconstruction and Development (EBRD).

4 See for a comparison between the Model Law and English Law G. McCormack and F. Dahan [1999] *Company, Financial and Insolvency Law Review* 65 and more generally J. Norton and M. Andenas (ed.), *Emerging Financial Markets and Secured Transactions*.

5 *Siebe Gorman v Barclays Bank* [1979] 2 Lloyd's Rep 142; *Re Brightlife Ltd* [1987] Ch 200; *Agnew v Commissioner of Inland Revenue* [2001] 2 AC 710.

6 See generally on the history and development of the floating charge R. Pennington, (1960) 23 *Modern Law Review* 630.

7 *Holroyd v Marshall* (1862) 10 HL Cas 191.

the charge to dispose of a clean title to the assets which form the subject matter of the charge until some event occurs which causes the charge taker to intervene. Such an event is called a 'crystallising' event. Put another way, the corporate debtor has management autonomy with respect to the category of assets covered by the floating charge. The centrality of the floating charge was acknowledged in *Agnew v Commissioner of Inland Revenue*[8] where Lord Millett said:[9]

> 'The floating charge is capable of affording the creditor, by a single instrument, an effective and comprehensive security upon the entire undertaking of the debtor company and its assets from time to time, while at the same time leaving the company free to deal with its assets and pay its trade creditors in the ordinary course of business without reference to the holder. Such a form of security is particularly attractive to banks, and it rapidly acquired an importance in English commercial life which ... should not be underestimated.'[10]

7. Thirdly, in *England* (and also in *Ireland*) statute has supplemented the common law by publicising the existence of security interests over property through the registration of company charges regime. There is general hostility to the recognition and enforcement of secret security interests and this hostility is based on the avoidance of detriment to other creditors. Such creditors may advance credit to a company on the basis that its assets are unencumbered and are prejudiced if it later emerges that the company has in fact given security for some or all of its existing debts. The register is open to public inspection and, in this way, third parties are alerted to the scope of a company's secured borrowings.

8. The registration regime does not apply to possessory security interests – pledges and common law liens – but the fact that the creditor has possession of the items used as security may be taken as the functional equivalent of notice. There are also no notification or registration requirements in the case of security interests arising by operation of law, i.e. equitable liens. This is a gap in the system and is, perhaps, the main reason why the judiciary have set their face against any extension of the category of equitable liens.

---

8 [2001] 2 AC 710.

9 *Ibid.* at para. 8.

10 The *Agnew* case is often also referred to as *Re Brumark Ltd.* It is a decision of the Judicial Committee of the Privy Council. The Judicial Committee of the Privy Council which normally sits in London hears appeals from certain British Commonwealth countries and territories (principally in the Caribbean) – see <www.jcpc.uk> accessed 17 May 2016. There is a strong equivalence of membership between the Privy Council and the UK Supreme Court which under the Constitutional Reform Act 2005 replaced the appellate committee of the House of Lords as the UK's highest court.

9. The registration regime applies to 'charges' and not to legal instruments that might in economic terms be regarded as the functional equivalent of security, i.e. title-based mechanisms such as finance leases, factoring of receivables and retention of title clauses in sale of goods contracts. In economic terms, there are many strategies for taking what would be regarded as the functional equivalent of security but which do not, in a legal sense, involve the creation of a charge or a security interest. These alternative legal devices may help a creditor to improve its position in the event of the debtor's insolvency.[11]

10. Fourthly, English law generally provides for effective methods of recovering secured debts from secured assets. From the point of view of a charge holder there has been a traditional and especially efficacious method of enforcing security rights through the out-of-court appointment of a receiver pursuant to a facility contained in the instrument of charge.[12] Although nominally the agent of the borrowing company to which he was appointed, the basic function of the receiver is to realise the secured assets for the benefit of the secured creditor. For most cases, the Enterprise Act 2002 changed the procedure by taking away the power to appoint an administrative receiver, i.e. a receiver of the whole, or substantially the whole, of a company's property. The holder of a general floating charge may however appoint an administrator out-of-court though the administrator must perform his functions with the objective of rescuing the company as a going concern where this is reasonably practicable and even in circumstances where it is not, the administrator must not unnecessarily harm the interests of company creditors as a whole.

11. Fifthly and finally, under English law the cost of creating, maintaining and exercising security interests appear to be at reasonable levels in that there are no notarisation fees or other levies payable on instruments of charge. Registering a charge and searching the register are subject to payment of a small fee but there are no other transaction costs apart, of course, from lawyer's remuneration.

12. If English law is judged against the benchmark of the EBRD principles then it scores quite well. The main advantages are the freedom to create security interests in almost all classes of assets and the general absence of procedural barriers in respect of the creation of security interests. The disadvanatages, on the other hand, are based around the fact, firstly, that there is no single reference point for determining priorities between competing security interests in the same property;

---

11 See generally on the company charge registration system W. Gough, *Company Charges*; G. McCormack, *Registration of Company Charges*.

12 As far as floating charges created after a certain date are concerned, the Enterprise Act 2002, in the generality of cases but subject to certain exceptions, removes the power of a floating charge holder to appoint an administrative receiver over a company's assets. Section 250 Enterprise Act inserts a new section 72A into the Insolvency Act 1986 to this effect.

secondly, a tension with the goals of corporate rescue and rehabilitation; thirdly, the relatively formalistic preoccupations of the law coupled with the fact that the law is not contained in a single source but in a mixture of common law and statute, and for this reason is not easily saleable internationally.

13. Firstly and on the issue of priorities, unlike the position in the United States under Article 9 of the Uniform Commercial Code, registration of security interests does not, of itself, determine priorities between more than one security interest over the same asset and seeking satisfaction out of that asset. As far as charges are concerned, while failure to register a charge will result in the invalidation of the charge in the event of the corporate debtor entering insolvency proceedings, once registration has been duly effected then the basic rule is that priority among competing charges turns on the date of creation. Whether the charge is fixed or floating, however, may also have a role as well as whether the floating charge instrument contains a 'negative pledge' or 'restrictive' clause, i.e. a clause forbidding the creation of any subsequent security having priority to the floating charge.

14. Where there is more than one assignment of the same debt, then priority among competing assignments is determined by the order in which notice of the assignments is given to the debtor unless a subsequent assignee has actual or constructive notice of an earlier assignment at the time that the subsequent assignment is made. In the latter situation priority is governed by a simple 'first-in-time-has-priority' rule.

15. The complexities in the law governing priorities has often led to the negotiation of priority agreements between secured parties in particular cases.

16. Secondly, there is a view that the enforcement of security should not conflict with the goal of corporate restructuring. In consideration of a business rescue objective, the Enterprise Act 2002 has watered down some of the enforcement rights of security interest holders. There have been suggestions however, for a wider stay on the enforcement of security in the context of 'pre-insolvency' restructuring proceedings.[13]

17. Thirdly, the fact that the English law of security interests consists of some statutory encrustations on a thick base of judge-made law means that the law sometimes appears less than transparent to a foreign observer. The fact that it is not written down in a single statute may obscure understanding and lead to the conclusion that the law is more complex that it actually is.[14] The lack of something

---

[13] See the proposal for a restructuring moratorium which was never implemented: <http://webarchive.nationalarchives.gov.uk/+/http:/www.insolvency.gov.uk/insolvencyprofessionandlegislation/con_doc_register/RestructuringMoratoriumConsultationDocument.pdf> accessed 17 May 2016.

[14] For proposals for a Secured Transactions Code by the Financial Law Committee of the City of London Law Society, see <http://www.citysolicitors.org.uk/index.php?option=com_content&view=category&id=129&Itemid=469> accessed 17 May 2016.

in the nature of a comprehensive code attracts unfavourable comparisons with Article 9 of the US Uniform Commercial Code and the Personal Property Securities Acts in *Canada*, *Australia* and *New Zealand*, though there is a separate and distinct body of law in these countries applying to real estate.[15] By and large, however, the law of personal property security interests in these jurisdictions is set out in a single statute though the underlying principles and statutory language may be complex and there may also be a complex and multi-faceted interaction with insolvency law.

18. There have been periodic calls to reshape the English law of security interests along North American and Australasian lines.[16] These regimes also adopt a wider, functional, approach towards classification of security interests by 'recharacterising' title-based mechanisms as security interests, or at least applying many of the same rules to them.

19. Lawyers in *England*, however, generally feel comfortable with the existing legal principles and these advantages of familiarity are not easily forsaken.[17] Moreover, and more importantly, the credit industry as a whole, and banks in particular, see no obvious merits in moving over to a new system. This reluctance seems well-founded, at least from their point of view. It may be that writing a new legislative blueprint risks reopening old controversies on the scope of secured creditor rights that have long been resolved in favour of banks. When the alternatives remain to be determined, the attractions of the 'tried and trusted' are obvious. As far as practitioners are concerned, and to use a colourful metaphor, one might safely sacrifice theoretical perfection at the altar of practical utility.

B. CREATION OF SECURITY RIGHTS

Question 1: In general terms to what extent is it possible in your legal system to create security rights (rights in rem) over assets?

20. English law provides for the granting of security in the widest possible range of circumstances. Security rights under English common law are rights in rem.

---

15 See generally J. De Lacy (ed.), *The Reform of UK Personal Property Security Law*.

16 See generally G. McCormack, 'Pressured by the paradigm: the Law Commission and company security interests' in J. De Lacy (ed.), *The Reform of UK Personal Property Security Law*, 83–116; H. Beale, (2006) 43 *Canadian Business Law Journal* 178; J. Ziegel, [2006] *Lloyds Maritime and Commercial Law Quarterly* 110. More recently, see the work done by the Secured Transactions Law Reform project: <http://securedtransactionslawreformproject.org/> accessed 17 May 2016.

17 Strong opposition to US style reform proposals have been mounted by the Financial Law Committee of the City of London Law Society. Its views can be found at <www.citysolicitors.org.uk> accessed 17 May 2016 and see also the article by its chair, R. Calnan of the law firm Norton Rose Fulbright, (2005) 20(1) *Butterworths Journal of International Banking and Financial Law* 25 which summarises the views of the Financial Law Committee.

In other words, they are enforceable against third parties and not just inter partes, i.e. between debtor and creditor.

21. There are many different types of security right recognised under English law but the main feature of the secured credit industry has traditionally been the charge – whether the fixed charge or the floating charge.

22. Under the floating charge it is possible to create security over the entirety of a company's business operations by simply charging the company's undertaking. It is also possible to create an additional or alternative security – the fixed charge over almost any asset belonging to a debtor company – provided that the company is restricted in the manner that it can deal with the assets that form the subject matter of the security. For instance, the courts have acknowledged the possibility of creating a fixed charge over future receivables, i.e. income flows from contracts, provided that the charge giver pays the proceeds of the receivables into a special bank account under the control of the charge taker.[18]

23. It is appropriate to consider the different types of security right under English law and the extent to which these make it possible to 'collateralise' assets.

1. Basic distinctions

24. The main types of security interest are mortgages, charges, pledges and liens. There are three basic distinctions: firstly, between possessory and non-possessory security interests; secondly, between consensual and non-consensual security interests; and thirdly, between legal and equitable security interests. These various distinctions cut across one another.

25. The distinction between possessory and non-possessory security interests is highly significant in practical terms. Mortgages, charges and equitable liens are non-possessory security interests; in other words, the lender does not have possession of the assets used as security whereas the pledge and the common law lien are possessory in nature, i.e. the lender is entrusted with possession of the assets used as security or at least documents of title to these assets. Finally, mortgages, charges and pledges are consensual security interests i.e. in other words they are created by agreement between the parties. Liens, on the other hand, are non-consensual, i.e. they arise by operation of law, irrespective of the agreement of the parties, in certain defined circumstances.

26. The distinction between legal and equitable security interests is perhaps most confusing to a non-common lawyer but it is easy to exaggerate the importance of

---

18 *Siebe Gorman v Barclays Bank* [1979] 2 Lloyd's Rep 142; *Re Brightlife Ltd* [1987] Ch 200; *Agnew v Commissioner of Inland Revenue* [2001] 2 AC 710; *National Westminster Bank plc v Spectrum Plus Ltd* [2005] 2 AC 680.

the distinction in practice. The distinction stems from the historical distinction between the separate systems of common law and equity and the fact that certain kinds of security right were only recognised in courts of equity, as distinct from courts of common law, prior to the unification of the court structure in the 1870s. For example, a mortgage of future property was void at common law and consequently, any security interest in future property must necessarily be equitable in nature.[19] The distinction retains some importance in the context of priorities. Legal interests are said to bind the whole world whereas equitable interests are said to bind all, save for a bona fide purchaser of a legal interest in the same property for value without notice of the prior equitable interest. The priority issue is, however, affected by the question of registration because, generally speaking, a charge created by a corporate debtor is invalid in the event of the debtor going into liquidation. Moreover, if an equitable security interest on property requires registration then the fact of registration should infect the holders of subsequent legal security interests in the same property with notice.

27. A brief description of each of the different types of security right is appropriate.

2. Mortgages and charges

28. The words 'mortgage' and 'charge' are used interchangeably in many contexts[20] whereas in other settings 'charge' is defined so as to encompass a 'mortgage'.[21] There is however a distinction between the two concepts. As Slade J explained in *Re Bond Worth Ltd*[22] the technical difference between a 'mortgage' and a 'charge' lies in the fact that a mortgage involves a conveyance of property subject to a right of redemption, whereas a charge conveys nothing and merely gives the chargee certain rights over the property as security for the loan.[23] In other words, a mortgage involves the transfer of rights of ownership whereas the phrase 'charge' is a general umbrella expression to cover a right of recourse to property for security purposes.[24] The chargee has certain rights over the

19 See e.g. *Lunn v Thornton* (1845) I CB 379; *Tailby v Official Receiver* (1888) 13 App Cas 523.

20 See *Re Leyland Daf Ltd; Buchler v Talbot* [2004] 2 AC 298.

21 The Companies Act 2006 in what is now s. 859A(7)(a) provides that 'charge' includes 'mortgage'. The Law of Property Act 1925, s. 205(1)(xvi) states that 'mortgage' includes any charge or lien on any property for securing money or money's worth; and see also Insolvency Act 1986, s. 248.

22 [1980] Ch 228.

23 *Ibid.* at 250.

24 See also the comments of Buckley LJ in *Swiss Bank Corporation v Lloyds Bank Ltd* [1982] AC 584 at 595: 'An equitable charge which is not an equitable mortgage is said to be created when property is expressly or constructively made liable or specifically appropriated, to the discharge of a debt or some other obligation, and confers on the chargee a right of realisation by judicial process, that is to say, by the appointment of a receiver or an order for sale ….'

property of the chargor to ensure the payment of money due or the performance of some other obligation. The chargee is entitled to resort to the property only for the purpose of satisfying some liability due to him, and, whatever the form of the transaction, the chargor has an equity of redemption to get the property back free from the charge once the liability has been cleared.

29. In *Re BCCI (No 8)*[25] Lord Hoffmann described an equitable charge as 'a species of charge, which is a proprietary interest granted by way of security. Proprietary interests confer rights in rem which, subject to questions of registration and the equitable doctrine of purchaser for value without notice, will be binding upon third parties and unaffected by the insolvency of the owner of the property charged. A proprietary interest provided by way of security entitles the holder to resort to the property only for the purpose of satisfying some liability due to him (whether from the person providing the security or a third party) and, whatever the form of the transaction, the owner of the property retains an equity of redemption to have the property restored to him when the liability has been discharged.'

30. In *Re TXU Europe Group plc*[26] Blackburne J suggested that to create an equitable charge what must be shown is: '(1) that a particular asset (or class of asset) has been appropriated to the satisfaction of a debt or other obligation of the charger or a third party and (2) that the chargee has a specifically enforceable right to look to the asset (or class of asset) or its proceeds for the discharge of the liability.'

31. He added that whether a particular transaction gives rise to a charge depends upon the intentions of the parties, ascertained on the basis of what they have done. The intention may be express or inferred but an expression of intention would not be determinative of the legal effect of the transaction. It was equally irrelevant that the parties did not realise that the legal effect of the transaction was to create a charge, if that was in fact its effect upon a proper understanding of the evidence. The decisive consideration is whether or not an asset has been made available as security for the performance of an obligation rather than for some other purpose.

32. For instance, in *Re Cosslett (Contractors) Ltd*[27] it was held that the right of an employer under a construction contract to retain possession of equipment

---

25 [1998] AC 214.

26 [2003] EWHC 3105 (Ch), [2004] 1 P & CR D20 at para. 35. See also the comments of J. Parker LJ, speaking for the Court of Appeal, in *Edwards v Flightline Ltd* [2003] 1 WLR 1200 at paras. 47, 48 and Lord Wrenbury in *Palmer v Carey* [1926] AC 703 at 706–707 that '[a]n agreement for valuable consideration that a fund shall be applied in a particular way may found an injunction to restrain its application in another way. But if there be nothing more, such a stipulation may not amount to an equitable assignment. It is necessary to find, further, that an obligation has been imposed in favour of the creditor to pay the debt out of the fund.'

27 [1998] Ch 495.

brought onto its premises by the contractor and use it to complete the works did not constitute a charge. The employer was not given a proprietary interest in the equipment but only rights of possession and use and these rights were not by way of security. Millett LJ said:[28] 'It is of the essence of a charge that a particular asset or class of assets is appropriated to the satisfaction of a debt or other obligation of the chargor or a third party, so that the chargee is entitled to look to the asset and its proceeds for the discharge of the liability. This right creates a transmissible interest in the asset. A mere right to retain possession of an asset and to make use of it for a particular purpose does not create such an interest and does not constitute a charge.'

33. In *Re Lehman Brothers International (Europe)*[29] it was held that it was not inherent in the nature of a charge that the charge holder should be the creditor, or a trustee or fiduciary for, the creditor. It was only necessary that the charge holder should have a specifically enforceable right to have the relevant property appropriated to the payment or discharge of the relevant debt or other obligation. That right of specific enforcement transforms what might have otherwise been a purely personal right into a proprietary interest in the charged property.

34. This pragmatic nature of the charge is illustrated by the decision of the House of Lords in *Re BCCI (No 8)*[30] where a unanimous court categorically rejected the doctrine that it was conceptually impossible for a security interest to be taken by a creditor over his own obligations to the debtor, e.g. for a bank to be granted a charge over its own indebtedness to a customer.[31] In Lord Hoffmann's view, the law should be slow to declare a practice of the commercial community to be commercially impossible given the fact that the law was fashioned to suit the practicalities of life. He added that legal concepts like 'proprietary interest' and 'charge' were no more than labels given to clusters of related and self-consistent rules of law. Such concepts did not have a life of their own from which the rules were inexorably derived.

35. The difference between a fixed and floating charge lies in the degree of control exercised by the person taking the benefit of the charge though it must be recognised that the concept of 'control' is somewhat problematic. If the charge giver has the authority to sell or dispose of assets covered by the charge in the ordinary course of business, without having to get the consent of the charge taker, then the charge is a floating charge. If, however, the charge giver has no such authority, then the charge is a fixed charge.

---

28 [1998] Ch 495 at 508.

29 [2012] EWHC 2997 (Ch) at para. 43.

30 [1998] AC 214.

31 As was held by Millett J in *Re Charge Card Services Ltd* [1987] Ch 150.

3. Pledges

36. A pledge involves the actual or constructive delivery of possession of an asset to a creditor by way of security. In the case of a pledge, the pledgee (lender) is given possession of the items pledged whereas ownership of the items remains with the pledgor (borrower).[32] As possessor, the pledgee is said to enjoy a 'special property' in the goods but the general property however, or what might be termed 'ownership', still belongs to the pledgor.[33] The actual or constructive delivery of possession is necessary to the creation of a pledge but the delivery of possession need not be contemporaneous with the making of the loan. The requirement of delivery means that the class of assets capable of forming the subject matter of a pledge is confined to goods and to documentary intangibles, i.e. documents of title where the entitlement to the asset can be transferred by delivery of the document with any necessary indorsement.[34] Pledges may be created in respect of documents of title to goods but not over common commercial contracts. Bills of lading, i.e. shipping documents, are regarded by mercantile usage as documents of title in respect of the cargo referred to in the documents and the fact that a bill of lading may be pledged suggests the usefulness of pledges for the financing of international trade.[35] The requirement, however, that a creditor takes a pledge over a document which is actually a document of title implies the limitations of the pledge as a security vehicle. Warehouse receipts are not, for example, documents of title nor are certificates relating to registered shares.[36] Bearer share certificates are, however, documents of title.

37. The usefulness of the pledge mechanism has been extended by judicial validation of three techniques. The first is that of 'constructive delivery of possession'.[37] The second is that of attornment and the third technique is the 'trust receipt'. The concepts of 'constructive delivery of possession' and 'attornment'

32 See generally Willes J in *Halliday v Holgate* (1868) LR 3 Ex 299.

33 The pledgee has an inherent right to sell unredeemed chattels after the loan period has expired. In *Matthew v TM Sutton Ltd* [1994] 4 All ER 793 it was held that a pledgee who sells unredeemed chattels for more than the sum owed by the pledgor holds the surplus as a fiduciary on trust for the pledgor.

34 In *Armstrong DLW GmbH v Winnington Networks Ltd* [2012] EWHC 10, [2013] Ch 156 the judge suggested (at para. 47) that documentary intangibles were 'documents of title to the payment of money (instruments) (including bills of exchange, promissory notes and cheques), to negotiable securities (e.g. bearer bonds and notes) and to goods (e.g. bills of lading). Documentary intangibles that can be transferred by endorsement (rather than mere delivery) are termed "negotiable"'.

35 For an explanation of some of the historical background to bills of lading see *Sewell v Burdick* (1884) 10 App Cas 74.

36 *Harrold v Plenty* [1901] 2 Ch 314.

37 The example was given in *Hilton v Tucker* (1888) 39 Ch D 669 of delivery of a key as the symbol of possession where the transfer of possession itself was practically impossible.

were explained by the court in *Official Assignee of Madras v Mercantile Bank of India Ltd*:[38] 'At common law a pledge could not be created except by a delivery of possession of the thing pledged, either actual or constructive. It involved a bailment. If the pledgor had the actual goods in his physical possession, he could effect the pledge by physical delivery; in other cases he could give possession by some symbolic act, such as handing over the key for the store in which they were. If, however, the goods were in the custody of a third person, who held for the bailor so that in law his possession was that of the bailor, the pledge could be effected by a change of the possession of the third party, that is by an order to him from the pledgor to hold for the pledgee, the change being perfected by the third party attorning to the pledgee, that is acknowledging that he thereupon held for him; there was thus a change of possession and a constructive delivery; the goods in the hands of the third party became, by this process, in the possession constructively of the pledgee.'

38. As the judicial statement shows, where goods are in the possession of a third party rather than the debtor, the third party can 'attorn' to the creditor, i.e. undertake to hold the goods for the benefit of the creditor. For instance, if the debtor is an art dealer who has deposited works of art with an auction house, the latter can, by 'attorning' in favour of the creditor, transfer constructive possession of the art works to the creditor and create a pledge in the creditor's favour.

39. On the third technique, the 'trust receipt' permits a pledgee to release goods to his pledgor as agent for sale and trustee of the proceeds but simultaneously maintaining the pledge interest.[39] The fact that goods are released back by the 'pledgee' to the 'pledgor' will not prejudice the claim to a pledge where the release takes place on the basis of a trust receipt. Trust receipts received the approval of the courts in *North Western Bank Ltd v Poynter, Son and Macdonalds*.[40] It was held that a pledgee may redeliver the goods to the pledgor for a limited purpose without thereby losing its rights under the contract of pledge. Pledgees of a bill of lading representing a specific cargo returned the bill of lading to the pledgors to obtain delivery of the merchandise and sell it on the pledgees' behalf and account for the proceeds towards satisfaction of the debt. The court took the view that the pledgees' security was not affected and that they were entitled to the proceeds of the cargo as against the general creditors of the pledgors.

38 [1935] AC 53 at 58–59. In this statement, the bailor is the pledgor.

39 See generally *North Western Bank Ltd v Poynter, Son and Macdonalds* [1895] AC 56; *Re David Allester Ltd* [1922] 2 Ch 211.

40 [1895] AC 56.

4. Liens

40. There are three forms of lien: common law lin, equitable liens and contractual liens. The common law lien is a right to retain possession of an asset until discharge of an outstanding debt. It is founded on possession and, except as modified either by statute or by contractual agreement between the parties, merely confers a right to retain the asset until payment.[41] The equitable lien, on the other hand, is essentially a form of non-possessory security interest arising by operation of law. The equitable lien is not dependent on possession and the holder of the lien has the right to request an order of sale from the courts.

41. In *Tappenden v Artus*[42] Diplock LJ compared the common law remedy of a possessory lien with other 'primitive remedies' such as abatement of nuisance, self-defence or ejection of trespassers to land. The remedy was said to be a self-help one. Diplock LJ said the possessory lien was a remedy in rem exercisable on the goods and its exercise required no intervention by the courts, for it was exercisable only by a person who had actual possession of the goods subject to the lien. A common law lien afforded a defence to an action for recovery of the goods by a person who, but for the lien, would be entitled to immediate possession.

42. Common law liens are non-consensual in nature and are confined to historically determined situations. For instance, in *Your Response Ltd v Database Business Media*[43] it was held that it was not possible to have a common law lien over intangible property. This meant that when the parties to a database-hosting contract did not provide in the agreement what was to happen to the database when the contract ended, the service provider had to return the database to the customer. The provider could not claim a common law lien over the database to ensure payment of its fees.

43. Statute however has sometimes brought into existence lien-type rights. Section 88 Civil Aviation Act 1982,[44] which was considered in *Bristol Airport plc v Powdrill*,[45] serves as a case in point. The section confers on airport authorities the right to detain aircraft to force payment of unpaid airport charges. The Court of Appeal took the view that the statutory right of detention was a 'lien or security'

41 There is a procedure laid down for the disposal of uncollected goods including those deposited for storage and repair in s. 12 and Schedule 1 of the Torts (Interference with Goods) Act 1977.

42 [1964] 2 QB 185.

43 [2014] EWCA Civ 281.

44 For an Irish equivalent see section 40 of the Air Navigation and Transport (Amendment) Act 1998.

45 [1990] Ch 744.

over property within the meaning of section 248 of the Insolvency Act 1986. In general a common law lien equals a passive power of detention. The lienee may, however, have a power of sale in the case of a statutorily-conferred lien as is the situation with section 88 Civil Aviation Act 1982. Moreover, statute sometimes gives the holder of the lien a power of sale in other circumstances.[46]

44. An equitable lien is a form of equitable charge arising by operation of law.[47] In other words, it is a right against property which arises automatically in certain circumstances to secure the discharge of an actual or potential indebtedness. The equitable lien may be enforced by obtaining an order for the sale of the property from the court.[48] The best-known equitable liens are the vendor's lien for unpaid purchase money and the purchaser's lien; both arising in the case of contracts for the sale of land.[49] The former is founded on the principle that 'a person, having got the estate of another, shall not, as between them, keep it, and not pay the consideration.'[50] The purchaser's lien rests on the converse principle that a person who has agreed to convey property in return for a purchase price should not be allowed to keep the price if he fails to convey the property as agreed.[51]

Question 2: Is it possible to create security rights over all assets of the debtor?

45. A distinction should be drawn in this connection between corporates and individuals. As far as corporates are concerned, English law permits 'all-assets' security through the medium of the floating charge and this facilitates lending.

46. As the Law Commission has pointed out, it is also possible for consumers to borrow on the security of assets but significant legal obstacles exist in the way of this:[52] 'If a lender wishes to take a charge or mortgage over a consumer's existing goods, they must comply with the complex requirements laid down in the Bills of Sale Acts. Some of the restrictions imposed by those Acts are valuable.

---

46 See, for example, Torts (Interference with Goods) Act 1977, sections 12 and 13. Moreover, under the Civil Procedure Rules, r. 25.1(1)(c)(v) the court has power to order the sale of any property which is the subject of a claim or as to which any question may arise on a claim and which is of a perishable nature or which for any other good reason it is desirable to sell quickly.

47 See generally on equitable liens the decision of the High Court of Australia in *Hewett v Court* (1983) 149 CLR 639.

48 *Bowles v Rogers* (1800) 31 ER 957; *Re Stucley* [1906] 1 Ch 67.

49 Under sections 41–43 Sale of Goods Act 1979 an unpaid seller of goods has a possessory lien and also a right to stop goods in transit but the courts have refused to recognise equitable liens in sale of goods transactions that operate independently of the legislation – *Re Wait* [1927] 1 Ch 606.

50 *Mackreth v Symmons* (1808) 15 Ves 329 at 340; 33 ER 778 at 782.

51 See *Rose v Watson* (1864) 10 HL Cas 672 at 684.

52 Law Com (2005) 296 *Company Security Interests* at para. 1.50. The report is available at <www.lawcom.gov.uk/> accessed 17 May 2016.

For example, the requirement that all the consumer's property be listed in the documents prevents consumers from charging goods that they may acquire in the future and from creating a floating charge over their goods.'

47. The Bills of Sale Acts date from the 19th century and essentially require that charges over goods granted by individuals should be in a certain prescribed form and registered at court offices.[53] The requirements of the Acts are difficult to comply with in practice but non-compliance with the statutory requirements means that the security granted by the documentation is void; not only against the grantor's trustee in bankruptcy but also against the grantor himself. The obscure and archaic statutory provisions[54] mean that consumer finance in *England*, when done on a 'secured' basis, is generally done through 'quasi-security' arrangements such as the hire-purchase/conditional sale agreement. Bills of Sale lending, however, has increased, particularly with respect to loans over motor vehicles and the rise of specialist lenders. This has led to calls for reform of the Bills of Sale Acts and the implementation of new measures of consumer protection.[55] For example, the Consumer Credit Act 1974 provides that where a debtor under a hire-purchase or conditional sale agreement has paid more than a third of the price, the creditor may not repossess the goods except by means of a court order. This procedural safeguard does not apply in respect of bills of sale. If a debtor defaults on a loan that is secured by a registered bill of sale, the lender, on serving a default notice, may obtain possession of the goods (an example being a motor vehicle) without any court order.[56]

---

53 The main Acts are the Bills of Sale Acts of 1878 and 1882. The registration requirement is laid down in s. 8 of the 1878 Act. The prescribed form is set out in a schedule to the 1882 Act. See generally G. McBain, (2011) 5 *Journal of Business Law* 475. There is similar Bills of Sale legislation in Ireland.

54 See the comments of Vos J in *Chapman v Wilson* [2010] EWHC 1746 (Ch) at para. 129: 'The twists and turns of the Bills of Sale Acts have already been the subject of much judicial and academic comment ... The issues raised in these proceedings have been complicated by their outdated provisions. One cannot help but think that the introduction of a modern system of registration offering protection and clarity to creditors, consumers and chattel-owners alike, is long overdue.'

55 See the Department for Business, Innovation and Skills consultation on proposals to ban the use of bills of sale for consumer lending: <https://www.gov.uk/government/uploads/system/uploads/attachment_data/file/31481/a_20better_20deal_20for_20consumers_20consultation_20on_20proposals_20to_20ban_20the_20use_20of_20bills_20of_20sale_20for_20consumer_20lending.pdf> accessed 17 May 2016. In the event, the proposals were never implemented and instead an industry Code of Practice was put in place instead – see: <https://www.gov.uk/government/uploads/system/uploads/attachment_data/file/31484/11-516-government-response-proposal-ban-bills-of-sale.pdf> accessed 17 May 2016. See now the Law Commission proposals on Bills of Sale: <http://www.lawcom.gov.uk/project/bills-of-sale/> accessed 17 May 2016.

56 Bills of Sale (1878) Act (Amendment) Act 1882, sections 7 and 7a as amended by the Consumer Credit Act 2006.

48. The Agricultural Credits Act 1928 exempts 'agricultural charges' as defined in the Act from the requirements of the Bills of Sale legislation. Essentially, the Act permits individual farmers to grant fixed or floating charges over their livestock and machinery without having to adhere to the burdensome Bills of Sale Acts conditions.[57] The Act is designed to facilitate lending but is of marginal significance since extensive farming in the *UK* is often carried out under the corporate umbrella.[58]

49. For corporates, the floating charge developed in the 19th century. It is essentially a charge on a class of assets, both present and future, which permits the company creating the charge to dispose of a clean title to the assets which form the subject matter of the charge until some event occurs which causes the holder of the charge to intervene. Such an event is called a 'crystallising' event. Put another way, the corporate debtor has management autonomy with respect to the category of assets covered by the floating charge. The centrality of the floating charge in English lending practice was acknowledged in *Agnew v Commissioner of Inland Revenue*.[59] Lord Millett said:[60] 'The floating charge is capable of affording the creditor, by a single instrument, an effective and comprehensive security upon the entire undertaking of the debtor company and its assets from time to time, while at the same time leaving the company free to deal with its assets and pay its trade creditors in the ordinary course of business without reference to the holder. Such a form of security is particularly attractive to banks, and it rapidly acquired an importance in English commercial life which … should not be underestimated.'

50. In *Re Spectrum Plus Ltd*[61] Lord Scott explained the history and development of the floating charge. He said: 'By the middle of the 19th century industrial and commercial expansion in this country had led to an increasing need by companies for more capital. Subscription for share capital could not meet this need and loan capital had to be raised. But the lenders required security for the loans. Traditional security, in the form of legal or equitable charges on the borrowers' fixed assets, whether land or goods, could not meet the need.

---

57 See section 5 of the Act.

58 In Ireland, the Agricultural Credit Act 1978 applies. Sections 23 and 26 of the Act requires that charges, whether fixed or floating, over agricultural stock cannot take effect unless they are registered in local courts offices. The Act applies to charges created both by individuals and by companies. In *Re Castlemahon Poultry Products Ltd* (13 December 1985, unreported) it was held that registration with the Companies registry means that a company does not have to register a second time in the chattel mortgage register under the Agricultural Credit Act though there is no express statutory basis for this decision. In the UK, the Agricultural Credits Act 1928 only applies to charges granted by individual farmers – see s. 5(7).

59 [2001] 2 AC 710.

60 *Ibid.* at para. 8.

61 [2005] 2 AC 680 at paras. 95, 97.

The greater part of most entrepreneurial companies' assets would consist of raw materials, work in progress, stock-in-trade and trade debts. These were circulating assets, replaced in the normal course of business and constantly changing. Assets of this character were not amenable to being the subject of traditional forms of security.'

51. Lord Scott pointed out that by the last decade of the 19th century the 'floating security' had become firmly established and was in regular use. This new form of security was not created by statute but had been developed by lawyers and judges out of the needs of the commercial and industrial entrepreneurs of the time.

52. Floating charges have been the subject of statutory regulation for over a century, although there is no statutory definition of a floating charge. The expression 'floating charge' bears the meaning attributed to it by judicial decision. A leading account of the floating charge is contained in the judgment of Romer LJ in *Re Yorkshire Woolcombers Association Ltd*[62] and this description refers primarily to the nature of the assets over which the security is taken.[63] Romer LJ said:[64] '[If] a charge has the three characteristics that I am about to mention it is a floating charge. (1) If it is a charge on a class of assets of a company present and future; (2) if that class is one which, in the ordinary course of the business of the company, would be changing from time to time; and (3) if you find that, by the charge, it is contemplated that, until some future step is taken by or on behalf of those interested in the charge, the company may carry on business in the ordinary way as far as concerns the particular class of assets I am dealing with.'[65]

53. Normally a fixed charge is taken over 'fixed' or specific assets, and a floating charge over circulating assets. The essence of the distinction however, is the autonomy of the charge giver in dealing with the assets charged. If the charge giver has freedom to deal with the assets charged in the ordinary course of business then the charge is a floating charge but if the charge giver has no such freedom then the charge is a fixed charge. The distinction nevertheless becomes somewhat blurred in that the floating charge is compatible with some restrictions on the debtor's conduct and such restrictions are common in floating charges.[66] In *Re Cosslett (Contractors) Ltd*[67] it was held that the fixed/floating charge

62 [1903] 2 Ch 284.

63 The nature of the floating charge was first set out by the Court of Appeal in *Re Panama, New Zealand and Australian Royal Mail Co* (1870) 5 Ch App 318.

64 [1903] 2 Ch 284 at 295.

65 It should be stressed that it is the members of the class rather than the boundaries of the class that is changing.

66 The leading cases are *Re Brumark Ltd; Agnew v Commissioner of Inland Revenue* [2001] 2 AC 710 and *National Westminster Bank plc v Spectrum Plus Ltd* [2005] 2 AC 680.

67 [1998] Ch 495.

distinction turned on the question of control over the charged assets. Millett LJ observed:[68] 'The chargor's unfettered freedom to deal with assets in the ordinary course of business free from the charge is obviously inconsistent with the nature of a fixed charge; but it does not follow that his unfettered freedom to deal with the charged assets is essential to the existence of a floating charge … The question is not whether the chargor has complete freedom to carry on his business as he chooses, but whether the chargor has control of the charged assets.'

54. Apart from the fact that the security giver has a greater liberty to dispose of the assets in the ordinary course of business, there are many other reasons for distinguishing between fixed and floating charges over property.[69]

55. First, under the provisions of the Insolvency Act dealing with the avoidance of transactions, the floating charge is more vulnerable to challenge in a liquidation than a fixed charge. Both fixed and floating charges as well as other forms of transaction are subject to attack under section 239 of the Insolvency Act, which renders voidable acts or things done by an insolvent company in the six-month period immediately prior to liquidation or administration that have the effect of putting a creditor in a better position than it would occupy in the event of the company's insolvent liquidation and where the company was influenced by a desire to prefer the creditor or a guarantor for the debt. The 'influenced by a desire' criterion has been interpreted as requiring a subjective wish to improve the creditor's position[70] and means that in practice there is very little chance of setting aside transactions unless the benefit has gone to a connected person.[71] On the other hand, floating charges alone are caught by the more draconian and far-reaching section 245 of the Insolvency Act 1986. This provision invalidates floating charges granted by insolvent companies to secure past indebtedness in the 12-month period prior to liquidation or administration.

56. Secondly, the fixed charge outranks the floating charge for priority purposes. Where there are two charges over the same property, one fixed and one floating,

68 [1998] Ch 495 at 510. The decision of the Court of Appeal was upheld by the House of Lords – see *Smith (Administrator of Cosslett (Contractors) Ltd) v Bridgend Borough Council* [2002] 1 AC 336.

69 Both fixed and floating charges (and indeed the other forms of security interest) exist in the Republic of Ireland and it is necessary to make the distinction for largely similar reasons though tax claims still have preferential status in Ireland in certain circumstances and there is no carve out of floating charge realisations for the benefit of unsecured creditors. The legislation relating to insolvency is also largely similar though there is no exact equivalent to administration. Instead, there is an 'examinership' procedure introduced by the Companies (Amendment) Act 1990 which performs broadly similar functions. See generally on this procedure T. Courtney, *The Law of Companies*, Chapter 22.

70 *Re MC Bacon Ltd* [1990] BCC 78.

71 The company is presumed to have been influenced by a desire to prefer if the preference was given to a connected person and there is also a longer two-year vulnerability period.

the fixed charge holder will generally prevail over the floating charge holder in any priority battle. This has given rise to the expression 'the fixed charge for priority; the floating charge for control'.

57. Thirdly, under what is now section 176A of the Insolvency Act 1986, introduced by section 252 of the Enterprise Act 2002, a proportion of set floating charge recoveries are set aside for the benefit of unsecured creditors.[72] The percentage is calculated on a sliding scale basis and constitutes 50% of the first £10,000, then 20% of the remainder but subject to an overall ceiling of £600,000 so that the fund for unsecured creditors will not in any case exceed £600,000.[73] The set aside provisions, however, only operate in respect of floating charges. If a security taker has the benefit of a fixed charge, its security will not be subject to the carve-out for unsecured creditors.

58. Fourthly, preferential claims are payable out of floating charge assets in priority to the floating charge holder, though the latter can recoup itself out of the free assets of the company to the extent that these assets are sufficient to satisfy the claims secured by the floating charge.[74]

59. Fifthly, in an administration it appears that under Schedule B1, paragraph 99(3) of the Insolvency Act 1986 the administrator's remuneration and expenses are payable out of floating charge assets in priority to the floating charge holder, but these items cannot be paid in the same way out of fixed charge assets.[75]

60. Finally, under the Insolvency Act 1986 the holder of a floating charge over the whole or substantially the whole of a company's assets has certain powers in relation to the appointment of an administrator, including the power to make an appointment out of court.[76]

61. A floating charge 'crystallises', i.e. becomes fixed, upon the happening of certain events. The effect of crystallisation is to terminate the company's management authority, i.e. its freedom to dispose of assets in the ordinary course of business clear of the security interest. It seems, however, on the basis of normal agency principles that a third party who is unaware that crystallisation has occurred

---

[72] The Enterprise Act abolished Crown Preference and the fund for unsecured creditors was established as a balancing measure to ensure that the benefits of the abolition did not go exclusively for the benefit of unsecured creditors. The fund has its origins in a recommendation of the Cork Committee on Insolvency Law and Practice (1982 Cmnd 8558 at para. 1538) that 10% of net realisations of property subject to a floating charge should be set aside for unsecured creditors.

[73] SI 2003/2097 Insolvency (Prescribed Part) Order 2003, SI 2003/2097.

[74] Insolvency Act 1986, ss. 40 and 175.

[75] See also Insolvency Act 1986, s. 19.

[76] Insolvency Act 1986, ss. 72A–H (which were added by Enterprise Act 2002, s. 250) and Schedule B1 of the Insolvency Act which contains the substantive law on 'new' administrations.

pursuant to an automatic crystallisation is entitled to assume the continuance of a company's managerial authority implied by the floating charge until cessation of that authority has been brought explicitly to its attention.[77]

62. The floating charge crystallises upon the charge holders, or their trustees, taking possession or appointing a receiver. It also crystallises if certain events occur which, under the instrument of charge, renders the security enforceable. If the company goes into liquidation the charge will also crystallise.

63. In *Re Woodroffes (Musical Instruments) Ltd*[78] it was decided that the cessation of a company's business had the same effect. This was because cessation removed the raison d'être of the floating charge, which was to permit the company to carry on business in the ordinary way insofar as the class of assets charged was concerned.

64. Then, in *Re Brightlife Ltd*,[79] Hoffmann J held that notice given by the charge holder to the chargor could convert a floating charge into a fixed charge. He said it was not open to the courts to restrict the contractual freedom of parties to a floating charge. He pointed to the limited and pragmatic interventions by the legislature in the area and suggested that these rendered it wholly inappropriate for the courts to impose additional restrictive rules on grounds of public policy.

65. The decision in *Re Brightlife Ltd* opens the door for clauses that stipulate for crystallisation on the occurrence of events such as borrowing of the company exceeding a certain level or its assets falling below a stated sum. These events may take place at a time unknown to the chargee, so that he is not aware that crystallisation has occurred.

66. One of the objectives of widely drafted crystallisation clauses is to secure the charge holder as prominent a place as possible in the queue of creditors. The Insolvency Act 1986 has, however, reduced the attractions of automatic crystallisation clauses in this respect. According to sections 40 and 175 of the Insolvency Act, preferential debts are payable in priority to the claim secured by a floating charge in a receivership or liquidation.[80] A floating charge is defined in section 251 of the Insolvency Act, for the purpose, inter alia, of these provisions,

---

77 See the comments of McGarvie J in the Australian case *Horsburgh v Deputy Commissioner of Taxation* (1984) 54 ALR 397 at 413 who doubted whether 'modern equity would be forced to run in such established grooves that if employees received pay and customers bought goods from a company, while reasonably unaware that the property of the company, had become subject to a fixed equitable charge, they would be losers'.

78 [1986] Ch 366.

79 [1987] Ch 200.

80 In Ireland, the equivalent provisions – now sections 440 and 621 Companies Act 2014 – have now been interpreted by the Supreme Court in the same way – see *Re JD Brian Ltd* [2015] IESC 62 – overturning the decision of the High Court at [2011] IEHC 113.

as a charge that, as created, was a floating charge.[81] So even if a floating charge has crystallised automatically prior to receivership or liquidation, it still ranks after the preferential creditors. A crystallised floating charge will still, however, take priority over a prior ranking floating charge, a subsequently created equitable fixed charge and execution creditors.

Question 3: Is it possible to create security rights over assets not yet owned by the debtor at the time of the creation of the security interest?

67. It is possible to create security rights over assets not yet owned by the debtor at the time of the creation of the security interests by means of both fixed and floating charges. In respect of the extensiveness of security interests, English law earns a reputation for being favourably disposed towards the secured creditor.[82]

68. In the 19th century legal practitioners and the courts responded to the growing needs of commerce by the development of an all-encompassing form of security – the floating charge. The transition from an agricultural to an industrial economy brought about by the Industrial Revolution meant that only a small proportion of a company's wealth might be tied up in buildings and fixed equipment. The bulk of a company's assets could now be in the form of raw materials, manufactured goods or goods in the process of manufacture, stock-in-trade and debts owed to the company by trade customers. The existing fixed forms of security could not capture fully these assets and the advent of the limited liability company meant that bank lending on a totally unsecured basis was an even more hazardous proposition.[83] There were two major developments in response to this state of affairs.

69. Firstly, the validity of fixed charges on after-acquired property – both goods and receivables – was recognised.[84] *Holroyd v Marshall*[85] is the leading House of Lords authority from the 19th century concerning goods. Lord Westbury said in the case that 'if a vendor or mortgagor agrees to sell or mortgage property, real or personal, of which he is not possessed at the time, and he receives the consideration for the contract, and afterwards becomes possessed of property answering the description in the contract, there is no doubt that a Court

81 See also the Insolvency Act 1986, s. 29(2).

82 See generally on the history and development of the floating charge R. Pennington, (1960) 23 *Modern Law Review* 630.

83 Limited Liability Act 1855.

84 *Holroyd v Marshal* (1862) 10 HL Cas 191 and *Tailby v Official Receiver* (1888) 13 App Cas 523.

85 *Holroyd v Marshall* (1862) 10 HL Cas 191 at 209 and *Tailby v Official Receiver* (1888) 13 App Cas 523. According to M. Bridge, L. Gullifer, G. McMeel and S. Worthington, *The Law of Personal Property*, 178 the House of Lords in *Holroyd v Marshall* 'insisted that it was merely applying established principles of law, although the facts suggest this rather underplays the decision's significance'.

of Equity would compel him to perform the contract, and that the contract would, in equity, transfer the beneficial interest to the mortgagee or purchaser immediately on the property being acquired.' The contract binds the property as soon as it comes into existence.

70. In *Tailby v Official Receiver*[86] the House of Lords confirmed the validity of an assignment of future receivables by way of security. The case concerned a security instrument that purported to assign all the book debts due and owing, or which might, during the continuance of the security, become due and owing to the security provider.[87] It was held that the assignment of future book debts, though not limited to book debts in any particular business, was sufficiently defined. It transferred to the security taker the equitable interest in book debts that arose after the date of the assignment, whether these debts arose from the business carried on by the security provider at the time of the assignment or in any other business. Lord Macnaghten said[88] that it 'has long been settled that future property, possibilities and expectancies are assignable in equity for value. The mode or form of assignment is absolutely immaterial provided the intention of the parties is clear. To effectuate the intention an assignment for value, in terms present and immediate, has always been regarded in equity as a contract binding on the conscience of the assignor and so binding the subject matter of the contract when it comes into existence, if it is of such a nature and so described as to be capable of being ascertained and identified.'

71. Secondly, the floating charge received approval from the courts and this form of security makes it possible to create a security interest over the entire existing and future assets of a corporation with relative ease. In *Re Panama, New Zealand and Australian Royal Mail Co*[89] an instrument of charge (debenture) purported to charge a company's undertaking. It was held that the word 'undertaking' referred to all the property of the company, not only that existing at the date of the debenture, but also including property that might be acquired by the

86 (1888) 13 App Cas 523.

87 There is not a statutory definition of book debts but they are generally defined as debts that could or would be entered as books of account as debts owing to the business – *Paul and Frank Ltd v Discount Bank (Overseas) Ltd* [1967] Ch 348. They are an asset of the business in the same way as land or buildings. The meaning of the word 'receivable' depends on the particular contractual or statutory context but it may potentially encompass assets or income flows that are not caught by the expression 'book debts'. Lending agreements may purport to create a charge over both 'book debts and receivables'.

88 (1888) 13 App Cas 523 at 543 and see also his comments at 546 that '[l]ong before *Holroyd v. Marshall* was determined it was well settled that an assignment of future property for value operates in equity by way of agreement, binding the conscience of the assignor, and so binding the property from the moment when the contract becomes capable of being performed, on the principle that equity considers as done that which ought to be done...'

89 (1870) 5 Ch App 318.

company subsequently. Moreover, the word 'undertaking' was taken to infer that the company could carry on business in the ordinary way without interference by the charge holder.

Question 4: Is it possible to create security rights over assets that are not yet in existence at the time of the execution of the security agreement?

72. Yes. This can be done in the same way as it is possible to create security rights over assets not yet owned by the debtor at the time of the creation of the security interest.

Question 5: Is it possible to have a 'global security agreement', i.e. covering all assets of the debtor?

73. This can be done by means of the floating charge. Corporate debtors can create a floating charge over their entire business operations if they simply charge their 'undertaking'.

74. The requirements of the Bills of Sale Acts means that it is not practicable for individuals to create 'all assets' security.[90]

Question 6: In general terms, what are the formalities in your legal system for the creation of a security interest over assets?

75. In theory and in general there are no special requirements under English law for the creation of a security interest. Both charges and pledges may be created orally though invariably there will be a written security agreement which may be long and detailed.

Question 7: Do the rules for the creation of security rights vary depending on the nature of the asset in question?

76. There are some variations depending on the nature of the asset in question.

77. Under section 2 of the Law of Property (Miscellaneous Provisions) Act 1989 a contract for the sale of an interest in land must be in writing and the wording is sufficiently broad to include the creation of a security interest over land.[91] So oral security interests of whatever type over land are impermissible.

---

90 Law Com no 296 *Company Security Interests* (2005) at para. 1.50. The report is available at <www.lawcom.gov.uk/> accessed 17 May 2016.

91 In Ireland the relevant provision is s. 2 Statute of Frauds (Ireland) Act 1695 which requires an agreement for the sale of an interest in land to be evidenced in writing.

78. The different types of security interest that may exist have somewhat different formality requirements. Since 2003 the only way of creating a legal mortgage over registered land is by what is referred to by statute as a charge by deed expressed to be by way of legal mortgage.[92] The shorthand for this is a legal charge and the deed simply states that the property in question has been charged with the debt by way of legal mortgage.[93]

79. An equitable mortgage over land can arise in two situations. The first is where the 'owner' has merely an equitable rather than a legal interest in the property. In this circumstance any mortgage is necessarily equitable in character. The second situation is where there is a contract to create a legal mortgage. Equity regards as done what ought to have been done and an equitable mortgage is deemed to come into existence as soon as there is a specifically enforceable contract for the creation of a legal mortgage.

80. No specific form or language is required for the creation of an equitable charge on land, although the effect of section 53(1) Law of Property Act 1925 may be that such a charge can only be created in writing, signed by the chargor or his agent. Apart from this, it suffices if language is used which makes it clear that the creditor has a right to look to the property for payment of the debt.

81. There is also a special form for mortgages of ships. In accordance with the Merchant Shipping Act 1995 and the Merchant Shipping (Registration of Ships) Regulations 1993[94] legal mortgages of ships must be in a prescribed form[95] and there is also provision under the legislation for a centralised register for ships, divided into separate Parts for different kinds of ship. It should be noted however that the requirement for a prescribed form only applies to legal mortgages and not to equitable mortgages.

82. In respect of intellectual property rights, section 30(6) of the Patents Act 1977 provides that any assignment or mortgage of a patent is void unless it is in writing and signed by or on behalf of the assignor or mortgagor.[96] It is laid

---

92 See generally R. Megarry and W. Wade, *The Law of Real Property*, Chapter 24. With registered land, title to the land is registered at the Land Registry. It is to be contrasted with unregistered land where there is no statutory register of title. Nearly all urban land is now registered land – see generally <www.landregistry.gov.uk/> accessed 17 May 2016.

93 See s. 87 Law of Property Act 1925 and s. 23 Land Registration Act 2002. In Ireland, under s. 89 of the Land and Conveyancing Law Reform Act 2000, all mortgages can only be created by way of charge. This provision applies to unregistered titles what previously, under s. 62 of the Irish Registration of Title Act 1964, was the position in respect of registered titles under the Irish Land Registry and see also the Property Registration Authority in Ireland <www.prai.ie/> accessed 17 May 2016.

94 SI 1993/3138. For the Irish provision see s. 50 Merchant Marine Act 1955.

95 Merchant Shipping Act 1995, s. 16 Sch. 1.

96 In Ireland, s. 79 Patents Act 1992 provides that the rules of law applicable to the ownership and devolution of personal property shall apply in relation to patent applications and patents as they apply in relation to other choses in action.

down in the Trade Marks Act 1994 that a charge on a registered trade mark is not effective unless it is in writing signed by or on behalf of the chargor.[97] Similar requirements apply in respect of security over registered designs.[98]

C. ENFORCEMENT OF SECURITY RIGHTS

Question 8: To what extent is it possible for the secured party to enforce the security without having to use formal court procedures?

83. Traditionally under English law, secured creditors have had great freedom and flexibility in relation to the enforcement of their security interests. The enforcement of security has been seen largely as a self-help remedy to be exercised by the secured creditor in accordance with the provisions of the security agreement. The enforcements rights vary somewhat, however, depending on the nature of the security and the type of secured asset (collateral).

1. Pledges and pawns

84. In the case of a pledge, if the pledgor defaults in respect of the loan agreement, then the pledgee has authority to sell the goods pledged and to apply the proceeds in discharge of the debt.[99] There is no requirement that the sale should be by way of public auction but, nevertheless, the sale must be a provident one. If, however, the proceeds of sale are insufficient to discharge the debt, then the pledgee has a right of action against the pledgor in respect of the balance. In *Jones v Marshall*[100] it was explained that if the item pledged does not realise the amount lent on it, the pledgee may bring an action for the deficit. The converse case was examined in *Matthew v TM Sutton Ltd*[101] and it was held that a pledgee who sells unredeemed chattels for more than the sum owed by the pledgor holds the surplus as a fiduciary on trust for the pledgor.

85. There appears to be a statutory exception to this in section 120 Consumer Credit Act 1974 which applies where the loan period is at least six months; the pledge has not been redeemed and the amount of the credit does not exceed £75. This seems to be a pragmatic response to the situation where low-value items are pledged to a 'pawnbroker' and the pledger takes no steps to redeem the pledge.

---

97 Section 24(3) and (4). Section 28 of the Irish Trade Marks Act 1996 is in similar terms.

98 Registered Designs Act 1949, s. 15B. For Ireland see s. 76(3) Industrial Designs Act 2001.

99 See Bowen LJ in *Re Hubbard ex parte Hardwick* (1886) 17 QBD 690 at 698.

100 (1890) 24 QBD 269.

101 [1994] 4 All ER 793.

Effectively the pawnbroker is allowed to take the items in satisfaction of the debt but, in theory, the items could be worth a lot more than the outstanding debt.

86. The expression 'pawnbroker' connotes somebody who makes small loans in return for the pledge of domestic goods. The services of a pawnbroker were often availed of by persons denied conventional sources of credit, and in 19th-century literature a strong association was made between pawn broking and the driving of harsh bargains.[102] The recent financial crisis may have witnessed a revival of this rudimentary form of credit though pawn broking has long been subject to statutory controls which contain a measure of consumer protection including the Pawnbrokers Acts 1872–1960. These Acts have now been replaced by the Consumer Credit Act 1974. Sections 114–122 of the Consumer Credit Act lay down various requirements that must be complied with in respect of transactions of pawn or pledge but the regime covers only 'articles taken in pawn under a regulated consumer credit agreement'.[103] All consumer credit agreements are now regulated by the 1974 Act unless specifically exempted, regardless of the amount of the credit. The Act does not apply, however, to cases where the pledgor is a body corporate.

2. Possessory liens

87. In the case of a possessory lien, the remedies of the holder of the lien (lienee) are in general much more restricted than would be the case if the transaction was in the nature of a pledge. The distinction between the two types of transaction is well established. In *Donald v Suckling*,[104] for instance, it was observed:[105] 'In the case of a simple lien there can be no power of sale or disposition of the goods, which is inconsistent with the retention of the possession by the person entitled to the lien; whereas in the case of a pledge or pawn of goods, to secure the payment of money at a certain day, on default by the pawnor, the pawnee may sell the goods deposited and realise the amount, and become a trustee for the surplus for the pawnor; or even if no day of payment be named, he may, upon waiting a reasonable time, and taking the proper steps, realise his debt in like manner.'

88. The powers of a lien holder, however, may be expanded either by contract between the parties or by statute. For instance, in relation to the statutory lien

102 See C. Dickens, *Sketches by Boz* and K. Chesney, *The Victorian Underworld*. See generally N. Palmer, *Bailment*, 1380.

103 For Ireland see the Pawnbrokers Act 1964, which remains in force, and in particular ss. 29 and 30.

104 (1866) LR 1 QB 585.

105 *Ibid.* at 604.

granted by the Civil Aviation Act 1982 in respect of unpaid airport charges, section 82 provides that the airport authority may sell the aircraft in order to satisfy the charges if the charges are not paid within 56 days of the date when the detention begins.

3. Mortgages and charges

89. With the pledge and the possessory lien, the creditor already has possession of the assets that are subject to the security interest. Mortgages and charges are non-possessory security interests but the charge holder may seek possession of the property as a prelude to sale and obtaining satisfaction of the debt from the proceeds of sale of the property. In fact, it has even been held in respect of a legal mortgage that the mortgagee 'may go into possession before the ink is dry on the mortgage unless there is something in the contract, expressly or by implication, whereby he has contracted himself out of that right'.[106] No such power exists in relation to a charge.[107] But a well-drafted security agreement would typically contain extensive provisions specifying circumstances of default in which the creditor may take control of, and ultimately sell, the debtor's property.

90. The Consumer Credit Act contains detailed measures on protection for consumers in respect of credit transactions including mortgages and charges over land and goods. But the Act is subject to a number of exemptions which means that most mortgages for house purchase or commercial finance are excluded though second mortgages on residential property securing consumer loans would be included. Where the consumer credit legislation does apply, the creditor must serve a default notice specifying the nature of the alleged breach. If the breach is capable of remedy, the debtor must be given at least 14 days to remedy the breach. If the breach is not capable of remedy, then the default notice should specify the sum that is required to be paid as compensation for the breach and give the debtor at least 14 days to pay.[108]

91. The debtor is also given the right to redeem the loan early at any time and the court, if it appears just to do so, may suspend any possession order and/or provide for the payment by instalments of any sums owed having regard to the

106 *Four Maids Ltd v Dudley Marshall (Properties) Ltd* [1957] Ch 317 at 320.

107 In respect of equitable mortgages of land, s. 90 Law of Property Act 1925 provides that the court may make an order of possession in favour of the secured party as a preliminary to sale. In Ireland, under s. 97 Land and Conveyancing Law Reform Act 2009, a mortgagee may not take possession of mortgaged property unless the mortgagor consents in writing to such taking at least 7 days beforehand.

108 See ss. 87 and 88 Consumer Credit Act 1974.

means of the debtor.[109] Also in the cases of land mortgages subject to the Act, a court order is needed for enforcement.[110]

92. More generally, in cases where the secured property consists of or includes a dwelling house, the court is given a wide statutory discretion in possession actions either to adjourn those proceedings, suspend the execution of any possession order, or postpone the date for delivery of possession for such period as it thinks fit.[111]

93. Leaving aside these provisions, the common law is pretty tolerant of self-help enforcement of security rights under mortgages and charges. Under the standard charge of corporate assets, once payment is due under the terms of the loan agreement,a demand for payment has been made and sufficient time has elapsed to allow the debtor to implement the mechanics of payment,[112] the secured creditor may enforce the security by taking possession of the secured assets. The more normal practice, however, would be to appoint a receiver over the charged assets and section 101 Law of Property Act 1925 confers an express power to appoint a receiver of the income of the charged property. The Insolvency Act 1986 also introduced the concept of an 'administrative receiver' defined as a receiver of the whole, or substantially the whole of a company's property, appointed by a floating charge holder.[113]

---

109 Section 94 Consumer Credit Act 1974.

110 Section 126 Consumer Credit Act 1974. In Ireland there is the Consumer Protection Code produced by the Central Bank under various statutory powers including section 8H of the Consumer Credit Act 1995. Entities regulated by the Central Bank must comply with the code. Failure to comply may result in the Central Bank using its administrative sanctions procedure and culminating in the entity losing its licence to operate in Ireland. Failure to comply with the code will not however, automatically invalidate a loan or mortgage contract, or render it unenforceable – *Friends First Finance Ltd v Cronin* [2013] IEHC 59.

111 See s. 36 Administration of Justice Act 1970 and s. 8 Administration of Justice Act 1973. The effect of a possession order on 'family life' under the European Convention on Human Rights, implemented in the UK by the Human Rights Act 1998, must also be considered. For more general powers in Ireland to stay orders for possession and sale of mortgaged property, see s. 101 Land and Conveyancing Law Reform Act 2009. See also s. 2 of the Irish Land and Conveyancing Law Reform Act 2009, which permits the adjournment of possession proceedings affecting the mortgagor's principal private residence to facilitate the making by the mortgagor of a proposal for a personal insolvency arrangement. There has been some disagreement in the Irish courts about whether a failure to comply with the requirements of the Code of Conduct on Mortgage Arrears (CCMA) promulgated by the Irish Central Bank might affect a mortgagee's ability to obtain a possession order in relation to residential mortgage property – compare *Stepstone Mortgage Funding Limited v Fitzell* [2012] IEHC 142 with *Irish Life & Permanent plc v Duff* [2013] IEHC 43. In *Irish Life and Permanent plc v Dunne* [2015] IESC 46 it was held by the Irish Supreme Court that so far as a breach of the Code involves a failure by a lender to abide by the moratorium period referred to in the Code, but in no other circumstances, non-compliance with the Code affects, as a matter of law, a lender's entitlement to obtain an order for possession.

112 See *Bank of Baroda v Panessar* [1987] Ch 335.

113 Section 29(2) Insolvency Act 1986.

4. Receivership as a security enforcement remedy

94. Receivership as a remedy developed historically in the context of real property. The remedy developed because secured creditors were reluctant to take possession of mortgaged property due to the potential risks of incurring a liability to the mortgagor.[114] A secured creditor who went into possession was liable on the basis of 'wilful default'. In consequence, the practice developed of the mortgagee instead appointing a receiver and manager who would take possession of the mortgaged business and proceed to run its operations with a view to using the proceeds so as to reduce the secured debt.[115] Also, contracts of loan began to specify that any receiver appointed would be deemed to be the agent of the mortgagor rather than the mortgagee. This state of affairs has received statutory endorsement. Section 109(2) of the Law of Property Act 1925 provides that any receiver appointed pursuant to that statute is deemed to be the agent of the mortgagor who is solely responsible for the receiver's act or defaults unless the mortgage deed provides otherwise.[116] Section 44 of the Insolvency Act 1986 lays down that an administrative receiver is deemed to be the company's agent unless and until the company goes into liquidation.[117]

95. Hoffmann J commented however in *Gomba Holdings (UK) Ltd v Homan*[118] that while nominally the agent of the company, the receiver's primary duty is to realise the assets in the interests of the charge holder and its powers of management are really ancillary to that duty.

96. The peculiar incidents of the agency were stressed by the Court of Appeal in *Silven Properties Ltd v Royal Bank of Scotland*:[119] 'In particular: (1) the agency is one where the principal, the mortgagor, has no say in the appointment or identity of the receiver and is not entitled to give any instructions to the receiver or to dismiss the receiver … (2) there is no contractual relationship or duty owed in tort by the receiver to the mortgagor: the relationship and duties owed by the

---

114 *Gaskell v Gosling* [1896] 1 QB 669 and [1897] AC 575.

115 The historical development of the law was explained by Rigby LJ in *Gaskell v Gosling* [1896] 1 QB 669 at 692–693. This judgment was approved by the House of Lords in the same case: [1897] AC 575. For the distinction between a receiver on the one hand and a receiver and manager on the other, see Jessel MR in *Re Manchester & Milford Rly Co* (1880) 14 Ch D 645 at 653.

116 For the Irish provision see s. 108 Land and Conveyancing Reform Act 2009.

117 The Republic of Ireland does not have the administrative receiver/non-administrative receiver distinction but the same basic law on receiverships applies. Section 439 Companies Act 2014 provides that: 'A receiver, in selling property of a company, shall exercise all reasonable care to obtain the best price reasonably obtainable for the property as at the time of sale.' See also s. 103 Land and Conveyancing Law Reform Act 2009.

118 [1986] 3 All ER 94 at 97.

119 [2004] 1 WLR 997 at para. 27.

receiver are equitable only … (3) the equitable duty is owed to the mortgagee as well as the mortgagor. The relationship created by the mortgage is tripartite involving the mortgagor, the mortgagee and the receiver; (4) the duty owed by the receiver (like the duty owed by a mortgagee) to the mortgagor is not owed to him individually but to him as one of the persons interested in the equity of redemption … (5) not merely does the receiver owe a duty of care to the mortgagee as well as the mortgagor, but his primary duty in exercising his powers of management is to try and bring about a situation in which the secured debt is repaid … (6) the receiver is not managing the mortgagor's property for the benefit of the mortgagor, but the security, the property of the mortgagee, for the benefit of the mortgagee ….'

97. A receiver, in realising the secured property, has a duty to exercise reasonable care to obtain the best price reasonably obtainable at the time of sale. This is a duty owed to the debtor, subsequent creditors and guarantors of the secured debt[120] but the duty does not extend to a guarantor who has not been called to pay under the guarantee.[121]

98. On the other hand, it seems to follow from the Privy Council decision in *China and South Sea Bank Ltd v Tan*[122] there is no duty owed to exercise reasonable care about the timing of sale. This view was endorsed by the Court of Appeal in *Silven Properties Ltd v Royal Bank of Scotland*[123] and applied in *Bell v Long*.[124] In the latter case it was held that receivers were entitled to sell four properties in a portfolio at a discount to their individual valuations. The receivers were entitled to choose the time of sale and the portfolio sale produced a guaranteed disposal of all the properties compared with the uncertainties of a longer period of marketing against a background of changing market conditions.

99. The administrative receiver/receiver distinction was introduced in 1986 by the Insolvency Act. Administrative receivers are, broadly, receivers appointed under floating charges on the whole or substantially the whole of the company's

---

120 *Standard Chartered Bank v Walker* [1982] 1 WLR 1410. Alternatively, it may be argued that where a secured creditor, or his receiver, sacrifices or impairs the security or by his neglect or default allows it to be lost or diminished, the surety is entitled to be credited with the deficiency in reduction of his liability.

121 *Burgess v Auger* [1998] 2 BCLC 478. See also *Raja v Austin Gray* [2002] EWCA Civ 1965, [2003] BPIR 725.

122 [1990] 1 AC 536.

123 [2004] 1 WLR 997. See also *Den Norske Bank ASA v Acemex Management Co Ltd* [2003] EWHC 326 (Comm), [2003] 2 All ER (Comm) 318; *Saltri III Ltd v MD Mezzanine SA* [2012] EWHC 3025(Comm), [2013] 1 All ER (Comm) 661 and *Alpstream AG v PK Airfinance* [2015] EWCA Civ 1318. It seems there is no difference in this connection between a receiver appointed under the Law of Property Act and an administrative receiver – see *Raja v Austin Gray* [2002] EWCA Civ 1965, [2003] BPIR 725.

124 [2008] EWHC 1273 (Ch), [2008] BPIR 1211.

property. Schedule 1 to the Insolvency Act 1986 confers various implied powers on an administrative receiver including power to carry on the business of the company. Essentially, the appointment of an administrative receiver will displace the board of directors from its management functions though the directors remain in office and are still empowered to carry out various non-management tasks.

100. The role of administrative receivers is considerably more important than that of other types of receiver, though the Enterprise Act 2002 introduced reforms to the Insolvency Act by abolishing the right to appoint administrative receivers in the generality of cases. A non-administrative receiver of part of the company's business may also be required by the administrator to vacate office.[125]

101. There are still however a significant number of residual cases where administrative receivers may be appointed. These are set out in sections 72B–72GA of the Insolvency Act 1986 and, in the main, cover high-end financing transactions and sector-specific financing, particularly in the context of public-private partnerships. Section 72B refers to capital market investments where a party incurs or, when the agreement was entered into, was expected to incur, a debt of at least £50m under the arrangement. The remaining sections relate to the following areas: section 72C: public-private partnerships with step-in rights; section: utilities; section 72DA: urban regeneration projects; section 72E: financed project companies including step-in rights; section 72F: charges in connection with financial markets; section 72G: registered social landlords; section 72GA: protected railway companies.

102. Perhaps the greatest potential is offered by the capital markets exception in section 72B and the project finance exception in section 72E, although reliance on the latter provision failed in *Feetum v Levy*.[126] Section 72E(2)(a) provides that a project is a 'financed project' if under an agreement relating to the project a project company incurred, or when the agreement was entered into, expected to incur, a debt of at least £50m for the purposes of carrying out the project. In *Feetum v Levy* there was no expectation that the company would borrow at least £50m and therefore the exception was held not to apply. Moreover, it was held that there were no 'step-in rights' within the meaning of the provision. Under section 72E, a project has step-in rights if a person who provided finance in connection with the project had a conditional entitlement under an agreement to: (a) assume sole or principal responsibility under an agreement for carrying out all or part of the project, or (b) make arrangements for the carrying out of all, or part of, the project. The lending agreement stated that any administrative receiver appointed was the agent of the company and not of the lender. Therefore,

125 Para. 41(2) Schedule B1 Insolvency Act 1986.
126 [2005] EWCA Civ 1601, [2006] Ch 585.

if the receiver decided to carry out the project, the borrower would be treated in law as carrying it out or as making the necessary arrangements to do so. The lender was not entitled to make the arrangements to carry out the project for it was dependent on the discretionary decision of the receiver. Consequently, the project was not one in which there were step-in rights. The case holds that the power to appoint an administrative receiver should not be equated with step in rights. Otherwise, the inclusion of a requirement for step-in rights would become superfluous.[127]

5. Foreclosure and 'appropriation' as security enforcement remedies – financial collateral

103. The expression 'foreclosure' is sometimes used as a journalistic shorthand for sale of charged property and paying the charge holder out of the proceeds of sale with the surplus going to lower-ranking charge holders in order of priority and then any balance becoming available to the debtor (chargor). The chargor is said to have an 'equity of redemption', i.e. a right to any balance that remains after the secured debt(s) plus any expenses of realisation have been paid.

104. But the expression 'foreclosure' has a traditional and somewhat different technical meaning denoting a process whereby the creditor takes the mortgaged property in satisfaction of the secured debt and the borrower's equity of redemption is extinguished.[128] Foreclosure actions require a court sanction and today the court would invariably order a sale of the property rather than authorising foreclosure in the strict, technical sense.[129] In *Palk v Mortgage Services*[130] Nicholls VC remarked that 'foreclosure actions are almost unheard of today and have been so for many years. Mortgagees prefer to exercise other remedies. They usually appoint a receiver or exercise their powers of sale.'

105. The Financial Collateral Arrangements (No 2) Regulations 2003, however, introduced a remedy of appropriation into English law and this remedy has some similarities with the foreclosure remedy. Appropriation may be defined as the sale by the secured party to itself of the collateral at a price that is commercially reasonable. The regulations are designed to implement the EU

127 See Jonathan Parker LJ at para. 93.

128 For a small scale statutory equivalent of forfeiture see s. 120 Consumer Credit Act 1974.

129 In Ireland, s. 96(2) Land Conveyancing Law Reform Act 2009 abolishes the mortgagee's right of forfeiture.

130 [1993] Ch 330 at 336.

Financial Collateral Directive,[131] which is part of the EU's Financial Services Action Plan,[132] and contain a number of provisions that impact on the English law of security interests. The Directive makes provision for the establishment of a Europe-wide regime under which cash, financial instruments, and now credit claims,[133] may be used as collateral under both security interest and title transfer structures.[134] According to the preamble, this will aid in the 'integration and cost-efficiency of the financial market as well as to the stability of the financial system in the Community, thereby supporting the freedom to provide services and the free movement of capital in the single market in financial services.'[135]

106. Member States may exclude the application of the Directive where one of the parties to the collateral transaction is neither a public authority nor a financial institution.[136] In fact, the *UK* in the Financial Collateral Arrangements (No 2) Regulations 2003 not only did not avail itself of the opt-out, but 'gold plated' the Directive and applied the new regime to all cases where the collateral provider and the collateral taker are both non-natural persons.[137] In *Ireland* the financial

---

131 Directive 2002/47/EC on financial collateral arrangements (OJ 2002 L168). The SI 2003/3226 Financial Collateral Arrangements (No 2) Regulations 2003 have been amended by the Financial Markets and Insolvency (Settlement Finality and Financial Collateral Arrangements) (Amendment) Regulations 2010, SI 2010/2993, which, inter alia, introduce a new definition of possession of financial collateral. In Ireland the implementing regulations are now the European Communities (Financial Collateral Arrangements) Regulations 2010, SI 626/2010.

132 COM (1999) 232. The Financial Services Action Plan is designed to contribute to the creation and maintenance of more efficient and competitive financial markets in Europe.

133 The extension to cover credit claims was made in the 2010 Amendment Regulations. These are essentially loans or, more technically, pecuniary claims which arise out of an agreement whereby a credit institution grants credit in the form of a loan. In Ireland under the European Communities (Financial Collateral Arrangements) Regulations 2010, SI 626/2010, financial collateral is also defined as meaning cash, financial instruments or credit claims but it does not include shares in a company whose exclusive purpose is (a) to own means of production that are essential to the collateral provider's business or (b) to own real property.

134 For a definition of cash and financial instruments see Art. 2 of the Directive. See generally on this whole area of security over shares and investment property the website of the Financial Markets Law Committee <www.fmlc.org> accessed 17 May 2016.

135 Paragraph 3 of the preamble.

136 Article 1(3).

137 SI 2003/3226, reg. 3. The discussion paper 'Implementation of the Directive on Financial Collateral Arrangements' (July 2003) at para. 2.4 canvassed the possibility of going further and applying the same principles to all financial collateral arrangements, including those involving individual natural persons: 'However, our view is that this is unlikely to be legally feasible using the implementing powers in the European Communities Act 1972.' In *R (Cukurova Finance International Ltd) v HM Treasury* [2008] EWHC 2567, [2009] EuLR 317, leave to challenge the Regulations as being ultra vires s. 2(2) European Communities Act 1972 was refused on the ground of delay in bringing the application. Moses LJ also commented, however, that the challenge was unlikely to succeed on its merits. See now, however, *US v Nolan* [2015] UKSC 63 where the comments of Lord Mance cast doubt on the regulations. But s. 255 Banking Act 2009 gives power to make regulations about financial collateral arrangements even if it is not required to do so under the Collateral Directive. These may provide that the Regulations, and anything done in reliance on them, will be treated as having had effect despite any lack of vires.

collateral regime is more limited in that it only applies where both parties to the transaction are either public authorities, financial institutions or a 'bondholder or the holder of any other form of securitised debt.'[138]

107. The Financial Collateral Directive seeks to resolve the main problems affecting cross-border use of collateral in wholesale financial markets, inter alia, by restricting the imposition of onerous formalities on either the creation or enforcement of collateral arrangements.[139] Recital 17 of the preamble states that the Directive 'provides for rapid and non-formalistic enforcement procedures in order to safeguard financial stability and limit contagion effects in case of a default of a party to a financial collateral arrangement.' But the recital also refers to 'a posteriori control which the courts can exercise in relation to the realisation or valuation of financial collateral and the calculation of the relevant financial obligations. Such control should allow for the judicial authorities to verify that the realisation or valuation has been conducted in a commercially reasonable manner.'

108. Article 4 provides that where an enforcement event has occurred, a collateral taker should be able to realise or appropriate any financial collateral by applying it in discharge of the financial obligations. Appropriation is only possible if it has been agreed by the parties in the security financial collateral arrangement and the parties have also agreed on the valuation of the financial instruments. Regulation 17 of the UK regulations provides that a collateral taker may exercise the remedy of appropriation in accordance with the terms of the security financial collateral arrangement without any foreclosure order from the courts.[140] Regulation 18 provides that the collateral taker must account to the collateral provider for any surplus and also that the collateral provider remains liable for any deficiency.

109. In *Cukurova Finance International Ltd v Alfa Telecom Turkey Ltd*[141] the appropriation remedy was considered by the Privy Council. The case originated in an offshore Caribbean jurisdiction, the British Virgin Islands, and stemmed from a battle for control of *Turkey*'s largest mobile phone operator between Turkish and Russian interests. The resultant litigation was long drawn out and gave rise to a number of Privy Council appeals. In *Cukurova (No 1)*, the

---

[138] European Communities (Financial Collateral Arrangements) Regulations 2010, SI 626/2010, para. 3(2).

[139] Furthermore, the Directive, inter alia, permits the re-pledging of collateral and provides limited protection of collateral arrangements from some rules of insolvency law that might inhibit the use of top-up or substitute collateral.

[140] The Irish provision is regulation 6 of the European Communities (Financial Collateral Arrangements) Regulations 2010, SI 626/2010. It is drafted somewhat differently and refers to the realisation of financial collateral.

[141] [2009] UKPC 19.

court pointed out that the drafters of the regulations wrongly assumed that appropriation was already a self-help remedy known to English law. Lord Walker said that this remedy, in practice, was possibly available in relation to charges over funds of cash that were either payable on demand, or held on short-term deposit.[142] In relation, however, to charges over shares in a company, particularly an unlisted company where valuation of the shares was difficult, 'the notion of appropriation by the unilateral act of the collateral taker was a novel concept … Before the Directive it would have been open to attack not only as self-dealing but also as a clog on the equity of redemption, an old-established but not obsolete doctrine of equity ….'[143]

110. The court also pointed out that if 'the power of appropriation is exercised the collateral taker takes the collateral as his own property, at its value under the agreed mechanism, subject (if that value exceeds the secured debt) to a liability to pay the excess to the collateral-provider, and with a claim for the balance of the debt if the value is less than the secured debt. In these respects (as well as in not needing an application to the court) appropriation differs from the traditional (but now obsolescent) English remedy of foreclosure.'[144]

111. In subsequent litigation,[145] the collateral taker was held to have exercised the remedy of appropriation in respect of the financial collateral. This consisted of shares in a company ultimately giving control of *Turkey's* largest mobile phone enterprise. The collateral provider committed some largely technical acts of default under a loan agreement and the collateral taker in fact had made available the loan thinking that the borrower would default and would thereby have to yield up the shares. The lender's intention all along was to take control of the shares and gain control of the mobile phone company. But it was held that this secondary purpose did not vitiate enforcement of the security. The court said that enforcement of the security purely for a collateral purpose would be ineffective between mortgagor and mortgagee. In this particular case, the charge holder had enforced the security for the proper purpose of satisfying the debt and the fact that it might have additional purposes did not invalidate the enforcement.

112. The Privy Council held, however, that the new statutory regime did not preclude application of the ancient equitable principle of relief against forfeiture. This meant that the debtor recover the property free from the security on

142 Reference was made in this connection to the discussion by Lord Hoffmann in *In re Bank of Credit & Commerce International SA (No 8)* [1998] AC 214 at 226–227.

143 [2009] UKPC 19 at para. 11. Reference was made in this connection to see *Jones v Morgan* [2001] Lloyd's Rep Bank 323.

144 [2009] UKPC 19 at para. 13.

145 [2013] UKPC 2. See also [2013] UKPC 20 where the court settled the terms of relief, i.e. the amount that the borrower would have to pay to have the appropriation of the shares reversed.

repaying the loan plus interest. The court said that repayment of the loan was secured by charges over the shares. The prime objective of the transaction was to secure the repayment of the loan along with contractual interest. The power to appropriate the shares was essentially a forfeiture provision and was added to secure that result. The court's jurisdiction to grant relief against forfeiture could not, in principle, be limited to particular types of collateral and there was nothing in the Financial Collateral Regulations that excluded the possibility of such relief. The court recognised the need for commercial certainty but suggested that the present case combined a number of unusual features that were unlikely to be repeated.

Question 9: Is the secured party affected by a 'stay' on the enforcement of security rights if the debtor enters insolvency proceedings?

113. It is necessary for this purpose to distinguish between 'administration' and 'liquidation'. Administration and liquidation are similar procedures, to the extent that they both involve the appointment of a qualified insolvency practitioner to a company and the displacement of the company's existing board of directors from their management function.

114. Liquidation and administration differ significantly, however, in terms of intended purposes.[146] Liquidation of a company involves the cessation of its business, the realisation of its assets, the payment of its debts and liabilities, and the distribution of any remaining assets to the members of the company. At the end of a liquidation, a company is wound up and ceases to exist.

115. Administration, in contrast, was designed primarily as a rescue procedure aimed at facilitating the survival of the company's business, either in whole or in part. In practice, however, it has been used to achieve a more advantageous realisation of the company assets than can be achieved in a winding up.[147] Often, more advantageous realisation of assets is accomplished by means of a 'pre-pack' administration whereby a deal has already been agreed for the sale of company assets prior to the company entering administration.[148] The buyer may be the incumbent management team and the sale takes place immediately after the company is placed into administration. The assets are transferred to a new company but the unsecured debt is left behind in the old corporate structure. The result of the process may be that the business of the company, but not the

---

146 See *Re MF Global UK Ltd* [2013] 1 WLR 903.

147 See the empirical evidence presented on the Insolvency Service website: <www.insolvency.gov.uk/>

148 See generally P. Walton and M. Wellard, (2012) 21 *International Insolvency Review* 143; V. Finch, (2006) 6 *Journal of Business Law* 568.

old corporate vehicle itself, survives but it will have managed to jettison some or all of the unsecured debt and therefore should be in a stronger financial position. The procedure effectively needs the support of the company's secured creditors, i.e. bankers, since the security will continue to attach to the assets. Pre-packs are however not explicitly recognised in the Insolvency Act though they are subject to extra-statutory regulation.[149]

116. The Insolvency Act states that an administrator must perform his functions with the objective of: (a) rescuing the company as a going concern, or (b) achieving a better result for the company's creditors as a whole than would be likely if the company were wound up (without first being in administration), or (c) realising property in order to make a distribution to one or more secured or preferential creditors.[150] There is this hierarchy of objectives and an administrator can only go down the list of objectives if he thinks that it is not reasonably practicable to achieve any of the preceding objectives.

117. Under the administration regime, secured creditors are however in a strong position. For instance, an administrator can be appointed by the holder of a floating charge over substantially the whole of a company's property out of court, by the court, or by the company itself upon giving prior notice to the floating charge holder. During the notice period, the floating charge holder may step in and make its own appointment.[151] The strong position of the floating charge holder is also seen in two provisions relating to court appointment of administrators.[152] Firstly, where an administration application is made by somebody other than a qualified floating charge holder, the latter may intervene in the proceedings and suggest to the court the appointment of a specified person as administrator. The court is obliged to respond positively to this intervention unless it thinks it right to refuse the application 'because of the particular circumstances of the case'.[153] Secondly, where an administration application is made by a qualified floating charge holder, there is no threshold insolvency requirement.[154]

---

149 See Statement of Insolvency Practice 16 (SIP 16) and the *Graham Review into Pre-pack Administration* (2014) <https://www.gov.uk/government/publications/graham-review-into-pre-pack-administration> accessed 17 May 2016. See now <https://www.prepackpool.co.uk/> accessed 17 May 2016.

150 For the list of statutory objectives see Schedule B1 Insolvency Act 1986, para. 3.

151 See in particular Schedule B1 Insolvency Act 1986, paras. 15 and 18.

152 Schedule B1 Insolvency Act 1986, para. 36. See also para. 37 which enables a qualifying floating charge holder to apply to have an existing liquidation converted into an administration but the court is not obliged to accede to such an application. Paragraph 38 enables the liquidator to make a similar application.

153 See also *Re Super Aguri F1 Ltd* [2011] BCC 452 and more generally on challenges to the appointment of particular administrators *Finnerty v Clark* [2011] EWCA Civ 858, [2011] BCC 702.

154 Schedule B1 Insolvency Act 1986, para. 35.

118. One of the most important features of administration is the moratorium. The commencement of the administration procedure imposes a freeze on proceedings or executions against the company and its assets. This provides a breathing space during which the company has an opportunity to make arrangements for the sale of its assets and/or the rescheduling of its debts and the restructuring of its affairs.[155] By virtue of the moratorium, no steps may be taken to enforce any security over the company's property[156] or to repossess goods in the company's possession under any hire-purchase agreement[157] and no legal process[158] including distress[159] may be instituted or continued against the company except with the leave of the court and subject to such terms as the court may impose; and or else with the consent of the administrator. Furthermore, when a company is in administration, any administrative receiver of the company shall vacate office, as well as a receiver of part of the company's property, if the administrator so requires.[160] It should be noted, however, that these restrictions on the enforcement of security do not apply to any security interest created or otherwise arising under a financial collateral arrangement.[161]

119. While the Enterprise Act 2002 has modified and restricted the traditional enforcement rights of secured creditors in the context of company administration, it does not affect the secured creditor's enforcement powers in liquidation. A secured creditor may continue to enforce its security notwithstanding the fact that a company has gone into liquidation.

120. In the *Republic of Ireland*, there is the liquidation procedure which functions in roughly the same way as in *England*. There is, however, no exact equivalent of administration. Instead, there is the examinership procedure. This procedure was introduced in 1990 by the Companies (Amendment) Act 1990 and has since been amended more than once by statute with a view to

---

155 The administration moratorium does not apply in relation to the enforcement of market charges under s. 173 Companies Act 1989. Basically there are charges in favour of a recognised investment exchange, for the purpose of securing debts or liabilities arising in connection with the settlement of market contracts.

156 Schedule B1 Insolvency Act 1986, para. 43(2).

157 *Ibid.* at para. 43(3) and defined by para. 111 as including conditional sale agreements, chattel leasing agreements and retention of title agreements.

158 The proceedings in question are legal proceedings or quasi-legal proceedings such as arbitration: *Bristol Airport v Powdrill* [1990] Ch 744. A 'legal process' requires the assistance of the court and therefore the service of a notice making time of the essence is not within this category: *Re Olympia and York Canary Wharf Ltd* [1993] BCC 15; *McMullen & Sons v Cerrone* [1994] BCC 25. See now on 'legal process' for the purpose of the moratorium *Re Railtrack plc* [2002] 2 BCLC 755 and see also *Environment Agency v Clark* [2001] Ch 57.

159 The essential feature of distress is that the assets distrained are seized and detained by the distrainor: *Bristol Airport v Powdrill* [1990] Ch 744.

160 Schedule B1 Insolvency Act 1986, para. 41.

161 Reg. 8 of the Financial Collateral Regulations 2003, SI 2003/3112.

improving its effectiveness.[162] The relevant provisions are now contained in the Irish Companies Act 2014. Examinership is, in effect, intended as a form of 'debtor-in-possession' type restructuring and the procedure is, in some respects, a 'halfway house' between administration and restructurings under Chapter 11 of the US Bankruptcy Code.

121. Section 509(1) Companies Act 2014 prescribes the initial task of the examiner as being to examine the state of the company's affairs. Section 509(2) of the Act provides that the court shall not order the appointment of an examiner unless it is satisfied that there is a reasonable prospect of the survival of the company, and the whole or any part of its undertaking, as a going concern.[163] The legislation sees the examiner as a sort of company doctor who analyses the patient, prescribes remedies and gets the parties concerned to try to agree.

122. During the period of examinership, a company enjoys protection from its creditors like a company in administration. The key elements in the system are the appointment of an examiner by the court and the placing of the company concerned under the protection of the court for an initial period of 70 days. During this period of protection the company may not be wound up, a receiver may not be appointed, debts cannot be executed against it and no security can be enforced against the company.[164] Moreover, the directors of a company have a three-day grace period from the appointment of a receiver to decide whether or not to seek to place the company into examinership. Section 512(4) Companies Act provides that the court shall not give a hearing to an examinership petition if a receiver stands appointed to the company and the receiver has stood so appointed for a continuous period of at least three days prior to the presentation of the petition.

123. If the examiner is of the view that the company, or a part of it, can be saved and that this would be more advantageous than a winding up, he will prepare a draft rescue plan. This will be put to appropriate meetings of creditors and members, and, if approved, will go to the court for confirmation. If the court

---

162 On the procedure see generally T. Courtney, *The Law of Companies*, Chapter 22.

163 There is provision for an independent accountant's report to assist the court in deciding whether the company has a reasonable prospect of survival. In *Re Gallium Ltd* (2009) 8 IESC Fennelly J stated at para. 47 that the 'entire purpose of examinership is to make it possible to rescue companies in difficulties. The protection period is there to facilitate examination of the prospects of the rescue. However, the protection may prejudice the interests of some creditors. The court will weigh the existence and degree of any such prejudice in the balance. It will have regard to the report of the independent accountant.'

164 Section 520(4) Companies Act 2014. Reg. 7 of the European Communities (Financial Collateral Arrangements) Regulations 2010, SI 626/2010 provides that a financial collateral arrangement has effect in accordance with its terms notwithstanding the commencement of winding up or reorganisation proceedings in respect of either the collateral provider or the collateral taker.

approves the plan, it will become binding on those concerned and the examiner's appointment will be terminated. It should be noted that the appointment of an examiner does not entail automatically the suspension of the management powers of the company directors. The examiner, however, is given the option of applying to the court for an order that all or any of the functions or powers which are vested in or exercisable by the directors shall be performable or exercisable only by the examiner.[165]

Question 10: Can the secured party apply to have any stay lifted?

124. Yes. With the leave of the court or with the administrator's consent, security may be enforced, goods may be repossessed and other legal processes may be instituted or continued notwithstanding the fact that the company is in administration.[166]

Question 11: Under what circumstances can the stay be lifted?

125. There have been a number of test cases in which the courts have had an opportunity to spell out their approach to the lifting of the administration stay. The leading authorities are the decisions of the Court of Appeal in *Bristol Airport plc v Powdrill*[167] and *Re Atlantic Computer Systems plc (No 1)*.[168] In the former case it was held that the exercise by an airport authority of its rights under the Civil Aviation Act 1982 to detain an aircraft for non-payment of landing charges constituted a 'step taken to enforce security' and thus came within the statutory moratorium. Leave was refused to enforce the security. Particularly telling factors against the airports were that none of the company's aircraft were on their runways at the commencement of the administration and had only arrived there subsequently because of the administrator's decision to continue the business; the airports had acquiesced in the administrator's proposal to sell the business as a going concern, which detention of the aircraft would prevent; and the airports had benefited financially from the continuation of the business by the administrator because they had received payment of substantial fees. Having supported the administration when it suited them, the airports could not later seek to enforce a right which was inconsistent with the achievement of the purpose of the administration.[169]

---

165 Section 528 Companies Act 2014.

166 Schedule B1 Insolvency Act 1986, para. 43(6). In Ireland, the examinership moratorium may be relaxed with the consent of the examiner or the court.

167 [1990] Ch 744.

168 [1992] Ch 505.

169 [1990] Ch 744 at 767, per Browne-Wilkinson V-C.

126. The Court of Appeal in *Powdrill* accepted that its reasoning would extend to a case where the holder of a possessory lien[170] on chattels was requested by an administrator to give up the chattels. Refusal to comply with the request would amount to a step taken to enforce security and fall within the statutory moratorium. The Court of Appeal accepted that it would be practically inconvenient and costly for the holder of every lien to have to apply to court for leave but thought that these potential difficulties would be mitigated in practice by the fact that the administrator and the holder of the lien could simply agree the matter between themselves without the intervention of the courts.

127. *Re Atlantic Computer Systems plc (No 1)* set out in general terms the approach of the court in leave applications. The underlying principle is that an administration for the benefit of unsecured creditors should not be conducted at the expense of those who have proprietary rights except to the extent that this may be unavoidable.[171]

(a) The onus is on the applicant to establish a case for leave to be granted.
(b) The moratorium is intended to assist in the achievement of the purpose for which the administration order was made. If granting leave to the applicant is unlikely to impede that purpose, leave should normally be given.
(c) In other cases, the court should balance the legitimate interests of the applicant and the legitimate interests of the other creditors of the company.[172]
(d) In carrying out the balancing exercise, great importance is normally to be given to the proprietary interest of the applicant. In general, so far as possible, the administration procedure should not be used to prejudice those who were secured creditors or lessors at the commencement of the administration.
(e) It will normally be sufficient ground for the grant of leave if significant loss would be caused to the applicant by the refusal. But if substantially greater loss would be caused to others by the grant of leave, or loss which is out of all proportion to the benefit which leave would confer on the applicant, that may outweigh the loss to the applicant caused by a refusal.

---

170 Under s. 246, liens and similar rights on the company's books, papers or other records are unenforceable against 'office-holders', a category which includes administrators. On lien-holders, see also *Re Sabre International Products Ltd* [1991] BCLC 470.

171 See also *Mackay v Kaupthing Singer* [2013] EWHC 2533 (Ch) where the court said at para. 75 that the court was only required to balance the interests of secured and unsecured creditors if the relevant property was required for the purposes of the administration.

172 For an example of the operation of this balancing process, see *Re Meesan Investments Ltd (Royal Trust Bank v Buchler)* (1988) 4 BCC 788, [1989] BCLC 130.

(f) In assessing the respective losses, the court will have regard to matters such as:
  - the financial position of the company;
  - its ability to pay rental arrears and continuing rentals (or, in the case of security, to meet its obligations under its loans);
  - the administrator's proposals;
  - the period for which the administration order has been in force and is expected to remain in force;
  - the effect on the administration if leave is given and on the applicant if it is refused;
  - the end result sought to be achieved by the administration;
  - the prospects of that result being achieved; and
  - the history of the administration so far.

(g) In considering these suggested consequences it will often be necessary to assess how probable they are.

(h) Other factors, such as the conduct of the applicant, may also be relevant.

(i) The above conditions also apply to a decision to impose terms if leave is granted and to impose terms as a condition for refusing leave. An example of refusal to grant leave on terms is provided by *Re Meesan Investments*,[173] where leave to enforce security was refused but the administrator was ordered to return to court in two months' time if the secured property had not been sold by then. The guidelines envisage refusal on terms becoming a common phenomenon.

(j) On applications to enforce security, an important consideration will often be whether the applicant is fully secured. If he is, delay in enforcement is likely to be less prejudicial than in cases where his security is insufficient.

(k) Unless the issue can easily be resolved, it is not appropriate on a leave application for the court to resolve a dispute about the existence, validity or nature of a security which the applicant seeks leave to enforce. The court needs to be satisfied only that the applicant has a seriously arguable case.

128. Wrongful refusal by an administrator to enforce security could render the administrator liable to pay compensation.[174]

---

173 [1989] BCLC 130.

174 *Barclay Mercantile Business Finance Ltd v Sibec Development Ltd* [1992] 1 WLR 1253.

Question 12: In insolvency proceedings, can an insolvency practitioner (IP) 'enforce' the security, i.e. realise the secured assets, without the consent of the secured party.

129. In many cases, in order to achieve the purposes of administration, the administrator will need to be able to use or dispose of all the company's property, including that part of it which is charged to a third party, e.g. the company's bankers. Schedule B1, paragraphs 70–72 give the administrator certain powers to deal with property that is charged to third parties and also chattels owned by third parties but in the company's possession, irrespective of the wishes of the charge holders or owners.[175] These provision do not apply however with respect to financial collateral.[176]

Question 13: Are there any conditions that must be satisfied before an IP may 'enforce' the security?

130. In this connection, there is a distinction between, on the one hand, assets subject to a fixed charge (or to hire-purchase agreements),[177] and, on the other hand, assets subject to a floating charge. In the case of assets subject to a floating charge, the administrator is given power to dispose of such assets or otherwise exercise his powers in relation to them as if the assets were not subject to the floating charge. Accordingly, the administrator can deal with such assets and dispose of them without being fettered by any contractual restrictions contained within the floating charge, for example by a negative pledge clause prohibiting the grant of other security over the assets. The reference to a floating charge means a charge which, as created, was a floating charge.[178] Consequently, the crystallisation of the floating charge prior to the administration order would not prevent the administrator from exercising these wide powers.

131. Where the administrator disposes of floating charge assets, the holder of the floating charge is given the same priority in respect of any of the company's property that directly, or indirectly, represents the assets disposed of as he would have had in respect of the assets subject to the floating charge. If, for example, the administrator sells plant and machinery subject to the floating charge, the proceeds of the sale will fall within the floating charge and the holder of the charge will be entitled to the same priority as against third parties (e.g. holders

---

175 For Ireland see s. 530 Companies Act 2014.

176 Financial Collateral Arrangements (No 2) Regulations 2003, reg. 7 and for Ireland see reg. 7 of the European Communities (Financial Collateral Arrangements) Regulations 2010, SI 626/2010.

177 This term includes conditional sale agreements, chattel leasing agreements and retention of title agreements: Insolvency Act Schedule B1, para. 111.

178 *Ibid.*

of subsequent floating charges) in respect of the proceeds as he had in respect of the plant and machinery.

132. As regards assets subject to a fixed charge (as created), or goods which are in the possession of the company under a hire-purchase agreement, the administrator may apply to court in accordance with Schedule B1, paragraphs 71 and 72, for an order authorising him to dispose of the property. The court may make such an order if it is satisfied that the disposal (with or without other assets) of the fixed charge assets or goods acquired on hire purchase would be likely to promote the purpose, or one or more of the purposes, specified in the administration order. The court order will authorise the administrator to dispose of the assets or goods as if they were not subject to the fixed charge or, as the case may be, as if the owner's rights under the hire-purchase agreement were vested in the company. Schedule B1, paragraphs 71(3) and 72(3) provide that the court must make it a condition of any such order that:

(a) the net proceeds of the disposal; and
(b) a sum equalling the deficit between the net proceeds of disposal and the net amount which would be realised by a sale of the assets at market value as determined by the court, must be applied towards discharging the sums secured by the fixed charge or payable under the hire-purchase agreement.

133. The operation of this provision was considered in *Re ARV Aviation Ltd*[179] where it was held that the task of the court in leave applications was to balance the prejudice that would be felt by the secured creditor by the making of an order against the prejudice that would be felt by those interested in the promotion of the administration purpose if it were not made. The view that the court takes of the open-market value of the assets is extremely important because this is the amount that the administrator is required to discharge as a condition of obtaining leave. In *ARV Aviation*, the court proceeded on the assumption that the purpose of this condition was to protect, to the maximum practicable extent, the secured creditor.[180] It was held that the granting of leave could be a two-stage process, with the open-market valuation being assessed at some point after the making of the order granting the administrator leave to dispose of the assets.

134. Leave may be sought in circumstances where the administrator and the secured creditor[181] are unable themselves to agree on a valuation; but such a

---

179 (1988) 4 BCC 708, [1989] BCLC 664. See also *Re Capitol Films Ltd* [2011] BPIR 334 and *O'Connell v Rollings* [2014] EWCA Civ 639.

180 The same underlying purpose would exist where the administrator seeks leave to dispose of goods in the possession of the company under a hire-purchase agreement.

181 Or supplier of goods on hire purchase, as the case may be.

dispute is not an essential prerequisite of the jurisdiction. Where a secured creditor consents to the sale of the charged assets,[182] the administrator may not use the statutory mechanism to retain the proceeds of the sale but must deal with these proceeds in accordance with the terms on which the secured creditor has agreed to release its security.[183]

135. Where assets are subject to more than one fixed charge and the court makes an order authorising the disposal of such assets, the proceeds of sale must be applied towards discharging the sums secured by the securities in their order of priority.[184]

Question 14: Do the rules or conditions differ depending on the nature of the insolvency proceedings in question?

136. Yes. There is a clear difference in this respect between administration and liquidation. In liquidation the secured creditor's rights are unaffected and a liquidator cannot dispose of a clear title to the assets that form the subject matter of the security interest without the consent of the charge holder. The liquidator can only dispose of the borrower's 'equity of redemption', i.e. the encumbrance on the property represented by the security interest will remain unless the secured creditor consents to a sale.

137. The secured creditor is free to realise its security without reference to the liquidator. Thus, where the value of the security is more than sufficient to discharge the debt or the security is a floating charge on all of the company's assets, the secured creditor may simply choose to enforce its security outside the liquidation. It is possible for a secured creditor voluntarily to surrender his security and prove for its debt as if it were unsecured[185] but it is very unlikely to be advantageous for a creditor to give up its security in this way.

138. If a secured creditor realises its security but the amount so realised is insufficient to discharge the debt, then it may prove for the balance in the liquidation.[186] A secured creditor also has the option of valuing its security and submitting a proof for the balance. In that case, the liquidator can offer to redeem the security at the value stated in the proof.[187] It may choose to do

---

182 Or a supplier of goods on hire purchase consents to the sale of those goods.

183 *Re Newman Shopfitters (Cleveland) Ltd* [1991] BCLC 407.

184 Schedule B1, para. 71(4).

185 Rule 4.88(2) Insolvency Rules. Note r. 4.96 which deems a secured creditor to have voluntarily surrendered its security (unless the court grants relief) if it omits to disclose its security in its proof.

186 Rule 4.88(1).

187 Rule 4.97.

this where it considers that the value stated in the proof is less than the value which the assets subject to the security could fetch on a disposal. Because, however, there is some scope for the secured creditor to revise the value stated in its proof,[188] the matter may then become one for negotiation between the liquidator and the creditor.

Question 15: Is a secured party liable to pay the general costs, i.e. costs apart from those incurred in connection with the realisation of security, of insolvency proceedings affecting the debtor?

139. A fixed charge holder is not liable to pay the general costs of administration or liquidation. The position is different in the case of the floating charge holder. In the context of administration, paragraph 99(3) Schedule B1 Insolvency Act 1986 provides that where a person ceases to be an administrator, his remuneration and expenses shall be charged on, and payable out of, property of which he had custody or control immediately before cessation and will be payable in priority to any floating charge.

140. Rule 2.67 of the Insolvency Rules sets out the order in which the expenses of the administration are payable though the court may adjust this order of priority. Under the Rule 'necessary disbursements' by the liquidator are payable in priority to the administrator's own remuneration. In the *Bloom v Pensions Regulator*[189] Briggs J at first instance considered the interaction between the Insolvency Act and rules, and the scheme under the Pensions Act 2004 for meeting unfunded pension fund liabilities of insolvent companies. It was held that the imposition of a 'financial support direction' by the Pensions Regulator under the Pensions Act upon companies in administration or insolvent liquidation created necessary disbursements, and therefore expenses within rule 2.67. Therefore, these expenses had prima facie priority over the administrator's own claim to remuneration and a fortiori, the unsecured debts of the company. Briggs J took the view that the liability was not a provable debt under rule 13.12 of the Insolvency Rules and as result had to be a 'necessary disbursement' because the liability could not fall into a statutory black hole.

141. The decision was confirmed by the Court of Appeal[190] but was reversed by the Supreme Court.[191] The court held that the mere fact that an event occurred during the administration which gave rise to a statutory debt on the part of the company was not enough to render payment of the debt 'an expense of the administration'. It

---

188 Rules 4.84 and 4.95.
189 [2011] BCC 277.
190 [2012] BCC 83.
191 [2014] AC 209.

was suggested that a disbursement fell within rule 2.67 if it arose out of something done in the administration (normally by the administrator or on the administrator's behalf), or if it was imposed by a statute which made it clear that the liability to make the disbursement fell on an administrator as part of the administration. This could be due either to the terms of the statute or the nature of the liability.

142. In liquidation, it is provided that the 'expenses of winding up ... so far as the assets of the company available for payment of general creditors are insufficient to meet them, have priority over any claims to property comprised in or subject to any floating charge created by the company and shall be paid out of any such property accordingly'.[192]

143. Rule 4.218 of the Insolvency Rules 1986 defines the liquidation expenses and the order in which they are payable. The liquidator's own remuneration is included in the list. The courts have also expanded the concept of 'liquidation expenses' to include liabilities incurred before the liquidation in respect of property afterwards retained by the liquidator for the benefit of the insolvent estate. Consequently, rent or hire-purchase charges in respect of land or goods in the possession of the company which the liquidator continues to use for the purposes of the liquidation are included within the concept of liquidation expenses.[193]

144. Among the items listed in rule 4.218 are 'any necessary disbursements by the liquidator'. In *Re Toshoku Finance (UK) plc*[194] it was held that the liability to corporation tax is a sum which, by statute, is payable by a company in respect of profits or gains arising during a winding up. Therefore it is a 'necessary disbursement' which the liquidator had to make and was payable as a liquidation expense. Costs incurred by a liquidator in an unsuccessful attempt to recover assets were not originally included in the concept of liquidation expenses[195] but the position has been altered somewhat. It is now only possible for a liquidator to pursue such proceedings with the sanction of creditors and the costs of such proceedings are now deemed to be a liquidation expense.[196]

---

192 Section 176ZA Insolvency Act 1986 which effectively overturns the decision in *Re Leyland Daf Ltd: Buchler v Talbot* [2004] 2 AC 298 on the interpretation of earlier legislation. According to s. 176ZA(3), however, rules may be made restricting the application of this provision in such circumstances as may be prescribed, to expenses authorised or approved (a) by the holders of debentures secured by, or holders of, the floating charges and by any preferential creditors entitled to be paid in priority to them, or (b) by the court. See also rr. 4.218A–4.218E of the Insolvency Rules.

193 *Re Lundy Granite Co* (1871) LR 6 Ch App 462; *Re Atlantic Computer Systems plc* [1992] Ch 505 where the earlier authorities are reviewed.

194 [2002] 1 WLR 671.

195 *Re M C Bacon Ltd (No 2)* [1991] Ch 127.

196 Rule 4.218(3) of the Insolvency Rules now refers to expenses or costs which are properly chargeable or incurred by the official receiver or the liquidator in preserving, realising or getting in any of the assets of the company or otherwise relating to the conduct of any legal proceedings.

145. In *Ireland* the relevant statutory provisions are sections 554(4) and 617 Companies Act 2014. Section 554(4) deals with examinership and section 617 with liquidation. Essentially, section 554(4) lays down that the costs and expenses of examinership are paid ahead of claims secured by a floating charge but after claims secured by a fixed charge. Section 617 provides that all 'costs, charges and expenses properly incurred in the winding up, including the remuneration of the liquidator ... shall be payable out of the property of the company in priority to all other claims'. It has been held that this provision is to be interpreted as meaning that general expenses of liquidation are payable in priority to claims secured by a floating charge.[197]

Question 16: Is the secured party liable to 'set aside' any portion of the amount realised from the enforcement of security for the benefit of (a) preferential or (b) unsecured creditors of the debtor?

146. In certain circumstances 'yes' but it is necessary for this purpose to distinguish between (a) preferential and (b) unsecured creditors.

In *Re Nortel GmbH*[198] Lord Neuberger said: 'In a liquidation of a company and in an administration (where there is no question of trying to save the company or its business), the effect of the insolvency legislation ... as interpreted and extended by the courts, is that the order of priority for payment out of the company's assets is, in summary terms, as follows:

(a) Fixed charge creditors;
(b) Expenses of the insolvency proceedings;
(c) Preferential creditors;
(d) Floating charge creditors;
(e) Unsecured provable debts;
(f) Statutory interest;
(g) Non-provable liabilities; and
(h) Shareholders.'[199]

147. Preferential debts rank equally among themselves after the expenses of the winding up and must be paid in full, unless the assets are insufficient to meet

---

197 See generally *Irish Bank Resolution Corporation Ltd v DTZ Debenham* [2013] EWHC 596 (Comm), [2013] All ER (D) 155. The court followed the English decision in *Re Barleycorn Enterprises Ltd* [1970] Ch 465 in preference to that in *Re Leyland Daf Ltd* [2004] 2 AC 298.

198 [2013] UKSC 52, [2013] 3 WLR 504 at para. 39 and see also David Richards J in *Re Lehman Brothers International (Europe)* [2014] EWHC 704 (Ch) at para. 15.

199 Sections 107 and 115 (voluntary liquidations) and 143 and 156 (compulsory liquidations) and s. 175 and r. 4.218 (both types of liquidation).

them, in which case they abate in equal proportions.[200] Also, whilst preferential debts rank behind debts secured by fixed charges, so far as the assets of the company available for payment of general creditors are insufficient to meet them, they have priority over claims secured by a floating charge created by the company and must be paid accordingly out of any property comprised in or subject to that charge.[201] The fact that the floating charge may have crystallised prior to the commencement of the winding up does not deprive the preferential debts of this special priority, because it is expressly provided by section 251 of the Insolvency Act that a floating charge for this purpose means a charge created as such.[202]

148. Schedule 6 of the Insolvency Act sets out the categories of preferential debts. As amended by the Enterprise Act 2002,[203] this now covers only up to four months' back-pay to employees and former employees (up to a prescribed maximum limit per employee) as well as unpaid holiday pay and contributions to state and occupational pension schemes.[204] Giving these claims preferential status in a liquidation, administration or receivership, is a way of protecting the interests of 'vulnerable' creditors, i.e. creditors who are not in a position to negotiate an enhanced position for themselves, whether by means of security or otherwise.[205]

---

200 Section 175(2)(a).

201 Section 175(2)(b).

202 In Ireland s. 621 Companies Act 2014 provides that preferential debts should be paid ahead of floating charge realisations. There is no statutory equivalent of s. 251 of the Insolvency Act and it has recently been held by the Irish Supreme Court that a floating charge holder will gain priority over preferential creditors if the floating charge has crystallised prior to liquidation or receivership – see *Re JD Brian Ltd* [2015] IESC 62. In Ireland however, the implications of what is now s. 1001 of the Taxes Consolidation Act 1997 should be noted. This section provides that if a chargor is in arrears on certain tax obligations to the Revenue, the tax authorities can serve a notice on any creditor of the chargor which has a fixed charge over the chargor's book debts to the effect that any monies received by the creditor from the chargor from the time of the notice, not only in respect of book debts, must be remitted to the tax authorities in or towards the discharge of the arrears of PAYE or VAT.

203 Which abolished preferences that the Crown used to have in respect of unpaid taxes of various sorts.

204 It should be noted that under part 12 of the Employment Rights 1996 Act, the National Insurance Fund pays certain entitlements (subject to limits) owed to former employees of insolvent companies. The Act implements the EU Insolvency Directive 80/987/EEC and guarantees a basic minimum payment to employees of insolvent employers, who might otherwise have to wait some considerable time for payment, or receive no payment at all in their capacity as creditors in the insolvency proceedings. Once they have made these payments, the employee rights in the insolvency proceedings are statutorily transferred to the National Insurance Fund. In Ireland there is a similar scheme – the Insolvency Payments Scheme – and the statutory foundation for this is the Protection of Employees (Employers' Insolvency) Acts, 1984–2004 and associated regulations.

205 See generally, L. Bebchuk and J. Fried (1996) 105 *Yale Law Journal* 857 but for criticism of redistributive provisions see J. Armour 'Should we Redistribute in Insolvency' in J. Getzler and J. Payne (eds.), *Company Charges: Spectrum and Beyond.*

149. The Enterprise Act introduced a new provision into the Insolvency Act setting aside a proportion of floating charge recoveries for the benefit of unsecured creditors.[206] The provision operates when the company is in liquidation, administration or receivership. The amount set aside is a percentage share of the company's net property as defined by statutory instrument and the percentage may be different for different classes of property.[207] The percentage may also be altered by statutory instrument from time to time. At the moment, under the Insolvency Act 1986 (Prescribed Part) Order 2003,[208] the proportion of floating charge recoveries set aside for the benefit of unsecured creditors of a company is based on a sliding scale. It is calculated as 50% of the first £10,000, then 20% of the remainder but subject to an overall ceiling so that the fund for unsecured creditors shall not exceed £600,000 in a particular case. It should be noted, however, that the provision may not apply if the cost of making a distribution to unsecured creditors would be disproportionate to the benefits. The court disapplied the rights of unsecured creditors on this ground in *Re Hydroserve Ltd*.[209]

150. In *Re Courts plc*[210] the court rejected the proposition that it could make a partial disapplication order. It attached importance to the principle of pari passu distribution, which meant that, subject to the claims of preferential creditors, the company's unsecured creditors were to rank equally between themselves. This was the case even though the claims of some creditors were small compared with others. The fact that, averaged out, the liquidator's expenses of processing each claim exceeded the distribution to a particular creditor was irrelevant. The fact that the actual cost of processing a particular creditor's claim could exceed the distribution to that creditor was also irrelevant. There was nothing in the legislation indicating that Parliament intended to treat, as a material consideration, the balance of cost and benefit on an individual creditor basis.

151. In *International Sections Ltd*[211] it was held that the court should not be too ready to disapply the prescribed part because the dividend for unsecured creditors as a result would be small. This was often the case irrespective of the costs of making any distribution. Disapplication should be the exception, and

---

206 The Enterprise Act abolished preference for unpaid tax claims and the fund for unsecured creditors was established as a balancing measure to ensure that the benefits of the abolition did not go exclusively for the benefit of unsecured creditors. The fund has its origins in a recommendation of the Cork Committee on Insolvency Law and Practice (1982 Cmnd 8558 at para. 1538) that 10% of net realisations of property subject to a floating charge should be set aside for unsecured creditors.

207 There is no equivalent of this provision in Ireland.

208 SI 2003/2097.

209 [2008] BCC 175.

210 [2009] 1 WLR 1499.

211 [2009] EWHC 137 (Ch), [2009] BCC 574.

not the rule. In *QMD Hotels Ltd Administrators*[212] it was reiterated that the court should not be too ready to disapply the prescribed part provisions. But the court also said that it should endeavour to ensure that the already small dividend payable to the unsecured creditors out of the prescribed part was not further reduced by an overzealous approach to the adjudication of such claims.

152. There has been considerable debate about whether the holders of a floating charge can receive any payment from the prescribed part in respect of a deficiency under the floating charge. In *Re Permacell Finesse Ltd*[213] this question was answered in the negative with the court holding that the prohibition on distributing the prescribed part to a floating charge holder was absolute. The Enterprise Act created a fund out of the floating charge holder's security to which unsecured creditors could have recourse and, in return, floating charge holders benefited by the abolition of the preferential status of tax claims. The prescribed part should not then be diluted by secured creditors having an effective 'second bite at the cherry'. In *Re Pal SC Realisations 2007 Ltd*[214] it was held, however, that a charge holder was entitled to participate in the prescribed part if it surrendered its entire security in accordance with rule 4.88(2) of the Insolvency Rules. Consequently, it was entitled to prove as if its debt was unsecured.

Question 17: Can the secured party be bound against its wishes by a restructuring plan that negatively affects either the secured debt or the enforcement of the security interest?

153. Yes, in practice this can be done through a scheme of arrangement under the Companies Act though not in the administration procedure alone nor in a company voluntary arrangement under the Insolvency Act.[215]

154. In the *UK* generally, there are certain statutory possibilities for overcoming holdouts among minority creditors in a corporate restructuring context. These procedures are premised on the assumption that for a company with a large number of creditors, reaching agreement with all of them may not be practicable.[216] There may be considerable coordination costs in assembling the

---

212 [2010] CSOH 168.

213 [2008] BCC 208. See also *Thorniley v Revenue and Customs Commissioners* [2008] EWHC 124 (Ch), [2008] 1 WLR 1516.

214 [2011] BCCC 933.

215 In Ireland there is no equivalent to company voluntary arrangements under Insolvency legislation but schemes of arrangement under the Irish Companies Act function in a broadly similar way to their UK counterparts and enable 'holdouts' to be overcome.

216 Many large company rescues are accomplished outside formal insolvency procedures by means of consensual 'workouts'. This is the so-called 'London Approach' on which see J. Armour and S. Deakin, (2001) 1 *Journal of Corporate Law Studies* 21. See also more generally J. Payne, (2014) 130 *Law Quarterly Review* 282; S. Paterson, (2014) 14 *Journal of Corporate Law Studies* 333.

necessary parties and obtaining their agreement. There is also the free-rider issue in that some parties have incentives to hold out for a better deal for themselves or to 'free ride' on other parties by remaining outside the agreement in the expectation that others would sign up to it, thus leading to an improvement in the company's fortunes from which they would also benefit. Thus some concession to majority rule seems appropriate but a simple majority rule principle appears to involve too great an infringement on the rights of individual creditors.

155. In the administration procedure, the administrator manages the company's affairs while formulating proposals to achieve the statutory goals, including the goal of rescuing the company as a going concern. The legislation is based on the principle that, in exchange for the moratorium, creditors are to have an important say in the conduct of the administration and should normally be afforded the opportunity of considering and reviewing what the administrator proposes to do. The basic model of creditor consultation and approval of proposals ignores, however, the possibility of circumstances arising where the administrator should act before there is an opportunity to convene a meeting of creditors. For instance, the administrator might be offered a favourable price for the business that is conditional upon a sale being concluded in accordance with a tight timetable. The administrator is given wide powers, even before approval of proposals by creditors, and it has been judicially affirmed that these powers extend to selling off the company's business prior to the holding of the creditors' meeting.[217]

156. Creditor approval of proposals requires a simple majority of votes cast, as measured by the amount of the outstanding indebtedness,[218] although the proposals may not result in non-preferential entitlements being paid ahead of preferential entitlements or one preferential creditor of the company being paid a smaller proportion of his debt than another.[219] More generally, it is specifically provided that an administrator's statement of proposals may include any action which affects the right of a secured creditor of the company to enforce its security. Secured creditors' rights are inviolate in this respect. Moreover, changing the substantive rights of creditors of whatever kind cannot simply be done by means

217 See *Re Transbus International Ltd* [2004] 2 All ER 911.

218 See rule 2.43(1) of the Insolvency Rules which provide that 'at a creditors' meeting in administration proceedings, a resolution is passed when a majority (in value) of those present and voting, in person or by proxy, have voted in favour of it.' The resolution however is invalid if more than half of creditors not connected with the company voted against it. A secured creditor may note for the amount of his secured debt only where there is insufficient property to make a distribution to unsecured creditors apart from the prescribed part. Normally, at a creditors' meeting under rule 2.40 a secured creditor is 'entitled to vote only in respect of the balance (if any) of his debt after deducting the value of his security as estimated by him.'

219 Schedule B1, para. 73(1)(a) and (b).

of approval of proposals in the administration context. Something more has to be done before creditors' rights can be discharged or varied without their consent.

157. If a company is in administration and it is decided that corporate restructuring is the best way forward rather than the sale of assets, then there are the options of a company voluntary arrangement (CVA) under the insolvency legislation or a scheme of arrangement under the Companies Act. The use of CVAs has certain advantages – the process is administratively simple with no need for multiple court applications. Indeed, the matter does not come before the court at all unless a dissenting creditor brings a challenge either on procedural grounds or on grounds of unfair prejudice.[220]

158. Company voluntary arrangements under Part 1 Insolvency Act 1986 are based upon a proposal to the company and its creditors for a composition in satisfaction of its debts, or a scheme of arrangement of its affairs. The proposal must provide for some person to act as trustee, or otherwise to supervise its implementation. That person is referred to as the 'nominee' and must be a licensed insolvency practitioner.[221] While not required to do so, an administrator may be designated as the nominee and this is usually the case.[222] The nominee must then summon meetings of the creditors and shareholders[223] to decide whether to approve the proposal.[224] The meetings may modify the proposal in certain respects, but the modifications must not be so extensive as to change the character of the proposal so that it is no longer a composition in satisfaction of the company's debts or a scheme of arrangement in respect of its affairs.[225]

220 Section 6(7). There is a tight timescale for bringing a challenge. A procedural irregularity does not invalidate the approval given at a meeting unless it is the subject of a successful statutory challenge. Where the court is satisfied that grounds for challenge are made out, it may revoke or suspend approvals given by the meetings and direct the summoning of further meetings, either to consider a new proposal from the original proposer or to reconsider the original proposal. The court itself has no power to devise a new proposal for consideration.

221 Section 1(2).

222 Section 1.

223 Section 3. Where the nominee is not the liquidator or administrator, the summoning of meetings is subject to directions from the court: section 3(1). The procedural aspects of the meetings are governed by the Insolvency Rules 1986, Part 1, chapter 5.

224 Section 4. Failure to provide sufficient and accurate information to enable the creditor to consider the merits of the proposed arrangement with a view to determining if and how to cast her vote at the meeting is a material irregularity entitling the court to revoke approval of the arrangement under section 6(4) of the Insolvency Act – see *Re Trident Fashions* [2004] 2 BCLC 35. Lewison J added however, at para. 39: 'It seems to me that the court should only interfere if a judgment made by the administrator about the material to be placed before the creditors was a judgment to which no reasonable insolvency practitioner could come. The judgment should I think be made on the basis of the material available to the administrator at the time and not with the benefit of hindsight.'

225 Section 4(2).

159. In the CVA context, there are no separate classes and so there is no need to sort out potentially tricky issues concerning the proper composition of a class of creditors. Approval of a CVA requires a majority in excess of 75% in value of creditors present at the creditors' meeting so long as those voting in favour include more than half in value of independent creditors. A CVA, however, may not affect the rights of secured creditors without their consent or the rights of preferential creditors to be paid ahead of unsecured creditors. There is no procedure whereby the objections of secured creditors can be overcome.[226] Moreover, the lack of court sanction in the general run of cases may act as an obstacle to the recognition of CVAs abroad. Schemes of arrangement may be more easily 'saleable' internationally in this respect since they come with the judicial imprimatur of fairness.[227]

160. The scheme of arrangement procedure has proved popular as a restructuring vehicle for large companies and large corporate debt, though it has also been used as a takeover device. In effect, it serves as a form of 'debtor-in-possession' restructuring. The procedure enables a company, irrespective of solvency, to enter into a compromise or arrangement with any class of creditors. The statute requires that a majority in number representing 75% in value of the class of creditors affected must accept the scheme. Court sanction is also required and once these conditions are fulfilled, the arrangement binds abstainers or dissenters. In this way, the objections of a minority within a class of secured creditors may be overcome.[228] Schemes of arrangement do not necessarily involve an administration filing. Nor do they benefit from a statutory stay under the Insolvency Act though recently the court has fashioned a limited stay from the Civil Procedure Rules.[229]

161. The approval of a scheme of arrangement is a three-stage process.[230] Firstly, there must be an application to the court for an order that a meeting or meetings

---

226 Section 4(3) and (4). Some 'wriggle-room' is however introduced by the decision in *IRC v Wimbledon Football Club Ltd* [2005] 1 BCLC 66.

227 See generally J. Payne, (2013) 14 *European Business Organization Law Review* 563; L. Chan Ho, (2011) 26 *Journal of International Banking Law and Regulation* 434.

228 Under s. 895 Companies Act 2006 it has been held that the court has authority to sanction a scheme of arrangement in respect of a foreign incorporated company provided that sufficient connection with England is shown – see *Primacom Holdings GmbH v Credit Agricole* [2011] EWHC 3746. In *Re Rodenstock GmbH* [2011] EWHC 1104, [2011] WLR (D) 150, for instance, where a scheme of arrangement was approved in respect of a German incorporated company, sufficient connection with England was found to exist by virtue of the fact that the credit facilities extended to the company contained an English choice of law clause and an English jurisdiction clause. Moreover, there was expert evidence to the effect that the German courts would recognise the English court order.

229 *BlueCrest Mercantile BV v Vietnam Shipbuilding Industry Group* [2013] EWHC 1146. In Ireland there is provision for a court ordered stay under s. 451 Companies Act 2014.

230 *Re Hawk Insurance Co Ltd* [2001] 2 BCLC 480.

should be summoned. Secondly, the scheme proposals are put to the relevant meetings with a view to obtaining the appropriate level of approval. Thirdly, if approved, there must be a further application to the court for its sanction. At the first stage, the court tries to ensure that those affected have a proper opportunity of being present (in person or by proxy) at the meetings. The second stage ensures that the proposals are acceptable to the necessary majorities and, at the third stage, the court tries to ensure that the views and interests of scheme opponents receive impartial consideration.

162. In *Re Telewest (No 2)*[231] it was held that in deciding whether to sanction a scheme, the court must be satisfied that it is a fair scheme – one that 'an intelligent and honest man, a member of the class concerned and acting in respect of his interest, might reasonably approve.' The scheme proposed need not be the only fair scheme however, or even in the court's view, the best scheme. There is room for reasonable differences of view on these issues and, on matters of finance, shareholders or creditors are superior judges of their own interests than the courts. Lewison J in *Re British Aviation Insurance Co Ltd*[232] pointed out that the test is not whether the opposing creditors have reasonable objections to the scheme. A creditor may be equally reasonable in voting for or against the scheme and, in these circumstances, creditor democracy should prevail.

163. It has also been held by the courts that under the statutory procedure, it is only necessary to get the consent of classes of creditors with an economic interest in the proposed restructuring. Schemes of arrangements can therefore be used to squeeze out intermediate creditors – so-called 'mezzanine' creditors. *Re Bluebrook Ltd*[233] is a case in point where the 'squeeze out' of mezzanine creditors was held not to constitute unfair prejudice and ground for the court refusing to confirm a scheme.

164. In *Ireland*, a secured creditor may be deprived of all or part of its security or have the value of its claim written down in the context of a scheme of arrangement[234] and there is a special truncated procedure for the approval of schemes of arrangement under the examinership legislation.[235] The entire rationale of an examinership is the preparation and approval of proposals for a scheme of arrangement. In *Re Clare Textiles Ltd*[236] Costello J said that the only

231 [2005] BCC 36.

232 [2005] EWHC 1621 at para. 75. The judge added: 'Where, as here, those who voted in favour of the scheme are large and sophisticated corporations, the rigid application of this test as the sole criterion would rarely, I think, enable the court to refuse to sanction the scheme.'

233 [2009] EWHC 2114. See also *Re MyTravel plc* [2004] EWCA Civ 1734, [2005] 2 BCLC 123.

234 See ss. 449–454 Irish Companies Act 2014. In Ireland the procedure for approving a scheme is simpler in that the company itself may summon the relevant meetings of creditors rather than the court.

235 Sections 539–544 Companies Act 2014.

236 [1993] 2 IR 213 at 220.

proposals that an examiner was permitted to formulate were those which made it more likely that (a) the company and (b) the whole or part of its undertaking would survive as a going concern. He added that an examiner had no authority to prepare proposals involving the sale of the company's assets and its business, or its liquidation, and indeed the court had no power to confirm such proposals.

165. A bare majority of votes cast in person, or by proxy, is all that is required for acceptance of proposals in the case of meetings of members whereas at creditors' meetings a majority in number representing a majority in value of claims represented at the meeting is necessary. After the relevant meetings, the examiner's proposals must come before the court for final sanction. Those entitled to attend are (a) the company (b) the examiner and (c) any creditor or member whose claim or interest would be impaired if the proposals were implemented. The court may confirm, confirm subject to modifications, or reject the examiner's proposals.There must, however, be at least one consenting class of members or creditors whose interests or claims would be impaired by the proposals. Moreover, the court may not give approval unless it is satisfied that the scheme proposed is fair and equitable in relation to impaired classes who do not affect the proposals and there is no unfair prejudice in relation to any interested party.[237]

166. It is specifically provided that where the court confirms proposals, these proposals shall, notwithstanding any other enactment, be binding on all the creditors or the class or classes of creditors affected by the proposals in respect of any claims against the company.[238]

Question 18: Can an under-secured creditor claim from the insolvency estate in respect of any deficiency arising as a result of the enforcement of the security?

167. Yes. If a secured creditor realises his security but the amount so realised is insufficient to discharge the debt, he may prove for the balance in the liquidation.[239]

---

237 Section 541(4) Companies Act 2014.
238 Section 541(6) Companies Act 2014.
239 Rule 4.88(1).

D. REGISTRATION OF SECURITY RIGHTS

Question 19: To what extent must security rights over assets be publicised by registration or filing to ensure the effectiveness of the security interest over parties other than the debtor and in the event of insolvency proceedings?

168. In the *UK* details of the main types of charge created by companies have to be registered at the Companies registration office – Companies House. The main consequences of non-registration are suffered by the charge holder who loses its priority where the company goes into administration or liquidation. The registration obligation is now laid down in the Companies Act 2006 (Amendment of Part 25) Regulations 2013[240] which came into force on 6 April 2013. Schedule 1 to the Regulations is inserted as Chapter A1 at the beginning of Part 25 of the Companies Act 2006.[241]

169. It should be noted that the obligation only applies to charges strictly so-called and does not cover other security mechanisms nor 'quasi-securities'. The latter are functionally equivalent legal devices such as finance leases, retention of title clauses in sale of goods contracts or factoring arrangements, i.e. the absolute assignment of receivables. 'Quasi-securities' may involve many of the same economic consequences as charges but have different legal characteristics and effects.[242]

170. The company charge registration system does not apply to security agreements executed by individuals but there is a parallel system in place; namely,

---

240 SI 2013/600.

241 SI 2013/600 Schedule 1 sets out the new CA 2006 Part 25, Ch. A1 of the Act containing CA 2006 sections 859A to 859Q.

242 In Ireland the system for the registration of charges operates in roughly the same way to that in the UK. As far as companies are concerned, the registration obligation is now contained in Part 7 Companies Act 2014 and applies to all charges subject to certain stated exceptions. There are now two separate procedures for registration of charges. A one-stage procedure requires that particulars of all charges created be delivered to the Companies Registration Office (CRO) within 21 days of their creation while a new two-stage procedure provides that a notice may be sent to the CRO stating the company's intention to create a charge, followed up by a further notification within 21 days of the creation and stating that fact. The CRO is required to issue a certificate of due registration which is stated to be conclusive evidence that there has been compliance with all the requirements of the Act as to registration (s. 415) but if the particulars of a charge delivered to the CRO omit the required particulars in respect of one or more properties to which the charge relates, the evidential effect of the certificate shall not extend to these properties.

There is a facility of applying to the court for late registration of a charge (s. 417). An unregistered charge becomes void in the event of the company creating the charge going into liquidation and it is also provided that the time of registration rather than the time of creation becomes the priority determinant point in respect of two charges of the same type (s. 412).

the Bills of Sale Acts 1878–1882 as amended.[243] Moreover, as far as individuals engaged in business are concerned, section 344 Insolvency Act 1986 provides that a general assignment of existing or future book debts, or any class of them, has to be registered under the Bills of Sale Act. If the individual is subsequently adjudged bankrupt, then an unregistered assignment is void against the trustee of the bankrupt's estate in respect of book debts which were not paid before the presentation of the bankruptcy petition.

171. The 1878 Act has the long title 'An Act to consolidate and amend the law for preventing frauds upon creditors by secret Bills of Sale of Personal Chattels'. The rationale of this Act and of the Act of 1882 was explained by Lord Herschell in *Manchester, Sheffield and Lincolnshire Railway Co v North Wagon Railway Co.*[244] He said the former enactment was designed for the protection of creditors, and to prevent their rights being affected by secret transfers of chattels that were permitted to remain in the ostensible possession of a person who had parted with the legal title in them. Under the statutory scheme, a bill of sale has to be attested and registered in a public register within seven days. Failure to comply with the registration requirement renders the bill void but only as against creditors or their representatives. As between the parties thereto, an unregistered bill of sale remains perfectly valid.

172. As regards the rationale of the 1882 Act, Lord Herschell said:[245] 'It was to prevent needy persons being entrapped into signing complicated documents which they might often be unable to comprehend and so being subjected by their creditors to the enforcement of harsh and unreasonable provisions. A form was accordingly provided to which bills of sale were to conform, and the result of non-compliance with the statute was to render the bill of sale void even as between the parties to it. But this being the object, the enactment is, as we have seen, limited to bills of sale given "by way of security for the payment of money by the grantor thereof."'

173. The 1882 Act requires that security bills of sale should be in a certain form so that the nature and terms of the loan and security are clearly marked out. The insistence on the statutory form has the consequence that certain categories of security cannot be employed as they are by nature incompatible with the statutory form. Section 9 of the 1882 Act also renders invalid a security bill of sale that is not in accordance with the statutory form. The implications of this edict were spelled out in *Smith v Whiteman*[246] where it was held that derogation

243 See generally G. McBain, (2011) *Journal of Business Law* 475. There is similar Bills of Sale legislation in Ireland.

244 (1880) 13 App Cas 554.

245 *Ibid.* at 560–561.

246 [1909] 2 KB 437. See also *Davies v Rees* (1886) 17 QBD 408; *Smith v Whiteman* [1909] 2 KB 437; and *Bradford Advance Co Ltd v Ayers* [1924] WN 152.

from the statutory form avoided a bill even as regards the grantor's personal covenant contained in the bill to repay the principal lent and interest thereon. The money advanced together with reasonable interest was however recoverable in a restitutionary action.

174. The cumbersome nature of the Bills of Sale Acts means that this form of lending has traditionally not been that common in practice though it seems that lending by means of a bill of sale on motor vehicles – 'logbook' lending – has become fairly popular in recent years.[247] Consumer purchases in *England* are often funded instead through hire-purchase agreements. Technically speaking, these are agreements for the hire of goods coupled with an option to purchase the goods at the end of the hire period.

175. The Bills of Sale Acts have a consumer protection aspect to them albeit one which is imperfectly and inappropriately realised. The company charge registration system has a different orientation, however. Its main rationale is the provision of information for persons such as credit reference agencies and prospective charge holders who wish to assess the creditworthiness of the company. For instance, prospective charge holders are able to ascertain from the register whether or not security has already been created over the assets of the company. In consequence, they are better informed about making a lending decision and structuring the terms of any loan.

Question 20: Can you describe briefly the nature of the filing or registration system and whether it is publicly accessible?

176. The Companies Act 2006 (Amendment of Part 25) Regulations 2013[248] introduce a new UK-wide registration system that applies to all UK incorporated companies irrespective of the place of incorporation of the company within the *UK*. Instead of a list of charges requiring registration, the requirement to register applies to all charges, subject to specified exceptions. Either the charge holder or the company creating the charge may affect registration and there is a 21-day

---

247 See the Department for Business, Innovation and Skills consultation on proposals to ban the use of bills of sale for consumer lending: <https://www.gov.uk/government/uploads/system/uploads/attachment_data/file/31481/a_20better_20deal_20for_20consumers_20consultation_20on_20proposals_20to_20ban_20the_20use_20of_20bills_20of_20sale_20for_20consumer_20lending.pdf> accessed 17 May 2016. In the event, the proposals were never implemented and instead an industry Code of Practice was put in place instead: <https://www.gov.uk/government/uploads/system/uploads/attachment_data/file/31484/11-516-government-response-proposal-ban-bills-of-sale.pdf> accessed 17 May 2016.

See now the Law Commission proposals on Bills of Sale – see <http://www.lawcom.gov.uk/project/bills-of-sale/> accessed 17 May 2016.

248 SI 2013/600.

time limit from the date of creation for registering particulars of a charge. If the charge is not registered within that period it becomes invalid in the event of the company creating the charge going into administration or liquidation. There is however the possibility of going to court and obtaining an order that permits late registration. The civil consequences of failure to register, impacting severely on the charge holder, means that in practice, it is likely that the charge holder will attend to registration matters as was the former practice.

177. Under the new law, specified particulars of the charge are provided to Companies House along with a certified copy of the instrument of charge although 'personal information' may be redacted from the security instrument. The company's file that is available for public inspection at Companies House contains both the particulars and the security instrument itself (minus the redacted information). The Registrar allocates a unique reference code to the charge and there is also provision for the issue by the Registrar of a certificate of registration of the charge. The certificate must state (a) the registered name and number of the company in respect of which the charge was registered and (b) the unique reference code allocated to the charge. The certificate is stated to be conclusive evidence that the required documents were delivered to the Registrar before the end of the relevant period allowed for delivery.

178. The new law also requires registration of a so-called negative pledge clause: 'whether any of the terms of the charge prohibit or restrict the company from creating any further security that will rank equally with or ahead of the charge'. This may impact on priorities between fixed and floating charges, however, unlike in previous drafts of the regulations, there is nothing specific to say that a 'person taking a charge over a company's property shall be taken to have notice of any matter requiring registration and disclosed on the register at the time the charge is created'.[249]

179. Section 859(A) provides that Companies House must register a charge if, before the end of the period allowed for delivery, the company or any person interested in the charge delivers to Companies House for registration a section 859D statement of particulars of the charge alongside a certified copy of the instrument of charge. The period allowed for delivery is 21 days beginning with the day after the date of creation of the charge, unless an order allowing an extended period is made under section 859F(3). For the first time, there is a statutory definition of the date of creation of a charge. In the standard case where a charge has been created or evidenced by an instrument, the date of creation is defined as the date of delivery of the deed where the instrument is a deed that has been executed and has immediate effect on execution and delivery.

249 In Ireland, s. 412 Companies Act 2014 deems particulars of a negative pledge clause to be extraneous material which should not be registered – s. 412(6).

180. The new section 859D deals with the statement of particulars that has to be delivered to the Registrar alongside a certified copy of the instrument of charge. In the standard case where the charge has been created or evidenced by an instrument, the statement of particulars must contain the following information:

(a) the registered name and number of the company;
(b) the date of creation of the charge;
(c) the name of each of the persons in whose favour the charge has been created or of the security agents or trustees holding the charge for the benefit of one or more persons; or,
(d) whether the instrument is expressed to contain a floating charge and, if so, whether it is expressed to cover all the property and undertaking of the company;
(e) whether any of the terms of the charge prohibit or restrict the company from creating further security that will rank equally with or ahead of the charge;
(f) whether (and if so, a short description of) any land, ship, aircraft or intellectual property that is registered or required to be registered in the *UK*, is subject to the charge;
(g) whether the instrument includes a charge over:
    (i) any tangible or corporeal property, or
    (ii) any intangible or incorporeal property, not described in the previous head.

It should be noted that a company which holds charged property as a trustee can file a statement to that effect.[250] The filing however is optional rather than compulsory.

181. Section 859B deals with the situation where a series of secured debentures has been issued to which the holders are entitled pari passu. In this case the section 859D statement of particulars must also contain the following information; namely:

(a) the name of each of the trustees for the debenture holders, or where there are more than four such persons, the names of any four persons listed in the charge instrument as trustees for the debenture holders, and a statement that there are other such persons;
(b) the dates of the resolutions authorising the issue of the series;
(c) the date of the covering instrument (if any) by which the series is created or defined.

---

250 Section 859J.

Section 859G makes provision for the redaction of information. It provides that the certified copy of an instrument delivered to the Registrar need not contain:

(a) personal information relating to an individual (other than the name of an individual);
(b) the number or other identifier of a bank or securities account of a company or individual;
(c) a signature.

There is no provision, however, for the redaction of any other information even if it is of a commercially sensitive nature.

182. The changes to the system introduced in 2013 should improve transparency and streamline the practical operation of the registration process. The main practical change sees the introduction of electronic registration and it is envisaged that this will supersede paper-based registration though a facility for the latter is still retained. Despite the changes, however, the UK system is still essentially a transaction-based system of registration and it should be contrasted with the notice filing system under Article 9 of the United States Uniform Commercial Code (UCC) and the Australian, New Zealand and Canadian Personal Property Security Acts (PPSAs).[251] The main difference between notice filing and traditional systems of registration is that notice filing is party specific rather than specific to a particular transaction. The notice filed does not record details of a particular security but rather the fact that certain parties have entered into, or may, in the future, enter into, a secured transaction in relation to specified property. The nature of the notice filing system means that notice may be filed before a transaction and the contemplated transaction may never in fact materialise. The same notice may also operate in respect of a series of transactions between the same parties. Furthermore, the notice on the register is, of necessity, generic rather than specific in character and functions more as an invitation to make further inquiries rather than being a full description of the security right. Article 9-type regimes also apply to all security interests, regardless of whether the security provider is an individual or a business entity.

183. Security rights over certain types of asset are subject to 'dual' registration requirements, i.e. registration at the company charges register and registration at a separate 'assets-based' or 'ownership' register.[252] This dual registration

---

251 Scottish Law Commission discussion paper *Registration of Rights in Security by Companies* (October 2002), 8.

252 For more details see the Law Commission Consultative Report No 176 *Company Security Interests* (2004) at para. 3.324 <http://www.lawcom.gov.uk/wp-content/uploads/2015/03/cp176_Company_Security_Interests_Consultative_Report.pdf> accessed 19 May 2016; and see also W. Gough, *Company Charges*, Chapter 35.

requirement applies in respect of certain security rights over land, ships, aircraft and intellectual property rights.

184. The Land Registration Act 2002 establishes a register of title to land and, in general, charges over land must be registered with the Land Registry as well as with the Companies Registry.[253] The Merchant Shipping Act 1995 and the Merchant Shipping (Registration of Ships) Regulations 1993[254] provide that legal mortgages of ships should be in a prescribed form and also provide for the registration of legal mortgages of ships in a register for ships.[255]

185. Section 86 of the Civil Aviation Act 1982 requires the registration of mortgages of aircraft in a 'Register of Aircraft Mortgages' to be maintained by the Civil Aviation Authority.[256]

186. Charges on patents,[257] trade marks[258] and registered designs[259] must, in addition to registration with the Companies Registry, be notified to the Intellectual Property Office.[260]

Question 21: To what extent does 'possession' or control of the secured assets serve as an alternative method to registration or filing in ensuring third party effectiveness of the security interest?

187. Under the original version of Part 25 of the Companies Act 2006, and Companies Acts going back to 1900, the registration requirement applied only to a statutorily defined list of charges. While the categories of registrable charge

---

253 For the equivalents in Ireland see the Registration of Deeds and Titles Act 2006 which established a property registration authority, see <www.landregistry.ie/> accessed 17 May 2016.

254 SI 1993/3138.

255 See Merchant Shipping Act 1995, Schedule 1 'Private Law Provisions for registered ships' and Part VII of the 1993 Regulations dealing with mortgages of ships. For the Irish equivalents see Merchant Marine Act 1955 and in particular s. 52.

256 In Ireland, the International Interests in Mobile Equipment (Cape Town Convention) Act 2005 gives effect to the Cape Town Convention and Aircraft Protocol Convention under Irish law. Aircraft mortgages or charges with an international interest must be registered on the international registry established pursuant to the Convention. This registry is supervised by the International Civil Aviation Organisation (ICAO) and is maintained in Dublin by Aviareto (a joint venture with the Irish government). The UK has now implemented the Convention though the International Interests in Aircraft Equipment (Cape Town Convention) Regulations 2015 SI 912/2015.

257 Patents Act 1977, s. 33(2). For Ireland, s. 85 Patents Act 1992.

258 Trade Marks Act 1994, s. 25(2). For Ireland, s. 29(2) Trade Marks Act 1996.

259 Registered Designs Act 1949, s. 19(1) as amended by Copyright, Designs and Patents Act 1988, Sch. 3, para. 18. For Ireland, s. 41 Industrial Designs Act 2001.

260 See generally I. Davies, (2006) 26 *Oxford Journal of Legal Studies* 559.

have been broadened over the years, the basic statutory approach remained the same until the 2013 amending regulations. The registration obligation now covers all charges save for those on the narrow itemised list of exclusions. The registration obligation does not cover pledges and liens. The fact, however, that in the case of pledges and liens the creditor generally has possession of the items used as security might be taken as the functional equivalent of notice to third parties of the existence of the security.

188. Millett LJ in *Re Cosslett (Contractors) Ltd*[261] referred to the four types of security interest known to English law: mortgages, charges, pledges and liens. The mortgage/charge is a non-possessory security whereas the pledge is a possessory security. As we have seen, a pledge may be described as the actual or constructive delivery of possession of an asset to a creditor by way of security.[262]

189. The registration obligation also does extend to liens. Liens fall into three categories: common law liens, equitable liens and contractual liens. The first two types come into existence by operation of law in certain circumstances and not by agreement between the parties and therefore may be said to fall outside registration requirements on this basis. The third type of lien (the contractual lien), however, depends on contractual agreement, but it has been held that the existence of a power of sale over the secured property in the relevant contract does not turn a contractual lien into a charge.[263]

190. *In Re Lehman Brothers International (Europe) (In Administration)*[264] it was common ground between the parties that one could not have contractual lien on anything other than tangibles and old-fashioned bearer securities. More recently however, in *Your Response Ltd v Database Business Media,*[265] it seems to have been implied that the parties to a contract could make express provision in their contract for a lien over at least certain types of intangible property, in that case a database.

191. Apart from the general absence of party consent to their creation, one could also justify the absence of any registration requirements pertaining to liens on the pragmatic basis that they are likely to be short term in duration. Pragmatism is at the heart of what is now section 859A(6) Companies Act 2006 which exempts

---

261 [1998] Ch 495 at 508. In *Re Lehman Brothers International (Europe) (In Administration* [2012] EWHC 2997 at para. 47, Briggs J suggested that 'there may be rare cases in which security rights fall wholly outside the recognised categories of lien, pledge, mortgage or charge, and into a residual, purely contractual, category sometimes categorised as turning the grantor's property into a form of "flawed asset"'.

262 See generally Willes J in *Halliday v Holgate* (1868) LR 3 Ex 299.

263 See *Re Hamlet International plc* [1999] 2 BCLC 506.

264 [2012] EWHC 2997 at para. 34.

265 [2014] EWCA Civ 281.

certain categories of charge from the company charge registration requirements, namely:

(a) a charge in favour of a landlord on a cash deposit given as a security in connection with the lease of land;[266]
(b) a charge created by a member of Lloyd's (within the meaning of the Lloyd's Act 1982) to secure its obligations in connection with its underwriting business at Lloyd's;
(c) a charge excluded from the application of this section by or under any other Act.

192. According to the Financial Collateral Arrangements (No 2) Regulations 2003, the registration of charge provisions do not apply in respect of a security financial collateral arrangement, or any charge created or otherwise arising under a security financial collateral arrangement. These regulations are designed to implement the EU Financial Collateral Directive[267] and the preamble refers to the need to achieve a balance between market efficiency and the safety of the parties to the arrangement, and of third parties. Consequently, the Directive is limited in its application to those financial collateral arrangements which provide for some form of dispossession, i.e. 'the provision of the financial collateral, and where the provision of the financial collateral can be evidenced in writing or in a durable medium, ensuring thereby the traceability of the collateral'.[268] The Financial Collateral Arrangements (No 2) Regulations 2003 apply the new regime in all cases where the collateral provider and the collateral taker are both corporates.[269]

193. In *Cukurova Finance International Ltd v Alfa Telecom Turkey Ltd*[270] the Privy Council pointed out that the assumption underlying the Directive that 'full ownership' is with either the collateral provider, or the collateral taker, did not apply very easily to a legal or equitable English mortgage or charge where each

266 In CA 2006, s. 859A(7) 'cash' is defined as including foreign currency. In Ireland the relevant exemptions are contained in s. 408(1) Companies Act 2014 and include cash, shares, bonds or debt instruments.

267 Directive 2002/47/EC on financial collateral arrangements (OJ 2002 L168). The SI 2003/3226 Financial Collateral Arrangements (No 2) Regulations 2003 have been amended by the Financial Markets and Insolvency (Settlement Finality and Financial Collateral Arrangements) (Amendment) Regulations 2010, SI 2010/2993 extending the collateral subject to the regulations to 'credit claims' and introducing a new definition of possession of financial collateral. In Ireland the implementing regulations are now the European Communities (Financial Collateral Arrangements) Regulations 2010, SI 626/2010.

268 Paragraph 10 of the preamble.

269 SI 2003/3226, reg. 3.

270 [2009] UKPC 19, [2009] 3 All ER 849 at para. 5.

party had a proprietary interest in the collateral as long as the security was in place.[271] The UK implementing regulations are also problematic in practice.[272] According to regulation 4 of the Financial Collateral Arrangements (No 2) Regulations, the registration of charge provisions in the Companies Act does not have any application in respect of a security financial collateral arrangement or any charge created or otherwise arising under a security financial collateral arrangement. To constitute a security financial collateral arrangement there mustbe, inter alia, an agreement or arrangement, evidenced in writing, where:

(a) the purpose of the agreement or arrangement is to secure the relevant financial obligations owed to the collateral taker;
(b) the collateral provider creates or there arises a security interest in financial collateral to secure those obligations.[273]

194. Many aspects of this definition were considered by Briggs J in *Re Lehman Brothers International (Europe)*[274] including the 'purpose' aspect. He suggested that where there is an express contract for the creation of a security, the purpose test is automatically satisfied. He noted that the Directive itself did not contain any 'purpose' test and he seemed sympathetic to the view that the additional 'purpose' requirement in the regulations might reasonably be regarded as mere surplusage. The judge also avoided a strictly literal interpretation of the requirement that a security financial collateral arrangement was limited to securities given for obligations owed to the collateral taker, holding that this part of the definition should be treated as descriptive rather than restrictive. Otherwise, and contrary to the purpose of the Directive, it would appear to 'exclude security given to a debenture trustee for debts owed by the collateral giver to a class of investors, where the collateral taker would not to any significant extent be likely to be a creditor at all.'[275]

195. 'Financial collateral' is defined as meaning either cash or financial instruments. There is also a lengthy definition of 'financial instruments' which includes shares in companies, and other securities equivalent to shares

---

271 It was accepted in the case however that an English charge of shares must be regarded as a security financial collateral arrangement. See also *Cukurova Finance International Ltd v Alfa Telecom Turkey Ltd* [2013] UKPC 2 at para. 101.

272 On the effect of gold-plating of the Directive by the Financial Collateral Arrangements (No 2) Regulations 2003, see *Cukurova Finance International Ltd v Alfa Telecom Turkey Ltd* [2013] UKPC 2 at paras. 100–102.

273 See reg. 3 of the Financial Collateral Arrangements (No 2) Regulations 2003.

274 [2012] EWHC 2997 (Ch) at para. 94. See also para. 98 cautioning against the subjective investigation of the parties' motivation in a scheme that was meant to encourage the reliable creation of security with minimum formality and minimum risk of uncertainty or unenforceability.

275 [2012] EWHC 2997 (Ch) at para. 99.

in companies as well as bonds. The expression 'security interest' is defined to include fixed charges as well as 'a charge created as a floating charge where the financial collateral charged is delivered, transferred, held, registered or otherwise designated so as to be in the possession or under the control of the collateral-taker or a person acting on its behalf; any right of the collateral-provider to substitute equivalent financial collateral or withdraw excess financial collateral shall not prevent the financial collateral being in the possession or under the control of the collateral-taker ...'.

196. According to the UK consultation document on implementation of the regulations, the definition of 'security financial collateral arrangement' and of 'security interest' in the regulations means that they do 'not apply to floating charges before the charge has crystallised and some control over the collateral has passed to the charge holder. Serious thought was given to extending the regulations to all floating charges. However, we have rejected this extension in the interests of providing appropriate protection for third parties, particularly unsecured creditors who appear after the floating charge has been taken.'[276]

197. It is not clear, however, whether the regulations, as drafted, accomplish the professed legislative objective. In support of this interpretation, however, one might say that the essence of the floating charge is that the charge giver and not the charge taker should have control of the charged assets and therefore the regulations only apply where the floating charge crystallises and control passes to the charge taker.

198. In *Gray v G-T-P Group Ltd*,[277] the judge accepted that the requirement for control in the regulations meant that the collateral taker should have the legal right to deal with collateral as distinct from having merely administrative control over the collateral. In the case of an uncrystallised floating charge, it is the collateral giver and not the collateral taker who has the legal right to deal with the collateral. Therefore, one could infer from the judgment that the regulations only take effect in when the floating charge has crystallised, though the judge did not make this point explicitly. He said that if the collateral taker could not prevent the collateral provider from dealing with the charged assets, then he did not, in any legal sense, have control though he might have control in an administrative or practical sense which was insufficient for the application of the regulations.

199. In coming to this interpretation, the judge looked to the totality of the regulations. For example, it was stated specifically that a right to withdraw

276 'Implementation of the Directive on Financial Collateral Arrangements' (July 2003) at para. 2.10.

277 [2011] BCC 869.

excess financial collateral would not prevent the regulations applying but, if the regulations applied anyway, then the collateral provider could withdraw the entirety of the collateral as a matter of legal right. The judge also looked at the preamble to the Directive which made it clear that the Directive was only intended to cover those financial collateral arrangements which provided for some form of dispossession. 'Dispossession' under the Directive seemed to signify a situation where the legal right to the charged asset was removed from the collateral provider.

200. The 'dispossession' requirement under the Directive and Regulations has also been considered in *Re Lehman Brothers International (Europe)*[278] – a case where the LBIE administrators sought directions on the interpretation, characterisation, validity and effect of security provisions in a master custody agreement (MCA) that had been used between LBIE and an affiliated company, namely LBF. LBIE held assets as custodian for clients and affiliates and the documentation provided that LBIE as custodian had a security on property held by it until the satisfaction of all obligations owed by the other party to LBIE or any Lehman Brothers entity. The judge decided that the security created by the MCA was a floating charge even though the MCA had referred to it as a 'general lien'.

201. He went on to decide, however, that the floating charge was not a 'security financial collateral arrangement' because the collateral provider, LBF, had not been sufficiently dispossessed.[279] The MCA provided that LBIE had the right to prevent the other party, LBF, from withdrawing assets beyond those which LBIE considered necessary to pay LBF's debts to LBIE, but this right did not extend to LBF's debts to other Lehman Brothers entities. With regard to the debts owed to LBIE, LBIE was considered to have sufficient possession and control, but not with regard to the debts owed to the other entities. Apart from its debts to LBIE, LBF could do what it liked with the property pending crystallisation of the floating charge, regardless of its liabilities to the other entities.

202. The judge broadly agreed with the analysis that 'control' means legal control, rather than administrative control[280] stating that what needs to be

---

278 [2012] EWHC 2997 at para. 34.

279 Nevertheless, the judge rejected the proposition that there was a 'bilaterality' test in the Regulations – the argument that the MCA charge failed to qualify as a 'security financial collateral arrangement' because it was multilateral to the extent that it created security for the debts of other Lehman Brothers entities, rather than for LBIE alone – [2012] EWHC 2997 at para. 86.

280 Note that the Financial Collateral Arrangements (No 2) Regulations 2003 have been amended by the Financial Markets and Insolvency (Settlement Finality and Financial Collateral Arrangements) (Amendment) Regulations 2010, SI 2010/2993, which, inter alia, introduce a

shown is that that there is 'sufficient possession or control in the hands of the collateral taker for it to be proper to describe the collateral provider as having been "dispossessed". There will be cases in which the collateral is sufficiently clearly in the possession of the collateral taker that no further investigation of its rights of control is necessary. In other cases … it will be necessary to analyse the degree of control thereby conferred on the collateral taker. There may be some cases, in particular where there is no delivery, transfer or holding to or by the collateral taker, but merely some form of designation, where the collateral remains wholly in the possession of the collateral provider, but on terms which give a legal right to the taker to ensure that it is dealt with in accordance with its directions.'[281]

E. PLURALITY OF SECURITY RIGHTS

Question 22: Is it possible to have more than one set of security rights (security interest) over the same asset?

203. Under the common law, it is theoretically possible to create multiple security interests over the same asset. Effectively what the charge giver is doing is creating a security interest over its 'equity of redemption', i.e. its stake in the property after the encumbrance represented by the prior security interest has been discharged.

Question 23: What are the rules for determining priority between competing security interests in the same property?

204. Under current English law the question of priorities between competing security interests is, in theory, fairly complex since one must make do with a system that consists of a mixture of inherited common law and equity, occasionally supplemented by statute. The existing priority rules have been succinctly summarised in the Diamond Report,[282] which states: 'Fixed legal charges which are registered within 21 days of creation rank with one another according to the time of creation and fixed legal charges created before a floating charge crystallises have priority over the floating charge, but subject to this the

new definition of possession of financial collateral. It is provided that 'possession' includes the case where financial collateral has been credited to an account in the name of the collateral taker, provided that the rights of the collateral provider are limited to rights to substitute equivalent collateral or withdraw excess collateral.

281 [2012] EWHC 2997 at para. 136.

282 A. Diamond, *A Review of Security Interests in Property*, 124.

rules are complicated, resting on the distinction between legal and equitable charges and involving questions of notice.'

205. The asset-based property and security registers also establish priority rules of specialised application. In respect of land, priority between registered charges is determined by date of registration rather than date of creation.[283] The Merchant Shipping Act 1995 and the Merchant Shipping (Registration of Ships) Regulations 1993[284] also lay down a statutory scheme of priority for registered mortgages based on the order of registration.[285] Priority is by date of registration irrespective of the date of creation of the security agreement and a registered mortgage will take priority over any other mortgage or charge that is either not registered or registered subsequently. It appears to be irrelevant that the mortgagee had notice of an earlier charge through its registration at the Companies Registry.[286]

206. The same broad principles apply to aircraft mortgages.[287] Section 86 of the Civil Aviation Act 1982, as well as making provision for the registration of mortgages of aircraft in a 'Register of Aircraft Mortgages' to be maintained by the Civil Aviation Authority, makes provision for the priority of registered mortgages. The details of the law, embodied in the Mortgaging of Aircraft Order 1972 (MAO),[288] have been succinctly summarised in the Law Commission Consultative Report on Company Security Interests as follows:[289] 'The MAO provides that an aircraft registered in the UK nationality register, or such an aircraft together with any store or spare parts for that aircraft, may be made security for a loan or other valuable consideration.[290] Registered mortgages have priority over unregistered mortgages and charges, and priority between

283 Land Registration Act 2002, s. 48.

284 SI 1993/3138.

285 See Merchant Shipping Act 1995 Schedule 1 para. 8. In Ireland s. 50 of the Mercantile Marine Act 1955 makes provision for the registration of mortgages over Irish flagged ships with priority determined by the order of registration – s. 52.

286 Schedule 1 para. 8(1) stating that priority shall be 'determined by the order in which the mortgages were registered (and not by reference to any other matter)'. Regulation 59 of the Merchant Shipping (Registration of Ships) Regulations creates however a system of priority notices. This system allows an intending mortgagee to lodge a priority notice signifying the intention to take a mortgage and provided that substantive registration takes place within 30 days, priority of the mortgage is backdated to lodgement of the priority notice.

287 For Ireland, under Article 29 of the Cape Town Convention (implemented in Ireland by the International Interests in Mobile Equipment (Cape Town Convention) Act 2005) there is a similar principle of priority by order of registration irrespective of notice of an earlier unregistered interest.

288 SI 1972/1268; and for a more detailed treatment see P. Thorne, 'Aircraft mortgages' in N. Palmer and E. McKendrick (eds.), *Interests in Goods*; N. Meeson, *Ship and Aircraft Mortgages;* and most comprehensively G. McBain, *Aircraft Finance: Registration, Security & Enforcement.*

289 Law Commission Consultation Paper No 176, para. 3.314.

290 MAO, Art. 3.

registered mortgages is decided by reference to the date of registration, although nothing in the priority rules is to be construed as giving a registered mortgage any priority over any possessory lien for work done to the aircraft or statutory right of detention.[291] Priority notices may also be entered in the mortgage register.'[292]

207. On the other hand, with the patent[293] and trademark[294] registers, priority is not determined strictly by the order of registration. It appears that actual knowledge of an earlier registered charge in the Companies Registry will prevent a subsequent charge holder from obtaining priority, even if the earlier charge is the second to be registered, or not registered at all, in the patent and trademark registers.

208. Leaving aside the specialist asset registers, there is no single reference point for determining priorities under English law. Unlike the position in the *US* under Article 9 of the Uniform Commercial Code, registration is not per se a priority determinant between competing security interests in the same property.[295] Under English law, interests that involve the use of absolute title by way of security, such as interests under trusts and 'simple' retention of title clauses,[296] enjoy super-priority status and, moreover, they are not subject to any requirement of registration. As far as charges, strictly co-called, are concerned, while failure to register a registrable charge will result in the invalidation of the charge in the event of the corporate debtor going into liquidation, once registration has been duly affected, then priority among competing charges turns on the date of creation. In other words, fixed charges rank amongst themselves according to the order of creation but, on the other hand, a floating charge is postponed, priority-wise, to a fixed charge, irrespective of the order in which the two charges were created.[297] This is the position unless it appears that the

291 MAO, Art. 14.

292 MAO, Art. 5(1).

293 According to s. 33(1) Patents Act 1977 priority is determined by the date of registration, but a later transaction will have priority over an earlier transaction if (a) it is not registered, (b) notice has not been given to the comptroller, or (c) in any case the party to the later transaction was unaware of the earlier one. In Ireland, s. 79 Patents Act 1992 provides that the rules of law applicable to the ownership and devolution of personal property apply in relation to patents as they apply in relation to other choses in action.

294 Section 25(3) Trade Marks Act 1994 provides that a later transaction will have priority over an earlier one if the party to the later transaction is ignorant of the earlier one. In Ireland, s. 30(2) Trade Marks Act 1996 states that equities in respect of a registered trade mark may be enforced in like manner as in respect of other personal property.

295 Unlike also the position in Ireland under s. 412 Companies Act 2014 where time of registration is established as the reference point for determining priority between two charges of the same type over the same property.

296 Put shortly, the property never comes into the beneficial ownership of the insolvent entity.

297 See G. McCormack, [1994] *Journal of Business Law* 587.

floating charge instrument contains a 'negative pledge' or 'restrictive clause', i.e. a clause forbidding or restricting the creation of any subsequent security having priority to the floating charge and particulars of the restrictive clause have been duly registered.

209. The complexities in the law governing priorities has led to calls for legislation that clarifies the position, or at least for private law solutions negotiated amongst secured parties. As one commentator has said:[298] 'The priority rules are a potential minefield for secured creditors. The rules vary depending on the nature of the assets concerned, floating charges are governed by a different set of rules altogether, and there is yet another set of rules for money lent after the creditor has received notice of a subsequent charge … For all these reasons, it is common practice for secured creditors to enter into a priority agreement with any other secured creditor of which they become aware.'

210. As far as charges are concerned, the priority rules may be stated in more detail in point form as follows:

(a) A duly registered charge (charge A) takes priority over a previously or subsequently created unregistered charge (charge B).
(b) There is an exception to the foregoing rule if charge B is prior in point of time to charge A and charge B was duly registered within 21 days of its creation even though in actual fact it was registered after the registration of particulars of charge A. This is despite the fact that charge holder A may have relied on the absence of any charges appearing on the register when advancing its money. Therefore it is clear that registration is not a reference point for determining priorities.
(c) A registered charge ranks after a prior unregistered charge over the same property where the registered charge takes expressly subject to the first unregistered charge.
(d) Where particulars of a charge (charge A) are delivered for registration outside the 21-day period from the date of the charge's creation and a second charge (charge B) is created before actual registration of charge A, charge B takes priority over charge A, irrespective of whether charge B was created within, or outside, the period of 21 days from the date of creation of charge A.[299]
(e) While the statement of the foregoing four rules was premised on the assumption that all the charges were fixed legal charges, in fact there is

[298] See R. Calnan, 'Taking Security in England' in M. Bridge and R. Stevens (eds.), *Cross-Border Security and Insolvency*, 17 at 33.

[299] In the Companies Act 1989 the issue was specifically addressed in s. 95. This particular provision was never implemented.

little modification of the priority rules if a later legal charge is competing against an equitable fixed charge which is prior in point of time. A holder of a legal interest takes free from the holder of an earlier equitable interest in the same property, provided that the subsequent holder of the legal estate is bona fide, has paid value, and is without notice, actual or constructive of the earlier equitable interest.[300] Since registration is deemed to constitute notice, the holder of the subsequent legal interest will be postponed to the holder of the prior equitable interest.

(f) In certain circumstances, earlier charge holders may be able to make subsequent advances that rank in priority to any loans made by intervening charge holders.

(g) A duly registered fixed charge ranks ahead of a duly registered floating charge irrespective of the respective dates of creation of the two charges except where the floating charge contains a restrictive clause.

(h) It appears that a floating charge has priority over a subsequent fixed charge (assuming due registration in both cases) where the subsequent fixed charge holder has notice of a restrictive clause in the earlier floating charge.[301] A restrictive clause (sometimes called a negative pledge clause) is a provision in the debenture containing the floating charge which prohibits or restricts the creation of subsequent fixed charges ranking prior to, or pari passu, with the earlier floating charge.

(i) The new registration of company charge regime introduced in 2013 makes details of a restrictive clause compulsorily registrable and this ought to give a subsequent fixed charge holder notice of the restrictive clause.

(j) If a fixed charge holder has priority over a floating charge holder in a particular case because the fixed charge holder has actual notice of a restrictive clause, then this gives rise to a circularity problem that also implicates the preferential creditors who, in terms of priorities, are in between the fixed and floating charges. The issue has provoked judicial disagreement, with one view suggesting that, by coming after the floating charge, the fixed charge should therefore come after the preferential creditors.[302] On the other hand, it was also suggested in this case that a different result would follow if the respective secured parties had agreed to exchange their proprietary rights. Another possible solution is to apply the doctrine of subrogation and to hold that, by virtue of the altered priorities between them, the floating charge holder stands in the shoes of the fixed

300 For a discussion of the meaning of 'notice' see *Gray v Smith* [2013] EWHC 4136 (Comm) at paras. 128–138.

301 See generally *Wilson v Kelland* [1910] 2 Ch 306; *Cox v Dublin City Distillery Co* [1906] IR 446; *Coveney v HS Perse Ltd* [1910] 1 IR 194; *G and T Earle Ltd v Hemsworth Rural District Council* (1928) 44 TLR 605.

302 *Re Portbase Clothing Ltd* [1993] Ch 388.

charge holder to the extent of the amount secured by the fixed charge and therefore the floating charge holder will be paid ahead of preferential creditors by the degree to which liabilities are secured by a fixed charge.[303]

(k) A crystallised floating charge takes priority over a subsequently created equitable fixed charge (assuming both charges have been duly registered within the 21-day period from the date of creation). A floating charge is taken to be a fixed equitable charge from the moment of crystallisation.

(l) The priority rules are further complicated by apparent judicial acceptance of the proposition that where a second floating charge covers only part of the assets covered by a prior floating charge, then the second floating charge will have priority, provided that the first instrument of charge authorises the creation of subsequent charges having this effect.[304] In principle, however, the question should be whether the first floating charge authorises the creation of superior ranking subsequent floating charges, and not whether the second floating charge is over part only of the assets covered by the first.

(m) Charge holders can agree to alter the priority between them, but such an agreement does not affect the rights or entitlements of a person who is not party to the agreement.

211. Some of these priority rules warrant further explanation and elaboration. For instance, priority rule 6 raises the issue of the priority of further advances. Often a charge is taken to secure further advances, such as a charge to secure a bank account.[305] The question arises whether a charge holder may make further advances ranking in priority to an intervening charge holder. This is known as 'tacking'. As far as registered land is concerned, the rules on tacking are contained in section 49 Land Registration Act 2002.[306] This provision enables the holder of a registered charge to make a further advance ranking in priority to a subsequent charge in four situations:

---

303 See *Re Woodroffes (Musical Instruments) Ltd* [1986] Ch 366.

304 *Re Automatic Bottle Makers* [1926] Ch 412; *Re Benjamin Cope & Co* [1914] 1 Ch 800. See also *Griffiths v Yorkshire Bank plc* [1994] 1 WLR 1427; *Re H & K Medway* Ltd [1997] 1 WLR 1422.

305 In this case the security will have to be expressed to be a continuing security. Otherwise, under the rule in *Clayton's Case* (1816) 1 Mer 572 and the principle of 'first in, first out' in relation to bank amounts, the security becomes discharged on repayment of the amount of the initial advance.

306 In Ireland, s. 111 of the Land and Conveyancing Law Reform Act 2009 provides that the right to tack in any form is abolished. The section also provides, however, that where 'a mortgage is expressed to be created on any land for the purpose of securing future advances (whether with or without present advances), the mortgagee is entitled, in priority to any subsequent mortgage, to the payment of any sum due in respect of any such future advances, except any advances which may have been made after the date of, and with express notice in writing of, the subsequent mortgage.' The provision in the 2009 Act applies more generally what was the position in respect of registered land under s. 75 Registration of Titles Act 1964.

(a) if he has not received from the subsequent charge holder notice of the creation of the subsequent charge; or
(b) if the further advance is made pursuant to an obligation which was entered in the register at the time of creation of the subsequent charge – under rule 108 of the Land Registration Rules 2003 a person applying to be registered who is under an obligation to make further advances, may apply to the registrar for such obligation to be registered on the register; or
(c) the parties to the prior charge have agreed a maximum amount for which the charge is security and such agreement was entered in the register at the time of creation of the subsequent charge.
(d) by agreement.

212. In *Re Black Ant Co Ltd*[307] the court suggested that the four rules basically codified the common law position as laid down by the House of Lords in *Hopkinson v Rolt*[308] and the argument in the case centred on whether the conditions specified in the rules had been met. The court pointed out that where an obligation to make further advances is noted on the register, the extent of the obligation and the circumstances in which it arises are not noted. Therefore a person who contemplates the making of an advance secured by a second charge needs to ascertain these matters either from the first charge holder or the borrower, in order to establish what equity, if any, is potentially left in the property.

213. The court said that 'further advance' meant, prima facie, the provision of further or additional funds but there might be a 'further advance' within these provisions without any new money being lent. The example was given of a revolving credit facility where earlier loan amounts were repaid and the facility was replenished with fresh funds though the lender's overall exposure to the borrower did not increase. The holder of the first registered charge would have priority in terms of the further advance under the revolving credit facility even though there was no increase of the total funds available to the borrower.

214. In relation to point 9, under the old registration of company charge regime, English authority suggested that actual rather than just constructive notice of a restrictive clause in an instrument of charge was required before the priority of a subsequent fixed charge holder loses priority to a floating charge

307 [2014] EWHC 1161 (Ch) and for the Court of Appeal judgment see [2016] EWCA Civ 30 where David Richards LJ said at para. 1: '"Tacking" describes the means by which a creditor, with a charge securing an original advance, is able to use the charge to secure a further advance and so obtain priority for the further advance over sums secured by any second or subsequent charge. Because of the potential prejudice to the interests of the holders of second or subsequent charges, first equity and then statute have severely restricted the circumstances in which tacking will be permitted.'

308 (1861) 9 HL Cas 514, 11 ER 829.

holder. A case in point is *English and Scottish Mercantile Investment Co Ltd v Brunton*[309] where the lawyer acting for the subsequent charge holder knew of the existence of the earlier floating charge, but was misled by the grantor of the charge into believing that there was nothing in the charge to affect its client's security. The subsequent charge holder obtained priority.

215. In *Wilson v Kelland*,[310] the court took the view that registration of the particulars of a charge pursuant to the company charge registration provisions amounted to constructive notice of a charge affecting the property, but not of any special provisions in the charge that restricted the company from dealing with its property in the usual manner when the charge was a floating security. The same view was clearly articulated in *G & T Earle Ltd v Hemsworth Rural District Council*[311] with the court stating: 'it has never been held that the mere fact that persons … have constructive notice of the existence of debentures also affects them with constructive notice of the actual terms of the debentures or that the debentures are subject to the restrictive condition to which these debentures were subject. No doubt it is quite common for debentures to be subject to this limiting condition as to further charges, but that fact is not enough in itself to operate as constructive notice of the actual terms of any particular set of debentures.'

216. In order to give greater protection to floating charges, the practice developed, which the registrar accepted, of including details of any negative pledge in the particulars of charge delivered for registration. If a subsequent charge holder actually consulted the register he would discover the existence of the restrictive clause and thereby become infected with actual notice. It was debatable, however, whether inclusion among the registered particulars gave constructive notice of the negative pledge. This issue was not tested in the courts in *England* and the proposition was rejected in *New Zealand*.[312] There is a strong view that registration only constitutes constructive notice in respect of those matters where registration is compulsorily required and not in respect of optional 'additional' matters.

217. Section 859D(2)(c) now makes details of a restrictive or negative pledge clause in a floating charge compulsorily registrable. The section provides that the statement of particulars of the charge submitted for registration should include

309 [1892] 2 QB 700. See also *Re Standard Rotary Machine Co* (1906) 95 LT 829; *Siebe Gorman v Barclays Bank* [1979] 2 Lloyd's Rep 142; and *ABN Amro Bank NV v Chiyu Banking Corp Ltd* [2001] 2 HKLRD 175, CFI (Hong Kong).

310 [1910] 2 Ch 306.

311 (1928) 44 TLR 605. Perhaps the fullest discussion of the authorities in modern times comes from the Irish Supreme Court in *Welsh v Bowmaker (Ireland) Ltd* [1980] IR 251 where the same view was taken.

312 *Dempsey v The Traders Finance Corporation Ltd* [1933] NZLR 1258.

details of any of the terms of the charge that prohibit or restrict the company from creating further security that will rank equally with or ahead of the charge. The new provision, however, does not say anything directly about constructive notice and the effect of registration of details of a restrictive clause on priorities between fixed and floating charge holders. There is nothing equivalent to section 103 of the Companies Act 1989 which was never implemented. That provision stated that a person taking a charge over a company's property shall be taken to have notice of any matter requiring registration and disclosed on the register at the time the charge is created. But by an apparent side sweep, the new section 859D(2)(c) seems, prima facie, to have altered the priorities between fixed and floating charges.

218. Priority rule 13 derives from the judgment of the Privy Council in *Cheah v Equiticorp Finance Group Ltd*[313] Lord Browne-Wilkinson made it clear that where there were two charges over the same property, the chargees could agree to alter the priority of their security interests without the consent of the debtor. He pointed out that in the ordinary case a mortgagor was not affected by the order in which the debts were satisfied. A mortgagor was bound to satisfy all the debts secured on the property before the property could be recovered, and priority of mortgages affected only the rights of the mortgagees inter se, in particular where the security was inadequate to pay all the secured debts in full. Lord Browne-Wilkinson added:[314] 'There may be cases (for example where the successive mortgages carry differing rates of interest) where the mortgagor has a genuine interest in ensuring that the debts are satisfied in a particular order. In such a case it will be for the mortgagor to insist upon a specific contractual provision precluding the alteration of the priorities of the mortgages.'

219. Debt subordination agreements were upheld by the court in *Re Maxwell Communications Corp plc (No 2)*.[315] Here a company, Maxwell Finance Jersey (MFJ), issued bonds that were guaranteed by another company, MCC, under a guarantee which provided that MCC's liability to the bondholders was subordinated to MCC's liabilities to other unsecured creditors. In other words, if MCC became insolvent, the rights of the bondholders against MCC were

313 [1992] 1 AC 472. See generally R. Nolan, [1995] *Journal of Business Law* 485. In Ireland s. 412(5) Companies Act 2014 seems to validate priority agreements between charge holders.

314 [1992] 1 AC 472 at 477.

315 [1994] 1 All ER 737. See also *Re SSSL Realisations (2002) Ltd* [2004] EWHC 1760 where Lloyd J suggested that the effect of a subordination agreement did not involve the diversion of an asset of the junior creditor, but rather its suppression by subordination. See now the decision of the Supreme Court in *Belmont Park Investments Pty Ltd v BNY Corporate Trustee* [2011] UKSC 38, [2012] 1 AC 383 and that of the Court of Appeal on the 'Lehman Waterfall 1 application' – see *Re Lehman Brothers International (Europe) (In Administration)* [2015] EWCA Civ 485 at para. 38.

subordinated to all other unsecured liabilities owed by MCC. It was held that the subordination agreement was a valid contract. The court took the view that since a creditor could waive his debt or decline to submit to proof, there was no reason why he should not, prior to any insolvency proceedings, agree to subordinate his claim to that of other creditors in the event of the debtor company's insolvency. Subordination did not undermine the pari passu principle which was understood to preclude a creditor from obtaining some advantage in the winding up of a company to which he was not entitled by virtue of insolvency principles. This principle was not contravened, however, where the performance of an agreement between various parties could not affect the entitlement of creditors who were not parties to the agreement. A liquidator might distribute in accordance with an agreement between the parties where to do so could not adversely affect any creditor not a party to the agreement.

220. The court in *Maxwell* considered the House of Lords decision in *National Westminster Bank Ltd v Halesowen Presswork and Assemblies Ltd*[316] on the principles governing the set-off of mutual debts in respect of insolvent companies. The House of Lords held that persons who had dealings with an insolvent company could not validly contract out of the statutory set-off provisions. Bankruptcy set-off was said to be part of a 'code of procedure whereby bankrupts' estates ... are to be administered in a proper and orderly way.'[317] This case was distinguished on the basis that the rationale underlining the set-off regime was one of public policy. The court drew attention to the inconvenience and potential unfairness to the liquidator and other creditors if a creditor was entitled either to exercise or, at his option, not to exercise the right of set-off. It said:[318] 'An agreement between the debtor and the creditor excluding the creditor's right of set-off, or the waiver by the creditor of his right of set-off, even after the commencement of the bankruptcy or winding up, might thus equally hinder the rapid, efficient and economical process of bankruptcy.' On the other hand, private rights were considered to be the basis of the pari passu doctrine.

Question 24: Are there special rules privileging the position of an acquisition financier, i.e. a secured party whose advance of funds funded the acquisition of a particular asset and who may be in a priority competition with an earlier general creditor whose security interest extends to all assets of the debtor whenever acquired?

221. In certain circumstances a creditor who has made a loan that enables the debtor to acquire property may outrank an earlier creditor with a security

316 [1972] AC 785.
317 *Ibid.* at 809.
318 [1994] 1 All ER 737 at 746.

interest that includes property afterwards acquired by the debtor. Basically, for this to happen the property must be fettered at the outset by the security interest in favour of the enabling or purchase money lender. There cannot be a moment of time in which the debtor is the unencumbered owner of the property, for, if this were to happen, the earlier creditor's afterwards acquired property clause would bite and therefore trump the purchase money security interest.

222. In the main, the English cases on 'purchase money security interests' have concerned land, although the reasoning employed in the cases is, in principle, applicable in other contexts.[319] The leading authority is the decision of the House of Lords (Supreme Court) in *Abbey National v Cann*[320] but this decision is best understood in the light of the earlier authorities such as *Re Connolly Bros Ltd (No 2)*[321] and *Wilson v Kelland.*[322]

223. In *Re Connolly Bros Ltd (No 2)*[323] a company created a floating charge upon their undertaking and all their property, including both present and future property. The floating charge contained a condition that the company should not be at liberty to create any other mortgage or charge with priority over it. A couple of years later, the company wished to purchase property but did not have the money for that purpose. Consequently, it borrowed a sum from a purchase money lender to facilitate the acquisition upon terms that the lender should have a charge upon the premises when purchased. The Court of Appeal held that the floating charge holder ranked after the purchase money lender on the basis that when the company purported to purchase the property it, in fact, acquired only an equity of redemption, subject to the equitable charge of the purchase money lender. 'Full' ownership never constituted part of the company's assets, insofar as the charge in favour of the floating charge holder was concerned, because the purchase money lender acquired an interest in the property that coincided with its acquisition by the company.[324]

224. Another case in point is *Wilson v Kelland*[325] where a vendor of land gave up the lien in respect of the unpaid purchase price in return, inter alia, for a contractual promise of an equitable charge over the property. The subsequently created charge was held to prevail over a floating charge over all the assets, present and future of the company, which was prior in point of time. The rationale of the decision was that the company had only acquired an equity of redemption in

---

319 See generally J. De Lacy, [1991] *Lloyds Maritime and Commercial Law Quarterly* 531.
320 [1991] 1 AC 56; on which see generally G. Goldberg, (1992) 108 *Law Quarterly Review* 380.
321 [1912] 2 Ch 25.
322 [1910] 2 Ch 306.
323 [1912] 2 Ch 25.
324 *Ibid.* at 31.
325 [1910] 2 Ch 306.

the property. Any equity which attached to the purchased property in favour of the floating charge holder was subject to the paramount equity of the unpaid vendors.

225. The problem with many of these old cases is that they turn on quite narrow distinctions rather than on the underlying economic realities.[326] The courts have examined the facts in some detail to determine whether or not there has been a split second of time (scintilla temporis) in which it could be said that a borrower has been the unencumbered owner of property. If there is such a period of time, however minute, then an earlier security interest extending over the borrower's after-acquired assets will have time to bite and, consequently, outrank a secured lender whose advance enabled the property in question to be acquired.

226. In *Abbey National Building Society v Cann*[327] the House of Lords appeared to give wider scope for the recognition of purchase money security interests by rejecting the doctrine of scintilla temporis. In other words, a purchaser of domestic property who relied on a bank or building society mortgage for completion could not be said to be the unencumbered legal and equitable owner of the property for a split second of time. In the court's view, the acquisition of the legal estate and the charge were not only precisely simultaneous, but indissolubly bound up together.[328]

227. The Court of Appeal decision in *Whale v Viaystems Ltd*[329] also signifies a wider recognition of the concept of a purchase money security interest. The court said:[330] 'it must now be taken as settled law that, in the context of an issue as to priorities between equitable interests, the court will have regard to the substance, rather than the form of the transaction or transactions which give rise to the competing interests; and in particular that conveyancing technicalities must give way to considerations of commercial and practical reality ... [T]his approach is not limited to cases involving the purchase of a property coupled with the grant of a mortgage or charge to secure repayment of the funds which were required to enable completion of the purchase to take place ... [I]t falls to

---

326 But for recognition of the purchase money security interest in Malaysia on the basis of the old English authorities see *United Malayan Banking Corp v Aluminex* [1993] 3 MLJ 587.

327 [1991] 1 AC 56. See also the judgments of the Supreme Court in the 'North East Property Buyers Litigation' – *Scott v Southern Pacific Mortgages Ltd* [2014] UKSC 52 interpreting *Cann*.

328 [1991] 1 AC 56 at 92. Lord Oliver also pointed out that in many, if not most, mortgage cases there will have been a formal offer of acceptance of an advance which will ripen into a specifically enforceable agreement immediately the funds are advanced, which will normally be a day or so before completion. See also the comments of Lord Jauncey at 101. Differing views were expressed on the significance of this by Lord Sumption and Lady Hale in *Scott v Southern Pacific Mortgages Ltd* [2014] UKSC 52.

329 [2002] EWCA Civ 480.

330 *Ibid.* at [72].

be adopted generally, in every case where an issue arises as to priority as between equitable interests.'

228. The court suggested that it would be inequitable to allow the previous charge holder a windfall increase in the value of its security that was brought about not with the debtor's money or new funds that had been injected by the charge holder but with new financing provided by a later charge holder.

229. There has been a lot of discussion about the theoretical basis for recognising purchase money security interests (PMSIs) in the *United States*. It has been suggested that the super priority of the PMSI can be thought of as a mechanism which alleviates the situational monopoly created by an after-acquired property clause.[331] The debtor is in a better position to access alternative lending streams and any dependence on the original lender for additional funds is lessened. Another justification rests on the fact that the release of funds by the purchase money creditor increases the debtor's total pool of assets.[332] The debtor is enabled, in consequence, to acquire new assets as distinct from merely rolling over existing debt. Whereas a security interest granted by the debtor over property that it already owns is potentially harmful to existing creditors, a security interest granted over newly acquired property to secure the price paid for that property is neutral in its effect on existing creditors. The debt incurred to pay for the property is offset by the addition of the property. Moreover, if an earlier creditor could rely on a provision in the instrument of charge that catches after-acquired property to the prejudice of a PMSI holder, the earlier creditor would gain an undeserved windfall, for it was the advance of funds by the later creditor that enabled the property to be acquired.[333]

230. On the other hand, providing privileges to the holder of a PMSI in this manner seems premised on the assumption that the release of funds to facilitate the acquisition of new assets is more valuable to a debtor's business than making advances which enable existing employees to be paid, for example. There is a question mark about whether one of these advances is necessarily of greater social benefit than the other.

---

331 T. Jackson and A. Kronman, (1989) 88 *Yale Law Journal* 1143 at 1171–1178.

332 See also A. Schwartz, (1984) 37 *Vanderbilt Law Review* 1051 who argues that whereas a general financier takes account of average risk, the PMSI lender may have particular skills and is able to lend on particularly advantageous terms because of its special knowledge of the collateral.

333 See the discussion at para. 17.7 of the A. Diamond report *A Review of Security Interests in Property*; and for a law and economics perspective see H. Kanda and S. Levmore, (1994) 80 *Virginia Law Review* 2103 at 2138–2141.

231. In the *United States*, under the Uniform Commercial Code, Article 9, there is an exception to the general first-to-file-has priority rule in the case of purchase-money security interests (PMSIs).[334] A PMSI will rank ahead of a prior security interest with an after-acquired property clause. If a debtor has granted an all-assets security interest that extends over future property then, notwithstanding the general first-to-perfect priority rule, a creditor whose advances funded the acquisition of 'new property' in the debtor's hands will outrank the earlier financier in respect of the collateral represented by the new property.[335] There is a fairly convoluted definition in Article 9-103 which requires a close nexus between the acquisition of the collateral and the security interest. Basically what is required is the giving of value 'to enable the debtor to acquire rights in or the use of the collateral if the value is in fact so used.' There are, however, special perfection requirements applicable to PMSIs under Article 9 and compliance with these requirements is necessary to obtain super-priority status. Article 9-324 distinguishes between inventory and other goods with a claim to PMSI status in inventory being more difficult to establish.

F. QUASI-SECURITY AGREEMENTS

Question 25: Does your legal system have any rules equating the treatment, in whole or in part, of security interest and 'quasi-security' agreements, i.e. agreements that in legal terms do not involve the creation of security interests but have many of the same economic consequences? Examples of quasi-security include the factoring or sale of receivables and finance leases, hire-purchase agreements and retention of title clauses in sale of goods contracts.

232. English law recognises the possibility of having the functional equivalent of a security interest over property through the use of other legal techniques. In *Chow Yoong Hong v Choong Fah Rubber Manufactory*[336] Lord Devlin observed that there are many ways of raising cash besides borrowing. To adjust the statement slightly, there are many ways in which a person who has 'advanced' money might

334 Article 9-324 deals with the priority of purchase-money security interests. For an argument against the PMSI super-priority rules see A. Schwartz, (1989) 18 *Journal of Legal Studies* 209.

335 Under Article 9-324(g) the holder of a purchase money security interest that secures the unpaid purchase price of collateral will prevail over the holder of a conflicting purchase money security interest that enables the collateral to be acquired. Translated into English law terms, this means that a retention of title seller has priority over a lender that makes an enabling loan. There is some possible inconsistency with Article 9-328, which deals with investment property. Priority in investment property is given to the secured party who has control. Article 9-328(2) provides that if two or more secured parties have control, priority is determined by who obtained control first.

336 [1962] AC 209 at 216.

enhance its prospects of recovery in the event of the debtor's insolvency besides being party to the creation of a charge. These methods include the following: (1) sale and leaseback/hire purchase; (2) title retention/conditional sale; (3) agency sales financing; (4) factoring/assignment of receivables; (5) Quistclose trusts; (6) trust receipts. These are all 'quasi-security' devices and will now be considered.[337]

1. Sale and leaseback/hire purchase

233. One financing technique involves the sale of goods or land followed by a leaseback. In all probability, the vendor will never have parted with possession and, in practice, it may be difficult to distinguish a genuine sale and leaseback from the creation of a charge over the property in question. In a leading case, *Re George Inglefield Ltd*,[338] Romer LJ attempted to explain the essential differences. He said:[339] 'In a transaction of sale the vendor is not entitled to get back the subject-matter of the sale by returning to the purchaser the money that has passed between them. In the case of a mortgage or charge the mortgagor is entitled, until he has been foreclosed, to get back the subject-matter of the mortgage or charge by returning to the mortgagee the money that has passed between them. The second essential difference is that if the mortgagee realises the subject-matter of the mortgage for a sum more than sufficient to repay him, with interest and the costs, the money that has passed between him and the mortgagor he has to account to the mortgagor for the surplus. If the purchaser sells the subject-matter of the purchase, and realises a profit, of course he has not got to account to the vendor for the profit. Thirdly, if the mortgagee realises the mortgage property for a sum that is insufficient to repay him the money that he has paid to the mortgagor, together with interest and costs, then the mortgagee is entitled to recover from the mortgagor the balance of the money ... If the purchaser were to resell the purchased property at a price which was insufficient to recoup him the money that he has paid to the vendor, of course he would not be entitled to recover the balance from the vendor.'

234. These distinctions, while easy to state on paper, may become blurred in practice. For example, sale agreements may include options to repurchase and

337 See generally S. Worthington, *Proprietary Interests in Commercial Transactions*. Ireland recognises the same form of quasi-security.

338 [1933] Ch 1.

339 *Ibid.* at 26–27. It was made clear in *Durham Bros v Robertson*, however, [1898] 1 QB 765, that once the security nature of a transaction is established, equity will imply a right of redemption; see at 772 per Chitty LJ. Having regard to this fact, F. Oditah, [1992] *Journal of Business Law* 541 at 546 argues that the judgment of Romer LJ gives very little, if any, useful guidance.

also profit sharing clauses under which the original vendor shares in profits from resales as well as provisions whereby the vendor agrees to indemnify the buyer in respect of any losses incurred on a resale.

235. The hire-purchase agreement in relation to goods builds on the clear theoretical distinction between a sale and a lease or hire of goods. Hire purchase entails a hiring coupled with an option to purchase. In legal terms, however, there is a lot to be said for the view that this description is, in reality, a legal fiction that bears little or no relation to economic reality.[340] In legal terms there is a contract for the hiring of goods coupled with an option on the part of the hirer to purchase the goods.[341] While the agreement subsists, the property in the goods remains in the owner and the hirer has no power to dispose of them. Moreover, although the hirer has an option to purchase the goods, it is not under a binding obligation to do so.

236. Normally a hire-purchase transaction involves three parties, namely, a dealer, finance house and hirer. Goods are sold by the dealer to the finance house who then lets them on hire-purchase terms to a hirer who had no prior interest in the goods. The tripartite nature of the transaction makes it difficult to argue that in reality it constitutes a loan. But the essential principle remains the same, irrespective of the fact that there are only two parties, as when the owner of goods sells them to a finance house and takes a lease-back under a hire-purchase agreement.

2. Retention of title clauses

237. Title retention clauses may take many forms but basically the clause refers to a situation where the seller of goods retains title to those goods until they have been paid for.[342] This is the simplest and perhaps the most common form of title retention clause but more complicated variants are possible. Under a 'current account' clause, the seller retains title until all debts owing by the buyer to the seller have been paid and not just indebtedness arising under the particular contract of sale. A 'proceeds' or 'tracing' retention of title clause permits the buyer to resell the goods in the ordinary course of business before the original debt has been discharged but transfers the seller's claim to the proceeds generated by the resale. 'Products' clauses are used in quite complex factual scenarios where the goods supplied have formed all or part of the raw materials in a process of

340 See generally Crowther Committee Report on Consumer Credit (1971, Cmnd 4569), 175–176.
341 For a modern analysis see *Forthright Finance Ltd v Carlyle Finance Ltd* [1997] 4 All ER 90.
342 For a comprehensive analysis see G. McCormack, *Reservation of Title.*

manufacture. With such a clause the supplier of the raw materials is claiming all or part of the finished article.

238. 'Simple' retention of title clauses and current account clauses have received judicial approval but the more complex variants – namely, 'proceeds' and 'products' clauses have recently met with judicial disfavour. The analysis goes like this: with a simple clause and a current clause the seller is merely retaining ownership of the goods until satisfaction of some condition. Until this condition is fulfilled the buyer does not acquire any bit of ownership which he can hand back to the seller by way of a security interest.[343] On the other hand, where goods have been sold, the seller's claim does not translate readily into the resale proceeds. Originally the courts were prepared to recognise the seller's claim on the basis that in reselling the seller was acting in a dual capacity, i.e. as an agent vis-à-vis the original seller but as a principal as far as the resale buyers were concerned so that the latter were not brought into direct contractual relations with original sellers.[344] More recently, however, the courts have moved away from this analysis holding that a seller's entitlement to resale proceeds is a limited interest by way of charge since it comes to an end upon the discharge of the original purchase price.[345] Likewise 'product claims' have attracted the disapproval of the courts. The dominant view is that where there is a mixture of heterogeneous goods in the manufacturing process a new product – nova species – is created which belongs, initially at least, to the manufacturer, so to speak.[346]

3. Assignment of receivables

239. In *England*, receivables financing may take the form of either the creation of a charge, whether fixed or floating, on receivables (debts) or else the outright assignment of receivables which is referred to as factoring. Factoring, or the absolute assignment of receivables, serves as the functional economic equivalent of taking a charge over the receivables. Factoring of debts is a well-recognised and established activity with many of the major financial institutions having factoring subsidiaries. A factoring transaction does not have to be registered but

343 See *Clough Mill Ltd v Martin* [1985] 1 WLR 111; *Armour v Thyssen Edelstahlwerke AG* [1991] 2 AC 339.

344 *Aluminium Industrie Vaassen BV v Romalpa Aluminium Ltd* [1976] 1 WLR 676.

345 See, for example, *Pfeiffer Weinkellerei-Weineinkauf GmbH Co v Arbuthnot Factors Ltd* [1988] 1 WLR 150; *Compaq Computer Ltd v Abercorn Group Ltd* [1991] BCC 484 but see, more recently, *Caterpillar (NI) Ltd v John Holt & Co* [2013] EWCA Civ 1232.

346 *Borden v Scottish Timber Products Ltd* [1981] Ch 25; *Re Peachdart Ltd* [1984] Ch 131.

where a company creates a charge over its debts, registration is a necessity.[347] Of course, the factoring of debts equates to a loan of money on the security of debts to the extent that ready cash is released to the assignor. The latter receives money upfront rather than having to wait for the debts to mature, or to be collected. Factoring, however, can serve functions other the immediate release of funds. For instance, if it is done on a notification basis then the factor is relieved of the responsibility of collecting the debts. The factor may also take over the burden of accounts administration. Factoring may also take on some of the features of credit insurance if the factor assumes the responsibility for the debtor failing to pay as distinct from the assignor being under an obligation to accept a reassignment of bad debts.

240. Receivables financing is, however, often carried out in a manner that blurs the distinction between the factoring (outright sale of receivables) and their transfer by way of security. For instance, a charge may be accompanied by a power of attorney by the chargor in favour of the charge holder which enables the latter to execute an assignment in the chargor's name. In circumstances of default by the chargor, the charge holder can then give notice of assignment to the account debtor and intercept payment before it reaches the assignor thereby providing a speedy and effective means of enforcement of the charge.

241. Because charges over debts executed by companies have to be registered, as distinct from assignments, it remains vitally important at the outset, however, to distinguish between the factoring of book debts and the creation of a charge over such debts. In *Bexhill Ltd v Razzaq*[348] the Court of Appeal made a clear distinction between, on the one hand, an absolute assignment of a thing in action which transfers rights in the thing in action from A to B, and, on the other hand, an assignment 'by way of charge only' which is, effective only as a right to exercise a claim on some identified property in certain identified events, as opposed to an absolute transfer of a property right.[349]

242. An absolute assignment can take the form of either (a) a legal assignment or (b) an equitable assignment. This was made clear in *Bexhill Ltd v Razzaq*[350] where the alternative possibilities were discussed. It was commented that a legal assignment would need to be in accordance with the Law of Property Act 1925 and 'would be a completed transfer of the equitable and legal title to the thing in action from A to B', whereas with an assignment taking effect in equity only 'the

---

347 The distinction between factoring and the creation of a charge over debts was explored at length by the House of Lords in *Lloyds & Scottish Finance v Cyril Lord Carpet Sales Ltd* [1992] BCLC 609.

348 [2012] EWCA Civ 1376 at para. 34 per Aikens LJ.

349 See also *Lloyds TSB Bank plc v Clarke (Liquidator of Socimer International Bank Ltd)* [2002] UKPC 27, [2002] 2 All ER (Comm) 992.

350 [2012] EWCA Civ 1376 at para. 34 per Aikens LJ.

assignee becomes the beneficial owner of the thing in action, but the legal title of the thing in action remains with the assignor'.

243. Section 136 Law of Property Act 1925[351] specifies the following conditions which must be met before an assignment of debts or other choses in action[352] can operate as a legal assignment:

(a) the assignment must be absolute and not by way of charge;
(b) the assignment must relate to the whole of the debt;
(c) the assignment must be in writing under the hand of the assignor;
(d) notice in writing of the assignment must be given to the debtor.

244. The assignee becomes legal owner of the debt and in the words of the section is entitled 'to pass and transfer from the date of such notice – (a) the legal right to such debt or thing in action; (b) all legal and other remedies for the same; and (c) the power to give good discharge for the same without the concurrence of the assignor'. An assignment passes to the assignee 'all legal and other remedies for the same'. To use the words of Peter Gibson LJ in *Camdex International Ltd v Bank of Zambia*,[353] it is apparent from the wording of the statute that Parliament sanctioned not only the assignment of debts and choses in action but also the transfer of the concomitant right to sue in respect of the same.

245. The legal/equitable assignment distinction has some practical consequences in terms of actions against the debtor. Basically a legal assignee can sue a debtor in its own name without involving the assignor in the proceedings, whereas in the case of an equitable assignment the assignor should be joined as a co-plaintiff if he is willing and as a co-defendant if he is not.[354] In certain circumstances, however, this rule may be waived.[355]

246. For an effective equitable assignment, there is no need for compliance with all or any of the statutory conditions in the Law of Property Act. For instance, notice to the debtor is not required to make an equitable assignment effective and it is not necessary to assign the whole debt – assignments of part of the debt are possible. Consideration for the assignment must, however, have been provided and the intention to assign must be clear. The validity of equitable assignments

---

351 In Ireland the equivalent provision is s. 28(6) Supreme Court of Judicature (Ireland) Act 1877.

352 In *Torkington v Magee* [1902] 2 KB 427 at 430, Channell J said that 'chose in action' is a known legal expression used to describe all personal rights of property which can only be claimed or enforced by action, and not by taking physical possession.

353 [1998] QB 22 at 40.

354 *Weddell v JA Pearce & Major* [1988] Ch 26 at 40–41.

355 See *William Brandt's Sons & Co v Dunlop Rubber Co Ltd* [1905] AC 454; *Hendry v Chartsearch Ltd* [1998] CLC 1382.

was confirmed at the highest judicial level in the 19th century in *Tailby v Official Receiver*.[356] Lord Macnaghten remarked that it has long been settled that future property, possibilities and expectancies are assignable in equity for value. In his view, the mode or form of assignment was absolutely immaterial provided that the intention of the parties was clear. The judge added that to effectuate the intention: 'an assignment for value, in terms present and immediate, has always been regarded in equity as a contract binding on the conscience of the assignor and so binding the subject-matter of the contract when it comes into existence, if it is of such a nature and so described as to be capable of being ascertained and identified'.

247. In commercial practice, factoring of debts is often done on a non-notification basis and this necessarily involves equitable assignment. The distinction between notification factoring and non-notification factoring is quite crucial in practical terms. With the former, notice of the assignment is given to the debtor and the factor invariably collects the debts. In the second situation, the assignor maintains direct relations with its customers by continuing to collect the debts. The factor remains in the background with the proceeds of the debts being remitted to it.

4. Agency sales financing

248. Agency sales financing is a fairly complicated form of financing technique that basically involves the entity requiring finance selling property to a financier without ever parting with physical possession to the financier and then purporting to resell the property as agent for, and on behalf of, the financier to third party buyers. A case in point is *Welsh Development Agency v Export Finance Co Ltd*[357] where an exporter of computer software financed its export trade transactions by selling the software in question to a financier and then fulfilling the overseas orders as the financier's agent. The financier acted as an undisclosed principal with the foreign buyers dealing at all times with the software supplier. The buyers made payment into a bank account that was in the name of the software supplier but which was under the complete control of the financier. The price that the financier paid the software supplier for the goods was not fixed at the outset but was subject to variation depending on the speed with which the foreign buyers paid for the goods. The financing arrangement also had a termination clause

356 [1888] 12 App Cas 523.

357 [1992] BCLC 148. Contrast *Re Curtain Dream plc* [1990] BCLC 925.

under which, on cessation of the agreement, the supplier would satisfy all claims owing to the financier by the foreign buyers and, once this payment had been made, the financier would transfer all interests it had in the goods to the supplier. It is important to note that the financing technique purported to involve a sale of goods rather than an assignment of debts.

249. It seems that, in the particular case, this form of financing arrangement was used because of a clause in a prior lending agreement under which the supplier covenanted not to factor, discount or assign its debts. Breach of this undertaking would entitle the lender to appoint a receiver. Unfortunately, the software supplier experienced financial difficulties and it was argued that the financing arrangement was invalid on the basis that, in reality, it represented a charge over goods rather than an absolute sale and that the requisite charge registration requirements had not been fulfilled.[358] The Court of Appeal rejected this proposition. The transaction was not a sham because there was no evidence that the parties intended themselves to have different rights and obligations from those set out in the agreement. Moreover, looking at the internal workings of the transaction, there was nothing therein that was necessarily incompatible with the transaction being one of sale. The termination clause was like a repurchase agreement and options to repurchase were not uncommon in sales transactions. Furthermore, price variation clauses were often found in sales contracts.

5. Quistclose/conditional purpose trusts

250. Some trusts may be regarded as serving a security type function and, in particular, the conditional purpose or 'Quistclose' trust.[359] Under a 'Quistclose' trust money is advanced subject to the condition that it is applied for a particular purpose. If this purpose is not fulfilled, or is no longer capable of being achieved, the money is said to be held on a secondary trust for the payer rather than being part of the debtor's assets available for payment to the debtor's general

---

[358] See also the comments of Lawrence LJ in *Re George Inglefield Ltd* [1933] Ch 1 at 23: 'As the law stands at present, there is nothing to prevent a limited company from selling its assets without giving notice of that sale to the public or to anyone else, remaining in possession of the assets so sold, with the consent of the buyer, and obtaining credit on the faith of that possession. If such a state of things ought to be remedied it is for Parliament to supply the remedy. All that the Court has to do … is to ascertain whether there has, in fact, been a sale of the assets and to give effect to the transaction if that be the case.'

[359] See the leading case *Barclays Bank Ltd v Quistclose Investments Ltd* [1970] AC 567 and see now *Twinsectra Ltd v Yardley* [2002] 2 AC 164.

creditors.[360] The courts have held that debt and trust can coexist – in other words, that the same transaction can give rise to the legal relationship of debt and also to a trust. It has been contended that a Quistclose trust constitutes a security interest in that the 'payer is to be protected from the claims of other creditors of the payee' on the latter's insolvency and thus 'clearly evinces an intention to seek and provide security'.[361] The Quistclose trust secures performance of the debtor's obligation to carry out the purpose of the advance.

251. On the other hand, it must be recognised that the Quistclose trust is not a conventional security interest. In the typical advance, the secured assets and the monies advanced are quite clearly separate and the former secures the latter. With a Quistclose trust, the payer is asserting a de facto security interest in the advance itself and it is not the failure to repay that is secured but rather the execution of the purpose. If the purpose is carried out, the payer is converted from a secured into an unsecured creditor.[362] Under a 'Quistclose' trust, the payee (debtor) never acquires beneficial ownership but is rather a trustee – a conduit for the transmission of funds.

G. TRANSACTIONAL AVOIDANCE

Question 26: Are there rules in your legal system that operate once the debtor enters insolvency proceedings and that provide for the invalidation of transactions entered into by the debtor prior to the commencement of the insolvency proceedings?

252. Yes. There are a number of rules under English law that operate once a debtor enters insolvency proceedings and that serve to invalidate certain

---

360 This was the analysis adopted in the *Quistclose* case itself, but Lord Millett in *Twinsectra Ltd v Yardley* [2002] 2 AC 164 took a different approach. He said at para. 100 that the *Quistclose* trust was: 'an entirely orthodox example of the kind of default trust known as a resulting trust. The lender pays the money to the borrower by way of loan, but he does not part with the entire beneficial interest in the money, and in so far as he does not it is held on a resulting trust for the lender from the outset … When the purpose fails, the money is returnable to the lender, not under some new trust in his favour which only comes into being on the failure of the purpose, but because the resulting trust in his favour is no longer subject to any power on the part of the borrower to make use of the money. Whether the borrower is obliged to apply the money for the stated purpose or merely at liberty to do so, and whether the lender can countermand the borrower's mandate while it is still capable of being carried out, must depend on the circumstances of the particular case.' See also *Gore v Mischon de Reya* [2015] EWHC 164 (Ch) at paras. 30–38 and *Bieber v Teathers Ltd* [2012] EWHC 190 (Ch), [2012] 2 BCLC 585 at para. 16.

361 See M. Bridge, (1992) 12 *Oxford Journal of Legal Studies* 333 at 345–346 and 360–361.

362 See the comments of Lord Millett in *Twinsectra Ltd v Yardley* [2002] 2 AC 164 at para. 72: 'Arrangements of this kind are not intended to provide security for repayment of the loan, but to prevent the money from being applied otherwise than in accordance with the lender's wishes. If the money is properly applied the loan is unsecured.'

'pre-'insolvency transactions entered into by the debtor.[363] In setting out the avoidance rules one must distinguish between insolvency proceedings affecting corporates and individuals though broadly similar rules apply in both instances except for the fact that section 245 on the invalidation of floating charges granted by companies has no 'individual' equivalent.

253. As far as corporates are concerned these transactions are as follows:

(a) transactions at an undervalue under section 238 Insolvency Act';
(b) 'preferences' under section 239 Insolvency Act;
(c) extortionate credit transactions under section 244 Insolvency Act;
(d) invalidation of floating charges under section 245 Insolvency Act;
(e) putting assets beyond the reach of creditors under section 423 Insolvency Act.

254. For individual debtors section 339 Insolvency Act deals with transactions at an undervalue, section 340 with 'preferences', and section 343 with extortionate credit transactions.[364] Section 423 Insolvency Act, on undervalue transactions that put assets beyond the reach of creditors, applies to individual debtors as it does to corporates.

255. In respect of individuals engaged in business are concerned, there is a special provision in section 344 of the Insolvency Act providing for the invalidation of unregistered general assignments of book debts. The section applies where a person engaged in any business makes a general assignment of his existing or future book debts, or any class of them, and is subsequently adjudged bankrupt. The assignment has to be registered under the Bills of Sale Act. If this is not the position, then the assignment is void against the trustee of the bankrupt's estate insofar as book debts which were not paid before the presentation of the bankruptcy petition are concerned.

Question 27: Do these transactional avoidance rules catch security and quasi-security type transactions?

256. Yes, in principle these transactional avoidance rules apply in respect of security and quasi-security arrangements as well as to other types of transaction.

---

363 J. Armour and H. Bennett (eds.), *Vulnerable Transactions in Corporate Insolvency*.

364 Outside insolvency, the court had power to re-open the majority of loans granted for non-business purposes as 'extortionate credit bargains' under ss. 137–140 Consumer Credit Act 1974. But, as explained by Lord Sumption in the Supreme Court in *Plevin v Paragon v Personal Finance* [2014] UKSC 61, this test was considered to set too high a bar for debtors wishing to challenge the terms of their agreements. Consequently, the 'extortionate credit bargain' test was replaced by a new test of 'unfair relationships' between creditors and debtors under provisions which became s. 140A Consumer Credit Act 1974. The court has the power to set aside any credit agreement or related security if it is unfair to the debtor because of various factors.

The term 'transaction' is defined in section 436 of the Insolvency Act to include 'a gift, agreement or arrangement'.

Question 28: If so, describe briefly these rules highlighting in particular (a) the rationale for the rules; (b) the conditions for the application of the rules; (c) the length of the 'suspect period'; (d) whether the rules apply to transactions with a cross-border element; (e) whether the rules operate more stringently in respect of transactions that favour parties who are connected to the debtor; and (f) any defences that may be availed of by a counterparty to the transaction, i.e. the defendant in an avoidance action.

1. Transactions at an undervalue under section 238 Insolvency Act

257. An administrator or a liquidator has the power to make an application to court in respect of undervalue transactions. If the application is successful, the court must make such order as it thinks fit for restoring the position to what it would have been if the company had not entered into the transaction.[365] The purpose of the provision is to prevent the assets of the company being depleted by gratuitous or near gratuitous transactions in the run up to formal insolvency proceedings.

258. A transaction at an undervalue is one where:

(a) the company makes a gift to a person or otherwise enters into a transaction with a person on terms that provide for the company to receive no consideration; or
(b) the company enters into a transaction with a person for a consideration the value of which, in money or money's worth, is significantly less than the value, in money or money's worth, of the consideration provided by the company.

259. The first part of the definition envisages a total absence of any consideration passing to the company, while the second part covers the case where there is some mutual consideration but significantly differing in amounts.

260. In terms of 'suspect period' or 'relevant time' there are two issues to be considered.[366] Firstly, the transaction must be entered into within two years before the onset of the administration or liquidation or at a time between the making of an administration application in respect of the company and the

365 Section 238(3).
366 Section 240.

making of an administration order on that application.[367] Secondly, it is only a 'relevant time' if, at the time, the company is unable to pay its debts or if it becomes unable to pay them in consequence of the transaction.

261. In principle, the transactions at an undervalue provisions apply to transactions with an international element since there are no territorial qualifications on the operation of the section. The leading English case is *Re Paramount Airways Ltd*[368] where the court held that the statutory provisions were sufficiently wide that the court had an overall discretion, if justice so required, to make an order against any other party to the impugned transaction, irrespective of location. But it would need to be satisfied that the party was sufficiently connected with *England* for it to be just and proper to make the order against him despite the foreign element. The court said that[369] 'in considering whether there is a sufficient connection … [it] will look at all the circumstances, including the residence and place of business of the defendant, his connection with the insolvent, the nature and purpose of the transaction being impugned, the nature and locality of the property involved, the circumstances in which the defendant became involved in the transaction or received a benefit from it or acquired the property in question, whether the defendant acted in good faith, and whether under any relevant foreign law the defendant acquired an unimpeachable title free from any claims even if the insolvent had been adjudged bankrupt or wound up locally. The importance to be attached to these factors will vary from case to case.'

262. For transactions with a person who is connected with the company, the 'suspect period' is not any longer than the standard two-year period but there is a reversal of the burden of proof in relation to the 'inability to pay debts' requirement. The company is deemed to have been unable to pay its debts unless the contrary is shown by the defendant to the avoidance action.[370]

263. In terms of defences, the court may not set aside a transaction at an undervalue if it is satisfied that: (a) the company entered into the transaction in good faith and for the purpose of carrying on its business; and (b) at the time when it did so, there were reasonable grounds for believing the transaction would benefit the company.[371] Good faith, propriety of purpose and reasonableness

---

367 Section 240(3).

368 [1993] Ch 223.

369 *Ibid.* at 240. It should be noted that in *Rubin v Eurofinance SA* [2012] UKSC 46 at para. 130 some scepticism was expressed about a sufficient connection test in connection with the enforcement of foreign judgments – a person who might have connections with a foreign territory that were only arguably 'sufficient' would have to actively defend foreign proceedings which could result in an in personam judgment against him.

370 Section 240(2). For the definition of a person connected with the company, see sections 249 and 435.

371 Section 238(5).

must all be established to the satisfaction of the court; if any of these elements is missing, the transaction remains vulnerable.

2. Voidable preferences under section 239 Insolvency Act

264. Section 239 Insolvency Act provides for the invalidation in certain circumstances of transactions that favour one creditor of a debtor company over another – 'improper preferences'. An administrator or liquidator may apply to the court for an order on such terms as the court thinks fit, for restoring the position to what it would have been if the company had not given a preference.

265. There are at least three possible bases for the preference provision. One goal is to achieve a level playing field amongst creditors, i.e. to stop one creditor gaining an advantage over another creditor in the immediate run up to formal insolvency proceedings. The Cork Committee on Insolvency Law and Practice pointed out that the 'bankruptcy code ... is directed towards achieving a pari passu distribution of the bankrupt's estate among his creditors. The justification for setting aside a disposition of the bankrupt's assets made shortly before his bankruptcy is that, by depleting his estate, it unfairly prejudices his creditors; and even where the disposition is in satisfaction of a debt lawfully owing by the bankrupt, by altering the distribution of his estate it makes a pari passu distribution among all the creditors impossible.'[372]

266. A second legislative goal is to prevent the premature dismemberment of a debtor company's estate and consequent collapse of the business. If creditors can keep what they can recover from ailing businesses just prior to the institution of formal liquidation proceedings, then a business that needs to be nurtured may have its life support withdrawn. Moreover, if creditors race to collect what they can from available company assets this may lead to the dissipation or destruction of economic value. Even if all the recoveries are aggregated, a piecemeal break up and sale of company assets is likely to produce less value than if the process is collectivised through formal insolvency proceedings. Protecting the collective

---

[372] (1982) Cmnd 8558 at para. 1209. There are equivalent US provisions in Article 547 of the Bankruptcy Code and according to a US House of Representatives committee report: 'the preference provisions facilitate the prime bankruptcy policy of equality of distribution among creditors of the debtor. Any creditor that received a greater payment than others of his class is required to disgorge so that all may share equally' (HR Rep No 595, 95th Congress, 1st Session 177 (1977)).

nature of insolvency proceedings is a third goal of the preference provisions. Liquidation is a collective process in that creditors no longer have the right to take individual enforcement actions. Everything is collectivised in the person of the liquidator who assumes responsibility for collecting in the assets of the company and then paying its debts. The collective nature of the process is diminished if particular creditors are paid before others in anticipation of liquidation.

267. It is questionable, however, whether the relevant provisions accomplish their goals. This has led to calls for reforms of the section along the lines of section 547 US Bankruptcy Code which provides for the strict avoidance of preferences subject to defences such as the fact that the transaction is in the ordinary course of business.[373]

268. A company is deemed to give a preference to a person if (1) that person is one of the company's creditors or a surety or guarantor for any of the company's debts or other liabilities; and (2) the company does anything, or suffers anything to be done, which has the effect of putting that person into a position which, in the event of the company going into insolvent liquidation, will be better than the position he would have been in if that thing had not been done.

269. The court may not make an order to reverse the preference unless the company was influenced in deciding to give it by a desire to put the recipient in a better position in an insolvent liquidation than it would have been in if the preference had not been given. A desire to prefer is narrower than intention in that a person may be held to have 'intended' the necessary consequences of his acts even though he does not desire them to happen. To prove the requisite desire, the company must be shown positively to have wished to improve the creditor's position in its insolvent liquidation. A company is 'influenced' by a desire to prefer where it is a motivating factor, but it need not be the only or predominant one.[374] The desire must be present at the time when the preference is given.[375]

270. A company gives a preference by providing an unsecured creditor with security. Another example is the decision to pay some debts but not others. The creditors whose debts are paid are obviously placed in a much better position than those whose debts remain unpaid and become obliged to prove for their debts in the company's liquidation.

---

373 See e.g. G. McCormack, (2006) 6 *Journal of Corporate Law Studies* 39: A. Walters, 'Preferences' in J. Armour and H. Bennett (eds.), *Vulnerable Transactions in Corporate Insolvency*.

374 *Re MC Bacon Ltd* [1990] BCC 78; *Re Beacon Leisure Ltd* [1991] BCC 213; *Re Fairway Magazines Ltd* [1992] BCC 924; *Re Agriplant Services Ltd* [1997] BCC 842.

375 *Wills v Corfe Joinery Ltd* [1997] BCC 511.

271. The court is given a very wide discretion to make orders for the purpose of restoring the position to what it would have been if the company had not given the preference. The proceeds of an action to set aside a preference are held for the benefit of general creditors and do not fall within the scope of a floating charge on company assets.[376] The underlying reasoning is that the power to attack a preference is granted only to the liquidator and administrator, and is not available to the company itself. Therefore the proceeds of a preference avoidance action cannot be the subject of a charge granted by the company on its assets.

272. The preference is vulnerable only if it was given at a relevant time. This means generally a period of six months before the onset of the administration or liquidation. In addition, the time between the presentation of a petition for the making of an administration order and the making of such order is a relevant time. A time will be a relevant time, however, only if the company is unable to pay its debts when the preference is given or becomes unable to pay its debts in consequence of the preference.

273. Where the preference is given to a person connected with the company (otherwise than by reason only of being its employee) then the relevant period is two years rather than six months and the company is presumed, unless the contrary is shown, to have been influenced in deciding to give the preference by the requisite desire.[377]

274. There are no explicit statutory defences to a preference avoidance action. It seems, however, that the pressure exerted on the debtor by the recipient of the preference – whether through seeking security or otherwise – the greater the likelihood that the action will be unsuccessful. For instance, in *Re MC Bacon Ltd*[378] where the security was granted to avert the calling-in of the company's overdraft and the immediate liquidation which would have followed if the bank had withdrawn its support, the requisite desire to prefer was not established and so the action failed. It is worth emphasising however, that the language of section 239 focuses exclusively on the state of mind of the debtor and there is no reference to the position of the creditor. The latter is not required to know of the debtor's insolvency or to have reasonable cause to believe that the debtor is likely to become insolvent.

---

[376] See *Re MC Bacon Ltd (No 2)* [1991] Ch 127 at 137.
[377] Section 239(6).
[378] [1990] BCC 728.

3. Extortionate credit transactions under section 244 Insolvency Act

275. This section allows a liquidator or administrator to challenge an extortionate credit transaction to which the company is party. The section is intended to act as a curb on excessively high interest rates. A transaction is regarded as extortionate if, having regard to the risk, the company is required to make grossly exorbitant payments or the transaction otherwise grossly contravenes ordinary principle of fair dealing. There is a three-year reach back period under the section which is not extended if the transaction is in favour of a connected party. In principle, the section can catch transactions with an international element provided that there is deemed to be sufficient connection with *England*. There are no defences available under the section apart from the counterparty establishing that the conditions for the operation of the avoidance provision have not been made out. Among the orders for relief that the court may grant is an order varying the terms of the transaction or varying the terms on which any security for the purpose of the transaction is held.

4. Avoidance of floating charges under section 245 Insolvency Act

276. Floating charges created by the company within a specified period prior to the commencement of the administration or the liquidation are rendered invalid in certain circumstances. Section 245 is limited to floating charges with fixed charges outside its ambit. The Cork Committee rationalised the provision and its express limitation on the basis that the floating charge was an excessive security because it extended to future assets that were not yet paid for by the company. In its view, it was acceptable for a lender to take a fixed charge over existing assets as the price of allowing the company to continue to trade instead of taking steps to have the company put into liquidation. It was unacceptable, however, for the lender to take a floating security over existing and future company assets.[379] But this justification should not go unquestioned for a fixed charge may also extend to future assets that have not yet been paid for by the company.

277. The invalidating rule in section 245 operates except to the extent that the consideration for the creation of the charge consists of 'new money'. 'New money' must have been provided at the same time as, or after, the creation of the charge

[379] *Review Committee on Insolvency Law and Practice* (1982, Cmnd 8558) at para. 1553.

and may consist of money paid or goods or services supplied to the company or the discharge or reduction of any debt of the company.[380] The phrase 'at the same time as' which is used in section 245 was considered by the Court of Appeal in *Re Shoe Lace Ltd*.[381] It was held that whether the consideration for the charge was given at the same time as the creation of the charge is a mechanical issue determined solely by the clock, subject only to de minimis delays.

278. In the standard case, the length of the suspect period under section 245 is 12 months but the company, at the time of creating the charge, must have been unable to pay its debts or become unable to do so in consequence of the transaction under which the charge was created.

279. In principle, section 245 should apply to transactions with an international element but no doubt the court would take into account the kind of factors referred to in *Re Paramount Airways Ltd*[382] in deciding whether or not to make an order under the section. These factors focus largely on the extent to which the transaction is connected with *England*.

280. If the floating charge has been granted to a person connected with the company, the relevant period is two years rather than 12 months and it is not necessary to establish that the company was unable to pay its debts at the time of granting the charge. Transactions in favour of persons connected with the company are still challengeable under section 245 even though the company may have been solvent when the transaction was entered into.

281. There are no defences as such to a challenge under section 245. A floating charge in the circumstances described in section 245 is automatically invalidated. The section is much more draconian in its operation than the preference avoidance provision in section 239, i.e. there is no need to establish a desire to prefer and this is one of the many reasons why an insolvency office holder may wish to go down the section 245 route rather than rely on a preference avoidance action under section 239.

---

380 Section 245 preserves (contrary to the recommendations of the *Review Committee on Insolvency Law and Practice* (1982, Cmnd 8558) paras. 1561–1562) the decision in *Re Yeovil Glove Co Ltd* [1965] Ch 148, whereby in respect of a floating charge created in favour of a bank to secure an overdrawn account, if payments are made into the account after the creation of the charge, these will, under the rule in *Clayton's Case* (1816) 1 Mer 572, go to reduce the pre-charge indebtedness, so that cheques drawn on the account after the creation of the charge will be money paid to the company thereafter and the charge will therefore be valid to this extent.

381 [1993] BCC 609.

382 [1993] Ch 223.

5. Putting assets beyond the reach of creditors under section 423 Insolvency Act 1986

282. Section 423 is a general provision enabling the court to set aside transactions at an undervalue where it is satisfied that the transaction was entered into by the company for the purpose of putting assets beyond the reach of any person who is making, or may at some time make, a claim against the company or of otherwise prejudicing the interests of such a person. The section aims at protecting creditors who are trying to obtain payment or judgment from a company.

283. Section 423 applies both inside and outside formal insolvency proceedings. As well as liquidators and administrators, any person making, or who may at some time make, a claim against the company has standing to seek an order under this section. If, however, the company is in administration or liquidation, the leave of the court must be sought.[383] Whoever brings the claim, it is treated as made on behalf of every victim of the transaction.[384] The applicant need only show that a substantial purpose, rather than the dominant purpose, was to achieve one of the proscribed aims though the courts have stressed the need to distinguish between the result of a transaction and the purpose behind it.[385]

284. There are no time-limits on applications under section 423. Therefore the suspect period extends indefinitely back in time though it would be difficult to satisfy the requirements of the section in respect of a transaction that was very distant. Moreover, it was held in *Hill v Spread Trustee Co Ltd*[386] that there was a general six-year limitation period in relation to claims under the section. It seems that where a claim is made by a liquidator, the limitation period only starts to run once the company enters liquidation.

285. Section 423 in principle applies to transactions with an international element and indeed one of the claims in *Re Paramount Airways Ltd*[387] was a claim under section 423. The potential extra-territorial effect of section 423 was confirmed in *Fortress Value Recovery Fund v Blue Skye Special Opportunities Fund*[388] where it was held that whether there was a sufficient connection with *England* to justify relief under the section depended on all the circumstances of the case. It was not a threshold question of jurisdiction.

286. There are no special rules that apply to transactions with connected parties. If the beneficiary under the transaction is in some way connected with the debtor,

383 Section 424(1)(a).
384 Section 424(2).
385 See *Hashimi v IRC* [2002] EWHC Civ 981, [2002] BPIR 974.
386 [2007] 1 WLR 2404.
387 *Re Paramount Airways Ltd (No 2)* [1993] Ch 223.
388 [2013] EWHC 14 (Comm), [2013] 1 All ER (Comm) 973.

this may be a factor that ends to show the existence of the necessary purpose but there are no presumptions or evidential aids in the section to facilitate the task of the applicant.

287. In terms of defences to a claim under section 423, the interests of third parties are protected. It is provided, inter alia, in section 425(2) that an order shall not prejudice any interest in property that was acquired from a person other than the debtor and was acquired in good faith, for value and without notice of the relevant circumstances. It has also been held in *4 Eng Ltd v Harper*[389] that a change of position defence may be available to transferees.

288. There are however no special defences available to the debtor that puts assets beyond the reach of creditors. It has even been held that the fact that the debtor had acted on the basis of legal advice does not preclude the debtor from having the necessary improper purpose.[390]

289. In *Ireland*, the preference avoidance rules follow the same general pattern as in the *UK* though there are some significant differences in terms of detail.

290. For corporates the relevant provisions are contained in section 604 Companies Act 2014 (preferences), section 597[391] (invalidation of floating charges) and section 608 (fraudulent dispositions of company property). The provisions do not apply to the Irish equivalent of the UK company administration procedure – examinership. For individuals, the relevant provisions are contained in the Bankruptcy Act 1988 as amended by the Personal Insolvency Act 2012 and serve to invalidate fraudulent preferences (s. 57); transfers at an undervalue (s. 58) and settlements of property not made in good faith and for valuable consideration (s. 59).

291. Section 604 of the Irish Companies Act 2014 invalidates improperly preferential acts or things done by a company prior to the commencement of winding up. In general, acts or things done by a company in relation to its property within six months of the company's winding up are invalid. The impugned act must have taken place at a time when the company was unable to pay its debts and the act must be done in favour of any creditor of the company with a view to giving such creditor, or any surety or guarantor for the debt due to such creditor, a preference over the other creditors. From case law, it is established that the company must have the 'dominant intention to prefer' and the act must have been done voluntarily as distinct from being coerced by pressure.[392] The six-month

389 [2009] EWHC 2633 (Ch), [2010] BCC 746.

390 *Arbuthnot Leading v Havelet Leasing (No 2)* [1990] BCC 636.

391 See also s. 598 on the invalidation of payments made under floating charges that were granted to secure debts owed to connected persons.

392 See generally *Parkes & Sons Ltd v Hong Kong and Shanghai Banking Corp* [1990] ILRM 341; *Corran Construction Co v Bank of Ireland Finance Ltd* [1976–1977] ILRM 175.

period is extended to two years in the case of transactions with persons connected with the company. The onus of establishing the legitimacy of the transaction is also placed on the connected person. A transaction is regarded as having been made with a view to giving such person a preference over the other creditors and to be a fraudulent preference, unless the contrary is shown.

292. Section 597 of the Irish Companies Act 2014 provides that a floating charge created within 12 months prior to the commencement of winding up is rendered invalid by the fact of the company going into liquidation. The suspect period extends to two years in the case of a floating charge given to a person connected with the company. Such invalidity operates except to the extent of cash paid to the company at the time when the charge is created or subsequently. The 'cash paid' exception covers money actually advanced or paid and the actual price or value of goods or services sold or supplied. It is a condition of the operation of the invalidating rule that the company be insolvent at the time of creation of the floating charge. The Irish Supreme Court in *Re Creation Printing Co Ltd*[393] said that the test of solvency in this context was whether immediately after the floating charge was given, the company was able to pay its debts as they became due. The question was not whether its assets exceeded the estimated value of its liabilities, or whether a businessman would have regarded it as solvent.

293. Section 608 Irish Companies Act 2014 provides for the setting aside and restoration of fraudulent dispositions of company property. The section, however, does not apply to any property that has been the subject of a fraudulent preference. The court is empowered to order the restoration to the liquidator of corporate property, or the proceeds of its sale of development, that has been disposed of in such a way as to perpetrate a fraud on the company, its creditors or members. The order may be made on the application of a liquidator or any creditor or member of the company. In deciding whether it is just and equitable to make such an order, the court is obliged to have regard to the rights of persons who bona fide and for value acquired an interest in the property.[394]

294. For individuals, following amendments made by the Personal Insolvency Act 2012, the relevant transactional avoidance provisions in the Irish Bankruptcy Act 1988 now contain more or less a uniform three-year reach back period. There is not a longer 'suspect' period for connected parties. Section 57 of the 1988 Act strikes at fraudulent preferences and follows the same lines as its corporate equivalent. Section 58, however, does not have an exact corporate equivalent. Essentially it applies to undervalue transactions. The provision operates if a debtor either sells any of his property at a price substantially below its market

[393] [1981] IR 353 at 358–359 (Kenny J).

[394] It seems that a fraudulent conveyance or mortgage can also be challenged under the Conveyances (Ireland) Act 1634 – see *Re Kill Inn Motel Ltd* [1978–1987] 3 ITR 706.

value or enters into a transaction which has the effect of substantially reducing the sum available for distribution to the creditors. The transaction is rendered void as against the Official Assignee in bankruptcy unless it was entered into bona fide and the other party, at the relevant time, had no notice of any prior act of bankruptcy committed by the bankrupt. Section 59 strikes at settlements of property. Basically, a settlement not made in favour of a person who acts in good faith and for valuable consideration, is rendered void if the settlor is adjudicated bankrupt within three years of the date of the settlement. There is no requirement that, at the date of the settlement, the settlor should have been unable to pay its debts as they fell. There is, however, a longer five-year reach back period if the settlor was unable to pay all of its debts without the aid of the property comprised in the settlement.

CHAPTER 7

SECURITY RIGHTS AND INSOLVENCY LAW IN THE ROMAN LEGAL SYSTEM

Marta Carballo Fidalgo, Laura Carballo Piñeiro and Renato Mangano

A. INTRODUCTION

1. The regulations on security rights in rem in *France*, *Italy* and *Spain* converge to a great extent, but also have some divergences. The similarities are due, on the one hand, to the common origin of all three regulations as they all stem from Roman law and its subsequent developments, and on the other hand to the fact that all three systems have transplanted some quasi-security rights as evolved in common-law jurisdictions, while following worldwide accepted principles on insolvency law. Concerning the similarities lying in their historical origin, it would be interesting to research whether the main features of these systems such as the fact that security rights in rem closely follow the property right's model, derive from classic Roman law or whether it is an outcome of its medieval and post-medieval evolution.[1] Last but not least, the reader of this report has to take into account that this report was updated on 1 May 2016 and that, in *Italy*, some reforms of insolvency law and security rights law are in progress. These reforms inter alia include the introduction of a form of non-possessory pledge. However, this regulation is not operational, since the planned register has not yet been established. In the following pages these reforms will not be dealt with, while footnote 14 will provide for further information in this respect.

1. Creation of security rights

2. *France*, *Italy* and *Spain* converge in the fact that security rights in rem involve the right to expropriate the encumbered assets with a view to satisfying the

---

1 See, for example P. Frezza, *Le garanzie delle obbligazioni. Corso di diritto romano. Garanzie reali*, vol. 2.

secured claim on the proceeds of the sale, and the right to have preferential satisfaction over other unsecured creditors. Each of the above-mentioned systems ensures that the right in rem is effective even against third parties in possession of the secured asset, i.e. it can be claimed against a purchaser for example.

3. All three jurisdictions distinguish two categories of security rights in rem, namely, mortgage and pledge classified in accordance with the nature of the encumbered assets: mortgage refers to immovable assets – but also to movable ones susceptible to registration – while pledge is created over movable assets, including intangible assets such as claims. Noteworthy is that *France* and *Spain* maintain a particular security right in rem, the antichresis.[2] According to both legislations, antichresis is a security right in rem over immovables by which the secured creditor gains possession over the immovable asset and is entitled to acquire its 'fruits' under the obligation to allocate them to paying the secured claim. *Italy* also regulates the antichresis (Arts 1960–1964 of the Civil Code); nevertheless, this contract, which is totally unusual, is considered as not creating a right in rem.[3] Additionally, the retention of title clause has made its way to the category of security right in rem in *France* and to a certain extent in *Spain*. As a matter of fact, *France* has undertaken a thorough modernisation of its system and e.g. transfer of ownership by way of security is now included in the kind of security rights under discussion here. This matter is not settled in *Spain* where transfer of ownership by way of security have not found its way yet.

4. Regard should be had to the conceptual distinction between preference and privilege, i.e. while the first one is usually contractually concluded and focuses on the payment of a claim over a specific asset, the second one is established ex iure legis granting preference either over the proceeds of a specific asset or over the whole debtor's estate – giving rise to a further distinction between special and general privileges. The debate has been open in all three countries on the nature of privileges, i.e. whether they are security rights or not to the extent that they do not grant the right of separate realisation over encumbered assets in possession of a third party. Currently, *Spain* has departed from the above-mentioned distinction and only distinguishes between, on the one hand, special privileges comprising

2 The term 'antichresis' is found in the *US Black's Law Dictionary* which reads as follows: 'antichresis [Latin: in place of interest] Roman & civil law. A mortgage in which the mortgagee retains possession of the mortgaged property and takes the "fruits" (such as rents) of the property in lieu of interest on the debt. La. Civ. Code Art. 3176. Under the Civil Code of Louisiana, taken from the Code Napoleon, there are two kinds of pledges: the pawn, when a movable is given as security, and the antichresis, when the security given consists in immovables or real estate. Under the latter the creditor acquires the right to take the rents and profits of the land, and to credit, annually, the same to the interest, and the surplus to the principal or the debt, and is bound to keep the estate in repair, and to pay the taxes. Upon default upon the part of the debtor, the creditor may prosecute the debtor, and obtain a decree for selling the land pledged'.

3 G. Persico, 'Anticresi' in *Enciclopedia di Diritto*, vol. 2, 531.

among others security rights in rem and on the other hand general privileges, while *France* and *Italy* acknowledge the distinction and place privileges at a more central place in their insolvency legal systems and thus in the ranking of creditors.

5. Each of the above-mentioned systems is characterised by the fact that security rights are featured by being an accessory in nature meaning that the security right always follows the secured obligation, with the right being indivisible and not to be split in the case of the asset's division. While several obligations can be secured and several assets be encumbered, the security right at stake is created indicating the distribution of obligations among the relevant assets. There is one divergence with regard to *Spain*, however, where 'floating' mortgages and pledges are accepted, i.e. although several obligations are secured by the same immovable assets, security is not fragmented among them and thus, it 'floats' indiscriminately over the encumbered assets; the same applies in the event of secured obligations unspecified in its amount.

6. All three jurisdictions make it possible to create security rights over all res in commercio to the extent that the provider of collateral is the owner and holds the right of disposal. In *Italy* it is debatable whether the prescriptions of the Code of Civil Procedure (see Arts 514 and 534) excluding seizure of some personal assets of the debtor could be interpreted as meaning that these assets might not be encumbered by a pledge. All three systems are based on the principle of specialty, i.e. it is mandatory to clearly specify the encumbered assets at the time of the security's creation. Accordingly and in general terms it can be said that the above-mentioned systems do not allow the creation of security rights over assets not yet owned by the debtor at the time of the creation of the security interest, over assets that are not yet in existence at the time of the execution of the security agreement, and do not allow either the creation of a global security agreement covering all assets of the debtor. Nevertheless, there are significant exceptions in each system and, in particular, the pledge of future claims is admitted in all of them.

7. *Italy* and *Spain* veto the pactum commissorium, i.e. the agreement allowing automatic appropriation by the creditor of the thing pledged or mortgaged upon the failure of the debtor to pay the secured obligation; but there are some exceptions making it clear that the secured creditor can take over the asset in those cases in which there is a balance between both parties to the security right. *France* has gone a step further, however, and permits it if suitable provision is made for it in the security agreement, considered by the other countries as the typical case of pactum commissorium.

8. Foreclosure proceedings are judicial in principle; but non-judicial ones are also provided for by the three legal systems. Notwithstanding, the Italian one restricts the availability of the latter to pledge while the Spanish one does not provide for such a possibility in the case of antichresis, the aforementioned security right in rem over immovable assets, also laid down in *France* (see para. 3).

2. Enforcement in insolvency proceedings

9. As a general rule security rights continue to be effective and enforceable after the opening of insolvency proceedings. Nevertheless, *France*, *Italy* and *Spain* all provide for a stay which – exceptionally and for a restricted period of time – limits the enforceability of the securities. However, there are concessions to secured creditors depending on the type of proceeding and whether it pursues liquidation or restructuring purposes. The most liberal system is the Spanish one, which authorises the enforcement of security rights as long as they are not over assets necessary for the running of a debtor's enterprise before the liquidation phase. In contrast, *France* applies the stay to all insolvency creditors regardless of their status with two exceptions, that of title retention and transfer of ownership by way of security which are almost immune to the opening of an insolvency proceeding.

10. Secured creditors can be bound by restructuring plans to a certain extent which diverges in each country under consideration. Hybrid proceedings are already laid down by Spanish insolvency law and debtors are allowed to commence negotiations before the opening of an insolvency proceeding with a view to concluding a restructuring plan. The enforcement of specific security rights is stayed and, where appropriate, secured creditors are bound by the said restructuring plan.

3. Publicity

11. All three systems distinguish between non-possessory and possessory security rights. Where security rights are non-possessory, each jurisdiction provides for a system of registration. At any rate, registries also play a significant and similar role in the three countries when it comes to immovable assets. In contrast, registration of security rights over movable assets plays a paramount role in *Spain* while *France* does resort to registration for publicity purposes as regards to non-possessory pledge.

12. A pledge over claims is permissible in the three legal systems provided that the debtor is notified subject to certain exceptions. *Spain*, however, does not generally require such a notification save the case of the Catalan pledge of claims, whose creation depends on its recording in a public document and debtor notification of the pledged claim.

13. Where security rights are possessory, every system under consideration regards debtor's dispossession of the secured assets as an alternative method to registration which also allows determining priority between competing security interests in the same assets. To this end, the usual system for determining priority relies on the date on which the possessory security right is created being specifically mentioned in a public document.

14. All systems make it possible to create several and different security rights over the same assets.

15. The strength of the registration system in these countries means that priority between competing security rights over the same asset is determined in accordance with priority of order provided by the relevant registry. In the case of securities that are not registrable in the relevant registers, priority is generally determined on the basis of establishing the date of the relevant security right's creation.

4. Quasi-security

16. All three systems acknowledge the so-called 'quasi-security' agreements, i.e. agreements that in legal terms do not involve the creation of security interests but have many of the same economic consequences. For example, all three jurisdictions permit and regulate sales with repurchase clauses and retention of title clauses in hire-purchase contracts. Factoring and finance leases have been imported from common law systems as well. Some of these operations were considered in the past as violating the principles governing security rights, such as the prohibition of the pactum commissorium. In this vein, the Italian reception of sale and lease back is a case in point. However, the debate has faded away in the light of the market's needs. It is also debatable whether, in all three jurisdictions, these agreements could grant the creditor a priority in the case of the insolvency of the debtor.

17. Some jurisdictions have created additional quasi-security rights which are strongly shaped by the context in which they are employed. For example, Italian banks have created special forms of assignment of claims for guarantee purposes by which the bank is entitled to collect the claim as a debtor's trustee. This, compared to pledge of claims, has the obvious advantage of allowing the lending institution to demand the claim assigned without the lender having to establish that the financed party has not fulfilled the terms of the lending agreement. For taxation reasons, again the Italian banks have created the so-called '*mandato irrevocabile all'incasso*' (irrevocable order to collect) which identifies the agreement by which the main debtor (client) issues to the agent-creditor (bank) an irrevocable order to collect one or more claims, with a power for the agent to receive the payment and to retain the sums received until fulfilment of the agreement, or to impute the sums received to paying off the debt in case of default. However, it is debatable whether this agreement can survive the client's insolvency proceedings.

5. Transactional avoidance

18. The French, Italian and Spanish jurisdictions have set up rules which operate once a debtor enters insolvency proceedings and which provide for the invalidation or non-enforceability of transactions entered into by the debtor prior to the commencement of the insolvency proceedings. Transactional avoidance covers security and quasi-security rights as well. In general, such provisions usually deal with transactions performed by the debtor himself; but they may exceptionally cover acts performed by a third party such as the creation of a security right which may be detrimental to the general body of creditors.

19. None of the three systems distinguishes between preferences and fraudulent transactions, but rather focuses on the detriment to the general body of creditors and envisage transactional avoidance as a remedy to it, more specifically as a way of preventing the debtor from damaging its creditors. In *Italy*, case law departs from the rules established in contract and tort law.

20. The operability of transactional avoidance differs from country to country. While *Spain* grants standing to the IP to challenge suspected transactions with a view to making them ineffective against the estate, *Italy* pays regard to the degree of fraud involved in the transaction and, where appropriate, either provides for the automatic ineffectiveness of legal transactions towards the insolvency proceedings (automatic transactional avoidance) or entitles the IP to challenge these transactions and to make them ineffective towards the insolvency proceedings (judicial transactional avoidance). In a similar vein, *France* also distinguishes between automatic and non-automatic transactional avoidance.

21. Should the transaction be avoided, Italian law and Spanish law consider the transactions affected by avoidance as relatively ineffective, i.e. ineffective only towards the insolvency estate, i.e. the same transaction is considered to be valid and effective among their parties. The same does not apply in *France* which modulates transactional avoidance as a case of nullity, either absolute or relative.

22. The length of the suspect period also differs from jurisdiction to jurisdiction. As a matter of fact, it can even vary within the same jurisdiction according to the type of proceedings and the act involved. On this point Italian law seems to be the most permissive because the suspect period established for challenging the most usual acts is fixed in at six and twelve months. *Italy* and *Spain* consider as the *dies a quo* or day as of which the suspect period runs, the date of the opening of insolvency proceedings while *France* fixes it at the date on which the debtor defaults in payment.

23. As expected, avoidance rules are naturally applicable when it comes to liquidation. But their enforceability is also feasible in the framework of restructuring proceedings save for some exceptions in *France*. As a matter of fact, the Spanish insolvency law only distinguishes between a restructuring and a liquidation phase in the framework of the same insolvency proceeding for which reason its rules on transactional avoidance are always applicable. Italian law lays down that in Marzano proceedings these transactional avoidance rules can be proposed by the IP even if the execution of a restructuring programme has been authorised (Art 6.1 Decree-Law 347/2003).

6. EBRD

24. To a great extent all three systems seem to comply with the Core Principles for a Secured Transactions Law drawn up by the European Bank for Reconstruction and Development. In particular, the French, Italian and Spanish jurisdictions all enable creation of security rights in rem allowing secured creditors a position of priority over unsecured creditors, which is enforceable even when insolvency proceeding affect the debtor. Moreover, all three feature effective systems of publicity or, in the case of possessory security rights, alternative regulations determining priority between competing security interests in the same assets and preventing conflicts between the various interests involved.

25. Nevertheless, the aforementioned systems still appear quite rigid and extremely debtor-oriented. This means, firstly, that they still contain many restrictions concerning the nature of the assets encumbered, and these assets must already be owned by the debtor or by the third party; secondly, that most security rights on movable assets are possessory with the result that their creation deprives the debtor of the use of his assets. In this regard, some reforms aiming at distinguishing between a regime of security transactions applicable to individuals and a regime suitable for companies would be welcome and would make the company regulation on security rights more flexible and creditor-oriented. Probably, these changes will increase the availability of credit. Nevertheless, it has to be borne in mind that every effort aimed at improving the system has to take into account the role of path-dependence and the negative influence of some other factors limiting credit availability. This is the case, for example, with excessively high tax pressure which, in *France*, *Italy* and *Spain*, forces companies to be small in size – the expression is intentionally non-technical – meaning that on the one hand they have a tiny equity share capital while on the other they have restricted assets; or, to use German terminology, which is very common in the Continent, in the sense that they are both *nominell unterkapitalisiert* and *materiell unterkapitalisiert*. Certainly, if companies have not much equity finance then surely they are likely to have relatively more debt finance. Nevertheless, the terms on which a loan is made available also depend on the amount of the share capital, on the whole size of the company and – especially after the adoption by the EU of Regulation 575/2013 and Directive 36/2013 (CRR/CRD IV) – on the degree of risk which a specific lender is able to take with respect to specific borrower.

26. Finally, it must be mentioned that all three countries have signed the Cape Town Convention on international interests in mobile equipment. So far, the Convention is only in force in *Spain* after the latter's ratification of its Aircraft Protocol. The point to be made now is that the principles on which the Convention features those security interests clash with those typical of the Roman legal systems. It is worth noting that the Convention is in line with the system of registered secured transactions set out e.g. in Article 9 of the UCC, by which the security is registered but the filing is very brief and not subject to the scrutiny of the person in charge of the registry. Accordingly, there is no presumption as to the accuracy of the file for which reason acquisitions by third parties in good faith, also known as acquisitions *a non domino* in Roman legal systems, are not protected and registration only grants to the first secured creditor priority over other creditors. The Convention is applicable to both international and national transactions in *Spain* whose system has to be modified to meet the features of the Convention. Nevertheless, this clash is a limited one given that the Cape Town Convention only deals with a particular class of movable assets.

B. CREATION OF SECURITY RIGHTS

Question 1: In general terms, to what extent is it possible in your legal system to create security rights (rights in rem) over assets?

1. France

27. French law embraces a broad concept of security interests in rem (*sûreté réelle*), including three kinds of security interest over assets: privilege general or special; security rights in rem stricto sensu, i.e. pledge over movable tangible assets, pledge over intangible assets, mortgage and antichresis;[4] and transfer or retention of title by way of security. Each of these types of security diverges as to their origin and functioning.

28. Privilege is created by operation of law and grants the secured creditor the right to receive priority payment from the debtor's encumbered assets (*droit de préference*).

[4] Antichresis is also classified by French law as an immovable pledge. See above fn. 2.

29. Security rights in rem – with the exception of what is known as 'legal mortgage' – are contractual, and grant the holder not only the above-mentioned preference but also the right to separate realisation (*droit de suite*) over the encumbered assets no matter who is in possession of the assets.

30. As to the different ways in which ownership can be used as security it must have a contractual origin, grant their holder an exclusive right over the asset, namely, its ownership, and so may be claimed without the risk of competing with other creditors.

31. The French Civil Code (CC) classifies the various types of security interests in rem according to the nature, movable or immovable, of the encumbered assets. Title II of Book IV entitled 'Security interest in rem' is divided into three sub-titles, dedicated to 'general provisions' (Art. 2373 et seq.), 'security interests over movable' (Art. 2339 et seq.), and 'security interests over immovable' (Art. 2373 et seq.). Within each category, the law regulates the various types of security interests mentioned above, namely privileges; security rights in rem, and ownership as security. The 'right of possessory retention' is not included in this Title, but the Code regulates it in its general provisions, common to both personal security interests and security interests in rem, making clear that such a right is an effective de facto method of securing the creditor's right to payment.

32. Book IV of the Code was drawn up following the law No 2006-346, of 23 March 2006, which substantially modified the previous regulation in an attempt to modernise, simplify, and enhance security interests. Nevertheless, this law has not managed to eliminate the multiplicity of special regimes that still coexist, both within and outside the Civil Code. A brief description of the different security interests in rem is appropriate.

1.1. Privileges

33. Privileges can be defined as the right of certain creditors to be paid in preference to other creditors from the encumbered asset. Granted by law on the basis of the 'quality of the claim' (Art. 2324CC), the classification of privileges as a security interest in rem is debated in legal literature, as most of them do not confer on the holder a right of separate realisation in respect of the encumbered assets. However, the fact that legislation has classified them as a security interest in rem as shown by Articles 2329 and 2373 CC on the one hand, and their effects vis-à-vis third party creditors on the other hand, justifies their characterisation as security interests in rem for our purposes.

34. Privileges may affect a whole class of the debtor's assets (general privileges, that can be movable or immovable) or certain particular assets, in which case privilege is deemed as special, either movable or immovable (Arts. 2328, 2330, 2374 and 2375 CC).[5]

35. It must be noted that privileges over movable and immovable assets differ in terms of publicity requirements.

36. In the case of movable privileges, the security interest clearly meets the defining features of privilege, i.e. movables assets are encumbered ex iure legis to satisfy the privileged claim. Whether they be general or special, movable privileges are not subject to publicity, which does not undermine their effectiveness against other creditors of the debtor.[6]

37. By contrast, immovable privileges in general do not relieve the secured creditor from the burden of registering it once a document has been drawn up clearly indicating which the encumbered assets are. This registration must be made within a period of two months after the date of the act creating the privilege, which takes ranks from this latter date. Only the special privilege of a property owners association and general privileges associated with legal costs and wage claims are exempt from the registration requirement, acting – as in the case of movable privileges – as tacit legal securities (Arts. 2377 and 2378 CC). A practical comparison can thus be made between immovable privileges subject to registration and legal mortgage (Art. 2400(5) CC).

38. Special mention should be made of the so-called *privilèges de la procédure*, in general claims against the estate privileging claims arising after the opening of insolvency proceedings to cover the needs of the latter, such as payments to insolvency practitioners, or in exchange for a loan or a supply of goods or services granted to the debtor during the observation period in *sauvegarde* and *redressement* proceedings, i.e. the French insolvency proceedings targeting the debtor's restructuring (Art. L. 622-17 Code de commerce, CComm.) or in general arising after the opening of liquidation proceedings (Art. L. 641-13 CComm.).

---

5 General privileges over movable assets are basically listed in Article 2331 CC (legal costs, funeral costs, expenses related to last illness, wages claims concerning the last six months and others of lesser importance), in tax legislation (privileges of the Public Treasury) and in the Social Security Code (privileges of the Social Security Administration for the payment of contributions). Privileges associated with legal costs and wage claims are extended to all immovable assets of the debtor as 'fully general privileges', where there are no movable assets (Arts. 2375–2376 CC). Special privileges over movable assets are described in Article 2332 CC, and privilege over immovables in Article 2374 CC.

6 Social security and public treasury privileges, which must be registered in a special registry kept by the Commercial Court, are exceptions to the rule, as in the absence of registration they are considered to be unsecured claims.

1.2. Security rights in rem over movables

1.2.1. Pledge over tangible assets

39. Article 2333 CC defines the pledge as a contract whereby the pledgor grants the creditor the right to be paid in preference to other creditors from a movable asset or a group of present or future movable assets. Traditionally, its creation required the creditor to take physical possession of the asset, but since the 2006 reform, pledges can be either possessory or non-possessory. In the latter case, the pledge agreement must be registered to be effective against third parties.

40. Despite the fact that the wide scope of this pledge could have covered all special pledges laid down in and out of the Civil Code, French legislation has retained and even extended all of them.

41. The common pledge (*gage de droit commun*). *Creation:* According to Article 2334 CC, the pledge can be created by the debtor himself or by a third party whose assets may be encumbered in order to satisfy the other's debt. At any rate, the provider of collateral must be the owner of the encumbered asset as well as have the right of disposal over it (Question 3).

42. The pledge may secure any present or future obligation, provided that it is determinable, and can encumber any movable asset or group of fungible or non-fungible assets, as long as they are *in commercio* (Question 2).

43. The pledge must be created in writing. If it is non-possessory, it must be publicised via registration to be effective vis-à-vis third parties (Questions 6 and 19).

44. *Effects:* Before the secured claim becomes mature: where pledges are possessory, the creditor or a third party must act as a depositary of the encumbered asset and is responsible for its deterioration (Arts. 2343–2344 CC). There is no right of disposal or of use, although the secured creditor may enjoy beneficial use of the assets and any 'fruits' arising out of the asset may be counted against the debt (Art. 2345). The pledgee in possession of an asset has the right of possessory retention as long as the secured claim is not paid in full, which allows him to refuse to transfer it to possible subsequent acquirers.

45. In cases of a non-possessory pledge, the pledgor remains in possession of the property but subject to a series of restrictions. He must maintain the asset in good condition, and in case of breach of this obligation, the creditor may request early payment of the secured claim or an additional pledge.[7] Article 2286 CC grants

[7] According to Article 2344.2 CC: 'When the pledge is made without dispossession, the creditor may avail himself of the forfeiture of the term of the secured debt or request an

the secured creditor who is not in physical possession of the encumbered asset a right of fictive retention, but in practice, it does not prevent the debtor from transferring the asset to a third party. Since 2006 the requirement to register the non-possessory pledge limits the scope of Article 2276 CC indicating that *en fait de meubles, la possession vaut titre*, and for which reason the pledgee can recover the asset from third parties.

46. *Enforcement of the pledge:* When the secured claim matures and it is not paid, the creditor has two ways of enforcing his claim, in addition to the right to retain possession of the pledged asset, i.e. either by selling the asset or by its appropriation.

47. *Sale of the pledged asset:* the pledgee can force the sale in order to use the proceeds to satisfy the secured claim according to his position in relation to other competing creditors (Art. 2346 CC). To this end, enforcement proceedings as laid down by the Civil Procedure Act must be taken, given that an agreement by the parties to directly sell the pledged asset, namely a *de voie parée* clause, is forbidden by law.

48. *Appropriation of the pledged asset:* The creditor may also request of the courts that the encumbered asset should be transferred to him by way of payment (Art. 2347 CC). If the asset's value is above that of the secured claim, the difference must either be paid to the debtor or paid to later ranking pledges if there are other pledgees. In contrast, should the value of the asset be insufficient to pay the claim in full, the pledge is terminated, but not the claim and thus, the creditor retains his right to the outstanding amount, but as an unsecured creditor.

49. The law permits the pledgor and pledgee to agree, either when creating the pledge or subsequently, to a pactum commissorium or *pacte commissoire* whereby the creditor assumes ownership of the asset in the case of default on the secured debt (Art. 2348 CC). The clause cannot be either concluded or enforced after the opening of insolvency proceedings (Art. L. 622-7.I CComm.).

50. *Special regulations regarding pledge over movable tangible assets.* The common pledge coexists with other pledges over movable assets which depart to some extent from the above-mentioned general regulation. The Civil Code itself regulates the pledging of motor vehicles, whose effects vis-à-vis third parties is subject to the formality of making a statement before an administrative body.

---

additional pledge if the pledgor does not carry out his obligation of preservation of the pledge'. The English version of the Civil Code as of 1 July 2013 follows the translation by David W. Gruning and revision by Juriscope. Expert Committee: A. Levasseur and J. Trahan, 'French Civil Code' (*Legifrance*, 1 July 2013) <http://www.legifrance.gouv.fr/Traductions/en-English/Legifrance-translations> accessed 26 May 2016. All Articles of the French Civil Code that will be literally quoted in this report are taken from this translation.

The document recording the said statement must be delivered to the pledgee, making possible by this means the transfer of the fictive possession of the pledged motor vehicle. Otherwise, the enforcement of the pledge is subject to the general rules (Arts. 2351 and 2352 CC).

51. Similarly, the above-mentioned general rules are complementary to those commercial law provisions dealing with pledge (Art. 2353 CC), of which there are three types, namely the commercial pledge, the pledge over industrial machinery, businesses and mobile equipment and the pledge over stock.

52. The *commercial pledge* is characterised by the commercial nature of the secured claim (Art. L. 521-1 CComm.), has distinctive features of form (Question 6) and enforcement (Art. L. 521-3 CComm. which basically simplifies the formalities required to enforce the security interest).

53. The pledge over industrial machinery, businesses and mobile equipment (*nantissement de l'outillage et du materiel d'équipement*) encumbers professional tools and equipment with the sole objective of securing the claim arising from the financing of the equipment's acquisition. Regulated by Articles L. 525-1 to L. 525-20 of the Commercial Code, it is a non-possessory pledge subject to specific form and publicity requirements, which determine its effects vis-à-vis third parties (Questions 6 and 19).

54. The pledge over stock is regulated by Articles L. 527-1 to L. 527-11 CComm. as amended in 2000, in order to enhance companies' access to credit, by allowing them to create a security interest over their raw materials, merchandise and products. Intended to secure any claim, it is limited to the relationships that link a credit entity or a financing company with the secured creditor – and a business owner (either a natural or legal person), who must be the owner of the encumbered assets. The pledge is non-possessory with powers of control over the appropriate maintenance of stocks conferred on the creditor, and its creation is bound by strict norms of documentation and registration (see Questions 6 and 19). The forced sale or judicial assignment of the secured assets is subject to the above-mentioned common rules, with the exception of the express prohibition of the pactum commissorium (Art. L. 527-2 CComm.).[8]

---

8 The Court of Cassation has decided that special regulation of pledge over stocks excludes the option to create a non-possessory common pledge over this kind of assets (Cass. Comm. 19.2.2013). See M. Bourassin, *La force d'attraction du gage des stocks*, 1363. Noteworthy is that Article 240 of Law No 2015-990 of 6 August 2015, *pour la croissance, l'activité et l'égalité des chances économiques*, authorises the government to harmonise by decree the pledge of stocks as established in the Commercial Code and the pledge on tangible assets laid down in the Civil Code with a view to making the interaction between both regimes clear and making the pactum commissorium feasible as well as possessory and non-possessory pledge over stocks favouring by this means corporate financing.

1.2.2. Pledge over intangibles (nantissement)

55. Article 2355 CC defines *nantissement* as the security interest over an intangible movable asset or group of intangible movable assets, whether present or future. The provision distinguishes between the pledge of claims which is subject, in the absence of special provisions, to Articles 2356 et seq. CC, and the pledge of other intangible movable assets subject, in the absence of special provisions, to the provisions on pledge over tangible assets.

1.2.3. Pledge over claims

56. *Creation: a* pledge over claims can be agreed to secure any present or future indebtedness as well as to encumber any current or future claim or a part of a claim. It is possible to pledge a group of present and/or future claims in a single agreement, provided that the pledge agreement clearly identifies them. Specifically, the pledge may encumber a bank account, in which case the pledged claim is security for the credit balance at closure, or in the event of insolvency proceedings, at the time of the opening of these proceedings (Art. 2360 CC). Under penalty of nullity, the agreement must be set down in writing, and is enforceable against third parties from the date of its creation as recorded in the document, save for the account debtor of the encumbered claim who must be notified of the pledge agreement in order for the pledge agreement to be enforceable against him (see Question 19).

57. *Effects before the secured claim becomes mature:* Once the debtor of the pledged claim has been notified, he is obliged to pay only the pledgee. The latter is entitled to enforce the pledged claim where appropriate and duly notifying other pledgees (Art. 2363 CC). Should the secured claim not be mature, the pledgee is not entitled to retain the amount paid and he is obliged to transfer any payments to a special account held at an authorised establishment. The latter will repay them to the debtor-creditor of the pledged claim if he meets his obligations. Otherwise, the pledgee can be paid from those funds eight days after the pledgor has defaulted.

58. *Enforcement of the pledge:* Once the secured obligation is due, the secured creditor has different alternatives to enforce the pledge depending on whether the pledged claim is due or not. If it is not yet due, the creditor can have the claim attributed to him 'judicially or under the conditions set out in the agreement' without waiting for it to mature (Art. 2365 CC, which implicitly allows the pactum commissorium). Once the pledged claim is mature, the secured creditor may appropriate the sums owed by the account debtor and use them to reduce his own claim, with an obligation to repay any amounts received that are in excess of what is owed (Art. 2366 CC).

1.2.4. Pledge over other intangible assets

59. Several provisions in various laws make provision for different types of pledge over intangible rights other than claims. Noteworthy are the pledge of a business (*nantissement du fonds de commerce*), a non-possessory security that encumbers the totality of movables associated with a business (Art. L. 142-1 et seq. CComm.), as well as a pledge over a marketable securities account (*nantissement de comptes-titres*), which encumbers the account in which the debtor's securities are held (Art. L. 211-20 of the Monetary and Financial Code).

60. The following assets, including those under construction, can be subject to a mortgage provided that they can be clearly identified and thus registrable: ocean vessels and other maritime structures (*hypothèque maritime*: Arts. 244 et seq. of the Customs Code), inland waterway vessels of a certain size (*hypothèque fluvial:* Art. L. 4122-1 of the Transport Code) and aircrafts (*hypothèque aérienne*: Arts. L. 6122-1 et seq. of the Transport Code). This kind of mortgage is a conventional, non-possessory security and, to the extent that it is registered, grants the holder a right of priority payment and separate realisation even against third parties in good faith and in possession of the asset.

61. *Creation:* It must be created in writing and registered in a public registry, kept by the Customs Office in the case of a maritime mortgage; by the commercial court in whose jurisdiction the ship is registered in the case of a waterway mortgage and by the Ministry of Civil Aviation in the case of a mortgage over aircrafts.

62. *Effects:* Secured creditors are assimilated with mortgagors and have the rights of the latter over the encumbered assets. But their priority rights are reinforced, since mortgages over movables are preferred to common privileges (Arts. L. 4122-15, L. 5114-14, L. 6122-15 Transport Code).

1.3. Security rights in rem over immovable property

63. A mortgage is a security right in rem over immovable assets (Art. 2393 CC). It is a non-possessory security interest that gives the creditor a priority right over the encumbered asset, and is enforceable whoever the owner may be. There are also special privileges over immovable assets, which should now be considered as 'legal mortgages'.

64. *Creation:* Mortgages can be created contractually, by operation of law or judicially (Arts. 2395 and 2396 CC). Whatever the origin of the security right, they must be registered at the Land Registry to be effective against third parties (Question 19).

65. *Conventional mortgage:* This is the usual type of mortgage and arises from a contract between a creditor and a debtor or a third party who is not the debtor, but the owner of the mortgaged immovable asset, the latter case known as *caution réelle*. A mortgage may secure present or future obligations provided they are determinable and the source of the obligation is documented when the contract is created, e.g. a debit balance on a current credit account.

66. The mortgage agreement is a formal contract, the validity of which is subject to recording in a notarised deed which must contain a number of matters because of the principle of specialty (Question 6). An agreement for a mortgage can be contained in a private agreement, but the agreement creates no more than a positive obligation, breach of which gives rise to a right to compensation.

67. A legal mortgage is defined in the Civil Code as a mortgage created by operation of the law (Art. 2396). Despite its origin, a legally recognised mortgage does not apply automatically in favour of certain creditors, but requires registration for the security right to be effective vis-à-vis third parties (Art. 2401 CC). The main legal mortgages are listed in Article 2400 CC, such as the mortgage that one spouse can create over the other's assets, the one that minors or adults in guardianship can set up over their tutor or guardian's property, or that of the state. Other privileged claims are laid down in sections 2, 3, 5, 7 and 8 of Article 2331 CC.

68. *Judicial mortgage*: Despite its name, a judicial mortgage is not created by the court but by law to the extent that it provides for the registration of a mortgage over all a defendant's assets in favour of a creditor who has obtained a favourable judgment (Art. 2412 CC). In any event, the mortgage is effective only after registration. The so-called *hypothèque judiciaire conservatoire* can be requested by the creditor-plaintiff as an interim measure (Arts. L. 511 et seq. Code des procedures d'exécution). The granting of this interim measure results in a provisional registration so that once there is a firm ruling, the creditor-plaintiff can request definitive registration which is effective from the date of the provisional registration.

69. *Effects of the mortgage: Security period:* Before defaulting on a secured debt, the debtor continues to have use, enjoyment and rights of disposal over the asset. The owner is only barred from actions that might compromise the value of the asset, and failure to comply may result in early enforcement of the secured claim (Art. 1188 CC).

70. *Mortgage enforcement.* Should the debtor default, the creditor is entitled to realise the encumbered asset according to the provisions of foreclosure proceedings (*saisie immobilière*), the formalities of which cannot be circumvented by means of a *voie parée* clause (Art. 2458 CC).

71. In the case of conventional mortgages, Article 2458 CC entitles the secured creditor to request the court to transfer the encumbered asset, as seen in the event of pledge enforcement. Similarly, Article 2459 CC allows the inclusion of a pactum commissorium in the mortgage agreement, except when the property is the debtor's habitual residence. In any case of payment in kind, the property must be valued by an expert designated by mutual agreement or by the court. If the value is greater than the secured claim, the creditor must return the difference to the debtor or to other secured creditors if there are other security rights subsisting with respect to the property.

72. *Antichresis or gage immobilier* is a security right over an immovable asset whose possession must be transferred by the provider of collateral (Art. 2387 CC), being the secured creditor entitled to use the asset and be paid with its 'fruits'. This security right shares features of both mortgage, since it is over an immovable, and possessory pledge, since it requires taking possession of the immovable asset, for which reason it is subject to both regulations.

73. *Creation:* Subject to strict formalities, namely notarisation and registration, the existence of the right is dependent on the transfer of possession of the asset to the secured creditor.

74. *Effects: Security period:* Antichresis grants the secured creditor possession and use of the asset, including the right to collect its 'fruits' and pay the secured claim with them. The creditor may lease the asset, either to a third party or to the debtor himself, without ceding legal or fictive possession (*antichrèse bail*).

75. *Enforcement:* In the case of default, the secured creditor may exercise his right in the same way as a mortgagee, i.e. by forced sale or direct attribution of the encumbered immovable asset. Similar to pledgees, he is allowed to retain possession until full performance of the secured obligation (Art. 2391 CC). This right is not enforceable against mortgagees who have previously registered their rights.

1.4. Ownership by way of security

76. Along with the typical security rights in rem and with a view to promoting access to credit, modern French law has now regulated the retention or transfer of ownership by way of security, i.e. the secured creditor remains or becomes owner until the secured claim is paid in full, in which case the debtor recovers ownership or becomes owner over the encumbered assets, i.e. should the secured claim not be paid, the creditor acquires full ownership over the assets.

77. Accordingly, the use of ownership as a form of security is found in two types of security interest. The first one is typical of operations for financing the acquisition of an asset, and consists of the creditor retaining ownership of the supplied asset until the debtor has paid the price in full, namely by including in the contract a retention of title clause. The second one can be found in the framework of any credit transaction to the extent that the debtor transfers ownership of one of his assets to the creditor with agreement to recover it once the secured claim has been satisfied. In this way, there is a transfer of ownership by way of security. Both types of security interest may be over movable and immovable assets (Arts. 2329 and 2373 CC), and are thus dealt with together here.

1.4.1. Retention of title

78. The retention of title clause is an agreement by which the transfer of ownership of assets is delayed until payment for them has been made in full [Art. 2367(1) CC]. It can be included in any contract which involves the transfer of ownership, particularly the sale of goods, and it implies derogation from the French principle of transfer of ownership on the sole basis of the parties' agreement.[9]

79. Under French law, the retention of title clause does not secure any claim other than that resulting from the contract in question. Under the terms of Article 2367(2) CC, it is an accessory to the secured obligation and the transfer or termination of the latter implies the transfer or termination of the former (Art. 1692 CC).

80. *Creation:* The Civil Code reduces the formalities for creating this security interest by simply requiring it to be set down in writing, which is enough to make it effective against third parties (Art. 2368 CC).

81. *Effects:* The clause is a particularly effective type of security interest, such that if the obligation is not fully satisfied when due, the creditor may demand restitution of the asset, recovering his right of disposal over it. The value of the asset is set off against the outstanding debt, and thus the creditor is obliged to reimburse the excess to the debtor, that is, the amount of the asset's value which is over and above the secured claim (Art. 2371 CC).

82. The asset may be recovered whatever its nature and situation. Protection is enhanced by the mechanism of subrogation in rem; according to Article

9 According to Article 1583 CC: 'It is perfect between the parties, and ownership is acquired as of right by the buyer with regard to the seller as soon as they have agreed on the thing and on the price, although the thing has not yet been delivered nor the price paid'.

2372 CC, the property right of the secured creditor is extended to the debtor's claim against third parties who may have acquired the asset in question from him as well as to compensation for damage to the encumbered asset arising from insurance policies.

83. However, this security interest does have limitations. If the clause has not been registered, the action for recovery of a movable asset might be neutralised by the application of Article 2276 CC, i.e. when a third party has taken possession of the asset in good faith. In the case of conflict with a subsequent pledgee, the Court of Cassation gives preference to the latter's rights over those of the unpaid seller.[10] Moreover, the secured creditor's action for the recovery of the asset may be stayed by another creditor exercising a right of possessory retention over the asset.[11]

1.4.2. Transfer of ownership by way of security: fiducie-sûreté

84. Under modern French law, a claim can be secured by a debtor transferring one or several of his assets to the creditor, who acquires ownership over them limited in scope and time. If the secured claim is satisfied, the debtor recovers ownership, otherwise the creditor acquires full ownership of the asset, depending on the value of the claim.

85. Transfer of ownership by way of security (*fiducie-sûreté*) can proceed as to all types of asset and for any type of debt. A type of fiduciary contract, it is thus regulated by both provisions on fiduciary contracts in general (Arts. 2011 et seq. CC), and those laid down in particular in Title II of Book IV of the Civil Code (Arts. 2372-1 to 2372-5 in respect of movables and Arts. 2488-1 to 2488-5 in respect of immovable assets).

86. *Creation:* Transfer of ownership by way of security is created through a written contract (Question 6). Even when it essentially involves transfer of ownership [Arts. 2329, 2372.1, 2373, 2488(1) CC], transfer of possession might not take place, in which case the provider of collateral retains the use and enjoyment of the asset transferred by way of security. Even in the event that possession has been transferred, it is nevertheless a temporary and incomplete transfer of ownership, i.e. without the right of disposal and dependent on the non-payment of the secured claim. Articles 2372-3 and 2488-3 CC do not provide for the full

10 This is the understanding of the Court of Cassation, giving precedence to the pledgee acting in good faith over the interests of the holder of a retention of title clause over the pledged asset (Cass. Comm. 28.11.1989; Cass. Comm. 26.11.2006; Cass. Comm. 26.5.2010; Cass. Comm. 11.9.2012).

11 Cass. Comm. 3.10.1989.

transfer of ownership and thus, for acquisition of the right of disposal over the encumbered assets, save for the case of realisation of the security.

87. The collateral may be provided by one or more natural or legal persons, whilst the fiduciary (*fiduciaire*), who can be the secured creditor or a third party, must be a financial institution or a practising lawyer (Arts. 2011, 2015, 2016 CC). According to Article 2017 CC, the debtor may name a 'protector' of his interests to ensure the proper enforcement of the contract.

88. *Effects: Before the secured claim becomes mature*: The *fiducie-sûreté* results in a temporary, purpose-oriented transfer of ownership of one or several assets, which are separate from the fiduciary's personal assets and form a separate estate. In this period, the absence of legal provisions on the powers of the fiduciary can be complemented assimilating him to a pledgee: he cannot use the assets although he may appropriate their 'fruits', and cannot dispose of the assets unless they are fungible, in which case goods must be replaced. As to claims, the fiduciary is considered to be a holder of a pledge of claims.

89. *Enforcement of the transfer by way of security*: Articles 2372-3 (as regards movable assets) and 2488-3 (as regards immovable assets) of the Civil Code recognise two ways for a creditor to enforce his rights.

90. If the creditor is in possession of the assets, in the case of non-compliance and unless otherwise agreed, he acquires the full right of disposal of the asset or the claim transferred by way of security. In contrast, should he not be in possession of the asset, he can claim from the person in possession of the asset either the delivery of the secured assets, or, if stipulated in the contract, the sale of the assets and satisfaction of his claim from the sale proceeds.

1.5. Right of possessory retention

91. The right of possessory retention entitles the creditor who is in material or fictive possession over immovable or movable, tangible or intangible assets belonging to the debtor, to retain them until the debtor has fulfilled his obligations. The right grants the secured creditor a purely defensive but highly effective means of exerting pressure on the debtor and against other unsecured or preferential creditors.

92. *Cases in which the right is granted*: Article 2286 of the Civil Code grants the right of possessory retention over assets to four types of creditor:

(1) The person to whom an asset is delivered until the obligation is fulfilled. This case covers the right of retention of the pledgee and that of the

creditor in antichresis, as well as cases of right of retention created by a specific and autonomous contract, which can target an asset unrelated to the secured claim and are exempt from formal requirements.

(2) Where retention is associated with an existing legal connection between the claim and the physical control over an asset, e.g. retention by a garage-owner, a depositary, a cash seller, a business manager, or a builder on third-party land.

(3) The person whose claim arises due to possession of the asset. Retention is associated with the material connection between the asset retained and the claim, such as retention by the usufructary, i.e. who has the right to enjoy all 'fruits' produced by the thing in usufruct, or a bona fide possessor.

(4) The pledgee of a non-possessory pledge. This covers the 'fictive retention', which is characteristic of certain non-possessory security rights over movables and was introduced in French law in 2008. The Court of Cassation has limited the scope of Article 2286.4 to securities over tangible assets, excluding the pledge over intangibles which is subject to special provisions.[12]

93. *Effects: Powers not conferred by this right*: as a temporary holder, the secured creditor has no power of intervention over the asset, i.e. no use, enjoyment or disposal. He does not have a right of separate realisation; retention does not confer *droit de suite* nor the option to request the courts for transfer of the asset by way of payment.

94. *The right to refuse the return of an asset:* The only power conferred by the right of possessory retention is the right to refuse the transfer of the asset, freezing de facto the exercise of other security rights in rem and privileges that may exist over it. To counteract this, the secured creditor is obliged to maintain the asset in good condition, being liable for its loss or culpable deterioration. The option of refusing return of the assets is indivisible; thus one may retain all encumbered assets until full payment of the secured claim is made.[13]

---

12 See, in relation to pledge of a business, Cass. Comm. 26.11.2013. In the framework of gage over tangibles, legal literature extends the fictive retention to common and special pledges. See R. Damman and G. Podeur, *Le nouveau paysage du droit des sûretés: première étape de la réforme de la fiducie et du gage sans dépossession*, 2300; O. Buisine, (2011) 6 *Revue des procédures collectives* étude 31.

13 The Court of Cassation has defined the right of possessory retention as a right over rem, in consideration of its effectiveness against third acquirers of the asset (Cass. civ. 24.9.2009).

2. Italy[14]

95. Italian law does not provide a legal definition of 'security rights'. Traditionally this term is used to describe any right that aims to ensure the performance to the

---

[14] As said, this report was updated on 1 May 2016. Therefore, it takes into account d.l. 27.6.2015 No 83, which was converted – with amendments – into L. 6.8.2015 No 132. By contrast, this report does not contain any reference to a Bill of a Delegating Law 25.11.2015 which was prepared by the Rordorf Commission (so-called after the name of its Chairman, Dr R. Rordorf), or to the more recent L. 30.6.2016 No 119.

Bill 25.11.2015 is addressed to the Italian Parliament, which should pass it and enable the Italian Government to achieve a comprehensive reform of Italian domestic insolvency law. This text is still subject to parliamentary hearings, which might suggest some changes. Moreover, it is not predictable when the reform will enter into force and to what extent it will concretely affect present insolvency law. This reform should affect most parts of Italian domestic insolvency law and, as such, it is not easy to summarise it here. Nevertheless, its key points include: an increasing alignment of Italian insolvency law with Regulation (EU) 2015/848 on insolvency proceedings, with the EU Recommendation of 12 March 2014 on a new approach to business failure and insolvency, and with the UNCITRAL Model Law on Cross-Border Insolvency and other related documents; the adoption of a criterion similar to that of the COMI to ascertain territorial competence to open insolvency proceedings; the introduction of a comprehensive legal framework to tackle group insolvencies; the introduction of specific measures aimed at anticipating the time when a debtor or his creditors may intervene to prevent a situation of crisis, which is still reversible, from becoming irreversible; a simplification of the system of privileges and their ranking; a softening of the prohibition of the agreement of forfeiture; the introduction of a form of non-possessory security right.

L. 30.6.2016 No 119 contains both urgent prescriptions concerning individual and insolvency proceedings, and prescriptions in favour of savers having invested their money in banks which are now in liquidation (*Disposizioni urgenti in materia di procedure esecutive e concorsuali, nonché a favore degli investitori in banche in liquidazione*; http://www.normattiva.it). This statute, converting d.l. 3.5.2016 No 59 with some amendments, unpacked the contents of the much more ambitious project endorsed by the Rordorf Commission, and only introduced into Italian jurisdiction a form of non-possessory pledge which allows the pledger of some assets to maintain possession of them. In particular, L. 30.6.2016 No 119 lays down that a businessman who is registered in the firm register may grant a non-possessory pledge in order to secure both his obligation and a third party obligation; that the secured claim may be both existing and future, both determined and determinable, provided that this claim refers to the grantor's business and that the pledge agreement provides a cap on the maximum amount guaranteed (Art. 1.1). The pledge agreement must be concluded in writing (Art. 1.3); the pledge right may encumber both movables, even intangibles, referring to the grantor's business, and claims either deriving from the grantor's business or related to it. The encumbered assets may be both existing and future, both determined and determinable by reference to one or more product categories or to a total value (Art. 1.2). L. 30.6.2016 No 119 moreover establishes that, unless otherwise provided, the debtor or that third party who grants the pledge may both sell and transform the encumbered assets and that, if it is the case, the security right automatically passes to the sales proceeds and to that product resulting from the transformation of the original item, respectively, in order to encumber them. Prescriptions are provided for the case where assets, encumbered by different pledges and belonging to different creditors, are commingled, as well as for the case where the debtor or the pledge grantor abuses their powers (Art. 1.2). The non-possessory pledge is effective against both creditors and third parties by means of registration in a digital register, specifically designed for non-possessory pledges. This register will be held by the

creditor of an obligation of the debtor. It is appropriate to consider that for this purpose Italian law provides for several legal instruments. First of all, Italian law provides creditors with a 'generic security' consisting of all present and future assets of their debtor (principle of the debtor's general liability: Art 2740 Civil Code). On the debtor's assets all his creditors may obtain satisfaction of their claims, in competition with each other according to the principle of pari passu (Art 2741 Civil Code). In addition to this 'general security', Italian law provides creditors with a system of 'specific securities' that aim to strengthen further the likelihood of fulfilment of the secured claims.[15]

96. Italian law distinguishes between 'personal' and 'real' security rights (rights in rem). Through personal security rights, a third party assumes liability for the payment of another person's debt: the most important example is the guarantee (*fideiussione*: Art 1936 Civil Code). Hence, personal security rights strengthen the probability of fulfilment of the secured claims as they increase the number of those liable persons and, therefore, the number of the estates on which the secured creditor may obtain satisfaction in the event of default. However, they create neither rights in rem enforceable erga omnes nor rights of preference against other creditors. On the contrary, real security rights make it more probable that the secured claims will be fulfilled by creating a creditor's right in rem over a specific asset, either of the debtor or of a third party, which, in the event of the debtor's default, allows the creditor to have it sold

---

Italian Revenue Authority (Art. 1.4). Registration expires after 10 years; renewal is allowed, provided that the previous registration has not already expired (Art. 1.6). Registration gives to the pledge priority over third parties in accordance with the 'first-in-time rule' (Art. 1.4). This rules applies, unless otherwise provided. In fact, L. 30.6.2016 No 119 provides two exceptions to this rule. The first exception could be summarised as follows: the retention of title by the seller over a specific movable property devoted to the firm always prevails over a non-possessory pledge, even if the retention of title is successive to the creation and registration of the non-possessory pledge (Art. 1.5). The second exception consists in the fact that a pledge, both possessory and non-possessory, which was granted to a creditor who financed the purchase of a specific movable property devoted to the firm, prevails over a prior non-possessory pledge, provided that, at the time of the registration, the registering creditor informed those creditors who had previously registered their non-possessory pledges (Art. 1.5). Regulation concerning the Italian non-possessory pledge is innovative as regards enforcement too. In this respect the secured creditor enjoys many powers of self-help; he may – without any court intervention – either sell the assets, or enforce the encumbered claims; moreover, if it is provided by the pledge agreement and if this clause is registered, the secured creditor may either rent out the encumbered assets and employ the rental fees to satisfy his claim, or become the proprietor of them (Art. 1.7). Further, some prescriptions ensure that these forms of enforcement are carried out in a context of transparency and fairness – the secured creditor has a multi-direction duty of communication; he has to hand over the surplus to the debtor, or to the pledge grantor (if this is a different entity) (Art. 1.7), while both the debtor and the pledge grantor may challenge the enforcement before a court and claim against creditor abuses (Art. 1.7-*bis*). As said, this reform is not operational since the planned register has not yet been established.

15 V. Roppo, 'La responsabilità patrimoniale del debitore' in P. Rescigno (ed.), *Trattato di diritto privato*, vol. XIX, 363.

and to use the proceeds obtained from the sale for his preferential satisfaction (Art 2741 Civil Code). This report focuses on this second category of security rights. Hence, when in the following paragraphs reference is made to 'security rights', the reference is always to security rights in rem.

97. Security rights are regulated by a set of common principles. First of all, they are considered as a numerus clausus: the creation of security rights other than the types provided by law is not allowed.[16] They show a direct and immediate relationship with the asset to which they relate, which remains bound (until the debt has been satisfied) although no longer part of the debtor's estate. This feature conveys the idea of the absolute nature of security rights, which are enforceable erga omnes and not just inter partes (i.e. between the debtor and the creditor). This implies that the security right's holder can protect it against anyone who interferes with his right without his consent. Furthermore, this implies that, in the event of default, the security right's holder has the power to have the encumbered asset expropriated (*ius distrahendi*), even against the third party purchaser (*ius sequelae*), and to obtain preferential satisfaction from the proceeds of this asset against debtor's other unsecured creditors (*ius prelationis*). However, under Italian law the security right's holder cannot automatically acquire ownership of the encumbered asset as a result of default: the agreement that pursues this purpose (*patto commissorio*: for its implications see below the answer to Question 25) is banned by law (Art 2744 Civil Code).[17] Another common principle is that security rights can be created only over individual and specific assets and as collateral for certain claims ('specificity principle': for its implications see below the answer to Question 5). In principle, security rights are indivisible: they subsist for the total amount of the secured claim over each encumbered asset and over its every part, and they guarantee the claim until it is fully paid. Finally, security rights have an accessory nature in relation to the guaranteed claim. This means that the security rights strictly follow the secured claim: hence, the extinction of the claim entails the extinction of the security right; the non-existence of the claim or the invalidity of the agreement from which it arises entails the invalidity of the security right agreement.[18]

98. Italian private law system distinguishes between two types of security rights, namely pledge (*pegno*) and mortgage (*ipoteca*), depending on the nature of the assets to which they are related and, then, depending on the formalities required for their creation. A further ground of preference, whose validity as a security right proper is debated in the literature, is the privilege (*privilegio*).

---

16 App. Milano 28.9.1998, [1999] C 555.

17 Cass. civ. 2.2.2006 no 2285, [2006] MGC 2.

18 G. Gorla and P. Zannelli, 'Del pegno. Delle ipoteche' in A. Scialoja and G. Branca (eds.), *Commentario del codice civile*, 221.

There follows a brief description of each of the different types of security right and some general considerations on the extent to which these make it possible to 'collateralise' assets.

2.1. Pledge

99. In general terms, pledge is a security right which can be granted by a debtor or by a third party over movable assets as collateral for a claim (Art 2784 Civil Code). The pledge object will be further dealt with in the answers to Questions 2–5.

100. The contract aimed at creating a pledge is a 'real agreement': this means that its conclusion necessarily requires the delivery of pledged assets by the pledgor (debtor or third party) to the pledgee (Art 2786 Civil Code).[19] However, if the security is validly constituted between the parties simply by way of delivery without further formalities, these formalities are nevertheless required in order to enforce the preferential right on the pledged assets. The formalities relating to creation of a pledge will be further dealt with in the answers to Questions 6–7.

101. Generally speaking, the creation of a pledge has the following effects. First of all, the pledgee acquires possession of the assets: unless otherwise agreed, he has the power to hold the asset's 'fruits' and to apply them first to expenses and interest and then to the capital; on the other hand, to protect the pledgor, the pledgee is legally bound to keep the pledged assets in his custody and is liable for any loss or deterioration. Further, he may not use the pledged assets without the debtor's consent and may not dispose of them, whether by way of pledge (*subpegno*), or by allowing third parties to dispose of them (Arts 2790–2792 Civil Code). Above all, the pledgee acquires the power to have the pledged assets expropriated, even against the third party purchaser, and to obtain preferential satisfaction from the proceeds of these assets against a debtor's other creditors (Art 2796 Civil Code). He may also apply to the court for the assets to be transferred to him by way of payment; if this occurs, the value of the assets in excess of the amount required to discharge the debt is returned to the debtor (Art 2798 Civil Code). The possibility for the pledgee to enforce the security without having to use formal court procedures will be dealt with in the answer to Question 8.

102. It is appropriate to consider that the above rules regarding custody, use, preservation and disposal of the pledged assets do not apply to the so-called 'irregular pledge' (*pegno irregolare*: Art 1851 Civil Code). This type of pledge

[19] Cass. civ. 24.6.1995 no 7158, (1995) I GC 2633.

is characterised by the fact of having as its object fungible assets (e.g. a sum of money), granted by the debtor as collateral for a claim. In this case, the assets given as a pledge become the property of the creditor who will have to return, at the time of the fulfilment of a guaranteed claim, assets of the same genus and quantity. Vice versa, in case of non-fulfilment, he will have to return the part of them that exceeds the amount of the claim, determined in relation to the value of the assets at the time of maturity of the secured claim.[20]

103. In addition to pledge over movable assets, the Civil Code specifically regulates the pledge over claims. This is a security frequently required by banks: they finance enterprises against the pledge of their claims towards their clients. The formalities relating to the creation of this type of pledge will be dealt with in the answer to Question 7. It is appropriate to point out here the effects produced by its creation. In this case, the pledgee is obliged to collect the interest on the claim or the other periodic services, ascribing the amount firstly to the expenses and the interest and then to the capital. He is also obliged to bring the actions for preserving the claim received as a pledge (Art 2802 Civil Code). At maturity, the pledgee is required to collect the claim received as a pledge. If this relates to money or other fungible assets, at the request of the debtor, the pledgee must deposit it in a place determined by agreement or otherwise determined by the court. At maturity of the secured credit, the pledgee may hold back the received money to satisfy his claim and return the residual amount to the pledgor. If it comes to assets other than money, the pledgee may sell them or request the assignment of them as a form of payment (Art 2803 Civil Code). The unsatisfied pledgee may in any case ask that the pledged claim should be assigned to him as a form of payment, up to the full amount of his claim (Art 2804.1 Civil Code).

2.2. *Mortgage*

104. In general terms, a mortgage is a security right which can be granted by the debtor or by a third party over immovable or registered movable assets as collateral for a claim. Also a mortgage, as well as a pledge, provides to the mortgagee the power to have expropriated, even against the third party purchaser, the individual assets mortgaged and to obtain preferential satisfaction from the proceeds of these assets (Art 2808.1-2 Civil Code). What may form the object of a mortgage will be dealt with further in the answers to Questions from 2 to 5.

105. In general terms, the constitution of the mortgage necessarily implies entry in the public register (called *iscrizione*), which has a constitutive effect

---

20 M. Di Marzio, 'Artt. 2784-2807' in P. Cendon (ed.), *Commentario al codice civile. artt. 2740-2906*, 544–547. In judiciary, see Cass. civ. Sez. Un. 14.5.2001 no 202, (2001) I FI 2511.

(Art 2808.2 Civil Code). The Italian Civil Code distinguishes between statutory mortgage, judicial mortgage and voluntary mortgage, depending on the origins of the right conferred by the mortgage (Art 2808.3 Civil Code). The statutory mortgage is provided for by law (Art 2817 Civil Code). The judicial mortgage derives from a court's decision (including one not immediately operative) ordering the debtor to pay a sum of money or fulfil another obligation, in order to secure the fulfilment of those obligations. (Arts 2818–2820 Civil Code). The voluntary mortgage is granted by the debtor or by a third party mortgagor whether by agreement or by unilateral act done inter vivos. It has to be done by deed: otherwise, the act will be null and void (Art 2821 Civil Code). It is appropriate to observe that the act granting the mortgage provides the creditor only with the right to apply for entry in the public register; the mortgage itself is only constituted by the public entry. The formalities relating to the creation of mortgage will be further dealt with in the answers to Questions 6–7.

106. The mortgage takes its ranking from the date of its entry (Art 2852 Civil Code). Entry retains its effect for 20 years from its date of entry, unless it is renewed before the expiration of that period (Art 2847 Civil Code). Once that period has expired, the mortgagee may perform a new entry but in this case the mortgage takes its ranking from the date of the new entry (Art 2848 Civil Code).

2.3. (Special) privilege as a security right

107. Privilege is the ground of preference which law provides to creditors because of the ground of their claim (Art 2745 Civil Code). Italian law considers certain claims deserving of greater protection and, in accordance with that evaluation, attributes to the holders of these claims the right of preferential satisfaction against a debtor's other unsecured creditors.

108. Privilege can be either general or special. General privilege concerns all movable assets of the debtor (Art 2746 Civil Code), but it takes effects only if at the date of the attachment (or the opening of insolvency proceedings) there are movable assets in the debtor's assets (Art 2747.1 Civil Code). Before then, the position of the holder of the privileged claim is analogous to that of unsecured creditors.[21]

109. Special privilege is profoundly different from the general. Special privilege concerns only certain debtor's assets, movable or immovable (Art 2746 Civil Code), and presents the peculiarity of opposability to third parties that have

21 A. Patti, 'I privilegi' in A. Cicu, F. Messineo and L. Mengoni (eds.), *Trattato di diritto civile e commerciale*, 26.

purchased rights over the asset after the rising of the privilege. Therefore, special privilege provides to the creditor the right to pursuit the assets on which it is constituted, thus it appears and is predominantly considered as a security right.[22]

110. However, it is appropriate to stress that the privilege, including the special one, is structurally different from security rights. The privilege, indeed, is not born as a separate right aimed at strengthening the credit right, but rather is a way of being of the latter.[23] The identification and the evaluation of the ground (of claim) deserving of privilege, both general and special, is exclusively reserved to the law which normally, on this basis, states also the ranking of privileged claims. This implies that privileges are a numerus clausus: private people cannot create, with an act of contractual autonomy, other privileges beyond those provided by law.[24] This implies also that, in principle, the claim arises as a privileged claim solely through policy choice, without the need for an agreement between the parties or for particular forms of advertising.

111. The law establishing the privilege can exceptionally state that the constitution of privilege requires agreement between the parties (consensual privilege: *privilegio convenzionale*) or also particular forms of advertising (advertising privilege: *privilegio iscrizionale*) (Art 2745 Civil Code). Nevertheless, the source of the privilege is always the law which provides for it with mandatory rules.[25] Private autonomy has a completely marginal role: it only sets out the condition which carries into effect the will of the law.[26]

112. By reason of all foregoing, and especially by reason of the peculiar nature of these rights, the general considerations regarding special privileges are limited to this answer.

3. Spain

113. In accordance with Article 1911 of the Spanish Civil Code (CC), debtors are liable for debts and obligations with regard to all their present and future assets. In addition to this general liability rule, creditors may seek additional guarantees, i.e. security rights. Although security rights in *Spain* can be both in rem and personal, such as assumed joint liability, this report focuses on the former, for which reason this narrow meaning of security rights must be understood in future references. The concept of security rights in rem in

---

22 D. Di Sabato, *I privilegi*, 30. In judiciary, see Cass. civ. 10.10.1967 no 2387, (1967) I GC 1947.
23 F. Gazzoni, *Manuale di diritto privato*, 644.
24 Cass. civ. 26.8.2005 no 17396, [2005] MGI.
25 D. Di Sabato, *I privilegi*, 45–46.
26 F. Parente, *Nuovo ordine dei privilegi e autonomia privata*, 306.

Spain implies both the right to realise an encumbered asset regardless of who is in possession of it with a view to paying the secured debt – *rei persecutio erga omnes* complemented by the *ius distrahendi* – and the right to take priority over other creditors where payment is concerned.

114. In *Spain* all security rights in rem are accessory in nature, meaning that they are created to secure an obligation whose non-existence, invalidity or termination involves the termination of the security right. Nevertheless, security rights can be created to secure future and conditional obligations as well as a number of obligations (Art. 1861 CC), including those whose amount is not established at the time the security right is created – such as bank credit accounts – provided that the security is subject to an upper limit for the purpose of protecting third parties, i.e. this limit is not applicable inter partes, but only when third parties claim their rights in competition with the secured creditor. While partial payments of secured claims lead to a corresponding reduction in the security right, the security right is indivisible. This means that those acquiring part of the encumbered asset from the debtor are not proportionally affected by the security right nor can a secured creditor transfer a portion of the security right with the secured claim from the creditor (Art. 1860 CC). By the same token, any transfer of the security right is dependent on the transfer of the secured claim (Art. 1528 CC).

115. In general, all assets deemed to be *res in commercio* can be subject to a security right, whose features vary depending on the type of asset involved. The main distinction is the classic one between immovable and movable assets and the latter category is classified into tangibles and intangibles, such as claims, shares, patents, trademarks, intellectual rights and so on. However, the Spanish legal system has developed a further categorisation of assets based on the extent to which they can be identified and whether they can be registered for publicity purposes.

116. The debtor or a third party can provide collateral as long as he has ownership and a right of disposal of the asset or assets to be encumbered (Art. 1857 CC). Acquisition by a third party in good faith of a security right is also possible under Spanish law provided that the creditor acts in good faith and the specific requirements are met – which is not always feasible as pledge of claims illustrates.

117. Secured creditors are entitled to *ius distrahendi*, even in the event of insolvency proceedings over the debtor. To this end, while pactum commissorium is prohibited in *Spain*, judicial and non-judicial foreclosure proceedings are available. Priority rights depend, however, on the framework in which they are claimed, such that Law 22/2003 of 9 July on Insolvency Proceedings (*Ley Concursal*, LC) establishes an order of creditors which differs from that applicable in individual enforcement proceedings, i.e. before the opening of pre-insolvency or insolvency proceedings (see Arts. 1922, 1923, 1926 and 1927 CC).[27] At any rate, the basic principle governing security rights is order of priority.

118. The main consequence of this distinction is that only secured claims listed as such by insolvency law can be taken into account when establishing creditor priority in the framework of insolvency proceedings. It needs to be noted that Spanish insolvency law does not follow the classic distinction between preferences and privileges, according to which the latter are legally established to provide satisfaction over the whole of the debtor's estate in priority to other creditors (general privileges) or over a particular asset (special privileges). All claims secured by a right in rem are deemed privileged according to this law, but a distinction is established between special privileges i.e. satisfaction out of a specific asset or assets (Art. 90 LC) and general privileges, i.e. secured creditors have preference over other creditors and their satisfaction may be out of the whole of the debtor's estate (Art. 91 LC). Nevertheless, the principle of speciality means that special privileges prevail over general privileges (Art. 156 LC). This report only addresses the former.

119. The Spanish legal system for security rights in rem is spread over several laws, the core being the Civil Code and its provisions on mortgages, pledges and antichresis. Further laws established other security rights such as chattel mortgages and non-possessory pledges. The retention of title clauses and prohibitions on disposal are controversial:[28] although generally resorted to in practice, there is no comprehensive regulation or definition of these clauses in the Spanish system, with the exception of that laid down in a regional law, i.e. Law 483 of the *Fuero Nuevo de Navarra*. As a matter of fact, only the clauses included in the scope of application of Law 28/1999 of 13 July on Hire Purchase Agreements (*Ley de Venta a Plazos de Bienes Muebles*,[29] LVPBM) can be deemed to be security rights to the extent that both sellers and/or financiers have the right to realise the secured claim over the asset subject to retention of title and/ or of prohibition on disposal, in priority to other creditors and regardless of whether the asset belongs to a third party.

120. Before examining each security right in more detail, it should be pointed out that several private laws exist side by side in *Spain* to the extent that some

---

27 For example, while a pledge-secured claim is paid following workers' claims as laid down in Art. 32(1) and (2) of the Workers' Statute [Art. 1926(1) CC], it is granted preference vis-à-vis other creditors, including claims against the estate, workers and tax payment in the framework of insolvency proceedings [Art. 90(1)(6), 91(4) and 154 LC].

28 See, for all, A. Carrasco Perera, E. Cordero Lobato and M.J. Marín López, *Tratado de los derechos de garantía*.

29 BOE No 167, 20.7.1998.

regional Parliaments have legislative competence on private law matters apart from the Spanish Parliament. In this regard, Chapter IX of Title V of the Catalan Civil Code (CCCat) is of special interest as it provides for rules on mortgages, antichresis, pledges and the right to possessory retention, which will be briefly addressed in this report for the purpose of highlighting features of special interest. The CCCat does not contradict the general principles mentioned above, such as this type of right's accessory nature (Art. 569-1 CCCat). In fact, it seeks to avoid incompatibilities by retaining its supplementary nature in relation to state commercial law – for example, Article 569-7.2 CCCat submits the enforcement of the pledge of marketable securities to the relevant legislation issued by the Spanish Parliament without prejudice to the application of the CCCat, should there be legal loopholes in commercial laws.

121. The applicable inter-regional conflict rule is Article 16 CC, which subjects the issue to domestic private international rules and thus to Article 10 CC, the lex rei sitae being the basic rule for both movable and immovable assets. Specific provisions laid down for goods in transit enable both sender and receiver to agree to subject the creation and assignment of rights over these assets to the law of the place of destination instead of the place of departure [Art. 10(1)(III) CC]; for ships, aircraft and railway transport this issue is subject respectively to the law of the flag, or registration, with the exception of automobiles and other means of road transport, which are subject to the lex rei sitae [Art. 10(2) CC]; for securities it is subject to the place of issue [Art. 10(3) CC]. Nevertheless, Spanish law does not address the question of which law is applicable to the assignment of claims and its effectiveness against third parties, a relevant issue given that the CCCat also deals with the pledging of claims – which is the usual way of assigning claims by way of security in both Spanish and Catalan civil law. In short, although these private international law provisions aim to solve the inter-regional conflict of laws, they are clearly insufficient.

122. The Cape Town Convention on international interests in mobile equipment has been in force since October 2013 and applicable in *Spain* following the entry into force of the Aircraft Protocol on March 2016. This report will not address this convention, but it should be noted that it is applicable to both international and internal transactions (Art. 50 thereof), and that the lack of formalities featuring this security interest displaces the national security rights when it comes to getting financing over aircrafts [Art. 2(3)].

123. Spanish insolvency law operates on the basis of the principles of legality and typicality, for which reason only the security rights listed in Article 90 LC are granted special privilege. Consequently, security rights in rem have to be legally acknowledged to be effective in the framework of insolvency proceedings that are opened in *Spain*, despite the fact that the Spanish system for rights in rem is a numerus apertus, i.e. the number of rights in rem is not limited.

124. The presentation of security rights follows the basic distinction between immovable and movable assets. As mentioned above, Article 90 LC does not specify all security rights and not all the special privileges listed there can be deemed to be security rights. Some of them are considered quasi-in rem securities and will therefore be addressed in Question 25, in particular sale under resolutory condition, retention of title clauses and prohibitions on disposal not subject to the LVPBM. Others are truly (special) privileges inasmuch as they have been created by law and focus on specific assets which cannot be realised by the holders when they are in the possession of a third party. This is the case with the security granted to claims arising from the construction, re-construction, repair and improvement of assets over those assets, which will be addressed in this question.

3.1. *Security rights over immovable assets*

3.1.1. *Mortgage*

125. *Mortgages* (*hipoteca*) can be contractually and legally created over immovable assets, but mortgage agreements must be recorded in public documents and registered in the Land Registry (Art. 1875 CC and 145 of *Ley Hipotecaria*,[30] LH). 'Legal mortgages' are rights granted to creditors in respect of whom certain persons designated by law are obliged to take out mortgages in their favour. Most legal mortgages are listed in Article 168 LH, including the right of minors or incapacitated persons to mortgage their legal guardians' assets with a view to securing the liability of guardians arising out of their obligation to administer the minors' assets in good faith. There are other legal cases, however, such as those provided for Article 569(36) CCCat. Articles 193–197 LH also cover what are called 'tacit legal mortgages'; these cannot be classified as real mortgages as they are created by operation of law, basically in favour of government bodies and insurance companies for the payment of taxes and insurance premiums on a particular asset and neither notarisation nor registration is needed. These types of security right are given by law priority over prior mortgages created by agreement.

126. During the security period, the mortgagor remains in possession of the asset and is obliged to maintain the asset's value. To this end, Article 117 LH provides the mortgagee with special powers for preventing the asset's deterioration, including what is known as 'devastation action', whereby a court may not only order preventive measures but also the transfer of the asset to judicial administration.

---

30 Approved by Decree 8.2.1946 (BOE No 58, 27.2.1946). See Arts. 104–197 LH.

Once the secured claim matures, realisation of the asset may proceed by special non-judicial and judicial enforcement proceedings and the secured creditor is granted a priority right [Arts. 1923(3), 1927(2) CC and 90(1)(1)] LC].

3.1.2. Antichresis

127. Antichresis is a creditor's entitlement to acquire the 'fruits' of an immovable asset under the obligation to allocate them to paying first the interest and second the capital of the secured claim (Art. 1881 CC). Article 1881 CC seems to imply that the creditor is in possession of the asset, for which reason he is obliged to maintain it in good condition by paying taxes and expenses, thereby increasing the secured claim (Art. 1882 CC). The CC systematically regulates antichresis with mortgages and pledges and it is included among special privileges in Article 90(1) LC. However, doubts arise as to whether this is really a security right in rem. On the one hand, the debtor's non-payment does not pave the way for specific foreclosure proceedings, and Article 1884 CC simply refers to the general rules of the Spanish Civil Procedure Act for realisation purposes (*Ley de Enjuiciamiento Civil*, LEC). On the other hand, the law contains no requirement for a special formality when creating this right for which reason such creditors do not really enjoy specific preference over third parties save for the fact that they are supposedly in possession of the immovable asset. Anyway, antichresis is listed in Article 90(1)(2) LC as a special privilege and thus grants secured claims specific preference over the 'fruits' of the asset. It must be noted that, in addition to antichresis, parties to mortgage or pledge contracts may agree on what is referred to as the '*efecto anticrético*' (antichresis effect) and the creditor is thus entitled to be paid interest and capital with the asset's 'fruits' in the order given above (specifically, Art. 1868 CC). Surprisingly, however, Article 569(2)(2) CCCat vetoes this effect beyond antichresis itself, which otherwise involves the rights of possessory retention and separate realisation of the asset.

*3.1.3. Right of possessory retention (*derecho de retención*)*

128. Although the Spanish CC does not consider right of possessory retention a security right, Article 569(3) CCCat lays down that persons who hold an immovable or a movable asset in good faith may retain possession by way of security in relation to debts listed in the subsequent provision, such as necessary expenses, compensation for damage and payment for work or of interest. The creditor must notify the debtor of the retention decision through a public notary for this right to be created and the debtor may only challenge its creation during the two-month period following the date of notification. The right can be registered in the Land Registry [Art. 2(2) LH], but registration is only for publicity purposes against third parties.[31]

129. The creditor can retain possession against third parties until full payment is received [Art. 569(6)(1) CCCat] and is obliged to maintain the asset in good condition [Art. 569(6)(2) CCCat]. Non-payment triggers the enforcement of the security right by specific enforcement proceedings provided for by Article 569(8) CCCat. However, nothing is said as to priority rights or the right of separate satisfaction in the framework of insolvency proceedings because of the lack of legislative competence on the Catalan side. The general rules are therefore applicable, i.e. Article 90 LC which does not mention this right for which reason there is no priority in the event of debtor's insolvency.

3.2. Security rights over movable assets

*3.2.1. Chattel mortgage and ship mortgage (*hipoteca mobiliaria, hipoteca naval*)*

130. The previous and rather unsuccessful non-possessory pledge regulations combined with the need to obtain credit without compromising key assets of the debtor's enterprise, triggered the issuance of the 1954 Law on Chattel Mortgage and Non-Possessory Pledge (*Ley de Hipoteca Mobiliaria y Prenda sin Desplazamiento*, LHMPSD).[32] The explanatory introduction highlights the law's innovativeness, in that it emphasised the nature of a given asset and in particular its ability to be identified and thus entered in a public registry. In accordance with this feature, a distinction is made between movable assets that are similar to immovable ones, to which chattel mortgage law is applicable, and those over which a non-possessory pledge can be created. It should be noted that this law contains a complete list of the assets that can be subject to either one or the other (see Question 2). This restriction – that only listed assets can be subject to one of these security rights – has been criticised on the grounds that other assets could also meet the registration requirements.

131. The mortgage agreement only refers to assets listed in Article 12 LHMPSD – such as businesses, aircraft, automobiles and other motor vehicles or intellectual and industrial property rights – provided that the mortgagor both owns them and holds the right of disposal. The security right is only created once the

---

31 See P. Pozo Carrascosa, A. Vaquer Aloy and E. Bosch Capdevila, *Derecho Civil de Cataluña. Derechos reales* 431–432.

32 *Ley de 16 de diciembre de 1954, de Hipoteca Mobiliaria y Prenda sin Desplazamiento* (BOE No 352, 18.12.1954), complemented by a regulation with the same title, approved by Decree 17.6.1955.

mortgage agreement has been recorded in a public document and registered in the Personal Property Registry.

132. During the security period the mortgagor is obliged to maintain the encumbered asset in good condition (Arts. 27 and 44 LHMPSD) and in particular to avoid its deterioration (Arts. 17 and 44 LHMPSD); otherwise, the mortgagee is entitled to undertake action to remedy the mortgagor's (in)activity by seeking judicial administration over the asset [Art. 18(II) LHMPSD] and the mortgagee is thus allowed to check the asset wherever it is located [Art. 22(3) LHMPSD]. Following any non-payment, the mortgagee may avail himself of judicial and non-judicial enforcement proceedings, and the secured claim is granted specific preference over other creditors either in the framework of individual enforcement proceedings or insolvency proceedings [Arts. 10 LHMPSD, 1922(2), 1926(1) CC and 90(1)(1) LC].

133. Secured claims over aircraft also have priority rights [Arts. 41 LHMPSD, 133 *Ley 48/1969, de Navegación Aérea*, LNA] and creditors may realise the aircraft regardless of insolvency proceedings, as with ship mortgages. According to Article 126 of Law 14/2014, of 24 July on Shipping (*Ley de Navegación Marítima*, LNM),[33] ships, barges and marine artefacts in general can be subject to mortgages whose creation requires their recording in a public or private document and registration in the Personal Property Registry (Art. 128 LNM). The opening of insolvency proceedings over the mortgagor authorises the mortgagee to realise his security separately without being affected by any stay or effect triggered by the proceedings [Arts. 140(b) LNM and 76(3) LC].

3.2.2. *Pledge* (prenda)

134. Creating a pledge involves the concluding of a valid agreement[34] followed by the transfer of the asset's ownership from the pledgor to the pledgee or a third party (Art. 1863 CC). The date on which the pledge is created must be specifically mentioned in a public document if the pledge is to be effective against third parties, as it is essential for determining priority rights [Art. 1865 CC or Art. 569(13)(2) CCCat]. The pledgor cannot be in possession of the asset during the pledge's life. This requirement is there in an effort to ensure that third parties are aware of the existence of the pledge. Accordingly, only assets that can be possessed can be pledged. When assets are represented by a negotiable

---

33 BOE No 180, 25.7.2014.

34 Pledges are created contractually except in the cases laid down in Art. 79(2) of *Ley 58/2003, de 17 de diciembre, General Tributaria* (BOE No 302, 18.12.2003) – the General Tax Law – by which a legal pledge securing taxes on transmissions, acquisitions or imports over assets subject to the taxed operations is created.

document, a pledge of the assets can be created by transferring possession of the negotiable document to the pledgee or a third party. Examples of this are warehouse receipts, transport documents, bills of lading and agriculture warrants.

135. As discussed in Question 2, the pledging of claims is also recognised, although not legally regulated, by the Spanish Civil Code.[35] Their creation depends in practice on the agreement being recorded in a public document (Art. 1865 CC by analogy) and the debtor in the pledge claim (account debtor) being notified (Art. 1863 CC by analogy). While claims can also be subject to non-possessory pledge and such pledges must therefore be registered (Art. 54 LHMPSD), this is considered an alternative to the possessory pledge.[36] In *Spain*, the transposing of Directive 2002/47/EC of the European Parliament and of the Council of 6 June 2002 on financial collateral arrangements[37] by Royal Decree 5/2005 led to a specific regime for the transfer of ownership by way of security or pledge of claims – specifically, marketable securities, financial instruments and money credited to an account – arising from such arrangements and in favour of a financial entity.[38] The CCCat regulates the pledge of claims requiring a public document and debtor notification of the pledged claim [Art. 569(13)(3)] and securities, including portfolios [Art. 569(16)(3)]. In order to be considered special privilege, Article 90(1)(6) LC distinguishes between a pledge of claims whose effectiveness is only made dependent on a written form stating the date of creation, and a pledge of futures claims that requires public document save the case of this type of pledge being submitted to the above-mentioned Royal Decree 5/2005.

---

35 See Spanish Supreme Court (TS) judgments 19.4.1997 (RJ 1997/3429); 7.10.1997 (RJ 1997/7101).

36 See RDGRN 18.3.2008 (BOE No 77, 29.3.2008) and A. Carrasco Perera, E. Cordero Lobato and M.J. Marín López, *Tratado de los derechos de garantía*, 233–234. Art. 201 of Law 30/2007 of 30.10.2007 on Public Contracts allows the assignment of claims arising out of this type of contracts specifically requiring the Public Administration to be notified. The Third Additional Disposition of Law 1/1999 of 5.1.1999 regulating venture capital entities and their management companies (BOE No 5, 6.1.1999) deals with the global assignment of claims arising from both government and commercial contracts for cases in which the assignee is a credit institution or a securitisation fund. The Sixth Additional Disposition of Law 13/1994 of 1.6.1995 on the autonomy of the Bank of Spain (BOE No 131, 2.6.1994) also deals with the pledge of claims in favour of the Bank of Spain, the Central European Bank or any other European national central banks.

37 Amended by Directive 2009/44/EC of the European Parliament and of the Council of 6 May 2009 amending Directive 98/26/EC on settlement finality in payment and securities settlement systems and Directive 2002/47/EC on financial collateral arrangements as regards linked systems and credit claims, OJ 2009 L146/37.

38 Real Decreto Ley 5/2005, de 11 de marzo, de reformas urgentes para el impulso a la productividad y para la mejora de la contratación pública (BOE No 62, 14.3.2005).

136. While in possession, the pledgee is obliged to maintain the asset in good condition [Art. 1867 CC or Art. 569(12)(2)][39] and is entitled to exercise all actions, including those typical of owners, to defend the asset against third parties (Art. 1869 CC), even when the asset is in the possession of a third party that is acting as a depositary. The pledgee is also entitled to any interest or 'fruits' accruing from the asset – it can even be agreed that the asset will be assigned to be used by a third party (Art. 1870 CC) – and use these to pay off first the interest and then the capital (Art. 1868 CC).[40] Should claims other than the secured claim arise between pledgor and pledgee, the latter holds a right of retention over the asset until these are all paid (Art. 1866 CC). Nevertheless, this right of retention cannot be deemed a security right inasmuch as the creditor is not granted preference over other creditors.

137. Non-payment of the secured claim entitles the pledgee to initiate non-judicial or judicial foreclosure proceedings. The secured claim is preferential over other claims as established by Articles 1922(2), 1926(1) CC and 90(1)(6) LC referring to the pledge of tangible assets; by Articles 1922(3) CC, 221 LCCH, 320 et seq. CCo and 90(1)(6) LC to the pledge of securities or marketable securities that can be traded in official secondary markets, and in general the pledge of claims and future claims; by Article 90(1)(5) LC that addresses the pledge of book-entry securities.

3.2.3. Non-possessory pledge

138. The current legislation was preceded by specific attempts to establish the non-possessory pledge: firstly on agricultural products, equipment and livestock, by Royal Decree 22 of September 1917, whose Title II which deals with warehouse receipts is still in force; secondly on oil products, by Decree 29 of November 1941; thirdly on industrial machinery by Law 17 of May 1940 and fourthly in general by Law 5 of December 1941 amending the Spanish Civil Code, now abrogated by the 1954 Law. Articles 52, 53 and 54 LHMPSD contain a full lists of assets on which non-possessory pledges are allowed (see Question 2), the creation of which requires their recording in a public document or a commercial agreement to be concluded before a public notary (Art. 3 LHMPSD);

[39] Expenses incurred to maintain the asset can be recovered and are also secured. Should the pledgee not fulfil his obligations, he is liable for damages in accordance with Arts. 1101, 1182 and 1183 CC. One such case was decided by TS 1.4.1996 (RJ 1996/2877) where the pledgee did not seek payment of a bill of exchange and the corresponding action was lost.

[40] This provision only mentions interest, but a broad interpretation including fruits is preferred as the provision's scope would otherwise be limited to pledges of claims and securities. Furthermore, a strict interpretation would not be in accordance with the role of party autonomy acknowledged by the same provision. On this debate, see A. Carrasco Perera, E. Cordero Lobato and M.J. Marín López, *Tratado de los derechos de garantía*, 192–194.

the second type benefits from tax exemption. Registration in the Personal Property Registry is only necessary to make the pledge effective against third parties.

139. During the security period, the pledgor is neither dispossessed of the pledged asset nor does he have to retain possession of it, as the asset can be entrusted to a third party. However, the pledgor or a third party in possession of the pledged asset is considered to be a depositary and is obliged to maintain the asset in good condition (Art. 50 LHMPSD). In addition to being prohibited from disposing of the asset without the creditor's consent (Art. 4 LHMPSD), the pledgor is also forbidden from moving it from the immovable property mentioned in the pledge agreement without the creditor's consent (Art. 60 LHMPSD) and the latter is entitled to carry out inspections (Art. 63 LHMPSD). Any deterioration of the asset may entitle the pledgee to take early enforcement action in respect of the secured claim where this is agreed in the contract (Art. 62 LHMPSD) and even to request judicial administration in the terms of Article 117 LH.

140. A non-possessory pledge is deemed a possessory pledge for priority purposes [Arts. 56 and 66 LHMPSD, 1922(2), 1926(1) CC and 90(1)(1) LC], but there are significant limitations on this provision in respect of third parties. Enforcement of security does not proceed in cases in which the debtor is not in possession of the asset and it has not been handed over to the creditor for purposes of realisation [Art. 94 LHMPSD and 687(3) LEC]. In other words, the pledgee cannot enforce security against third parties who are acting in good faith [Art. 464 CC and 85 of the Spanish Commercial Code (*Código de comercio*, CCo)]. Third parties, however, can only act in good faith if the pledged assets have been moved from their status loci or rather from the territorial demarcation of the registry where the pledge is registered.[41]

3.2.4. *Retention of title clauses and prohibition on disposal provisions* (reserva de dominio y prohibiciones de disponer*)*.

141. Retention of title clauses and prohibition on disposal provisions included in hire-purchase agreements or financing agreements for tangible, non-perishable and identified assets either in favour of the seller – who is entitled by Article 4 LVPBM to assign his claim including retention of title to a financier – or the financier, grant sellers and financiers both rights of separate satisfaction and priority. This is provided that the contract in question is registered in the Personal Property Registry though registration is only necessary to make the security effective against third parties. The security rights are validly created between

41 See J. Lacruz Berdejo, (1956) *Anales de la Academia Matritense y del Notariado* 349, 386.

the parties with the concluding of the contract in question. The prohibition on disposal is implied by law in every contract though the retention of title must be agreed independently.

142. The seller or financier can enforce the security against the buyer in possession in accordance with the summary procedure laid down in Article 16(2) LVPBM, but only if the contract has been registered in the Personal Property Registry. If the contract is registered, the seller can also proceed against third parties in possession [Art. 16(3) LVPBM]. The seller can also request the termination of the contract by a specific summary procedure laid down in Article 250(1)(11) LEC, but such procedure also implies that each party should return what they have received under the contract. Secured creditors have priority rights [Arts. 1922(2) and 1926(1) CC, and 90(1)(4) LC] and have the right to separate satisfaction in the framework of insolvency proceedings in the terms of Article 56 LC.

3.2.5. *Right of possessory retention*

143. As stated above, Article 569(3) CCCat provides for this security right, with Article 569(7)(1) establishing a specific enforcement regime when the right is exercised over a movable asset.

3.2.6. *Fixed asset claims* (créditos refaccionarios)

144. Claims arising from activities connected with the construction, reconstruction, repair and improvement of assets – known as *créditos refaccionarios* – or fixed asset claims, are also granted a specific privilege over a particular asset provided that this right is registered [for construction work contracts over immovable assets see Art. 42(8) LH].[42] Registration is not necessary, however, [Art. 90(2) LC] in the case of work claims whose security is provided by the specific assets built, produced, manufactured or repaired by workers who are also creditors, as long as they are owned by the employer [Arts. 90(1)(3) LC and 32(2) of the Workers' Statute]. For example, if the assets have been subject to a sale and lease back, this privilege is no longer operative, as it is not operative if the employer concludes a hire-purchase agreement over the assets including a retention of title clause or a financial lease.[43] For this reason, neither type of fixed asset claims is considered a security right, but a special privilege in the strict sense of the legal term.

---

42 SSTS 19.4.1975; 5.7.1990 have understood that this specific privilege includes of construction work financers.

43 See J. Garrido, 'Article 90' in A. Rojo and E. Beltrán, *Comentario de la legislación concursal*, 1606 at 1622.

Question 2: Is it possible to create security rights over all assets of the debtor?

1. France

145. All a debtor's assets, immovable and movable, tangible and intangible, can be subject to a security right in rem or a transfer of title by way of security, provided that they are in commercio. Likewise, both immovable and movable assets, with the exception of intangibles, can be subject to a retention of title clause.

146. It should be pointed out here that legal privileges are not addressed in these questions nor in Questions 2, 3 and 4 on the grounds of their legal origin. Accordingly, the following answers only deal with conventional security rights.

147. Following the 2006 reform, a pledge may encumber one or more present or future tangible assets or a group of assets, i.e. *sub specie universalitatis* [Art. 2331(1) CC]. The pledged asset must be tradable, i.e. available for sale or to be assigned to the creditor if the secured claim is not satisfied. Consequently, assets that are non-tradable by law cannot be pledged, while temporary prohibitions, deriving from clauses prohibiting the disposal of the asset, do not prevent a secured asset from being encumbered.

148. Pledge over fungible assets is laid down in Articles 2341 and 2342 CC. When a possessory pledge is created, the creditor must keep the assets separate from similar ones in his possession unless the agreement specifically states otherwise. If there is a waiver, the creditor acquires ownership of the delivered assets and is responsible for returning the same quantity of similar assets [Art. 2341(1) CC]. When a non-possessory pledge is created, the agreement may entitle the provider of collateral to dispose of the assets that he possesses, but he is obliged to replace them. A type of 'floating' pledge (*tournant* or *flottant*) is thus established by contractual agreement.

149. The above-mentioned provisions are similar to those governing a pledge over intangible assets, which can encumber a present or future asset or group of assets [Art. 2355(1) CC]. Non-tradable claims by law or by agreement cannot be pledged unless the prohibition on disposal is only temporary.[44]

150. A mortgage may encumber any of a debtor's immovable assets and appurtenances – and improvements – provided they are in commercio and can be sold [Art. 2397(1) CC].[45] Although a mortgage is generally created on

[44] Cass. Comm. 30.9.2008, which holds the validity of pledge of shares subject to a temporary prohibition of transfer.

[45] Cass. civ. 29.6.1983; Cass. civ. 23.2.2012, holding the invalidity of mortgage of assets subject to a temporary prohibition of transfer.

the right of ownership, it may also encumber other rights in rem, such as bare ownership, usufruct or right of superficies. However, non-transferable rights in rem, such as the right to use and habitation or easements cannot be mortgaged as they cannot be transferred regardless of the immovable asset to which they are related. Antichresis encumbers a productive immovable asset over which the secured creditor enjoys a full right of disposal (Art. 2413 CC).

151. A retention of title clause can be agreed in contracts transferring movable and immovable assets (Arts. 2329 and 2373 CC). However, the fact that the clause is rarely used with respect to immovable justifies the lack of any specific regulation.

152. Where the encumbrance of fungible assets is concerned, a retention of title clause can be enforced up to the total of the outstanding debt over assets of a similar kind and quality in the debtor's possession (Art. 2369 CC). This provision therefore allows the recovery of fungible assets, which is an exception to the principle that requires the identification of the property that is the object of ownership.

153. Transfer of ownership by way of security applies to any immovable or movable, tangible or intangible, asset or groups of assets, personal or in rem rights, including security rights in rem (Art. 2011 CC).When fungible assets are transferred, the provisions on pledge are applied, meaning that once the security is terminated by payment, the provider of collateral must be reimbursed with an equal quantity of assets. If the transfer includes claims, the powers of a creditor can be compared with those of a pledgee (*créancier nanti*) in the absence of specific provisions to the contrary.

2. Italy

154. Under Italian law, not all assets of the debtor can be constituted by parties as the object of the security right, as will be seen from what will be said below.

2.2. Pledge

155. Article 2784.2 of the Italian Civil Code states that the pledge can be constituted over movable assets, bulk of movable assets (*universalità di mobili*, Art 816 Civil Code), claims and other rights attached to movable assets. This regulation is more concise than the detailed Articles 2810–2811 of the Civil Code, dictated regarding mortgage. However, the application of these two rules also to pledge is generally recognised. It follows that: (a) the pledge cannot be constituted over assets *extra-commercium*;[46] and (b) the pledge includes the appurtenances, the usufruct, the improvements and other rights related to the pledged assets.[47]

156. It is debatable whether a pledge may be created over those assets (such as personal effects) which, according to Article 514 of the Civil Procedure Code, are not subject to attachment, i.e. to that process by which a court, at the request of a creditor, designates specific property owned by the debtor to be sold for the benefit of the creditor. Nevertheless, the prevailing opinion is in the affirmative. In effect, the fact that some assets are by law not attachable does not rule out the possibility that those assets may be freely transferred, and especially that a debtor, or a third party, may pledge them voluntarily.[48]

157. The pledge over assets capable of being mortgaged is not allowed because the law provides for the creation of security right by entry in public registers, not by delivery of assets. Therefore registered movable assets cannot be the object of a pledge.[49] For the same reason, it is doubtful whether one can establish a pledge over all the assets of a firm including immovable or registered movable assets. It is generally accepted however that one can create a pledge over all the assets of a firm provided that these assets consist only of movable assets that are capable of being pledged individually.[50]

158. As already mentioned, the pledge can be constituted over claims and other rights attaching to movable assets. This implies that the pledge cannot be constituted over rights attaching to immovable assets.[51] Regarding the pledge over other rights, the regulation concerning copyrights is a case in point. Article 111 L. 22 April 1941 No 633[52] states that the rights of publication of the work and the rights of use of the work published cannot be the subject of pledge until they belong to the author personally. The proceeds of the use and the copies of the work may instead be pledged.

159. It should be noted that the pledge created on fungible assets takes the form of the so called 'irregular pledge' (see above the answer to Question 1).

---

46 Of course Italian law provides, as a rule, for free saleability of assets. Exceptions to the rule are the *res extra-commercium*, which are not capable of property. Traditionally, they are the *res communes omnium* (e.g. air, sunlight), unavailable State-owned assets, the human body and its parts. Also *res extra-commercium* are those rights that, because of the close connection with the person, are by their nature unavailable and unselleable (e.g. personality rights).

47 F. Realmonte, 'Il pegno' in *Rescigno*, 806.

48 M. Di Marzio, 'Artt. 2784-2807' in P. Cendon (ed.), *Commentario al codice civile. artt. 2740-2906*, 506.

49 Cass. civ. 12.2.1951 no 370, [1950] MGI 95.

50 M. Di Marzio, 'Artt. 2784-2807' in P. Cendon (ed.), *Commentario al codice civile. artt. 2740-2906*, 513–514.

51 D. Rubino, 'La responsabilità patrimoniale. Il pegno' in F. Vassalli (ed.), *Trattato di diritto civile*, 213.

52 Available via <www.normattiva.it> accessed 26 May 2016.

2.2. *Mortgage*

160. Article 2810 of the Civil Code states that a mortgage can be constituted over the following: immovable assets in commerce and relative appurtenances; the usufruct of the assets themselves; the right to build; the right of the inheritable tenancy and the right of the grantor on the inheritable tenancy; state revenues; ships, aircraft and motorcars. According to prevailing opinion, this list of assets capable of mortgage is not exhaustive. However, it can be extended only by express statutory provision. Consequently, it is not possible by contractual provision to make assets, other than those specified by law, capable of mortgage.[53]

161. In any case, the mortgage cannot be constituted over assets that are *extra-commercium* and, among others, over unavailable state-owned assets.[54]

162. The mortgage on immovable assets certainly covers their appurtenances (Art 817 Civil Code). This rule is subject to an exception in the case of assets of a firm. The mortgage over assets of a firm, in fact, does not automatically extend to movables which are incorporated in it (e.g. machinery, equipment and the like). This is because it is commonly accepted that the various goods organised by a businessmen – but not necessarily belonging to him – for the running of a firm are in a position of absolute parity, which prevents one from considering immovable assets as *res principales* and movable assets as *res accessoriae*, unless it is clearly established otherwise.[55]

163. Regarding the object of a mortgage on movable assets, reference should be made to special statutes (Art 2810.2 Civil Code) and exactly: for the mortgage over state revenues, to d.P.R. 30 December 2003 No 398; for the mortgage over the ships and aircraft, to r.d. 30 March 1942 No 327 (Maritime Code); for the mortgage over motorcars, to r.d.l. 15 March 1927 No 436 and to r.d. 29 July 1927 No 1814.[56]

3. Spain

164. Spanish law makes it possible to create security rights over all assets to the extent that they are in commercio,[57] and the collateral provider is the owner and

---

53 A. Ravazzoni, 'Le ipoteche' in A. Cicu, F. Messineo and L. Mengoni (eds.), *Trattato di diritto civile e commerciale*, 88.

54 G. Gorla and P. Zannelli, 'Del pegno. Delle ipoteche' in A. Scialoja and G. Branca (eds.), *Commentario del codice civile*, 228. Concerning the *res extra-commercium*, see also above fn. 46.

55 Cass. civ. 29.9.1993 no 9760, (1994) I FI 1840.

56 Available via <www.normattiva.it> accessed 26 May 2016, except for r.d.l. 15.03.1927 No 436, and to r.d. 29.07.1927 No 1814.

57 The pledging of merchandise that is subject to market restrictions such as pharmaceutical products is also possible. See RDGRN 30.11.1992 (RJ 1992/9496).

has the right of disposal (Art. 1857 CC). To this end, many provisions seek to ensure this right of disposal, one example being Article 1 LHMPSD, which lays down that if bare ownership and usufruct are in different hands, both holders have to consent to the chattel mortgage; otherwise, this security right is not effective erga omnes.

165. Article 2 LHMPSD vetoed the creation of chattel mortgages and non-possessory pledges over encumbered assets or assets whose price had not been fully paid by the collateral provider, but this provision was amended in 2007 and the restriction no longer applies. However, a debtor cannot dispose of the mortgaged or pledged asset without the creditor's consent (Art. 4 LHMPSD). The same restriction seems to apply in the event of a second possessory pledge being created over an asset insofar as the transfer of possession is mandatory and this requirement can only be met by naming a depositary with the first pledgee's consent.[58]

166. Mortgages can be created on all rights in respect of immovable assets, including usufruct, superficies or the right to mortgage itself. A few restrictions are listed in Article 108 LH, namely easements, except for water easement and the mortgaging of the easement along with the related beneficial immovable property; legal usufructs, with the exception of those in the favour of a widow or widower; and the right of use and habitation are not subject to mortgage on the grounds that they cannot be sold, or at least only with difficulty. Other provisions such as Article 107 LH and Article 569(39) to 569(42) CCCat deal with particular mortgages by their object insofar as they are created over rights or legal situations on the verge of termination, ineffectiveness or imminent change, such as mortgages on assets subject to a condition subsequent, on rights arising from contractual pre-emptive rights and even on the right of the auctioneer.

167. Only businesses, automobiles and motor vehicles, trams and train carriages, aircraft, industrial machinery and intellectual and industrial property rights can be subject to a chattel mortgage (Art. 12 LHMPSD). Business chattel mortgage always implies the right to use the premises where the business is located (Art. 20 LHMPSD), thereby the creation of this right involves a lease contract whereby enforcement of the asset is made possible – although the lease itself is not subject to chattel mortgage. A chattel mortgage automatically extends to the business's appurtenances such as intellectual or industrial property rights or machinery for professional or industrial purposes (Art. 21 LHMPSD). However, the right to realise these erga omnes only exists if they are clearly identified in the public document and registration in the Personal Property Registry by which the chattel mortgage is created.

---

58 See A. Carrasco Perera, E. Cordero Lobato and M.J. Marín López, *Tratado de los derechos de garantía*, 173–174.

168. As a pledge requires the transfer of possession, intangible assets are not subject to this security right unless the assets may be said to be represented by documents of title, as is the case with securities, shares and capital shares in private limited companies (Arts. 1872 CC, 320 et seq. CCo and 106, 132 of the Law on Companies)[59] or in the event that bank endorsement by way of security is considered to be transfer of possession (Art. 22 of the Exchange and Cheque Law).[60] In contrast, a pledge can be created over all tangible assets, including perishable goods, the specification of which takes place while transferring possession.[61] By the same token, the pledging of rights in rem over tangible assets is only feasible provided these are in the pledgor's possession, a good example being the pledge of securities held in usufruct, or the pledge of the right of pledge. Book-entry securities may also be subject to a pledge in accordance with specific legislation.[62]

169. Pledge of claims is not addressed in Spanish civil law, but it is commonly accepted and it is of some significance in Spanish practice. There is no concept of fiduciary transfer of claims under the Spanish tradition and therefore the pledge is used to achieve the intended outcome, the assignment of claims by way of security. As there cannot be any effective formality with publicity purposes, the pledgor must be the owner of the pledged claim; thereby acquisition *a non domino*, i.e. by third parties in good faith, of pledge of claims is not feasible. Furthermore, should the parties to the contract agree on the non-assignability of the claim, the creditor is not entitled to pledge it.[63] Any claim can be pledged, even those dealing with non-monetary obligations. As long as insurance policies can be assigned, the pledging of claims arising from them is also feasible, and the pledging of life insurance policies is specifically addressed by the relevant legislation.[64]

170. Article 3 LHMPSD replaced dispossession of the pledgor with registration. A non-possessory pledge is in principle only possible over certain designated assets. These are set out in Articles 52, 53 and 54 LHMPSD; namely, pending

---

59 Royal Decree-Law 1/2010 of 2 July approving the recast text of the Law on Companies (BOE No 161, 3.7.2010). Likewise, see Law 35/2003, 4.11.2003, on collective investment institutions (BOE No 272, 5.11.2003) and Royal Decree 1309/2005, 4.11.2005 (BOE No 267, 8.11.2005) approving its regulation.

60 *Ley 19/1985, de 16 de julio, Cambiaria y del Cheque* (BOE No 172, 19.7.1985).

61 See A. Carrasco Perera, E. Cordero Lobato and M.J. Marín López, *Tratado de los derechos de garantía*, 172.

62 See Arts. 10–12bis of the Law 24/1988, 28.7.1988, on the Securities Market (*Ley del Mercado de Valores*, LMV) and Royal Decree 878/2015, 3.10.2015. on clearing, settlement and registration of book-entry securities, on Central Securities Depositories and Central Counterparties, and on transparency requirements imposed on issuers of securities admitted to trading on a regulated market.

63 See STS 26.9.2002 (RJ 2002/7873).

64 See Art. 99 of Law 50/1980, 8.10.1980, on Insurance Contracts. On the assignment of insurance policies which can be paid nominative to order or to the bearer, see Art. 9 thereof.

'fruits', anticipated fruit crops in the agricultural year in which the contract is concluded, and fruit or products; animals, their offspring and products; machines and other agricultural equipment; machinery and machines identified by serial number or otherwise, not inextricably linked to professional or business exploitation; stored goods and raw materials; assets or collections of assets with artistic and historical value, such as paintings, sculptures, porcelain or books, either whole or partial; and claims. The pledge agreement has to include detailed specifications, including the immovable property where the goods are stored or deposited, from whose production they originate or to whose exploitation they are intended [Art. 57(2) LHMPSD], given that the status loci is important for specification and publicity purposes.

171. As stated in Question 1, only the retention of title clauses and prohibitions on disposal included in the relevant hire-purchase or financing agreements for tangible, non-perishable and identified assets are deemed to be security rights. Accordingly, neither intangibles nor consumables are subject to this security. Secured assets must be identified, e.g. by serial number [Art. 1(2) LVPBM], which means that this security cannot be construed over an asset that does not yet exist. A collection or group of assets can be subject to these clauses, and groups made up of physically and legally independent assets are accepted, as well as groups made up of assets that constitute an economic unit of production or exploitation, either because parties to the contract have agreed to this or because they are fungible.[65]

Question 3: Is it possible to create security rights over assets not yet owned by the debtor at the time of the creation of the security interest?

1. France

172. In general terms, the validity of security rights in French law requires the provider of collateral, either the debtor or a third party, to have ownership and full disposal rights over the assets.

173. Article 2335 CC states that pledges over others' property are invalid, without prejudice to the right of a creditor acting in good faith to be compensated for any loss caused by the invalidity of the security. The rule is applicable by analogy to pledges of claims, for which there is no provision in the law, and directly applicable to pledges of intangible assets other than claims [Art. 2355(5) CC].

---

65 See Art. 8 of the Order of 19 July 1999 approving the regulation of the hire-purchase contract registry.

174. The incoherence of the rule in Article 2335 CC has been criticised to the extent that the Code accepts the pledge of future assets (Question 4). However, the wording of the provision is clear, but the contradiction can be explained by understanding that it lays down a rule of relative nullity and the rule only applies against a creditor who realises that the asset belongs to someone else.[66] This interpretation is parallel to that upheld by the jurisprudence establishing a prohibition on selling others' assets (Art. 1599 CC).[67] In accordance with this interpretation, the prohibition in Article 2335 CC does not preclude the application of Article 2276 CC in respect of the bona fide pledgee, who is protected against the real owner.[68]

175. Pledges created over undivided property are different from those over another person's asset, and the former must be authorised by all co-owners. If consent is not unanimous, the effects of the pledge are limited to the pledgor's rights after the division, i.e. the pledge only takes effect if the asset is wholly or partially assigned to the pledgor.

176. According to Article 2413 CC, also applicable by reference to antichresis, mortgages can only be created over assets owned by the mortgagor and in respect of which he has the right of disposal. Interpretations of this provision are guided by the rule prohibiting mortgages on future assets and hold that a mortgage over another person's asset is absolutely null and void and cannot be regularised by the mortgagor subsequently acquiring the asset.[69] Similarly, a mortgage created by the purchaser of an asset whose ownership is later annulled is also invalid, except in cases where an apparent right caused the mortgagee to make a bona fide error.[70]

177. With regard to undivided assets, Article 2414 CC distinguishes between mortgages consented to by all parties and thus fully valid, and those only consented to by some co-owners, which are valid only if the asset is assigned to the co-owner who consented to the creation of a mortgage over the asset.

178. The fact that any sale of assets by a person other than the owner is invalid in French law (Art. 1599 CC) means that retention of title clauses included in contracts transferring another's asset are invalid.

---

66 See P. Crocq, 'Gage' in *Répertoire de Droit Civil*, No 6–7. Contra, D. Legeais, (2006) 6 *Contrats Concurrence Consommation* 13.

67 The relative nullity of the sale of another's property is defended by constant jurisprudence (Cass. civ. 8.12.1999; Cass. civ. 9.3.2005).

68 See above fn. 10.

69 See M. Bourassin, V. Brémont and M.-N. Jobard-Bachellier, *Droit des sûretés*, 565.

70 Cass. civ. 24.9.2003.

179. With regard to the transfer of ownership by way of security, the lack of any express prohibition and the fact that transfers are possible in respect of future assets might open the door to the creation of security interests over an asset that is not yet owned by the provider of collateral at the time of its creation. The same applies to an asset subject to a retention of title clause and not yet owned by the debtor at the conclusion of the contract. This interpretation may find support in the practical comparison between the transfer of a not yet existing asset and the transfer of an asset not yet owned by the debtor. However, this solution is difficult to uphold in *France* due to the invalidity of the sale of another person's asset (Art. 1599 CC), and the provisions on pledge and mortgage of assets not owned by the provider of collateral.

2. Italy

180. In the Italian civil law system it is commonly accepted that the debtor or a third party can make an agreement with a creditor for the purpose of constituting a pledge right or a mortgage right having as their object assets belonging to others. According to the prevailing opinion, such an agreement is valid but has merely inter partes effects, as will be seen from what will be said below.

2.1. Pledge

181. Italian law does not provide for any specific regulation on this subject. Nevertheless, it is held that such an agreement is valid but has merely inter partes effects according to Article 2822 of the Civil Code, which actually refers to the subject of the mortgage (see afterwards, para. 183). This means that this agreement binds the grantor to acquire the property of the assets to which the pledge right will refer and, then, to put in place all the necessary measures in order to allow the creditor to acquire the pledge right. Only when the grantor purchases the asset's property and possession, the *traditio* will be able to take place and the pledge right can arise.[71]

182. If a pledgee obtains possession of the pledged assets irrespective of the fact that the pledgor is not the owner of the pledged assets, the status of the pledgee cannot be impeached by the property owner, according to Article 1153.3 of the Civil Code.[72]

---

[71] F. Realmonte, 'Il pegno' in *Rescigno*, 808.

[72] *Ibid.*

2.2. *Mortgage*

183. The constitution of a mortgage over other people's assets is expressly regulated by Article 2822 of the Civil Code. This establishes that 'if the mortgage is granted by someone that is not the owner of the asset, its entry can only be validly made when the asset is purchased by the grantor'. From this provision emerges the proposition that granting a mortgage on other people's assets is allowed. The constitutive act is valid but it has merely inter partes effects, in the sense that the grantor is obliged to acquire the assets to which the mortgage refers. It is only when the assets have become the grantor's that the entry can be validly made.[73]

3. Spain

184. The Spanish legal system on security rights is subject to the principle of specialty and for this reason it is not possible in principle to create such rights over assets not yet owned by the debtor at the time the security interest is created. Article 1857 CC in particular lays down that the security provider must be the asset's owner and have the right of disposal over it; otherwise, the security right is not effective against third parties. For this reason, a collateral provider who expects to become the owner can conclude a security agreement, although the security right will be effective erga ommes only once ownership is acquired and the other requirements of creation, such as the transfer of possession, are met [see Art. 107(6), (7) and (10) LH]. In such cases the mortgage or pledge agreement is deemed to be a promise by which the promisor is obliged to undertake any action needed to create the security right or pay the promisee damages (Art. 1862 CC).[74] This would occur with an agreement by which the client promises his bank that all securities handed over to the bank in future would be subject to a pledge that secures the claims by the bank against him; a pledge is created once the securities have come into the bank's possession and there is no need for further formalities, as the formality requirements are deemed to have been met by the existing agreement.[75]

185. A creditor may, in good faith, acquire a security right over an asset not yet owned by the debtor at the time the security right is created, provided that specific requirements are met. This can occur with mortgages (Art. 34 LH), pledges (Arts. 464 CC and 85 CCo) such as a pledge of securities (Art. 545 CCo), even book entry securities (Art. 9 LMV), and bills of exchange as well as any other

73 M. Fragali, 'Ipoteca (dir. priv.)' in *Enciclopedia del diritto*, vol. XXII, 785.

74 A. Carrasco Perera, E. Cordero Lobato and M.J. Marín López, *Tratado de los derechos de garantía*, 160–170.

75 *Ibid.* at 174–176.

claim that can be transferred by endorsement such as shares or warrants (Art. 19 LCCH). However, chattel mortgages, ship mortgages and non-possessory pledges cannot be acquired *a non domino*, as the Personal Property Registry is in principle only a charges registry and does not operate on the basis of the principle of registration in good faith. A pledge of claims cannot be acquired *a non domino* either, given that its creation relies on the pledgor being the owner of the claim.

Question 4: Is it possible to create security rights over assets that are not yet in existence at the time of the execution of the security agreement?

1. France

186. The answer to this question differs with respect to movable and immovable assets.

187. Article 2333 CC makes provision for a pledge of future movable assets. The future asset or assets and their nature or type have to be described in the pledge agreement (Art. 2335 CC).[76] Similarly, Article 2355 CC provides for the encumbrance of an asset or group of intangible assets, present or future to secure an obligation. In the specific case of a pledge of future claims, its creation depends on the possibility of setting out the claim in the agreement creating the pledge [Art. 2356(3) CC which requires either the individualisation of the claim, or the indication of the elements that make this individualisation possible: the debtor, place of payment, the value of the debt, and the due date].

188. The creditor will not have effective rights over the asset until it exists and becomes part of the pledgor's estate, at which point it automatically becomes encumbered as security, without the requirement of any further formalities. This principle is established in Article 2357 CC on a pledge of future claims and is also applicable to a pledge over movable tangible assets. This provision is complemented by Article 2361 CC, according to which the pledge of claims, including future ones, takes effect between the two parties and is enforceable against third parties from the date of the agreement. Mutatis mutandis, a common pledge over future assets is effective from the date of the act creating the collateral.

---

76 The admissibility of pledge over future assets is implied in the very nature of pledge over stock, which, according to the principle of subrogation in rem is extended to the assets substituting the stocks disposed of by the debtor, namely pledge extends to assets not yet owned or not yet in existence at the moment of its creation [Art. L. 527(5)(2) CComm.].

189. In contrast, a mortgage can only be created over assets that exist and form part of the debtor's estate at the time it is created. Article 2419 CC prohibits and invalidates mortgages over future assets. However, there are a fair number of exceptions to this principle (Art. 2420 CC).[77]

190. The transfer of possession which is fundamental in pledge over immovable assets prevents this right being created over future assets.

191. The transfer of ownership by way of security can refer to future movable tangible or intangible assets provided that they are determinable according to the criteria laid down in the contract, which must also mention their estimated value [Arts. 2011 and 2018, 2372(2) and 2488(2) CC].

192. By analogy with the sale of future assets, it could be understood that the security interest does not come about until the asset exists, provided that it existed prior to the commencement of insolvency proceedings. However, the implementation by analogy of the provisions regarding a pledge over assets and claims might imply that future assets, as well as those 'replacing' the original assets must be considered part of the encumbered estate ab initio.[78]

2. Italy

193. In the Italian civil law system such an agreement is commonly considered valid but has merely inter partes effects in a similar way to a security agreement on assets belonging to others.

---

77 More specifically, Article 2419 CC lays down that: 'In principle, a hypothec may be granted only on existing immovables' while Article 2420 reads as follows: 'By exception to the preceding Article, a hypothec may be granted on future immovables in the following circumstances and subject to the following conditions:
(1) He who does not possess existing and unencumbered immovables or who does not possess sufficient quantity of them to secure the claim may agree that each immovable he will acquire in the future will be assigned to the payment of the claim, as each acquisition occurs;
(2) He whose existing immovable is burdened with a hypothec has perished or suffered deteriorations so that it has become insufficient for the security of the debt may do so likewise, without prejudice to the right of the creditor to enforce at once his reimbursement;
(3) He who possesses an existing right that entitles him to build for his benefit on another's property may grant a hypothec on the buildings whose construction has begun or is merely planned; in case of destruction of the these buildings, the hypothec is transferred as of right onto the new buildings constructed on the same place.'

78 See R. Damman, *Fiducie-sûreté et droit des procédures collectives: évolution ou révolution.*

2.1. *Pledge*

194. The Civil Code does not expressly regulate the pledge on future assets, but it is considered permissible on the basis of general principles.[79] In this hypothesis the pledge agreement between creditor and debtor (or third provider of the security) is immediately valid, but it merely produces inter partes effects. The pledge right will arise only with the asset coming into existence and being delivered.[80]

2.2. *Mortgage*

195. The case of a mortgage on future assets is expressly regulated by the Italian Civil Code under Article 2823. This provision simply lays down that 'entry of mortgage on future assets can only be validly made when the assets that form its objects have come into being', which is similar to Article 2822 of the Civil Code regarding the mortgage over other people's assets (see above the answer to Question 3).

3. Spain

196. As stated in Question 3, the principle of specialty establishes the answer to this question. However, there are some significant exceptions.

197. The first concerns as yet unbuilt apartments and business premises. These can be mortgaged although they are not yet in existence, as the building plans can be registered in the Land Registry, and the mortgage is effective *erga omnes* from the time of registration. The same applies to ships or aircraft under construction, provided that a third of the total budget has already been invested and the ship or chattel mortgage has been registered in the Personal Property Registry [Arts. 131 LNM, 38(III) LHMPSD and 187 Regulation of the Business Registry approved by Decree 14 December 1956 (RRM 1956)[81] on ships and aircraft].[82] A chattel mortgage over a future cinematographic work is also possible as long as the filming permit has been issued; the security right

---

79 F. Realmonte, 'Il pegno' in *Rescigno*, 640.

80 G. Gorla and P. Zannelli, 'Del pegno. Delle ipoteche' in A. Scialoja and G. Branca (eds.), *Commentario del codice civile*, 19. In judiciary, see Cass. civ. 26.3.2010 no 7257, [2010] RN 1566.

81 BOE 7.3.1957.

82 A. Carrasco Perera, E. Cordero Lobato and M.J. Marín López, *Tratado de los derechos de garantía*, 92–93 also consider the case of industrial machinery under construction provided it is fully described while registering the chattel mortgage, as indicated by Art. 43(1) LHMPSD.

has to be preventively annotated in the Personal Property Registry, and the annotation expires at the end of a two-year period (Arts. 4 and 9 of Decree 3837/1970, 31 December).

198. A chattel mortgage over a business covers its appurtenances, including goods and raw materials intended to be exploited in the mortgaged business (specifically Art. 22 LHMPSD). While third party bona fides in the acquisition of rights over the latter cannot be challenged by the mortgagee, the mortgagor is obliged to have goods and raw materials to the same or a greater amount and value in the business than those specified in the mortgage deed, and is entitled to substitute them in accordance with commercial practices. Accordingly, this security right covers assets that are not yet in existence at the time the security agreement is executed, i.e. a chattel mortgage is created on that date, even for goods and raw materials acquired by the mortgagor in the future.

199. The same right of substitution seems to apply to either possessory or non-possessory pledges *sub specie universalitatis*, i.e. a collection of goods or assets whose specification can only proceed by reference to its quantity and/or quality. Should the pledged assets be perishable commodities, this entitlement stems from the obligation to maintain the asset in good condition (Art. 1867 CC); otherwise, it must be agreed on by the parties to the contract, given the general prohibition on use laid down in Article 1870 CC – Article 569(17)(1) CCCat specifically mentions the permissibility of such agreements. With the exception of pledges on collections as described in Article 54 LHMPSD, the right of substitution ought to operate implicitly in cases of non-possessory pledges over fungible assets such as agricultural products, livestock, merchandise and raw materials, or automobiles before their specification by registration. The costs attached to registering new assets in the Personal Property Registry are thereby avoided.[83] Similarly to Article 22 LHMPSD, pledges are considered to be created from the time that the security agreement is executed. Nonetheless, neither chattel mortgages nor non-possessory pledges are given priority over unpaid sellers (see Question 23).

200. It should be noted that while Article 569(16)(3) CCCat provides for pledges to be created over portfolios, i.e. consisting of different types of security, Article 569(17)(2) entitles parties to pledge contracts to agree on their substitution as if they were fungibles, i.e. although they are not in fact fungible assets, they are considered as such by agreement and so can be traded by the collateral provider during the security period.

Other assets cannot benefit from this interpretation as their ownership is registered in specific administrative registries and certification thereof must be provided when registering a chattel mortgage in the Personal Property Registry.

83 See A. Carrasco Perera, E. Cordero Lobato and M.J. Marín López, *Tratado de los derechos de garantía*, 367–370.

201. The pledging of future claims is admitted in Spanish legal practice but was only addressed legally by the Third Additional Disposition of Law 1/1999, 5 January 1999, regulating private equity entities and their management companies and dealing with blanket assignments or the pledging of future claims to immunise them against transactional avoidance proceedings in relation to the assigned debtor or assignor's insolvency proceedings. This provision is the basic regulation for factoring in *Spain*, for which reason it is addressed in Question 25. Over and above this, the pledging of future claims is allowed, although there is no reference to how those assets should be specified. Basic principles would suggest, however, specification by reference to the relationships from which these claims may arise. This same protection insists on ensuring that there is consideration on the side of the pledgee; otherwise, the pledge must be deemed to be in abuse of law.[84] With regard to the date of the pledge's creation, the principle seems to be as that which operates in chattel mortgages over businesses, i.e. the time that the pledge agreement is executed, although pledged claims cannot be enforced until they become part of the debtor's estate.[85] By the same token, a pledge is only effective if the contract from which the claim arises was concluded before the opening of insolvency proceedings: claims arising prior to and after the opening of proceedings but arising from contracts which have been reinstated by the insolvency practitioner, or claims over which pledges were registered prior to the opening of proceedings, are deemed to have special privilege [Art. 90(1)(6) LC].

Question 5: Is it possible to have a 'global security agreement', i.e. covering all assets of the debtor?

1. France

202. In *France*, genuine 'global' security rights are created by legal provisions and can affect a class of movable assets, namely general privileges over movable assets ex Article 2331 CC, or movable and immovable assets, i.e. general privileges such as those securing legal costs or wage claims as laid down in Articles 2331 and 2375 CC.

203. Within the scope of conventional security rights, specific security rights in rem can be created over a group of tangible assets that form a functional entity, thus a security right is enforced over the entity as a whole. In addition to such cases, the device of security ownership as security make possible a global encumbrance over a group of present or future assets, whatever their nature, to secure the payment of one or more claims.

84 *Ibid.* at 267–271.
85 *Ibid.* at 274.

204. A group of assets can be pledged *sub specie universalitatis*, as a global entity. This applies to specific pledges such as pledge over stock, which includes all raw materials, products and goods belonging to the debtor, i.e. a group of assets that are deemed to be a whole item whose composition can be changed, either by the principle of subrogation in rem, or by agreement between the parties to reduce the encumbered stock in proportion to payments received by the creditors [Arts. L. 527(5)(2), L. 527(8) CComm.].

205. A pledge over intangible assets can also encumber a group of assets. The pledge of marketable securities (*nantissement d'un compte-titre*) is created over what is deemed a single asset, namely the account in which the financial instruments are registered, and whose transfer in exchange for new shares causes the immediate encumbrance of the latter by operation of the principle of subrogation in rem [Art. L. 211(20)(IV) CMon. and Fin.]. Similarly, in a pledge over a business, the subject of the security right is the totality of movable assets that make up a single entity at the service of the business activity, namely different tangible and intangible elements such as clients, merchandise, material, equipment, leases and industrial property rights [Art. 142(2) CComm.]. Enforcement of the pledge must be over the proceeds of the sale of the business as a whole; isolated elements cannot be realised.

206. With respect to immovable assets, the principle of specialty does not exclude the creation of a mortgage over all of a debtor's present assets, provided they are described individually in the deed of creation. However, it is not clear that this can be referred to as a 'global' security interest as the assets need to be specified separately.

207. Transfer of ownership by way of security allows the transfer of any tangible and intangible movable and immovable assets, personal rights and rights in rem, and even security rights (Art. 2011 CC). Assets, rights or security rights transferred are kept separate from assets belonging to the provider of collateral and that of the fiduciary, and this separate estate only responds for the debts arising from its maintenance and management but not for other claims.[86]

---

86 Article 2025 CC reads as follows: 'Without prejudice to the rights of the creditors of the grantor holders of a right to follow property that derives from a security right published before the contract of fiducia was executed and outside cases of acts in fraud of the rights of the creditors of the grantor, the fiduciary patrimony may only be seized by the holders of claims arising from the preservation or the management of that patrimony. If the fiduciary patrimony is insufficient, the patrimony of the grantor is the common pledge of these creditors, unless the contract of fiducia makes all or part of the liabilities the obligation of the fiduciary. The contract of fiducia may also limit the obligation of the fiduciary liabilities to the fiduciary patrimony exclusively. Such a clause is ineffective against creditors unless they have expressly accepted it'.

2. Italy

208. In Italian civil law, the so-called 'principle of specificity of rights in rem' applies. This principle stipulates that only specific individual assets can be subject to rights in rem. The creation of a security right in rem over assets in its entirety without specifying the individual assets would therefore not be permissible. It follows that a global security agreement intended as a constitutive act of security right in rem covering all assets of the debtor would similarly not be permissible.[87]

2.1. Pledge

209. Concerning pledge, the 'principle of specificity' is embodied in Article 2787.3 of the Civil Code. This rule, in setting out the requirements of a pledgor, provides that it must contain sufficient indication of the movable assets on which the security right is constituted, as well as of the claim to which the security refers.[88]

210. The necessary compliance with Article 2787.3 of the Civil Code raises the issue of the permissibility of collateral extension clauses. Banking practice leads to the inclusion in the pledge agreement of so-called *omnibus* clauses, not only in relation to the guaranteed claims, but also in relation to the pledged assets (*pegno omnibus*). In this last respect, the *omnibus* clause is intended to extend the guarantee to future assets and even all of the debtor's assets that are in every way, and for any reason, held by the bank or that are received subsequently by the bank. The validity of such clauses is the subject of debate. The prevailing opinion argues for the validity and effectiveness of the *omnibus* clause relating to the pledged assets inter partes only: this clause obliges the grantor to put in place all the necessary measures in order to provide the creditor with the right of pledge. The rights under the pledge will only accrue to the secured creditor when the new assets, to which the security extends, are sufficiently indicated in a written form that has a 'certain date' specified along with an indication of the secured claim (Art 2787.3 Civil Code).[89]

211. Banking practice has created another clause, the 'rotatory' clause, whose permissibility has long been debated because of the alleged conflict with the

---

87 P. Gorla and P. Zannelli 'Del pegno. Delle ipoteche' in A. Scialoja and G. Branca (eds.), *Commentario del codice civile*, 221. In judiciary, see Cass. civ. 27.8.1996 no 7859, [1997] *CG* 336.

88 Cass. civ. 22.6.1972 no 2056, (1973–9) II *BBTC* 236.

89 E. Gabrielli, 'Il pegno' in R. Sacco (ed.), *Trattato di diritto civile*, 143–144. In judiciary, see Cass. civ. 27.4.1999 no 4208, (2000) II *DF* 1203.

'principle of specificity'. The rotatory clause allows replacement of the pledged assets with others without entailing a novation of the security. The validity of the rotatory pledge (*pegno rotativo*) is now firmly established in the case law, on condition that: the rotatory clause is drawn up in writing having a certain date; the possibility of replacing the pledged assets is expressly provided for; the assets delivered in substitution of the original ones do not have a higher value. If these conditions are fulfilled, the pledge covers the new assets with effect from the date of the pledge agreement.[90]

2.2. Mortgage

212. The 'specificity' of mortgages is expressly stated in Article 2809.1 of the Civil Code. This establishes that 'entry of mortgage must be made on specifically indicated assets and for a specified amount in money'.

213. With specific regard to voluntary mortgage, the 'principle of specificity' is strengthened by Article 2826 of the Civil Code. This establishes that 'in the act granting the mortgage the assets must be specifically designated with an indication of their nature, of the municipality in which they are located, as well as of their cadastral identification data'.[91]

3. Spain

214. Personal security rights such as assumed joint liability cover all the debtor's assets, but this does not apply to security rights in rem, as the principle of specialty applies. Nevertheless, some concessions have been made recently with a view to promoting credit, i.e. the provision of security to cover unspecified present and future obligations is possible as long as a maximum liability is set. This maximum operates as a third party protection rule, i.e. informing third parties of their exposure in the event of debtor insolvency, but it does not work inter partes, meaning that secured claims may be enforced against assets whose whole amount is secured. Legally speaking, this type of 'unspecified' security agreement is addressed in two cases – that of mortgages over immovable assets as laid down by the Spanish LH and that of pledges under Catalan law.

215. Although it has been contended that secured future obligations must arise from a legal relationship between the parties to the mortgage contract that

---

[90] Cass. civ. 5.03.2004 no 4520, [2005] *F* 547.

[91] G. Gorla and P. Zannelli, 'Del pegno. Delle ipoteche' in A. Scialoja and G. Branca (eds.), *Commentario del codice civile*, 317–318. In judiciary, see App. Milano 7.4.1978, (1978) I *FP* 270.

exists at the time that the security right is created,[92] Article 153bis LH makes it clear that such a degree of specificity is not necessary and a description of the business from which secured obligations arise or may arise is sufficient. It is worth noting that a mortgage produces effects from the date it is created, regardless of whether the secured obligation eventually comes into existence or not; when it eventually comes into existence, the mortgage is immediately effective, but priority is granted to the mortgagee from the date of creation of the mortgage. In addition to maximum liability mortgages (*hipoteca de máximo*), which are characterised by the fact that they secure an unspecified amount in their obligation, 'floating mortgages' are also allowed. These are mortgages that at any time indiscriminately secure more than one obligation of a determined amount at the time of their creation, i.e. security is not fragmented among secured obligations but 'floats' indiscriminately over them. 'Global mortgages' are a combination of the two types, and they secure more than one obligation, at least one of which is an unspecified obligation. There is, however, a proviso: Article 153bis LH stipulates that floating mortgages can only be created in favour of either the financial entities detailed in Article 2 of Law 2/1981, or government creditors for the payment of taxes or social security contributions.[93] Against this background, it must be noted that it is possible to create a mortgage over several immovable assets insofar as the secured claim is distributed among them (Art. 119 LH), but this proviso is not applicable in the event of a maximum liability mortgage.[94]

216. In Catalan law pledges may also be created to secure all kinds of present and future obligations, insofar as maximum liability is established at the time of creation [Art. 569(14)(2) CCCat]. Global pledges over several assets are legally covered by Article 569(17), which deals with the right to substitute fungible assets or securities and other financial instruments that are included in a portfolio: while several present and future obligations can be secured, a class of assets, present and future, can be subject to pledge.

Question 6: In general terms, what are the formalities in your legal system for the creation of a security interest over assets?

1. France

217. In general terms, French law requires the agreement creating security rights in rem to be in writing and, in accordance with the principle of specialty,

---

92 See RDGRN 17.1.1994 (RJ 1994/239).

93 On the basis of the supplementary nature of LH it is contended the establishing of floating chattel mortgages and non-possessory pledges. See F. Vegas, *La hipoteca flotante*, 527.

94 See RDGRN 27.8.1912 (CL 150).

it should at least describe the secured claim and the asset encumbered by the security, otherwise the agreement will be invalid (*ad solemnitatem* form).

218. In a pledge over tangible assets, the contract's validity is dependent on the issuing of a deed that specifies the secured claim, the assets pledged and their type or nature (Art. 2336 CC). Since 2006, the pledgee taking possession is no longer a condition for the creation of the pledge. Today, the transfer of possession of the pledged assets is no longer a condition of the effectiveness of the pledge against third parties. One can publicise the non-possessory pledge by registration and this serves as an alternative to transfer of possession for ensuring the effectiveness against third parties of the pledge.

219. Unlike the common pledge, there are no formal requirements for the commercial pledge [Art. L. 521(1) CComm.], while registering the security right is necessary for inter partes recognition of some special non-possessory pledges. Thus, a pledge over stock where the retention of assets is fundamental for the company-pledgor must be registered within a maximum of 15 days from the date of written agreement between the parties setting out the collateral [Arts. L. 527(1) and L. 527(4) CComm.]. A pledge over equipment is also subject to this requirement; in this case a public or private pledge contract must be made in writing within a maximum of two months from the delivery of material and registered in 15 days of the day of the constitutive instrument [Arts. L. 525(2) and L. 525(3) CComm.].

220. To be valid a pledge of claims must be in writing (Art. 2365 CC), and must include a series of references (claims secured and claims pledged); in case of future claims, specification shall make claim individualisation possible and thus include elements such as the identification of the debtor, the place of payment or the amount of the claims.[95] The pledge becomes effective between the parties and against third parties from the date of creation. To be effective with respect to the account debtor, he must be notified of the pledge contract or be present at the conclusion of the contract [Arts. 2362 CC, L. 525(2) and L. 525(3) CComm.].

221. The mortgage agreement is a written contract, whose validity is subject to it being notarised and the principle of specialty requires that certain information should be clearly set out including the nature and situation of each mortgaged asset, and precisely what indebtedness is secured (Arts. 2416, 2418 and 2421 CC).

---

95 More specifically, Article 2356 Civil Code reads as follows: 'Under penalty of nullity, the pledge of a claim shall be concluded in writing. Claims secured and claims pledged are specified in the act. If they are future claims, the instrument must allow for their individualisation or contain the elements that provide for it, such as the identification of the debtor, the place of payment, the amount of the claims or their evaluation, and if appropriate the date their payment is due'.

222. The contract creating antichresis must also be a public document (Art. 2416 CC by reference to Art. 2388 CC). Delivery of the asset is also a requirement as dispossession forms part of the structure of this kind of security in rem (Art. 2387 CC).

223. The Civil Code only requires the retention of title clause to be in writing with a view to making it effective against third-parties [Arts. 2368 CC; L. 624(16) CCom.]. It has been noted that this is not an *ad solemnitatem* form, nor is there any publicity obligation as Article 2368 CC contains no provisions comparable to Articles 2336 and 2356 CC. Moreover, the fact that the retention of title clause is in writing is not to inform third parties, but to entitle the secured creditor to exercise his rights as owner should insolvency proceedings be opened (Questions 10 and 11).

224. The agreement constituting the transfer of ownership by way of security is subject to the formalities required for any fiduciary contract by Articles 2018(8) and 2019 CC; otherwise, it is deemed null and void. The agreement must be in writing and include the following information: assets, transferred rights and security rights; the duration of the transfer of ownership that can be no longer than 90 years; the identities of debtors, secured creditors and beneficiaries, or, alternatively, rules that allow their appointment; and the scope of their administrative and dispositive powers over assets. To this information should be added the particulars provided for in Articles 2372-2 and 2488-2 CC on the subject of *fiducie-sûreté*, regarding both movables and immovables, namely the secured claim and the estimated value of an asset or right transferred to the separate estate.

225. In addition to the written form and as a measure to avoid tax fraud, the validity of contractual transfer of ownership by way of security requires the registration of the act of creation as well as any complementary acts, at the offices of the tax authorities in the place of the secured creditor's domicile within one month. In the case of immovable assets, the contract must also be registered at the Land Registry within two months (Art. 2019 CC), an exceptional case of mandatory registration in order to create the security.

226. A *fiducie* may secure claims other than those specifically mentioned in the contract by which it is created provided that there is a specific agreement and it is publicised in the same way as the transfer of ownership by way of security itself [Arts. 2372(5) and 2488(5) CC]. This is known as rechargeable transfer of ownership by way of security.

227. A national registry for transfers of ownership by way of security (*Registre National des Fiducies*) was created by Article 2020 CC, and further established by Decree No 2010-19 of 2 March 2010. It centralises the information in these contracts and thus facilitates control over tax evasion, money-laundering and the financing of terrorism. The provision does not establish any sanctions for failure to register but it is likely that the one applicable in other cases are applicable to this case, i.e. invalidation of the contract.

2. Italy

228. In Italian private law, the creation of security rights is informed by a series of requirements of a formal character which may refer, on one side, to the security agreement and, on the other side, to its publicity.

2.1. Pledge

229. In accordance with Article 2786 of the Civil Code, the contract aimed at creating a pledge is considered a 'real' agreement: hence, it can be provided for in any form, including orally, but its constitution requires the delivery of the movable assets (or the delivery of the document that attributes the exclusive control and availability of the asset) by the pledgor (debtor or third party) to the pledgee (Art 2786 Civil Code).[96] The assets (or the document) may also be delivered to a third party designated by the parties, or be placed in the custody of both the parties, but in a way that the pledgor is unable to dispose of them without the cooperation of the pledgee (Art 2786 Civil Code).

230. The delivery of the pledged assets and consequent dispossession of the debtor also fulfil an advertising function. However, they are not enough to give rise to the pledgee's preferential right. For this purpose it is also required that the pledge agreement is drawn up in written form with a certain date and containing sufficient indication of the claim and of the pledged asset (Art 2787.3 Civil Code).[97] In any case, the preferential right cannot be enforced if the pledged assets have not remained in the possession of the pledgee or by the third party designated by the parties (Art 2787.2 Civil Code).

231. The formalities relating to the creation of a pledge on movable assets others than the tangible ones will be further dealt with in the answer to Question 7.

2.2. Mortgage

232. The mortgage on immovable assets comes into being and takes its ranking from the date of its entry in the office of the Real Estate Registers at the place

96 Cass. civ. 5.9.2006 no 19059, [2006] *MFI.*
97 *Ibid.*

where the immovable assets lie (Art 2827 Civil Code). Article 2839 of the Civil Code is expressly indexed as 'formalities for mortgage entry'. This establishes that, to perform a mortgage entry, the constitutive title must be presented together with a note containing certain prescribed information. The features of this advertising system will be further dealt with in the answer to Question 20.

233. With specific regard to a voluntary mortgage, Article 2821 of the Civil Code also establishes that a constitutive act, an agreement or a unilateral act of granting, must be drawn up through a public or private deed, without which it will be a nullity.[98] If the title for entry is a private deed, the signature of the mortgagor must be authenticated or confirmed by the court in order to satisfy mortgage publicity requirements (Art 2835.1 Civil Code).

234. The formalities relating to the creation of a mortgage on assets other than immovable ones will be further dealt with in the answer to Question 7.

3. Spain

235. As in any other Roman law system, formalities are necessary to make third parties aware of security rights and the risk to their own rights that these involve. With this in mind, the mechanism preferred by Spanish law for conferring erga omnes effect to a security interest over assets is recording in a public registry. The Personal Property Registry, which brings together the former Chattel Mortgage and Non-Possessory Pledge Registry and the Hire Purchase Contracts Registry among others, was set up for publicity purposes alongside the Land Registry. Mortgages over immovable assets have to be notarised and registered in the Land Registry to be created and be effective erga omnes. The same applies to chattel and ship mortgages as well as non-possessory pledges; they have to be registered in the Personal Property Registry, but only to be effective erga omnes. The creation of chattel mortgage agreements relies on the agreements being recorded in a public document, which can be a commercial agreement enforced by a public notary in the case of non-possessory pledge (see Art. 3 LHMPSD) or a private document in the case of ship mortgages (Art. 128 LNM).

236. Likewise, in Catalonia the creation of the right to possessory retention and antichresis both require recording in a public document, while registration in the Land Registry – should the rights be created over immovable assets – is only for publicity purposes [Art. 569(24)(2) CCCat]. In addition to this formality, the creation of the right to possessory retention and the pledging of claims are contingent on the account debtor being notified by a public notary of the retention or pledge.

---

98 C. Cicero, 'Artt. 2808–2899' in P. Cendon (ed.), *Commentario al codice civile*, 767.

237. Retention of title clauses and prohibitions on disposal also have to be registered in the Hire Purchase Agreements Registry set up by the 1998 law of the same name, now included within the Personal Property Registry. Registration is only possible if the contract is drafted in a form approved by the institution that supervises the Spanish Registry System, the General Directorate of Registries and Notaries (*Dirección General de los Registros y del Notariado*, DGRN). There is no official form, but all interested parties can request approval. Although this single condition is burdensome and expensive, it is less so than the requirement for the contract to be recorded in a public document required for other security rights such as chattel mortgages or non-possessory pledges.

238. For cases in which registration is not possible, dispossession of the collateral provider is the sole formality required to make the secured claim effective erga omnes. Pledges also have to be recorded in a public document, in particular the date they were created for priority purposes, but what is essential is the dispossession of the collateral provider, without which the security right is presumed to be cancelled [Art. 1191 CC and Art. 569(19(3) CCCat]. Should the pledged asset be in possession of a third party against the pledgee's will, he can take action to recover it and his priority over other creditors (Art. 1922 *in fine* CC).

239. As the pledging of claims is not addressed legally by the Spanish CC or similar, there are no specific formalities for its creation. Nevertheless, practitioners usually notarise the pledge agreement and notify the assigned debtor. The latter requirements are mandatory in the CCCat.

Question 7: Do the rules for the creation of security rights vary depending on the nature of the asset in question?

1. France

240. In general terms, the answer to this question is no. As seen, the rules governing the creation of security interests vary little; validity depends on the rights of disposal and ownership of the provider of collateral, whether he is the debtor or a third party.

241. Regarding form – and with the exception of the retention of title clause and some special pledges – the creation of security rights must be in writing and the contract must include the information required by law, otherwise it will be void. Exceptionally, transfer of the asset's possession (antichresis), or where there is no dispossession, the registration of the collateral (pledge over stock or a business) can be required as conditions of validity and effectiveness of the security right inter partes.

242. From a time perspective, the opening of insolvency proceedings ends the possibility of creating new security rights unless there is legal authorisation to do so (Question 9). Article L. 622(7) CComm. allows the insolvency judge within the observation period of the proceedings of *sauveguarde* and *redressement* to create security rights in line with the objectives of the insolvency proceeding, in particular company restructuring.

2. Italy

243. Yes. They do. Under Italian law the rules governing the creation of security rights vary depending on the nature of the specific assets in question. These rules, indeed, are generally modulated on the rules governing the transfer of ownership of the specific kind of assets which constitute their object. Since the legal rules governing the contractual transfer of ownership of assets vary depending on the nature of the assets, the rules governing the creation of security rights do so as well.

244. This explains why the general rules described under Question 6 relating to the creation of the pledge (on movable assets) and of the mortgage (on immovable assets) differ. This explains also why the same general rules undergo some further variations due to the peculiar nature of some of 'collateralisable' assets, as will be seen from what will be said below.

2.1. Pledge

245. Concerning claims, the impossibility of their material delivery is overcome by requiring the notification of the pledge agreement to the debtor of the pledged claim or the acceptance by the latter in writing and with a certain date. The agreement in writing and its notification (or acceptance) is expressly required by Article 2800 of the Civil Code for the right of preferential satisfaction, similarly to what is provided for the transfer of claims (Art 1264 Civil Code). However, case law seems to consider notification (or acceptance) a necessary requirement for the very existence of the pledge right, in the same way as for delivery of the item for the pledge over tangible assets.[99]

246. Concerning rights other than claims, the pledge is constituted in the form respectively required for the transfer of the rights themselves. A written agreement for a pledge having a certain date, provided for in Article 2787.3 of the Civil Code, is however a necessary condition for the existence of a preferential right (Art 2806 Civil Code).

---

[99] Cass. civ. 24.6.1995 no 7158, (1995) I *GC* 2633.

247. Concerning negotiable instruments, the pledge is constituted as the pledge over tangible assets, i.e. as a pledge over the document which is regarded as a tangible good.[100] The pledge constitution requires, therefore, the delivery of the document in accordance with the rules on its transfer (Arts 1997, 2003, 2008, 2014, 2021, 2024, 2026 Civil Code).[101] Anyhow, a pledge in writing having a certain date (Art 2787.3 Civil Code) is a necessary condition for the preferential right.[102]

248. These rules do not apply to 'dematerialised financial instruments' for which there are specific laws and regulations.[103]

2.2. Mortgage

249. Mortgage over registered movable assets is governed by special statutes. As far as ships and aircraft, mortgage is governed by the Maritime Code. The constitutive title may only be a voluntary act (Arts 565, 1027). This must be drawn up through a public or private deed, otherwise it will be null (Arts 565, 1027). Nevertheless, the private deed has to be authenticated by the signature of a notary to obtain the mortgage advertising, called 'transcription' (*trascrizione*) (Arts 569, 1032) by the Civil Code. This transcription is performed in various ways and mostly: by registration and annotation on the deed of nationality if the ship is major in seize; by entry into the Register of ships if the ship is minor in seize or is a barge; by entry into the Register of ships being built if it is a ship being built (Art 567); by entry into the National Aeronautical Register (RAN) and annotation on the certificate of matriculation if it is an aircraft; by entry into the Register of aircraft being built if it is an aircraft being built (Art 1030). Mortgage publicity has to be requested from the ship or barge or aircraft registration office (Arts 568, 1031) presenting the same documents stipulated in Article 2839 of the Civil Code and those eventually required by Articles 569, 1032. The primary effect of the publicity is the constitution of the mortgage right, which only arises as a result of it and from its date takes ranking (Arts 574, 1035).

250. As for motorcars, the security right is still governed by r.d.l. 15 March 1927 No 436, followed by r.d. 29 July 1927 No 1814. They establish motorcars

---

100 Cass. civ. 27.4.1999 no 4208, [2000] *F* 1317.

101 Cass. civ. 23.10.1998 no 10526, (1999) I *GC* 2115.

102 Cass. 19.3.2004 no 5561, [2004] *GDir* 18, 63.

103 See Arts 83-*octies*, 85, 87 and 90 d.lgs. 24.02.1998 No 58 <www.normattiva.it> accessed 26 May 2016. See also the Regulation of the Monte Titoli S.p.A. on the centralised management system and the related and instrumental activities <http://www.lseg.com/sites/default/files/content/04%20MT%20Regolamento%20GA%20aggiornato%20con%20ev_0.pdf> accessed 26 May 2016.

'privilege', but Article 2810.3 of the Civil Code expressly states that such a privilege must be deemed a mortgage. This mortgage can be voluntary, statutory or judicial.[104] The constitutive title must be set out in writing, otherwise it will be null. The mortgage is constituted through entry in the Public Automobile Register (PRA), held by the Italian Automobile Club, and annotation in the certificate of ownership. The date of entry determines the priority of the mortgage.

251. Special statutes also govern mortgages of state revenues. Article 2810.2 of the Civil Code provides that state revenues can also be mortgaged in the manner determined by the statute relating to public debt.[105]

3. Spain

252. As already set out in Questions 1, 2 and 7, the significance the Spanish security rights system attaches to registration has led to assets being classified on the basis of their ability to be identified and thus registered.

C. ENFORCEMENT OF SECURITY RIGHTS

Question 8: To what extent is it possible for the secured party to enforce the security without having to use formal court procedures?

1. France

253. In the case of security rights in rem, non-judicial enforcement is made possible by the acceptance of the pactum commissorium, whereby the parties agree that if the secured obligation is not satisfied, the creditor becomes the owner of the encumbered asset [Art. 2348 CC: common pledge; Art. 2352 CC: pledge over motor vehicles; Art. 2365 CC: pledge over claims, Art. 2355 CC: pledge over intangibles other than claims; Art. 2459 CC: mortgage; Art. L. 521(3) CComm.: commercial pledge].The pactum is not permitted in the case of pledge over stocks [Art. L. 527(2)], mortgage over movable assets nor in mortgages over immovable when the immovable asset is the debtor's habitual residence, save the case of the *prêt viager hypothécaire*, i.e. a reverse mortgage by which an

[104] Cass. civ. 13.5.1971 no 1378, (1971) I *FI* 1191.

[105] See Art 15 d.P.R. 30.12.2003 No 398, Art 90 d.lgs. 24.02.1998 No 58, and, for the previous legislation, Arts 38, 40, 41 d.P.R. 14.02.1963 No 1343 <www.normattiva.it> accessed 26 May 2016. See also the Regulation of the Monte Titoli S.p.A. on the centralised management system and the related and instrumental activities, above fn. 103.

immovable property occupied by the debtor is created to secure a loan which is repaid after his death by his heirs [Art. L. 314(1) et seq. CComm.].

254. To avoid the dangers of the *pactum*, Articles 2348(2) and 2460 CC establish that the value of the assets must be assessed by an expert designated by agreement or by the courts. If the value is higher than the value of the secured claim, the creditor must return the difference to the debtor or to the third-party provider of collateral, or make the difference available to the other creditors. A pactum cannot be made or become effective where insolvency proceedings have commenced [Art. L. 622(7)CComm.].

255. The enforcement of the pledge of shares or securities takes place essentially out of court. If the debtor defaults, after eight days the creditor can directly appropriate cash in the account where securities are registered, or can sell any listed securities on the relevant stock market and thus be paid with the exchange value, or become the owner of securities according to their value at closure of the previous trading session [Art. D.211(12), developing Art. R-211(12) of the *Code Monetaire*].

256. Once the debtor defaults on the secured claim, retention of title clauses give the creditor-owner the right to claim in and out of court the property of the asset, whose value is used to discharge the outstanding secured claim (Art. 2371 CC).

257. In *fiducie-sûretée*, if the secured creditor is the fiduciary of the asset, the debtor's default entitles the former to become the full owner and thus to have the right of disposal over the secured asset. If the fiduciary is not the secured creditor, the latter acquires full ownership of the assets and thus is entitled to claim for the transfer of possession against the fiduciary once the secured claim matures. However, parties to the deed creating the security interest may agree on the right of the secured creditor to request the fiduciary to sell the asset and pay all or part of the value received [Art. 2372(3) CC on *fiducie* over movables; Art. 2488(3) CC on *fiducie* over immovable assets]. In any case, the assets must be valued by an expert appointed by agreement or by the courts, and the secured creditor must reimburse the difference between this value if it is greater than the claim [Arts. 2372(4) and 2488(4) CC].

2. Italy

258. Before addressing the specific issue in question, some preliminary considerations are appropriate.

259. The secured creditor, as a means of self-protection, has prerogatives on the encumbered assets the exercise of which does not necessarily require using formal court procedures. These prerogatives arise not only in the case in which the debtor has not fulfilled his obligation but also in a prior period in order to safeguard the continued existence and effectiveness of the security itself.

260. In this regard, it is worth mentioning the following general prerogatives enjoyed, without any distinction, by the pledgee and mortgagee and privileged creditor. Article 2742.1 of the Civil Code establishes that, if the assets subject to privilege or pledge or mortgage have perished or deteriorated, the sums owed by indemnity insurers in respect of the loss or deterioration are paid to the secured creditors according to their ranking, unless the sum is used to repair the loss or deterioration.

261. In addition, Article 2743 of the Civil Code establishes that, if the assets given as a pledge or submitted to a mortgage perish or deteriorate so as to be insufficient for the security of the creditor, the latter can ask that a suitable security be given to him on other assets and, in default, can ask for immediate payment of his claim.

262. As to the possibility for the secured party to enforce the security without having to use formal court procedures the following is observed.

2.1. Pledge

263. The pledgee has the power to enforce the security without having to use formal court procedures. The Civil Code provides 'out of court' enforcement proceedings implemented through the forced sale. To this end, the pledgee has to turn to a bailiff and, through him, must notify the debtor of the order to pay the debt, warning him that otherwise he will proceed with the sale. If within five days of receiving the order no opposition is made known, or if the latter is rejected by the court, the pledgee can have the pledged assets sold at public auction. If the assets have a market price, the pledgee can also have these assets sold at the current price through a person or a body authorised to carry out such acts (Arts 2796–2797 Civil Code). It is appropriate to stress that a further simplification of this 'out of court' procedure for the enforcement of the security is allowed. Indeed, Article 2797.4 of the Civil Code states that parties may agree different forms for the sale of the pledged assets.[106]

[106] C. Bianca, 'Le garanzie reali. La prescrizione' in C. Bianca, *Diritto civile*, vol. VII, 208–209. In judiciary Cass. civ. 28.5.2008 no 13998, (2009) I *GC*. 176.

2.2. *Mortgage*

264. In principle, the mortgagee has no powers to enforce the security without having to use the formal court procedures.[107]

2.3. *Special privilege*

265. Normally, the holder of a special privilege has no powers to enforce the security without having to use formal court procedures. Only exceptionally does the law provide the power directly to have the encumbered assets sold. This occurs, for example, with respect to special privilege established by Article 2756 of the Civil Code which makes express reference to the provisions for this purpose laid down concerning pledge (see above in this answer).[108]

3. Spain

266. In addition to ordinary judicial proceedings, judicial and non-judicial foreclosure proceedings are available in Spain. Article 681 et seq. of the Spanish Civil Procedure Law (*Ley de Enjuiciamiento Civil*, LEC) lays down specific enforcement proceedings aimed at either auctioning (by electronic means) the mortgaged or pledged asset (Art. 643 et seq. LEC), selling it through a specialist (Art. 641 LEC) or concluding an agreement between creditor and debtor about the asset's destiny (Art. 640 LEC). The grounds for refusal of enforcement are restricted to the security right or secured claim having ceased to be effective, the existence of a prior security right over movable assets and the inclusion of unfair terms in the mortgage or pledge agreement, for which reason either the enforcement must be terminated or the secured claim recalculated (Art. 695 LEC). Foreclosure proceedings are suspended when criminal proceedings concerning false executive title are opened (Art. 697 LEC).

267. Non-judicial foreclosure proceedings supervised by a public notary are also available prior to this judicial phase for all security rights except antichresis (see Question 1). Opposition to enforcement should be allowed in all these proceedings on similar grounds to those provided by Articles 695 and 697 LEC. In fact, Article 88 LHMPSD concerning a chattel mortgage and Article 164 RRM 1956 concerning a ship mortgage subject this issue to Article 695 LEC. This is not true of pledge (Art. 1872 CC) or non-possessory pledge (Art. 94 LHMPSD)

---

107 Bianca, 'Le garanzie reali. La prescrizione' in C. Bianca, *Diritto civile*, vol. VII, 467.

108 *Ibid.* at 25, 45.

since both laws are silent on the matter, but it seems that in these situations foreclosure may also be suspended on the grounds detailed above.[109] A third party may undertake other actions, for example claiming priority rights over the enforcing creditor or for the surplus from a forced sale; the seized court may then be requested to order the securing of the outcome of the forced sale for the benefit of the plaintiff [for example, Arts. 236(a) RH, 88 LHMPSD, and 165 RRM 1956 subject this issue to Art. 698 LEC]. Ownership rights cannot be claimed in non-judicial proceedings. The enforcing creditor is entitled to suspend non-judicial proceedings before foreclosure without prejudice to other actions that remain open.

268. Parties to the mortgage or the chattel mortgage contract must agree to the non-judicial forced sale of the mortgaged asset. The procedure is laid down in Articles 129 LH, 234 et seq. RH and 86 et seq. LHMPSD and requires the agreement to be recorded in the public document that creates the right including the following: the debtor's representative on the days of the sale to be nominated, an address for notification purposes and the reserve price for the asset at the public auction. At the mortgagee's request, the public notary asks the debtor, the mortgagor and the asset's owner, where appropriate, for payment. Those requested to must either pay or release the asset for auction. Should the asset not be sold at the first auction, the mortgagee is entitled to acquire it for the asking price at the auction, or 50% of the reserve price if there are no bids.

269. Any breach of contract entitles the pledgee to realise the pledged asset under the supervision of a public notary (Art. 1872 CC). The forced sale of the asset proceeds by public auction and the debtor and/or the pledgor must be notified in advance so that they are in a position to place bids. The pledgee is only entitled to appropriate the asset if there are no bids at the second auction, and the secured claim is then deemed to be paid in full. The same applies to non-judicial enforcement of non-possessory pledge (Art. 1872 CC is also applicable here), retention of title clauses and prohibitions on disposal [Art. 16(2) and 16(3) LVPBM].

270. The non-judicial enforcement of the pledge of marketable securities is subject to Articles 322 et seq. CCo, according to which their forced sale is undertaken by the institutions in charge of the respective official secondary market with the help of a broker. Forced sale is even possible in cases in which the debtor may argue that the secured claims still need to be liquidated [Art. 323 CCo referring to Art. 572(2) LEC]. However, it is not necessary to notify the debtor and/or pledgor of the foreclosure in these proceedings as the market value of the securities is already granted. The same applies to book-entry securities (Arts. 12 of Law 24/1988, and 26 RD 878/2015), collateral for payment and security settlement

109 A. Carrasco Perera, E. Cordero Lobato and M.J. Marín López, *Tratado de los derechos de garantía* 213–214.

systems,[110] and joint stock company shares. The pledgee is entitled to exercise actions arising from bills of exchange once the underlying obligation matures, with the aim of offsetting the secured claim against the amount due, although he is not entitled to endorse them (Art. 1870 CC). Likewise, the secured claim can be offset against pledged claims, and so enforcement proceedings are not necessary here; however, it is advisable to include a clause on this issue in the pledge contract.

271. The CCCat is more expeditious and entitles the parties to the security contract to agree on the direct sale of the asset, either by one of them or by a third party (Arts. 569–7 and 8 on right of possessory retention, 569–26 on antichresis and 569.20 on pledge). In cases of default, the asset can be auctioned under the supervision of a public notary; should this fail to produce results, the creditor is entitled to appropriate the asset in specific circumstances.

272. As can be seen here, the secured creditor can appropriate the asset in certain circumstances on the understanding that this does not infringe the general prohibition on pactum commissorium (Art. 1859 CC). This is clear when the secured creditor participates in public auctions as a bidder. It is also clear that any agreement on the transfer of the asset by payment of the debt that is concluded when the security right is created is a pactum commissorium and is thus null and void, save the case of agreements concluded after financing has been granted or the secured obligation has matured. In a similar vein, contractual offsetting must be accepted in all cases in which the price of the mortgaged or pledged asset can be established objectively. This is accepted in Article 11(3) of Royal Decree 5/2005 by which creditors may appropriate securities and other financial instruments by way of payment and offset them against their claims, as long as this enforcement method and the way of establishing their market price were agreed in the financial collateral arrangement. By the same token, any surplus amounts must be returned to the debtor – a rule which is clearly provided for in Article 569-20.5 CCCat concerning pledges of money, also known as irregular pledges.

Question 9: Is the secured party affected by a 'stay' on the enforcement of security rights if the debtor enters insolvency proceedings?

1. France

273. Modern French insolvency law aims at business restructuring, as highlighted by the Explanatory Memorandum of the Law No 2005–845, of 26

110 Art. 14(5) of Law 41/1999, 12.11.1999 on payment and security settlement systems (BOE No 272, 13.11.1999) subjects the enforcing of security rights to Art. 322 CCo.

July 2005, named *Loi de sauvegarde des entreprises*, which reforms Articles L. 610(1) to L. 680(7) of the Code de commerce. To this end, the law regulates three distinct proceedings, namely the rehabilitation proceedings (*procédure de sauvegarde*), applicable when the business has difficulties in meeting its financial commitments; the restructuring proceedings (*redressement judiciaire*), applicable in the case of suspension of payments; and the liquidation proceedings (*liquidation judiciaire*), applicable when the insolvent business is clearly not viable. The first two proceedings aim to favour the continuity of the business, maintain employment and reduce the company's liabilities, whereas the aim of the third one is the realisation of assets and the winding up of the insolvent business.

274. The opening of any of the above proceedings directly affects creditor rights, which are downgraded to the extent that priority is given to rescuing the business (*sauvegarde* and *redressement*) or will abate proportionately if there are insufficient assets to be in the estate (*liquidation*). The same applies to secured creditors who are also affected by the opening of any type of insolvency proceedings.

275. The opening of insolvency proceedings affects the effectiveness of the security rights in two ways. Firstly, the registration of security rights is barred after the opening of the insolvency proceeding; secondly, the security right is only effective provided it is lodged, verified and admitted in the insolvency proceeding.

276. Insolvency law forbids registration of privileges and security rights, movable and immovable, including leasing (Cass. Comm. 11 May 2010), created before proceedings began. The prohibition also applies to any registration of acts and decisions concerning the transfer or creation of rights over property, for which reason it is understood that the same applies to the *fiducie-sûreté* unless it has been notarized before the opening of the insolvency proceeding [Arts. L. 622(30)(1), L. 631(14) CComm.].[111]

277. It is not clear whether the rule applies to claims arising after the opening of the insolvency proceedings, although it seems obvious that security rights authorised by the insolvency judge in accordance with Article 622(7) CComm. are not subject to the above-mentioned prohibition, in so much as they require publicity.

278. The bar on registration implies that a security right is not effective during the insolvency proceedings, namely, the secured creditor does not have any priority rights over the proceeds of the sale of a debtor's assets.[112]

111 See F. Macorig-Venier, (2013) 310 *Répertoire Droit des Sociétés*.

112 Cass. Comm. 7.11.20016. See P. Le Corre, *Droit et pratique des procédures collectives*, 1895.

279. Once insolvency proceedings have commenced, the effectiveness of security rights in rem requires their holder or his representative complying with the obligation to declare his claim and security rights to the insolvency practitioner, declaring his intention of collecting his claim [Arts. L. 622(24) to L. 622(27): *sauvegarde*; L. 631(14): *redressement*; L. 641(3): *liquidation*]. To this end, the secured creditor must bring his claim before the insolvency court and thus, after the due process of verification and admission, a decision will be made either recognising the claim or not.

280. All existing creditors prior to the commencement of insolvency proceedings are obliged to declare. Exceptions are made for wages and maintenance claims, and insofar as liquidation is concerned, claims already included in previous rehabilitation or restructuring proceedings.

281. Subsequent claims not mentioned in Article L. 622(17)(I) CComm. should also be declared, which implies parity between previous creditors and non-privileged subsequent creditors.

282. The declaration must be made within two months of the commencement of proceedings, or, in the case of subsequent creditors, from the due date.

283. Creditors holding a security right that must be registered, or creditors connected to the debtor through a registered contract such as is the case of a financial lessor, a fiduciary or a seller in a sale contract including a retention of title clause, are notified personally of the insolvency proceedings and their obligation to declare their claims in the time period calculated from the date of notification.

284. The declaration of claims must indicate any security rights, excluding the right of possessory retention and the retention of title clause: in the absence of a declaration, the claim can only be admitted as an unsecured claim.

285. Non-declared claims do not become invalid, but do lose their effects during the insolvency proceedings, and so the creditor is excluded from the distribution of dividends and the right of retention granted by some security interests becomes ineffective. The sanction applies until the rehabilitation or restructuring plan has been implemented and the commitments laid down in it or decided by the court have been fulfilled [Art. L. 622(26)(2) CComm.].

286. Once insolvency proceedings have commenced, French insolvency law prohibits partial or total payment of any claims arising prior to the opening of the insolvency proceedings, as well as non-privileged claims borne after it. The prohibition, imposed on both the debtor and the IP, is both automatic and of a general scope, being applicable to all insolvency proceedings [Arts. L. 622(7)(I) CComm.: *sauvegarde*; L. 631(14) CComm.: *redressement*; L. 641(3) CComm.: *liquidation*] and affecting all liabilities, irrespective of their nature and whether they are secured or not. Similarly, it affects all payments, direct or indirect, which explains the suspension of any pactum commissorium after proceedings have commenced.

287. Despite its breadth, the rule on prohibiting payments is not absolute. On the one hand, legislation expressly authorises the offsetting where appropriate, after proceedings have commenced [Art. L. 622(7) CComm.], while on the other, specific privileged claims and security ownership devices can be paid once the secured claim matures (see Questions 10 and 11).

288. The opening of insolvency proceedings triggers a stay on all judicial and non-judicial actions as well as the suspension of ongoing proceedings with a view to ensuring the parity of treatment of creditors and determining all debtor's liabilities. Accordingly, Articles L. 622(21)) *sauvegarde*, L. 631(14) *redressement*, and L. 641(3)(1) *liquidation* require this effect to be applicable ex officio by the insolvency judge.[113]

289. The stay has a wide scope to the extent that, on the one hand, it covers any prior claims save maintenance payments and wage claims, as well as any claims subsequent to the opening of the insolvency proceeding save the cases laid down in Article 622(17)(1) privileging specific claims; the source, nature or type of claim, whether it is conditional or not, secured or unsecured, is irrelevant. On the other hand, the stay covers all declaratory proceedings, including the action for termination of the contractual relationship on the grounds of non-performance, and any enforcement proceedings. This entails the suspension of any ongoing foreclosure proceeding.

290. As regards security rights, they are in principle affected by the stay, although there are significant exceptions.

291. In the case of pledge, *nantissement* and mortgage, the stay is without exception during the rehabilitation and restructuring proceedings, thus the secured creditors are deprived of their right to enforce them by selling the encumbered assets and having priority over the proceeds of the sale. It is only where liquidation proceedings begin and the IP is inactive for three months that are the holders of these rights that have declared their claims entitled to request the realisation of the asset and to be paid in accordance with the order for payment established by Insolvency law [Art. L. 643(2) CComm.].

292. The pactum commissorium cannot be enforced either and is also stayed by the opening of insolvency proceedings [Art. L. 622(7)(I) CComm.], as well as the judicial transfer of the pledged or mortgaged asset by way of payment. Once liquidation has started, the law grants holders of possessory or non-possessory

113 Cass. Comm. 12.1.2010; Cass. Comm. 15.6.2011.

pledges who have declared their claims the right to seek judicial transfer of the encumbered asset by way of payment before the pledge is realised [Art. L.642(20)(1) CComm.]. This right is not granted to mortgagees, but creditors in antichresis do have it on the grounds that they are in possession of the asset.

293. In contrast to the aforementioned typical security rights in rem, the stay does not affect security rights based on retention or transfer of ownership by way of security. Sellers who have included a retention of title clause in the contract can claim as owners the encumbered asset subject to limitations that will be addressed later on, while the rights of a secured creditor in possession of the transferred assets remain unaltered. Only where the provider of collateral retains use and enjoyment of the assets and rights transferred by way of security, transfer of them by the fiduciary is prohibited during the periods of observation, approval and enforcement of a rehabilitation or restructuring plan in the framework of *sauvegarde* and *redressement* proceedings (Art. L. 622-23-1 CComm.).[114] The holder of a right of possessory retention also maintains his blocking power in insolvency proceedings, save in the case of fictive retention, which is not effective during the observation period and during the implementation of a rehabilitation or restructuring plan [Art. L. 622(7) I al. 2 CComm.]

2. Italy

294. In general terms, it can be said that the secured party is affected by a 'stay' on the enforcement of security if the debtor enters insolvency proceedings. However, the extent of the 'stay' differs according to the nature of the insolvency proceedings in question.

295. In this regard, it is appropriate to point out that Italian insolvency law had historically the purpose of regulating the failure of medium-large entrepreneurs. Small entrepreneurs and farmers remained subject to individual enforcement proceedings. It was only in 2012 that the Italian legislator introduced specific insolvency proceedings designed for debtors other than the medium-large entrepreneur (i.e. small entrepreneur, farmers, independent professionals and consumers) in order to allow them to settle their relationships with all creditors and to have, under certain conditions, a fresh start (see below, paras. 315–318).

296. At present, Italian insolvency law system provides for six different proceedings addressed to the medium-large entrepreneurs and for three different proceedings addressed to other types of debtors. With regard to the first group

[114] See O. Gout, (2012) 40 *La Semaine Juridique Notariale et Immobilière* 1339.

of insolvency proceedings, four of them are regulated by the so-called *Legge Fallimentare* (r.d. 16 March 1942 No 267 and subsequent amendments, L.Fall. hereafter).[115] They are: *Fallimento, Concordato preventivo, Accordi di ristrutturazione dei debiti* (hereafter referred to as '*Accordi di ristrutturazione*' for reasons of uniformity with Annex A of Regulation (EU) 2015/848 of the European Parliament and of the Council of 20 May 2015 on insolvency proceedings) and *Liquidazione coatta amministrativa.* A fifth proceeding, the *Amministrazione straordinaria delle grandi imprese in stato di insolvenza* (hereafter referred to as '*Amministrazione straordinaria*' for the same reasons as above) was introduced by L. 3 April 1979 No 95[116] and subsequently radically reformed by d.lgs. 8 July 1999 No 270.[117] A sixth and final proceeding, a special variant of the *Amministrazione straordinaria*, was added to the catalogue by d.l. 23 December 2003 No 347, converted into L. 18 February 2004 No 39.[118] These insolvency proceedings can be classified as follows: liquidation proceedings designed to satisfy the creditors only (*Fallimento*; *Liquidazione coatta amministrativa*); insolvency proceedings designed to combine the satisfaction of creditors with the rescue of the firm (*Amministrazione straordinaria*); and insolvency proceedings designed to avoid bankruptcy through a negotiated settlement of the financial difficulties (*Concordato preventivo*; *Accordi di ristrutturazione*).

297. The second group of insolvency proceedings is regulated by L. 27 January 2012 No 3, and includes a liquidation procedure and two procedures to settle the crisis. These three proceedings respectively are: *Liquidazione del patrimonio* (hereafter referred to as *Liquidazione dei beni* for reasons of uniformity with the cited Annex A) and *Procedura di composizione della crisi da sovraindebitamento*, which is actually divided into *Accordo di composizione della crisi* and *Piano del consumatore* (hereafter referred to as *Procedure di composizione della crisi da sovraindebitamento* (*Accordo* o *Piano*) in accordance with the above mentioned Annex A).

298. All these insolvency proceedings, although different from each other, have some common features: they aim to encompass all the debtor's assets; moreover, they aim to encompass all creditors of the debtor at the time of opening of the proceedings and at ensuring, in principle, equal treatment among them. This means that individual enforcement proceedings are by law replaced by collective forms of enforcement the basic objective of which is to distribute the debtor's assets among all his creditors.[119]

---

115 <www.normattiva.it> accessed 26 May 2016.
116 *Ibid.*
117 *Ibid.*
118 *Ibid.*
119 G. Campobasso, *Diritto commerciale*, vol. III, 336.

299. Having made this general introduction, it is appropriate to examine the relevant rules on the issue in question with respect to each Italian insolvency procedure.

2.1. Fallimento *(bankruptcy)*

300. *Fallimento* is a judicial proceeding, reserved for the medium-large entrepreneur, excluding public bodies (see Art 1 L.Fall. laying down three co-existing quantitative prerequisites, which could be updated by means of a decree), which aims to pay those who are creditors at the time of its opening by liquidating the debtor's assets and distributing the proceeds among them, according to the principle of pari passu.

301. The opening of *Fallimento* affects, first of all, the procedural rules to realise the claims. Individual enforcement proceedings on the debtor's assets are indeed replaced by the law with bankruptcy's collective enforcement procedure, in which creditors must find satisfaction. In this respect L.Fall. lays down the following general principles:

(a) *Fallimento* gives creditors the right to participate in the distribution of the debtor's assets. Each claim, as well as each right in person and each right in rem, on movable or immovable assets, has to be verified within the proceedings (Art 52 L.Fall.); and
(b) unless otherwise provided by law, from the time of the opening of *Fallimento*, no individual enforcement proceedings or individual precautionary proceedings can be started or pursued on the bankruptcy estate, even for claims that arise during the insolvency proceedings (Art 51 L.Fall.). If such individual enforcement proceedings have been started by a creditor before the time of the opening of *Fallimento*, the IP can take the place of the applicant creditor in order to maximise the bankruptcy assets; otherwise, on application of the IP, the court declares that the individual enforcement proceedings may not be pursued (Art 107.6 L.Fall.).[120]

302. The ban on individual enforcement proceedings does not imply the dismissal of such proceedings, but rather their statutory conversion into bankruptcy's unitary enforcement procedure essentially managed by the IP.[121] The rationale is not only to ensure equal treatment among creditors, but also to enable the IP

120 C. Esposito, sub Art 51 in G. Lo Cascio (ed.), *Codice commentato del fallimento*, 578–579.
121 R. Rosapepe, 'Effetti nei confronti dei creditori' in V. Buonocore and A. Bassi (eds.), *Trattato di diritto fallimentare*, 272.

to choose the time and manner of the realisation of the debtor's assets in the interest of all the bankruptcy creditors for the maximisation of the bankruptcy assets, if necessary by sacrificing the interests of the secured creditors in an immediate realisation of the collateral.[122]

303. The rationale of the ban, laid down in Article 51 L.Fall., explains its exceptions too. As already mentioned, in certain cases individual enforcement proceedings are exceptionally allowed. This is to give certain secured creditors the benefit of immediate realisation of the assets to which their preferential rights are related, without prejudice to the rules governing the lodging, verification and admission of their claims against the bankruptcy estate and the priority order of distribution of proceeds from the realisation of assets in question. These exceptions mainly concern the following categories of creditors:

(a) creditors secured by a pledge or special privilege on movable assets with a retention right (Arts 2756, 2761 Civil Code). After their priority claims against the bankruptcy estate have been lodged, they can be judicially authorised to enforce their security through the sale of the encumbered assets within the time and according to the procedures that the court has established. The court, however, may refuse authorisation if this would conflict with the interests of bankruptcy proceedings. In this case, however, the court authorises the IP to satisfy the claim whether by realising the assets or otherwise. In any event, the proceeds of the sale must be distributed according to the priority order stated by law[123] (Art 53 L.Fall.);[124]
(b) banks may start or pursue individual enforcement proceedings on immovable assets mortgaged to secure particular types of bank financing. However, the IP has the power to intervene in the enforcement proceedings and the proceeds exceeding the amount due to the bank are part of the insolvency estate (Art 41.2, 42.4 and 44.5 Unified Banking Code).[125] In any case, the proceeds of enforcement cannot be retained by the bank when there are other bankruptcy creditors of a superior rank.[126]

304. Beyond these exceptions, creditors may not start or pursue individual enforcement proceedings against the bankruptcy estate, even for the individual

---

122 L. Guglielmucci, *Diritto fallimentare*, 184–185.

123 Cass. civ. 18.12.2006 no 27044, [2007] *F* 391.

124 For a derogation from Art 53 L.Fall. see Art 4 d.lgs. 21.5.2004 No 170 <www.normattiva.it> accessed 26 May 2016, which has implemented Directive 2002/47/EC on the financial collateral arrangement extending the power of self-protection of the pledgee also in case of opening of a reorganisation or a liquidation proceedings. On the issue see T. Di Marcello, (2011) II *BBTC* 528 et seq.

125 D.lgs. 1.9.1993 No 385 <www.normattiva.it> accessed 26 May 2016.

126 App. Torino 5.9.2007, [2008] *F* 186.

enforcement of security rights. However, this does not mean that the collateral cannot be realised. Rather, it means that this realisation is no longer the responsibility of the secured party. Indeed, from the time of the opening of *Fallimento*, the realisation of the bankruptcy estate, then also of the collateral, is the responsibility of the IP who proceeds according to the time frame and the procedures laid down by him in the liquidation programme. The fact remains that once the collateral is realised, sooner or later, the IP must distribute to the secured creditors the proceeds from this realisation up to the amount of the secured claims, according to the priority order stated by law (Arts 54, 55, 111, 111-*quater* L.Fall.).

2.2. Liquidazione coatta amministrativa *(compulsory administrative liquidation)*

305. *Liquidazione coatta amministrativa* is an administrative proceeding which applies to special categories of company (determined by law) with a view to excluding them from the economic system, including for reasons other than insolvency. In fact, insolvency is not necessarily required.

306. L.Fall. regulates this proceeding providing a general scheme of rules (Art 194 et seq. L.Fall.) which normally apply only if the other specific laws in this area do not provide otherwise. Some rules laid down by L.Fall. are, however, mandatory and, among these is Article 201. This transposes the effect of *Fallimento* in respect of creditors (Arts 51–63 L.Fall.) including the ban on individual preservation measures and the ban of individual enforcement proceedings as well as the exceptions to these bans.

2.3. Amministrazione straordinaria *(extraordinary administration)*

307. *Amministrazione straordinaria* is a proceeding which is both administrative and judicial. It is designed with the goal of combining the satisfaction of creditors with the rescue of the business complex of a large insolvent company. *Amministrazione straordinaria* is actually governed by two different sets of rules and, consequently, can be implemented according to two different proceedings: *Prodibis* proceedings, introduced in 1999 by d.lgs. 270/1999, and *Marzano* proceedings, introduced in 2003 by d.l. 347/2003 in order to meet the specific needs resulting from the insolvency of the larger companies.

308. For the specific purpose intended by this question, in *Prodibis* proceedings a distinction must be drawn between the opening of the preliminary stage of ascertaining the insolvency requirement, the proceedings that follow this decision and the opening of *Amministrazione straordinaria* proper. During the preliminary stage, individual enforcement proceedings against the debtor's assets are still possible. By way of contrast, however, with the decision which declares the insolvency, individual preservation measures or individual enforcement proceedings against the debtor's assets cannot be started or pursued by previous creditors. Such proceedings are declared null and void (Art 18 d.lgs. 270/1999).[127] Furthermore, from the time of the opening of *Amministrazione straordinaria* proper this ban becomes more absolute as it applies to all such proceedings including proceedings for which provision has been made in a separate statute (Art 48 d.lgs. 270/1999). This rule has its rationale in the function of *Amministrazione straordinaria* which is aimed at maintaining the unity of the business complex.[128]

309. In *Marzano* proceedings there is no preliminary stage. Consequently, the ban laid down by Article 48 d.lgs. 270/1999 starts immediately from the time of the opening of the *Amministrazione straordinaria* (Art 2.2-*bis* d.l. 347/2003).

2.4. Concordato preventivo *(preventive settlement)*

310. *Concordato preventivo* is a judicial proceeding that allows an entrepreneur in financial distress (*state of crisis*) to avoid bankruptcy by way of a negotiated settlement of its distress (Art 160 et seq. L.Fall.).

311. From the publication of the application of *Concordato* in the Register of Firms and until the approval decision becomes definitive, a 'stay' prevents all previous creditors irrespective of their title and cause from starting or pursuing individual enforcement proceedings or individual preservation measures on the debtor's assets, under the penalty of nullity (Art 168 L.Fall.).

312. This 'stay' provides the debtor with a so-called 'protective umbrella' necessary to prevent opportunistic behaviour that could hinder the agreed settlement of the crisis,[129] in addition to ensuring the integrity of the assets intended for execution of the *Concordato* and safeguarding the principle of pari passu distribution of available assets.[130]

---

127 Art 18 d.lgs. 270/1999 transposes Art 168 L.Fall.

128 G. Campobasso, *Diritto commerciale*, vol. III, 458.

129 L. Guglielmucci, *Diritto fallimentare*, 331.

130 F. Filocamo, sub Art 168 in M. Ferro (ed.), *La legge fallimentare*, 905.

2.5. Accordi di ristrutturazione *(restructuring agreements)*

313. *Accordi di ristrutturazione* are out-of-court agreements between the debtor (merchant or even farmer)[131] and his creditors representing at least 60% of the total debts aimed at the restructuring of those debts (Art 182-*bis* of L.Fall.). Nevertheless, such agreements may be deemed to be insolvency proceedings because, once they are approved by a court, they also produce effects against 'outsider' creditors, i.e. against creditors who have not concluded that agreement.[132] Recently, this regime was supplemented by Article 182-*septies* of L.Fall., which is indexed as '*Accordi di ristrutturazione con intermediari finanziari e convenzione di moratoria*' (Restructuring agreements with financial intermediaries and a moratorium agreement). In particular, where a firm owes debts to banks and other financial intermediaries to the extent of at least 50% of its total debts, Article 182-*septies* of L.Fall. lays down that the '*accordo di ristrutturazione*' may provide many classes of creditors; creditors with the same or similar types of claims and interests may be put in the same class; and those creditors who, within a specific class, have voted against the agreement may be crammed down, provided that all the creditors have been thoroughly informed of the content of the agreement and that the banks or other financial intermediaries, having voted in favour of the agreement, represent at least 75% of the claims in that class. Finally, the same Article 182-*septies* of L.Fall. regulates the '*Convenzione di moratoria*' (moratorium agreement). This is an agreement between the debtor and his creditors who are banks and financial intermediaries and represent a qualified majority of the claims (75%) of the same class/classes, with the purpose of regulating the effects of the crisis through a temporary moratorium on the claims. Although this is an agreement concluded between private parties, it also binds 'outsider' creditors on condition that the agreement is certified by a qualified professional and communicated to 'outsider' creditors. However, Article 182-*septies*.6 L.Fall. lays down that 'outsider' creditors may challenge the agreement before a court, in order to prevent that agreement from producing effects against them.

314. Among these effects is that of the 'stay' which, in these proceedings, aims to provide the debtor with a limited 'protective umbrella' necessary to prevent opportunistic behaviour that might hinder the conclusion of the agreements; implementation of such agreements and ultimately the goal of debt restructuring.[133] Specifically, Article 182-*bis*.3 L.Fall. states that, for 60 days

---

131 See Art 23.43 d.l. 6.07.2011 No 98 enacted into L.15.07.2011 No 111 <www.normattiva.it> accessed 26 May 2016.

132 E. Frascaroli Santi, *Gli accordi di ristrutturazione dei debiti*, 81 et seq.

133 G. Fauceglia, sub Art 182, in G. Lo Cascio (ed.), *Codice commentato del fallimento*, 2164.

starting from the date of publication in the Register of Firms of the agreements filed in court for approval, all previous creditors of whatever type cannot start or pursue individual enforcement proceedings or individual preservation measures on the debtor's assets. As already mentioned, this 'stay' may also cover the negotiation phase, before the formalisation of the agreements. To this end, the debtor has to file an application to the court and publish it in the Register of Firms. From this date, the provisional effects of the 'stay' continue until its confirmation by the court (Art 182-*bis*.6-7-8 L.Fall.).

2.6. Liquidazione dei beni *(liquidation of assets)*

315. In the new system of insolvency proceedings reserved for debtors other than the entrepreneurs capable of insolvency proceedings, *Liquidazione dei beni* performs the function which, in the traditional system, is covered by *Fallimento*. Indeed, *Liquidazione dei beni* is a judicial proceeding which aims to pay those who are creditors at the time of its opening by liquidating the debtor's assets and distributing the proceeds among them, according to the principle of pari passu (Art 14-*ter* et seq. L. 3/2012).

316. The opening of *Liquidazione dei beni* stops any race between creditors to take control of the debtor's assets. From this moment and until the closure of the insolvency proceedings, a 'stay' prevents all previous creditors from starting or pursuing individual enforcement proceedings or individual preservation measures on the assets subject to liquidation, under penalty of nullity (Art 14-*quinques*.2 letter b L. 3/2012).[134] As seen in relation to *Fallimento*, this does not mean that the collateral cannot be realised. It means, rather, that the realisation of the assets subject to liquidation, including collateralised assets, is the responsibility of the IP who proceeds according to the liquidation programme (Art 14-*novies* L. 3/2012).

2.7. Procedure di composizione della crisi da sovraindebitamento (accordo o piano) *[procedures for composition of crisis from over-indebtedness (settlement or plan)]*

317. In the new system of insolvency proceedings reserved for debtors other than the medium-large merchant, *Procedure di composizione della crisi da sovraindebitamento* through *Accordo* are judicial proceedings comparable to the proceedings of *Concordato preventivo* and *Accordi di ristrutturazione*. Indeed,

---

[134] Also creditors with a subsequent cause or title cannot proceed executively on the insolvency estate (Art 14-*duodecies*.1 L. 3/2012).

the proceedings in question aim to achieve a settlement of the crisis from over-indebtedness agreed between the debtor and creditors. To this end, proceedings provide the former with a 'protective umbrella' from the date of publicity of the decision to proceed to an *Accordo* until the approval decision becomes definitive. In this period, a 'stay' prevents all previous creditors by title and cause from starting or pursuing individual enforcement proceedings or individual preservation measures on the debtor's assets, under the penalty of nullity (Art 10.2 letter c L. 3/2012).[135]

318. As an alternative to the proposal of *Accordo*, a 'no-fault' consumer debtor can present a *Piano*. The proceeding is very similar to that of *Accordo* and is governed, to a large extent, by the same rules. The substantial difference is the following: the *Piano* proposal is addressed by the debtor to the court which is the only one that must approve it, without the need for approval by creditors. For the intended purpose of the question, it must also be stressed that the decision to proceed to a *Piano* does not bring about a generalised ban on individual enforcement proceedings. In this connection, Article 12-*bis*.2 L. 3/2012 allows the judge to order the suspension of proceedings right down to the moment when approval becomes definitive, but only of the specific individual enforcement proceedings pursuance of which can jeopardise the feasibility of the plan. From the date of the approval decision, a 'stay' prevents all creditors of whatever type by title and cause from starting or pursuing individual enforcement proceedings or individual preservation measures on the debtor's assets (Art 12-*ter*.1 L. 3/2012).[136]

3. Spain

319. All the debtor's liabilities and assets have to be established once insolvency proceedings have been opened (Arts. 49 and 76 LC). The debtor's creditors include all secured creditors including cases where the security has been provided not by the debtor itself, but by a third party. Nevertheless, the creditor is entitled to enforce its security since the asset in question is not affected by the insolvency procedure as it is owned by a third party; if the latter pays, he becomes an insolvency creditor. The debtor may be in possession of an asset that secures another debtor's liability; this asset cannot be included within the debtor's estate if the latter is not the owner, and so the secured creditor may proceed to realise

135 Moreover, from the approval decision a 'stay' prevents creditors with a subsequent cause or title from starting or pursuing individual enforcement proceedings on the assets that are the object of the *Accordo* (Art 12.3 L. 3/2012).

136 Moreover, from the approval decision a 'stay' prevents creditors with a subsequent cause or title from starting or pursuing individual enforcement proceedings on the assets that are the object of the *Piano* (Art 12-*ter*.2 L. 3/2012).

his claim over the asset separately [Art. 56(4) LC]. In contrast, cases in which the debtor has provided security but is not the debtor in the secured claim, meaning that the asset is owned by the debtor, are treated differently; the asset must be included in his estate and is thus affected by the opening of insolvency proceedings.

320. The opening of insolvency proceedings implies a stay on all judicial and non-judicial enforcement proceedings over the debtor's assets, including the suspension of current enforcement proceedings (Art. 55 LC). However, section 4 of this provision omits security rights from this stay, and so the general rule is that creditors who are granted a security right in rem have the right to separate realisation even in the event of insolvency proceedings.

321. Nevertheless, Spanish insolvency legislation seeks to strike a balance between conflicting interests, namely those of secured creditors in enforcing their rights and those of other creditors in achieving the insolvency proceedings' main objectives, i.e. either restructuring of the enterprise in difficulty or liquidation. To this end, Article 56 LC provides for a stay or suspension of enforcement proceedings arising from security rights over assets necessary for the running of debtor's enterprise. It must be highlighted at this point that Articles 5bis and 235 LC, which provide for pre-insolvency proceedings to conclude a refinancing or restructuring plan, moves this stay or suspension forward to the time at which the debtor informs the court where the insolvency proceedings are to be opened that he intends to conclude such an agreement. The conditions required for stays in this framework are addressed in Question 14.

322. Once a secured claim has matured, therefore, the creditor is not allowed to initiate judicial or non-judicial proceedings to enforce his security right over assets necessary for the running of the business in difficulties. Furthermore, Article 56(1) LC does not only refer to enforcement, but includes other actions intended to remove these assets from the debtor's estate on the grounds of in rem or quasi-in rem security, namely action to terminate either a hire-purchase or related financing agreement that includes a retention of title clause registered in the Personal Property Registry [Art. 250(1)(11) LEC], action to terminate the sale of immovable assets that includes a condition subsequent to non-payment of the deferred price registered in the Land Registry [Art. 1504 CC], and action to recover the leased asset in the framework of financial leasing, provided that the contract has been registered in the Personal Property Registry or recorded in a public document (First Additional Disposition LVPBM).

323. The key concept is 'assets necessary for the running of the debtor's enterprise', which is a question of fact and is thus determined by the insolvency court [Art. 56(5) LC]. The only legal remark on this concept is laid down in Article 56(1) LC: 'In particular, company shares intended exclusively for the holding of assets and liabilities necessary for their funding provided that the enforcement of the security right created over them does not give rise to cause for the termination or modification of the contractual relationships that enable the debtor to maintain the operation of the asset, are not considered necessary for the running of the activity'. In the case of a stay granted in relation to a pre-insolvency refinancing agreement, the debtor shall indicate which enforcement proceedings are pending at that time over assets necessary for his enterprise. Should his characterisation be disputed, the final decision is taken by the court where the insolvency proceeding are to be opened if the negotiations failed.[137]

324. Should the insolvency court consider that a particular asset is necessary for the running of the debtor's enterprise, security cannot be realised: (1) until there is some change of circumstance that triggers a change in the characterisation of the asset; (2) until a restructuring plan that is not binding on the secured creditor is achieved; or (3) until a year has passed since the opening of the insolvency proceedings and the liquidation phase has still not been opened [Art. 56(1) LC]. The stay also applies when creditors with a security over an asset that is necessary for the running of the debtor's enterprise have already initiated enforcement proceedings at the time the insolvency proceedings are opened, i.e. suspension is mandatory even when the forced sale of the asset has reached the point at which the auction is about to be announced; in these circumstances, resumption is only possible once a copy of the insolvency court's decision confirming that the asset at stake is not necessary for the debtor's enterprise has been provided in the relevant proceedings, or any of the other conditions are met.

325. It must also be highlighted that the right of separate realisation can only be enforced once the insolvency court decides whether the asset is necessary for the running of the debtor's enterprise (see further Question 10). With a view to ensuring that the provisions of the stay are fulfilled, the principle of *vis attractiva concursus* comes into play and all enforcement proceedings have to be brought before the insolvency court [Arts. 8 and 57(1) LC].

326. However, there are some exceptions to the general rule that the debtor's estate comprises all the debtor's assets, namely secured claims over ships and aircraft [Art. 76(3) LC]. Following the 1993 Convention on maritime liens and mortgages, maritime creditors are not affected by the opening of insolvency proceedings over their debtors and can proceed to the forced sale of the ship regardless of the proceedings, i.e. enforcement proceeds before the competent authority according to the relevant legislation, but not in the insolvency court. Any money that remains after payment must be included in the debtor's estate. There is, however, one proviso, which is that enforcement must begin within a year starting from the date on which the insolvency proceedings are opened;

137 See Art. 5bis.4 LC as amended by Law 9/2015 of 25 May (BOE No 125, 26.5.2015).

otherwise, it cannot begin and maritime claims will be ranked in accordance with LC. The same applies to security rights over aircraft; more specifically, to the rights securing these claims laid down by Article 133 LNA.[138]

327. Likewise, Articles 13 and 14 of Law 41/1999 as amended by Law 7/2011 and 12bis LMV establish the right of separate realisation over financial instruments covered by these laws in the event of the opening of insolvency proceedings over a debtor participating in a payment and clearance system or in an official securities market, or over the entity in charge of the system or registry of securities.

328. Following the Commission Recommendation on a new approach to business failure and insolvency,[139] Spanish insolvency law has been amended to make possible a second chance (fresh start) for natural persons. In addition to further requirements to ensure that the debtor natural person is in good faith, the granting of a debt discharge is made dependent on him having paid in full all claims against the estate, the privileged claims and, in case he had not tried to reach an out-of-court restructuring plan, at least 25% of the ordinary claims.[140] Alternatively, he may agree on a five-year payment plan provided that he had complied with the cooperation duties established in Article 42 LC, another discharge had not been granted in the last 10 years and he had not rejected a suitable job offer in a four-year period before the opening of the insolvency proceedings.[141] In this alternative case, debt discharge comprises all ordinary and subordinate claims pending at the time of concluding the proceedings as well as the part of the secured claim included in Article 90(1) LC not paid after the realisation of the security right.

Question 10: Can the secured party apply to have any stay lifted?

1. France

329. There are several exceptions to a stay of security rights' enforcement deriving from the opening of insolvency proceedings.

330. Due to their nature, some privileged claims grant their holders a right to be paid once their claim is due, such as wages claims for the last two months [Art. L. 625(8) CComm.], maintenance claims [Art. L. 622(7)(I) CComm.] and claims against the estate or *privilèges de la procédure* [Art. L. 622(17)(1) CComm.].

---

138 *Ley 48/1960, de 21 de julio, de Navegación Aérea* (BOE No 176, 23.7.1960)

139 COM(2014) 1500 final.

140 Art. 178bis(3)(4) LC as amended by Royal Decree-Law 1/2015, 27.2.2015 (BOE No 51, 28.2.2015).

141 Art. 178bis(3)(5) LC.

331. During the observation period of the *sauvegarde* proceedings, the insolvency judge can authorise payment of a debtor's obligations that arose prior to the commencement of proceedings in order to recover assets necessary for the running of the debtor's enterprise [Art. L. 622(7)(II) CComm.]. The same applies to the *redressement* proceedings as laid down by Article L. 631(14) CComm. entitling the IP to assume the debtor's position, as well as to liquidation proceedings where the recovery of the asset is only authorised should its subsequent sale provide for a sum higher than the now authorised payment of the secured claim [Art. L. 641(3) al. 2 CComm.]. There are two conditions governing the authorisation of payment, which are set out in the paragraphs that follow.

332. Firstly, the recovery of the said assets must be in line with the relevant insolvency proceeding's objectives, either because they are necessary for the running of a debtor's enterprise, in the case of *sauvegarde* or *redressement* proceedings, or because their sale contributes to the discharge of liabilities, i.e. in the case of liquidation proceedings.

333. Secondly, the security right must also grant the secured creditor an exclusive right over the asset, consisting of either a right of effective retention such as the one attributed to a possessory pledgee or a simple retainer, or a right of limited ownership, such as the one provided by a possessory *fiducie-sûreté* whereby the asset is transferred to the secured creditor. Furthermore, creditors secured by a retention of title clause over the encumbered assets and financial lessors can be paid with the aim of preventing them from enforcing their right to terminate the contract in the event of non-payment, and thereby to enable recovery of an asset that is necessary for the debtor's enterprise [Arts. L. 624(16), L. 631(18), L. 641(14) CComm.].

334. Payment to creditors who have a right of possessory retention aims to neutralise their blocking power based on the material possession of the asset and can be done in each type of insolvency proceeding. The only exception is that of the holders of a right based on a fictive possession of the asset that are not paid in advance during the observation period and the enforcement of a rehabilitation or restructuring plan [Arts. L. 622(7)(I) and L. 631(1) CComm.]. But the payment of the right of retention, including that of fictive retention, is granted in the case of transfer of activity or the total business.[142]

335. The satisfaction of creditors in possession of the secured assets, secured by a transfer of ownership, is not feasible during the liquidation proceedings.

336. Creditors who, by way of their security interests, are the owners of movable assets in possession of the debtor at the opening of the insolvency proceeding

142 See L. Aynès, (2009) 9 I *La Semaine Juridique. Édition Générale*, 119.

can either claim that they are the owners of the asset and thus have the right to recover it, providing proof of their right (revendication action); or apply directly for them to be transferred without providing proof of their right provided that the contract had been registered before the opening of the insolvency proceeding, as laid down by Articles L. 624(9) to 624(18) CComm., applicable to all three proceedings (restitution action). In both cases, the recovery of assets amounts to satisfaction of the secured claim so that should the asset's value exceed the claim, the difference must be paid to the estate.

337. The rule benefits three types of creditors: parties to a contract including a retention of title clause provided that the assets actually exist and the clause has been agreed upon in writing at the time the assets were transferred to the debtor [Art. L. 624(16)(2) CComm.]; fiduciary creditors, when it has been agreed that movable assets transferred by way of security remain in the debtor's possession [Art. L. 624(16)(1) CComm.]; the financial lessor, who may apply for restitution first to the IP, and secondly to the insolvency court if the IP has not given permission; in accordance with Article L. 313(10) of the *Code monetaire et financiere*, the financial lessor's right must be registered before the commencement of insolvency proceedings; otherwise, the right would not be effective against third parties and it is not possible to claim for restitution in respect of the leased asset.

338. In general, one may say that 'owners' are not affected by the stay imposed by the opening of the insolvency proceedings, although the enforcement of their recovery rights is subject to significant limitations.

339. A claim for revendication must be brought within three months running from the opening of the insolvency proceedings. The IP can agree to it and thereby deliver the asset to the secured creditor. If the IP opposes the action, the claim must be brought before the insolvency judge within one additional month [Art. L. 624(17) CComm.]. If the action is not brought in accordance with the aforementioned conditions, the IP may sell the 'unclaimed' asset according to the established channels for the realisation of assets, with the creditor having no preferential right in the distribution of the proceeds.[143]

2. Italy

340. Generally speaking, the secured party cannot apply to have the 'stay' lifted until the date of the closure of the proceedings or, if different, until the final date of the 'stay', save in cases where the insolvency proceedings have been

---

143 Cass. Comm. 15.10.2013.

annulled. That is the situation both where the 'stay' implies a real 'moratorium' on the enforcement of security and also where the 'stay' implies rather a statutory change in competence in relation to who may realise the encumbered assets.

341. In the latter case, however, individual enforcement proceedings are exceptionally allowed by law in order to give to certain secured creditors the benefit of immediate realisation of the assets to which their preferential rights are related – see answer to Question 9. Nevertheless, the case concerning creditors secured by pledge or special privilege on movable assets with a retention right (Arts 2756, 2761 Civil Code) merits further attention. Article 53 L.Fall. establishes that the secured party may apply to the court to regain competence in relation to the realisation of collateral. Normally, the judge grants the secured party authorisation to sell the encumbered assets when this does not conflict with the interests of the insolvency proceedings. Otherwise, the judge may refuse authorisation but he must also authorise the IP either to sell the secured assets and pay the secured creditor out of the sale proceeds or otherwise to satisfy the claim of the secured creditor.[144]

3. Spain

342. As stated in Question 9, only security rights over assets necessary for the running of the debtor's enterprise are affected by stays imposed by Article 55(1) LC. Nevertheless, with the exception of security rights over ships, aircraft and specific financial instruments, the secured party has to apply for a judicial decision stating that enforcement can begin or proceed if the asset is not classified as being necessary for the debtor's enterprise. The competent authority is the insolvency court before which enforcement proceedings are to be brought, because of the application of the principle of *vis attractiva concursus* [Arts. 8 and 57(1) LC]. The decision can only be challenged in the same court without prejudice to further discussion in a specific insolvency action or in any immediate appeal.

343. In the course of insolvency proceedings assets may prove not to be necessary for the debtor's enterprise, in which case the secured party may apply for the stay to be lifted. The same applies when a restructuring plan that is not binding on the secured creditor in question is concluded [Arts. 123(1) and 134(2) LC]; should it be binding, the fate of the security right will depend on the restructuring plan's provisions (Art. 136 LC). In any case, the stay is lifted when the liquidation

---

144 For a derogation from Art 53 L.Fall. relating to the financial collateral arrangement in the form of pledge see above fn. 124.

phase begins or if a year from the opening of the insolvency proceedings elapses without the liquidation phase beginning. The latter entitles the creditor to lift the stay and enforce his security right in the insolvency court; should enforcement not begin before liquidation, the secured creditor can no longer enforce his right individually, but only collectively [Art. 57(3) LC]. Whether enforcement is individual or collective, secured creditors are paid from the sale of the secured asset up to the secured amount [Art. 155(1) LC].

344. Noteworthy is that a secured party can only initiate enforcement proceedings once the requirements laid down in the relevant legislation are fulfilled, in particular the maturing of the secured obligation. Accordingly, the stay referred to above is in principle not relevant until then because beginning insolvency proceedings does not cause the claims to mature; this only happens when the liquidation phase begins (Art. 146 LC). Opening insolvency proceedings does not prevent interest accruing on the amounts owing either, although these will only be payable within the limits of the secured claim [Art. 59(1) LC].

Question 11: Under what circumstances can the stay be lifted?

1. France

345. See the answer given to Question 10.

2. Italy

346. As a rule the secured party cannot apply to have the 'stay' lifted, both in the case where the 'stay' implies a real 'moratorium' on the enforcement of security and in the case where the 'stay' implies rather a statutory change in competence in relation to who may realise the encumbered assets. In the latter case, however, individual enforcement proceedings are exceptionally allowed by law to provide certain secured creditors with the benefit of immediate realisation of the assets to which their preferential rights are related. Cases and circumstances in which this can occur have been briefly illustrated in the answers to Questions 9 and 10, to which the reader is referred.

347. As to the present question it is appropriate to add the following: As far as *Fallimento* proceedings are concerned, Article 104-*ter*.7 states that the IP, with the approval of the creditors' committee, may waive his right to liquidate certain assets, where a liquidation of the assets appears manifestly not to be convenient. In this case, the IP shall inform the creditors who, as an exception to the ban by

Article 51 L.Fall., may start enforcement or preservation measures in relation to these assets.

3. Spain

348. The circumstances under which a stay can be lifted are set out in Question 10, namely the secured asset is not or is no longer necessary for the debtor's enterprise; the secured creditor is not bound by a restructuring plan, and the liquidation phase has still not begun a year after the opening of the insolvency proceedings.

349. During the one-year period established by Article 56 LC for the temporary stay of the secured creditors' right to separate satisfaction or the stay granted before the opening of the insolvency proceedings in order to reach a refinancing agreement, the IP has the option to pay the amount due to secured creditors that are affected by the stay, without the assets subject to the security being realised [Art. 155(2) LC], i.e. by this means ensuring that the asset in question remains at the disposal of the proceedings and ensuring achievement of its objectives. Once the secured creditor has been notified that this option will be exercised, the IP has to pay off the debt immediately, either by paying it in full or by paying all due instalments and accrued interest and committing himself to pay the remaining instalments. From then on these are classified as claims against the estate up to the secured amount, which must be calculated in accordance with Article 94 LC. If the IP does not fulfil the obligation to pay, any secured assets will be enforced immediately, i.e. without waiting either for the liquidation phase to begin or for a year to elapse in which it does not begin.

Question 12: In insolvency proceedings, can an insolvency practitioner (IP) 'enforce' the security, i.e. realise the secured assets, without the consent of the secured party?

1. France

350. The insolvency practitioner can enforce the security over the encumbered assets with or without the consent of secured creditors insofar as the IP does it in the interests of the debtor in difficulties, and in particular with a view to carrying out the plan approved in the insolvency proceedings.

351. The observation periods in *sauvegarde* and *redressement* proceedings are characterised by the fact that the debtor's enterprise is still running. To this end, the debtor may sell assets with the insolvency judge's authorisation. When these assets are encumbered by a security right such as a mortgage, pledge over tangibles, intangibles or real immovable, the value of the encumbered assets' sale corresponding to the secured claim is deposited at the Bank for Official Deposits (*Caisse des dépôts et consignations*) in the form of a restrictive fund [Art. L. 622(8) CComm.]. Creditors are not reimbursed immediately, nor can they exercise their right over the said fund until the observation period is over, and always following the established order of payment depending on the type of insolvency proceeding. This order is the same in *sauvegarde* and *redressement* proceedings but different in the liquidation proceeding (see Question 16). The insolvency judge may exceptionally authorise the payment of a claim prior to the termination of the observation period in advance of maturity provided that the secured creditor presents a bank guarantee. The judge may also impose on a secured creditor the substitution of his collateral for another security right.

352. Once the observation period is over, *sauvegarde* and *redressement* proceedings result in the approval and implementation of a plan that seeks to keep the business running, to restructure it and to pay debts and other liabilities. If implementation of a restructuring plan requires the sale of assets encumbered by a special privilege or a security right in rem, the sale proceeds representing the secured claim are set aside for satisfaction of the claim, as is the case with sales that take place during the observation period. However, payment is not immediate: the money is deposited in the Bank for Official Deposits while verification and admission of liabilities proceeds and the order of creditors is determined.[145] The IP responsible for the plan's implementation divides the proceeds giving priority to unpaid 'super-privileged' wage claims and general privileges; makes the payments and then cancels the registration of the security rights. If, as a consequence of this rule, a secured creditor receives early payment, Article L. 626(22) CComm. entitles the IP to reduce the total to be received by

145 According to Article L. 626–22 CComm.: 'In the event of a sale of an asset charged with a special privilege, a pledge of corporeal movables, a pledge of incorporeal movables or a hypothec, the portion of the proceeds corresponding to the claims secured by these guarantees will be placed on a deposit account with the Caisse des Dépôts et Consignations and the creditors secured by these guarantees or by a general lien shall be paid out of the proceeds after payment of those claims secured by the lien provided for in Articles L. 3253-2 to L. 3253-4, L. 742-6 and L. 7313-8 of the Labour Code. They shall receive dividends to fall due pursuant to the plan, reduced according to the advance payment, following their order of priority. If an asset is charged with a special privilege, a pledge of corporeal movables, a pledge of incorporeal movables or a hypothec, another guarantee may be substituted for the said asset, where necessary, if it grants equivalent benefits. In the absence of agreement, the court may order this substitution.' The English version of the Commercial Code as of 1 July 2013 has been translated by M. Fillastre, A. Kyeremeh and M. Watchorn, and revised by Juriscope. Expert committee: J. Ball, M. Séjean and A. Deysine, September 2014 <http://www.legifrance.gouv.fr/Traductions/en-English/Legifrance-translations> accessed 26 May 2016. All Articles of the CComm. quoted word-for-word in this report are taken from this version.

the secured creditor according to the plan, taking into account the dividends to be distributed. There is much controversy as to how this rule operates in practice since its meaning is not clear and to date there have been no leading cases.[146] It must be noted that even without the creditor's consent, his right to be paid out of the sale proceeds can be substituted by the grant of new and equivalent security rights.

353. In the proceedings of *redressement* and judicial liquidation, the insolvency judge may agree on the transfer of the business to a third party with a view to continuing the business, i.e. a recovery plan by transfer. In this case, when the transfer includes assets encumbered by a special privilege or a security right in rem, the secured creditor has no rights against the acquirer of the company in difficulties [Art. L. 642(12) al. 2 and 3 CComm.]. In contrast, they are entitled to enforce their rights over the price paid for the transfer, depending on their rank (Question 14). Exceptionally, secured creditors can also enforce their right against a third party acquiring an asset from the assignee who has sold the asset without having paid the full price for the transfer.[147]

354. During the first three months after the opening of liquidation proceedings and although the opening causes all debts to become immediately payable, the liquidator is the only person responsible for realising the company's assets. If he makes no sales during this period, creditors with a special privilege, pledgees over tangible and intangible assets, mortagees and the public treasury are granted again the right to bring an individual action [Art. L. 643(2) CComm.]. In any case, the liquidator must distribute the sale proceeds among the creditors, depending on the priority order established by law (see Question 16).

2. Italy

355. In general terms, it can be said that if the IP has the power and the responsibility to realise the secured assets, he can do so without the consent of

---

146 See C. Saint-Alary-Houin, *Droit des entreprises en difficulté*, 352–648; P. Le Corre, *Droit et pratique des procédures collectives*, 1213.

147 Article L642-12.1 and 3 CComm. reads as follows: 'Where the assignment includes assets charged with a special privilege, a pledge of corporeal movables, a pledge of incorporeal movables or a hypothec, a portion of the price will be set aside by the court for each asset for the distribution of the price and the exercise of preferential rights. The payment of the price of the assignment shall bar the exercise against the assignee of the creditors' rights attached to the assets. Until full payment of the price entailing the removal of the rights registered over the assets included in the assignment, creditors holding a right to sue the asset-holder (*droit de suite*) may exercise it only where the asset assigned is alienated by the assignee'.

the secured party. Further details on this issue will be mentioned in the answer to Question 13.

3. Spain

356. The payment of claims granted special preference in Article 90 LC takes priority over secured assets, irrespective of whether they are individually or collectively enforced [Art. 155(1) LC]. Collective enforcement proceeds once the liquidation phase has begun, either according to the approved plan (Art. 148 LC) or the applicable default rules (Art. 149 LC). The individual and thus separate enforcement of security rights proceeds in the terms described in Question 9; although secured creditors have the right to separate realisation under the circumstances detailed above, enforcement proceeds in the insolvency court and under the conditions required by Article 155(3) LC. The same provision grants the IP the power to satisfy the secured creditor without the realisation of secured assets, inasmuch as the IP understands that releasing the assets from security is financially beneficial for the purposes of the insolvency proceedings [Art. 155(2) LC]. As mentioned in Question 11, the IP is only granted this option during the period of stay or the suspension of the enforcement of the security rights, and its exercise cannot be questioned by the secured creditor, who is simply notified of the IP's intentions and is only entitled to immediate separate enforcement when payments due fail to be made.

357. The IP may also realise secured assets during the course of the insolvency proceedings without the creditor's consent, with a view to protecting all creditors. This may occur in two types of cases. The first is because of the nature of the assets: they are perishable or prone to quick deterioration or devaluation, or because their maintenance or storage costs are high compared with the value of the assets, and the second is because of the insolvency proceedings themselves, i.e. where there is a lack of liquidity and realising the assets is a way to fill the gap.[148] The IP may realise assets without judicial authorisation in a number of cases [Art. 43(3) LC] on the grounds that their realisation is essential to ensure the company's viability or if funds are needed to continue the insolvency proceedings; also if their realisation is essential for the running of the debtor's enterprise or because an offer has been received for a secured asset which is not necessary for the debtor's enterprise and the offer substantially matches the price given to the asset in the inventory.

---

[148] J. Garrido, 'Article 155' in Á. Rojo and E. Beltrán, *Comentario de la legislación concursal*, 2441, 2456.

Question 13: Are there any conditions that must be satisfied before an IP may 'enforce' the security?

1. France

358. See the answer given to Question 12.

2. Italy

359. Yes. There are some conditions that must be satisfied before an IP may 'enforce' the security. These conditions vary depending on the insolvency proceedings in question, as will be seen from what will be said below.

2.1. Fallimento *(bankruptcy)*

360. In general, the IP must carry out the sales and other acts of liquidation of assets in accordance with the liquidation programme he has drawn up and that is approved by the creditors' committee and communicated to the delegated judge who authorises the implementation of acts that are in compliance with the liquidation programme. The IP may anticipate in the liquidation programme that sales should be carried out by a designated judge according to the provisions of the Civil Procedure Code. Otherwise, the IP must carry out sales through competitive procedures and ensuring, through adequate forms of publicity, maximum information and participation by interested parties. With specific regard to the sale of immovable assets and registered movable assets, the IP must give notification to each of the mortgagee and privileged creditors before the completion of the sales operations. As regards the sale of intellectual property licences, rights in respect of industrial inventions, of trademarks and databases, the IP must comply with the respective statute laws (Arts 104-*ter*, 107, 108-*ter* L.Fall.). Before completing sale operations, the IP must inform the delegated judge and the creditors' committee of the outcome of the process, by filing the documentation at the court registry. The designated judge, on application of one of the parties, may suspend the sale where there are serious and justified reasons to do so and he may also prevent the sale if the price offered is significantly lower than might be expected given the market conditions (Arts. 107.5, 108 L.Fall.).

361. It is appropriate to stress that before the approval of the liquidation programme, the IP may proceed with the liquidation of assets only when the delay may jeopardise the interests of the creditors and, in all cases, with the previous authorisation of the designated judge and having consulted with the creditors' committee (Art 104-*ter*.6 L.Fall.).

2.2. Liquidazione coata amministrativa *(compulsory administrative liquidation)*

362. In general, the IP has all the powers necessary for the liquidation of assets, within the limits established by the authority that oversees the liquidation and under the control of the supervisory committee. With specific regard to the sale of immovable assets and movable assets in whole, the IP needs the previous authorisation of the aforesaid authority and to have consulted the supervisory committee (Art 210 L.Fall.).

2.3. Amministrazione straordinaria *(extraordinary administration)*

363. In general, the IP must carry out the sales and other acts of liquidation of assets in accordance with the provisions of the programme authorised by the Ministry for Economic Development and having consulted the supervisory committee. In any case, the IP must carry out the sales after the determination of the value of the assets by one or more experts and with procedures adequate to the nature of the assets and aiming at better realisation, in accordance with the general criteria established by the aforesaid Ministry. With specific regard to the sale of firms and branches of firms, of immovable assets and movable assets in whole, the IP needs the authorisation of the Ministry and to consult the supervisory committee. The IP can then carry out the sale after ensuring that it has been appropriately publicised (Arts 42, 57, 62 d.lgs. 270/1999).

2.4. Liquidazione dei beni *(liquidation of assets)*

364. In general, the IP must carry out the sales and other acts of liquidation of assets in accordance with the liquidation programme he has drawn up. The IP must perform sales through competitive procedures, on the basis of estimates and ensuring, through adequate forms of publicity, the maximum information and participation of the interested parties. Before completing the sale operations, the IP must inform the debtor, the creditors and the court of the outcome of the procedure. The court verifies whether the acts done in the liquidation process comply with the programme and may suspend the process where there are serious and justified reasons to do so (Art 14-*novies* L. 3/2012).

365. *Other proceedings.* The resolution of financial difficulties through a restructuring plan will be widely dealt with in the answer to Question 17, to which the reader is referred.

3. Spain

366. The IP is obliged to request judicial authorisation to realise any of the debtor's assets with the exception of the cases laid down in Art. 43(3) LC mentioned above (see Question 12) provided that the IP immediately communicates the acts of disposal undertaken to the court and provides due justification.

367. Secured assets must be realised through public auction in the terms established by Article 155(4) LC. Nevertheless, it is also laid down that, at the request of the IP and with a prior hearing for interested parties, the insolvency court can authorise the sale of assets with the continuation of the security right and the acquirer obtains the asset subject to the debtor's obligation [Art. 155(3) LC]. In these circumstances the secured creditor would be excluded from the insolvency proceedings. The IP can also dispose of the security right without the creditor's consent in the case of sale of the debtor's business or a productivity unit and these rights attach to that business during the liquidation phase. In this case, secured creditors are paid their security in full, unless the payment does not satisfy the secured claim, in which case at least 75% of this type of creditors has to agree on that sale to the extent that they lose part of their security [Art. 149(2) LC]. However, this provision only mentions secured creditors entitled to individual realisation, i.e. apparently excluding those secured creditors who were not able to realise their security before the opening of the liquidation phase and thus are submitted to collective enforcement of their rights. While in the light of the protection granted to secured creditors, Article 149(2) ought to be interpreted as referring to all secured creditors, the issue has not been so far settled.

368. At the IP's request or the request of a secured creditor according to a restructuring plan, secured assets can be realised through direct sale – assignment in payment – or appropriation by the secured creditor or another person named by the latter, provided that these realisation methods terminate the security right; where appropriate, the excess of the claim not covered by the security is to be classified either as an ordinary or subordinated claim [Art. 155(4) LC].

369. Direct sale is also feasible when these conditions are not met, but potential purchasers must offer a higher price than the minimum agreed for the assets in the insolvency assets inventory and make a down payment. The only exception to these conditions is when the debtor and secured creditor agree to accept a lower price for the asset provided that it is sold for a market price that has been objectively determined, monitored by an officially authorised body in the case of immovable assets, and assessed by specialists in the case of movable assets.

370. All in all, judicial authorisation to proceed with one of these methods of asset realisation and their conditions must be announced in similar terms to those used for public auctions. Following the last announcement, a 10-day period is open for other bidders to make an offer; should there be a better offer, the court must open the bidding to all potential purchasers and establish the deposit that they must provide in order to take part in the bidding process.

371. Finally, it must be noted that these realisation rules are designed to apply throughout the insolvency proceedings, meaning that they are not only applicable before the liquidation begins but also during it, should individual realisation of the assets in question be agreed on.

Question 14: Do the rules or conditions differ depending on the nature of the insolvency proceedings in question?

1. France

372. The similarity between the objectives of *sauvegarde* and *redressement* proceedings explain why they are subject to the same rules, including provisions dealing with the fate of security rights during the observation period, namely prohibition of payments, stay, mandatory declaration of claims, etc. The order of priority among preferential rights is common to both proceedings.[149]

373. The *redressement* proceeding has, however, two special features. First, the opening of the proceedings triggers the duty of insolvency practitioners to challenge acts and payments made by the debtor during the suspect period (see Question 27). Second, and unlike the *sauvegarde* proceedings, the observation period can lead either to a restructuring plan or a plan for total transfer of the business [Arts. L. 631(13) and L. 631(22) CComm.].

374. The situation of creditors varies within the framework of the liquidation proceedings, the aim of which is to realise assets and pay the company's liabilities once the non-viability of the company has been established. The opening of

149 Namely: 'super-privileged' wage claims including wages for the last two months; legal costs; claims secured by settlement privilege, that benefit the grantor of a loan and supplier of goods and services during the pre-insolvency period; specific claims against the estate or *privileges de la procedure*; prior secured claims; unsecured claims (see Question 16).

liquidation proceedings involves the divestment of the debtor's powers and produces similar effects to other proceedings, namely, a bar on the enforcement of pactum commissorium [Art. L. 641(3) CComm.] and a stay, in principle, on payments, enforcement and registration of security rights. These effects will be prolonged until the liquidator realises the assets, either by approval of a plan transferring the business to a third party, or through the separate sale of assets [Art. L. 640(1) CComm.].

375. Once a plan transferring the business, including assets encumbered by a special privilege or a security right in rem, has been approved, secured creditors cannot take action against the third party who buys the business. They are paid from the sale price in accordance with the order of priority, as mentioned above. To this end, the full price paid for the business is divided by the insolvency court among the secured creditors in accordance with the order of priority. Such a payment terminates their security rights [Art. L.642(12) CComm.]. These provisions do not apply, however, to holders of a right of possessory retention, who are entitled to assert their rights against the third party taking on the business or assets and thus, try to obtain full payment of the claim [Art. L. 642(12)(5) CComm.].[150] According to Article L. 642(12)(4) CComm., the same provisions apply to acquisition financiers in the event that the financed assets are included within the transfer of the business, meaning that they can realise their right over those assets even after the transfer (see Question 24). Fiduciary creditors are, however, exempt from the transfer agreement: where assets have been transferred by way of security, these assets cannot be assigned along with those owned by the debtor as they do not form part of the debtor's estate. In the case of a non-possessory transfer of ownership by way of security, where the debtor retains the use and enjoyment of the encumbered assets, such assets cannot be transferred to third parties without the secured creditor's agreement [Art. L. 642(7) CComm.].

376. In the event of the sale of single assets, the liquidator divides the sale proceeds according to the order of priority laid down by Article L. 643-13 CComm. The possessory or non-possessory pledgee has the right to request the judicial transfer of the pledged assets before they go on sale [Art. L. 642-20.1 al. 2 CComm.].[151] Should there be a sale of assets subject to any type of right of possessory retention, the insolvency court can authorise the payment of the claim in order to rescue the asset (Art. L. 641-3 to 2 CComm.). In the absence of this payment, the asset must be realised within six months from the opening of

[150] This rule applies also to those holding a right to fictive retention despite the many problems that it poses. See P. Crocq, (2009) 4 *Cahiers de droit de l'entreprise* 21.

[151] The Court of Cassation denies the benefit of the judicial transfers of the asset to retainers which are not pledgees (Cass. Comm. 9.6.1998).

the liquidation phase, and the amount obtained must be invested to satisfy the holder of the right of possessory retention [Art. L. 642-20.1 to 3 CComm.].[152]

377. As a final remark, it should be noted that the order of payment of competing creditors is different in the framework of liquidation proceedings from that in the event of rehabilitation or restructuring proceedings. In liquidation proceedings, absolute priority is given to those creditors holding a right of possessory retention and to mortgagees and immovable privileged creditors that take priority even over privileged claims against the estate.

2. Italy

378. Yes. The rules or conditions that must be satisfied before an IP may 'enforce' the security vary depending on the nature of the insolvency proceedings in question. This is illustrated in the answer to Question 13, to which the reader is referred.

3. Spain

379. In contrast to the previous insolvency system, Law 22/2003 on Insolvency sought to unify legal systems, disciplines and insolvency proceedings (see Explanatory Introduction to the Law). In general, the only differences in the treatment of security rights are those mentioned in connection with the realisation of secured assets in the event of a restructuring plan or liquidation (see Question 13). Nevertheless, comparative law has introduced some new features, in particular the establishment of hybrid proceedings to conclude a voluntary restructuring plan (Arts. 5bis, 71bis, 231 and the Fourth Additional Disposition LC). These are begun by informing the competent insolvency court of the debtor's intentions to conclude a refinancing or restructuring plan. From then on, a stay or suspension is imposed in judicial or non-judicial enforcement proceedings with regard to assets necessary for the debtor's enterprise until either: (1) the plan laid down by Arts. 71bis(1), 238 or Fourth Additional Disposition has been concluded; or (2) the petition for court approval has been admitted; or (3) the agreement has been adopted; or (4) the debtor has obtained the necessary acceptances for a proposed agreement to be accepted; or (5) the insolvency proceedings are begun. Should no plan be reached, the debtor must in general request insolvency proceedings following the conclusion of the three-month period that the law allows for negotiation of an agreement [Art. 5bis(4) LC].

---

152 The Court of Cassation has denied the right over the price in the cases of right of retention created by an autonomous contract (Cass. Comm. 23.4.2013).

380. Enforcement proceedings over assets necessary for the debtor's enterprise are therefore affected by any stay or suspension. For this reason and although Article 5bis(4) provides that secured creditors may realise their security right, it also indicates that they can be subject to the aforementioned stay. The same applies to enforcement proceedings brought by financial creditors, provided that at least 51% of them have expressly approved opening negotiations to sign a restructuring plan and have agreed not to initiate or continue individual enforcement against the debtor during the negotiations. In contrast, the stay or suspension never applies to holders of public law claims.

Question 15: Is a secured party liable to pay the general costs, i.e. costs apart from those incurred in connection with the realisation of security, of insolvency proceedings affecting the debtor?

1. France

381. General costs of insolvency proceedings such as the IP's remuneration, taxes, fees payable to officials, lawyers' and experts' remuneration, notifications, publicity, expenses arising from the settlement or modification of the plan, etc., have to be paid in priority over all other claims, whether they are secured or not, save the case of 'super-privileged' wage claims, i.e. wages for the last two months. Hence, secured creditors are only paid out of the proceeds of the encumbered assets after the general costs have been paid (Arts. L. 622-8; L. 626-22; L. 641-13; L. 643-8).

2. Italy

382. As a general rule, the secured party is liable to pay pro rata the 'general costs' (i.e. costs apart from those directly incurred in connection with the administration and realisation of security) provided they have been directly or indirectly incurred also in its interest. The remuneration of the IP and the costs necessary for the progression of the insolvency proceedings up to its completion are amongst these. These costs must be deducted from the proceeds of the encumbered assets in an amount proportional to their actual utility for the secured creditor or, if such a quantification is not de facto possible, pro rata to the proceeds of the encumbered good compared to the proceeds from all others.[153] This therefore means that the amount due to the secured creditor is the net amount, i.e. what is left of the proceeds of the encumbered assets after these

[153] Cass. civ. 12.5.2010 no 11500, [2010] *F* 1271.

costs have been paid. These propositions express the general judicial consensus and are embodied in the new Article 111-*ter*.3 L.Fall.

3. Spain

383. As mentioned in Question 12, creditors with special privilege are paid out of the specific secured assets [Art. 155(1) LC]. In general, payments to creditors may only proceed after payment of claims against the estate. However, Article 154 LC makes it clear that this rule does not apply to secured creditors, i.e. they are not liable to pay any general costs. They do pay realisation costs, but the law does not mention any other contributions to the insolvency proceedings.

Question 16: Is the secured party liable to 'set aside' any portion of the amount realised from the enforcement of security for the benefit of (a) preferential or (b) unsecured creditors of the debtor?

1. France

384. French law establishes an order of payment of competing creditors that the IP has to observe when he distributes the sale proceeds of the debtor's assets. That means that in the case of preferential creditors over security rights in rem according to the ranking, the preference granted to the holders of security rights may not serve the purpose of satisfying the secured claim given that the sale proceeds will be invested in paying those first ranked. In order to avoid benefiting some privileged creditors disproportionately over other secured ones, the rule in practice, albeit unwritten, is that the IP gathers all dividends arising from any assets' sale, total or individual, and proceeds to their distribution at the same time and in a proportionate way with the aim of satisfying to a certain extent all secured creditors regardless of their ranking and the moment in which they are paid.[154]

385. The order of payment of competing creditors is different in the framework of liquidation proceedings, where holders of a right of possessory retention take absolute priority and mortgagees take priority over privileged claims against the estate (Arts. L. 641-13-II and L. 642-20-1 CComm.) in the order of the framework of rehabilitation or restructuring proceedings. In the latter type of proceedings' regulation the fact that security rights in rem are paid later than other privileges is more evident than in the liquidation proceedings. The ranking

154 See P. Le Corre, *Droit et pratique des procédures collectives*, 1665–1666.

of distribution among creditors is laid down in Article L. 622-17, which reads as follows:

(a) the 'super-privilege' laid down in Articles L. 3253-2, L. 32534 and L. 7313-8 of the Labour Code, granted to the two months' wages before the opening of the proceeding;
(b) legal costs arising after the opening of insolvency proceedings to cover the needs of the latter;
(c) claims secured by settlement privilege, which benefit the grantor of a loan and/or the supplier of goods and services during the pre-insolvency period (Art. L. 611-11 CComm.);
(d) specific claims against the estate or *privileges de la procedure*, borne after the opening of insolvency proceedings to cover their needs or the observation period or in exchange for a loan or a supply of goods or services granted to the debtor during this period. Article L. 622-17.III establishes an order among these posterior privileged creditors: (1) wages and salaries resulting from the continuation of business; (2) loans and claims arising from the running contracts; (3) other claims according to their priority;
(e) secured claims by pledge, mortgage or privilege. Their holders must be satisfied from the proceeds of assets to which their rights are related, in accordance with the priority order established by law (see Question 23);
(f) unsecured claims (Art. L. 643-8-1 CComm.), whose holders compete among themselves and with secured creditors who are not fully paid out of the proceeds of the encumbered asset for the remaining amounts due to them (Arts. L. 643-6 and L. 643-7 CComm.).

2. Italy

386. Before answering this question, a general premise should be stated. Italian insolvency law basically distinguishes between three different classes of creditor following the basic distinction between three different categories of claims and precisely:

(a) preferential claims (*crediti prededucibili*), i.e. those so qualified by law or that have arisen on the occasion/as a function of the insolvency proceedings. Their holders must be fully satisfied (capital, interest and expenses) before other creditors. (Arts 111.2, 111-*bis* L.Fall.);
(b) secured claims (*crediti privilegiati*), i.e. those ensured by pledge or mortgage or privilege. Their holders must be satisfied with priority from the proceeds

of assets to which their rights are related and for an amount equal to capital plus interest and expenses; only if not fully satisfied, they compete with unsecured creditors (Arts 54, 55, 111.1, 111-*quater* L.Fall.);

(c) unsecured claims (*crediti chirografari*). Their holders compete amongst themselves and with unsatisfied secured creditors in the distribution of the remaining assets (Arts 54, 55, 111.1 L.Fall.).

387. The hierarchy among the three classes of creditors in the order of distribution of the amount realised from the liquidation of the insolvency estate is clearly defined by Article 111.1 L.Fall. This hierarchy is expressly regulated concerning *Fallimento*; but this regulation applies also in *Liquidazione coatta amministrativa* and in *Amministrazione straordinaria*.[155] Consequently, it can generally be said that when an IP has the responsibility to liquidate the debtor's assets and distribute the proceeds among creditors, he must perform the distribution according to the order laid down by Article 111.1 L.Fall. and precisely:

(a) for the payment of the holders of preferential claims; this implies that, if there is a preferential claim and a secured claim on the same asset, the preferential claim is paid first (Art 111-*bis* L.Fall.);
(b) for the payment of secured creditors, from the proceeds of assets to which their security rights are related and according to the priority order stated by law;
(c) for the payment of unsecured creditors and secured creditors, the latter if not yet satisfied or left unsatisfied by the realisation of security, in accordance with the principle of pari passu.

388. As a result, secured creditors do not have to give any portion of the amount realised from the enforcement of their securities for the benefit of other classes of creditors, of course up to the amount of the secured claims. Legal restrictions are only made by the imposition of specific costs (i.e. costs of administration and realisation of the collateral) and of pro rata general costs (see the answer to Question 15 above).[156]

3. Spain

389. Article 155(1) LC applies, and thus the secured party is not liable to set aside any portion of the amount realised from the enforcement of security but is paid in full, including any accrued interest where appropriate.

155 See Art 212 L.Fall. and Art 67 d.lgs. 270/1999, respectively.

156 Cass. civ. 14.1.2004 no 335, [2005] *F* 294.

Question 17: Can the secured party be bound against its wishes by a restructuring plan that negatively affects either the secured debt or the enforcement of the security interest?

1. France

390. The objective of rescuing a business in difficulties justifies the creditors being affected by various measures that aim to reduce the debtor's liabilities.

391. In general terms, the opening of *sauvegarde, redressement* or *liquidation* proceedings implies that claims cannot accrue interest, be it remunerative or moratory [Arts. L. 622(28), L. 31(14), L. 641(3) CComm.]. The rule affects preferential as well as unsecured claims, with the exception of claims arising after the opening of proceedings.

392. In particular, the discharge of liabilities included within the *sauvegarde* or the *redressement* plan can waive secured claims or convert the debt into shares, provided that the affected creditors agree on it; defer payments for a maximum of 10 years that the insolvency court may impose on any creditor; or contain reductions linked to shorter periods of payment that also may be accepted by the concerned creditors.

393. In the case of companies with more than 150 employees or a volume of business that exceeds €20 million, the restructuring plan must be approved by two thirds of the members of the two creditors' committees that have to be created, one made up of financial creditors and the other of trade creditors. Approval of the plan for the said qualified majority by each of the committees is binding on those of the same group not agreeing to the plan. The plan may include debt reduction or release, debt postponement or conversion into financial instruments. Creditors not integrated in any of the committees are notified by the IP of the plan: if they do not express rejection of the plan, their silence is understood as approval save in the case of the plan imposing on debt release or conversion into shares in which case silence means non-acceptance.

394. In some cases the existence of the security right itself might be compromised, namely, in the event that a security interest created during the suspect period is declared null and void (Question 27), or when an encumbered asset is sold in the course of the enforcement of a *sauvegarde* plan and thus, those security rights over it have to be substituted by other equivalent rights.

395. Finally, the effects of insolvency proceedings on the realisation of security rights has already been dealt with: those creditors secured by privileges, mortgagees and pledgees cannot enforce their security interests while those secured by a retention of title clause or a transfer of ownership by way of security to a fiduciary other than the secured creditor who is thus not in possession of the asset, have their rights temporarily limited. It must be noted, however, that secured creditors in possession of the asset whose ownership has been transferred by way of security are not affected by the opening of an insolvency proceeding.

2. Italy

396. Under Italian insolvency law it is possible that the secured party is bound against his wishes by a plan that negatively affects the secured claim and/or the enforcement of the creditor's security interest. This can occur in *Fallimento, Liquidazione coatta amministrativa, Amministrazione straordinaria, Concordato preventivo, Accordi di ristrutturazione* and *Procedure di composizione della crisi da sovraindebitamento (Accordo o Piano),* as will be seen from what will be said below in the order suggested for reasons of simplicity and brevity.

2.1. Concordato preventivo *(preventive settlement)*

397. As said in the answer to Question 9 (para. 310), *Concordato preventivo* is a judicial proceeding that allows an entrepreneur in financial distress to avoid bankruptcy by way of a negotiated settlement of the crisis.

398. The proceedings are divided into the three phases of proposal, acceptance and approval. The debtor initiates the proceedings by filing an application to the court with a proposed plan that aims at the restructuring of debts and the satisfaction of claims. The plan may also contemplate the division of creditors into classes according to the nature of their claims, and different treatment for each class of creditors. The plan can never have the effect of altering the ranking of secured rights. Nevertheless, it may provide also that secured creditors are only partially satisfied as long as this is not less than the proceeds achievable in the case of the liquidation of the encumbered assets (Art 160 L.Fall.). After an initial hearing, if applicable, the court declares the opening of the proceedings during which the creditors will be asked to accept the *Concordato* (Art 163 L.Fall.).

399. Article 177 L.Fall. states that the *Concordato* must be accepted by the creditors that represent the majority of the claims admitted to the vote. Where different classes of creditors are contemplated, the settlement is accepted if the majority of classes is favourable, so that a class as a whole can be crammed down. Secured creditors, of which the proposed plan contemplates payment in full, do not have the right to vote unless they forego the preferential right totally or partly. If, instead, the proposed plan does not contemplate their full satisfaction, they are treated in the same way as unsecured creditors for the residual part of the claim (Art 177.2-3 L.Fall.).

400. If the *Concordato* has been accepted, the court holds the approval hearing. The court verifies the regularity of the procedure and the result of the vote. As a rule, instead, it does not evaluate how advantageous the *Concordato* is for creditors. An exception is the case where a creditor belonging to a dissenting class or (if there are no classes) the dissenting creditors that represents 20% of the claims admitted to the vote contest the advantageousness of the *Concordato*. If this occurs, the court must give its approval it if considers that creditors will receive at least as much under the plan as under the available alternatives. By contrast, the court may not consider eventual prejudice to particular creditors or groups of creditors. (Art 180 L.Fall.). The approved *Concordato* is binding on all those who were creditors at the time of publication of the *Concordato* application in the Register of Firms (Art 184 L.Fall.).

2.2. Procedure di composizione della crisi da sovraindebitamento (accordo o piano) *[procedures for composition of crisis from over-indebtednes (settlement or plan)]*

401. As said in the answer to Question 9 (para. 317), *Procedure di composizione della crisi da sovraindebitamento (Accordo o Piano)* are united by the fact that they aim to overcome the crisis of the debtor through the implementation of a plan that has been proposed by the debtor himself. Despite the presence of several distinctive features, the contents of the proposal, the treatment of secured creditors, the nature and effects of the judgment of approval by the court are all governed by rules similar to those described in respect of the *Concordato preventivo*.

402. The *Accordo* proposal may contemplate a moratorium lasting up to one year after the approval for payment of secured creditors, unless it foresees liquidation of the encumbered assets (Art 8.4 L. 3/2012).[157] The proposal must be accepted by creditors representing at least 60% of claims (Art 11.2 L. 3/2012) though any interested party may contest the plan in terms of how advantageous it is and, in this case, the court must be satisfied that a creditor must receive at least as much under the plan as in a liquidation (Art 12.2 L. 3/2012).

403. As far as the *Piano* in concerned, a distinctive feature compared to the *Accordo* is worthy of mention: there is no requirement to obtain the consent of creditors before court approval. Creditors may, however, challenge the *Piano* in court, arguing that a liquidation would be more beneficial to them. (Art 12-*bis* L. 3/2012).

---

157 G. Campobasso, *Diritto commerciale*, vol. III, 480.

2.3. Fallimento *(bankruptcy)*

404. It is possible that *Fallimento* might be closed through a negotiated settlement accepted by creditors and approved by the court. This settlement is called *Concordato fallimentare* (Bankruptcy settlement) and, despite the presence of some distinctive features, is governed by rules similar to those described in respect of *Concordato preventivo*. This holds true, in particular, for the contents of the proposal, especially concerning the treatment of secured creditors; for the voting rights of secured creditors; for the majority required for acceptance; and for the nature and effects of the judgment of approval by the court (Arts 124-141 L.Fall.).

2.4. Liquidazione coatta amministrativa *(compulsory administrative liquidation)*

405. *Liquidazione coatta amministrativa* might also be closed through a settlement called *Concordato* which can have the same content as the *Concordato fallimentare*. The proceedings, however, have considerable differences. The *Concordato* proposal is approved by the court without requiring acceptance by creditors. The creditors can only assert their rights through opposition filed with the court before approval. Nevertheless, the court can approve the *Concordato* proposal even if all the creditors oppose it, by weighing the correspondence of the proposal with the public interest as preeminent (Art 214 L.Fall.).[158] Theoretically, this implies that the court could approve the proposal even if 100% of creditors are opposed.

2.5. Amministrazione straordinaria *(extraordinary administration)*

406. The possibility of closing the proceedings through a settlement called *Concordato* is also contemplated in the *Amministrazione straordinaria*, but the rules differ significantly depending on whether the relevant proceedings are *Prodibis* proceedings or *Marzano* proceedings.

407. In the first case, i.e. in the *Prodibis* proceedings, the *Concordato* proposal is governed by the same regulations laid down concerning *Liquidazione coatta amministrativa* (Art 78 d.lgs. 270/1999).

408. By contrast, in *Marzano* proceedings the *Concordato* proposal presents autonomous features. The *Concordato* proposal can contemplate the division of creditors into classes, according to the nature of their claims, and different

158 *Ibid.* at 452.

treatment for each class of them; the *Concordato* proposal must be accepted by the creditors representing the majority of the claims admitted to the vote; where different classes of creditors are contemplated, the *Concordato* proposal is accepted if this majority is also present in all classes; the court can approve the *Concordato* proposal despite the dissent of one or more classes, if the majority of classes has approved the proposal and if it is determined that the creditors belonging to the dissenting classes will receive at least as much under the plan as they would do under the alternative procedures (Art 4-*bis* d.l. 347/2003).

2.6. Accordi di ristritturazione *(restructuring agreements)*

409. *Accordi di ristrutturazione* are out-of-court agreements between the debtor and his creditors representing at least 60% of the total debts. Nevertheless, they may be deemed to be insolvency proceedings because, once approved by court, they also produce effects against 'outsider' creditors. Among these effects is that of a limited 'stay' on the enforcement of security, as illustrated in the answer to Question 9 (para. 314) to which the reader is referred.

3. Spain

410. The general rule is that secured creditors can only be bound by a restructuring plan if they have voted in favour of the proposal or their signature or acceptance to it has been considered a favourable vote [Art. 134(2) LC]. The same provision makes it clear that they can always voluntarily join the plan provided that their acceptance has been judicially acknowledged and the plan has not already been completed.

411. Nevertheless, and with a view to reinforcing the viability of businesses, this provision has been amended[159] to make a restructuring plan binding on secured creditors under specific conditions [Art. 134(3) LC]. In particular, the restructuring plan has to be approved by a given majority of the respective class of creditors. Article 94(2) provides for the relevant classification of secured creditors and distinguishes between four categories, namely creditors holding (1) work claims, (2) public law claims, (3) financial claims, and (4) others not included in the first three categories, including claims arising from commercial operations.

412. The majorities required to approve a restructuring plan depend on the measures included therein and how they affect the insolvency claims, i.e. the

[159] Royal Decree-Law 11/2011, 5 September, on urgent in insolvency matters (BOE No, 6.9.2011).

significance of deductions and refinancing measures. Accordingly, secured creditors can be bound by a restructuring plan when 60% of the relevant class of creditors vote in favour and the plan includes measures laid down by Article 124(1(a) LC, or 75% vote for measures contained in Article 124(1)(b) LC (the greater majority refers to maturity postponement of more than five years or more than 50% deduction of or release from debt, conversion of the debt into shares in the debtor who is a legal person or into participation loans, or asset assignment by way of payment). It should be noted that the majorities needed to bind creditors with special privileges are calculated on the basis of the total amount of security rights granted within each of the aforementioned categories (see para. 411), while the calculations for creditors with general privilege are carried in respect of the total liability secured by the type of privilege within each class.[160]

413. As explained in Question 14, pre-insolvency proceedings have been set up and the Fourth Additional Disposition LC in particular addresses the conditions that a restructuring plan agreed on prior to the opening of the insolvency proceedings must contain before being approved by the competent court. The agreement must be concluded with the holders of financial liabilities, including secured liabilities, who are then bound by the agreement whether they wish to be or not, provided that the scheme has either 65% or 80% approval, calculated on the basis of the proportion of security right holders that have approved the agreement in relation to the total value of the existing security rights. The difference between one majority and the other follows the type of measures that bind the secured creditors, as explained with regard to Article 124.

414. A similar rule has been established in the event that a debtor natural person with liabilities under €5m, or a legal person whose insolvency is not especially complex as indicated by Article 190 LC, attempts to reach an out-of-court plan with their creditors: secured creditors are only bound if they are in favour of the settlement [Art. 238bis(2)]. However, those creditors that are not in favour are also bound if the plan has obtained either 65% or 80% approval depending on the type of measures agreed on. The greater majority, 80%, is applied when the settlement contains reductions in the amount of the debt of more than 25%, debt extensions over five years but up to 10 years of the repayment period, asset assignment by way of payment, conversion of the debt into participation loans, or similar [Art. 238bis(3)]. Less aggressive measures only require 65% approval.

160 These rules have to be read along with the ones established by Article 94 and the Fourth Additional Disposition LC to determine the value of secured assets. While there can be several secured creditors over the same asset, privilege can only be granted to those creditors who can actually be paid over the asset. If the total debt secured by the asset exceeds its value, the remaining claims cannot be classified as privileged, i.e. those creditors not covered by the security right are not taken into account while voting a restructuring plan.

Question 18: Can an under-secured creditor claim from the insolvency estate in respect of any deficiency arising as a result of the enforcement of the security?

1. France

415. Secured creditors must be paid with the sale proceeds of the assets that are subject to their charge, up to the amount of the secured claim and according to the priority order established by law (Question 16). If claims are not fully satisfied by the proceeds of the encumbered assets, they are classified as under-secured and their holders will compete with other under-secured creditors for the amounts due to them (Arts. L. 643-6 and L. 643-7).

2. Italy

416. As described in the answer to Question 16, the creditors admitted with priority against the insolvency estate must be satisfied with preference in the net proceeds of the sale of the assets that are the object of their right, up to the amount of the secured claim (capital, interest and expenses) and according to the priority order stated by law. For the part of their claim that has not been satisfied, such creditors qualify as unsecured creditors and must compete with the other unsecured creditors in the distribution of the assets remaining according to the pari passu principle.

417. It is appropriate to add that the same creditors (whose priority claim against the insolvency estate has been established) have the right to participate as unsecured creditors in distributions made even before the distribution of the proceeds from the encumbered assets. In this situation, however, the amount they will receive from the encumbered assets is reduced by the amount they have received under the prior distribution (Arts 54.2, 111.1 no 3 L.Fall.).[161]

3. Spain

418. Creditors with special privilege are paid up to the secured amount from the realisation of secured assets regardless of the realisation method. Their role in the insolvency proceedings is mainly to request the enforcement of the security right, except for cases in which the IP can realise the asset without their consent. Should realising the asset not satisfy the claim in full, the remaining

161 L. Guglielmucci, *Diritto fallimentare*, 246.

debt must be reclassified as an ordinary or subordinate debt [Art. 90(3) LC]. The same applies when, once the value of the secured asset has been calculated in accordance with the rules provided by Article 94 LC, it becomes apparent that some secured creditors will not be satisfied from the distribution of the proceeds of the encumbered asset. Hence, the IP shall determine the value of the security rights in order to classify all the debtor's liabilities and electronically communicate the inventory to all creditors who are entitled to challenge it. The secured creditor is allowed to provide another valuation report at his own expense, including in those cases in which he argues a change in circumstances that modify the value of the secured asset.

D. REGISTRATION OF SECURITY RIGHTS

Question 19: To what extent must security rights over assets be publicised by registration or filing to ensure the effectiveness of the security interest over parties other than the debtor and in the event of insolvency proceedings?

1. France

419. As a general rule, where there is no transfer of possession, the effectiveness of security rights against third parties stems from them being publicised by their registration in official registers established for this purpose (Question 20).

420. In the event of non-possessory security rights, the effectiveness of a common pledge depends on it being registered, which halts the effects of Article 2276 CC [Art. 2337(1) and (3) CC]. Publicity is effected by the pledge being entered in a special register administered by officials of the commercial court and corresponding to the place where the pledgor is domiciled, or has its seat or the place of its central administration. As regards a mortgage over movable assets, registration is a requirement of effectiveness of the security right, both against third parties and against other creditors.

421. Entry in a special registry is not only a condition for the effectiveness of non-possessory pledges against third parties, it is also required for the validity of the pledge concluded between the parties to it in the case of certain special types of non-possessory pledge in which the pledgor's retention of the asset is crucial. This applies for pledge over stock [Art. L. 527(4) CComm.] or pledge over industrial machinery, businesses and mobile equipment, whereby entry in the register corresponding to the seat of the company grants the secured creditor a priority right over the pledged assets for five years as regards to the capital of his claim, and for two years as regards the corresponding accrued interest [Arts. L. 525(3)(2) and L. 525(11) CComm.].

422. Where immovables are concerned, the security right must be registered in the Land Registry to be effective against third parties (*Conservation des hypothèques*) regardless of whether the right is possessory or non-possessory.

423. With regard to mortgages, registration is a condition *sine qua non* for the secured creditor to have priority rights in relation to other creditors, as well as the right to separate realisation of the mortgaged assets in possession of a third party. Registration determines a creditor's rank in relation to other registered creditors. If registration has not occurred, the mortgage becomes ineffective even against unsecured creditors, although they may have known of its existence by other means.

424. The registration requirement is also applicable to legal mortgages whereby the law grants a creditor the right to have the benefit of a mortgage over immovable assets which it describes and indicates. The mortgage becomes effective by its registration over each immovable asset, according to the principle of specialty (Art. 2401 CC).

425. The publicity of the antichresis proceeds by the transfer of possession of an immovable asset in the creditor's favour (Art. 2387 CC), but it does not avoid the requirement of being entered in the Land Registry, for the right to be effective against third parties [Arts. 28(1) and 30 of Decree 4.1.1955]. Failure to comply with this requirement however does not prevent the secured creditor from exercising the right of retaining the asset until full payment of the secured claim.

426. Publicity of the transfer of ownership of immovable assets by way of security is also guaranteed by the obligation to register, which is also necessary for the contract to be valid (see Question 6). However, the transfer of ownership of movable assets by way of security is not subject to any form of registration.

2. Italy

427. As explained in the answers to Questions 1, 6 and 7, under Italian private law registration (in the form of entry, transcription and alike) is only required for certain security rights over certain assets. In any case, where the law requires the registration of a security right, this requirement is normally conceived in a way that the constitution of the security right depends on its registration, regardless of which party or against which party its existence is invoked.

428. As for *Fallimento*, Article 45 L.Fall. states that the necessary formalities to make security rights effective against third parties have no effect against creditors if carried out after the date of the opening of proceedings. The rule is the expression of a settled principle concerning the attachment provided by Articles 2914–2916 of the Civil Code. This principle establishes that transactions involving the sale of assets or the creation of unavailability constraints on attached assets, as well as mortgages and privileges relating to the same, have no effects on creditors participating in the procedure if the necessary formalities to make these rights effective against third parties are carried out after the attachment.[162]

429. Article 45 L.Fall. must be considered in close connection with Article 44 L.Fall., which protects the bankruptcy estate, and with the pari passu principle.[163] Once again, the regulatory device is that of relative ineffectiveness that concerns any formalities, carried out by bankrupt or third parties, relating to deeds of disposition. Hence, the formalities in question are fully valid and effective between the parties, even though they cannot be effective against bankruptcy. By contrast, they fully recover their effectiveness even against the creditors and third parties after the closure of the insolvency proceedings.

430. The rule established by Article 45 L.Fall. applies to the *Liquidazione coatta amministrativa* (Art 200 L.Fall.). The same rule also applies to the *Amministrazione straordinaria* (Arts 18 and 36 d.lgs. 270/1999) and to the *Concordato preventivo* (Art 169 L.Fall.), in this case beginning with the filing of an application of the *Concordato*. With respect to these proceedings, Article 168.3 L.Fall. also states that judicial mortgages entered during the 90 day period preceding the date of publication of the *Concordato* application in the Register of Firms are ineffective in relation to competing creditors. However, in the same proceedings Article 45 L.Fall. co-exists with other provisions that allow the constitution of preferential rights during the course of the proceedings (Art 168.3 L.Fall. and Art 18 d.lgs. 270/1999).

431. The *Accordi di ristrutturazione*, on this subject, are regulated by Article 182-*bis* L.Fall. Specifically, this provision establishes that, from the date of publication of the *Accordo di ristrutturazione* (or of the application to the court during its negotiation) in the Register of Firms, prior creditors of whatever type cannot acquire preferential rights if not agreed upon: in the first case, for 60 days; in the second case, during the proceedings and up to 60 days after the *Accordo di ristrutturazione* has been publicised.

432. The *Procedura di composizione della crisi da sovraindebitamento* through *Accordo*, on this subject, is regulated by Article 10.2, letter c, L. 3/2012. Specifically, this provision establishes that prior creditors cannot acquire preferential rights over the debtor's assets from the date of publicity of the decision of admission to the proceedings and until the approval decision becomes definitive. The same prohibition applies in the *Procedura di composizione della crisi da sovraindebitamento* through *Piano*, but only beginning with the date of publicity

---

162 S. Satta, *Diritto fallimentare*, 161.

163 L. Guglielmucci, *Lezioni di diritto fallimentare*, 117.

of the decision on plan approval (Art 12-*ter*.1 L. 3/2012), and in the proceedings of *Liquidazione dei beni*, beginning with the date of publicity of the decision of admission to the proceedings until the closure of the same (Art 14-*quinques*.2, letter b, L. 3/2012).

3. Spain

433. The significance of registration in the Spanish security rights system has already been addressed in Questions 1 and 6. It should be noted that all rights except pledges must be registered, and the significance of these formalities is underlined by Article 90(2) LC. This provision makes it clear that classifying claims as holding special privilege relies on the relevant security right being created in accordance with the requirements and formalities requested for their effectiveness against third parties as laid down by the relevant legislation. The only two exceptions are firstly, what are known as tacit legal mortgages, and secondly, worker-held fixed asset claims. Pledge is not specifically mentioned in Article 90(2) LC, but Article 90(1)(6) LC specifically recalls the formalities necessary for its effectiveness against third parties, i.e. recording the date of creation in a public document for priority purposes.

Question 20: Can you describe briefly the nature of the filing or registration system and whether it is publicly accessible?

1. France

434. Security rights over immovable assets are publicised by registration in a public registry, which is part of the Ministry of Finance: the *Conservation des Hypothèques*, i.e. the Land Registry of the property's location. According to the principle of specialty, the registration application must set out certain information including in particular the specific amount of the secured claim, ie the principal sum and interest payable, and a description of the encumbered asset(s).

435. Acts and contracts affecting ownership and other rights over immovable assets are registered at the Conservation des Hypothèques. In particular, the Land Registry centralises information and publicity for the various security rights over immovable assets mentioned in question 1 (privileges, mortgage, antichresis, transfer of ownership by way of security) as well as leasing contracts and sales with a retention of title clause [Arts. R. 313(12) C. Mon. and Fin.; R. 624(15) CComm.].

436. Acts that have to be registered must be correctly drawn up in public documents such as public deeds, judgments, etc. Once presented, they are entered in the *registre de dépôts* and when their formal validity has been certified, they are registered in the *registre de formalités*, according to their category. Together with registration, the security right in rem is catalogued in an archive organised in personal files according to the person's name, and property files according to the property's description. Any interested party may request information regarding property and obtain either a full copy of the entry or, more usually, an extract showing the information requested.

437. In comparison to the centralisation of publicity for immovable assets, security rights over movables are publicised by registration in various special registries on non-possessory pledge, pledge over stock and pledge over industrial machinery, businesses and mobile equipment, which are administered by commercial court officials (*greffiers du tribunaux de commerce*). For non-possessory pledge, the official in charge of the relevant registry sends information about the pledgor and the registered pledge to central computerised records administered by the *Conseil National des Greffiers des Tribunaux de Commerce*, which can be accessed free of charge on the Internet.[164]

438. Contracts of sale with a retention of title clause and leasing contracts are also publicised in open registries at the commercial court in whose jurisdiction the secured creditor is registered or his business is located [Arts. R.3131(4)-R313(5) C. Mon. and Fin.].

2. Italy

439. In *Italy* there is no general register for security rights. As a rule, their registration (if this is required) must be in the public register related to the kind of assets that constitute the object (for a different registration system see the answer to Question 24).

440. In Italian law the system of real estate registration is based mainly on the Real Estate Registers. Real Estate Registers are kept by a conservator at the Public Offices located in the main towns of the provinces of *Italy*. Unlike the German and Austrian systems, the Italian system of real estate registration is organised on a 'personal' basis. This means that each registration does not concern the plots of real estate but rather the person who has a right over a plot of real estate. Consequently, from Real Estate Registers it is possible to know what transcriptions or entries have been made chargeable to or in favour of a given natural or legal person, but not what legal events have concerned a given plot of real estate.[165]

164 See <http://www.cngtc.fr/fichier-national-gages.php>.

165 F. Gazzoni, *Manuale di diritto privato*, 294.

441. It is appropriate to stress that transcription (*trascrizione*) and entry (*iscrizione*) in Real Estate Registers do not have the same effect. As a rule, transcription has declarative effects, i.e. it makes an act, already valid and effective between the parties, enforceable against third parties. Entry, instead, has constitutive effects, i.e. as long as such formality is not observed, the act has no effect even between the parties. This is the case with a mortgage. As said, entry of a mortgage in the Real Estate Registers has a constitutive effect in respect of security rights.[166]

442. The Real Estate Registers are publicly accessible. Article 2673 of the Civil Code establishes that the conservator is obliged to issue to anyone that applies, a copy of the transcriptions, the registrations and the annotations, or a certificate confirming that there are none. The conservator also has to allow inspection of the Registers, in the manner and at the times laid down by law, and to issue a copy of the documents that have been deposited with him. The services of the Real Estate Registers have been computerised and it is possible to inspect them today through distance searches. The relevant web-addresses are: www.conservatoria.it and www.catasto.it.

443. It is appropriate to specify that in Italian law a system of registration on a 'real' basis, called the *tavolare* system, is also in force. This applies in the provinces of Trentino-Alto Adige which previously belonged to *Austria-Hungary* and which were attached to *Italy* after the First World War.[167]

444. The Italian system of movable assets registration has many areas of overlap with that of real estate, in regards to both the transactions to which it is subject and the effects of registration. However, the system of movable assets registration is distinguished by an essential aspect: while the organisation of Real Estate Registers is on a personal basis, movable assets registration is asset based. This means that an essential precondition of movable assets publicity is the registration of the asset in a particular register and on a page exclusively reserved for it, on which subsequent legal events are then marked.[168]

445. Nevertheless, such a system is provided by law only for high value movable assets such as ships, aircraft and motorcars (Art 2683 Civil Code).[169]

446. As far as Italian merchant ships, they are divided into major ships, minor ships, and barges (Art 136 Maritime Code). Normally, the major ships are

---

166 *Ibid.* at 290.

167 G. Gabrielli, 'Libri fondiari' in *Digesto civile IV*, vol. XI, 3.

168 F. Gentile, *La trascrizione mobiliare*, 1.

169 As far as industrial property rights, their registration system is managed by the Italian Office of Patents and Trademark (UIBM) at the Ministry of Economic Development. Sake of brevity impose to refer to the regulation on the matter and, in particular, to d.lgs. 10.2.2005 No 30 and d.m. 13.01.2010 No 33 <www.normattiva.it> accessed 26 May 2016.

entered in certain registers called '*Matricole*' which are kept at the relevant maritime direction headquarters (Art 146 Maritime Code); minor ships and barges are entered in the Registers kept at the district offices and by the other offices indicated by the regulation;[170] the Registers of ships and barges used for internal navigation are kept by the harbour inspectorates and by the other offices indicated by the laws and regulations (Art 146 Maritime Code); ships and barges being built must be entered in a specific Register kept by the relevant offices (Arts 233–234 Maritime Code).[171]

447. As far as Italian aircraft are concerned, they are entered in the National Aeronautical Register (RAN) kept by the ENAC (National Body for Civil Aviation: Art 687 Maritime Code). Aircraft being built are entered in the Register of aircrafts-building kept by the Ministry for aeronautics (Art 848 Maritime Code).

448. Motorcars are entered in the Public Automobile Register (PRA) kept by each provincial office of the Italian Automobile Club.

449. It is appropriate to observe that registration in the above-mentioned registers is established by various statutes with varying terminology (transcription, entry, annotation and such like). However, their function and effects are, in principle, similar to what was seen in the context of Real Estate Registers. In particular, registration relating to a mortgage has a constitutive effect: the security right arises only through the act of registration.

450. As with Real Estate Registers, all the Registers referred to above are publicly accessible. This means that registration and searching can be done electronically.

3. Spain

451. The Spanish Registry System, including the Land, Business and Personal Property Registries, is integrated in the Ministry of Justice which is in charge of the Land and Business Registries. Disputes are resolved by the General Directorate of Notaries and Registries (*Dirección General de los Registros y del Notariado*), an administrative body the case law of which is published in the Spanish official gazette, although it can be challenged in court. Nowadays all registries operate online, and *Spain* is part of the European Land Information Service (EULIS).[172] An Interactive Land Registry Information Service has been

170 See d.P.R. 15 February 1952 No 328 <www.normattiva.it> accessed 26 May 2016.

171 The advertising system of the pleasure ships is ruled by d.lgs. 18.07.2005 No 171 <www.normattiva.it> accessed 26 May 2016.

172 See <https://www.registradores.org/en/index.jsp> and <http://eulis.eu/> both accessed 26 May 2016.

set up and rights holders can apply for certificates online, while users with a legitimate interest can apply for land registry extracts, which are simple notes or location notes if they need information about the site of an immovable and its respective land registry (Art. 221 et seq. LH). The service is available in English.

452. The Land Registry is a registry of titles governed by the principles of public faith as regards what is published in the Registry, and publicity for which reason certainty is provided by the entries in the event that the registered situation is questioned, thus shifting the burden of proof onto the party that challenges the registry's content; acquisitions by a third party acting in good faith are upheld if they have been registered in the Land Registry (Art. 34 LH). Other principles that apply are those of legitimisation, constructing a rebuttable presumption that Registry entries are true, and the chain of succession, requesting that each new entry, i.e. right, is based on an old one. A priority in rule order is thus built up on the basis of these principles.

453. The Personal Property Registry brings together registries set up by different pieces of legislation in relation to movable assets, such as the chattel mortgage and non-possessory pledge registry and the hire-purchase agreement registry.[173] However, the registering of security rights follows the instructions laid down by the relevant legislation, namely RRM 1956, LHMPSD and LVPBM.

454. Unlike the Land Registry, the Personal Property Registry does not provide the assets' legal history, as it is a charges registry except where ships and aircraft are concerned. It cannot be otherwise, as subjecting the establishment of legal relationships over movables to registration would be disproportionately expensive. The registry's purpose is to protect secured creditors vis-à-vis third parties and/or other creditors. Its organisation is far from straightforward and it is divided into six sections, in which assets are mixed up with encumbrances: ships and aircraft (section 1); automobiles and other motor vehicles (section 2); industrial machinery, businesses and mobile equipment (section 3); other security rights (section 4); other movable assets requiring registration (section 5); and the general conditions of contract registration (section 6).

455. The Personal Property Registry functions uniquely as a title registry – and not only of encumbrances – as regards ships[174] and aircraft. A folio is opened for each ship or aircraft and the principles of chain of succession, legitimisation,

---

[173] The Personal Property Registry was set up by the Only Additional Disposition of Royal Decree 1828/1999, 3.12.1999, approving the regulation of the registry on general contracting conditions (BOE No 306, 23.12.1999). For a critical study see L. del Pozo, *El registro de bienes muebles*.

[174] The Registry covers all ships including those that operate for not-for-profit purposes, which are otherwise excluded from the Business Registry by Arts. 146 and 179 RRM/1956.

priority and registered public faith apply. In contrast, encumbrances other than those over ships and aircraft are entered in the relevant section, and a folio is opened for each registered asset which has security rights or contracts registered over it. As with the Land Registry, anyone with a legitimate interest can request information (Arts. 78 LHMPSD, 31 OVPBM). This Registry has been instituted as the national reference point for the purposes of complying with Article 18 of the Cape Town Convention. However, the Sixth Additional Disposition of Royal Decree 384/2015, 22 May on Registration of aircraft poses a number of issues, in particular that it may be in contradiction with the simplicity of the filing system laid down by the Cape Town Convention – for example, it lays down that international security rights on aircraft have to be registered in the Personal Property Registry – not yet solved by legislation or case law.

Question 21: To what extent does 'possession' or control of the secured assets serve as an alternative method to registration or filing in ensuring third party effectiveness of the security interest?

1. France

456. As regards pledge over movable tangible assets, whether common or commercial, provisions on its effectiveness against third parties varies according to whether the possession of a pledged asset is transferred or not. When the transfer of possession to a creditor or a third party designated in the contractual agreement occurs, the publicity granted by the debtor's dispossession determines the security right's effectiveness against third parties from that moment on. In the case of pledge over vehicles, the transfer of possession takes place once the creditor receives a document recording the mandatory declaration that the debtor must issue before the relevant administration body [Arts. 2351 and 2352 CC].

457. In pledge of claims, the date of creation determines its effectiveness vis-à-vis third parties (Art. 2361 CC). However, the debtor must be notified of the pledge for it to be effective against him, unless he has participated in the act creating the pledge. In all other cases, only the pledgor can receive payment of encumbered claims (Arts. 2361–2362 CC).

458. There is no generally accessible system for publicising a *fiducie* over tangible movable assets that are not put into the fiduciary's possession. Where there is no change of physical control of the assets, to which the parties can agree [Art. 2018(1) CC], the fiduciary runs the risk of the debtor selling the asset to a third party, who can avail himself of the protection provided by Article 2276 CC.[175]

---

175 See P. Ancel, *Droit des sûretés*, 232.

459. As regards the *fiducie* over intangible movable assets, Article 2018(2) CC establishes an identical provision to that stipulated in *nantissement* for the transfer of the ownership of claims by way of security. The rights conferred by the *fiducie* are thus effective against third parties from the date of the contract and against the debtor of the transferred claim from the time that he is notified of the contract.

2. Italy

460. Under Italian law there is no choice between registering the security right and transferring the 'possession' of the encumbered assets for ensuring third party effectiveness of the security interest. As widely explained, for certain types of assets and security rights Italian law requires the security registration. For other types, it requires the transfer of 'possession' of the encumbered assets.

461. The latter is the case with pledge, already examined in the answers to Questions 1–7, to which, for the sake of brevity, the reader is referred.

462. Particular types of special privilege on movable assets merit further discussion. Indeed, in some cases the existence of the privilege and the possibility of asserting the privilege against third parties depend on a certain de facto situation relating to the asset. This de facto situation may be that the assets are located with the creditor: reference is made, in this respect, to 'possessory privilege' (*privilegio possessuale*: e.g. Art 2760.1 Civil Code). The de facto situation may also be that the assets are at a place where the debtor can have access: reference is made, in this respect, to 'almost possessory privilege' (*privilegio quasi possessuale*: e.g. Arts 2757.2, 2759.1 Civil Code).[176] The fact that the assets are in some way 'detained' in these situations serves roughly the same publicity function as that performed by registration in public registers.[177]

3. Spain

463. As explained in Question 6, it is not possession or control of the secured assets that serves as an alternative method to registration to ensure third party effectiveness of the security interest, but the dispossession of the debtor on the grounds that nobody can transfer something that is not under his control to a third party, which corresponds to the French principle *en fait de meubles, possession vaut titre.*

---

176 C. Bianca, 'Le garanzie reali. La prescrizione' in C. Bianca, *Diritto civile*, vol. VII, 24 at 34.
177 F. Parente, *Il sistema dei privilegi del credito*, 49.

E. PLURALITY OF SECURITY RIGHTS

Question 22: Is it possible to have more than one set of security rights (security interest) over the same asset?

1. France

464. All assets of the debtor, either movable or immovable, can be subject to more than one general privilege, which can also compete with specials privileges. Privileges, security rights in rem and security-ownership devices can be created over the same asset.

465. The distinction between movable and immovable security rights in rem makes it clear that they cannot encumber the same asset, save the cases of mortgage and antichresis, which may encumber the same immovable. In general, assets can be subject to two or more security rights of the same type.

466. Retention of title clause and transfer of ownership by way of security can be created over pledged or mortgaged assets. In general, however, it is not possible to create a security right in rem over assets subject to security-ownership devices, without prejudice to the possible application of Article 2276 CC.

2. Italy

467. In general terms, it is possible to have more than one set of security rights over the same assets. In particular, it is possible to have multiple mortgages or multiple privileges and, according to the nature of the asset, a coexistence of privileges and mortgage or a coexistence of privileges and pledge.

468. By contrast, it is de facto unlikely that there will be multiple pledge rights over the same assets, at least for tangible assets. Indeed, the pledge is created through the delivery of the assets. Therefore, after the constitution of the first pledge, the 'dispossessed' constituent will no longer be able to deliver the same to other creditors. Nevertheless, scholars recognise, theoretically, the possibility of a pledge next in ranking. The second pledge would be over any surplus value remaining after the claim of the first pledgee to the pledged assets is fully satisfied. For a valid constitution, it would require that the first pledgee agrees to possess the pledged assets also for the benefit of the new creditor.[178]

---

[178] C. Bianca, 'Le garanzie reali. La prescrizione' in C. Bianca, *Diritto civile*, vol. VII, 188.

3. Spain

469. Encumbered assets can be subject to different security rights in *Spain*. The only exceptions were in respect of assets subject to chattel mortgages and non-possessory pledges, on the basis that Article 2 LHMPSD laid down that these types of security right could only be created over unencumbered assets. This provision was amended, however, in 2007. As a result, these security rights may exist side by side with another type of security right; this is especially true of mortgages over immovable assets, which also cover an asset's appurtenances such as movable assets or 'fruits', whichever is applicable [Art. 111(1) LH]. In fact, a movable asset such as industrial machinery may be subject to mortgage, chattel mortgage, non-possessory pledge, typical pledge and a title retention provision included in a hire-purchase agreement. The only rights that cannot co-exist over the same assets are chattel mortgage and non-possessory pledge, due to the prohibition contained in Articles 12 and 55 LHMPSD. Catalan law only lays down possessory pledges, despite the fact that the pledgor may retain material possession if the pledgee agrees.[179] This piece of legislation displaces Spanish CC provisions on pledge where appropriate, but not the 1954 law on chattel mortgage and non-possessory pledge given that the latter addresses different security rights. Accordingly, an asset may also be subject to both, the Catalan pledge and a chattel mortgage or a non-possessory pledge.

Question 23: What are the rules for determining priority between competing security interests in the same property?

1. France

470. The question of determining priority between competing rights requires the systemisation of existing cases, which are only occasionally resolved by the law.

471. *Conflicts between privileges.* Article 2331 CC establishes the priority order among general privileges over movables, which is complemented by tax and labour legislation. Privileges are paid according to the following priority ranking:

(a) legal expenses resulting from the administration and realisation of the debtor's assets, provided that they have been incurred in the collective interests of creditors;
(b) privileges granted to Public Treasury for certain tax claims;
(c) funeral and final illness expenses;

179 See P. Pozo Carrascosa, A. Vaquer Aloy and E. Bosch Capdevila, *Derecho Civil de Cataluña. Derechos reales*, 450.

(d) wages and other claims resulting from the last six months of the employment relationship;
(e) other privileges of minor importance, in the order established by the said provision.

472. When a general privilege conflicts with a special privilege over the same movable, the latter takes priority [Art. 2332(1) CC], save in the case of the general privilege granted to legal expenses and that of the Public Treasury for certain tax claims, which have always the priority of a special privilege.

473. Articles 2332 and 2332(3) CC establish the priority order among special privileges over movables. In respect of special privileges over immovable assets, priority is determined by the date of the claim, provided that they are registered.

474. *Conflict between pledges over tangible assets:* The conflict between various pledgees over a tangible asset is addressed by Article 2340 CC. This distinguishes between two basic situations: competition among various non-possessory pledges, which is resolved by order of registration, and competition between a non-possessory pledge and a subsequent possessory pledge (the reverse situation is not possible) which is resolved in favour of the former; the non-possessory pledge registered at an earlier date takes priority over a subsequent possessory pledge, despite the latter's right to retention [Art. 2340(2) CC].

475. *Conflict between pledges of claims:* In the absence of any specific regulations, it is possible to apply, mutatis mutandis, Article 2340 CC, under which notification of the pledge to the debtor is deemed to amount to transfer of possession of the asset. In the absence of notification, the earliest *nantissement* takes priority. If only the second pledge has notified the debtor in respect of the pledged claim (account debtor), the theoretical priority of the first pledgee loses any practical value in the sense that after receiving notification the debtor can only satisfy the claim by paying the pledgee who provides the notification.

476. *Conflict between mortgages*: Where mortgages are concerned, each creditor's position in the order of priority over the same asset is determined by the date of registration. Mortgagees may agree on transfers of priority order (Art. 2424 CC). Should more than one mortgage be registered on the same day, preference is given to the one deriving from a prior contract, and if the date is the same, the mortgagees have an equal position in the priority order (Art. 2425 CC).

477. *Conflict between mortgage and antichresis*: Due to the transfer of possession of an asset that is implied in antichresis, it is not possible to create two rights of the same type over the same asset. However, antichresis can be in opposition to a mortgage, and the conflict is resolved by the priority established according to the registration date rule. The right to retention granted by the law to the holder of antichresis is not effective against mortgagees who have previously registered (Art. 2340 CC by analogy).

478. *Conflict between privileges and security rights in rem:* In relation to security rights over movable assets, a pledge is ranked behind general privileges such as legal expenses and certain tax claims, and behind claims deriving from expenses incurred in keeping an asset in good condition. Conversely, mortgages over movables have priority over common privileges arising after the registration of the security right.

479. In respect of security rights over immovable assets, the preference over them is granted to legal expenses, wage claims and registered immovable special privileges arising before the registration of a mortgage (Art. 2324 and 2376 CC).

480. *Retention of title clauses versus security rights in rem*: Competition between a pledgee and a seller who had sold the asset including a retention of title clause in the hire-purchase contract is solved by the Court of Cassation in favour of the right of the subsequent pledgee who prevails over that of the unpaid seller on the basis of Article 2279, today Article 2276 CC. Furthermore, the creditor with a retention of title clause may find that his right to terminate the contract in case of breach on the side of the debtor and thus to recover the encumbered assets, is stayed by another creditor exercising a right to retention over the asset.

481. *Fiducie-sûreté versus security rights*: The *droit de suite* over the encumbered asset granted to creditors secured by security rights in rem can be exercised against secured creditors by a *fiducie* to whom pledged assets or mortgaged assets have been subsequently transferred. It must be noted that the conflict does not arise as regards to a previous antichresis on the grounds of its possessory nature. When the *fiducie* has been set up previously, the creation of subsequent security rights in rem over the same asset, either by the debtor or the secured creditor by the *fiducie*, will be deemed null and void on the grounds that none of them have powers of disposition over the asset. Publicising a *fiducie* suspends the effects of Article 2276 CC.

2. Italy

482. To answer this question, a distinction must be made depending on whether several security rights of the same type or several security rights of a different type coexist over the same assets.

2.1. Competing security rights of the same type

483. *Pledge.* As explained (see the answer to Question 22), the possibility of having competing pledge rights is de facto unlikely. If this occurs, the general principle for determining their ranking is that of priority in time (of the collateral constitution).

484. *Mortgage.* Italian law expressly allows the constitution of multiple mortgages over the same asset. Accordingly, it affords clear regulation of the order of priority among mortgages. The general rules provided on the subject by the Civil Code establish that the mortgage takes its ranking from the moment of its entry (and not from the date of the title: Art 2852 Civil Code). For this purpose, every entry receives an order number, and this number determines the 'ranking' of the mortgage. If several people simultaneously request an entry of a mortgage against the same person or over the same immovable assets, these mortgages are entered under the same number and have the same ranking. The creditors, therefore, will share with one another in proportion to the amount of their respective claims (Arts 2853–2854 Civil Code).

485. *Special privilege.* As explained above (see the answer to Question 1), a privilege is a preference granted by the law because of the basis of the claim. It follows that, in the case of coexistence of several preferential claims over the same assets or complex of assets, to establish the order of preference among privileges, reference is not made to time as a determining factor (as in the case for other security rights) but, rather, to the basis of the claim. As a rule, this evaluation is made by the law. The general regulation on the subject is contained in Articles 2777–2783-*ter* of the Civil Code, to which, for the sake of brevity, the reader is referred.

2.2. Competing security rights of different type

486. As mentioned, over the same assets, according to their nature, it is possible to have the coexistence of special privileges and mortgage or the coexistence of special privileges and pledge. The graduation among these different grounds of preference is set out by express legal provision.

487. *Coexistence of special privileges and mortgage.* If privileges and mortgage coexist over the same asset, Article 2748.2 of the Civil Code establishes that, unless the law provides otherwise, creditors that have privilege over immovable assets are preferred to mortgagees.

488. *Coexistence of special privileges and pledge.* If privileges and pledge coexist over the same asset, Article 2748.1 of the Civil Code establishes that, unless the law provides otherwise, special privilege over movable assets cannot be exercised to the prejudice of the pledgee.

3. Spain

489. Priority between competing security interests over the same asset depends in principle on the priority of order provided by the registry. The rule applies neatly to security rights of the same type. Competing mortgages over the same immovable asset are classified in accordance with either the date that registration was applied for (Art. 24 LH) or the time of registration where appropriate (Art. 25 LH). Nevertheless, all contractual mortgages take second place to tacit legal mortgages, as they arise automatically by operation of law and do not need registration, i.e. publicity, to produce effects against third parties. Priority on the basis of the date that registration was applied for also applies to chattel mortgages, ship mortgages, non-possessory pledges, retention of title clauses and/or prohibitions on disposal contained in hire-purchase or financing agreements as laid down by LVPBM, as they all have to be registered in the Personal Property Registry.

490. As it is dependent on the dispossession of the debtor, a second pledge is feasible provided that the first creditor is notified of the creation of the second pledge. In some cases this creditor acts as a depositary on the second pledgee's behalf; in others, a third party is the depositary for both creditors. The first always has to be notified of the creation of a second pledge, although notification does not prevent problems at the time of enforcement, which are reduced in the framework of insolvency proceedings.

491. Should there be different types of security rights over the same asset, conflicts are always resolved in accordance with the priority rule, generally taking either the date of registration in the respective registry or the date of the pledge's creation recorded in the public document as a reference. Nevertheless, some remarks need to be made as seen in the paragraphs that follow.

492. The conflict between a chattel mortgage or a non-possessory pledge and a mortgage over an immovable asset that extends to its appurtenances is addressed in Article 75 LHMPSD, which requires a marginal note to be made in the Land Registry to the effect that the former is to be given priority over the latter. The relevant date is the date on the note in the Land Registry. If a mortgage over an immovable is registered first, the issue arises as to whether it covers all appurtenances, and thus any subsequent chattel mortgage or non-possessory pledge has to take second place. Should the appurtenances be specifically detailed in the mortgage registration or be part of the immovable asset at the time of both the mortgage's creation and its enforcement, any subsequent chattel mortgage or non-possessory pledge is relegated in terms of priority. In contrast, a chattel mortgage or non-possessory pledge only takes priority in the event of the movable asset being specifically separate from the encumbered immovable property. The same applies to retention of title clauses and prohibitions on disposal registered in the Personal Property Registry, meaning that they are given priority over mortgages on immovable assets where movable assets that were only attached to the immovable after its creation are concerned.[180]

493. As mentioned above, a chattel mortgage or non-possessory pledge can now be created over encumbered assets or assets not yet fully paid for, and so prior encumbrances have to take priority over them, as well as the rights of an unpaid seller, even if the latter's contract containing a retention of title clause had not been registered (Arts. 21, 22 and 56 LHMPSD). In contrast, a possessory pledge is preferred in these cases, provided that the hire-purchase or financing agreement does not include a retention of title clause and/or a prohibition on disposal and was not registered prior to the creation of the pledge; otherwise, these security rights are given priority over pledges [Art. 16(5) LVPBM].

Question 24: Are there special rules privileging the position of an acquisition financier, i.e. a secured party whose advance of funds funded the acquisition of a particular asset and who may be in a priority competition with an earlier general creditor whose security interest extends to all assets of the debtor whenever acquired?

1. France

494. A claim only enjoys privilege if it is accompanied by the creation of a security right. An exception to this rule is the case of hire-purchase contracts, in particular when they are concluded over movable assets or *vente a tempèrement*, whereby the seller financing the acquisition retains ownership of the asset until all payments have been made; these sales can also be subsumed under the special privilege over movables in Article 2332(4) CC.

495. In the framework of insolvency proceedings, secured claims arising from contracts financing the acquisition of a particular asset benefit from a special rule; while security interests are terminated and thus do not follow the debtor's business or whole assets sold to a third party, the former do follow the assets acquired with such financing and included in the sold business or assets, i.e. the acquirer takes on the secured claim [Art. L. 642(12)(4) CComm.].

2. Italy

496. Under Italian law there are special rules privileging the position of an acquisition financier at the expense of earlier creditors. Of particular importance

[180] See SSTS 14.12.2000 (RJ 2000/10442) and 7.4.2001 (RJ 2001/2387).

among these, due to the quality of the financier and of the normative source, are Article 2762.4 of the Civil Code and Articles 44.2 and 46 of the Unified Banking Code.[181]

2.1. *Special privilege referred to by Article 2762.4 of the Civil Code*

497. This provision states that a bank, which has provided the purchase price to the buyer of machines (not entered in the public registers), has privilege for its claim over the machines sold and delivered. The privilege subsists on condition that the document proving the claim indicates the purpose, the amount and the maturity date of the claim, contains the exact designation of the machine object of privilege and is registered in the Register for transcriptions of sales with retention of title clause[182] kept in the office of the clerk of the court in the jurisdiction in which the machine is situated.[183]

2.2. *Special privileges referred to by Articles 44.2 and 46 of the Unified Bank Code*

498. Article 44.2 of the Unified Bank Code establishes that the financings of agrarian credit and fishing credit provided by the banks in the short and medium term are assisted by special privilege on financed enterprise's movable assets indicated by the same and, specifically: (a) on 'fruits' not separated from the object which they originate from, finished products and ones being processed; (b) on livestock, commodities, stocks, raw materials, machines, utensils and other assets however purchased with the financing granted; (c) on credits, also future ones, deriving from the sale of the assets indicated at letters (a) and (b). The mere legislative provision is sufficient to make this privilege effective.

499. Article 46 of the Unified Bank Code states that the granting of financings by the banks to firms in the medium and long term can be guaranteed by special privilege on movable assets that are destined for the firm's activities, not entered in the public registers. These assets must only be those indicated by legislative provision and, particularly: (a) plant and works both current and future, franchises and instrumental assets; (b) raw materials, products being processed, stocks, finished products, fruit, livestock and commodities; (c) assets purchased at any rate with the financing granted; (d) credits, also future, deriving from the sale of the goods indicated at the previous letters. The privilege in question has

---

181 D.lgs. 1.09.1993 No 385 <www.normattiva.it> accessed 26 May 2016.

182 See d.m. 27.03.2000 No 264 <www.normattiva.it> accessed 26 May 2016.

183 C. Bianca, 'Le garanzie reali. La prescrizione' in C. Bianca, *Diritto civile*, vol. VII, 105–108.

a consensual nature. Even if the privilege, as a general rule, is not born as a separate right aimed at strengthening the credit right, but rather is a way of being of the latter in accordance with a special evaluation provided by law (see paras. 107–110), Article 46 of the Unified Bank Code is not sufficient in itself to make the privilege effective: an agreement between the parties is required. Specifically, the privilege has to result from a written deed, otherwise it will be void, and has to contain the exact description of the assets and claims on which the privilege is constituted, the creditor bank, the debtor and the subject that has granted the privilege, the amount and the conditions of the financing, as well as the sum of money for which the privilege is taken on. The possibility of asserting such privilege against third parties is subordinated to the transcription of the deed in a special Register devoted to the transcriptions of sales with retention of title clause.[184]

3. Spain

500. There are no special rules privileging the position of an acquisition financier at the expense of earlier creditors. However, two controversial sets of circumstances may arise: there may be first a clash between a security right that is created over future assets and another right securing the same assets when they become part of the debtor's estate, and second the third party acquisition of a security right in good faith. The principle of order of priority operates for all other cases, as detailed in Question 23.

501. Both cases lack significance in practice, however. When it comes to security rights created over future assets, chattel mortgages and non-possessory pledges come to the fore in the event that these future assets, such as goods, raw materials, livestock and so on, are bought under a contract that includes a retention of title clause. It is common opinion that a security right over future assets cannot take priority over the right of the seller or financier. As to the acquisition of security rights by a third party in good faith, its feasibility is almost entirely restricted to pledges in view of the registration system, and the pledging of claims cannot be a matter for controversy as it always requires the pledgor to be the owner of the claim. The only troublesome case is the clash between non-possessory and possessory pledges. Despite the legal prohibition on creating a pledge after a non-possessory pledge has been created (Art. 55 LHMPSD), a possessory pledge can be acquired by a third party in good faith to the extent that the non-possessory pledge is not opposed to him as it is not legally foreseen how to establish the priority of a non-possessory pledge over the right of a third party

184 *Ibid.* at 113–115.

in good faith; the lacuna thereby makes possible the creation of a pledge after a non-possessory one. There is a proviso, however: acquisition by a third party in good faith is doctrinally restricted against this background to cases in which the asset is no longer found in the territorial demarcation of the Personal Property Registry's office where the non-possessory pledge is registered; otherwise, mala fides is always presumed in the third party's acquisition.[185]

F. QUASI-SECURITY AGREEMENTS

Question 25: Does your legal system have any rules equating the treatment, in whole or in part, of security interest and 'quasi-security' agreements, i.e. agreements that in legal terms do not involve the creation of security interests but have many of the same economic consequences? Examples of quasi-security include the factoring or sale of receivables and finance leases, hire purchase agreements and retention of title clauses in sale of goods contracts.

1. France

502. The Civil Code comprehensively regulates security rights in rem and barely deals with the concept of 'quasi-security'. However, *crédit-bail* or leasing can be considered an example: a leasing company, the *crédit bailleur*, acquires an asset to be leased to a third party, who can acquire ownership of it at the end of the contract. The lessor thus retains ownership of the asset until the end of the credit period and can demand its return in the case of default, even after the opening of insolvency proceedings.

503. Although it is not included in Title II of Book IV, leasing is treated as a security right by the *Code Monétaire et Financier*, which requires it to be publicised in a special register at the commercial court to be effective against third parties, and by the insolvency legislation, which grants the leasing company that has registered the contract a privileged position to the extent that it does not have to prove ownership over the assets and can bring a reclamation action even after the three-month period within which other similar actions must be brought once the insolvency proceedings have been opened. The insolvency court judge may provide that the debtor or the IP may exercise the option to purchase the asset on paying all due instalments. In the framework of the insolvency proceedings these payments may only be made if it is established that the asset is necessary for the running of the debtor's enterprise and that the payments are less than the asset's market value [Arts. L. 622(7)(II) and L. 631(14) CComm.].

185 See A. Carrasco Perera, E. Cordero Lobato and M.J. Marín López, *Tratado de los derechos de garantía*, 379–381, 383.

504. A second type of 'quasi-security' is known as the 'Dailly assignment' and consists of the transfer of professional claims, present or future, to a credit institution from their clients.[186] When this occurs by way of security and no price is given, the assignment transfers ownership of the claims to the financial institution and the claims are only recoverable by the client once the credit granted is satisfied. In the event of default, the institution pools ownership of the claims. The assignment functions through a form listing the assigned claims (the *bordereau Dailly*) being handed to the financial institution. The date on the document determines the third party effects of the assignee's right of ownership.[187]

2. Italy

505. Under Italian law it is possible to provide for agreements that in legal terms do not involve the creation of security interests but nonetheless have many of the same economic consequences. The contractual scheme used mainly consists in selling or, more generally, transferring a right: essentially, the sale of assets or the assignment of claims as a guarantee of the fulfilment of an obligation.

506. However, the development of such agreements (according to a widespread trend in international trade) has in *Italy* encountered an obstacle in the shape of the statutory ban on the 'forfeiture agreement' (*patto commissorio*). This ban is established by Article 2744 of the Civil Code and implies the nullity of the agreement whereby it is agreed that in default of the payment of the debt in the established term, the ownership of the assets given as a pledge or mortgaged is automatically transferred to the creditor.

507. In formal terms, the ban only covers a forfeiture agreement which is auxiliary to a security right encumbering given assets. Nevertheless, the rule established by Article 2744 of the Civil Code is universally deemed to be a general principle designed to penalise the unlawfulness of a certain economic result, i.e. the unlawful coercion of the debtor to submit to the will of the creditor, agreeing ex ante the transfer of ownership of certain assets as a result of non-payment of a debt regardless of the actual value of the assets which may potentially be greater than the amount of the debt. The courts will penalise as void (pursuant to Art 2744 of the Civil Code) any agreement, even one not auxiliary to a security

---

186 First regulated by the Dailly Law of 2 February 1981, it is presently laid down in Articles L. 313(23) et seq. of the C. Mon and Fin. These regulations are the basis of the present norms on pledge over claims.

187 The Court of Cassation has refused to recognise the assignment of claims as way of security beyond the case laid down by the Dailly Law (Cass. Comm. 19.12.2006; Cass. Comm. 26.5.2010).

right, even if otherwise lawful and whatever its content, which is used to pursue in practice the banned result.[188]

508. The invalidating provision of the Civil Code has been applied to sales for guarantee purposes (*alienazioni a scopo di garanzia*), both to cases in which it is agreed that the ownership of a given good of the debtor is transferred to the creditor in case of default as well as in cases in which it is agreed that the purchase is terminated in case of default;[189] trust for guarantee purposes;[190] preliminary sale agreement;[191] mandate to sell conferred by the debtor to the creditor;[192] 'sale and lease back' agreement (see below, para. 519);[193] sale with repurchase clauses (see below, para. 516).[194]

509. The extensive application of Article 2744 of the Civil Code has highlighted the importance of the 'Marcian agreement' (*patto Marciano*), i.e. the contract whereby it is agreed that the transfer of ownership of the collateral is subject to the estimate of its value made by a third party at default; so that if this value exceeds the amount of the secured claim, the creditor must repay the excess to the debtor. The Marcian agreement, then, is a sale for guarantee purposes, but it is characterised by the clause pre-estimating the likely loss for the secured creditor in the event of default by the debtor. For this reason the Marcian agreement escapes the ban under Article 2744 of the Civil Code and as such is widely deemed to be lawful.[195]

510. After this general premise, a description of the 'quasi-security' agreements follows. This description focuses, for the sake of brevity, only on the types considered of particular interest from the present question.

---

188 Cass. civ. 2.2.2006 no 2285, (2007) I GC 700.

189 Cass. civ. Sez. Un. 3.4.1989 no 1611, [1989] *MGC* 431–432.

190 Trib. Bologna 3.12.1996, (1998) II *BBTC* 177, which states this indirectly. Actually, Italy is a non-trust jurisdiction. Nevertheless, Italy has signed the Convention of 1 July 1985 on the Law Applicable to Trusts and on their Recognition. Moreover, some scholars, such as M. Lupoi, *Trusts*, 533 et seq., maintain that this Convention would allow an Italian resident to create a trust in Italy when the assets, located in Italy, have been placed under the control of an Italian trustee, provided the Italian settlor chooses the law of a trust jurisdiction as a law governing the trust. In fact, these writers state that the choice of a foreign law would suffice to apply the Convention and obtaining the recognition of the trust by the Italian jurisdiction. However, this position, which is followed by some local courts, is highly controversial. On the point, see F. Gazzoni, [2001] *RN* 1247 et seq.

191 Cass. civ. 23.10.1999 no 11924, [2000] *GI* 1599.

192 Cass. civ. 10.3.2011 no 5740, (2011) I *GC* 1449.

193 Cass. civ. 22.3.2007 no 6969, [2007] *MGC* 635.

194 Cass. civ. 20.6.2008 no 16953, [2008] *MGC* 1006.

195 N. Cipriani, *Patto commissorio e patto marciano*, 137.

2.1. *Sale with retention of title clauses*

511. Sale with retention of title clause is recognised by Article 1523 of the Civil Code. This states that, in hire purchase of movable assets with retention of title clause, the buyer takes on the risks relating to the perishing of the assets from the moment of delivery, but only acquires ownership of the assets with the payment of the final instalment.[196] It follows that the buyer, until that time, cannot sell the assets, nor they can be attached by his creditors, since they are still owned by the seller.

512. Therefore, the clause provides to the seller an effective means of protection against any default of the buyer. Nevertheless, to protect the buyer's creditors (who may not be aware of its existence), it is established that the retention of title clause may be asserted against them only if the clause is recorded with a certain date that precedes the attachment by the buyer (Art 1524 Civil Code), and the same also applies in relation to insolvency proceedings affecting the buyer.

513. Moreover, in the event of insolvency proceedings affecting the buyer, the seller enjoys some protection. Article 73.1–2 L.Fall. states that the sale contract remains suspended until the IP declares whether he wishes to assume or reject the contract. In the first case, the seller can ask for a caution unless the IP immediately pays the price; in the second case, the seller can ask for the recovery of the assets that are still owned by him. Nevertheless, the seller has to repay the instalments already collected but he has the right to an equitable remuneration for the buyer's use of the assets.[197]

2.2. *Sale with repurchase clauses*

514. Sale with repurchase clause is recognised by Article 1500.1 of the Civil Code. This states that the seller can reserve the right to recover ownership of the assets sold (right of repurchase) within a specified term through the repayment to the buyer of the price and expenses, without it being necessary to provide for a new contract.

515. A repurchase clause can concern both movable and immovable assets and it is used, as a rule, when the seller has to deprive himself of ownership of the assets to cope with a temporary financial difficulty. For the purpose of protecting the seller, the weaker party in this relationship, Article 1500.2 of the Civil Code lays down that the agreement to pay back a higher price than that stipulated for the sale is void as regards the excess amount.

---

196 Cass. civ. 8.4.1999 no 3415, [2001] *N* 473.

197 Cass. civ. 24.2.1998 no 1999, [1998] *F* 604.

516. This rule reflects the use that is made of this contract in commercial practice. Sale with a repurchase clause is often a financial operation in which payment of the purchase price corresponds to a loan; the subsequent repayment of the price corresponds to the repayment of the loan. From this perspective, sale with a repurchase clause acts as a 'real' security of the claim of the buyer-financier, protected through ownership of the assets that are the object of the transfer. However, if stipulated exclusively for the purpose of guarantee, this typology of sale (abstractly lawful) is deemed to be void as it is used by the parties to pursue the economic result banned by Article 2744 of the Civil Code.[198]

517. Without prejudice to the above, in the event of the seller's bankruptcy the position of the buyer is protected to an extent. Specifically, the seller's right of repurchase is transferred to the IP who can exercise it for the purpose of reconstituting the debtor's assets. The exercise of the right, however, entails the actual repayment to the buyer of the price that was paid by him, in addition to the expenses.[199]

2.3. Finance leasing/sale and lease back

518. Finance leasing is an agreement imported into *Italy* from foreign commercial practice. It is a trilateral operation which involves the leasing company (lessor), the entrepreneur interested in the use of the assets (lessee) and the entrepreneur that produces or distributes them (supplier). The lessor purchases from the supplier the assets desired by the lessee and grants him a right of use, providing for an agreement (leasing) that has the following features: (a) use is granted for a determined period; (b) the lessee has to pay to the lessor a periodical fee as compensation for use; (c) the lessee has the facility to acquire ownership of the assets on expiration of the agreement, paying a predetermined price. As a rule, the lessor contractually excludes his own liability for all risks connected to the use of assets but, on the other hand, grants to the lessee the right to exercise, against the supplier, the warranty rights arising from the sale.[200]

519. The vast and multifaceted category of leasing also includes the 'sale and lease back' agreement. In a *de qua* operation, an entrepreneur sells his own assets (movable, immovable, even all the assets of a firm) to a leasing company which pays their price. At the same time the leasing company stipulates with the seller a leasing agreement having as its object the same assets. The latter, therefore, remain

198 C. Bianca, 'Le garanzie reali. La prescrizione' in C. Bianca, *Diritto civile*, vol. VII, 290–293. In judiciary, see Cass. civ. 12.10.2011 no 20956, [2011] *C* 1144.

199 Cass. civ. 3.4.1991 no 3478, [1991] *F* 799.

200 G. Rescio, *La traslazione del rischio contrattuale nel leasing*, 182 et seq.

in use for the seller who must pay the leasing fees and may repurchase the assets on expiration of the agreement, by paying a predetermined price. A 'sale and lease back' agreement has its own specific structure and function, and is, in the abstract, considered lawful. However, as well as the sale with a repurchase clause, the 'sale and lease back' agreement is suitable, in practice, for obscuring a sale which does not have a 'leasing function' but a 'guarantee function'. The guarantee function is presumed, for example, when there is a clear disproportion between the value of the assets and the sums paid by the leasing company. Only if this and certain other features are present will the 'sale and lease back' agreement be considered void pursuant to Article 2744 of the Civil Code.[201]

520. Without prejudice to the above, in the event of the lessee's bankruptcy the lessor enjoys some protection. Article 72-*quater* L.Fall. states that the agreement remains suspended until the IP decides whether to assume or reject the contract. In the latter case, the lessor has a right to restitution of the assets. On the other hand, the lessor is obliged to repay to the IP the difference between the sale proceeds and the residual claim. If this claim is not satisfied by the sale, the lessor may lodge it in the insolvency proceedings. In any case, for the payments already collected, the lessor enjoys exemption from transactional avoidance in accordance with Article 67.3.a of the L.Fall. (see further the answer to Question 28).

2.4. *Assignment of claim for guarantee purposes*

521. Under Italian law the creditor can assign his claim with or without valuable consideration, also without the consent of the debtor, provided that the claim does not have a strictly personal character or the assignment is not banned by law (Art 1260 Civil Code). The transfer of ownership of a claim in favour of a is immediate, but becomes effective towards the assigned debtor only when it has been notified to him or accepted by him (Art 1264 Civil Code).

522. The assignment of claim can be stipulated also for guarantee purposes (*cessione del credito a scopo di garanzia*) and, in this case, acts as a security. This is broadly employed in the relationships between entrepreneurs and banks. In this context, the bank grants a loan to an entrepreneur making the sum available in a current account; at the same time, to guarantee the repayment of capital and interest, the bank obtains the assignment of certain claims that the entrepreneur has against third parties. In the event of default, the bank satisfies its claim against the entrepreneur from the claims assigned to it, with the obligation to repay any

201 Cass. civ. 9.3.2011 no 5583, [2011] *N* 259.

excess amount (otherwise the contract will be void pursuant to Art 2744 Civil Code).[202]

523. The assignment of a claim for guarantee purposes is distinguished from the pledge over claims because the former transfers to the assignee the ownership of the claims whereas the latter provides to the pledgee a security right on claims of which the pledgor remains owner. It follows that, in the case of the assignor's bankruptcy, the assignment of a claim for guarantee purposes, previously notified (or accepted), affords to the assignee the advantage of being able to obtain satisfaction from the assigned claims without the burden of having to lodge his claim in the insolvency proceedings.[203]

2.5. *Factoring*

524. The essential nucleus of the factoring contract is constituted by the assignment of claims (Art 1260 Civil Code). Generally speaking, factoring can be defined as a global assignment of monetary credits with valuable consideration. Under Italian law, this agreement is regulated by L. 21 February 1991 No 52.[204] The essential scheme of the contract contemplates an entrepreneur (assignor-supplier) assigning to another entrepreneur (assignee-factor) ownership of the claims derived or that will derive from the exercise of his business, with or without a guarantee of the debtor's solvency. In turn, the factor undertakes to manage and collect the assigned claims; he can also undertake the granting of advances on the amount of the same claims and to taking on the insolvency risk of the assigned debtor.

525. Specific regulation protects the factor against possible abuses by the assignor who, in breach of the agreement, assigns the same claims to third parties, as well as against the assignor's other creditors and against bankruptcy of the same. Indeed, the effectiveness of the assignment against third parties does not require notification to the assigned debtors when the following conditions occur: (a) the factor has totally or partly paid the price for the assignment; (b) the payment has a certain date that is prior to the title of third-party assignees of the assignor, to the attachment of other creditors or to bankruptcy proceedings (Art 5 L. 52/1991).[205]

526. Additionally, in the latter case the IP takes over the contract automatically and will have to fulfil its obligations entirely. He can withdraw from the contract,

---

202 C. Bianca, 'Le garanzie reali. La prescrizione' in C. Bianca, *Diritto civile*, vol. VII, 267.

203 Cass. civ. 3.2.1987 no 950, (1987) II *DF* 692.

204 <www.normattiva.it> accessed 26 May 2016.

205 For an exception to the opposability regime against insolvency proceedings of the supplier see Art 7.1 L. 52/1991.

but only with effect for the claims that have not yet arisen at the date of the opening of insolvency proceedings. Moreover, the IP will have to repay the factor the sums that have already been paid for the claims in question (Art 7.2-3 L. 52/1991).

3. Spain

3.1. Retention of title

527. Retention of title clauses that are included in contracts other than those laid down by the LVPBM cannot be held as security rights. As stated in Question 1, the Spanish system lacks thorough regulation of these clauses, but the matter is mentioned in a number of laws apart from the LVPBM already discussed, such as Article 17 of Law 7/1996 of 15 January on Retail Commerce,[206] and Article 10 of Law 3/2004 of 29 December on combating late payment in commercial transactions.[207] Laws 483–485 of the *Fuero Nuevo*, the private law in Navarre, do tackle its regulation on the grounds that ownership is not transferred to the buyer until full payment has been made. Accordingly, the seller is still the owner and as such may defend his right against third parties. Contracts that include a retention of title clause entitle the buyer to possess and use the asset, while the seller is obliged not to resell it; in the event of seller insolvency, the buyer is still entitled to become the owner after full payment of all instalments. Should the buyer not meet a number of instalments, the seller has the right to terminate the contract, i.e. each party's consideration is returned although the seller is entitled to compensation for the asset's loss of value. The *Fuero Nuevo* applies to contracts that contain a retention of title that was concluded or enforced in Navarre, as the inter-regional conflict of laws is resolved in accordance with Article 10(5) CC by reference to Article 16 CC.[208] Apart from the retention of title that is subject to this piece of legislation or the LVPBM, the matter of their effects remains unsettled; the general legal opinion is, however, that the seller is the owner until full payment has been made, and therefore the legal consequences are similar to those laid down by the *Fuero Nuevo*. At any rate, Article 90(1)(4) LC does grant special privilege to claims arising out of hire-purchase agreements that include a retention of title clause and/ or a prohibition on disposal. The same applies to sales under condition subsequent

206 BOE No 15, 17.1.1996.

207 BOE No 314, 30.12.2004. Transposing Directive 2000/35/EC, this law has been amended to transpose Directive 2011/7/EU of the European Parliament and of the Council of 16 February 2011 on combating late payment in commercial transactions (OJ 2011 L48).

208 As stated in Question 1, Article 16 CC is the one rule dealing with inter-regional conflict of laws in Spain and refers this issue to Spanish international conflict rules. In default of a specific declaration by the Spanish legislator, Regulation (EC) No 593/2008 on the law applicable to contractual obligations is thus not applicable here.

in the event of non-payment. This type of contract is not addressed by LVPBM, and it is therefore understood that the aforementioned special privilege only applies if the sale under condition subsequent refers to immovable assets; the granting of privilege thus depends on it being recorded in a public document and registered [Arts. 1504 CC, 9(2) and 23 LH]. In either case special privilege is restricted to claims arising from the contracts mentioned above for unpaid instalments.

3.2. *Financial lease*

528. As with retention of title clauses, the Spanish system addresses the financial lease in the Third Additional Disposition of Law 10/2014 of 26 June on Control of Credit Institutions,[209] while in accordance with the First Additional Disposition LVPBM financial leases on tangible, non-consumable and identified assets can be registered in the Personal Property Registry and terminated by the procedure laid down in Article 250(1)(11) LEC. This action is governed by Article 56(1) LC in the event of lessee insolvency and is thus affected by the stay following the opening of insolvency proceedings, provided that the asset in question is necessary for the debtor's enterprise. In general, financial leases over either movable or immovable assets grant the leasing company a priority right in the event of lessee insolvency proceedings for unpaid instalments and the compensation for the non-exercise of the purchase option [Art. 90(1)(4) LC].

3.3. *Lease back or sale and lease back*

529. Lease back or sale and lease back is not unknown in Spanish practice either and its registration in the Personal Property Registry is accepted. Nevertheless, there is no agreement on whether it is a type of financial leasing[210] or a transfer of ownership by way of security.[211] The latter has been the cause of even more debate as it is not clear whether the grantee becomes full owner of the transferred asset or not; transfer of ownership takes place for financing purposes and thus the grantee holds a limited right of ownership. The point is that the Spanish system does not provide an adequate legal construction for this restriction, as the Spanish system is not familiar with either trust or fiduciary contracts.[212] The resulting legal uncertainty has restricted the use of this financing method, which is in practice almost entirely restricted to business between private individuals. Law 466 of the *Fuero Nuevo* in Navarre on *fiducia en garantía* is the exception.

209 BOE No 156, 27.6.2014.
210 See STS 2.2.2006 (RJ 2006/494).
211 See STS 25.2.2005 (RJ 2005/1405).
212 See SSTS 15.7.2003 (RJ 2003/4462); 10.3.2005 (RJ 2005/1405); 2.2.2006 (RJ 2006/494).

Nevertheless, it must be noted that these are not covered by Article 90 LC and thus creditors secured by this means do not enjoy special preference in insolvency proceedings.

3.4. *Factoring*

530. Factoring or purchase of receivables is also practised in *Spain*. A distinction is made between non-recourse and recourse factoring according to whether the factor bears the risk of the transferred claim proving to be valueless because the debtor cannot pay the debt. The Third Additional Disposition of Law 1/1999 on private equity firms and their management companies provides for a special regime for the specific assignment of claims, i.e. (1) the assignor is a business and assigned claims arise out of his enterprise and (2) the assignee is a credit entity or a securitisation fund, (3) assigned claims already exist at the time of the assignment contract, or arise from the assignor's enterprise in the following year, or the future debtors' identity is stated in the assignment contract, (4) the assignee must pay the assigned claims to the assignor in cash or by instalments, with the respective discount for service costs, and (5) the assignee must pay the assignor the amount of the assigned claim partially or in full or before it matures unless it has been agreed that the assignor will be responsible for the assigned debtor's insolvency vis-à-vis the assignee. Section 2 of the Disposition makes it clear that factoring is effective against third parties from the date of the conclusion of the contract provided that it is recorded in a public document or by any other means that guarantees that the date can be ascertained. In addition, it provides for an exception to the application of avoidance transaction rules (see Question 27).

G. TRANSACTIONAL AVOIDANCE

Question 26: Are there rules in your legal system that operate once the debtor enters insolvency proceedings and that provide for the invalidation of transactions entered into by the debtor prior to the commencement of the insolvency proceedings?

1. France

531. With the aim of protecting creditors, the law entitles IPs in *redressement* or liquidation proceedings to challenge specific legal acts and payments that the debtor makes during the suspect period, which runs from the date of default on payments to the opening of the insolvency proceedings. It sanctions both the debtor's intent to diminish the value of his estate, and the infringement of the order of payment among creditors established by law; in general, it seeks to prevent the debtor from concluding any act detrimental to the general body of creditors.

532. The provisions on transactional avoidance are compatible with the actio pauliana laid down in Article 1167 CC, which allows one to challenge acts and contracts made outside the suspect period or not included in the range of avoidance proceedings laid down by the insolvency law.[213]

533. By regulating the *nullité de certains actes* carried out during the suspect period, the legislator distinguishes between cases of automatic avoidance, listed in an exhaustive way by the law but whose operation depends on the insolvency court stating the grounds of avoidance, and non-automatic avoidance, which requires the third party to be aware of debtor's default on payments and only proceeds by way of an avoidance proceedings before the insolvency court.

534. *Automatic avoidance:* According to Article 632(1) CComm., the following acts are null and void, although the insolvency judge has to declare that the relevant provisions are applicable;[214] detriment to the general body of creditors is presumed:

(1) not-for-profit acts that result in a transfer of movable or immovable assets;
(2) any bilateral contract under which the debtor's obligations significantly exceed those of the other party;
(3) payments of a debt which is not yet due;
(4) the payment of due debts by means that are unconventional in business relationships, such as giving an asset by way of payment, or conventional set-off of unconnected claims;
(5) court-ordered deposits and consignment of funds, effects or securities;
(6) the creation of security rights in rem over the debtor's assets for previous claims;
(7) preventive judicial guarantees adopted during enforcement proceedings (mortgage, pledge over business, pledge over shares, etc.), except if registration and the necessary notifications have been undertaken prior to the suspect period;
(8) operations of authorisation and enforcement of stock options;
(9) the assignment of goods or rights to a fiduciary fund, unless it guarantees a concomitant debt;
(10) any amendment to a fiduciary agreement assigning the rights or assets already transferred in a fiduciary fund as collateral for debts contracted prior to this amendment;

[213] Cass. Comm. 7.7.1987; Cass. Comm. 9.10.1996; Cass. Comm. 10.11.2009.
[214] Cass. Comm. 16.2.1993.

535. *Non-automatic avoidance*: According to Articles L. 632(1)(II) and L. 632(2)(I) CComm., non-automatic avoidance affects:

(a) any not-for-profit act occurring six months prior to cessation of payments, when the third party benefiting from the act in question knew of the debtor's difficulties;
(b) payments and onerous acts undertaken during the suspect period with third parties who knew of the debtor's default. The law does not stipulate that the acts need to objectively cause any detriment to the general body of creditors nor that there needs to be any bad faith on the part of the third party.[215] The latter only needs to know of the debtor's situation and this must be assessed by the insolvency court while declaring the nullity of the act;
(c) seizure of claims over a sum of money, in particular bank accounts, effected during the suspect period by creditors knowing the debtor's cessation of payments.

536. Avoidance proceedings result in an act or contract being declared null and void. Accordingly, transactional avoidance contributes to business restructuring in accordance with the objectives of *redressement* proceedings as well as to the discharge of liabilities in the case of liquidation to the extent that the debtor's estate benefits from the recovery of assets and from the non-recognition of preferences. The third party is obliged to return any payments or assets received, either the payments or assets themselves or by paying compensation where appropriate.

537. If a security right is rendered void, the secured claim becomes unsecured and the assets are 'liberated' from that particular security. If mortgages are declared invalid, this fact must be recorded in the Land Registry, while the invalidation of possessory security rights obliges the creditor to return the encumbered asset.

2. Italy

538. Italian law provides for such rules. These rules, in some cases, provide for the automatic ineffectiveness of legal transactions in the insolvency proceedings (automatic transactional avoidance) and, in others, entitle the IP to challenge these transactions and to make them ineffective in the insolvency proceedings

---

[215] Cass. Comm. 24.10.1995; Cass. Comm. 9.1.1996.

(judicial transactional avoidance). In insolvency law, the specific situations that bring about automatic invalidation of transactions are laid down in Articles 64–65 L.Fall. The specific situations enabling the IP to challenge a transaction are laid down in Articles 67–69 L.Fall.

539. These rules are provided for the case of *Fallimento*. Nevertheless, they also apply in *Liquidazione coatta amministrativa*, if the state of insolvency of the firm to be liquidated has been judicially declared (Art 203 L.Fall.), and in *Amministrazione straordinaria*. In this connection, however, a distinction must be made between *Prodibis* proceedings and *Marzano* proceedings. In *Prodibis* proceedings the transactional avoidance rules apply only if the implementation of a programme of liquidation of business complexes has been authorised (Art 49.1 d.lgs. 270/1999). In contrast, in *Marzano* proceedings the transactional avoidance rules apply even if the implementation of a restructuring programme has been authorised, provided that they produce an advantage for the creditors (Art 6.1 d.l. 347/2003).

3. Spain

540. Spanish insolvency law deals with avoidance proceedings in Chapter IV of Title III LC, which is entitled 'effects on acts detrimental to the general body of creditors'. Articles 71 et seq. lay down actions to challenge acts or omissions on the part of the debtor that benefit a third party – who may also be a creditor – to the detriment of the general body of creditors. Avoidance transaction is legally modulated and takes into account the relevant circumstances; the fact that the act is detrimental to the general body of creditors, which is usually presumed in the light of the circumstances in which the act was carried out; when it took place in relation to the opening of the insolvency proceedings, and collusion between parties to the challenged act. Acts that are detrimental to the general body of creditors are not declared null and void, but ineffective with respect to the insolvency proceedings. The person who benefited from the act or transaction has to restore the benefits to the debtor's estate, while the third party is granted a claim against the estate for his consideration in the challenged transaction unless he is proved to have acted fraudulently, in which case his claim is classified as subordinated [Art. 92(6) LC]. If it is not possible to restore the specific benefits received to the estate, the third party that benefited from the challenged act must pay compensation, in addition to damages if mala fides on his part is established (Art. 73 LC). The same applies if the actio pauliana laid down in Articles 1111 CC and 1291(3) CC – applicable by reference of Article 71(6) LC – proceeds.

Question 27: Do these transactional avoidance rules catch security and quasi-security type transactions?

1. France

541. Sections 6, 7, 9 and 10 of Article L. 632(1)(I) CComm. render the creation of security rights in rem during the suspect period automatically void provided that they aim to secure claims borne prior to them; should the claim and security be created at the same time, this avoidance rule is not applicable. This principle applies to pledge over tangible and intangible assets, mortgage, including the legal mortgage between spouses, and *fiducie-sûreté*, whether created ex novo or as a security by which claims other than those mentioned in the initial agreement are secured by a pre-existing *fiducie*. Security rights authorised by courts or the law as an interim measure in the enforcement of a claim and legal mortgages linked to an adverse judicial ruling can be also rendered invalid.

542. The above-mentioned voidability rule does not apply to retention of title clauses and the right of conventional retention stipulated in the suspect period given that they are not specifically mentioned in Article L. 632(1)(I) CComm. However, both rights can be declared null and void should court proceedings be initiated by the application of Article L. 632(2)(I) CComm.[216]

2. Italy

543. On the basis of the set of rules laid down by Articles 64–65 and 67–69 L.Fall., it can be said that any legal transaction that is detrimental to creditors may be subject to avoidance. More particularly, the wording of Article 67.1 points 3–4 and 67.2 L.Fall. expressly mentions the granting of securities as possibly subject to avoidance.

3. Spain

544. In principle, Articles 71 et seq. LC cover all transactions, including omissions such as the waiving of inheritance, but there are some exceptions to this general rule, as laid down in Article 71(5). In addition to transactions carried out in normal conditions during the ordinary course of the debtor's professional or business activity, the provision protects transactions concluded

216 The Court of Cassation does not apply either this rule to the transfer of professional claims by way of security and thus the so-called 'daily assignment' is not held as null and void on the grounds that it is not deemed an act of creation of a security right (Cass. Comm. 28.5.1996).

in the framework of settlement finality in payment and securities settlement systems. This exception is further regulated in Law 41/1999, Articles 13 and 14 of which stipulate that these transactions and the security rights over them are not subject to avoidance proceedings.[217] Likewise, collateral provided to secure public law claims (such as Articles 65(3) and 82 of the Law 58/2003 on General Taxation)[218] and in favour of the Spanish wage guarantee fund (*Fondo de Garantía Salarial* or FOGASA) for the concluding of restructuring agreements as laid down by specific legislation[219] cannot be challenged. Such agreements concern companies that are being driven into insolvency by wage claims and consist of FOGASA paying the wages during the agreed period; in exchange for this deferral of payment FOGASA usually requests security rights that are excluded from avoidance proceedings by Article 71(5) LC. In accordance with the Third Additional Disposition of Law 1/1999, the assignor's insolvency may trigger the application of Article 71 LC on avoidance transactions. In the event of the account debtor's insolvency, payments by the latter to the assignee are not subject to avoidance transaction. Transactional avoidance may however take place over the payment of claims that mature after insolvency proceedings have been opened, or if it is proved that the assignor or assignee knew about the account debtor's insolvency when the former paid the latter. Avoidance does not burden the assignee unless this has been agreed upon.

Question 28: If so, describe briefly these rules highlighting in particular (a) the rationale for the rules; (b) the conditions for the application of the rules; (c) the length of the 'suspect period'; (d) whether the rules apply to transactions with a cross-border element; (e) whether the rules operate more stringently in respect of transactions that favour parties who are connected to the debtor; and (f) any defences that may be availed of by a counterparty to the transaction, i.e. the defendant in an avoidance action.

1. France

545. *The rationale for the rules.* Transactional avoidance seeks to prevent the debtor in difficulties from undertaking any act detrimental to the general body of creditors, either by impoverishing his estate or by establishing preference in favour of specific creditors.

217 This law transposes Directive 98/26/EC of the European Parliament and of the Council of 19 May 1998 on settlement finality in payment and securities settlement systems. This exception was introduced into the Spanish legal system and has now been amended by Directive 2009/44/EC.

218 BOE No 302, 18.12.2003.

219 See Order 20 August 1985 supplementing Art. 32 of the Royal Decree 505/1985, 6 March on the conclusion of restructuring agreements on debts owed to the Wage Guarantee Fund (BOE No 206, 26.8.1985).

546. *The conditions for the application of the rules*. Whether it is a question of automatic or non-automatic avoidance, the declaration of an act being null and void is dependent on legal action being taken before the insolvency court against any creditor who has received payment from or entered into agreements with the debtor during the suspect period.[220] The IP and the public prosecutor are all able to take action independently and on an equal footing (Art. L. 632-4). Avoidance proceedings are feasible as long as those with standing are in charge of the relevant insolvency proceeding.[221]

547. Also in cases of both automatic and non-automatic avoidance, there are two conditions for the declaration of invalidity: the suspect period must have been established by the insolvency court and the act must have been made within this period.

548. In the particular framework of security rights, nullity is determined by the date of its creation in relation to the date of the secured debt; this requires further explanation. Firstly, transactional avoidance is restricted to the security rights created to guarantee previous claims and this legitimates the creation of security rights for new or concomitant debts. Secondly, the relevant date is that of the creation of a security right: the right will be rendered void if created during the suspect period even if the security right has been created on the basis of a pre-existing promise. But it will be deemed a valid one if created prior to the commencement of the suspect period even when the security right is finally registered during the suspect period, except in the case of security rights that require registration to be valid.[222] In particular, a pledge over future claims or a pledge over a group of present or future assets is not declared void where the substitution of an asset is considered to have been carried out on the date the pledge contract was signed. Finally, prior security rights substituted in the suspect period cannot be invalidated if the value of the new security right is not greater than the value of the old one.[223]

549. *The length of the 'suspect period'*. The suspect period runs from the day of cessation of payments until the opening of insolvency proceedings, for a maximum of 18 months. The law defines the debtor's cessation of payments as a situation in which a debtor cannot meet its current liabilities with current assets. The date of cessation of payments is initially established by the insolvency court

---

220 Even in the case of creditors whose claims had been admitted in the passive of the process (Cass. Comm. 19.3.2002; Cass. Comm. 16.3.2012).

221 Cass. Comm. 1.2.2000; Cass. Comm. 21.9.2010.

222 While in the case of a legal mortgage linked to a condemnatory judgment the relevant date is that of the judgment itself, in the case of an interim judicial mortgage and a pledge over companies it suffices that their provisional registration is prior to the default on payment.

223 Cass. Comm. 20.1.1998.

at the opening of the restructuring or the liquidation proceedings. If a date of cessation of payments cannot be established with certainty, it is deemed to be the date of the commencement of proceedings. This date may be changed for an earlier date during the course of proceedings at the request of the IP or the public prosecutor, up to a maximum of 18 months prior to the opening of the insolvency proceeding [Art. L. 631(8) CComm.].[224]

550. *Application of these rules to transactions with a cross-border element.* Articles 4(2)(m) and 13 of the Regulation (EC) No 1346/2000 on insolvency proceedings are applicable where appropriate. Accordingly, French rules on transactional avoidance are applicable qua lex fori concursus, save the case in which the law governing the challenged act does not make it ineffective by any means. Should the Regulation not be applicable, French conflict rules indicate that the lex fori concursus is applicable to transactional avoidance.[225]

551. *Special rules in respect of transactions that favour parties who are connected to the debtor.* Beyond the automatic invalidation of a legal mortgage between spouses created during the suspect period, there are no special, more rigorous regulations applicable to transactions made in favour of persons connected to the debtor. However, within the framework of non-automatic invalidation, jurisprudence makes it easier to prove a contracting third party's knowledge of the debtor's default when they are relatives or there is a business relationship.[226]

552. *Defences that may be availed of by a counter-party to the transaction.* With regard to automatic avoidance, there are no defences available, unless it can be proved that the transactions occurred prior to the suspect period or, in the case of security rights in rem, that they are concomitant or subsequent to the secured claim. Where non-automatic avoidance is concerned, the exception par excellence is the defendant's unawareness of the debtor's situation, which makes a possible ruling of invalidity less likely when the plaintiff cannot prove the contrary.

224 According to Article L. 631-8, 1–4: 'The court shall determine the date of the cessation of payments. If a date is not being determined, the date of the cessation of payments shall be deemed to be that of the issue of the commencement order. The date of the cessation of payments may be moved once or more times, without however going back more than eighteen months before the date of issue of the commencement order. Except in cases of fraud, it may not be moved to a date prior to the final decision endorsing an amicable agreement in compliance with Article L. 611-8 (II). An action may be filed with the court by the administrator, the court appointed receiver or the Public Prosecutor's Office to that effect. It shall rule upon the case after having heard or duly summoned the debtor. The petition for modifying this date must be filed with the court within a year from the issue of the commencement order'.

225 Cass. Comm. 2.10.2012.

226 See C. Saint-Alary-Houin, *Droit des entreprises en difficulté*, 749; Cass. Comm. 16.2.1993.

2. Italy

553. *Rationale.* The prescriptions within Articles 64–70 L.Fall. aim to set aside transactions, performed before opening insolvency proceedings, which are detrimental to the general body of creditors. These prescriptions usually refer to transactions performed by the debtor himself; they exceptionally include acts performed by a third party, such as the creation of a security right, which are detrimental to the general body of creditors.

554. Italian law does not distinguish between preferences and fraudulent transactions, and it is commonly accepted that Articles 64–67 L.Fall. provide a homogeneous device which is traditionally called *revocatoria fallimentare degli atti pregiudizievoli per i creditori* (insolvency transactional avoidance). The underlying rationale of these provisions has been vigorously debated. Case law considers the *revocatoria fallimentare* to be a remedy aimed at enforcing the principle of pari passu during the period between when a debtor has became insolvent and the date of the opening of insolvency proceedings.[227] On the other hand, academic opinion considers that the *revocatoria fallimentare* constitutes a remedy designed to provide redress against the damages caused by an insolvent debtor to his creditors.[228] Nevertheless, it is commonly accepted that this remedy is peculiar, that it has been cross-fertilised by other remedies (such as those concerning the avoidance of contracts), and that there is no strict test of causation proving that the debtor has concretely damaged his creditors.[229] Moreover, it is commonly accepted that the *revocatoria fallimentare* does not affect the validity of the transaction concerned and this means that the transaction is ineffective only vis-à-vis the general body of creditors and the IP who represents them. Finally, Article 69-*bis* L.Fall. lays down that all cases of transactional avoidance cannot be brought more than three years after the opening of insolvency proceedings and, in any case, no longer than five years after the performing of a transaction. Because of an express choice of policy resulting from the index of Article 69-*bis* L.Fall. (which is titled '*decadenza dall'azione*'), this temporal restriction does not consist in any limitation of action, but in an unusually long term for the expiration of the right. This means that the period of time laid down by Article 69-*bis* L.Fall. is not subject to any form of interruption (Art 2964 of the Civil Code).

555. Italian law also provides the actio pauliana, called *azione revocatoria ordinaria* (Art 2901 et seq. Civil Code), and lays down that an IP may file

227 Cass. civ. Sez. Un. 28.3.2006 no 7028, (2006) I *FI* 1718.

228 M. Libertini, (1977) I *GComm* 84 et seq. In judiciary, see Cass. civ. 16.3.2005 no 5713, [2005] *F* 713.

229 G. Terranova, [2010] *DF* 31.

it in accordance with the provisions of the Civil Code (Art 66 L.Fall.). This means that, if an IP intends to challenge a transaction within insolvency proceedings by means of the actio pauliana, he should prove the damage and the debtor's awareness that this transaction will be detrimental. Moreover, if the challenged transaction has been performed against for consideration, the IP should also prove that the defendant was aware that this transaction would be detrimental. Nevertheless, it is commonly accepted that filing the actio pauliana within insolvency proceedings is to the advantage of the general body of creditors.

556. *Conditions for the application/length of the suspect period. Judicial transactional avoidance.* The IP may challenge the debtor's transactions if it is proved that: (a) the debtor performed them when he was already insolvent (objective condition); and (b) the defendant was aware of his insolvency (subjective condition).

557. In proving the existence of such conditions, the position of the IP is facilitated. In effect, the prescriptions on judicial avoidance divide relevant transactions into two groups, which respectively refer to 'abnormal transaction' and 'normal transaction', and in this connection they provide that if an IP intends to challenge a transaction of the first group, the defendant's knowledge of the debtor's insolvency is presumed (Art 67.1 L.Fall.); however, if the IP intends to challenge a transaction of the second group, he has to prove the defendant's knowledge of the debtor's insolvency (Art 67.2 L.Fall.).

558. The first group, referring to 'abnormal transaction', consists of: (1) transactions for valuable consideration made in the year preceding the opening of insolvency proceedings, where the performance carried out or the obligations undertaken by the debtor exceed by over 25% what has been given or promised to him; (2) transactions to pay off monetary debts that have matured and are due and which are not performed by money or by other regular means of payment, if carried out in the year preceding the opening of insolvency proceedings; (3) pledges, antichreses and voluntary mortgages constituted in the year preceding the opening of insolvency proceedings for pre-existing debts that have not matured; (4) pledges, antichreses and judicial or voluntary mortgages constituted in the six months preceding the opening of insolvency proceedings for debts that have matured.

559. The second group refers to 'normal transactions' which have been performed in the six months preceding the opening of insolvency proceedings. They are: (1) payments of liquid and due debts performed by regular means of payment; (2) transactions constitutive of a preferential right for debts, even belonging to third parties, if the security was granted on the same date when the claim arose; (3) any other transaction for valuable consideration.

560. This regulation lays down many exemptions which may, in broad terms, be grouped into three categories: (1) protection for transactions performed during the ordinary management of the firm (Art 67.3, letters a–b, L.Fall.); (2) protection for transactions in connection with an attempted composition of a firm's debts (Art 67.3, letters d–e and g, L.Fall.); (3) protection for certain transactions deemed particularly worthy of protection for the subjective position of the addressee (Art 67.3, letters c and f, L.Fall.).[230] Also immune from avoidance are some specific forms of bank financing (Arts. 67.4 L.Fall., Arts 39.4, 42.4, 44.5, 48 Unified Banking Code). There are specific provisions for payment of bills of exchange (Art 68 L.Fall.), payments within a contract of factoring (Art 6 L. 52/1991) or those within a contract of securitisation (Art 4.4 L. 130/1999).[231]

561. *Automatic transactional avoidance.* Some groups of transactions become relatively ineffective, simply because the insolvency proceedings have opened. These are: (a) transactions without valuable consideration (Art 64 L.Fall.), and (b) payments of claims that mature on the day of the opening of insolvency proceedings or subsequently (Art 65 L.Fall.), both if those acts (i.e. the transactions without valuable consideration and the anticipated payments of claims) were performed by the debtor in the two years preceding the opening of insolvency proceedings.

562. *Avoidance of transactions with a cross-border element.* The only prescription in Italian insolvency law of any importance in this respect, is Article 9.3–4 L.Fall. This lays down that: 'an entrepreneur, the head office of whose firm is abroad, can be declared bankrupt in the Italian Republic even if a declaration of insolvency has been made abroad. International conventions and the legislation of the European Union are exempted'. In accordance with Articles 7 and 16 of Regulation (EC) No 848/2015 Italian avoidance law in European cross-border cases is applicable either as lex fori concursus, or as lex causae where the transaction is governed by Italian law not being lex fori concursus.

563. *Avoidance of transactions that favour parties connected to the debtor.* Italian avoidance law operates more stringently in respect of transactions that favour parties that are connected to the debtor. This happens particularly with respect to the debtor's spouse, to the shareholders of the debtor company and to the shareholders of the group of companies to which the debtor belongs.

564. *Spouses.* The insolvency rules on transactional avoidance operate more stringently in respect of transactions that have been made between spouses. This is because the spouse is unlikely to be unaware of the debtor's insolvency. Starting from these considerations, Article 69 L.Fall. operates in several ways:

---

230 N. Abriani and L. Quagliotti, [2008] *F* 379-380.

231 L. 30.4.1999 No 130 <www.normattiva.it> accessed 26 May 2016.

(a) it eliminates the time limit of one year/six months, so that all the transactions between spouses can be made relatively ineffective from the moment the debtor began his business; (b) it establishes that the spouse is always presumed to know of the debtor's insolvency.

565. *Shareholders.* Article 2467 of the Civil Code regulates the practice of 'financings' by members of limited companies without shares (*società a responsabilità limitata*). In the presence of an 'undercapitalised' company, this practice allows members to finance the company and, regarding this financing, to bypass their role of residual claimants and to take on the formal role of creditors and, therefore, to compete with other creditors in the liquidation of the company's assets. Therefore, Article 2467 of the Civil Code lays down that, if the financial situation of the company at the time of financing was critical, reimbursement of such financing is postponed to the satisfaction of creditors and, if it took place in the year before the opening of the insolvency proceedings, the payment must be returned.

566. This prescription, which is different from the German ones concerning capital replacing loans,[232] is considered an insolvency law prescription. Moreover, scholars maintain that this postponement of reimbursement represents the outcome of a form of a transactional avoidance, comparable to the automatic avoidance governed by Articles 64–65 L.Fall.[233]

567. *Groups of companies.* It is believed that the risk of opportunistic behaviour by the financier-shareholders to the detriment of the creditors is also present in the financing of companies belonging to a group. Accordingly, Article 2497-*quinquies* of the Civil Code extends the treatment of financing by members, provided by Article 2467 of the Civil Code and described above, to financing performed by a holding company to its subsidiaries or between companies belonging to the same group. It is appropriate to stress that the rule provides arguments in favour of the applicability of the treatment of financing by members to companies with shares (*società per azioni*), even in the absence of group links.[234]

568. The existence of a group is also a condition of application of a strengthened regime of transactional avoidance within proceedings of *Amministrazione straordinaria* and *Liquidazione coatta amministrativa.* Article 91 d.lgs. 270/1999 and Article 2.4 d.l. 233/1986,[235] indeed, extend the term of one year to five and the six-month term to three years for judicial avoidance under Article 67 L.Fall.

---

[232] See R. Bork, Germanic Report, Question 28.

[233] G. Terranova, 'Commento sub Art. 2467 c.c.' in G. Niccolini and A. Stagno d'Alcontres (eds.), *Società di capitali. Commentario*, vol. 3, 1449 et seq.

[234] G. Portale, (2003) I *BBTC* 663, 681.

[235] D.l. 5.6.1986 No 233 <www.normattiva.it> accessed 26 May 2016.

569. *Defences against avoidance actions.* There are no special defences against such actions by the IP. The general rules of the civil procedure law apply. The IP has to prove that the requirements for the specific avoidance situation on which his action is based were met. If he is successful or where the meeting of the requirements is legally presumed, the other party has to produce (counter) evidence that the requirements are not met.

3. Spain

570. The rationale for Spanish transactional avoidance rules rests on the maintaining of the legal order of creditors before insolvency proceedings are opened, and seeks to prevent debtors in difficulties manoeuvring to place certain creditors in a better position or removing assets from the estate with the aim of worsening creditors' chances of being paid. To this end, the legislation focuses on the combination of different conditions: the type of transaction concluded, e.g. whether it is for profit or not, whether it is the cause of detriment to the general body of creditors, whether intent to defraud can be perceived, the persons involved in the transaction, and the time at which the act was concluded in relation to the opening of the insolvency proceedings.

571. Article 71(1) considers avoidance transactions to be all acts detrimental to the general body of creditors that are concluded within a two-year period before the opening of the insolvency proceedings, even if there is no intent to defraud. The 'detriment to the debtor's estate' requirement is applied differently in different circumstances. The first one is not rebuttable; detriment is always presumed in the event of not-for-profit acts, with the exception of liberalities of use, i.e. expenses incurred due to social interaction such as the customary gifts (Art. 1041 CC), and payments or other acts that terminate obligations that will mature after the insolvency proceedings are opened. In any other case, in particular with respect to transactions involving a security right in rem, a rebuttable presumption is operative. Detriment to the general body of creditors is therefore presumed unless proved otherwise when the debtor concludes a for-profit transaction in favour of a person closely related to him, creates a security right in rem in favour of pre-existing obligations or new ones concluded to replace them, or pays or otherwise terminates obligations secured by a security right in rem and which mature after the opening of the insolvency proceeding. If the transaction is not within one of these categories, the applicant has the burden of establishing detriment to the debtor's estate. Regard should be paid to Article 10 of Law 2/1981, 25 March on the Mortgage Market that sets mortgages registered in favour of financial entities apart from the rebuttable presumption, for which reason the IP must prove detriment to the general body of creditors.

572. Following the English example of voluntary schemes of arrangements, specific hybrid proceedings have been set up to conclude a pre-insolvency restructuring agreement, and a special system for avoidance transaction has also been established (see Question 14). Accordingly, Article 71 LC does not apply if a scheme of arrangement is concluded prior to the opening of the insolvency proceedings, i.e. neither the scheme nor the transactions or security rights granted on this basis can be challenged, provided that the conditions laid down in Article 71bis LC are met, namely (1) the scheme increases the credit available, or modifies or terminates obligations either by extending maturity or establishing new obligations to replace the former, provided that the agreement is concluded on the basis of a viability plan for the debtor's enterprise that secures its continuity in the short and medium term; (2) the scheme is approved by a qualified majority of creditors representing three fifths of the debtor's liabilities on the date it is adopted; (3) the scheme is supervised by the debtor's auditor or, in default of this, by an independent auditor; (4) the scheme is recorded in a public document.

573. Article 71bis was amended in 2014[236] to exclude from avoidance proceedings any transactions intended to provide the debtor with a second chance but which cannot meet the above-mentioned conditions. Accordingly, avoidance proceedings cannot be opened against transactions made individually or jointly in the execution of a restructuring agreement that meet the following conditions: (1) the agreement increases the proportion of the debtor's assets over his liabilities; (2) the agreement increases the proportion of current assets in relation to current liabilities; (3) the value of the collateral in favour of the creditors that sign the agreement exceeds neither nine tenths of the value of the debt pending payment on their behalf nor the proportion of guarantees in relation to the outstanding debt which they had prior to the agreement; (4) the interest rate applicable to the surviving debt or the debt that results from the restructuring agreement in favour of the signing creditors does not exceed the rate applicable to the previous debt by more than one third; and (5) the agreement is formalised by a public instrument executed by all parties involved and expressly states the reasons underlying the various acts and transactions made between the debtor and creditors from a financial viewpoint, with special reference to the conditions laid down in points 1–4. Compliance with points 1 and 2 must be verified by examining all financial consequences including tax, early termination clauses and suchlike arising out of transactions carried out in the framework of the restructuring agreement, even if these consequences concern creditors who have not signed the agreement.

---

236 Law 17/2014, 30 September on urgent measures for the refinancing and restructuring of business debt. It was again amended by Law 9/2015, 25 May.

574. In both cases covered by Article 71bis, the conditions must be met on the date the public document recording the restructuring agreement is issued. In particular, both the debtor and the creditors may request that an independent expert is appointed to report on the fair and workable nature of the viability plan, the proportionality of the security rights under normal market conditions at the time the agreement is signed, and on any other issues mentioned by the applicable law where appropriate. Should the report contain restrictions or limitations of any kind, their significance must be explicitly assessed by the signatories to the agreement.

575. It must be highlighted that if any of the above conditions, as laid down in Article 71bis LC, are not met, these transactions can be challenged (only) by the IP.

576. The Fourth Additional Disposition LC excludes from transactional avoidance those out-of-court refinancing plans meeting the requirements therein established and approved by the court. On the grounds of this approval, it is almost impossible to challenge this type of plan and, whether appropriate, the IP is the only one who has standing to challenge the plan. In a similar vein, Article 238(4) LC excludes from transactional avoidance those out-of-court plans reached by the creditors listed in Article 231 LC referring to debtor natural persons with liabilities under €5m and legal persons whose insolvency would not be especially complex. Surprisingly, however, the general rules on standing apply and this is not only granted to the IP.

577. In accordance with Article 4(2)(m) of Regulation (EC) No 1346/2000, Article 7(2)(m) of Regulation (EU) No 848/2015 and Article 200 LC, Articles 71 et seq. are applicable as part of the lex fori concursus and thus apply to transactions with a cross-border element in all cases in which insolvency proceedings are opened in *Spain*. However, their application can be set aside by the law applicable to the act that is challenged if it does not allow the challenge by any means (Arts. 13 of Regulation No 1346/2000, 16 of Regulation 848/2015 and 208 LC).

578. Article 71(3) LC presumes detriment to the general body of creditors in the event of not-for-profit acts concluded by the debtor with a person who is closely related to him. Article 93 LC contains a detailed list of such persons and distinguishes between debtors who are natural persons and debtors who are legal persons. It is important to note that this provision is not only relevant for the application of avoidance transaction rules but also for classifying subordinate creditors (Art. 92 LC).

579. Should the debtor be a natural person, the following are considered to be closely related to him: (1) the debtor's spouse, civil partner or any person habitually living with the debtor, now or in the two years before the opening of the insolvency proceedings; (2) the ascendants, descendants or siblings of either the debtor or any of the persons designated in point 1; (3) the spouses of the persons indicated in point 2; (4) legal persons in the debtor's charge or one of the persons referred to in points 1–3 or de iure or de facto administrators; (5) legal persons belonging to the same group of companies as those persons indicated in point 4; (6) legal persons whose de iure or de facto administrators are the persons detailed in any of the previous numbers.

580. If the debtor is a legal person, the persons with a close relationship are the following: (1) the partners and where these are natural persons, those closely related to them as stipulated in Article 93(1) covering persons closely related to debtors who are natural persons, who in law are personally and severally liable for the company debts, and those who were directly or indirectly holders of at least 5% of the share capital at the time the claim originated, provided that the company declared insolvent was allowed to trade on official secondary securities markets; otherwise, those that hold at least 10% of the share capital; (2) its de iure or de facto administrators, the liquidators of debtors or legal persons and those with legal persons' general powers as well as those who have held them within a two-year period prior to the bankruptcy. Unless proven otherwise, creditors who have signed the restructuring agreement as laid down in Article 71bis or by the Fourth Additional Disposition, or an extrajudicial settlement or restructuring plan of LC cannot be held to be persons with a close relationship to the debtor when it comes to the classification of their claims arising from the refinancing of the debtor; creditors cannot be considered the de facto administrators either when they have signed a refinancing agreement, a restructuring plan or a non-judicial settlement for the obligations assumed by the debtor in relation to the viability plan unless proven otherwise; (3) legal persons that are members of the same group of companies as the debtor and their common partners provided that they meet the conditions mentioned in point 1.

581. There is a rebuttable presumption that the assignees or grantees of claims belonging to the persons mentioned as having a close relationship to the debtor are also closely related to him, provided that the acquisition took place in a two-year period prior to the opening of the insolvency proceedings, applies both to debtors who are natural or legal persons [Art. 93(3) LC].

582. There are no special defences available to the defendants, namely the debtor and the third party that benefited from the challenged act; a person that is not a party to the challenged transaction may also be sued if the plaintiff seeks to challenge an onward transmission of the benefit of the transaction to that person. The IP is primarily granted the standing to initiate avoidance proceedings in the framework of insolvency proceedings, but creditors are also entitled to challenge a particular act if they have specifically requested the IP to do so in writing and the IP has failed to act in a two-month period following the request [Art. 72(1) LC]. Nevertheless, only the IP is entitled to challenge an act arising from a voluntary scheme of arrangement. Where the presumptions mentioned above are applicable, the burden of proof is placed on the defendant, i.e. that the conditions for challenging the act have not been met. Otherwise, it is up to the IP to prove that the conditions have been met [Art. 71(4) LC].

CHAPTER 8

SECURITY RIGHTS AND INSOLVENCY LAW IN THE CENTRAL AND EASTERN EUROPEAN SYSTEMS

Tibor Tajti*

A. INTRODUCTION

1. The coverage of the report

1. This report adresses security rights and the avoidance of transactions from the perspective of a select number of national laws from the region of Central and Eastern Europe (CEE). The closure date for this Report was 30 March 2016, save the mention of the most important changes introduced by the June 2016 amendments of the 2013 Hugarian Civil Code.[1]

2. *Hungary* is herein the legal system discussed in most detail though the coverage of Lithuanian and Polish laws will also provide the reader with a fair insight into their security and insolvency laws not limited to their idiosyncratic features. It is to be noted as well that this report is not a commentary of national laws. It rather aims to provide a fairly in-depth insight into the Region's laws but without commenting on each provision of the analysed laws. Consequently, consulting local laws and counsel is essential whenever the application of these laws comes into the picture.

---

* The report was compiled with contributions by Prof. Lina Aleknaite van der Molen (Kazimieras Simonavičius University Law School, Vilnius, Lithuania), Krzysztof Kaźmierczyk (Dentons Law Firm, Warsaw, Poland), Catalin Gabriel Stanescu (SCPA Bordianu and Associates, Bucharest, Romania), Patricia Živković (doctoral (SJD) candidate at Central European University (CEU), Legal Studies, Budapest, Hungary), and Virág Ilona Blazsek (doctoral (SJD) candidate at Central European University (CEU), Legal Studies, Budapest, Hungary).

1 See Act No. LXXVII of 2016 on the Amendment of Act No. V of 2013 on the Civil Code (*2016. évi LXXVII. törvény indokolása a Polgári Törvénykönyvről szóló 2013. évi V. törvény módosításáról*).

2. Methodology caveats

3. As this project aimed to canvass not only the positive law (i.e. black-letter law in force) but also to collect information and indicia on how the targeted laws work in reality – in particular the EU Regulation 1346/2000 on Insolvency Proceedings – the following caveats in particular ought to be highlighted. Needless to say, much more is known about how national secured transactions and insolvency laws work in practice compared to their cross-border kin.

4. On a national level the frequent amendments or the substantial rewriting of law creates considerable uncertainty yet not just in terms of their practical application. Due to lack of understanding, inappropriate *travaux preparatoires* and the speed of change, omissions, imperfect drafting and similar defects plague local laws, as a result of which it is often hard (or impossible) to provide proper answers even to questions that in other jurisdictions might be easy to answer. The reader therefore should not be puzzled that occasionally no crystal clear answers can be provided to some questions.

5. Although the number of publicised domestic court cases (or decisions/ positions of regulatory bodies) has been growing in all the countries in the region during the last decade or so, the relatively small number of available reported cases continues to be an obstacle for the researcher.

6. The inadequacy and problems with access to empirical sources of law is even greater when we turn to the international scene, more precisely to cross-border insolvency cases and the recast Regulation 2015/848 on Insolvency Proceedings (Recast Regulation) or its predecessor Regulation 1346/2000. Here, the number of reported court cases are even fewer; some of the cases that reached the ECJ originate, however, in the region. What matters, however, is that often it is difficult to draw firm conclusions from these cases though some of the cases do reflect the emergence of issues known outside the region as well. Among these, the concept of the centre of main interest (COMI) seems to lead the way.[2] Not infrequently the problem is that simply no empirical evidence is available.[3] For these central reasons essentially it is impossible, or at least, difficult to pass

---

2 For example, the only book specifically devoted to cross-border insolvencies in Hungary written by A. Csőke mentions three COMI-related cases from Hungary. See A. Csőke, *A határokon átnyúló fizetésképtelenségi eljárások* [Cross-Border Insolvency Proceedings] (HVG/ORAC, Budapest, 1st ed., 2008), 98–100.

3 One may point again to the fact that A. Csőke in his treatise, given the lack of cases on cross-border insolvency generated in Hungary – was forced to resort to foreign judicial decisions. Out of 37 cases used to explain and illustrate the mechanics of Regulation 1346/2000 only four stemmed from Hungary. Although the book was published in 2008 and some additional cases have emerged in the meantime in Hungary, the general feature has hardly changed.

a verdict on the quintessential question whether the Recast Regulation or its predecessor works fairly and efficiently in practice.

7. Although no empirical studies seem to have been made of less fathomable factors influencing the efficiency of a law such as the intensity of the bankruptcy stigma or the lack of a proper understanding of relatively novel branches of law such as secured transactions and insolvency, these are very much present in the region. As Professor Bork quite aptly put it commenting on the intensity and the omnipresence of the bankruptcy stigma in Germany, '[although] [i]t may be tempting to disregard this factor as non-serious, but any earnest attempt to construct an efficient restructuring law must take it into account until there is a wide-ranging and sustained change in popular mentality.'[4] These factors still meaningfully impact the application of the EU cross-border insolvency regulatory regime. The most important caveat that follows from this is that the absence of court cases and other empirical evidence related to Regulation 1346/2000, should not be taken to mean that the Recast Regulation or domestic insolvency laws function impeccably in practice. Put simply, the fact that in a jurisdiction there are no, or only a few, cross-border insolvency-related cases should not be taken as meaning, therefore, that the law is perfect.

8. The caveats stated above should definitively be borne in mind when reading this report. Given these determinants, whenever the law is unclear on a point, this will be noted. Similarly, when no clear position could be taken as to whether a given provision or law properly works in practice, this will be clearly stated, although the empirical evidence is scarce.

9. From the perspective of CEE, however, a common EU insolvency and secured transactions law would be not just desirable but – in particular with respect to the similar paths of reforms and the many commonalities in the context of secured transactiond and insolvency laws – possible and desirable.

3. The geographic reach of the report

10. This report extends to those countries within Central and Eastern Europe (CEE or the region) which have, since the fall of the Berlin Wall, acceeded to the European Union. Geographically these include (proceeding from north to south):

(a) the Baltic States – namely *Estonia*, *Latvia* and *Lithuania*;
(b) *Poland*, the *Czech Republic*, *Slovakia*, *Hungary* and *Romania*; and

---

4 See R. Bork, *Rescuing Companies in England and Germany* (Oxford University Press, 2012), section 2.12.

(c) finally the two successor countries of the former Yugoslavia: *Slovenia* and *Croatia*.

11. The limits of this report, however, do not allow for providing equal attention to each of the jurisidictions.

12. The geographic proximity and the shared history of some of these countries is often of relevance to the topics touched upon in this report. For example, while the presence of Scandinavian banks is substantial in the Baltic States, that is not so in Central Europe, where German, Austrian, Italian and Spanish banks, together with a few domestic ones, dominate the market.

13. Needless to say, being part of the same state for decades meant also that many common elements of the legal super-structure were inherited by the successor countries – i.e. the *Czech Republic* and *Slovakia* on one hand and *Croatia* and *Slovenia* on the other. For example, the post-Yugoslav countries have no civil codes but property, contract and tort law are in separate statutory enactments. Consequently, while in *Hungary* and *Romania* secured transactions law is in the civil codes, in *Croatia* and *Slovenia* the applicable law can be found in distinct statutes.

14. However, no far-reaching conclusions should be drawn purely based on either geographic proximity or (more or less) shared common history with respect to fields of law covered by this Report.

4. Commonalities of the region's legal systems of relevance to the report

15. Primarily for the sake of orientation, two common features of the legal systems of the region ought to be stressed: first, these systems all belong to the civil law legal tradition (family) and, second, until the 1990s they were all socialist (communist) systems.

16. A few quite practical implications ensue from this for the purposes of this project.

4.1. The repercussions of belonging to the same legal family

17. *The legal origins:* Notwithstanding that fundamental differences exist among the systems of the region, a common ancestry remains of importance in some respects up until today. A few examples of relevance for this project ought to be mentioned.

18. First of all, this common ancestry is reflected in *the sources of law* relied on not just by courts and those applying the law but also by scholars. Similarly to German, but contrary to English law, the civil codes (or their equivalents) are the most important and thus most frequently referred to sources of law. Whilst according to conventional wisdom continental European civil codes are supposedly gap-less and answers to any and all disputes could be found in them, often what they contain are no more than general principles and rules rather than concrete answers. This is why of fundamental significance is the increasing importance of case law and the so-called 'unifying positions' of the supreme courts. Needless to say, this will be reflected in this report, as often key decisions close the gaps that arise in respect of new and fast-changing fields of law such as insolvency and securities law – both considered in this Report.

19. Although meaningful changes have occurred in most of the CEE states, what is the concrete rule of law is often obscure because only a small – though increasing – proportion of decisions gets reported.

20. Second, there is kinship which is due to the fact that *most of the legal categories, principles and rules – or lack of these – are shared.* Examples can easily be found among branches of law relevant to this report, such as the absence of the concept of 'tracing' known in common law systems, the conceptual unity of real and personal property law, or the accessory nature of in rem securities.[5]

4.2. The impact of the omnipresent bankruptcy stigma

21. The perception of insolvency, insolvency law and insolvency procedure, not only among the citizenry and businessmen, but also among lawyers, is negatively impacted by the stigmatisation of bankrupts. This feature is, unfortunately, such a commonality in the region that no analysis on insolvency law could disregard it. In this respect the region resembles, for example, such economically superior economies as that of *Germany*.

22. Another commonality of the region's countries is the absence of a business rescue culture. Although the insolvency laws have also been upgraded following Western models in the post-1990 period – including the introduction of the local (close or remote) version of US Chapter 11 reorganisations, though looking at German or French law (typically) as the direct models – one could hardly speak

5 See e.g. T. Tajti, 'Could Continental Europe Adopt a Uniform Commercial Code Article 9-Type Secured Transactions System? The Effects of the Differing Legal Platforms' (2014) 35 *Adelaide Law Review* 149–178.

of a major breakthrough in that respect as of yet. Obviously such a state of affairs is closely linked to the devastating effects of the omnipresent bankruptcy stigma.

23. As a consequence, if blue chip corporations (i.e. strategically important businesses) are being rescued, then they are bailed out by the government rather than finding a way out of insolvency through negotiations, workouts or other forms of private ordering.

4.3. *The socialist/communist past*

24. The socialist/communist past left its imprint on both the security and insolvency laws of the Region's jurisdictions. This is a factor the importance of which has significantly diminished now, yet it would be a mistake to think that it is of no relevance anymore. For example, in a number of CEE countries (e.g. Serbia, Bosnia and Herzegovina), a significant part of the former state- or employee-owned economic sectors have not yet been privatised. Here it suffices only to emphasise that in the eyes of communist systems, credit and credit security were despised ideological enemies. As a result, during the years of communism the law on credit-securities was clearly in decline, although admittedly attitudes began to change for the better from the end of the 1970s onwards in some countries in the region.

4.4. *The post-1990 transition towards market economy*

25. At the time of the fall of the Berlin Wall the law on securities was underdeveloped in the entire region due specifically to the hostility of the former regime. It was not without reason that the EBRD[6] itself was established precisely to help these countries to introduce (or reintroduce) market economy, and the reform of secured transactions laws became the EBRD's first priority project.

---

6 The European Bank for Reconstruction and Development (EBRD), seated in London, UK, was established at the beginning of the 1990s to assist CEE countries in their transition towards market economy. Its secured transactions law reform was among the first and began in 1992 and has been ongoing ever since; lately expanding also to the Maghreb countries. The Bank's objective has been 'to encourage countries to modernise their secured transactions laws and it offers assistance at all stages of the reform process'. See F. Dahan and J. Simpson, 'Legal Efficiency of Secured Transactions Reform' in F. Dahan and J. Simpson (eds.), *Secured Transactions Reform and Access to Credit* (Edward Elgar, 2008), 122. See also D. Dunnett, (1991) 28 *Common Market Law Review* 571–597 and A. Harmathy, 'The EBRD Model Law and the Hungarian Law' in J. J. Norton and M. Andenas, *Emerging Financial Markets and Secured Transactions* (Kluwer Law International, 1998), 197–209.

26. What this meant for the purposes of secured transactions law in particular is set out in the following paragraphs.

27. The available in rem (proprietary) security devices were essentially limited to possessory pledge and mortgage of immovables. As far as personal securities were concerned, especially in the 1980s and related to foreign trade, the use of bank guarantees and letters of credits were common.

28. The lack of a developed security law was mitigated in certain contexts by contractual penalties (though this was primarily characteristic of the USSR, less so of those countries that have in the meantime become Member States of the EU).

29. Primarily in the countries neighbouring *Germany*, some forms of non-registrable security devices (the so-called '*kautelarische Sicherheiten*') have become common in practice. As latent securities, these caused priority problems following the introduction of the registration-based security interests as part of the post-1990 reforms. This was the case, for example, in *Hungary* and *Poland*. For Hungarians, it took a while to realise that the two systems could not co-exist: changes ensued only with the new 2013 Civil Code. In *Poland*, for example, these security devices continue to play a meaningful role.

30. Needless to say, as time passes by, the socialist past is of less and less relevance, especially in the systems that have reformed their security and insolvency laws.

5. Reformed and unreformed legal systems of the region

31. While some cross-fertilisation is detectable in some of the region's countries, the rule is rather that each of the jurisdictions has had a distinct path of reform (where any reform has occurred) and post-1990 evolution of secured transactions and insolvency law.[7] As a result, the systems' solutions often differ quite significantly. For example, the operation of the newly introduced registers for security interests on movables have been entrusted to different bodies and have been subject to differing rules, which might be a problem should the EU decide to link these registries in the future.

---

7 See e.g. T. Tajti, *Post-1990 Secured Transactions Law Reforms in Central and Eastern Europe – Focus on Hungary and its Neighbors*, in Bulletin of the Chamber of Public Notaries of County Szeged (Hungary), vol. II, Nos. 3–4 (27 October 2013) 18 et seq. Also available via <http://www.ssrn.com> accessed 23 May 2016 and Researchgate.

32. Irrespective of the distinctions and without the pretension of completeness, some commonalities can be identified as well, as indicated in the paragraphs that follow.

33. Most of the systems that have embarked on reforming their secured transactions law have been *influenced by Anglo-Saxon laws*, typically English and/or US law (i.e. UCC Article 9). As a rule, the source of inspirations and support was critical in that respect. For example, while the Hungarian reforms were primarily influenced by the documents and instruments produced by EBRD, Article 9 of UCC[8] was the primary model in *Romania*.

34. There have been waves of reforms[9] each trying to make headway although backpedalling was not unheard of either, perhaps best illustrated by the new Hungarian (2013) and Romanian (2013) Civil Codes. While the Hungarians have decided to discard the nominated 'property encumbering charges' (i.e. the local equivalents of the English floating charges), the Romanians have reduced the self-help related rules originally introduced in 1999 directly based on UCC Article 9.

35. It is also common, and of importance from the perspective of secured transactions and insolvency laws, that none of the systems has introduced a comprehensive secured transactions law based on the unitary concept of security interests. This applies especially to what is referred to in this report as quasi-securities, which remains a concept largely foreign to CEE. As a result, various more advanced forms of leasing or factoring contracts remain legal

---

8 See e.g. V. Padurari and A. Burtoiu, 'Taking Stock of Romanian Secured Transactions after 15 years of Reform' in F. Dahan (ed.), *Research Handbook on Secured Financing in Commercial Transactions* (Edward Elgar, 2015), 403–421; N. de la Peña and H. Fleisig, (2004) 29 *Review of Central and East European Law* 133–217 at 164; I. Smeureanu and F. Giurgea, 'Enforcement of Contracts in Romania' in S. Messmann and T. Tajti (eds.), *The Case Law of Central and Eastern Europe – Enforcement of Contracts* (European University Press, Bochum, 2009), 723–731. The Romanian reform was assisted also by the United States Agency for International Development (USAID), which is a federal agency that assists low-income countries, among others, in achieving self-sustaining socioeconomic development. In Romania, this included the reform of secured transactions law.

9 In the case of Hungary, for example, the security law-related parts of the Civil Code were significantly revamped three times in the post-1990 period: in 1996, in 2000 and in 2013. While the 1996 amendments introduced the new regime, the ones from 2000 were limited essentially only to its upgrading and refinements. However, the 2013 new Civil Code not only expanded the system, but also made important advancements towards the Anglo-Saxon models and Book IX of the DCFR. For example, notice-filing was introduced and financial leasing contracts were subjected to registration. On the Hungarian developments see T. Tajti, *Post-1990 Secured Transactions Law Reforms in Central and Eastern Europe – Focus on Hungary and its Neighbors*, in Bulletin of the Chamber of Public Notaries of County Szeged (Hungary), vol. II, Nos. 3–4 (27 October 2013) 18 et seq. On the 1996 and 2000 amendments of the Civil Code see the 'Chapter on Hungary' in T. Tajti, *Comparative Secured Transactions Law* (Akadémiai könyvkiadó, Budapest, 2002), 293–315.

categories strictly distinct from security agreements. Changes can already be seen, however, to be taking place. For example, under the new 2013 Hungarian Civil Code financial leasing and factoring contracts – while remaining distinct legal categories – have become subject to registration in the registry of security rights on movables introduced as part of the reforms.

36. Consequently, one has to be cautious to determine which particular types of transactions or asset-types, have remained outside the reach of the newly introduced regime. Besides ships, aircraft, fixtures and some forms of intellectual property, this applies especially to receivables, transactions containing retained title (ownership), investment property and 'global' security extending to all (or substantially all) present and future assets of a debtor.

37. Put simply, compared not just to UCC Article 9, and the Australian or Canadian provincial PPSAs, but also to Book IX of the Draft Common Frame of Reference (DCFR), these systems still tend to be fragmented.

6. The synopsis of the secured transactions and insolvency laws of selected CEE jurisdictions

6.1. Hungary

38. The fall of the Berlin Wall brought about a new beginning for both secured transactions and insolvency law in *Hungary*.[10] This applies especially to the former, which was reformed with the assistence of the EBRD resulting in a system adopting common law concepts.

39. Secured transactions law is enshrined in the Civil Code and thus the three significant amendments to the Code involved further reform: while the first in 1996 introduced the new system,[11] and the second of 2000 aimed only at refining the law and filling the gaps left by the drafters of the first version,[12] that of 2013 – introduced by a brand new Civil Code[13] – brought about a major

10 See, for example, the 'Chapter on Hungary' in T. Tajti, *Comparative Secured Transactions Law*.

11 The 26th Law of Year 1996 on Amendment of Certain Provisions of the Hungarian Republic's Civil Code (hereinafter: the 1st Reform Act).

12 The 137th Law of Year 2000 on the Amendment of the Law Regulating Charges (hereinafter: the 2nd Reform Act).

13 The 5th Law of Year 2013 on the Civil Code *(A Polgári Törvénykönyvről szóló 2013. évi V. törvény)*. The law on security rights is in Book V on Property Law, Part III on Limited Proprietary Rights, Title VII on Security Rights, §§5:86 through 5:144. All the references to various paragraphs – unless otherwise specifically stated – will be related to this part of the 2013 Civil Code.

advance towards the unitary model of UCC Article 9. In particular, financial leasing, factoring and retained title (ownership) was made subject to registration in the charges register; a version of notice filing was also introduced, together with a milder version of self-help repossession. Needless to say, the ensuing report will state the law as per the 2013 Civil Code and will rely on the related Commentaries.[14]

40. It ought to be added, however, that in particular the National Organization of Public Notaries and the Banking Association requested meaningful changes to the 2013 Civil Code shortly after its passage, most importantly discarding the notice-filing system and re-introducing instead the old document-authentication system as well as the reintroduction of independent security rights. From these, only the latter was accepted and consequently the so-called independent (non-accessory) security (*önálló zálogjog*) was reintroduced with the June 2016 amendments of the Civil Code.[15]

41. Insolvency law was also amended significantly in the post-1990 period, following developments in *Germany* and other civil law countries in Europe rather than Anglo-Saxon systems. The core of the system is Law No. XLIX of 1991 on Insolvency and Liquidation Proceedings (as amended) (hereinafter: the Insolvency Act),[16] amended fundamentally five times in the meantime.[17]

---

14 Professor L. Vékás was at the helm of the team drafting the new Civil Code just as he was the editor of one of the Commentaries: L. Vékás (ed.), *Complex Commentary* (Complex, 2013). The other Civil Code Commentary is: G. Welmann, *HVG Commentary*.

15 Act No. LXXVII of 2016 on the Amendment of Act No. V of 2013 on the Civil Code (*2016. évi LXXVII. törvény a Polgári Törvénykönyvről szóló 2013. évi V. törvény módosításáról*). As the official justification states, the independent security (charge) was reintroduced because the implementation of Regulation 575/2013/EU on prudential requirements for credit institutions and investment firms and amending Regulation (EU) No. 648/2012 in Hungary required that. This Regulation actually introduced the recommendations of Basel III (the Third Basel Accord) on bank capital adequately, stress testing, and market liquidity. According to these recommendations, as enshrined in section 402 of the EU Regulation, non-accessory securities are considered to be less risky financial products and as such they lessen the exposure of banks possessing such securities in their portfolios. This is so since the non-accessory nature of independent securities makes their transfer (sale) easier.

16 *1991. évi XLIV. törvény a csődeljárásról és a felszámolási eljárásról.*

17 The literature speaks of these, due to their in-depth nature, as 'novellas' to differentiate them from other minor amendments. Notwithstanding the indeterminacy inherent to such classification, we will follow the established standards in this respect. In light of that, the list of the most important amendments in the post-1992 (passage of the Insolvency Act) – called novellas – are the following.

The first novella of 1993 (Act LXXXI of 1993) discarded the concept of mandatory insolvencies and the automatic conversion of reorganisations to liquidation. This was possible because after the 1992 passage of the Insolvency Act the national-level wave of insolvencies – caused by circular indebtedness amounting to more than a thousand billion Hungarian forints – subsided. The second novella of 1997 (Act XXVII of 1997), among others, increased the entitlements of the creditors' committee and of the equity holders. The third novella of 2004 (Act XXVII of 2004) was needed because Hungary joined the EU on 1 May 2004 and therefore

Besides these, the insolvency regime was affected (at different levels) by the three waves of secured transactions reforms mentioned earlier and also by various amending statutes, although some of these addressed only minor matters.[18]

42. Already these few sentences indicate how dynamic (if not hectic) the post-1990 development of Hungarian insolvency law has been. The hastily passed amendments and the large number of changes could only cause problems in the application of the law. As the transition of the economy from planned to market economy was completed in this period and essentially similar challenges exist in *Hungary* as in other Central European countries today, there is nothing to forestall the passing of a new consolidated Act enriched by the latest-generation experiences of developed legal systems. Unfortunately, no such initiative seems to be on the lawmakers' agenda save the issue of the bankruptcy of individuals – triggered by the systemic risk generated by the widely used Swiss Franc-denominated (primarily) housing mortgage loans. The first-ever Hungarian individual (consumer) bankruptcy Act was consequently passed in 2015 and entered into force on the 1 September 2015.[19] As the first consumer bankruptcy cases have only been launched, this report will not refer to the new Act.

6.2. Synopsis of the laws of Lithuania and Poland

43. Developments in the jurisdictions which follow cannot be scrutinised in the same level of detail employed with *Hungary*, the main jurisdiction herein. Still,

---

in effect this novella implemented EU law. The fourth novella of 2006 (Act IV of 2006) reconciled the Insolvency Act with the new Company Act and also refined the law on some key building blocks of the system (e.g. new criteria for insolvency, costs of insolvency). Finally, the fifth novella of 2009 (Act LI of 2009) again significantly revamped insolvency law, among others, by (1) introducing the institution of immediate 'moratorium', (2) subjecting the filing of creditor claims to payment of fees, (3) increasing the powers of the administrator (trustee), and (4) introducing once again the rule that unsuccessful reorganisations automatically convert to liquidation proceedings. See L. Juhász, *The Hungarian Insolvency Handbook* (Novotni Publishing House, Miskolc, 2014), 38–40.

18 Insolvency law was affected by the following acts: (1) Act LXI of 2007 (e.g. faster publication in the Bulleting of Companies, ranking of security interests); (2) Act LXXVIII of 2007 (aimed to deal with circular indebtedness but touched upon some insolvency issues); (3) Act CXV of 2009 on Sole Proprietors (made registered sole proprietorships subject to insolvency law); (4) Act XCVI of 2009 (introduced the duty of the debtor's CEO to file a tax return); (5) Act CXLIX of 2009 (changes to the system of criminal records and the related duties of the insolvency administrator); (6) Act CL of 2009 (changes in the laws regulating the financial system); (7) Act CXV of 2011 introduced the category of the 'enterprise of national importance' ('*nemzetgazdaságilag kiemelt gazdálkodó szervezet*'); (8) Act CXCVII of 2011; (9) Act CIV of 2012; (10) Act CCLII of 2013 (making the insolvency system compatible with the new 2013 Civil Code); and finally (11) Act XV of 2014 (modification of the rules on administrators). See L. Juhász, *The Hungarian Insolvency Handbook*, 39–40.

19 Act No. CV of 2015 on the Debt-Consolidation of Natural Persons (*2015. évi CV. törvény a természetes személyek adósságrendezéséről*).

as will be seen, the review of developments and some of the key – sometimes idiosyncratic – solutions demonstrates that the upgrading (modernisation) of secured transactions law has ranked high on the agenda of each of these countries, principally by borrowing from Anglo-Saxon systems. The introduction and gradual refinement of insolvency laws has also been an important agenda of law reforms in the region.

6.2.1. Lithuania

44. *Lithuania* was no exception in the CEE: it also modernised its mortgage and secured transactions law in the post-1990 period.

45. As part of that modernisation it established a centralised registry (the Central Mortgage Office) in 1998, a government-funded institution monitored by the Ministry of Justice, the work of which is now carried out electronically.[20] The Office maintains a separate registry for some specific types of contracts of relevance to this Report including, in particular, credit and financial leasing contracts.[21]

46. The main source of mortgage law is the Civil Code[22] of 2000 (last amended in April 2015)and its Book IV, Chapter XI (the last amendment is from 2011, which came into force on the 1 July 2012); parallel with which the earlier lex specialis Law on Pledge over Movable Assets was quashed.[23] One should mention also Resolution No 1246 of 18 October 2001 of the Government of the Republic of Lithuania on the Approval of the Regulations of the Mortgage Register of the Republic of Lithuania (Official Gazette, No. 90-3173, 2001), as amended by Resolution No. 571 of the Government of *Lithuania* of 23 May 2012.[24] Both the number of registrations (relative to the size of the country)[25] and the overall

---

20 The English language pages of the Central Mortgage Office are at <https://www.hipotekosistaiga.lt/index.php?2506114761> accessed 23 May 2016.

21 The English language pages of the Central Mortgage Office for these specific contracts are at <https://www.hipotekosistaiga.lt/index.php?1927692242> accessed 23 May 2016. Note that the register of real property and cadastre is maintained by another body, by the State Enterprise Centre of Registers at <http://www.registrucentras.lt/index_en.php#> accessed 23 May 2016.

22 The Civil Code of 18 July 2000, Law No. VIII-1864 (as amended). The English text of the Civil Code of the Republic of Lithuania is available at <http://www3.lrs.lt/pls/inter3/dokpaieska.showdoc_l?p_id=245495> accessed 23 May 2016.

23 Although not in force since 1 January 2003, one has to make mention of it because some sources mistakenly mention it as a key act on security rights. The act was part of the reform package and was enacted on 10 June 1997 as Law No. VIII-250.

24 The English text of the amended Resolution is available at <http://www3.lrs.lt/pls/inter3/dokpaieska.showdoc_e?p_id=450749&p_query=&p_tr2=2#> accessed 23 May 2016.

25 For statistics (though in Lithuanian language) on registrations by type of asset see <https://www.hipotekosistaiga.lt/Statistika/HR_statistika%28projektas2014%29.htm> accessed 23 May 2016.

achievements in reforming the system are meaningful although difficulties persist.[26]

47. In many respects, *Lithuania* faced the same problems as other CEE reform-oriented countries due to a civil law heritage. Perhaps the main problem was the reluctance to accept that the analogous application of rules applicable to real property (immovables) mortgage law is ill-suited to use of movables, rights and claims as collateral.[27] Although, undoubtedly the 2011 amendment of the relevant Civil Code provisions was a major advance – for example by recognising a form of enterprise mortgage (shifting stock as collateral) and a limited form of out-of-court enforcement – the drafters have nonetheless failed to go as far as the introduction of notice-filing (in contrast with *Hungary*). Under the present law, notaries are still entrusted with meaningful roles in the constitution and registration of security rights.[28]

48. The new Lithuanian insolvency law for businesses is encapsulated in the Enterprise Insolvency Act of 2001;[29] one could say a typical Continental European insolvency law.

49. A public register exists with data on business enterprise insolvencies; basic insolvency related information is searchable on the Internet.[30] In order to effect an advanced research, the searcher must be pre-authorised and payment of a modest fee is also required. The Ministry of Economy, through its Department of Enterprise Insolvency Management, publishes not only data related to business insolvencies[31] but also – since 2013 – to individual bankruptcies.[32]

---

26 For two cases dealing with security rights (with excerpts from the judgments themselves in English) see L. Aleknaite, 'Enforcement of Contracts in Lithuania' in S. Messmann and T. Tajti (eds.), *The Case Law of Central and Eastern Europe – Enforcement of Contracts* (European University Press, Bochum, 2009), 370–384.

27 See Article 4.199 of the Lithuanian Civil Code that imposes the duty to apply the rules on immovables mortgages mutatis mutandis to 'pledging' movables, rights and claims.

28 For a rundown of the main changes introduced by the 2011 amendments to the Civil Code see the brief commentary published by the Klaipeda City First Notary's Office from 2013 available at <http://www.notarius.lt/?en=1390464172> accessed 23 May 2016 or through the Oxford Secured Transactions Reform Project led by Prof. Gullifer at <http://securedtransactionslawreformproject.org/lithuania/> accessed 23 May 2016.

29 The Act was passed on 20 March 2001 as Act No IX-216 (last amended on 18 November 2014, amendments came into force on 1 January 2015 – XII-1309). The English text of the act is available at <http://www.doingbusiness.org/law-library/lithuania> accessed 23 May 2016. For an overview of the Act see the material compiled by the Department of Enterprise Bankruptcy Management operating under the Ministry of Economy at <http://www.bankrotodep.lt/Index.php>.

30 See the Centre of Registers at <http://www.jar.lt.> accessed 23 May 2016.

31 See the data for 2013 at <http://www.bankrotodep.lt/Doc/2013_00_en.pdf> accessed 5 January 2015.

32 See e.g. for 2014 at <http://www.bankrotodep.lt/Doc/FABIS_G.pdf> accessed 5 January 2015.

50. The restructuring of enterprises is regulated separately by the Law on Enterprise Restructuring, which was also passed in 2001.[33] The Law on Enterprise Restructuring governs the whole restructuring procedure, starting with the initiation of the restructuring of a case in court, through to the appointment of a restructuring administrator, the drawing up a restructuring plan, and finally to the approval and satisfaction of creditor claims. The law sets a definite framework according to which the restructuring procedure should be conducted. Ultimately, the procedure is creditor driven, as a restructuring plan can only be adopted upon creditor approval. The restructuring procedure is not available to companies that the court finds to be insolvent.

51. A methodological caveat: the analysis of Lithuanian law in this Report is based on the most recent English versions of the Civil Code and the Insolvency Act. This means, in the case of the Civil Code, the version valid at 1 October 2011[34] and in the case of the Insolvency Act, the version valid at 3 July 2012.[35]

6.2.2. Poland

52. *Poland*, similarly to *Hungary*, embarked on the modernisation of its secured transactions law right after the fall of the Berlin Wall. It passed a special statute named the Registered Pledge and Register of Pledges Act in 1996,[36] which extends to movables, rights and claims.

53. Three key determinants played a role in shaping the Act. First, the drafters tried to exploit the pre-WWII experiences with a number of laws allowing the

---

33 The Act was passed on 20 March 2001 as Act No IX-218 (last amended on 16 December 2014, amendments came into force on 1 August 2015 – XII-1456). The English text of the act is available at <http://www3.lrs.lt/pls/inter3/dokpaieska.showdoc_l?p_id=418092> accessed 23 May 2016. The list of amendments is available at <http://www3.lrs.lt/pls/inter3/dokpaieska.rezult_l?p_nr=&p_nuo=&p_iki=&p_org=&p_drus=1&p_kalb_id=1&p_title=%E1moni%F8%20restrukt%FBrizavimo&p_text=&p_pub=&p_met=&p_lnr=&p_denr=&p_es=0&p_tid=&p_tkid=&p_t=0&p_tr1=2&p_tr2=2&p_gal=&p_rus=> accessed 23 May 2016.

34 For the list of articles affected by subsequent amendments see <http://www3.lrs.lt/pls/inter3/dokpaieska.rezult_l?p_nr=&p_nuo=&p_iki=&p_org=&p_drus=1&p_kalb_id=1&p_title=civilinio%20kodekso&p_text=&p_pub=&p_met=&p_lnr=&p_denr=&p_es=0&p_tid=&p_tkid=&p_t=0&p_tr1=1&p_tr2=2&p_gal=&p_rus=1> or <http://goo.gl/2hlkgb> accessed 23 May 2016.

35 For the list of articles affected by subsequent amendments see <http://www3.lrs.lt/pls/inter3/dokpaieska.rezult_l?p_nr=&p_nuo=&p_iki=&p_org=&p_drus=1&p_kalb_id=1&p_title=%E1moni%F8%20bankroto&p_text=&p_pub=&p_met=&p_lnr=&p_denr=&p_es=0&p_tid=&p_tkid=&p_t=0&p_tr1=2&p_tr2=2&p_gal=&p_rus=1> or <http://goo.gl/hTdNmb> both accessed 23 May 2016.

36 The English translation of the original text of the act is available at <http://www.ebrd.com/downloads/legal/core/polandls.pdf> accessed 23 May 2016. Note that the act has been amended in the meantime. The Act will be hereinafter referred to as the Registered Pledge Act.

creation of registered pledges on some specific types of assets (timber, motor vehicles, equipment and agricultural registered pledge).[37] Second, the Act tried to incorporate into the Polish system a number of modern developments (e.g. by exploiting the EBRD's secured transactions law-related work). Finally, the Act yielded also to local expectations. As Spanogle aptly put it: 'Polish professors drafted the statute in their own style, using their own principles and civil law values.'[38] For example, the quasi-securities known as 'security transfers' (*przewlaszczeniena zabezpieczenie*) and 'security assignments' (*przelew na zabezpieczenie*) – not subject to registration with a public registry – were tolerated by the system, but could only negatively affect predictability on the market.[39] Leasing remains separate from the system of registered pledges until today.

54. Polish lawmakers – similarly to the Hungarians – have also struggled with the dictates imposed by the conceptual unity of security law, a characteristic of all continental European civil law systems. As the drafters did not dare to dispense with the concept, this had important consequences affecting the efficiency of the new system.

55. The greatest novelty of the reforms, the 'registered pledge' was looked upon as the weaker brother of the mortgage of immovables and consequently whenever possible (no matter how ill-suited) the same principles and solutions were applied also to the latter.[40]

56. This, most importantly, made the introduction of notice-filing impossible and rather entrusted courts and judges with maintaining the system. This made the system very cumbersome and slow because judges were entrusted with the

---

37 For short references to these laws see K. Kaźmierczyk and F. Kijowski, 'Chapter on Poland' in S. Messmann and T. Tajti (eds.), *The Case Law of Central and Eastern Europe*. note 162, p. 607. Keeping the strange designation combining pledge (inherently possessory) with registration (means of perfection of non-possessory securities) seems to stem from the pre-WWII period as well. Though as K. Kaźmierczyk and F. Kijowski noted, a better alternative was also known yet was eventually abandoned. *Id.*

38 See J. Spanogle, (2009) 31 *T. Jefferson L. Rev.* 279 at 279.

39 See the case II CK 409/2003 decided by the Supreme Court (excerpts from the decision and comments in English) in K. Kaźmierczyk and F. Kijowski in S. Messmann and T. Tajti (eds.), *The Case Law of Central and Eastern Europe*, 625–630.

40 Article 1.2. of the Registered Pledge Act proclaims that the provisions of the Civil Code apply to registered pledges if something is not regulated explicitly by the Act. Note, however, that mortgage law is regulated by the Act on Land and Mortgage Register and on Mortgages. Only the general rules applicable to all proprietary rights come into the picture. These include, in particular, rules on creation of proprietary rights (Article 245), rules on transfers of proprietary rights (Article 246), rules on expiry of proprietary rights (Articles 247–248), rules on changes to proprietary rights (Article 248) and priority rules (Articles 249–250).

'constitution' of registered pledges and the running of the registry.[41] The system is not faultless, yet it is fair to say that it works relatively smoothly and that the system of registered pledges has, indeed, contributed meaningfully to increasing access to finance.

57. Polish security law, however, is not only enshrined in the Registered Pledge Act. The rules on possessory pledges (also known as civil code pledge or ordinary pledge in Polish), some rules on 'pledging' of rights and claims as well as some generally applicable rules on securities are contained in the Civil Code.[42] The relationship between the Civil Code and the Registered Pledge Act is that of the lex generalis versus the lex specialis. In other words, for matters not regulated by the Registered Pledge Act one must consult the Civil Code. Furthermore, separate Acts cover mortgages on immovables[43] and financial collateral.[44]

58. As far as insolvency law is concerned, laws from 1934 were revived with the fall of socialism in *Poland*. These soon proved to be inadequate for modern times yet a brand new law – the Insolvency and Rehabilitation Act[45] – was enacted only in 2003 (hereinafter: the 2003 Insolvency Act). The Act seems to have been modelled primarily on German law.

59. The desire to promote the rescue of businesses was proclaimed as one of the primary functions of the Act[46] but this desire has not been fulfilled appropriately. This realisation led to the 2015 Restructuring Act (passed in May 2015), which entered into force on 1 January 2016.[47] As the Statement of Reasons attached to the Act puts it, the primary purpose is to boost restructuring instead of liquidations, as has been the predominant aim of insolvency prcedures. A *lex specialis* was opted for – instead of only amending the 2003 Act – to deal with the all-pervasive stigma of bankruptcy. Although pre-WW II law was also considered, the main source of inspiration was US Chapter 11 reorganisation

41 As per Article 36.2. the register of 'registered pledges' is kept by district (commercial) courts. Although as per Article 40.3. the court may reject an entry only if that would evidently violate the law, actually the judge must go into the merits as well as its mandate is to '[verify] only the form and content of the application and the documents on whose basis the entry is to be made and only within the scope of the data to be entered.' See also J. Spanogle, (2009) 31 *T. Jefferson L. Rev.* 279 at 288.

42 The Civil Code was originally enacted on the 23 April 1964 (hereinafter: Polish Civil Code) but has been in the meantime amended many times. For the general rules on securities see Articles 244–251, on possessory pledges Articles 306–326, and for 'pledging' of rights Articles 327–335.

43 See Act of 6 July 1982 on Land and Mortgage Registers and on Mortgage (as amended) (hereinafter: the Polish Mortgage Act).

44 See Act of 2 April 2004 on Certain Financial Collaterals (as amended).

45 Note that due to the changes introduced by the 2015 Restructuring Act, the restructuring-related provisions in the 2003 Act have been deleted. Consequently, the designation of the Act has been reduced to 'Insolvency Act'.

46 See Article 2 of the Polish Insolvency Act.

47 The Restructuring Law of 15 May 2015, published in (2015) 978 *Journal of Laws*.

proceedings. The Act also proposes to enhance the position of creditors and establish a Central Insolvency and Restructuring Register.[48]

60. The 2015 Restructuring Law introduced four types of restructuring proceedings: (1) pre-packaged arrangements (*postępowanie o zatwierdzenie układu*); (2) accelerated arrangement proceedings (*przyspieszone postępowanie układowe*); (3) arrangement proceedings (*postępowanie układowe*); and (4) rehabilitation proceedings (*postępowanie sanacyjne*).

61. A methodological caveat is that as with *Lithuania*, for the ensuing analysis of Polish law, this Report relied on the most recent English versions of the Civil Code and other cited Acts. Here, however, the central Act – the Registered Pledge Act – has undergone only technical changes in the mean-time[49] and thus the publicly available English version could have been worked with. As far as insolvency law is concerned, the entry into force of the previously mentioned lex specialis Restructuring Act and the Consolidated Insolvency Act (containing 268 changes) of 1 January 2016, were the main, obviously fundamental, developments.[50] Statistical data on insolvency proceedings is regularly published

---

48 As per the new Act, it is envisaged that the new Registry will commence its operations on the 1 February 2018.

49 In 2015 there were three amendments to the 2009 version on which the latest translation was based. First, on 28 July 2015 a technical amendment was added to Article 42(4a) concerning release of public entities from costs of registration proceedings. Second, on 18 November 2015 Article 42(4a) was again amended to specify the conditions for the release of public entities from payment of registration fees. Finally, the new Restructuring Law also made a technical amendment to Article 4(1)(3).

50 The English translations of the relevant Polish acts are as follows. *Private and commercial law*: (1) the Act on Registered Pledges – translation based on text published in (2009) 1663 (215) *Journal of Laws* 2009, three technical amendments since then; (2) the Civil Code – translation based on text published in (2014) 121 *Journal of Laws*, published on 23 January 2014, nine amendments since then; (3) Code of Civil Procedure – translation based on text published in (2014) 616 *Journal of Laws*, published on 1 July 2014, 27 amendments since then; and finally (5) the Act on Land and Mortgage Registers and on Mortgages – translation based on text published in (2013) 941 *Journal of Laws*, published on 1 December 2013, three amendments since then. *Insolvency law*: (1) the Insolvency Act – translation based on text published in (2013) 613 *Journal of Laws*, published on 12 June 2013, eight amendments since then; (2) based on the Insolvency Act, a distinct brand-new Restructuring Law (enacted on 15 May 2015). It ought to be noted that the new Restructuring Law has significantly amended the earlier insolvency act as well mainly by transposing the reorganisation-related law to the new Act.

The website of the Polish Parliament listing the amendments (in Polish) are: (1) for the Civil Code: <http://isap.sejm.gov.pl/RelatedServlet?id=WDU19640160093+2000%2412%2409&type=12&isNew=true>; (2) for the Code of Civil Procedure: <http://isap.sejm.gov.pl/RelatedServlet?id=WDU19640430296+2015%2401%2410&type=12&isNew=true>; (3) for the Insolvency Act <http://isap.sejm.gov.pl/RelatedServlet?id=WDU20030600535+2014%2412%2431&type=12&isNew=true>; (4) for the Registered Pledge Act: <http://isap.sejm.gov.pl/RelatedServlet?id=WDU19961490703+2010%2401%2418&type=12&isNew=true>; and (5) for the Mortgage Act <http://isap.sejm.gov.pl/RelatedServlet?id=WDU20130000941+2013%2412%2401&type=12&isNew=true> all accessed 23 May 2016.

by the Ministry of Justice as part of the report on the operation of general courts.[51]

6.3. *A brief look at selected other CEE reform jurisdictions*

6.3.1. *Croatia*

62. The Balkan wars delayed the reform of secured transactions law in *Croatia*, yet it became a reality in 2006 before the country's accession to the EU. The Law on the Registry of Court and Public-Notary Security Interests on Movables and Rights[52] was quite innovative and a trend-setter. It introduced an electronic public register and a version of floating (global or enterprise) security.[53] It made not only securities on movables – including the floating security – subject to registration[54] but also retained title and even negative pledge clauses.

6.3.2. *Slovakia*

63. *Slovakia*, similarly to *Hungary*, primarily relied on EBRD's work on secured transactions law. The common law inspired security law was introduced by an amendment to the Civil Code in 2002.[55] As with *Hungary*, the running of the brand new centralised and computerised register of security interests was entrusted to public notaries.[56]

---

51 Statistical report in insolvency and rehabilitation matters for 2014, available at the Ministry of Justice's website at <http://isws.ms.gov.pl/Data/Files/_public/isws/jednoroczne/2014/spr_zbior_2014/ms-s20un_2014.pdf.> accessed 23 May 2016.

52 The Croatian language text of the act is available at <http://www.zakon.hr/z/276/Zakon-o-Upisniku-sudskih> accessed 23 May 2016. The floating security is regulated by Article 38(1) of the Act. See also T. Tajti, *Post-1990 Secured Transactions Law Reforms in Central and Eastern Europe – Focus on Hungary and its Neighbours,* Bulletin of the Chamber of Public Notaries of County Szeged (Hungary), vol. II, No. 3 at 14–21 and No. 4 at 18–26, also available at <http://www.ssrn.com> and <http://www.researchgate.net> both accessed 23 May 2016.

53 See also P. Živković, *Floating Security Interest – Comparative Analysis of US, English and Croatian Approaches*, conference paper (Bratislava 2013), available at <http://papers.ssrn.com/sol3/papers.cfm?abstract_id=2243590> accessed 23 May 2016.

54 The register of security interests on movables and shares is maintained by FINA – the Financial Organisation – which provides other services as well <http://www.fina.hr/Default.aspx?sec=976> accessed 23 May 2016.

55 Articles 151a to 151md of the Civil Code contain the new law.

56 The register of pledges – with English, German, French and Hungarian pages (besides Slovak) – is available at <http://www.notar.sk/en/MainPage/Centralnotaryregisterofdeeds.aspx> accessed 23 May 2016.

6.3.3. *Romania*

64. *Romania* is a special case because the secured transaction law reforms were introduced here with assistance from the US. This was clearly reflected in Law No. 99/1999 on Security Interests in Movable Property that was closer to UCC Article 9 than any of the other CEE systems.[57] This included, not only the creation of a new registry system, but also the introduction of self-help repossesion. The subjection of leasing contracts (at least with respect to some classes of assets) to public notice was another such US-inspired revolutionary innovation that had not been widely followed elsewhere in the CEE. The drafters of the new Civil Code of 2011 have, however, backpedalled and made the security law more typical of Continental Europe; in particular as far as self-help repossession is concerned.[58]

B. CREATION OF SECURITY RIGHTS

Question 1: In general terms, to what extent is it possible in your legal system to create security rights (rights in rem) over assets?

1. Hungary

1.1. *The Hungarian spectrum of security devices*

65. The spectrum of security devices known to Hungarian law can be subdivided into the following: proprietary (in rem), personal (in personam), security devices as well as other creditors' position-enhancing devices.

66. While this report will focus exclusively on in rem security devices, it ought to be added that some of the devices belonging to the third group have quasi-in rem effects (like subordination or comfort letters) or are a source of receivables that may be used as collateral (e.g. letters of credit). Further, the law on suretyships and guarantees (as paradigm in personam security devices) was upgraded by the 2013 Civil Code as well,[59] a development that together with

---

57 See I. Smeureanu and F. Giurgea, 'Enforcement of Contracts in Romania' in S. Messmann and T. Tajti (eds.), *The Case Law of Central and Eastern Europe – Enforcement of Contracts*, 726 et seq.

58 On self-help in Romania see also K. Fabián and A. Horváthová and C. Stănescu, 4 *Journal of Eurasian Law* 83, also available at <http://www.SSRN.com> accessed 23 May 2016.

59 Suretyship and guarantee contracts (as in personam security devices) are regulated by Book VI: Obligations, Part Three: Individual (Nominated) Contracts, Title XXI of the Hungarian Civil Code.

the three times revamped secured transactions system is the best proof of the increased importance accorded to security devices in toto since the fall of the Berlin Wall.

1.2. The novelties introduced by the new 2013 Hungarian Civil Code

67. Turning to security rights (i.e. in rem or proprietary securities), *Hungary* has managed to upgrade its system from one that is conservative and minimalist, inherited from socialism, to one that is credit and security-friendly due to the common law inspired reforms launched in 1996. Notwithstanding the fluctuations, the data properly evidence meaningful growth.

68. Given that the new 2013 Civil Code introduced fundamental changes in security law – and prohibited two specific categories of – earlier widely exploited secured transactions, a brief look at the earlier law is needed. Before 2013 four main groups of in rem security rights were widely exploited: (1) real property (immovables)[60] mortgages; (2) security interests on movables, rights and claims; (3) the so-called fiduciary securities ('*fiduciáris hitelbiztosítékok*');[61] and (4) three specific devices that had their own isolated life: specifically, sales contracts with retained-ownership (clauses), financial leasing and factoring. In conclusion, omitting any of these categories when assessing the economic importance of in rem securities, would distort the overall picture.

69. Contrary to the law on real property (immovables) mortgages that also underwent some changes (especially with respect to computerisation of the registry), the law on securities on movables, rights and claims was at the centre of the three waves of reforms. Fiduciary securities were the products either of legal innovation or were transplanted financing patterns from Western legal systems.

70. Until the new 2013 Civil Code, the legal system looked only on real property mortgage and security devices on movables, rights and claims as being true in

---

60 For the purposes of this Report, it will be presumed that the common law category of 'real property' is equal (or substantially equal) with the civil law concept of 'immovables.' The two terms will thus be used interchangeably.

61 The three main forms utilised in practice were: (1) transfer of ownership (on an immovable), (2) assignment (transfer) of a claim, and (3) granting of an option to purchase (right of first refusal) an asset (typically an immovable, like a flat) – in each case as a security for a debt. The two main problems with these were that, on one hand, they gave considerably more entitlements to the creditor than what would be legally justified and, on the other hand, these contravened the prohibition of strict foreclosure (lex commissoria). As L. Vékás says in the Comments, through these devices 'the creditors ... acquired ownership as most complete forms of proprietary rights, or – based on their purchase options – could acquire it based on a unilateral declaration.' See L. Vékás (ed.), *Complex Commentary*, 574.

rem securities. As a result, they were placed in the same part of the Civil Code, both were subjected to registration, and the same principles applied to them unless something else followed from their different nature.

71. In comparison, fiduciary securities were looked upon as different kinds of legal institutions and the related provisions appeared in different parts of the Code. In fact, their exact legal status remained the subject of polemics and courts took no common position on whether to recognise them: some recognised them, others either declared them null and void or subjected them to registration and mortgage law.[62] Most importantly, however, no piece of legislation has ever required them to be subjected to registration and the strict priority regime applicable to genuine security rights. More because of the many abuses rather than because of their unclear legal status, the 2013 Civil Code prohibited them.[63] Foreseeably this change will not negatively affect the market given that the other avenues remain widely open.

72. The other novelty of the 2013 Code is the imposition of registration (filing) in the charge register requirement in respect of financial leasing,[64] factoring[65] and sales contracts with retained ownership (title)[66] clauses. This was introduced to prevent the bypassing of the registration system applicable to movables, rights and claims. In other words, the new system has come close to the unitary concept of security interests.[67]

73. The 2013 Civil Code, 'departs from the fact that credit is one of the vital elements of market economies and that the availability of efficient security devices is a crucial precondition of that.'[68] In line with such a policy goal, the Code declares that any asset can serve as collateral[69] – including after-acquired property[70] – that the collateral may be identified by description only and that the security right will extend to the parts, products, and proceeds of the collateral.[71]

62 See L. Vékás (ed.), *Complex Commentary*, 574.

63 See Book VI on Obligations, §6:99 of the Hungarian Civil Code.

64 See Book VI on Obligations, Part III on Specific Contracts, Title XX on Credit and Account-Contracts, Chapter LIX on Financial Leasing Contracts, §6:410 of the Hungarian Civil Code.

65 See Book VI on Obligations, Part III on Specific Contracts, Title XX on Credit and Account-Contracts, Chapter LVIII on Factoring Contracts, §6:406 of the Hungarian Civil Code.

66 See Book VI on Obligations, Part III on Specific Contracts, Title XIV on Contracts for Transfer of Ownership, Chapter XXXII on the General Rules on Sales contracts, §6:216(3) of the Hungarian Civil Code.

67 See L. Vékás (ed.), *Complex Commentary Comments,* 417.

68 *Ibid.* at 416.

69 See §5:101 of the Hungarian Civil Code. The restrictions stem from the nature of the asset used as collateral. Thus, possessory pledge can be constituted only on movables (§5:101(2)). Furthermore, security right cannot be constituted on an asset in condominium unless the ownership share of the debtor cannot be determined or in case of divisible obligations (§5:101(3)).

70 See §5:89(4) of the Hungarian Civil Code.

71 See §5:103(1)(2) of the Hungarian Civil Code.

74. A pro-credit novelty is the introduction of the notice-filing system instead of the earlier document-registration model that relied on the same principles that have remained valid for real property mortgages. With this measure the transaction costs of the constitution of security rights are significantly reduced, although the transition to the new system and ignorance of the notice filing requirement may generate unexpected risks and costs.

2. Lithuania

75. As a result of the post-1990 efforts aimed at the modernisation of Lithuanian secured transactions law (i.e. in rem rights on movables, rights and claims), it is now possible to grant securities in a wide range of circumstances.

76. The caveat is that the terminology and system of the Civil Code (in which security law is enshrined) and the available English translations might blur the picture. This applies especially to Book IV, Chapter XII, which contains possessory 'pledges' and known possessory securities. What makes *Lithuania* interesting is that besides the floating charge (security) covering the whole enterprise (Chapter XI),[72] a narrower version of floating security is also in existence. The latter extends only to some specific property such as equipment or goods for sale (inventory) and is regulated in a manner distinct from that in Chapter XII.

3. Poland

77. A wide range of securities – both in rem and in personam – may be granted in *Poland* today, too. As far as in rem securities are concerned this is to a great extent due to the reform efforts of the post-1990 transitory period. This includes mortgage of immovables, possessory as well as 'registered pledges' (i.e. non-possessory securities) on almost all kinds of assets from specific movables, through various rights and claims (receivables), to the encumbering of an enterprise as a whole[73] or a particular part of it.

---

72 See Article 4.202 of the Lithuanian Civil Code.

73 See Article 7.2(3) of the Registered Pledge Act, which refers to 'a set of movable things or rights that constitutes an economic unit, even if the constituent elements change'. Note that the definition of 'enterprise' here is different from the one in Article 55^1 of the Civil Code, which is a general private law definition of enterprise.

Question 2: Is it possible to create security rights over all assets of the debtor?

1. Hungary

78. The Code proclaims as a general principle that '[a]ny property [type] may be used as a collateral.'[74] Based on the definition of 'property' (*vagyontárgy*) this may include assets (things), rights and claims.[75] Further, a security interest may be created on more[76] and shifting assets,[77] as well as it automatically extends to the components, accessories, and proceeds of the assets used as collateral.[78]

79. These general rules must, however, be qualified. First, some methods of 'pledging' are limited to certain specific types of assets. For example, the objects of possessory pledge can only be movables and other tangible assets (e.g. certificated securities). Moreover, the sui generis possession and control-based security device – the security-bailment interest (*óvadék*) – can be instituted solely on some specific types of assets, specifically cash, investment property and payment accounts (*fizetési számla*).[79]

80. Second, certain assets may not be freely transferable and thus their use as collateral would also be restricted, due to some specific legal restrictions. Insolvency law lists a number of such assets including national parks, historic buildings, public waters, land separated for restitution, former church estates separated for restitution, trade union membership fees and unpaid taxes that have been deducted from an employee's wages before the opening of insolvency proceedings but have not been transferred to the tax authorities.[80]

81. Third, the Code foresees that as a general rule pledging parts of assets or of claims is not possible without pledging also the whole 'unit.' Pledging separable parts of movables or portions of a claim are nonetheless allowed through explicit exceptions: the part (e.g. an apartment) owned by the debtor in a condominium, the portion of a right held by more than one person (e.g. a patent held by the debtor and another person) and a specific part of a divisible claim.[81]

82. That Hungarian law is based on the all-asset policy is highlighted also by the few limitations set out in the Insolvency Act. These do not prohibit the use of some specific assets as collateral but rather only grant the right of first refusal (option to purchase) to some specific persons. These assets are, on the one hand,

---

74 See §5:101(1) of the Hungarian Civil Code.
75 See §8:1(1)(5) (Book Eight, Concluding Provisions – Part One, Interpretative Provisions).
76 See §5:105 of the Hungarian Civil Code.
77 See §5:104 of the Hungarian Civil Code.
78 See §5:103 of the Hungarian Civil Code.
79 See on security-bailment as well Question 6 below.
80 See §4(3) of the Insolvency Act (assets that are not part of the insolvency estate).
81 See §5:101(3) of the Hungarian Insolvency Act.

national parks and national monuments, in which case the right of first refusal belongs to the competent government bodies.[82] On the other hand, if part of the debtor's estate is residential property that has already been paid for fully or partially by a private individual yet ownership had not been transferred before the opening of the liquidation proceedings, such buyer will have the right of first refusal.[83]

2. Lithuania

83. A form of floating security is known in Lithuanian law as well. This device was introduced by an explicit provision in the Civil Code.[84] The available English language literature speaks of these floating securities, however, as 'company mortgages.'[85] As this device was introduced only recently, the exact features and structure of this security device are not yet fully known. Security interests can be created over a wide array of assets including movables and property rights such as receivables. Floating security over stock was introduced back in 2001.

84. Later amendments to the Civil Code expanded the provision to permit the use of any property complex constituted of movables as collateral, including stock, equipment and claims as specifically stated in the Civil Code. Finally, the 2011 amendments have introduced the possibility of creating a floating charge over the entire property belonging to an enterprise.

3. Poland

85. As indicated under Question 1, today one can use as collateral all types of transferrable assets. This includes fixtures (i.e. movables affixed inseparably to immovables),[86] commingled, processed or mixed assets[87] or enterprises (or organised parts thereof). Limitations exist, such as the prohibition of the constitution of registered pledges on assets that may be encumbered by either mortgages or maritime mortgages (which are subject thus to a distinct regime).[88]

---

82 See §49/C(1) of the Hungarian Insolvency Act.

83 See §49/C(2) of the Hungarian Insolvency Act.

84 See Lithuanian Civil Code Article 4.202.

85 See the brief commentary published by the Klaipeda City First Notary's Office from 2013, available at <http://www.notarius.lt/?en=1390464172> or through the Oxford Secured Transactions Reform Project led by Prof. Gullifer at <http://securedtransactionslawreformproject.org/lithuania/> both accessed 23 May 2016.

86 See Article 9 of the Registered Pledge Act.

87 See Article 8 of the Registered Pledge Act.

88 See Article 7.1. of the Registered Pledge Act.

Question 3: Is it possible to create security rights over assets not yet owned by the debtor at the time of the creation of the security interest?

1. Hungary

86. According to the new 2013 Civil Code (as was the case following the first secured transactions law reform of 1996), it is possible to create security rights over after-acquired property.[89] This includes assets that are not yet owned by the debtor at the time of the creation of the security interest.

2. Lithuania

87. Lithuanian law also allows for constitution of a security interest over after-acquired property (i.e. assets not yet owned by the debtor at the time of the creation of the lien). Moreover, this is explicitly provided for by the Civil Code.[90]

3. Poland

88. Similarly to Hungary and Lithuania, Polish law also explicitly provides for the possibility to encumber after-acquired property in the Registered Pledge Act.[91]

Question 4: Is it possible to create security rights over assets that are not yet in existence at the time of the execution of the security agreement?

1. Hungary

89. According to the new 2013 Civil Code (as was the case following the first secured transactions law reform of 1996), it is possible to create security rights over assets that are not yet in existence at the time of the execution of the security agreement.[92]

---

89 This is proclaimed explicitly by the second sentence of §5:89(4): 'The collateral must be indicated by type and quantity or by using another appropriate method of identification. Such assets may also be identified that are not yet in existence or with which the debtor cannot dispose of [at the time of the identification].'

90 See Article 4.201(1) of the Lithuanian Civil Code.

91 See Article 7.3 of the Registered Pledge Act.

92 See §5:89(4) of the Hungarian Civil Code.

2. Lithuania

90. The Civil Code states in Article 4.201(1) that any existing or future movable or other property right can be used as collateral.

3. Poland

91. The Registered Pledge Act has no explicit provision as to whether security interests can be constituted over assets not yet in existence at the time of the execution of the security agreement. However, it has rules making that possible indirectly in certain circumstances. These rules, in particular, are: (1) automatic extension of security interests to products and the proceeds of collateral;[93] (2) the possibility of pledging after-acquired property that exists at the time of execution of the pledge agreement;[94] and (3) the possibility of encumbering an enterprise in its totality (or a particular part of it).[95]

Question 5: Is it possible to have a 'global security agreement', i.e. covering all assets of the debtor?

1. The hectic saga of the Hungarian 'property encumbering charge'

92. A version of floating charge, allowing for an encumbrance of all present and future assets of a debtor, was first introduced in *Hungary* with the first secured transactions law reforms in 1996 under the designation 'property encumbering charge' (*vagyont terhelő zálogjog*).

93. The drafters relied on the EBRD Secured Transactions Model Law[96] rather than on any one single national model. The provision in the Model Law was, however, similar to the English floating charge and not the US floating lien. As a consequence, the exact priority point of the property encumbering charge was initially controversial as it was not clear whether the time of registration in the charge registry (maintained by public notaries) or rather the time of 'crystallisation' was the crucial time.

---

93 See Article 10.1 of the Registered Pledge Act.

94 See Article 7.3 of the Registered Pledge Act.

95 See Article 7.2(3) of the Registered Pledge Act.

96 EBRD, *Model Law on Secured Transactions* (1994), available at <http://www.ebrd.com/downloads/research/guides/secured.pdf> accessed 23 May 2016.

94. This was remedied first by a Supreme Court decision[97] and finally by an explicit provision in the 2000 amendments to the secured transactions provisions of the Civil Code.[98] According to this provision the secured creditor was entitled 'to exercise its enforcement right on the priority position he acquired on the date of the registration of the property encumbering charge.'[99]

95. Notwithstanding such initial problems, the property encumbering charge has become quite a popular security device in *Hungary* within a relatively short period of time. Exactly because of this, it came as a complete surprise when the drafters of the brand new Civil Code discarded the concept.[100] More precisely, the property encumbering charge – as a distinct nominated security device – was 'only' given up. According to the advice of the drafters of the Code, however, the same results can be achieved through a series of secured transactions, each encumbering a different class of assets and thus at the price of a string of separate registrations.[101] This is made possible, in addition, by the rule that allows for indicating the collateral by mere description[102] (except immovables and catalogued movables and rights)[103] and the rule permitting giving the debtor unfettered dominion over the collateral.[104] Eventually nothing seems to prevent the inclusion of such a string of encumbrances in the same security agreement. Admittedly, given that this is a brand new development, inevitably some dilemmas exist.

---

97 See BH 120/2006.

98 See §266(3) of the pre-2013 (old) Civil Code valid from 1 September 2001.

99 See §266(3) of the pre-2013 (old) Hungarian Civil Code. See also the article of I. Mándoki, 'A vagyont terhelő zálogjog ranghelye' [The Priority Position of the Property Encumbering Charge] in (July–August 2006) Nos. 7-8 *Bulletin of Public Notaries* 14–17 [in Hungarian]. I. Mándoki was the public notary acting in the case that was published eventually as case No. BH 120/2006.

100 See L. Vékás (ed.), *Complex Commentary*, 417.

101 See §5:101(1) of the Hungarian Civil Code which proclaims that any asset (type) may be used as collateral. See *also* L. Vékás (ed.), *Complex Commentary,* 417.

102 See §5:93(4) of the Hungarian Civil Code that foresees that entries into the charge register – contrary to the register of mortgages on immovables – may be made either by individualising the asset used as collateral or by describing it. See also §5:102 on collateral indicated by description. According to this section, if the collateral is indicated by description ('*körülírás*'), the collateral will be composed of those assets over which the debtor will have a right of disposal at any point in time. It is presumed that the right of disposal for the purposes of this paragraph will survive if the collateral was not disposed of through regular commercial channels or if it was not disposed of in good faith and without consideration.

103 See §5:93(3) of the Hungarian Civil Code according to which in case of mortgages on immovables and charges on catalogued chattel, the collateral must be individualised ('*egyedileg meghatározott zálogtárgy*').

104 See L. Vékás (ed.), *Complex Commentary*, 417. See also §5:108(1) of the Hungarian Civil Code, which contains the basic rule according to which the debtor has the right to possess the collateral, to use and exploit it in the ordinary course of business and to keep it in good condition. See §5:108(2) off the Code applicable to security agreements where the collateral is identified by description. In this case, 'the debtor is entitled to process, transform, assemble, commingle or dispose of the collateral in the ordinary course of business.'

96. In any event, one may legitimately question whether a proper comparison has been made, on the one hand, between the transaction costs accompanying the original, initially problematic but eventually satisfactorily functioning, system relying on a nominated single security device and, on the other hand, of the transaction costs that the new multiple-securities-based regime has introduced. As far as the latter is concerned, not only the costs associated with the creation of multiple security devices should be taken into consideration, but also the costs of the risk of possible conflict among these separate security devices.

2. Lithuania: the jurisdiction of two versions of floating security

97. Two versions of global security are foreseen by the Lithuanian Civil Code. The first is narrower and allows for pledging of shifting and complex asset classes including raw materials, equipment, receivables.[105] The other, the version that is all-encompassing, makes creation of a security interest over the whole company possible.[106] The fact that global security is possible is also apparent from the regulation on the running of the Mortgage Registry that requires the filing of a digital copy of the company's inventory for registration.[107]

3. The Polish 'registered pledge' over 'economic units'

98. A full and a limited version of global security has been introduced by the Registered Pledge Act, mentioned many times already. As the Act provides, a security right can be established on 'a set of movable things or rights that constitutes *an economic unit*, even if the constituent elements change.'[108] The assets that cannot be encumbered with a registered pledge (i.e. immovable property and other rights that may be subject to a mortgage or vessels that may be subject to a maritime mortgage) must, however, be excluded from the enterprise pledge and should be encumbered separately under the security interests applicable to them (i.e. mortgage or maritime mortgage).

---

105 See Article 4.202 of the Lithuanian Civil Code.

106 See Article 4.177 of the Lithuanian Civil Code.

107 See section 27 of the Resolution No. 571 amending Regulation 1246 on the Approval of the Regulations of the Mortgage Register of the Republic of Lithuania.

108 See Article 7.2(3) of the Registered Pledge Act.

Question 6: In general terms, what are the formalities in your legal system for the creation of a security interest over assets?

1. Hungary

1.1. The typology of formalities

99. The system imposes two groups of formalities for the creation of securities over assets: (1) requirements that apply to all security agreements (general requirements); and (2) collateral-specific ones (i.e. rules that differ depending on the asset class used as collateral). Here we will focus on the first category only and in considering the next question, on the asset-specific rules.

1.2. Caveats on the idiosyncratic terminology of the 2013 Civil Code

100. A preliminary qualification, however, should be added. Namely, the Code's language and structure may be misleading since it imposes specific preconditions for the validity of security interests but does not mention them as such. Three points need to be stressed here.

101. First, the Comments to the Civil Code speak of the written form of security agreements as the only formal requirement imposed by the system.[109] While under the pre-2013 Civil Code the validity of security agreements on movables, rights and claims was subject to a special form – the public document (*közokirat*) form[110] – this additional formal requirement was not included in the new 2013 Code and now a simple written form of security agreement suffices. The main reason for this simplification was that the public document requirement imposed significant transaction costs on the parties to security agreements, which deterred use of the new secured transactions system.[111] Today, the only exception (or rather alternative written form) recognised it he possibility of the issuance of a certificated form of investment property (i.e. shares, bonds),

---

[109] See L. Vékás (ed.), *Complex Commentary*, 428.

[110] This requirement was imposed by §262(2) of the old (1959) Civil Code. The public document requirement – something similar to a deed made by a public notary – was, interestingly and quite illogically, imposed only on security interests on movables, rights and claims but not on mortgages of immovables or security interests on special categories of movables for which specific registries have been in existence (ships, aircraft, some IP forms). See L. Vékás (ed.), *Complex Commentary*, 428.

[111] See L. Vékás (ed.), *Complex Commentary*, 428.

negotiable paper or documents of title[112] in lieu of a written security agreement. This option is available, however, only as a substitute of possessory pledge.[113]

102. Second, the Code imposes additional duties on the debtor, which are treated by the Code as 'mere' obligations of the debtor connected to the execution of security agreements. Such treatment and language may, however, be misleading because in some foreign systems these are looked upon as a distinct precondition for the creation of a security interest valid 'against the world.' For example, English or the secured transactions law of the United States (US) names this phase in the life of a security interest as 'perfection.'[114] In these laws, put simply, if a security interest is perfected for example by registration, then it is valid not only against the counter-party to a secured transaction but against all the other participants of the market. Hungarian law has no such distinct designation but simply speaks of the debtor's related obligations. For example, in case of using receivables as collateral, it speaks of 'the duty of the debtor' to, either *notify* the obligor (account debtor) on the security agreement in writing, or to issue a declaration on that to the secured creditor[115] – in lieu of speaking of it as a precondition for the creation of security interests.[116]

103. The difference between the two notification methods is that while in the first case the obligor is informed about the pledging before default and in the latter case later at the option of the secured creditor but typically on default. Note, however, that in the case of claims (receivables), in addition to the duty (obligation) to notify the account debtor, registration in the register of security interests on movables, rights and claims is also required.[117] Similarly, in the case of a possessory security (pledge), a duty (obligation) is imposed on the debtor *to transfer possession* or control (*hatalmat*) over the collateral.[118]

---

112 Note that for Hungarian law the category of 'securities' is broader than, for example, in US law because it encompasses negotiable instruments and documents of title as well; though the new Civil Code does not list the recognised securities by name. See §Book VI on Obligations, Part Five on securities. The drafters of the provision in question, for example, departed from the case of pawn receipts, which are routinely used by Hungarian pawn-shops and are in particular favoured because the name and other personal data of the debtors are not recorded (what would be the case if contracts would be made instead of the issuance of pawn receipts). See L. Vékás (ed.), *Complex Commentary,* 428–429.

113 See §5:89(6) of the Hungarian Civil Code. Such security (negotiable instrument) should entitle its holder to request the transfer of the collateral within the time specified therein and up to the sum specified in the security (negotiable instrument).

114 *Black's Law Dictionary* (DeLuxe 7th ed., West, 1999) defines perfection as follows: 'Validation of a security interest as against other creditors, usually by filing a statement with some public office or by taking possession of the collateral.'

115 See §5:89(c) of the Hungarian Civil Code.

116 To readers from common law systems this may be puzzling. However, it should be borne in mind that, as a civil law country, Hungary has never recognised 'equity' as a distinct legal category and thus the tandem of equitable and legal security interests (liens) is foreign. This is why the system rather speaks of creation versus the additional obligations of the parties.

117 See L. Vékás (ed.), *Complex Commentary,* 430.

118 See §5:89(2)(a) of the Hungarian Civil Code.

104. Third, even though the drafters of the reformed Hungarian secured transactions law have relied on Anglo-Saxon laws – especially the 2013 version of the Civil Code – and on UCC Article 9, the dualistic concepts of attachment and perfection have not been adopted, nor does the Code use such terminology. In fact, the Hungarian system has more than two phases in the life of a security right. What may be puzzling is that, in effect, attachment and perfection can be identified (and we will use such terminology), though some additional requirements also need to be satisfied in order to have a fully enforceable security right against third parties (i.e. erga omnes effect).

1.3. The three formal phases of the creation of security interests

105. As far as the generally applicable (i.e. applicable to all security agreements) preconditions are concerned, the new 2013 Civil Code (expressed somewhat non-transparently) differentiates three phases in the process of coming into being of security interests: namely, attachment, constitution (*alapítás*) and emergence (*létrejötte*) of security interests. That 'attachment' phase can be extrapolated from a distinct provision which states that the security agreement will be valid between the debtor and secured creditor even if the security interest was not properly constituted (i.e. perfected).[119] However, no distinct designation was attributed to such 'attached' security interests.

106. The situation is clearer with respect to 'constitution', which presumes either the transfer of possesion to the secured creditor by the debtor or registration in one of the existing registers, requirements that could be conveniently referred to as perfection.[120] A security interest, on the other hand, 'emerges' once it has been constituted and in addition the debtor can dispose of the collateral,[121] what one may conveniently name as a thick concept of perfection.

107. What further adds to the puzzle and makes comparison with other systems uneasy is that a distinct provision imposes the requirement that the collateral and the claim secured must be identified.[122] Even though the system is flexible and allows for identification of the collateral by any appropriate method and may include after-acquired property,[123] the language of the Code clearly speaks of this as a precondition for '*the coming into being of the security agreement*.'[124] This

119 See §5:91 of the Hungarian Civil Code.
120 See §5:88 of the Hungarian Civil Code.
121 See §5:87(b) of the Hungarian Civil Code.
122 See §5:89(3) of the Hungarian Civil Code.
123 See §5:89(4) of the Hungarian Civil Code.
124 See §5:89(3) of the Hungarian Civil Code.

remains a precondition of the validity of the security agreement notwithstanding that the secured claim may as well be determined by any appropriate method[125] (not only the identification of the collateral).

1.4. Formal requirements in consumer contracts

108. In case of consumer contracts[126] two further requirements are imposed for the sake of consumer protection: the exact value (sum) of the secured debt must also be specified[127] and the collateral must be individualised (i.e. collateral in this case cannot be determined only by description and after-acquired property cannot be pledged).[128]

1.5. Perfection by constructive possession: warehousing

109. To this list one has to add various forms of perfection by way of constructive possession,[129] i.e. when a third person holds possession of the collateral instead of the secured creditor. In such a case, the third party-possessor must be informed on the pledging of the asset held by him.[130]

110. This ought to be mentioned because of the popularity the local version of field warehousing – called 'artificial warehousing (*művi raktározás*)' – has gained during the last two decades.[131] In this case, it is not the collateral that is

---

125 See §5:89(5) of the Hungarian Civil Code.

126 The Code defines consumer contracts as forms of PMSIs – specific individual asset acquired by the debtor through the loan or trade-credit – and assets which are not used by the debtor for his professional or business activity. See §5:90 of the Hungarian Civil Code.

127 See §5:90(b) of the Hungarian Civil Code.

128 See 5:90(a) of the Hungarian Civil Code and L. Vékás (ed.), *Complex Commentary* Comments at 429.

129 See §5:94(1) of the Hungarian Civil Code.

130 See §5:94(2) of the Hungarian Civil Code.

131 Field warehousing is regulated by Act XLVIII of 1996 on Public Warehousing *(1996. évi XLVIII. törvény a közraktározásról)* (hereinafter: Warehousing Act 1996), as (meaningfully) amended in 2013 by Act LXVI of 2013 *(2013. évi LXVI. törvény a közraktározásról szóló 1996. évi XLVIII. törvény módosításáról)* (hereinafter: Warehousing Act 2013). Actually field (artificial) warehousing is now more often resorted to than public warehousing in Hungary As per the separate statute regulating both types of warehousing, both can issue negotiable warehouse receipts, pledging of the goods in the warehouse is subject essentially to the same rules: the warehouse receipts are pledged with the financing bank. Contrary to the typical American field warehousing arrangement, the debtor – e.g. his employee or agent – cannot be appointed as warehouseman in Hungary. Rather, only licensed and properly equipped warehousing companies and their staff may engage in field warehousing. In this way, the issue of whether dominion (possession) over the collateral was left with the debtor could not arise. See T. Tajti (2014) 55(3) *Acta Juridica Hungarica* 185–235.

transported to a public warehouse but the warehouse comes to the place where the collateral is located (e.g. farm, factory). The Code itself also recognises as a valid transfer of possession for the purposes of the creation of security interests a joint holding of the collateral by the secured creditor and the debtor (e.g. lockbox arrangements).[132] The precondition of validity in such cases is that the debtor cannot have unfettered dominion over the pledged asset in any circumstances.[133]

2. Lithuania

111. Lithuanian law conditions the validity of security agreements on two requirements: (1) written form and (2) notary certification and registration (the registration requirement does not apply to possessory securities). Requirement of a written form means that the validity of security agreements is conditional on some form of writing evidencing either the existence of the security agreement – made separately or as part of the credit agreement – or a unilateral declaration proving the intention to pledge certain assets.

112. For non-possessory securities, to which also the second requirement (of notary certification and registration) applies, before the 2011 amendments to the Civil Code came into force on the 1 July 2012, the written form requirement could have been satisfied only by using a special form approved by the Minister of Finance; today there is no such requirement.

113. Yet what makes Lithuanian law peculiar is that a written form is required even in case of possessory securities. Such written contracts on possessory pledges are not subject, however, to registration. Likewise, no registration is required when receivables (claims) are used as collateral for financing purposes under a factoring agreement.[134]

3. Poland

114. Two prerequisites apply: written form security agreements (except possessory pledges) and registration.[135] Separate rules apply to security assignments, where written agreement is required only if the assigned claim is evidenced in writing

---

132 For example, if the parties keep the collateral in a locked box which could not be opened either by the debtor or the secured creditor only. See L. Vékás (ed.), *Complex Commentary*, 431.

133 See §5:94(3) of the Hungarian Civil Code.

134 See chapter XLV of Book VI of the Civil Code on factoring. Registration is also not required when receivables (claims) are being sold.

135 For registered pledges see Article 2.1. of the Registered Pledge Act.

(however for the security to be effective in insolvency, a dated written form certified by a notary is required) and no registration requirement exists (security assignments are 'secret liens' perfected by a notice to the debtor of the assigned claims).

115. While the encumbering of immovables requires a special notarial written form, in case of registered pledges a simple written form agreement is required.[136] The agreement should, at least: (1) specify the date of the agreement; (2) identify the debtor and creditor (i.e. business name and registered office or address); (3) specify the collateral (based on its features); as well as (4) specify the claim secured by the pledge and the maximum amount secured.[137]

116. Polish law is idiosyncratic in two matters in respect of the securing of obligations from debt securities issued in a series (i.e. fixed-income securities such as bonds). First, the security agreement need not be concluded between the debtor and the secured creditor(s) but by the debtor (pledgor) and the pledge administrator.[138] Although the content of such agreements is not regulated by the Act, this may amount to a control agreement. Second, the securities are to be established for the benefit of all creditors,[139] who will be represented by a pledge administrator the appointment of whom is mandated by the issuer of the securities.[140] The administrator must not be one of the creditors in such cases.

Question 7: Do the rules for the creation of security rights vary depending on the nature of the asset in question?

1. Hungary

1.1. General comments on the three perfection methods of Hungarian law

117. If one departs from the specific titles of the paragraphs of the Code,[141] one may easily be misled into thinking that the Code does not impose any further

136 See Article 3.1. of the Registered Pledge Act, which stresses that 'provisions on special written form set forth elsewhere [i.e. other legal acts] do not apply to agreements to establish a registered pledge on claims and rights.' Registration is not required in case of financial pledges that are created by a written agreement and perfected by a notice.

137 See Article 3.2. of the Registered Pledge Act.

138 See Article 2.4. of the Registered Pledge Act.

139 See Article 4.3. of the Registered Pledge Act.

140 See Article 4.4. of the Registered Pledge Act.

141 For example, the above cited §5:87 of the Hungarian Civil Code is named 'Emergence of the Security Interest' ['*A zálogjog létrejötte*'] and that of §5:88 'Constitution of the Security Interest' ['*A zálogjog alapítása*']. Truth be told, all the referred to provisions are located in the relatively short Chapter XXI entitled also 'the Emergence of the Security Interest' ['*A zálogjog létrejötte*'].

formal requirements on the creation of security interests other than those listed under Question 6. In fact, however, through scattered provisions, the creation of security rights is subject to additional preconditions depending on the nature of the assets used as collateral and – in the case of the the distinct security device we will conveniently name as 'security-bailment' (*óvadék*) – tradition.

118. If these additional conditions are also taken into account, we can see that actually the Code sets out three (perfection) methods for the creation of security interests over assets: the transfer of possession (including constructive possession), registration in one of the public registers, and control – the last essentially disguised as the separate security device of 'security bailment.'[142]

119. Notification of an obligor (account debtor) is also a requirement – cast in the form of the debtor' obligation[143] – for security interests over rights and claims as well as registration in the register of security interests. In other words, perfection of security interests on rights and claims is by registration as well[144] as opposed to the old Civil Code's perfection method that took the form of notification only.

120. It should be emphasised that a written security agreement is a general condition applicable to all secured transactions, which can be substituted only by certificated securities (documents of title and negotiable paper satisfying the definition of 'security' under Hungarian law).[145] We will briefly summarise each perfection method.

1.2. Perfection by transfer of possession

121. The basic rule is that a possessory pledge can be created only on movable (tangible) assets[146] (or equivalents such as certificated securities) either by the possessor (*birtokos* or *főbirtokos*) or his agent (called the sub-possessor [*albirtokos*]). Two forms of joint constructive possession are recognised by the system as substitutes for the transfer of possession from debtor to secured creditor: (1) joint-possession by the debtor and secured creditor, and (2) possession by a third party as a pledge-holder for their account.[147]

---

142 See §5:95 of the Hungarian Civil Code.

143 See §5:89(2)(c) of the Hungarian Civil Code.

144 See L. Vékás (ed.), *Complex Commentary*, 424 which proclaims: '[The new Civil Code] makes a step ahead and extends [registration] to intangible assets, as well as to rights and claims. As a result, constitution of security rights by registration becomes a possibility for all kinds of assets.'

145 See §5:89(6) of the Hungarian Civil Code.

146 See §5:101(2) of the Hungarian Civil Code.

147 See §5:94(1) of the Hungarian Civil Code. The language of the Code is quite short and does not regulate the details of the contract between the third party and the parties to the security agreement. The Comments leave this to the parties and point to the provisions on deposit contracts. See L. Vékás (ed.) *Complex Commentary*, 432.

1.3. *Security bailments and perfection by control*

1.3.1. *The distinguishing features of the security bailment*

122. While the rules on perfection by transfer of possession are more or less common, this may not be so with respect to a specific type of secured transaction – or a specific method of pledging – called the 'security-bailment' (*óvadék*). This device has 'historically developed in parallel with [conventional] security interests and grew into a kin institution',[148] a process that ended with its integration into security law. The integration did not, however, end with the complete disapparance of this device: specific rules applicable to it alone are part of the 2013 Civil Code.

123. Two distinguishing features make the security-bailment special: first, only some specific types of assets may be used as collateral; and second, the secured creditor has a direct right of enforcement on the asset bailed. As far as the first aspect is concerned, only cash, investment property (securities), some bank accounts and similar forms of personal property may qualify.[149]

1.3.2. *Extra-judicial enforcement of security bailments*

124. The enforcement rules ensure direct enforcement and provide the secured creditor with strict foreclosure-like rights, i.e. he may upon default unilaterally declare to the debtor that he is acquiring title (ownership) on the bailed collateral, or if he has already acquired title, that he has no obligation to return to the debtor assets of the same quantity and type that had been transferred to him initially.[150] These rules are, however, less onerous compared to the generally applicable strict foreclosure rules. Namely, given that the value of the collateral subject to a security-bailment is always easily determinable, there is no need for the extra step of secured party offer and acceptance by the debtor.[151]

1.3.3. *Perfection of the security bailment*

125. Hungarian law allows for perfection of security-bailments by transfer of possession and control (though the Code does not use this term but rather describes what actions need to be taken).[152] The perfection rules follow the

[148] See L. Vékás (ed.), *Complex Commentary* Comments, 432.

[149] See §5:95 of the Hungarian Civil Code.

[150] See §5:138(1) of the Hungarian Civil Code.

[151] See L. Vékás (ed.), *Complex Commentary,* 474. For the offer and acceptance process applicable to other types of secured transactions see §5:137 of the Hungarian Civil Code.

[152] See §5:95(2)(a) of the Hungarian Civil Code.

nature of assets and hence in the case of cash and certificated securities – tangible assets that can be physically possessed – the perfection method is by transfer of possession, i.e. the rules on possessory pledges apply. As opposed to that, with bank accounts the method is by control.

126. Strangely, the Code talks of transfer of possession also in case of dematerialised securities, or forges an artificial concept of possession for this specific case.[153] Given the direct reliance on comparative law by the drafters of the 2013 Code, this formula is barely comprehensible.

127. The Comments speak of the perfection of security-bailment by way of registration only as a curiosity 'having little if any practical importance.'[154] Yet this possibility is not excluded either. As the Comments themselves admit, this may be the case whenever the collateral is identified through a wide-reaching description, such as all movables or receivables of a company.[155] Notwithstanding the cautionary language, the Code does have an explicit priority rule according to which, if the same asset is encumbered by both a security-bailment and a registered security right, the former enjoys priority.[156]

128. Perfection by control presumes a tripartite (the debtor-account-holder, the secured creditor and the service-provider with whom the account is maintained) written agreement according to which the service-provider proclaims that, while it will follow the instructions of the debtor only with the consent of the secured creditor, it will obey the instructions of the secured creditor without

---

153 See §5:95(1)(b) of the Hungarian Civil Code. This anomaly was also noted by G. Welmann, *HVG Commentary,* 125. The explanation provided by L. Vékás, editor-in-chief of the *Complex Commentary* – a Commentary that was written by the drafters of the Code – reads as follows (at 434): 'Creation of a security-bailment in case of dematerialized investment property occurs by way of transfer of possession so that a transfer is effected between the investment accounts of the parties (i.e., by charging the debtor's investment account and crediting the secured party's investment account). This can be looked upon as a form of possessory pledge because – based on the Civil Code and similarly to the earlier rules – the dematerialized security is also a security (investment property) to which the rules on "things" must be appropriately applied [§5:14(2)] and as a result of the here described account transactions the secured creditor acquires real control over the securities (investment property) [§5:3(1)].' In other words, the drafters – instead of introducing the concept of 'control' – opted for artificially stretching the concept of possessory pledge to extend also to physically clearly intangible goods: uncertificated securities. This was a strange choice especially as both the EU Directive on Financial Collateral Arrangements of 2002 and the Draft Common Frame of Reference (see Article IX.-3:204: Control over financial assets) have introduced the concept of 'control.' While the EU Directive is law also in Hungary as a Member States of the EU, the DCFR was used as a source of inspirations as stated by the drafters (see L. Vékás (ed.), *Complex Commentary*, Introduction, point 4, p. 20).

154 See L. Vékás (ed.), *Complex Commentary,* 433.

155 *Ibid.* at 433.

156 See §5:123 of the Hungarian Civil Code.

the approval of the debtor.[157] Where the secured creditor is the service provider itself (bank or broker), a bipartite contract guaranteeing the same right to the service provider would qualify.[158]

129. If one adds up all these elements, one can see that what is a semi-distinct nominated security device for Hungarian law, is actually contentwise equal to the rules on perfection by control in systems such as UCC Article 9.

1.4. Perfection of security interests by registration (filing)

1.4.1. The post-1990 history of registration

130. Prior to the first 1996 secured transactions reforms – save for some registers dealing with specific high value assets and IP rights (see below) – no register was in existence for the registration of security interests on movables, claims or rights in *Hungary*. This changed with the common-law-inspired reforms of 1996 and the ensuing implementing legislation; due to the latter a brand new electronic registry was introduced specifically for recording security interests on movables (but not for claims/receivables). The National Chamber of Public Notaries (*Országos Közjegyzői Kamara*) was entrusted with the running of the system.[159]

131. At that time, the registration system was structured to follow the system for registration of mortgages on immovables,[160] including the constitutive and authentic nature of entries.

132. This has radically changed with the 2013 Civil Code. On the one hand, the provision that entrusted the Chamber with the running of the system was deleted and no specific body was nominated in lieu. The intention was to give the government freedom to decide and to change the service-provider if necessary in the future.[161] Nonetheless, in 2014 (the year of the entry into force of the Civil Code), the right to operate the system remained with public notaries and at the moment no change is expected.[162]

---

157 See §5:95(2)(a) of the Hungarian Civil Code.

158 See §5:95(2)(b) of the Hungarian Civil Code.

159 The webpage of the Chamber is <http://www.mokk.hu> accessed 23 May 2016. See also §262(2) of the former Civil Code for the mandate given to the National Chamber.

160 See L. Vékás (ed.), *Complex Commentary*, 457.

161 *Ibid.* at 457.

162 See §2 of Act CCXXI of 2013 on the Register of Security Interests (entered into force 16 March 2014). See also Ordinance No. 18/2014 (III.13) of the Ministry of Justice and Administration on the Detailed Rules for the Operation of the Register of Security Interests.

1.4.2. Switch to notice filing by the 2013 Civil Code

133. A more meaningful change occurred, however, in respect of the perfection rules. The system has switched to notice-filing, a system originating in the American UCC Article 9. This means that now the entries in the register serve 'merely' to notify third parties on the existence of security interests and to ensure priorities.[163] In practical terms, while earlier the security agreement itself had to be made before a public notary whose duty it was also to check the data and to instruct the parties of their rights, now only a notice needs to be filed with the registry containing the basic data necessary for the identification of the transaction, the parties and the collateral.[164] The fact that an entry has been made is not now authentic proof of the existence of the security interest.[165] Besides these, the register also displays the date and the ranking of the entry.[166] Under the new system, the public notaries are not expected to check the contents of the entries.[167] To avoid misunderstandings, it should be noted that no new term was introduced for 'filing' instead of 'registration' to express the change.

1.4.3. Electronic registration by the 2013 Civil Code

134. At the same time, to ensure ease of access, the Act proclaimed that 'the register of security interests is public and its contents are freely accessible on the Internet without any identification.'[168] In brief, the system became electronic, linked on the Internet, and thus became quicker as well. While searching the database is free of charge,[169] a modest fixed fee is charged for entries.[170] Both

---

163 See L. Vékás (ed.), *Complex Commentary*, 458.

164 These include (1) the name and some other data determined by special statute of the debtor; (2) the name and some other data determined by special statute of the secured creditor; (3) name of the agent of a legal person or other association and data determined by special statute; as well as (4) the determination of the collateral either by specification or by description. See §5:115(1) of the Hungarian Civil Code. The entry may (but must not) specify also the amount of the debt the collateral secures. See §5:115(2).

165 As the L. Vékás (ed.), *Complex Commentary*, 459, says: 'the function of the register is not to authentically prove the existence of the security interest but rather to inform the public about the constitution of the security interest, ensure its validity against third persons (§5:91) and its priority position (§5:118) to enhance predictability (*'hozzájáruljon a forgalom biztonságához'*) on the market.'

166 See §5:116 of the Hungarian Civil Code.

167 See §5:113(1) of the Hungarian Civil Code.

168 See §5:112(2) of the Hungarian Civil Code.

169 See §5:112(2) of the Hungarian Civil Code.

170 As per the amended Ordinance of the Ministry of Justice on the Tariffs of Public Notaries No. 14/1991 (XI. 26) the fees payable (work and costs included) are: (1) HUF 6,000 for each entry (§30F(1)), and (2) in case of registration through a permanent representative HUF 6,000

the secured creditor and the debtor are entitled to file (creation, modification or deletion), however, only if first registered as users.[171] Prior registration as users ensures electronic identification of the parties.[172]

135. The entry process has become electronic and as such it is fast. First, entries can be made solely by way of electronic forms (the outlook and elements of which are fixed by law) on the webpage of the Chamber of Public Notaries.[173] Second, the parties are automatically informed electronically of any entry effected by the other party, although the Code does not specify the exact means of electronic information.[174] Third, although both the secured party and the debtor can make entries both of the creation and deletion of an entry, however, no entry on the creation of a security interest can be valid with the electronic signature of the debtor.[175] and vice versa – for deletion, the consent of the secured creditor is required.[176]

136. The secured creditor's consent (declaration) to delete the security interest is deemed to be given if the secured creditor has failed to make a declaration to the contrary within 30 days.[177] To ensure performance, the Code adds to this an obligation that the secured creditor should not withhold his consent if the secured transaction has ceased to exist, nor file an objection against deletion without a legal basis.[178] The secured creditor who breaches these rules is liable for all damage caused.[179]

137. Finally, the 2013 Civil Code expanded the reach of the register of security interests in two directions. First, contrary to the earlier position, the filing requirement has been extended from security interests on movables to cover also security interests on receivables (claims) and rights that are not subject to registration in a specific register.[180] This means that in the case of receivables, besides notification of the obligor (account debtor), filing in the security interest register is also essential (a perfection requirement).

---

for each hour of commenced work but not exceeding 18,000 HUF (even if when working more than three hours) (§30F(2)). As per the exchange rate in December 2014 (1 euro = HUF 307,277), 6,000 Hungarian forints were slightly less than 20 euros.

171 See §5:113(3) of the Hungarian Civil Code.

172 See §5:113(5) of the Hungarian Civil Code.

173 See §5:113(1) of the Hungarian Civil Code.

174 See §5:113(2) of the Hungarian Civil Code.

175 See §5:114 of the Hungarian Civil Code. This, in other words means, that while the electronic signature (consent) of the secured creditor is not a must, if the secured creditor began the filing, the entry will not become valid until consented to by the debtor electronically.

176 See §5:117(3) of the Hungarian Civil Code.

177 See §5:117(3)(b) of the Hungarian Civil Code.

178 See §5:117(4) of the Hungarian Civil Code.

179 See §L. Vékás (ed.), *Complex Commentary*, 460.

180 See §5:93(1)(b) of the Hungarian Civil Code. See also L. Juhász, *The Hungarian Insolvency Handbook*, 750.

138. On the other hand, financial leasing,[181] factoring[182] and contracts with retained title[183] are also subject to registration with the register of security interests.

1.5. *Perfection by constitutive registration*

139. Hungarian law does not recognise the real versus personal property securities divide of the common law and hence regulates both in the same part of the Civil Code and continues – even after the meaningful infiltration of common law concepts through the secured transactions reforms – to look upon them as two sides of the same coin. For this reason some attention should be given to security rights on immovables, i.e. mortgage law. As special registers exist for some specific classes of personal property (movables) (e.g. ships, aircraft) and as they typically function in a similar way to the real property mortgage registries, the two will be discussed together.

1.5.1. *Registration of mortgages on immovables*

140. In the case of mortgage law, instead of reforms, there have only been improvements as far as the new 2013 Civil Code is concerned. The most significant changes relate to the technical rules on the operation of the immovables registries given that the primary problems did not concern mortgage law itself (i.e. the applicable provisions of the Civil Code) but were rather of a technical and technological nature (e.g. delay in recording entries in the various files kept by the register and the need for modernisation). These, however, will not be discussed here.

141. As already mentioned, until the arrival of the new 2013 Civil Code, the legal regime for the registration of security interests on movables was intentionally structured to follow, so far as possible, the one applicable to mortgages of immovables. The two most important basic rules were that the entries in the register of mortgages of immovables had constitutive force and the entries were presumed to be authentic proof of the entries (*közhitelesség*). In the new 2013 Civil Code, these remain key features of the law in the context of immovables (as well as security interests on specific personal property registries) but not in the

---

181 See §6:409 of the Hungarian Civil Code.

182 See §6:405 of the Hungarian Civil Code. With this innovation the Hungarian system has come closer to the American UCC Article 9 that likewise extends to both sale of receivables (factoring) and use of receivables 'only' as a security. The crucial difference is that the Hungarian system linked factoring to the secured transactions system only through filing in the common security interest register. All the other possible rules are located outside secured transactions law.

183 See §6:216 of the Hungarian Civil Code.

case of the register of security rights on movables, rights and claims. The volte face occurred due to the realisation that the features of these asset categories require distinct legal treatment.[184]

142. Another key difference is that while the immovables register operates as an asset-based database (*reálfólium*), the register for security interests on movables, rights and claims uses a debtor-based listing (*perszonálfólium*). As a consequence mortgages could be registered, on the one hand, only on individualised and existing immovables and only on immovables that were already in the ownership of the debtor (and therefore had been entered in the books) at that point in time.[185] In the case of the immovables register, entries can be made either based on the security agreement itself or based on the permission of the debtor.[186] The system imposes a specific obligation on the debtor to provide the secured party with permission and this obligation gives the secured party some additional leverage.[187]

1.5.2. Perfection of security interests on specific registered (Lajstromozott) *movables*

143. It is not only in *Hungary* that certain high-value classes of personal property (movables) and the encumbrances that can be created on them are registered in distinct registers. In *Hungary*, the most important ones are the following: (1) ships; (2) aircraft; (3) patents; (4) trademarks; (5) specimens/models; and (6) shares in limited liability companies.[188] The perfection and other rules for these assets are all contained in lex specialis, which tend to be replicas of the immovables registry system.

2. Lithuania

144. There are some variations in Lithuania depending on the nature of the collateral although the basic division is along the lines of immovables versus movables-cum-rights and possessory versus non-possessory securities. Based however, on the language of the Code – which could be taken as an idiosyncratic feature of Lithuanian law – one may gain the impression that the main division is between so-called legal and contractual mortgages.[189] As this report focuses

184 See L. Vékás (ed.), *Complex Commentary*, 457.
185 See §5:93(3) of the Hungarian Civil Code.
186 See §5:93(3) of the Hungarian Civil Code.
187 See §5:89(2)(b) of the Hungarian Civil Code.
188 See L. Vékás (ed.), *Complex Commentary*, 430.
189 See Article 4.175 of the Lithuanian Civil Code.

on consensual (contractual) security rights, we will abstain from detailed analysis of the treatment of legal (statutory) mortgages. The variations depending on the nature of the asset used as collateral would be set out in the following pargraphs.

145. In the case of mortgages of immovables, registration has constitutive force and thus mortgages on immovables can come into existence only by registration in the appropriate public register.[190]

146. The situation is a bit more complex in the case of movables and rights. Formally the system does *not* recognise the dualism of attachment and perfection of security rights, i.e. there are no such distinct designations. Content-wise, however, the Code's provisions make such a differentiation in the case of non-possessory securities as it is provided that the security right is valid against third parties and bankruptcy administrator only after registration with the Register of Mortgages.[191] In the case of possessory securities, the situation is simpler, as perfection is linked to the transfer of possession plus conclusion of a written pledge agreement.[192] As already noted, the latter makes Lithuanian law distinctive.

147. The law provides specific rules when negotiable instruments are used in practice. Thus, for pledging with pawnshops, the Code requires the issue of a pawn-ticket.[193] In the case of documents of title granting rights to the holder, the transfer of possession may be substituted by transfer of the instrument (e.g. warehouse receipts).

148. The rules on pledging of receivables are somewhat obscure. Namely, the Civil Code regulates the use of claims (receivables) as collateral as part of the law on factoring[194] though without entering into details. The factoring rules, however, do not provide for registration of security rights as a precondition of creation but rather link that to notification of the obligor (account debtor).[195] On the other hand, the Civil Code rules on 'pledges' recognise the pledging of 'real rights'[196] – which includes claims (receivables)[197] – just as one could extend the company charge onto receivables;[198] both are subject to registration under this part of the Code.

---

190 See Article 4.187 of the Lithuanian Civil Code.
191 See Article 4.213 of the Lithuanian Civil Code.
192 See Article 4.213 of the Lithuanian Civil Code.
193 See Article 4.227(2) of the Lithuanian Civil Code.
194 See Article 6.903(2) of the Lithuanian Civil Code.
195 See Article 6.909(1) of the Lithuanian Civil Code.
196 See Article 4.204 of the Lithuanian Civil Code.
197 For pre-2011 court cases and scholarly analyses are of continued relevance. See on this L. Aleknaite, (2009) 34 *Review of Central and East European Laws* 257–258.
198 Reference is primarily made to Articles 4.202 and 4.177 of the Lithuanian Civil Code.

3. Poland

149. There are some variations depending on the nature of the asset used as collateral though the basic rules are typical to a reformed continental European civil law system.

150. First, constitution of a mortgage of immovables presumes execution of a notarised deed (in writing)[199] and registration in the land and mortgage register.[200]

151. Second, the rules on establishment of possessory pledges are somewhat peculiar under Polish law. Namely, transfer of possession over the collateral and the pledge agreement (which may be oral) makes the pledge valid only between the parties to the transactions.[201] In order to make it valid against third parties, besides transfer of possession, a written contract with a certified date is needed.[202] The requirement of a certified date was introduced only in 2009 (with effect from 20 February 2011) to prevent abuse of the possessory pledge due to its secret nature. As a result of this change the possessory pledge may 'compete' with other security interests in the distribution of enforcement proceeds[203] and therefore the moment of its creation becomes relevant.

152. Third, non-possessory security rights on movables, rights (on intangible property) and claims (receivables) as well as rights to financial instruments (with the exception of financial instruments covered by the relevant EU legislation) come into being if registered with a public register: the 'Register of Pledges.'[204] Enterprise (global) securities are treated as a variant of registered pledges and are subject to the same registration rules as movables, rights and claims.[205]

---

199 See Article 245 with reference to Article 158 of the Polish Civil Code, i.e. the rules on the transfer of ownership requiring a notarised deed apply mutatis mutandis, as do the establishment of limited proprietary rights. The requirement of a notarised form is limited only to the statement of the property ownership, however (Article 32.1 of the Polish Mortgage Act). Furthermore, in the event the mortgage is established as security for banking transactions (such as bank loans) for the benefit of a bank, the notarised form may be waived if a special form of 'banking documents' are used. These documents are to be duly certified and stamped by representatives of the bank (see Article 95.3 of the Banking Law, statute dated 29 August 1997, published in (2015) 128 *Journal of Laws*). The rationale of these simplifications is to make mortgages cheaper through decreasing the transaction costs.

200 See Article 67 of the Polish Mortgage Act.

201 See Article 307 of the Polish Civil Code.

202 See Article 307.3. of the Polish Civil Code.

203 See Articles 1025 and 1026 of the Polish Code of Civil Procedure.

204 See Article 7.2. of the Polish Registered Pledge Act.

205 See Article 7.2(3) of the Polish Registered Pledge Act.

153. Finally, two further registration-related principles of Polish law deserve mention. One of them is related to security interests on motor vehicles that are also subject to registration in the register of registered pledges; however, the pledge is additionally indicated on the registration document of the vehicle.[206] This is a peculiar yet useful principle of Polish law. Another such idiosyncracy of Polish law is that security interests on civilian aircraft and industrial property rights are also subject to registration with the register of registered pledges irrespective of the fact that distinct registers exist for those items. There is provision however for exchange of information between the two registers.[207] In both cases, registration with the register of 'registered pledges' enjoys primacy.

C. ENFORCEMENT OF SECURITY RIGHTS

Question 8: To what extent is it possible for the secured party to enforce the security without having to use formal court procedures?

1. Hungary

1.1. The changing attitude to out-of-court enforcement of security interests in Hungary

154. Similarly to other continental European civil law systems and contrary to common law systems,[208] Hungarian law also looks with suspicion on out-of-court enforcement. Hence, the basic rule is that security rights are to be enforced through formal court procedures. However, for a number of reasons, this approach began to change in the 1990s, notwithstanding the fact that on the face of it the basic rule remained essentially the same in the new 2013 Civil Code which provides among the fundamental principles that '[t]he enforcement of rights provided by the Act [i.e. the 2013 Civil Code] is through courts, *unless otherwise provided*'[209] (emphasis added).

---

206 See Article 12.1. of the Polish Registered Pledge Act.

207 See Article 41a. of the Polish Registered Pledge Act.

208 For common laws, encouragement of self-help is said to be one of the eight principles forming the 'philosophy of commercial law.' See R. Goode, 'The Codification of Commercial Law' (1988) 14 *Monash University Law Review* 136 at 148. This is definitively not so in civil law systems, which either prohibit or severely restrict out-of-court enforcement of rights based on private or commercial law. See also T. Tajti, 'Testing the Equivalence of the new Comprehensive Australian Personal Property Securities Act, its Segmented European Equivalents and the Draft Common Frame of Reference' (June 2012) 24 *Bond Law Review* 85 at 132.

209 See §1:7. of the new Hungarian Civil Code entitled: Guarantying Court Enforcement. The earlier formulation of the same principle in §7 of the 1959 Civil Code (Act IV of 1959 on

155. Perhaps the best expression of the shift are the provisions related to enforcement of security interests. That the drafters have attributed heightened importance to this novelty is visible from the fact that these essentially procedural rules have found their place not in the separate statute – which used to and continues to regulate court enforcement of security rights[210] – but in the Civil Code itself, a solution per se novel in *Hungary*.[211] Furthermore, the out-of-court enforcement system is now not only regulated in more detail compared to the earlier law[212] but the reach of the rules has expanded as well.

1.2. Enforcement of security interests by bailiffs

156. Judicial enforcement remains also available to secured creditors for enforcement of their security interests under the 2013 Civil Code. Yet in this domain meaningful changes have also occurred in the post-1990 period. Namely, judicial enforcement is no longer performed by bailiffs as employees of courts but by private, profit-making businesses and thus this means of enforcement might also be looked upon as a sort of quasi-private enforcement. In order to make enforcement more efficient, the system of so-called independent bailiffs was introduced more than a decade ago. These bailiffs were incentivised by allowing them to earn more if more was collected. While this increased their effeciency, however, the loose regulatory environment, led also to overreach and abuse of their powers. These problems have become visible in particular during the national crisis caused by the crash of the foreign currency-denominated housing mortgage market. The country was close to becoming bankrupt due, to a great extent, to the spill-over effects of the 2008 global financial crisis. Mass evictions ensued, often with media-reported overreaching of their powers on the part of the bailiffs, after the exchange rate of HUF suddenly drastically fell against all western foreing currencies causing thousands of consumer-debtors to default on their loans. To curb the abuses of bailiffs, control over the earlier Chamber of Hungarian Court Bailiffs (*Magyar Bírósági Végrehajtói Kamara*) was transferred to the Ministry of Justice on the 1 September 2015. The legal

---

the Civil Code) was: 'It is the duty of every state (governmental) body to protect the rights guaranteed by this act. Their enforcement – unless otherwise provided by law – is through courts.'

210 The court enforcement of security rights is regulated by Act LIII of 1994 on Court Enforcement.

211 As is widely known, out-of-court enforcement of security interests is an integral part of Article 9 of the American Uniform Commercial Code and all the other systems that have taken over the unitary security-interest-based system, in particular the Canadian common law provinces, New Zealand and Australia. Book IX of the European Draft Common Frame of Reference should also be added to the list.

212 See L. Vékás (ed.), *Complex Commentary* 465, which proclaims that the 2013 Civil Code 'enlarges and, compared to the earlier system, regulates in more detail the out-of-court enforcement of security rights.' See L. Vékás (ed.), *Complex Commentary*, 465.

successor to the Chamber is now the Bar of Hungarian Court Bailiffs (*Magyar Bírósági Végrehajtói Kar*).[213]

1.3. *Enforcement under the 2013 Civil Code*

157. The following features of the new rules should be mentioned to properly describe their contents and reach. First, the new regime for the enforcement of security rights is cumulative: a secured party may opt for any of the options[214] (court versus out-of-court or may shift from one to another form of self-help).[215] While these rights are not subject to limitations in the case of business finance, in the context of consumer contracts there are two limitations. On the one hand, the collateral may be disposed of only at a public sale (except if the parties have agreed[216] – in writing and after default – on another method of disposal). On the other hand, strict foreclosure is prohibited, i.e. the secured creditor may not acquire the title (ownership) to the collateral (save on cash, certificated and uncertificated securities as well as on some bank accouts).[217]

157. Second, the Code itself talks explicitly of three out-of-court enforcement methods only: disposition, limited version of strict foreclosure (i.e. acquisition of title/ownership by the secured creditor on the collateral), and collection of receivables or enforcement on a right (that was used as collateral).[218] To the mind-set of Hungarian law, repossession (i.e. retaking possession of the collateral) is not a distinct form of self-help but only a prerequisite of disposition.[219]

159. Finally, the 2013 Civil Code introduced a restrained and notification-conditioned form of self-help repossession.[220] This novel institution rests on more footings as follows. We will now take a look at each of these enforcement forms in the following sections.

1.3.1. *Repossession of the collateral according to the 2013 Civil Code*

160. It is proclaimed that the secured creditor is entitled to take possession (repossess) of the collateral upon default by the debtor, but only for the

213 See §42 of Act No. CVII. of Year 2015 on Amendment of the Act on Court Enforcement No. LIII. of year 1994 and on the Modification of other Laws in Connection to that (*A bírósági végrehajtásról szóló 1994. évi LIII. törvény, és ezzel összefüggésben egyes törvények módosításáról szóló 2015. évi CVII. törvény 42. §-a*).
214 See §5:126(3) of the Hungarian Civil Code.
215 See §5:127(2) of the Hungarian Civil Code.
216 See §5:128(a) of the Hungarian Civil Code.
217 See §5:128(b) of the Hungarian Civil Code.
218 See §5:127(1) of the Hungarian Civil Code.
219 See §5:132(1) of the Hungarian Civil Code.
220 See §5:132 of the Hungarian Civil Code.

sake of disposition.[221] This last precondition makes the Hungarian solution somewhat peculiar because – as the commentaries state – 'repossession is not to serve its own end [but] may be exercised solely for the purpose of disposition. Therefore, if the secured party would not be in the position to sell the collateral because of a lack of demand on the market, then he would not be entitled to take possession from the debtor.'[222] The same prohibition applies if disposition could not be effected without first repossessing from the premises (e.g. from the locked workshop or garage of the debtor) or hands of the debtor.[223] Such a solution is a clear example of the debtor-protective nature of the system as it fails to recognise the value inherent in the changed strategic position that repossession entails. It also disregards the realities of the market given that often nobody can readily foretell whether there is a market for the collateral or whether the market will have unexpectedly frozen by the time of the disposition unexpectedly.

161. It is also peculiar that the system somewhat naïvely departs from the presumption that debtors are normally willing to cooperate with the secured creditor. As the related commentaries and scholarly papers cite no empirical studies whatsoever on this point, one may conclude that this presumption of the drafters rested on purely theoretical projections. True, the Code imposes two related obligations on the debtor: on the one hand, to hand over (i.e. transfer the possession over) the collateral or to allow repossession by secured creditor,[224] and on the other hand, to refrain from any such action that might hinder disposition by the secured creditor.[225]

1.3.2. Debtor-protective counter-balances

162. Similar to the DCFR yet in stark contrast to UCC Article 9, the new Civil Code's most significant out-of-court repossession-weakening rules impose the duty to notify the debtor in advance related to his obligation to (re)transfer possession of the collateral. Although the rules are not entirely clear, such notification must contain a demand to the debtor[226] and also set a deadline within which to transfer possession. As far as the latter is concerned, the basic – somewhat vague – rule is that the deadline must be appropriate to the given circumstances.[227] This is then supplemented by further limitations according to

---

221 See §5:132(1) of the Hungarian Civil Code.

222 See G. Welmann, *HVG Commentary*, 188 referring to the reasoning of the amendment proposal that was transposed to the final formulation of this paragraph.

223 See L. Vékás (ed.), *Complex Commentary*, 468.

224 See §5:132(3) of the Hungarian Civil Code.

225 See §5:132)(3) of the Hungarian Civil Code.

226 See §5:132(3) of the Hungarian Civil Code mentioning the demand (*felszólítás*).

227 See §5:132(2) first sentence of the Hungarian Civil Code ('*a körülmények által indokolt határidő*').

which the deadline cannot be less than ten days in case of movables and twenty days if immovables were used as collateral.[228] Moreover, letting the creditor take possesion of vacated dwelling-immovables cannot occur in less than, at least, three months.[229]

163. Finally, the greater reliance on out-of-court enforcement is further counter-balanced – with respect to all out-of-court (self-help) forms – by two new court remedies aimed at protecting the debtor in addition to his right to damages caused by improper exercise of enforcement rights.[230] These are court orders (injunctions) either to suspend the out-of-court enforcement of security rights or to enforce them according to the terms and conditions determined by the court;[231] both presume the filing of a claim with the court by the debtor himself or by any other third person having a legal interest.[232] It is impossible to understand why only (one of the) Commentaries – and not the text of the Code itself – declared that these new tools were introduced to 'prevent irreversible harm and damage' since such guidance might have helped the courts better to understand the nature and intended function of these tools. Similar criticism could be made of the drafters' failure to ensure swift issue of these measures through specific prescriptive language,[233] for example in the form of summary or even ex parte proceedings. At the moment nothing seems to guarantee that.

1.4. *Recognised out-of-court enforcement forms*

1.4.1. *Private disposition (sale)*

164. Sale of the collateral – private or public[234] – after default is listed as one of the out-of-court forms of enforcement of security interests[235] for the exercise of which no special agreement is needed: it is a statutorily-granted right of the secured creditor.[236] This enforcement avenue can be exercised solely by public

228 See §5:132(1) of the Hungarian Civil Code.
229 See §5:132(2), second sentence of the Hungarian Civil Code.
230 See L. Vékás (ed.), *Complex Commentary*, 466.
231 See §5:130 of the Hungarian Civil Code.
232 What qualifies as legitimate 'legal interest' is not defined by the Code, nor is the list of persons who may have such interests. For example, as G. Welmann, *HVG Commentary* suggests, all persons that should have been notified of the secured creditor's intention to dispose of the collateral or all the secured creditors who have been harmed by the inappropriate – not satisfying the standards of commercial reasonable disposition – may qualify. See G. Welmann, *HVG Commentary*, 185.
233 See L. Vékás (ed.), *Complex Commentary*, 466.
234 See §5:134(2)(b) of the Hungarian Civil Code.
235 See §5:127(1)(a) of the Hungarian Civil Code.
236 See L. Vékás (ed.), *Complex Commentary*, 465.

sales in the case of consumer contracts, unless the parties make an agreement in writing on another method of disposition – and after default.[237]

165. The Code has tried to find a formula for balancing two contrasting goals: opening the doors more widely to private disposition yet providing the debtor, other affected creditors and third parties (e.g. a surety) with efficient counter-balances. While the secured creditor's position was strenghtened through reduction of the formal requirements tying the hands of the secured creditor (e.g. the right to choose the enforcement avenue), the debtor and other (junior) secured creditors are protected through a set of explicit rules, all originating in the standard of commercial reasonableness.[238]

166. The balance rests on six footings. First, it declares that dispositions must be undertaken in a commercially reasonable manner and that 'the interests of the debtor and of the surety must also be taken into account during disposition.'[239] The rebuttable presumption that the disposition was commercially reasonable is presumed only for sales on stock-exchanges and only if a quoted price exists for the given security-collateral (i.e. the market price at the time of sale) and for sale in the ordinary course of business (i.e. sale by a known method on a recognised market and in the ordinary course of business).[240] This standard – imported from US law – is in addition to the generally applicable principles of good faith and honesty (long known in Hungarian law) and the duty to 'act as it is expected in a given situation.'[241]

167. Second, disposition is subject to certain notification requirements; a requirement that can be disregarded only in case of quickly deteriorating as well as collateral the value of which would significantly fall due to delay inherent to notification or that is traded on commodities or stock exchanges.[242] Notwithstanding the good intentions of the drafters of the Civil Code, the notification requirements are quite burdensome since essentially they protect all

---

237 See §5:128 of the Hungarian Civil Code.

238 See L. Vékás (ed.), *Complex Commentary*, 466.

239 See §5:133(1) of the Hungarian Civil Code.

240 See §5:133(2) of the Hungarian Civil Code.

241 See L. Vékás (ed.), *Complex Commentary*, 469. The principle of good faith and honesty is defined by §1:3 of the Hungarian Civil Code. Subsection 2 of this provision contains the concrete example in civil law known as the maxim of *venire contra factum proprium, a* rough equivalent of the common law [equitable] estoppel. Concretely: 'It infringes the principles of good faith and honesty to act contrary to one's earlier behavior which the other party had reasonably relied on.'

The principle of expected behaviour, on the other hand, is contained by §1.4. of the Hungarian Civil Code. This is a general principle that reads: 'Unless a different standard of behavior is expected by this Code, one has to act as it would be normally expected in the given situation.' This, in other words, is a sort of rationality standard just expressed in different words.

242 See §5:131(4) of the Hungarian Civil Code.

parties that might have any kind of right to the collateral, from the debtor, surety (and his guarantor), other (junior) secured creditors, and all parties who either have registered rights or otherwise prove the existence of rights.[243]

168. Third, as explained above, the Code introduced a sui generis, debtor cooperation-presuming form of self-help repossession (retaking) of the collateral.[244] This is another meaningful departure from conventional civil law doctrines, which look with great suspicion on any form of out-of-court enforcement. It is strange that while Hungarian law looks on this 'merely' as a precondition for a private disposition – part of the law that transplanted the American doctrine of commercial reasonableness – it failed to heed the extremely rich US experience concerning self-help repossession. One of the issues that will presumably cause many problems in the future is that the system departed from the idealistic postulate that most of debtors are willing to cooperate and return the collateral voluntarily. As a result, the 'without the breach of peace' standard known to UCC Article 9 (or anything resembling that) was not adopted.

169. Fourth, more as an illustration and encouragement rather than a restriction, a few shorter provisions declare that the secured creditor is entitled – as a statutory agent of the debtor[245] – to sell (i.e. to transfer ownership) the collateral on behalf of the debtor,[246] in altered or unaltered form,[247] privately or publicly,[248] in bulk or separately (if the collateral is made of more assets).[249] The only limitation is that the secured creditor may acquire ownership of the collateral disposed of at a public sale only if that is done through an exchange.[250]

170. Fifth, the Code imposes the duty on the secured creditor to prepare without delay a written account for the disposal, which needs to contain five classes of information: (1) identification of the sold collateral; (2) the price received; (3) the proceeds collected by the secured creditor; (4) the costs of safekeeping, maintenance, processing, transformation and disposal; as well as (5) the ranking of the security interests and the respective claims secured by each (if known to the secured party).[251]

171. It is unclear why the Code uses different standards for, on the one hand, communicating the intention to dispose of the collateral and, on the other hand,

---

243 See §5:131(1) of the Hungarian Civil Code.
244 See §5:132 of the Hungarian Civil Code.
245 See L. Vékás (ed.), *Complex Commentary*, 469.
246 See §5:134(1) of the Hungarian Civil Code.
247 See §5:134(2)(a) of the Hungarian Civil Code.
248 See §5:134(2)(b) of the Hungarian Civil Code.
249 See §5:134(3) of the Hungarian Civil Code.
250 See §5:134(4) of the Hungarian Civil Code.
251 See §5:135 of the Hungarian Civil Code.

for making the written accounts and dispatching them to the debtor and all parties entitled to notification. Namely, while – as described above in the case of the former – fixed deadlines apply, in the latter case the Code speaks only of 'without delay'[252] for the preparation of the accounts and it does not specify a deadline for dispatching the information on the accounting.[253]

172. The other part of the duty to account is the duty to distribute the collected moneys according to the priorities of the security interests. First, however, the disposing secured creditor may deduct from the sales price and the collected proceeds the costs incurred in safekeeping, maintenance, processing, transformation and sales. If there is anything remaining after all the secured creditors have been paid, those funds should be returned to the debtor.[254]

173. Sixth, the Code counter-balances the secured creditor's self-help rights by explicitly granting to the debtor, surety and generally to any other person having a legal interest, a right to apply to the courts for an order suspending the enforcement stage or for enforcement subject to court-formulated conditions. These remedies may in principle be resorted to only where the secured creditor disregards any of his enforcement-related obligations specified in the Code.

174. A final concluding point ought to be made. Namely, the rules on private (out-of-court) disposition are obviously the product of a new – but clearly salutary – approach that yields to practical needs, empirical evidence and comparative law in lieu of theoretical considerations. Concretely, besides refining the earlier adapted American concept of 'commercial reasonableness',[255] the Code took into account the experiences with the earlier generation limited forms of private enforcement.[256] The new provision giving the right to senior secured creditors to take over the already commenced private (extra-judicial) disposition might be a further encouraging novelty pointing in the right direction.[257]

---

252 See §5:135(1) of the Hungarian Civil Code.

253 See §5:135(2) of the Hungarian Civil Code.

254 See §5:135(3) of the Hungarian Civil Code.

255 The standard of commercial reasonableness entered the Hungarian legal system from the Directive 2002/47/EU on financial collateral arrangements (6 June 2002), which was borrowed from the commercial law of the US. See L. Vékás (ed.), *Complex Commentary,* 470.

256 For example, as opposed to the earlier version of the Code, no provision is now devoted to joint disposition by debtor and secured creditor because this did not work in practice. See L. Vékás (ed.), *Complex Commentary,* 468.

257 See §5:129 of the Hungarian Civil Code. According to this the senior secured creditor may do so through a written declaration addressed to the junior secured creditor (who has already started the disposition) and if he defrays the related costs of the latter. The junior secured creditor, on the other hand, is obliged to appropriately inform the senior creditor of the steps already taken and of the concomitant costs.

1.4.2. *Collection of receivables*

175. The basic principle is that until the obligor (account debtor) is served with the so-called order to perform (*teljesítési utasítás*) – or collection order – by the secured creditor, he has to make payments to the debtor.[258] This order needs to identify the secured creditor[259] unless that has already been done with the notification on the 'pledging' of the receivables. In other words, although without using such vocabulary and rather resorting to obscure descriptive language, the system aims to recognise both notification and non-notification receivables financing.

176. Thus, when the Code states that the order to perform may be provided together with the notification on pledging,[260] it speaks of indirect (non-notification) receivables financing as the account debtor (obligor) is not informed of the fact that the receivables were used as collateral until default. The same provision also allows, however, for the possibility of notification of the account debtor (obligor) on the 'pledging' of the receivables at the time of the creation of the security interest, in which case – if the account debtor was informed as to who the secured creditor is – the order to perform may be issued solely by him.[261]

1.4.3. *Strict foreclosure*

177. The Code kept the prohibition of lex commissoria. Hence, the agreement of the debtor and secured creditor according to which the latter would automatically acquire ownership of the collateral upon the debtor's default, is null and void.[262]

178. However, as a form of out-of-court enforcement, the Code recognises the validity of agreements according to which the secured creditor acquires ownership of the collateral as a full or partial substitute for the (payment for the) secured claim, if concluded after default.[263] The system presumes that in that stage the debtor 'is not exposed to the [opportunistic behavior of the] secured

---

258 See §5:111(1) of the Hungarian Civil Code.

259 See §5:111(1) of the Hungarian Civil Code. The provision is somewhat ambiguous. It states that the legal entity needs to be identified but specifically mentions only the seat; this is obviously insufficient for identification. In contrast, in the case of physical persons, the domicile, habitual residence or the identification of the account is required. It is not clear whether the requirement of the identification of the account where the moneys are to be transferred to is a requirement in case of both, juridical and physical persons.

260 This follows from §5:111(2) of the Hungarian Civil Code.

261 See §5:111(2) of the Hungarian Civil Code.

262 See §5:136 of the Hungarian Civil Code.

263 See §5:137(1) of the Hungarian Civil Code.

creditor anymore and is in the position to make a [learned] decision whether to accept the purchase offer taking into account his own interests.'[264]

179. Resort to this form of enforcement is subject to a number of preconditions, some serving the interests of the strategically weaker party, the debtor, and others protecting third parties.

180. The debtor is intended to be protected by rules specifying the form such strict foreclosure may take: it is not only the secured creditor who must make an offer to purchase the collateral in written form[265] and by specifying all the key components of the offer[266] but the debtor must accept the offer also in written form, within a statutory fixed time limit.[267] Besides the debtor, the secured creditor must also notify other parties who may have an interest in the offer made to the debtor.[268]

181. Those third parties who have to be notified by the secured creditor of the intended offer to acquire the collateral may object if that might endanger their secured claims.[269] If the debtor accepts the offer in writing within 20 days and none of the interested third parties files an objection in writing (also) within 20 days, it will be presumed that a sales contract has been concluded between the debtor and the secured creditor.[270] It is also presumed that the secured debt will extinguish fully or partially as specified in the the secured creditor's offer. Based on this the debtor is obliged to transfer the collateral into the possession of the secured creditor and to issue permission for the registration (entry) of the

264 See L. Vékás (ed.), *Complex Commentary* Comments, 472.

265 See §5:137(2) of the Hungarian Civil Code.

266 As per §5:137(2) the secured creditor's offer must identify: (a) the debtor and the secured creditor; (b) the collateral (for which the offer has been made); (c) the amount of the outstanding debt secured by the collateral; and (d) the reason and the time of the default. The offer must also specify (e) what portion of the secured debt would be extinguished by the strict foreclosure (i.e. acquisition of title/ownership by the secured creditor), or, if the price of the collateral would be higher than the debt secured, it should specify what amount of money would be paid by the secured creditor in addition to acquiring the title/ownership on the collateral.

267 The time within which the debtor may accept such offer is twenty days counted from the receipt of the secured creditor's offer. See §5:137(5) of the Hungarian Civil Code.

268 See §5:137(3) of the Hungarian Civil Code which imposed the duty of notification on the following categories of third parties: (a) sureties and guarantors as well as those who have guaranteed performance by these; (b) secured creditors who have a security interest on the (same) collateral; (c) all those persons who have rights and interests (proprietary rights) on collateral subject to registration (*lajstromozott zálogtárgy*); and (d) all those other who claim to have rights on the collateral and have informed and provided the secured creditor with proofs about that – provided that such information has reached the secured creditor in writing and not later than the tenth day before the offer of the secured creditor.

269 See §5:137(4) of the Hungarian Civil Code.

270 See §5:137(5) of the Hungarian Civil Code.

secured party's ownership (in the case of assets for which a system of registration of ownership exists such as immovables).[271]

2. Lithuania

182. Until the 2011 amendments to the Lithuanian Civil Code, enforcement of security rights was exclusively by the courts and court-bailiffs. Changes have been introduced to increase the efficiency of the system, in particular by reducing the role of courts to deciding on challenges to the actions of the notary or the bailiffs. Under the new system, the creditor applies to the notary and receives the so-called executive entry, which he can then take directly to the bailiff for enforcement. The bailiff conducts the enforcement irrespective of whether the debtor cooperates or not. Empirical data are lacking on whether this works well in practice in *Lithuania*. Out-of-court repossession is illegal in *Lithuania*.

183. Strict foreclosure is also known in *Lithuania* in the case of both real property mortgages and pledges of movables.

3. Poland

184. *Poland* belongs to the continental European legal tradition and as such is hostile to self-help. Even the Registered Pledge Act – considered to be a modern statute comparable to the EBRD Model Secured Transactions Law – declares court enforcement to be the rule.[272] Court enforcement is required also for possessory pledges.[273] Yet this Act has already introduced some steps that represent some limited forms of out-of-court enforcement. A form of self-help was introduced for financial collateral based on EU law.

185. One such out-of-court enforcement method is the transfer of title on the pledged collateral to the secured creditor (strict foreclosure). It can be resorted to if so stipulated by the security agreement, without the involvement of courts.[274] The time of the transfer of the title differs for the different classes of collateral.[275] Special rules regulate the determination of the value of collateral in

---

271 See §5:137(5) of the Hungarian Civil Code.
272 See Article 21 of the Polish Registered Pledge Act.
273 See Article 312 of the Polish Civil Code.
274 See Article 22(1) of the Polish Registered Pledge Act.
275 See Article 22.2 of the Polish Registered Pledge Act.

such instances.[276] The Civil Code provides for a similar solution for possessory pledges.[277]

186. While sale of the collateral at a public auction held by a public notary or enforcement officer might also qualify as an out-of-court enforcement method,[278] enforcement of a registered pledge on an economic unit (enterprise or global security)[279] is perhaps the best example corroborating the claim that Polish law has also opened the doors to self-help (out-of-court enforcement). In this process the court gets involved only if the pledgor files a claim for an injunction to prevent enforcement. In practice, normally the security agreement will regulate such receivership (private enforcement) in great detail – moreover, normally on much harsher terms for the debtor than the default rules (compulsory administration) enshrined in the Code of Civil Procedure.[280]

187. Finally, enforcement of security assignments is also made outside courts: the assignee (secured creditor) notifies the debtor of the assigned claims that the receivables should be paid directly to him.

Question 9: Is the secured party affected by a 'stay' of the enforcement of security rights if the debtor enters insolvency proceedings?

1. Hungary

1.1. The three types of Hungarian insolvency moratoria

188. Although the position of Hungarian law has fluctuated post-1990 on this issue, the law in force does stay the enforcement of security rights in case of both reorganisation and liquidation proceedings. However, the system does not have a comprehensive concept of 'automatic stay' known, for example, to US law. The Hungarian system rather relies on a set of specific provisions which have the effect of a stay. Instead of a single broad concept, therefore, Hungarian law is based on a set of particular provisions. The underlying philosophy is that, first, security interests can be enforced solely as part of liquidation proceedings, second, the collateral becomes part of the estate and, third, the secured parties enjoy a somewhat limited right to separate satisfaction within bankruptcy proceedings.[281]

189. The Hungarian 'stay' formula could be said to be made of two building blocks: three forms of moratoria (called '*moratórium*' in Hungarian) and a

276 See Article 23 of the Polish Registered Pledge Act.
277 See Article 313 of the Polish Civil Code.
278 See Article 24 of the Polish Registered Pledge Act.
279 See Article 27 of the Polish Registered Pledge Act.
280 The procedure of enforcement by 'compulsory administration' is regulated by Articles 1064^1–1064^{13} of the Polish Code of Civil Procedure.
281 See L. Juhász, *The Hungarian Insolvency Handbook*, 760.

number of specific rules that have the effect of a 'stay.' As far as the latter category is concerned, of special importance is the general rule that enforcement of security rights can be effected solely within bankruptcy proceedings (both liquidation and reorganisation). The starting point of the stay is either the receipt of the notification on the opening of bankrutpcy proceedings by the creditor or the moment when the notice on the commencement of proceedings becomes public.[282]

190. The Hungarian moratorium is a limited device and is nothing more than extra time for performance of obligations applicable in the context of both liquidations and reorganisations with legal consequences.[283] Most importantly, during the moratorium, security rights cannot be enforced. In other words, it is not only that the opening of insolvency proceedings stays enforcement of security rights, but – if the moratorium arises automatically based on the law (normal moratorium) or if approved either by the bankruptcy court (provisional moratorium) or the majority of creditors (prolonged moratorium) – security rights cannot be enforced while the moratorium is in place either.[284] It causes some unease that the related provisions are somewhat obscure.

1.2. *Synopsis of the effects of 'stay' in Hungarian insolvency law*

The overview of the fragmented and thus incomplete substitute of 'automatic stay' could be exemplified[285] as follows:

The Hungarian 'Stay'	
Moratorium (extension of time for payment)	**Additional specific provisions exemplified**
A. Within reorganisation	**A. Within reorganisation**
§9(1): *provisional moratorium* (if requested by debtor)	§8(5): bank cannot enforce on bank account or privilege creditors
§11(1): *normal moratorium* (automatic upon opening the insolvency proceedings)	§9(2): the debtor must add 'cs.a.' (under reorganisation) to its name
§18(7): *prolonged moratorium* (if requested by debtor and if approved by the qualified majority of creditors)	§10(5): court will automatically reject requests for liquidation

282 See §4/A of the Hungarian Insolvency Act (rules introduced in 2013).

283 See primarily §11 for reorganisations and §§34–36 for liquidations; both references are to the Hungarian Insolvency Act.

284 In the case BH2013, 131, adjudicated by the Curia (Supreme Court), the enforceability of the fiduciary security of 'option to purchase' coupled with a mortgage on an immovable during a moratorium was the issue. As per the holding of the court, although default can be declared, securities cannot be enforced during a moratorium. This also includes when default occurred before a moratorium but the security remained unenforced until the declaration of the moratorium.

285 The chart is incomplete and does not contain a full list.

The Hungarian 'Stay'	
Moratorium (extension of time for payment)	**Additional specific provisions exemplified**
Corollary of moratorium (e.g.)	
§11(1): duty of debtor, administrator, financial institutions (with which the debtor has accounts) as well as creditors to refrain from any act that might frustrate the goals of the moratorium[286]	
§11(2)(a): prohibition of set-off	
§11(2)(f): new debt only if approved by administrator	
B. Within liquidation	**B. Within liquidation**
§26(3): court may approve a 45-day moratorium if requested by debtor	§35(1): all debts become due upon issuance of the decision on opening the proceedings
	§38: court enforcement stopped
	§49/D: sale of collateral by the administrator

1.3. 'Stay' in reorganisations

191. Three types of moratoria should be differentiated in the context of reorganisation. First, the provisional moratorium (*ideiglenes fizetési haladék*) is granted within one working day by the bankruptcy judge ex parte and is valid from the day it is made public on the website of the Bulletin of Companies (*Cégközlöny*).[287] Its function is to provide prompt protection to the debtor and is not linked to the opening of the reorganisation proceedings but it depends on an application for reorganisation proceedings.[288] As opposed to that, second, the so-called 'normal' (*rendes*) moratorium is automatic from the publication of the decision on the opening of insolvency proceedings[289] and is effective for 122 days.[290]

192. Finally, the statutory moratorium can be extended by the bankruptcy court though only if approved (counter-signed) by the bankrutpcy administrator[291]

286 This is similar to the effects of an injunction and also similar to the automatic stay under US law.

287 The moratorium is in principle granted automatically upon the filing of a related claim by the debtor. The qualification has to be added because it is not fully clear on what bases can the judge refuse grating it. The law says merely that 'unless granting is refused instantaneously' but it does not specify on what grounds. See §9(1) of the Hungarian Insolvency Act. The literature points to formal deficiencies. See L. Juhász, *The Hungarian Insolvency Handbook*, vol. II, 157.

288 See L. Juhász, *The Hungarian Insolvency Handbook*, vol. II, 157.

289 See §10(2)(e) of the Hungarian Insolvency Act.

290 See §10(4) of the Hungarian Insolvency Act.

291 See §10(4) of the Hungarian Insolvency Act.

and if supported by the qualified majority of creditors.[292] This is the third extended form of moratorium.[293] The majority of creditors, however, may condition the prolongation of the moratorium by imposition of further limitations on the powers of the debtor's directors. Concretely, they may require, on one hand, that all entries in the company register may only be made jointly by the chief executive officer (or another authorised person) and the administrator, and, on the other hand, conditioning the disposal with bank accounts upon the administrator's approval (counter-signing).[294] These restrictions make sense because in the case of Hungarian reorganisations an administrator must be appointed[295] notwithstanding that the debtor (i.e. chief executive officer, directors and officers) remains in possession, to exercise their governance and management powers save the duties imposed on them by the Insolvency Act. In other words, as opposed to some jurisditions (e.g. the US) where the normal course of events is that the management stays put in reorganisations (named as 'debtor-in-possession') and no trustee is appointed, in Hungarian law the powers over the insolvent company are divided in reorganisation proceedings.

193. Insolvency law tries to make the chief executive officer of debtors cooperate with the administrator by imposing monetary fines.[296] The function of the normal and extended forms of moratoria is to give sufficient time for reaching an agreement with the creditors,[297] but it may not be more than 365 days.[298]

1.4. 'Stay' in liquidations

194. Security rights cannot be enforced directly by the creditors after the opening of liquidation proceedings, save the so-called security-bailment. In the latter case, the secured creditor can enforce his security right notwithstanding the opening of the proceedings, but only if he does so within three months from the opening of the proceedings.[299] After that period his security right will be treated like other securities, i.e. the insolvency administrator will enforce them, deduct the amounts recognised by the Act (e.g. costs for the safekeeping or sale

292 See §18(8) of the Hungarian Insolvency Act.
293 See §10(4) of the Hungarian Insolvency Act.
294 See §18(10) of the Hungarian Insolvency Act.
295 See §13(1) of the Hungarian Insolvency Act. See also L. Juhász, *The Hungarian Insolvency Handbook*, 224.
296 See §13(2) of the Hungarian Insolvency Act.
297 See L. Juhász, *The Hungarian Insolvency Handbook*, vol. II, 170.
298 See §18(1) of the Hungarian Insolvency Act.
299 See §38(5) of the Hungarian Insolvency Act.

of the collateral, as well as the fees of the administrator) and will distribute the rest to creditors in accordance with their entitlements.[300]

2. Lithuania

195. Although the law does not use the term 'stay,' rules having such effect do exist in the case of court-run bankruptcy proceedings initiated against business enterprises. These presume first and foremost transfer of the management of the bankrupty enterprise into the hands of the court-appointed bankrutpcy administrator.[301] This also includes collateral and as the system provides for the enforcement of security rights primarily through the administrator, the stay affects also the security rights.

196. Moreover, acquisition (taking over) of the collateral by the secured creditor – as an alternative method to sales – may be exercised only if approved by the meeting of creditors after a failed auction.[302] In other words, private enforcement of security rights is unknown to Lithuanian law and all enforcement procedures take place as part of the insolvency proceedings.

197. The other rules having the effect of a 'stay' include, in particular:

(a) the prohibition (on creditors and other persons) otherwise than in accordance with the Bankruptcy Act to manage and dispose of the assets of the bankrupt company;[303]
(b) third parties holding the assets of the debtor are prohibited from entering into any transactions with third parties related to these assets;[304]
(c) court proceedings against the bankrupt company in other courts are stopped;[305]
(d) all debts become due;[306] and
(e) bailiffs (enforcement officers) have to transfer to the bankruptcy court all the enforcement cases in process.[307]

---

300 See §49/D of the Hungarian Insolvency Act. Somewhat different rules apply for shifting securities (see §49/D(2)).
301 See in particular Article 10.7(1) and (2) of the Lithuanian Enterprise Insolvency Act.
302 See Article 33(6) of the Lithuanian Insolvency Act.
303 See Article 14.1(1) of the Lithuanian Enterprise Insolvency Act. The bankruptcy administrator is appointed by the bankruptcy court as per Article 10.4(1) of the Act.
304 See Article 14.1(2) of the Lithuanian Enterprise Insolvency Act.
305 See Article 15.1. of the Lithuanian Enterprise Insolvency Act.
306 See Article 16 of the Lithuanian Enterprise Insolvency Act.
307 See Article 18.1. of the Lithuanian Enterprise Insolvency Act.

3. Poland

198. Given the separation of the insolvency (liquidation) and restructuring laws in 2015, we will discuss them separately. Both include the concept of stay yet with variations in their contents.

3.1. 'Stay' in liquidations

199. As far as insolvency law is concerned, once insolvency proceedings are opened, the debtor has to transfer all of its assets to the insolvency practitioner[308] because they automatically convert into and become part of the bankruptcy estate.[309] Based on explicit provisions, ongoing enforcement proceedings must be stayed.[310] The proceeds collected from disposition of certain collateral by the bankrupt but which have not been transferred to the creditors as of the date of the opening of the insolvency proceedings, will not become part of the estate.[311] The novelty introduced by the 2015 amendment is that the secured creditor's priority of satisfaction of proceeds from the sale of a collateral (whether sale occurred prior to or during the insolvency) will survive the opening of the insolvency procedure.[312]

200. Another important feature of the system is that Polish insolvency law does not recognise the private enforcement of security rights in the context of insolvency proceedings and thus security rights can be enforced only by insolvency practitioners or exceptionally as approved by the bankruptcy court.

201. This concretely means, that if the registered pledge (i.e. security) agreement does not provide for any out-of-court enforcement methods, it is for the insolvency practitioner to sell the collateral, in which case the pledgee will have priority over the proceeds of sale. If the pledge agreement provides for out-of court enforcement methods, only strict foreclosure or sale at public auction may be resorted to by the pledgee in insolvency.[313]

202. The insolvency judge may set a deadline for exercising strict foreclosure by the pledgee, upon the expiry of which the collateral is sold by the insolvency

---

308 See Article 57(1) of the Polish Insolvency Act. Note that with the passage of the new Restructuring Law (April 2015) this rule will apply only in case of liquidation proceedings. Under the new Restructuring Law, except the rehabilitation proceedings, all types of restructuring proceedings are debtor-in-possession type of proceedings.

309 See Article 61 of the Polish Insolvency Act.

310 See Article 146 of the Polish Insolvency Act.

311 See Article 63(1)(3) of the Polish Insolvency Act.

312 See Article 146(2a) of the Polish Insolvency Act.

313 See Article 327(1) of the Polish Insolvency Act.

practitioner. This is linked to the the insolvency practitioner's mandate to take control of the bankruptcy estate and start administering it immediately upon opening the proceedings.[314] This power extends also to the collateral although the law has specific rules for enforcement of possessory securities, i.e. collateral that is possessed by the creditor or third party at the time of the opening of the bakruptcy.[315]

3.2. *'Stay' in the 2015 Restructuring Act*

203. As far as the 2015 Restructuring Act is concerned, different rules apply to the various restructuring alternatives. While there is no stay in case of pre-packaged arrangements, enforcement is stayed in case of rehabilitation proceedings.[316] As opposed to these, rules similar to the ones described above with regard to insolvency proceedings apply to the arrangement and the accelerated arrangement proceedings.This means that the secured creditor may enforce its security interest but only against the collateral[317] notwithstanding that there is a stay of enforcement proceedings.[318]

204. Security rights are affected by the 'stay' also in respect of interests. While the general rule is that interests cease to run with the opening of insolvency proceedings, that is not the case with security rights. However, they are limited to the proceeds that may be obtained from the sale of the collateral.[319]

Questions 10/11: Can the secured party apply to have any stay lifted? Under what circumstances can the stay be lifted?

1. Hungary

205. It seems that under Hungarian law there is no formal option for a secured party to apply to have a stay lifted. Consequently, save the limited exception of the security-bailment mentioned above, satisfaction from the collateral is always to occur within the context of insolvency proceedings.[320]

---

314 See Article 173 of the Polish Insolvency Act. Note that with the passage of the new Restructuring Law (April 2015) this rule will apply only in case of liquidation proceedings.
315 See Article 327(2) of the Polish Insolvency Act.
316 Article 312(1) of the Polish Restructuring Law.
317 Articles 278–279 of the Polish Restructuring Law.
318 Article 259(1) of the Polish Restructuring Law.
319 See Article 92(2) of the Polish Insolvency Act.
320 See §4/A of the Hungarian Insolvency Act.

206. The only exception seems to be the security-bailment (*óvadék*), which due to its very nature – especially the nature of the collateral – ought to be treated differently. However, in this case, the right to enforce the security right is not dependent on any special approval either by the administrator or the bankruptcy court.[321] This is, in other words, rather a form of private realisation (out-of-court enforcement) than an example of stay being lifted. As a result, there seems to be a conflict between the general rule that all security rights must be enforced within insolvency proceedings and the said right to directly realise the security-bailment by the secured creditor; or it is not fully clear what is exactly meant under 'to be enforced exclusively within insolvency proceedings.' According to Juhasz, a leading expert on Hungarian insolvency law, given that the provisions on the security-bailment are specific (lex specialis), they apply rather than the general rule.[322]

207. This possibility is, however, subject to some restrictions. In particular, the secured creditor must account for the surplus with the administrator. Furthermore, he can exercise this direct-enforcement method only within three months from the day the decision on the opening of the liquidation proceedings has been publicised. Moreover, if the secured creditor is a person controlled by the debtor, this enforcement avenue is not available as in such cases the collateral must be handed over to the administrator immediately upon the commencement of the case.[323]

2. Lithuania

208. Lifting the 'stay' and allowing the secured creditor to enforce a security right outside the context of insolvency proceedings is not possible. In other words, enforcement of secured transactions is completely entrusted to the administrator. The system foresees the same process for all kinds of pledged and mortgaged assets.[324]

209. The basic disposal method is by auction; the secured creditors must be informed about them.[325] The secured creditors may acquire the collateral only if the auction has proved unsuccessful and they wish to acquire the collateral.

321 For liquidations see §38(5) of the Hungarian Insolvency Act. In the case of reorganisation, the exception is narrower as it applies only to netting transactions on the capital markets and among a group of qualified entities. See §11(2)(d).

322 See L. Juhász, *The Hungarian Insolvency Handbook*, 92.

323 See §38(5) of the Hungarian Insolvency Act.

324 This follows even from the definition of 'creditors' claims secured by a pledge and/or mortgage' in Article 2.7 of the Lithuanian Enterprise Insolvency Act.

325 See Article 33.6 of the Lithuanian Enterprise Insolvency Act.

From the collected funds, first the administration expenses[326] will be deducted and then they must be credited – no later than 10 days from the date of receiving the price – to the respective creditor's account.[327] The secured creditors are paid in priority from the funds obtained from the sale of the collateral. In respect of the unpaid part, they are treated as unsecured creditors.[328]

210. For quasi-securities (leasing and retained title), no specific rules are laid down in the Act on Enterprise Insolvency. Thus, the generally applicable enforcement rules, as supplemented by private law, will apply. In case of leasing, thus, the Civil Code comes first into the picture because the Insolvency Act introduces the principle that the rights of creditors granted by other laws remain intact to the extent they do not contradict any provisions of the Insolvency Act.[329]

211. Further, the administrator has the duty to inform creditors whether he intends to perform executory contracts or whether he will reject them.[330]

212. According to the Civil Code, retained ownership (title) in case of leasing contracts is looked upon as ownership rather than a mere security right, and therefore the owners are entitled to recover their property.[331]

3. Poland

213. As far as insolvency proceedings are concerned, the general rules is that a stay cannot be lifted in enforcement proceedings.

214. However, as already suggested above, certain methods of private enforcement of *registered pledges* are explicitly exempted from this general rule. If the underlying security agreement so provides, the creditor may take over (acquire) the collateral or turn to public notaries or bailiffs for its disposal – as provided for by the Act on Registered Pledges.[332] However, if the collateral is in the possession of the insolvency practitioner, engagement of notaries or bailiffs is no longer possible.

---

326 See Article 36 on administrative expenses of the Lithuanian Insolvency Act.
327 See Article 33.6 of the Lithuanian Enterprise Insolvency Act.
328 See Article 34 of the Lithuanian Enterprise Insolvency Act.
329 See Article 1.3 of the Lithuanian Enterprise Insolvency Act.
330 See Article 10.7(4) of the Lithuanian Enterprise Insolvency Act.
331 On the dilemmas and case law on leasing and retained title in Lithuania see L. Aleknaite, 'Leasing in Lithuania' in S. Messmann and T. Tajti (eds.), *The Case Law of Central and Eastern Europe – Leasing*, 240–263.
332 See Article 327(1) of the Polish Insolvency Act.

215. As far as the new 2015 Restructuring Law is concerned, given that enforcement of security interests in prepackaged and accelerated arrangements as well as arrangement proceedings cannot be stayed, Question 10 does not apply to them. As opposed to these, in case of rehabilitation proceedings it is not possible to lift the stay on enforcement proceedings.[333] This comes as a surprise because the possibility of lifting the stay exists even in insolvency proceedings.

Question 12: In insolvency proceedings, can an insolvency practitioner (IP) 'enforce' the security, i.e. realise the secured assets, without the consent of the secured party?

1. Hungary

216. *Hungary*'s distinctive solution is that the administrator (insolvency practitioner) can enforce security,[334] though this question may arise only in the case of liquidations in *Hungary*. The system sets as the basic rule that creditors – including secured parties – must file their claims with the insolvency practitioner within the fixed period of 40 days from the date of publication of the decision on the opening of the liquidation proceedings. Claims filed within this 40-day period enjoy full recognition. On the other hand, claims filed after 40 but before 180 days will be listed, but will only be paid if assets remain after preferential and secured creditor claims filed within the 40-day period.[335]

217. The same treatment also applies to secured claims: claims must be filed within 40 days of publication of the decision to open liquidation proceedings.[336] If the claim was filed with the administrator in time, the administrator will dispose of the collateral, deduct the preferential administration expenses (i.e. the costs of safekeeping, preservation of the collateral, as well as of enforcement and administrator's fee) and will then pay the secured party without delay.[337]

218. Now, where the secured party fails to file a claim within the statutory 40 days, the administrator may sell the collateral – or as the language of the statute says: 'this is not an obstacle to the sale.' In other words, the administrator may sell the collateral without the consent of the secured party given that failure to file the claim obviously denotes lack of consent. In such a case, however, the administrator has to separate the recovered monies but can pay the secured creditor only if, after having paid all the costs of liquidation, all secured creditors

---

333 Article 312(1) of the Polish Restructuring Law.
334 See e.g. C. Bridge, *Insolvency Office Holders*, 9.
335 See §37(1) of the Hungarian Insolvency Act.
336 See §28(2)(f) of the Hungarian Insolvency Act.
337 See §49/D(1) of the Hungarian Insolvency Act.

and a number of other preferential claims,[338] there are still funds available for distribution.[339] Different rules apply, however, where a settlement is reached within liquidation.[340]

2. Lithuania

219. There are no explicit provisions on whether the insolvency practitioner can sell the collateral without the consent of the secured party in the Lithuanian Act on Enterprise Insolvency.

220. There are however broad powers granted to the creditors meeting with respect to, on the one hand, the continuation of economic activities of the bankrut entity and, on the other hand, imposition of restrictions on the disposal of the enterprise's assets,[341] and these may also extend to restricting the use and disposal of the collateral.

3. Poland

221. As in restructuring proceedings, the arrangement does not extend to secured claims (i.e. mortgage, pledge, registered pledge, tax lien or maritime lien), unless the secured creditor consents,[342] the only instance where the insolvency practitioner may realise the assets contrary to the will of the secured creditor is the following – and applies only to insolvency proceedings. Namely, as Polish law prefers the sale of the bankrupt debtor's enterprise as a whole rather than piecemeal, when it is more profitable to realise an individual security by selling the entire enterprise, or an organised (i.e. separable economic or technological organisational unit of an enterprise which may but must not have legal entity status) part of an enterprise rather then enforcing each security independently, then the previous method will be given preference notwithstanding the wishes of the secured party. In such a case, however, the value of the asset subject to registered pledge must be put aside for the benefit of the secured party.[343]

---

338 See §57(1) of the Hungarian Insolvency Act. See also §57(2) for what qualifies as costs of the liquidation proceedings.

339 See §37(1) of the Hungarian Insolvency Act.

340 See §37(1) of the Hungarian Insolvency Act.

341 See Article 23.6 of the Lithuanian Enterprise Insolvency Act.

342 Article 151(2) of the Polish Restructuring Law.

343 See Article 330 of the Polish Insolvency Act.

Question 13: Are there any conditions that must be satisfied before an IP may 'enforce' the security?

1. Hungary

222. Presuming that the collateral still exists, besides the obvious requirement that the creditor must have a valid and recognised claim, the law imposes two further requirements on the enforcement of the security: the duty to file the claim with the insolvency practitioner and payment of a registration fee.[344] These preconditions apply both to reorganisation and liquidation proceedings although subject to somewhat differing rules mainly due to the distinct nature of the two proceedings.

223. Most importantly, while in the case of liquidations the secured creditors must file their claims with the insolvency practitioner within 40 days from the publication of the decision to open liquidation proceedings,[345] with reorganisations the deadline is 30 days for pre-reorganisation claims and eight days for those that come into being after the opening of the reorganisation proceedings.[346]

224. As for the payment of the so-called registration (filing) fee (*regisztrációs díj*), in the case of liquidations this is equal to 1% of the principal amount of the claim, which cannot be less than HUF5,000 and more than HUF200,000. Evidence that the fee has been paid must be presented to the administrator.[347] In the case of reorganisation, the upper limit is HUF100,000.[348]

2. Lithuania

225. First, the secured creditors must file their claims with the administrator within the time set by the bankruptcy court (maximum 45 days)[349] and the bankruptcy court must approve them within 45 days of receipt of the list from the administrator.[350]

226. Second, administrative costs are paid from all of the company's funds, including the monies received from the sale of the collateral.[351] What makes the Lithuanian system a bit peculiar is that the number of pertaining explicit rules is small. Thus, although not stated explicitly in the Act, normally once a creditor's claim is approved, the fee creditors have to pay as administrative costs are fixed

---

344 See L. Juhász, *The Hungarian Insolvency Handbook*, 770.
345 See §37(1) of the Hungarian Insolvency Act.
346 See §10(2)(f) of the Hungarian Insolvency Act.
347 See §46(7) of the Hungarian Insolvency Act.
348 See §12(1) of the Hungarian Insolvency Act.
349 See Article 10.4(5) of the Lithuanian Enterprise Insolvency Act.
350 See Article 26.1 of the Lithuanian Enterprise Insolvency Act.
351 See Article 36 of the Lithuanian Enterprise Insolvency Act.

pro-rata depending on the size of their claims. What makes the Lithuanian system further idiosyncratic is that it is the creditors' meeting that has the power to determine 'the sequence and procedure for covering administrative expenses.'[352] As far as the time of the payment of fees is concerned, if not fixed by the creditors' meeting, these will be deducted by the administrator upon the disposition of the collateral and before transferring the price collected from the sale of his collateral to the secured creditor.[353]

3. Poland

227. Besides the existence of a properly constituted (perfected) security right, the Polish Insolvency Act also requires the listing of the secured claim. The system is peculiar, however, in that it explicitly declares that secured creditors' claims are listed ex officio notwithstanding what the secured creditors have the right to file.[354] This seemingly redundant provision aims to allow for the secured creditor's active participation where there is disagreement with the insolvency administrator. Employees are the other such privileged class of creditors with equal entitlements.

228. The preconditions are logically most onerous if the entire enterprise, or organised part thereof, is the collateral. In such cases, first, the value of the enterprise as collateral, as well as the value of any individual security rights that exist, must be determined by experts.[355] Second, the terms and conditions of the public auction or tender for the realisation of the collateral must be confirmed by the bankruptcy judge before the insolvency practitioner may start the disposition (e.g. notification).[356]

Question 14: Do the rules or conditions differ depending on the nature of the insolvency proceedings in question?

1. Hungary

229. Even though both reorganisation and liquidation are centralised and no private enforcement of security rights is known under Hungarian law (save bailment-securities), the fate of security rights differ under the two regimes.

352 See Article 23.5 of the Lithuanian Enterprise Insolvency Act.

353 See Article 33.6 of the Lithuanian Enterprise Insolvency Act. The administrative expenses have to be paid in also in case the asset are acquired by secured creditors after unsuccessful auctions as per the same provision.

354 See Article 236(2) of the Polish Insolvency Act.

355 See Articles 318 and 319(3) of the Polish Insolvency Act.

356 See Article 320(1) of the Polish Insolvency Act. The 2015 amendment to the Insolvency Act discarded the possibility of disposition outside of the public tender process with the approval of the bankruptcy judge (Article 326 of the old Act was deleted).

230. In the case of reorganisations, no security right can be enforced with the exception of security-bailments granted to specific participants in capital markets while a provisional or normal moratorium is in force.[357]

231. If the secured creditor's claim has been filed and recognised by the administrator and he has paid the registration fees due, he will have a right to vote on the reorganisation plan.[358] The affirmative vote of the majority of both secured and unsecured classes should be acquired in order to prolong the moratorium for a maximum of 240 days from the starting date of reorganisation.[359]

232. On the other hand, in the case of liquidations, if the claim was filed with the liquidator within the prescribed 40 days, the secured claim will be separately satisfied. This means that the liquidator will sell the secured assets and then, after deduction of preferential administrative costs and his fee, the sums recovered from the sale of the collateral will be forwarded to the secured party. If the claim was filed late, the collateral will nonetheless be sold but the ranking of the claim will fall significantly – as described above under points 12 and 13.

2. Lithuania

233. The enforcement of security rights are, in theory, subject to the same regime in both reorganisations and liquidations, i.e. sale by the administrator at auctions.

234. As a supplementary method, the secured party may, if he so desires, acquire the collateral, however, only if the auction has failed for specified reasons.[360] These rules are contained in a chapter that applies to the 'bankruptcy process'[361] that extends to both judicial and out-of-court bankruptcy procedures. In other words, the system foresees this as the only enforcement method applicable to all types of recognised insolvency proceedings. Moreover, these rules apply even to out-of-court settlements of creditors and the debtor as a separate nominated insolvency proceeding, given that no specific enforcement rules are contained in this respect in the Act.[362]

---

357 The list includes the Hungarian and the national banks of other EU Member States, (commercial) banks and various other financial organisations. For the list see §11(3) of the Hungarian Insolvency Act.

358 See §18(4) of the Hungarian Insolvency Act.

359 See §18(8) of the Hungarian Insolvency Act.

360 See Article 33.6 of the Lithuanian Enterprise Insolvency Act.

361 See the title of Chapter Eight devoted – besides sale of assets of the bankrupt entity – to satisfaction of creditors' claims in the course of the bankruptcy process. The bankruptcy process is defined as 'the totality of judicial or extrajudicial enterprise bankruptcy procedures.'

362 See Article 13.1 of the Lithuanian Enterprise Insolvency Act.

3. Poland

235. The old 2003 Act contained no special enforcement rules for reorganisation except what follows from the nature of such proceedings. In other words, the reorganisation plan did not affect the secured party unless it chose to participate. For example, a security right could have been waived, changed or replaced[363] as a measure intended to contribute to the success of the restructuring, however, only with the consent of the secured creditor. In other words, collateral was included in the reorganisation plan only if the affected secured party agreed.

236. Thus, security rights were enforced as in the case of liquidations: unaffected by the plan unless the reorganisation plan provides for taking over (acquisition) of collateral by creditors.[364] This approach was adopted by the Restructuring Act as well.[365] The new 2015 Restructuring Act's basic principle is therefore that none of the arrangement proceedings extend to secured claims.[366]

Question 15: Is a secured party liable to pay the general costs, i.e. costs apart from those incurred in connection with the realisation of security, of insolvency proceedings affecting the debtor?

1. Hungary

237. The system makes participation in insolvency proceedings (both reorganisation and liquidation) contingent on payment of a registration fee in addition to the costs deductable for the safekeeping, preservation and sale (collection) of the collateral (if any).

238. In the case of reorganisations, failure to file (and prove) the claim as well as the failure to pay the registration fee results in refusal of the registration of the claim (creditor).[367] The registration fee is 1% of the registered claim, though not less than HUF5,000 and not more than HUF100,000.[368] According to the law the fees have to be kept on a separate account by the administrator, who can spend the money only in connection with costs incurred by him and for his remuneration. Moreover, if the monies collected as registration fees are

---

363 Article 270.1(5) of the Polish Insolvency Act was repealed from the Polish Insolvency Law with the 2015 changes. The (identical) rule was moved to Article 156(1)(5) of the Restructuring Law.

364 See Article 271 of the 2003 Polish Insolvency Act, repealed by the 2015 Restructuring Law.

365 Article 156(1)(5) in connection with Article 151(2) of the Restructuring Law.

366 Article 151(2) of the Restructuring Law.

367 See §12(1) of the Hungarian Insolvency Act.

368 See §12(1) of the Hungarian Insolvency Act.

insufficient to cover the costs and remuneration of the administrator, it is the debtor who is responsible for the difference.[369]

239. Two tools aim to control spending by the administrator. On the one hand, the administrator has to prove all such costs with invoices and the creditors' committee or creditor representatives are entitled to check the spending (if neither is in place, then the checking is done by the bankruptcy court).[370] On the other hand, all of the administrator's expenditure must be proven by invoices.

240. Even though sale of the collateral is the normal corrollary of liquidations (the cost of which is deducted from the sum recovered from the sale of the collateral), the secured party is expected to contribute to the general costs of the liquidation proceedings as well. This is 1% of the claim, or at least HUF5,000 or a maximum of HUF200,000.[371] Irrespective of the fact that the fee so paid is then listed as a recognised unsecured claim (though with a very inferior ranking position)[372] and theoretically the creditors could recover it, as in most liquidation cases there is insufficient money available to pay unsecured creditors, normally such fees are lost.

2. Lithuania

241. Lithuanian law foresees as well that the secured creditor must contribute to the coverage of the general costs of the proceedings. The Insolvency Act pronounces this to be a general rule and says that the expenses will be paid first from any type of funds available to the bankrupt entity – including pledged assets.[373] Then, through explicit language the Act provides that the administrative expenses are to be deducted by the bankruptcy administrator from the proceeds of sale of the collateral before any transfer to the secured creditor. If the assets are not sold but are acquired by the secured parties, they have to pay the administrative expenses as well.[374]

---

369 See §12(1) of the Hungarian Insolvency Act.

370 See §12(1) of the Hungarian Insolvency Act.

371 See §46(7) of the Hungarian Insolvency Act.

372 See §46(7) of the Hungarian Insolvency Act. For ranking of the residual category of unsecured claims – named other claims (*egyéb követelések*) – into which the registration fees fall, see §57(1)(f).

373 See Article 36.1 of the Lithuanian Enterprise Insolvency Act.

374 See Article 33.6 of the Lithuanian Enterprise Insolvency Act.

3. Poland

242. As per the Insolvency Act the secured creditor has to cover, from the proceeds of sale of the collateral, two types of costs: (1) the costs of the disposal of the collateral; and (2) the general costs of the insolvency proceedings. However, the latter is limited by two cumulatively applicable criteria: on the one hand, the costs deducted may not be more than one-tenth ($\frac{1}{10}$) of the proceeds generated by the sale of the collateral, and on the other hand, that amount may not exceed the amount that would be proportionate to the ratio of the value of the collateral versus the value of the entire estate.[375]

243. The debtor has to cover the costs of restructuring proceedings under the new 2015 Restructuring Law.[376]

Question 16: Is the secured party liable to 'set aside' any portion of the amount realised from the enforcement of security for the benefit of (a) preferential or (b) unsecured creditors of the debtor?

1. Hungary

244. Save for the narrow exception of security-bailment, Hungarian insolvency law does not recognise private enforcement of security rights. Hence, it is the liquidator who has to set aside portions of the amount realised from the enforcement of security. Moreover, this applies only in the case of floating securities, or – after 15 March 2014 when the new Civil Code entered into force in this respect and discarded the earlier nominated property-encumbering (enterprise or floating) charge – when the collateral is 'identified by description' and when the security right 'extends to all assets registrable in the register of security rights [on movables, rights and claims].'[377]

245. In such cases, after having deducted the costs of sale of the collateral, the liquidator may apply no more than 50% of the recovered funds exclusively for the payment of the secured claim (principal, contractual interest and concomitant costs), assuming the security right was constituted before the commencement of the proceedings.[378] If the recovered funds are insufficient to fully pay such a secured creditor, the claim for the residue will rank after administrative expenses. This is nevertheless a high priority position but ranking after the administrative expenses.

---

[375] See Article 345(1) of the Polish Insolvency Act.

[376] Article 208(1) of the Restructuring Law.

[377] See §49/D(2) Insolvency Act.

[378] See §49/D(2) Insolvency Act.

246. The Hungarian system also provides for an idiosyncratic solution aimed at punishing insiders. Namely, these rules do not apply if the secured party was either a director, officer (as well as a close relative, life partner of these or – in case of juridical persons – was controlled by the debtor)[379] or a controlling shareholder[380] of the debtor. The security rights of these creditors will not benefit from separate enforcement. Rather, their claims will be treated as mere unsecured claims with an extremely inferior ranking.[381]

2. Lithuania

247. This question does not arise in the context of Lithuanian insolvency law because enforcement of security rights is exclusively carried out by bankruptcy administrators. In other words, it is the task of the administrator to collect the administrative expenses.

248. As stated above (see previous question), the administrator will deduct the administrative expenses – as approved by the creditors' meeting – from the monies recovered from the sale of the collateral before transferring any monies to the secured party.[382] However, as the creditors meeting is empowered to decide on the sequence and procedure for covering administrative expenses,[383] there is the possibility that the administrator will be instructed to request advances from secured creditors though no such practice seems to have emerged in the country.

3. Poland

249. The basic principle is that monies collected from the sale of collateral are reserved for the secured creditors; only the surplus becomes part of the estate.[384] However, through specific rules, secured creditors are obliged to put aside a certain percentage of the recovered funds to cover the costs of enforcement and to contribute to the general costs of the proceedings.[385] (See the details under

379 See §49/D(4) Insolvency Act.
380 See §49/D(5) Insolvency Act.
381 See §57(1)(h). In fact, besides all the administrative costs (§57(2) – including but not limited to unpaid wages and other wage-like obligations, all costs corollary to the preservation of the estate and completion of the production of the debtor, costs of the sale of the estate's assets, costs of various liquidation-related court and administrative proceedings, costs imposed by data protection laws, all the other secured and unsecured claimants will enjoy priority.
382 See Article 33.6 of the Lithuanian Enterprise Insolvency Act.
383 See Article 23.5 of the Lithuanian Enterprise Insolvency Act.
384 See Article 336.1 of the Polish Insolvency Act.
385 See Article 345 of the Polish Insolvency Act.

Question 16 above.) The novelty introduced by the amended 2015 Insolvency Act is that, as explicitly stated, if the collateral generates income, such income becomes part of the estate and is not reserved for the secured creditor.[386]

250. Such (or a similar) situation arises only in the case of enforcement of a security right on an enterprise, or an organised part thereof. In such cases, an evaluation has to be made not only of the value of the enterprise-collateral but also of the specificindividualised assets encumbered by a mortgage, pledge or registered pledge. The function of such valuation is to determine (a) which of the securities will remain in effect after sale; (b) what their value is; and (c) the ratio of the value of the individual collateral to the value of the enterprise.[387] This is not a case, however, of setting aside monies for preferential or unsecured creditors.

Question 17: Can the secured party be bound against its wishes by a restructuring plan that negatively affects either the secured debt or the enforcement of the security interest?

1. Hungary

251. The Insolvency Act explicitly mentions the term 'forced agreement' (*kényszeregyeszség*)[388] and as a result it could be validly claimed that the system recognises a version of cram-down. These rules apply generally and not only in relation to secured creditors.

252. The following features of the system are determinative here. The first, explicitly stated rule is that the reorganisation plan applies also to those registered creditors, both secured and unsecured, that have not consented to the plan or have failed to participate in the related proceedings (notwithstanding having been properly summoned). The same applies to creditors with disputed claims.[389] Here, the reasons that led the secured creditor to reject the restructuring plan or not to participate at voting are irrelevant. However, through an explicit rule, these creditors are protected because the plan cannot impose on them terms and conditions that would be more onerous than the ones applicable to creditors of the same class.[390]

253. Second, the system tries to provide protection to all classes of creditors. As far as voting is concerned, the plan is accepted, not if the majority of all the

386 Article 336(3) of the amended Polish Insolvency Act.
387 See Article 319(4) of the Polish Insolvency Act.
388 See §20(2) of the Hungarian Insolvency Act.
389 See §20(2) of the Hungarian Insolvency Act.
390 See §20(2) of the Hungarian Insolvency Act.

creditors votes for it, but rather if the majority of each of the classes (secured and unsecured) in terms of value, casts an affirmative vote.[391] Theoretically thus neither the secured nor the unsecured creditors can impose the plan against the wishes of the other classes. Note, however, that this applies to the class as a whole and does not exclude the possibility that some individual creditors may lose out.

254. Third, besides this voting arrangement, the Act adds another balancing tool to ensure that none of the classes can impose its position on the other. This tool, however, rests on somewhat vague grounds given that – relying on the good faith principle – it proclaims that the restructuring plan may not contain provisions that obviously or conspicuously disadvantages all the creditors or only some specific classes.[392]

255. Fourth, the decisions ideally leading to the acceptance of the restructing plan are all passed by the majority of the classes – both secured and unsecured classes[393] – of creditors. In other words, the position of individual secured creditors is sacrificed in the hope of an easier approval of the plan; this notwithstanding that voting census is established proportionately to the value of recognised claims: one full vote is attributed to each HUF50,000 of recognised claims.[394]

256. Fifth, not only will the plan not apply to the the individual creditor who did not participate in the conclusion of the restructuring plan because of a failure to file the claim within the statutory deadlines (i.e. non-registered creditors), but he will additionally lose his enforcement rights as well.[395] In such cases the only possibility for realisation of his security right is through filing his claim in liquidations proceedings initiated by another creditor and only if the statute of limitations has not run out for his claim.[396] In this way the system obviously aims to incentivise creditors not only to file their claims but also to participate in reorganisation proceedings.

257. Finally, the creditor dissatisfied with the reorganisation plan, may file an appeal (within eight days of receipt of the court's decision approving the reorganisation plan or – if the decision was publicised on the Internet – from the date of the second such announcement).[397] In such a case, the bankruptcy

---

391 See §20(1) of the Hungarian Insolvency Act.

392 See §20(1a) of the Hungarian Insolvency Act.

393 The plan is accepted if the majority votes of each of the classes is obtained. In other words, the majority of unsecured creditors cannot impose on the secured creditors the plan against their wishes. See §20(1) of the Hungarian Insolvency Act.

394 See §18(5) of the Hungarian Insolvency Act.

395 See §20(3) of the Hungarian Insolvency Act.

396 See §20(3) of the Hungarian Insolvency Act.

397 See §21/C(3) of the Hungarian Insolvency Act.

court will make a decision[398] primarily based on the generally applicable rules on enforceability of agreements in the Civil Code.[399]

2. Lithuania

258. The Lithuanian Act on Enteprise Insolvency contains provisions for a loosely regulated settlement (literally: peace agreement) when the creditors agree with owners (shareholders) that the insolvency proceedings should not be completed.[400] This requires the consent of affected creditors.[401] The bankruptcy court has the task of checking whether the legally guaranteed rights and interests are dully recognised.[402] Hence, unless the secured party consents, his security interest or his enforcement rights may not be negatively affected. Lithuanian law contains no provisions for cram-down. This even includes out-of-court settlement proceedings because they are also subject, unless otherwise explicitly stated, to the Insolvency Act.[403]

259. However, as the creditors committee is empowered to appraise and fix the selling price of the collateral[404] and as sale is by auction, and if too high price is fixed, that may prolong the process of sale.

260. The procedure of company restructuring in *Lithuania* is regulated by the Law on Restructuring of Companies. According to this law, the restructuring plan is adopted if creditors with a value of claims comprising two-thirds of the value of all claims approved by the court vote in favour of it.[405] The plan is binding on all creditors.

261. However, it is only a right and not an obligation of the creditor to assist the debtor regarding his debts. A creditor may, in particular, agree on postponement of payment or the performance of obligations, the writing off, either fully or partially, of claims, or accept performance in kind instead of payment of

---

398 See §6(7)(a) of the Hungarian Insolvency Act.

399 See the decision of the Curia in the case BH2013, 131, stating that a reorganisation plan is null and void if it does not treat creditors equally. Concretely, in the case the reorganisation plan gave a freedom to the debtor to unilaterally fix different dates at which various creditors would be paid.

400 Only the relatively short Articles 28 and 29 regulate composition.

401 See Article 28.2 of the Lithuanian Enterprise Insolvency Act.

402 See Article 29.3 of the Lithuanian Enterprise Insolvency Act.

403 See Article 13.1 of the Lithuanian Enterprise Insolvency Act.

404 See Article 23.5 of the Lithuanian Enterprise Insolvency Act.

405 See Article 14 part 3 of the Lithuanian Law on Restructuring of Companies.

monies.[406] Therefore such assistance can be included in the restructuring plan with the consent of the creditor. Otherwise, creditor claims are satisfied in accordance with procedure specified in the law. Once the collateral is sold, the secured creditor receives the proceeds. For the remainder of the claim, the creditor is treated the same way as unsecured commercial creditors.

262. If the restructuring plan does not envisage the sale of the collateral, than an opinion on the value of collateral by an independent valuer must be obtained. In such a case secured creditors are paid together with first ranking creditors (employees), but only the amount up to the approved value of the collateral. If that is not sufficient to cover the claim, for the remainder of the claim they are treated the same as unsecured commercial creditors.[407]

3. Poland

263. As per the new 2015 Restructuring Act it is not possible to impose a reorganisation plan on a secured creditor against his will.

264. This means that the basic rule is that the secured claim is not subject to the restructuring plan unless the secured party consents to this, unconditionally and irrevocably.[408] In other words, the secured creditor could have been bound unwillingly only with respect the deficiency that could not be covered by the value of the asset used as collateral; this applies also to an unsecured creditor. Similarly, although an arrangement may foresee that the collateral is to be waived, changed or replaced, that can ensue only if consented to by the affected secured creditor.

265. If, however, the secured creditor consented to the inclusion of his secured claim in the reorganisation plan, he may be bound by the restructuring plan if outvoted. This may occurr irrespective whether joint voting or voting by classes of creditors is practised.[409] In other words, Polish law recognises a version of cram-down that is, however, not applicable only to secured creditors. It blurs the picture, however, that there are no detailed rules on the formation of classes.

---

406 See Article 24(3) of the Lithuanian Law on Restructuring of Companies.
407 See Articles 13(1), (3) and (4) of the Lithuanian Act on Restructuring Companies.
408 See Article 151(2) of the Restructuring Law.
409 See Article 161 of the Restructuring Law.

Question 18: Can an under-secured creditor claim from the insolvency estate in respect of any deficiency arising as a result of the enforcement of the security?

1. Hungary

266. Yes, the right to claim deficiency from the estate is generally granted.[410] However, the position of the secured creditor differs depending on whether the collateral is 'only' a specific, individualised asset, or rather a floating security, determined by description but extending substantially to all assets of the debtor.

267. Namely, if the collateral is a specific, individualised asset (right or claim), the residual claim will be treated as unsecured ('other claims' [*egyéb követelések*]).[411] The systems reckons with the fact that the secured creditor should be in the position to determine the right credit versus collateral value ratio. This being so as in the case of such collateral, in principle the secured creditor will recover 100% of his claim (principal, interest and costs) as the liquidator is entitled to deduct only the costs of the safekeeping, preservation and sale as well 5% as his remuneration.[412]

268. The situation is different in the case of global (enterprise or floating) security, where the main problem is that such all-encompassing securities can hardly be enforced without restrictions; it is also an issue whether an unrestricted monopoly should be given to a single, typically strategically powerful creditor. Consequently, the law affords the right of separate satisfaction – within insolvency proceedings – only up to 50% of the monies collected from the realisation of the collateral. Still, these secured parties enjoy a higher ranking in respect of deficiency claims compared to other secured parties with security rights over individual assets, whose deficiency claims are treated as mere unsecured claims preceded not just by administrative costs but also by a number of other specific classes of creditors. In respect of creditors with global security, their deficiency claims will be inferior only to the administrative expenses of the proceedings.[413]

269. As the new 2013 Civil Code discarded the nominated security device of 'property encumbering charge' (global, enterprise or floating security) the different treatment afforded to individualised and floating (all-encompassing) security by insolvency law may lead to opportunistic creditor behaviour. For example,

410 See §49/D(6) of the Hungarian Insolvency Act.

411 See §57(1)(f) of the Hungarian Insolvency Act.

412 See §49/D(1) of the Hungarian Insolvency Act.

413 See §57(1)(b) of the Hungarian Insolvency Act. In other words, while the deficiency claims based on floating securities will rank as point (b) of §57(1), the deficiency claims of creditors enforcing on single, individualised collateral will qualify only as point (f) in §57(1) – under the Insolvency Act.

by registering a security interest on almost all assets of a business debtor – but definitively leaving out some specific economically important assets – the secured party can ensure that he might ask for separate satisfaction through the sale of each of the individual assets resulting in full satisfaction, instead of recovering only 50% of his claims and risking non- or reduced payment of the residue.[414]

2. Lithuania

270. There is no explicit provision in the Insolvency Act as to whether the secured creditor can file as an unsecured creditor for the residue.[415] However, this follows from the language of the article devoted to enforcement of security rights, according to which 'the creditor's claims secured by pledge and/or mortgage shall be satisfied *first of all* from the proceeds obtained from the sale of the pledge assets of the enterprise or by transferring the pledged assets' (emphasis added).[416]

3. Poland

271. Claims secured by a mortgage, pledge, registed pledge, tax pledge or marine mortgage – in the amount in which they have not been satisfied from the collateral – are included in the plan for the distribution of the insolvency estate due to an explicit provision in the Polish Insolvency Act.[417]

D. REGISTRATION OF SECURITY RIGHTS

Question 19: To what extent must security rights over assets be publicised by registration or filing to ensure the effectiveness of the security interest over parties other than the debtor and in the event of insolvency proceedings?

1. Hungary

1.1. Publicity of security rights as the basic principle of the 2013 Civil Code

272. As described in more detail above under Questions 6 and 7, according to the new 2013 Civil Code, the basic principle is that security (in rem) rights

[414] See A. Csőke and L. Juhász, 'Az új Ptk. hatása a csődtörvényre' [The Impact of the new Civil Code on Insolvency Law] in *Csőd, Felszámolás, Reorganizáció*, Nos. 11–12, 2014/1–2, 13.

[415] See Article 34 of the Lithuanian Enterprise Insolvency Act.

[416] See Article 34 of the Lithuanian Enterprise Insolvency Act.

[417] See Article 340(1) of the Polish Insolvency Act.

can be validly asserted against the world (third parties) only if registered in public registers or if perfected by transfer of possession (including constructive possession).[418] The only exceptions are the security-bailments discussed above. This was also the rule before 2013 yet some specific transaction types (quite important segments of the economy) have remained outside the system and registration (provision of public notice) was a requirement in their case (e.g. leasing, factoring or the so-called fiduciary securities).

273. Although the new system significantly expanded the reach of the general perfection requirement and has tried to clarify the perfection-related rules, canvassing a full picture requires adding a few qualifications.

1.2. Prohibition of fiduciary securities

274. First, one of the advancements introduced by the drafters of the 2013 Civil Code was the prohibition of fiduciary securities (in fact quasi-securities).[419] Parallel with that, financial leasing, recourse-factoring and transactions containing retained title (ownership) were subjected to registration with the register of security rights. The idea was, indeed, to subject all transactions that perform a security function to one of the recognised perfection methods (even at the price of prohibiting some). The issue is that some economically significant transactions have been left out of scope. It is thus questionable whether this policy has been appropriately achieved when all other leasing-forms but financial leasing or non-recourse methods of receivables financing (including factoring) have been left out?[420]

1.3. Perfection of security interests on receivables, rights and claims

275. Second, it ought to be noted as well that the Hungarian system goes a step further in respect of claims (receivables). Namely, while it imposes as 'the obligation' of the debtor to inform the obligor (account debtor) about 'pledging' of a claim at the time of the constitution of the security interest or issue a declaration on that to the secured party,[421] such notification is insufficient for

418 See §5:88. As the *Complex Commentary* proclaims: '[The new Civil Code makes no changes as far as the constitution of security rights is concerned] and essentially recognized two methods of perfection: transfer of possession over the asset used as collateral and registration in the appropriate register.' See L. Vékás (ed.), *Complex Commentary*, 423.

419 See §6:99 of the Hungarian Civil Code.

420 See more on this below on Question 25 on quasi-securities.

421 See 5:89(2)(c) of the Hungarian Civil Code.

perfection: the pledging must be registered in the register of security rights as well.[422] Note that (as mentioned above) recourse-factoring is also subject to registration with the same registry of security rights.

1.4. Perfection by control

276. Third, the language and the system of the new Hungarian Civil Code might be misleading to those familiar with UCC Article 9 and other internationally renowned security laws. Namely, what these laws perceive as perfection by 'control' is not mentioned in Hungarian Civil Code as a method of perfection. Rather, under Hungarian law, control is disguised as a distinct nominated security device that was retained because of tradition. This is the already-mentioned 'security-bailment' (*óvadék*).[423]

277. The reason why security-bailment could not be fully equated with control is that security-bailments can be perfected in two other ways. Concretely, if cash or certificated securities (*értékpapír* – known also as investment property) are used as collateral, perfection is by transfer of possession.[424] Strangely, dematerialised securities (investment property) can also be perfected by 'transfer of possession',[425] a highly controversal fiction of the new Code, of little (if any) practical value. More importantly, however, security-bailment can be constituted on dematerialised securities and bank accounts as well, if the service provider with whom the account is held is also the secured creditor, purely based on the security agreement of such content.[426]

278. As there is no registration in such cases, the law requires such secured creditors to 'indicate that the account is encumbered by a security interest on each and every statements of accounts.'[427] It makes things more complicated that certain asset-types can be encumbered by both a security-bailment and a registered security interest at the same time.[428]

---

422 L. Vékás (ed.), *Complex Commentary* emphatically states: '[The new Civil Code], in order to ensure the full publicity of all security rights, contrary to the [earlier] Civil Code from 1959, requires registration also of security interests on rights and claims.' This follows also from §5:88 that recognises only two perfection methods: transfer of possession or registration with the competent registry.

423 See §5:95 of the Hungarian Civil Code. See on security-bailment in more detail above under Questions 6 and 7.

424 See §5:95(1)(a) of the Hungarian Civil Code.

425 See §5:95(1)(b) of the Hungarian Civil Code.

426 See §5:95(2)(b) of the Hungarian Civil Code.

427 See §5:95(3) of the Hungarian Civil Code.

428 See §5:123 of the Hungarian Civil Code on the priority between the two.

1.5. Perfection of security interests on motor vehicles

279. Fourth, given the truly heightened importance attributed to the reform (upgrading) of secured transactions law in the post-1990 period – including the new 2013 Civil Code – it is surprising that the 'pledging' of motor vehicles (obviously an important part of the economy) has escaped proper attention. Namely, unlike *Poland*– where the registration of security interests on motor vehicles is ex officio reported to the body issuing certificates of title – or *Lithuania*, there is no such synchronisation in *Hungary* as of yet.

280. In fact, two distinct systems of registration exist side by side for encumbering motor vehicles: on the one hand, by registering the security right on the certification of title (i.e. the document attesting who the owner of the motor vehicle is), and on the other hand, by filing with the register of security interests on movables, rights and claims operated by the National Association of Public Notaries.

281. This dualism generates practical and legal dilemmas. For example, as the fact that a motor vehicle serving as collateral (including being subjected to a retained title) is indicated on the face of the certificate of title (*jármű törzskönyv*), creditors (financiers) – especially in the case of newly acquired vehicles – may (and normally do) keep possession of the certification of title until repayment of the debt, and do not register it. If the debtor repays the debt, the financier issues a declaration whereby it allows deletion of the inscription from the certificate of title. The municipalities, in the territory of which the registered residence (or seat, in the case of companies) of the debtor is, are to effect such deletions. In other words, notwithstanding that the certificate of title registry system does not prove authentically the existence of a security right over motor vehicles, they may be used to bypass the registration system. It is an issue what happens then with the main effort of the new Civil Code system that wants to extend the requirement of publicity to all kinds of assets.

282. To make the situation even more convoluted, as empirical evidence shows, it seems also that especially for older motor vehicles still in use, no such certificates of title were issued (or often they were lost). While this does not seem to cause problems as far as the use of these motor vehicles is concerned,[429] it makes clear that security interests on such vehicles can be created only by registration in the register of movables, claims and rights operated by public notaries. Moreover, as the certificate of title in principle attests only the title but not the security interest if registered, the entry in the register of movables should yield priority

---

429 See Article 81(2) of the Act LXXXIV of 1999 on the Register of Data Concerning Public Traffic (*1999. évi LXXXIV. Törvény a közúti közlekedési nyilvántartásról*) (hereinafter: Public Traffic Registration Act).

ranking of the registered security interest.[430] However, whether this is the case is unclear at the moment. Obviously, the two systems should be syncronised as soon as possible given that motor vehicles represent one of the economically most important assety types today.

283. Finally, the new Civil Code also introduced the concept of 'trust', modelling the newcomer legal institution specifically after its Anglo-Saxon kin. The new transplant seems to have been employed in two different contexts. On the one hand, a new nominated contract – one could call it the 'trust agreement' (*bizalmi vagyonkezelési szerződés*) was introduced. This contract was designed to become the vehicle for inter-generational transfer of wealth and for use by financial institutions. On the other hand, the new category of 'security agent' or security trustee' (*zálogjogosulti bizományos*)[431] was added to the chapter on security rights. The security trustee is expected to 'hold' the security in lieu of multiple secured parties (syndicated loans)[432] and as such he takes over the rights and duties of the secured party. However, such security trustee's acts will be valid against third parties only if registered in the appropriate register.[433] Notwithstanding the obligation to register and the possibility of registering only the security trustee in lieu of the (single or multiple) secured creditor(s), this arrangement hardly amounts to another type of security.

284. In sum, save for the few exceptions mentioned, the obvious aim of the policy makers was to ensure that public notice is a prerequisite for the creation of all in rem security rights.[434] Although with financial leasing, recourse-factoring and retained title (ownership) being subject to registration, a major step has been made in that direction, dilemmas remain and presumably there will be a need to refine the system once again in the not too distant future. More transparent rules on the 'creation' of security rights may also be needed.

2. Lithuania

285. While mortgages of immovables cannot come into existence without being registered in the appropriate public registers, in case of 'pledging' of movables

---

430 More precisely, Article 81(4) of the Public Traffic Registration Act says only that it is presumed that the holder of the certificate of title is the lawful owner of the motor vehicle, until the contrary is proven. In other words, entries in the register and on the face of the certificate of title do not authentically prove ownership.

431 See §5:96 of the Hungarian Civil Code.

432 See L. Vékás (ed.), *Complex Commentary,* 421.

433 See §5:96(2) of the Hungarian Civil Code. The appropriate register may be either the register of immovables or the register for the concrete other asset type in question (i.e. movables, rights and claims).

434 See L. Vékás (ed.), *Complex Commentary,* 430.

and rights – besides registration – transfer of possession is another recognised method of perfection. In these respects Lithuanian law is not different from other CEE systems.

286. Lithuanian law is, however, specific with respect to (financial) leasing[435] contracts as the most important quasi-security. Namely, these contracts are also subject to registration in order to be valid as against third parties[436] or the bankruptcy administrator.[437] This applies primarily to the retained ownership of the lessor,[438] which will be valid either against third parties with adverse claims or the bankruptcy administrator if registered. Leasing contracts are, however, registered in a database other than the one on 'pledged' movables and rights although both databases are maintained by the same organisation, the Central Mortgage Office.[439] Installment contracts are subject to registration with the same office yet in a separate database.[440]

287. The common feature of both registration systems is that neither of them is a notice-filing but rather they are document-filing systems with somewhat differing yet quite cumbersome rules requiring entry of quite a long list of data.[441]

3. Poland

288. With the exception of possessory pledges, all other types of security rights must be registered. This includes immovables, movables (non-possessory security on tangible assets), rights and claims (receivables) – including enterprises (or their organised parts). If a possessory pledge, security assignment or security transfer is to be effective in insolvency, there is an additional requirement as to form: the security agreement must be executed in writing with a certified date.[442]

---

435 The financial leasing contract is defined as a tripartite contract involving the financing lessor, the debtor wanting to acquire an asset and the seller of the asset. See 6.567(1) of the Lithuanian Civil Code. The Code allows the financing lessor to transfer most of the risks related to the defects of the asset onto the lessee.

436 See Article 6.572(1) of the Lithuanian Civil Code.

437 See Article 6.572(2) of the Lithuanian Civil Code.

438 The text of the relevant provisions do not use identical formulations though. While Article 6.572(1) speaks specifically of the lessor's ownership rights, Article 6.572(2) goes broader to 'lessor's rights.'

439 The database named the 'Register of Contracts' contains registrations related to leasing. See <https://www.hipotekosistaiga.lt/index.php?1927692242> accessed 23 May 2016. A different governmental resolution details the registration of leasing contracts, the Resolution No. 1158 of 2002 on the Establishment of the Register of Contracts and on the Approval of the Regulations of the Register of Contracts.

440 See Articles 6.411, 6.417 and 6.572 in the Lithuanian Civil Code.

441 For financial leasing see Resolution No. 1158 of 2002, in particular section 13.3.

442 See answer under Question 7 above on why certified date requirement was introduced for possessory pledges in 2009.

Question 20: Can you describe briefly the nature of the filing or registration system and whether it is publicly accessible?

1. Hungary

289. As already explained above, three registration systems exist in *Hungary*: the registry for mortgages on immovables, the registry for security interest on movables, rights and claims (i.e. personal property) and the few specific registries for some specific types of movables (i.e. ships, aircraft and some IP rights). Each of these systems are publicly accessible although the operation of each is radically different.

290. As described in more detail under Question 7 above, the register of immovables and the registers for specific items of movables (ships, aircraft) are document-filing systems, where entries have constitutive effects. The register for security interests on movables, rights and claims used to be the almost complete replica of the register of immovables until 2013, when the new Civil Code introduced notice filing (known by UCC Article 9). Now, the entries have no constitutive force and the excerpts from them do not authentically prove the existence of a security interest.

2. Lithuania

291. The two registers (databases) of relevance[443] are publicly accessible and are not based on notice-filing but rather the entries into these registers have constitutive force toward third parties.[444] This means that while the security agremeent is valid between the parties from the moment of its conclusion (unless otherwise stipulated), it may be invoked against third parties only if registered in the Mortgage Register.[445]

292. A designated government agency, the Central Mortgage Office (established in 1997) registers all security interests. It maintains the three previously mentioned registers (databases). Whereas security rights on immovables as well as movables and rights are entered into the Mortgage Register of the Republic of Lithuania, leasing contracts are subject to registration in the Register of

443 In Lithuania mortgage of immovables and security interests on movables are registered in one database. Retained title, however, is registered separately – in the register of contracts.

444 See Article 4.187 for mortgages of immovables, Article 4.213 for 'pledging' of movables and rights, and finally Article 6.572(1) and (2) of the Lithuanian Civil Code for retained title in financial leasing contracts. Registration is not a pre-condition for validity of retained title agreements, but is needed for use of the agreement against third persons.

445 See Article 4.187(1) and (2) of the Lithuanian Civil Code for contractual mortgages and Article 4.213 for security interests over movables and other property rights.

Contracts.[446] Security interests are primarily to be registered with this body. However, as this body is linked to a host of other registers, entries are thereafter synchronised with the others. The result is that if one searches the Central Mortgage Office database for security rights over property of a company, the search will reveal all registered security interests (including those in other databases).[447]

3. Poland

293. *Poland* has made significant steps toward making various commercial registers available online and free of charge. Surprisingly, it is not the register of 'registered pledges' that has reached the farthest as far as becoming electronically accessable and applying the latest generation technology. All the registries of relevance are run under the auspices of the Ministry of Justice although the courts that are empowered to make entries are directly responsible for those registries. These are described briefly hereinafter.

294. The Land and Mortgage Register is a public register for immovable property containing information on owners and in rem rights (including mortgages). It is maintained pursuant to the Act on Land and Mortgage Register and on Mortgages (originally enacted in 1982). Online access has been available since 1 July 2014.

295. The Register of Pledges is a public register for security interests on movables, rights and claims. The list also includes security interests established on enterprises (economic units) which could be established only based on the Act on Registered Pledges. These registers are operated by district (commercial) courts.[448] Notwithstanding that the very essence of this Act was the introduction of a system of registration specifically for non-possessory securities and provision of public notice through registration, this register has not as yet been made available online and accessible free of charge yet. Thus, at the moment, the person interested in obtaining information from the register must file an

---

446 See the website of the agency, with English language pages, at <https://www.hipotekosistaiga.lt/index.php?2506114761> accessed 23 May 2016.

447 According to Articles 58 and 57 of the Regulations of the Mortgage Register, the Mortgage Register must within eight working hours after registration of the mortgage or security interest pass all relevant information to the following registers: (a) register of legal persons; (b) register of real estates (immovables); (c) register of marine ships; (d) register of internal water ships; (e) register of railway rolling stock and containers; (f) register of trademarks; (g) register of patents; (h) register of designs; (i) register of tractors, self-propelled and agricultural vehicles and their trailers; (j) register of civil aircraft; (k) register of road vehicles; and (l) register of arms.

448 See Article 36.2. of the Polish Registered Pledge Act.

application, either by visiting the court that maintains the register or on the Internet. In the latter case, the register will deliver a PDF of the entry supplied with a certified electronic signature of the Minister of Justice.

296. The register is not a notice-filing system. Rather it is a document filing system[449] where entries have constitutive force and the data entered are deemed to be authentic. This means, in particular, that no person may plead ignorance of data disclosed in the register and the data is presumed to be true.[450] The following data are registered: (1) the date of submission of the request; (2) identification of the debtor (pledger or a third party-debtor) and creditor, i.e. the name and surname (or business name), Polish identification number, place of residence (registered office), address (for foreigners, the contact address in Poland); (3) identification of the collateral (or the method of its marking if so provided in the agreement); (4) the maximum secured amount and its currency; (5) the pledge enforcement method as set out in the pledge agreement (where allowed by the Act); and (6) the negative pledge covenant (if any).[451]

Question 21: To what extent does 'possession' or control of the secured assets serve as an alternative method to registration or filing in ensuring third party effectiveness of the security interest?

1. Hungary

297. The new Hungarian Civil Code requires a written form for all kinds of security agreements, thus it is not a distinguishing factor. As a result, perfection by transfer of possession and by registration are nothing more than alternative methods of ensuring third party effectiveness. The possibility of substituting a written form contract by certificated securities (*értékpapír*) that entitles its holder to the collateral conditioned on payment of the amount defined therein makes no difference.[452]

298. Where it is not fully clear whether possession or control may be equated with registration is in the case of the idiosyncratic security device of security-bailment. Here, two perfection methods may come into the picture: transfer of possession or control. (See on this in more detail under Question 20 above.) Of these two perfection methods, it is the control-related rules that make answering the above question difficult. Namely, in the case of perfection of security

---

449 As per Article 39 of the Polish Registered Pledge Act, the registration request must be accompanied by the pledge agreement or another agreement that involves either a registered pledge or a collateral covered by a registered pledge.

450 See Article 38 of the Polish Registered Pledge Act.

451 See Article 40.1. of the Polish Registered Pledge Act.

452 See §5:89(6) of the Hungarian Civil Code.

bailments by control, specific formal requirements apply, i.e. conclusion of the tripartite control agreement (i.e. inclusion also of the service-provider with whom the bank or securities account is held)[453] and the obligation to indicate on all documents data the balance on the account.[454] As already mentioned, registration is not required in such a case.[455] In sum, the Hungarian version of 'control' may also qualify as equal with registration for the purposes of ensuring effectiveness against third parties.

2. Lithuania

299. The system treats possession of the collateral (or possession of the certificated documents of title or securities) only as one of the prerequisites of the validity of a possessory pledge. Where the collateral is transferred into the hands of the pledgee, besides transfer of possession, the pledge agreement must be concluded in written form.[456] Without the written form the transaction is rendered void.

300. Additional formal requirements apply in the case of indirect pledges, i.e. when the collateral is transferred either to a third person or is kept in the hands of the pledgor (debtor). In such cases, besides the pledge contract, a unilateral declaration of the owner of the collateral expressing his consent to pledge the asset, a pledge deed certified by a notary and registration with the Register of Morgages is a required.[457]

301. Control is not regulated explicitly by Lithuanian law but the use of control agreements in practice is not excluded either.

3. Poland

302. Under Polish law, conclusion of a possessory pledge contract (oral or written) and the transfer of possession on the collateral to the creditor or to a third party is sufficient only to make the contract valid between the parties.[458] To make it valid against the pledgor's (debtor's) creditors, furthermore, the contract must not only be executed in written format but the date of its execution must additionally be certified.[459] Due to these additional requirements for transfer

453 See §5:95(2)(a) of the Hungarian Civil Code.
454 See §5:95(3) of the Hungarian Civil Code.
455 See L. Vékás (ed.), *Complex Commentary*, 433.
456 See Article 4.209(1) of the Lithuanian Civil Code.
457 See Article 4.209(2) of the Lithuanian Civil Code.
458 See Article 307.1. of the Polish Civil Code.
459 See Article 307.3. of the Polish Civil Code.

of possession, such a transfer is not the exact equivalent of registration (filing). The requirement of certification of the date was introduced in 2009 (with effect from 2011) in order to prevent abuse by creation of 'fiduciary' pledges just for the purpose of improving ranking in pending enforcement (or insolvency) proceedings.

E. PLURALITY OF SECURITY RIGHTS

Question 22: Is it possible to have more than one set of security rights (security interest) over the same asset?

1. Hungary

303. Although little emphasised by commentators, under the new 2013 Civil Code it is now clearer that the same asset can be encumbered by more than a single security interest.

304. Perhaps the best example – besides the priority rules[460] themselves – is the introduction of the concept of 'security trustee' (*zálogjogi bizományos*),[461] which was conceptualised primarily to serve syndicated lending with more creditors and with more security agreements. The rules allow the security trustee to represent all the creditors. This is an ideal solution when the members of the lenders' consortium are often changing.[462] If the name of the security trustee is registered in the registers of security interests, then the true secured creditors' names cannot be indicated in the registers.[463] In such cases the security trustee is the holder of the rights and obligations of the secured parties and acts in his own name but for the benefit of the secured creditors.[464]

2. Lithuania

305. Lithuanian law provides for such an eventuality explicitly in the priority rules.[465] Thus, if the collateral was not handed over to the creditor based on a prior pledge agreement and the pledge agreement does not state otherwise,

460 See §§5:118–5:125 of the Hungarian Civil Code.

461 See §5:96 of the Hungarian Civil Code. As there is no established vocabulary for this new legal institution, it ought to be added that the designation 'security agent' might also qualify.

462 See L. Vékás (ed.), *Complex Commentary*, 435.

463 See §5:96(4) of the Hungarian Civil Code.

464 See §5:96(5) of the Hungarian Civil Code.

465 See Article 4.211(1) of the Lithuanian Civil Code.

creation of a subsequent pledge is allowed. In such cases the prior pledge remains in force.

3. Poland

306. The possibility of multiple-security interests encumbering the same assets is possible in Polish law and this is foreseen in the priority rules explicitly.[466] To make it valid against the pledgor's creditors the contract establishing the possessory pledge must be executed in written form with a certified date.[467] In other words, to that extent transfer of possession is not equal to perfection by registration.

307. The Registered Pledge Act refers to a control agreement – although with little detail – which must be concluded, however, where the registered pledge is to secure debt securities issued in a series (e.g. bonds).[468] However, such security interests must also be registered and thus the control agreement is an addition to the registration requirement.

Question 23: What are the rules for determining priority between competing security interests in the same property?

1. Hungary

308. Hungarian law is based on a system of priority rules resting on the central 'first in time, first in rights' rule,[469] and a few specific priority-affecting provisions.

309. The 'first in time, first in rights' rule links priority to the time of the perfection of security interests, although the official terminology uses the term 'constitution of security interests' (*alapítás*). Two qualifications ought to be added here. First, assets that substitute or supplement the asset(s) used as collateral do not affect priority, unless they are encumbered by another specific security interest.[470] Second, the fact that the assets making the collateral (movables, rights or claims) are shifting, does not affect priority either – though this rule is applicable solely

466 See Article 16 of the Registered Pledge Act. See also Articles 249 and 310 of the Polish Civil Code. See also Articles 11 and 12 of the Polish Mortgage Act.
467 See Article 307.3. of the Polish Civil Code.
468 See Articles 2.4 and 4.4 of the Registered Pledge Act.
469 See §5:118 of the Hungarian Civil Code.
470 See §5:119 of the Hungarian Civil Code.

where the collateral is made of more assets registered in the register of security interests on movables, rights and claims.[471]

310. Five specific priority-affecting rules should be mentioned. For the first, the possible super-priority attributed to acquisition finance (purchase-money security interests), see Question 25 below.

311. The second rule simply gives full recognition to contractual subordination (*ranghely-szerződés*). It merely spells out the key subordination-related internationally accepted standards. Namely, that the ranking of security interest can be changed only with the consent of all affected parties and never to the detriment of a third party registered as a secured party at the time of the modification of the ranking order.[472] The senior secured creditor will keep its advanced, by-subordination-generated priority position and will not revert back to its pre-subordination priority if the junior (subordinated) security interest ceases to exist due to, for example, having been paid after the subordination.[473]

312. The third rule is a prescriptive rule that merely clarifies the situation that where two security interests are constituted on the same collateral but the earlier registered secured creditor acquires the right of disposal (*rendelkezési jog*) only after the second security interest was registered, he will have priority.[474]

313. The fourth rule declares that if a registered security interest and a security-bailment encumbers the same asset, the priority belongs to the latter.[475]

314. The fifth specific priority rule makes reservation of a ranking position possible. Namely, the owner of an asset may register the fact (in any of the registers) that he intends to exploit the asset as collateral, either by specifying the future secured creditor or without doing that.[476] However, such entries must specify the sum the future security interest will secure.[477] Such reserved ranking will eventually acquire the priority position according to the time of its entry.[478]

2. Lithuania

315. The system rests on the first in time, first in rights rule. As the system obviously takes account of the fact that time is needed to effect the registration

---

471 See §5:120 of the Hungarian Civil Code.
472 See §5:124(1) and (2) of the Hungarian Civil Code.
473 See §5:124(3) of the Hungarian Civil Code.
474 See §5:121 of the Hungarian Civil Code.
475 See §5:123 of the Hungarian Civil Code.
476 See §5:125(1) of the Hungarian Civil Code.
477 See §5:125(2) of the Hungarian Civil Code.
478 See §5:125(3) of the Hungarian Civil Code.

of security rights and that registration may be refused for some reason (e.g. non-approval by the notary checking the mortgage contract), the priority rule is not linked to the time of registration of the security right but to the time of the filing of the request to register with the registry. More precisely, if two security rights were registered at the same time, the one for which the application had been filed first will enjoy priority.[479]

316. Note also that retained title in financial leasing contracts (quasi-security) is not part of this priority system.

3. Poland

317. In *Poland* also, the basic priority rule is the first in time, first in rights.[480]

318. Where the same assets are encumbered by more than one registered pledge, the order of priority is determined based on the date of submission of an application for registration in the register of pledges. The date of submission of an application is the date when the application was delivered to the court where the register of 'registered pledges' is kept. If two applications are filed on the same day, they will rank equally.[481]

319. As opposed to that, in the land and mortgage register, the moment of entry is the priority reference point. Since however two entries cannot be made simultaneously, where applications for registration have been filed at the same time, in such a case the secured parties will have equal ranking.[482]

Question 24: Are there special rules privileging the position of an acquisition financier, i.e. a secured party whose advance of funds funded the acquisition of a particular asset and who may be in a priority competition with an earlier general creditor whose security interest extends to all assets of the debtor whenever acquired?

1. Hungary

320. Acquisition financiers (purchase-money security interest-holders) are given super-priority by the new Civil Code, though the related rules are pretty short.

479 See Article 4.212(2) of the Lithuanian Civil Code.

480 See also Articles 249 and 310 of the Polish Civil Code. For mortgage of immovables see 12.1 of the Polish Mortgage Act. For registered pledges see Article 15 of the Registered Pledge Act.

481 See Article 16 of the Registered Pledge Act.

482 See Article 12 of the Polish Mortgage Act.

Both suppliers of sales-credits (credit for the puchase price of a new movable) and loan-credits (loan to acquire a new movable) may qualify as acquisition financiers.[483]

321. These creditors will enjoy super-priority (i.e. will rank ahead of earlier registered security interests) if two preconditions are satisfied: first, such security rights must be registered in the register for security interests on movables, rights and claims; and second, all those secured creditors who have a first ranking security interest in the same collateral must be notified in writing on the constitution of the new security right.[484] The Comments underline that these rules aim to foster acquisition of new assets by the debtor.[485]

2. Lithuania

322. Lithuanian law does not have specific rules granting super-priority to acquisition financiers. However, the retained ownership (title) under financial leasing is recognised as full 'ownership' that is valid against third parties[486] and the bankrutpcy administrator[487] if registered in the Register of Contracts maintained by the Mortgage Office.

3. Poland

323. The Registered Pledge Act contains no such rules (purchase-money super-priority). Note, however, that leasing and contracts with retained title, are not looked upon as forms of security rights, as in their case the 'full' ownership ensures a high level of protection equivalent, if not higher, to the super-priority of PMSIs.

324. Security transfers and assignments – if executed in proper form (notarisation to certify the execution date) – have by now become the equivalent of in rem security devices rather than devices ensuring super-priority.

---

483 See §5:122 of the Hungarian Civil Code.

484 See §5:122 of the Hungarian Civil Code.

485 See L. Vékás (ed.), *Complex Commentary* Comments, 462.

486 See Article 6.572(1) of the Lithuanian Civil Code.

487 See Article 6.572(2) of the Lithuanian Civil Code.

F. QUASI-SECURITY AGREEMENTS

Question 25: Does your legal system have any rules equating the treatment, in whole or in part, of security interest and 'quasi-security' agreements, i.e. agreements that in legal terms do not involve the creation of security interests but have many of the same economic consequences? Examples of quasi-security include the factoring or sale of receivables and finance leases, hire-purchase agreements and retention of title clauses in sale of goods contracts.

1. Hungary

1.1. 'Fiduciary securities' as 'quasi-securities'

325. In *Hungary*, quasi-securities have come to be known as 'fiduciary securities'; some were products of legal innovation, others were transplants from Western Europe (or a mixture). These were widely exploited devices which gained a significant position in the national economy. Unfortunately, they have generated some legal problems as well, including causing major social tensions (e.g. housing mortgages combined with the option to purchase)[488] and bypassing of such fundamental principles of property law as the prohibition of lex commissoria (or prohibition of strict foreclosure).[489] As some of these devices have not only become popular but have also satisfied genuine commercial needs, the reaction of the drafters of the new Civil Code was two directional.

326. On the one hand, some of the fiduciary securities were prohibited.[490] These were contracts that secured monetary claims by transfering ownership, assigning claims or establishing the right to purchase (options). These were prohibited because 'they gave to creditors more rights [and entitlements] to

---

[488] Contracts with an option to purchase were used by businesses as well. In the case BH2013, 131, for example, the parties concluded a loan contract that was first secured by a mortgage on an immovable. Later, the parties also concluded a contract designated as an 'Option Contract' (*Opciós szerződés*). This gave the creditor the right to purchase the mortgage immovable that could be exercised by the latter upon default of the loan contract, more precisely, if the creditor were to terminate the loan contract with immediate effect or if the contract were to be terminated for any other reason. In other words, through the combination of the mortgage and the right of option to purchase, the secured creditor could simply declare that he is 'purchasing' – or becoming the owner – of the immovable encumbered by the mortgage.

[489] See L. Vékás (ed.), *Complex Commentary,* 574.

[490] See §6:99 of the Hungarian Civil Code, which states that: 'Agreements that secure a monetary claim through transfer of ownership, right or claim, or through granting of a purchase option are null and void; with the exception of agreements allowed by the [EU] Financial Collateral Directive.'

the detriment of debtors than would have been in fact necessary or legally justified.'[491] Additionally, they were often infringing such debtor and other creditor-protective devices such as the prohibition of the lex commissoria.[492]

327. On the other hand, there were also some other, quite widely used novel transactions that played an economically useful function. In their case, it became clear that their subjection to registration (provision of public notice) would be desirable and sufficient to curb abuses (e.g. factoring). In other words, the new Code brought them closer to classical security devices by imposing the duty to register in the register of security rights.

328. Yet new rules apply only to three specific types of contracts, namely financial leasing, recourse-factoring and contracts with retained title. For example, other types of leasing arrangements have remained intact following these changes. This is a questionable solution resting on the presumption that the so-called 'operative leasing' is equal to traditional rent (and thus there is no need even to nominate it) and on the – somewhat contradictory – postulate that 'leasing contracts are so diverse that their subjection to common rules is impossible.'[493]

1.2. Financial leasing

329. In the case of financial leasing[494] – the only leasing type regulated by the Code for the very first time in Hungarian legal history[495] – the system presumes that retained ownership (title) really means retention of full ownership. This is reflected, for example, in the rules on termination of the contract: while the lessor is entitled to terminate the contract on the basis of any of the five explicitly

---

491 See L. Vékás (ed.), *Complex Commentary*, 574.

492 *Ibid.* at 574.

493 *Ibid.* at 873.

494 Financial leasing is looked upon by the Code as a financing device where the 'lessor typically provides financing for the acquisition of the object of leasing by the lessee.' See L. Vékás (ed.), *Complex Commentary*, 873. The lessee may either automatically acquire ownership by the end of the leasing term (closed-end leasing), or he may purchase the object for the residual value (open-end leasing).

495 In the post-1990 phase, 'leasing' became (in addition to franchise and factoring) one of the most popular imported contracts. From among the many sub-variants found in practice, the operative versus financial leasing were recognised as the main forms. In the perception of the drafters, in the case of operative leasing the parties' intention is not to acquire ownership but rather only to use the object of leasing for a specified period of time; therefore, they opted not to regulate it. Thus, in the case of operative leasing the rules on conventional rent and usufruct apply mutatis mutandis. See L. Vékás (ed.), *Complex Commentary*, 873.

formulated grounds,[496] the lessee can do that only for the lessor's failure to fulfill its warranty duties.[497]

330. This also includes the duty of the lessor to warrant that no third person has any such right in respect of the object of leasing that would limit or prevent the lessee from its use.[498] As opposed to that, the warranty for the proper functioning (*kellékszavatosság*) of the object of leasing is imposed on the lessor only if it participated in the selection of the object of leasing or if it has waived the warranties without the consent of the lessee.[499]

1.3. Factoring

331. Similar to leasing, factoring is another successful transplant that has had an explonential growth in the post-1990 period in *Hungary*,[500] notwithstanding that for the old Civil Code it was only an innominate contract. Today, it is utilised in almost all segments of the economy.

332. Due to its economic importance and yet to curb the legal uncertainties surrounding factoring, the drafters of the new Civil Code chose to introduce factoring as a nominated, sui generis type of contract.[501] Interestingly, the drafters took recourse-factoring as the paradigm. As the Complex Comments say without recourse, the transaction cannot be differentiated from sales.[502] As a consequence of this peculiar solution, non-recourse factoring transactions would be treated either as purchase (claim-purchase) or atypical transactions.[503] In other words, the possibility of bypassing the registration system through non-recourse factoring contracts has remained a real option and they remain quasi-securities.

---

496 Based on a grammatical interpretation of §6:415(1) of the Hungarian Civil Code, termination of financial leasing contracts is possible only based on the explicitly specified grounds and this is not left to be determined by the parties (for example, in a default clause). This follows also from L. Vékás (ed.), *Complex Commentary,* 878, which reads: '[The Code, given the differences that exist between leasing and credit contracts] instead of seven provides only for five grounds for immediate termination.' It should be noted that the title of §6:415 of the Hungarian Civil Code (Termination of the contract) does not contain the adjective 'immediate'.

497 See §6:415(3) of the Hungarian Civil Code.

498 See §6:411(1) of the Hungarian Civil Code.

499 See §6:411(2) of the Hungarian Civil Code. There is a qualification in such cases, however. In particular, the lessee may not ask for the substitution of the leasing object. See §6:411(2). This paragraph contains some further rules on warranties.

500 According to L. Vékás (ed.), *Complex Commentary,* 866, in 2011 gross HUF 888 billion were factored.

501 See §§6:405–6:408 of the Hungarian Civil Code.

502 See L. Vékás (ed.), *Complex Commentary,* 867.

503 *Ibid.* at 868.

333. Two factoring-related rules are important from the point of view of security rights. First, it is the factor's duty (obligation) to register the fact that a factoring contract has been concluded and to enter the necessary details for identification of the debtor, in the register of security interests on movables, rights and claims.[504] Second, in the absence of registration – and notwithstanding the assignment – it is presumed that the claim has not been transferred to the factor (creditor). In other words, the non-registered Hungarian recourse-factoring would not be perfected but would attach and could therefore be enforced solely between the parties to the factoring contract but would not be valid against third parties.[505]

1.4. Retained title (ownership) clauses in sales contracts

334. Retained title is regulated by the new Civil Code in the Chapter on sales contracts.[506] While ROT on immovables was subject to registration even under the old Civil Code, the great novelty is that the duty to register has been extended onto movables as well. The volte face ensued due to the realisation that ROT, in fact, performs a similar function as security interests (liens).[507] As the functional equivalent of security rights, thus ROT should be treated equally especially in respect of provision of public notice on the existence of ROT. Consequently, the existence of the ROT and the identity of the debtor must be registered either in the register for security interests on movables, rights and claims, or – if a distinct register exists for certain classes of movables (e.g. ships) – in that public register.[508]

335. This equalisation does not extend, however, only to the duty to register and to cast the agreement on ROT in written form.[509] Namely, on the one hand, the non-registered ROT will not prevent the good faith purchase of the asset encumbered by the ROT to acquire proper title. On the other hand, the security interest granted by the buyer for the benefit of a third-party creditor will be enforceable against the seller (protected by the ROT) notwithstanding that the debtor lacks the right of disposal.[510]

---

504 See §6:406 of the Hungarian Civil Code.
505 See L. Vékás (ed.), *Complex Commentary*, 839.
506 See §6:216 of the Hungarian Civil Code.
507 See L. Vékás (ed.), *Complex Commentary*, 684.
508 See §6:216(4) of the Hungarian Civil Code.
509 See §6:216(2) of the Hungarian Civil Code.
510 See §6:216(4) of the Hungarian Civil Code.

2. Lithuania

336. Lithuanian law contains provisions for quasi-securities that are regulated by the Civil Code in a manner that is separate from mortgage and 'pledge' law. These include retained title in financial leasing[511] as well as in installment sales contracts,[512] the special case of consumer hire-purchase contracts[513] and assignment of receivables (claims) as security – regulated as part of factoring law.[514] These transactions are not looked upon as security devices as a rule and thus Lithuanian scholarship does not talk of them as such.

337. Similarly to Hungarian law, validity against third parties or the bankruptcy administrator in case of retained title presumes registration in the Register of Contracts maintained by the Central Mortgage Office. As opposed to that, in case of factoring registration is not a requirement; it is rather a notification-based system. In other words, the Lithuanian system treats contracts containing retained title (including leasing) as equals only with respect to the duty to provide public notice.

338. Consumer hire-purchase contracts are subject to distinctive regulation under Lithuanian law and deserve a brief mention. The single applicable provision states only that if the ownership is retained in case of consumer purchase-sales contracts the parties may agree that until payment of full purchase price of the contract the buyer will be 'only' a lessee.

3. Poland

339. Polish law knows also some quasi-securities. These include not only leasing and retained title but also the somewhat idiosyncratic security transfers (*przewlaszczenie na zabezpieczenie*) and security assignments (*przelew na zabezpieczenie*).

340. Leasing is subject to a regime distinct from security laws, regulated by a separate title in the Civil Code.[515] In fact, Polish law does not look upon leasing as a form of security but rather only as a newcomer nominated contract where the emphasis is on letting the lessee use, or use and collect, profits of object of

511 See Article 6.572(1) and (2) of the Lithuanian Civil Code. Art. 6.567 is a more general article, providing definition of leasing.

512 See Article 6.441(1) of the Lithuanian Civil Code.

513 See Article 6.361 of the Lithuanian Civil Code.

514 See Article 6.903(2) of the Lithuanian Civil Code.

515 See Book Three on Obligations, Title XVII1 on the Contract of Leasing, Articles 709^{1}–709^{18} (altogether 18 new sections), which were all added as amendments.

leasing.[516] The parties may agree that the lessee may acquire title to the object of leasing, however, that is not looked upon by the system as a normal but rather as an optional yet tolerated feature of the contract.[517] This is reflected also in the Insolvency Act, which foresees, for example, that in case of lessee's insolvency the leasing contract will not expire yet the insolvency practitioner may terminate the contract upon consent of the judge.[518]

341. Retained ownership is likewise distinct from security rights and is perceived to be part of sales law. The validity of ROT towards the buyer's creditors is conditioned by the Civil Code on written form with a certified (authenticated) date. Dates in official documents, or in documents issued by a governmental body (including local governments) or notaries will qualify as containing certificated dates.[519] If executed with certified dates, the ROT will survive insolvency[520] and the seller may claim exclusion of the asset from the bankruptcy estate.

342. As oposed to leasing and retained title, security transfers and assignments have been for most of the post-1990 period rivals of registered pledges (especially in car finance). They were case-law-created fiduciary securities which, however, were not subjected to registration or other form of public notice.[521]

343. These securities survive the opening of insolvency proceedings provided the agreement was executed in writing with data certa, i.e. authenticated date of the execution of the agreement.[522] They are still known in *Poland* although the law applicable to them has changed, in particular with the 2009 amendment of the Insolvency Act. While prior to the amendments the creditor could claim exclusion of the property or rights transferred or assigned to him by way of these

516 See Article 709[1] of the Civil Code containing the definition of leasing.

517 See Article 709[16] of the Polish Civil Code specifying that if transfer of ownership was agreed upon, the lessee may demand the transfer within a month from the lapse of the agreed upon time.

518 See Article 114 of the Polish Insolvency Act.

519 See Article 81 of the Polish Civil Code. Polish case law differentiates additionally between data certa sensu stricto (narrower, strict sense) and data certa sensu largo (broader meaning). While in the first case the certification is focused precisely on the date of the execution of an act, in the latter cases the documents primarily certify some other facts yet the same document certifies also the dates on which those acts were performed. The data certa requirement primarily aims to prevent antedating of documents. For a Supreme Court case involving a security transfer and a discussion on what satisfies in that context the data certa requirement see K. Kaźmierczyk and F. Kijowski, 'Enforcement of Contracts in Poland' in S. Messmann and T. Tajti (eds.), *The Case Law of Central and Eastern Europe*, 633–638.

520 See Article 101 of the Polish Insolvency Act. The Insolvency Act refers to these as 'claims secured by transfer of ownership of property, claim or another right.'

521 See J. Spanogle, (2009)31 *T. Jefferson L. Rev.* 279 at 283 and K. Kaźmierczyk and F. Kijowski, 'Enforcement of Contracts in Poland' in S. Messmann and T. Tajti (eds.), *The Case Law of Central and Eastern Europe,* 633.

522 See K. Kaźmierczyk and F. Kijowski, 'Enforcement of Contracts in Poland' in S. Messmann and T. Tajti (eds.), *The Case Law of Central and Eastern Europe*, 634.

fiduciary security from the bankruptcy estate, since the 2009 amendments they are treated in insolvency in the same way as pledges.[523]

G. TRANSACTIONS AVOIDANCE

Question 26: Are there rules in your legal system that operate once the debtor enters insolvency proceedings and that provide for the invalidation of transactions entered into by the debtor prior to the commencement of the insolvency proceedings?

1. Hungary

344. The liquidator (acting on behalf of the debtor) or the creditor may proceed, either on the terms of the Civil Code (the actio pauliana)[524] or the Insolvency Act to invalidate such transactions.[525] With the latter, the reasons for invalidation are: (1) fraudulent transfers (*csalárd ügyletek*),[526] (2) gratuitous or conspicuously undervalue bilateral transactions (*ingyenes vagy feltűnően aránytalan visszterhes jogügyletek*);[527] and (3) preferential treatment of a creditor (*hitelező előnyben részesítése*).[528]

345. The Insolvency Act differentiates additionally a sub-type of the last item – provision of preferential services (performance) to a specific creditor (*szolgáltatás visszakövetelése egy hitelező előnyben részesítése miatt*).[529] The rationale for this is that a preference may consist also of performing a contract before that is due (especially if performance is due after opening of the insolvency proceedings). Put simply, the Hungarian lawmaker found it important to stress this by casting it in a separate provision.

346. These suits are known as 'avoidance litigation' (*megtámadási perek*). As no empirical data seem to exist as to which avenue is more frequently exploited and why, one may only presume that the tools offered by insolvency law are more regularly resorted to. No empirical analyses exist on the basis of which an evaluation could be made about the efficiency of the laws.

---

523 See the new Article 70^1 as well as Article 336.2. of the Polish Insolvency Act.
524 See §6:120 of the new Civil Code.
525 See L. Juhász, *The Hungarian Insolvency Handbook*, 541.
526 See §40(1)(a) of the Hungarian Insolvency Act.
527 See §40(1)(b) of the Hungarian Insolvency Act.
528 See §40(1)(c) of the Hungarian Insolvency Act.
529 See §40(2) of the Hungarian Insolvency Act.

2. Lithuania

347. Lithuanian law knows two types of avoidance avenues: that which is initiated by the bankruptcy court – the sui generis institution of fraudulent bankruptcy[530] – in which case the time limit for review of transactions is five years. The other is part of the statutory duties of the administrator who has to check transactions concluded 36 months before the start of the insolvency proceedings.[531]

348. Lithuanian law also recognises the actio pauliana.[532]

3. Poland

349. Besides the actio pauliana that is available to creditors outside[533] insolvency based on the Civil Code,[534] the amended Insolvency Act contains a number of avoidance rules of relevance only to liquidations. The basic rules additionally apply to both corporate and individual debtors and are applicable to:

(a) gratuitous and grossly undervalue transactions (including court settlements, waiver of claims);[535]
(b) granting of a security or payment of an immature debt;[536]
(c) non-gratuitous transactions with connected parties;[537]
(d) a security assignment of future receivables made without certified date;[538]
(e) excessive remuneration paid to a director or officer of the bankrupt corporate;[539]
(f) securing the debt of a third party at no or extremely low consideration (benefit) for the bankrupt; and[540]
(g) contractual penalties in situations where the non-pecuniary obligation secured by the penalty has been performed to a material extent or the penalty is manifestly high.[541]

350. The novelties and changes introduced by the amended Insolvency Act are as follows:

---

530 See Article 20 of the Lithuanian Insolvency Act.
531 See Article 11.5(8) of the Lithuanian Insolvency Act.
532 See Article 6.66 of the Lithuanian Civil Code.
533 Under Polish law, actio pauliana is very rarely available after declaration of insolvency. This would be possible only if the avoidance rules would not provide protection in a particular case but actio pauliana would do. See also Article 131 of the Insolvency Act and para. 357 of this report.
534 Articles 527–534 of the Polish Civil Code.
535 See Article 127(1)(2) of the Polish Insolvency Act.
536 See Article 127(3) of the Polish Insolvency Act.
537 See Article 128(1) of the Polish Insolvency Act.
538 See Article 128a of the Polish Insolvency Act.
539 See Article 129(1) of the Polish Insolvency Act.
540 See Article 130(1) of the Polish Insolvency Act.
541 See Article 130a of the Polish Insolvency Act.

First, a new avoidance rule foresees that the assignment of future receivables is ineffective in insolvency if it comes into existence after the opening of insolvency proceedings unless the receivable assignment agreement was executed no later than six months prior to the filing of the bankruptcy petition in written form with certified date (data certa).[542] Second, the rules on avoidance of transactions with connected persons (i) have been expanded to include also unmarried yet cohabitating persons as well as companies with a single shareholder; (ii) the rules on avoidance of transactions with connected persons will not operate based on the law but will require a decision of the bankruptcy judge who may issue such decision at his/her discretion or on the application of the insolvency practitioner; and (iii) the burden of proving that the transactions is not harming the interests of the creditors is on the connected person. However, if the connected person proves that the transaction causes no damage to creditors, it cannot be declared void by the court.[543] Third, the rules allowing for challenge of the bankrupt's directors excessive remuneration were extended also to the so-called shadow directors, who may be either employees performing managerial activities, or persons providing managerial or supervisory services.[544] Finally, a rule aimed at faster recovery of assets from avoidable transactions was introduced. Accordingly, if the transfer of such property is avoided, there is no need to lodge a claim against the suspected transferee but the decision declaring the transaction void itself will qualify as an enforcement title against such person.[545]

351. Under the 2015 Restructuring Act the following avoidance rules apply: (1) gratuitous and grossly undervalue transactions (including waivers and settlements);[546] (2) granting of a security at no consideration or if the value of the collateral exceeds the secured claim by more than half;[547] and (3) excessive remuneration paid to a director or to an executive.[548]

Question 27: Do these transactional avoidance rules catch security and quasi-security type transactions?

1. Hungary

352. Granting of a security to a creditor in the suspect period of 90 days preceding the arrival of the request for liquidation to the court would qualify as a preference.

---

542 Article 128a(1)(2) of the Polish Insolvency Act.
543 Article 128 of the Polish Insolvency Act.
544 Article 129(1) of the Polish Insolvency Act.
545 Article 134 of the Polish Insolvency Act.
546 Article 304(1)(2) of the Polish Restructuring Law.
547 Article 304(3)(4) of the Polish Restructuring Law.
548 Article 305 of the Polish Restructuring Law.

The same regime also applies to modification of an existing contract for the benefit of a creditor or otherwise providing preferential treatment to a creditor.[549]

353. The language of the avoidance provisions in the Insolvency Act is otherwise neutral and speaks generally of 'a contract or a legal declaration' ('*[az adósnak] a szerződését vagy más jognyilatkozatát*') of the debtor. Therefore, quasi-security agreements may also qualify, just as all other contracts or legal declarations, if two additional requirements are present. On the one hand, it should be proven that the intention of the debtor was to defraud a creditor (or creditors) and, on the other hand, the avoidable contract (or legal declaration) led to the decrease in value of the debtor's estate.[550]

2. Lithuania

354. Both provisions (avenues for invalidation) are neutral and talk of 'transactions' rather than being limited to security rights. Thus, in principle, they cover both security and quasi-securities.

3. Poland

355. Secured transactions, i.e. the granting of in rem security (mortgage, pledge, registered pledge, or maritime pledge), may be avoided using a special provision in the Insolvency Act.[551] These, however, apply only to liquidations under the Polish Insolvency Act.

356. The regime applicable to fiduciary transfers as quasi-securities is essentially the same but whether fiduciary transfers are to be treated as 'securities' equal to mortgages and pledges for the purpose of avoidance law or rather as general transactions, is not easy to determine. There is no explicit formula for determining whether a transaction involving transfer of a movable or a claim qualifies or involves a security transfer or assignment.

357. The qualification is of importance because the suspect period for 'securities' is shorter than for other (general) transactions (six months as opposed to one year).[552]

358. Moreover, transactions that serve as security may be challenged only on the basis of a particular provision that contains a six-month suspect period.

---

549 See §40(1)(c) of the Hungarian Insolvency Act.

550 See §40(1)(a) of the Hungarian Insolvency Act.

551 See Article 130(1) of the Polish Insolvency Act.

552 The period was extended from two to six months by amendment of Article 127(3) of the Polish Insolvency Law introduced by the 2015 Restructuring Act.

As the Supreme Court ruled in a case, in order to determine whether such transactions could qualify as a security for the purpose of the avoidance rules, the interpretation of the parties' agreement is needed to determine the intent and thus the true nature of the contract (e.g. whether receivables were sold or rather used only as collateral). It also ruled that whenever the Insolvency Act is to be applied, the application of the Civil Code's rule on actio pauliana is excluded.[553]

Question 28: If so, describe briefly these rules highlighting in particular (a) the rationale for the rules; (b) the conditions for the application of the rules; (c) the length of the 'suspect period'; (d) whether the rules apply to transactions with a cross-border element; (e) whether the rules operate more stringently in respect of transactions that favour parties who are connected to the debtor; and (f) any defences that may be availed of by a counterparty to the transaction, i.e. the defendant in an avoidance action.

1. Hungary

1.1. The rationale of the rules

359. The Insolvency Act contains, neither a detailed preamble, nor is there an official comment on the Insolvency Act.[554] Hence, the rationale of the Hungarian avoidance rules does not seem to differ from those underlying the avoidance rules of most other European insolvency systems.

360. This in particular means the following:

(a) In the case of fraudulent transfers, the law allows for avoidance of transactions because, on the one hand, the debtor's intention was to defraud a creditor or creditors, and on the other hand, the party with whom the debtor concluded such transactions knew, or should have known, about the debtor's fraudulent intent.[555] Here, the system does not want to reward fraud, and aims to provide adequate and equal protection to all creditors.
(b) The protection of the estate and the equal protection of creditors also underlies the rules allowing for avoidance of gratuitous and conspicuously

553 For an analysis of the case III CZP 104/2005, with excerpts from the judgment in English and Polish, see K. Kaźmierczyk and F. Kijowski, 'Enforcement of Contracts in Poland' in S. Messmann and T. Tajti (eds.), *The Case Law of Central and Eastern Europe*, 638–645.

554 The short preamble of the Hungarian act posits the reorganisation of the debtor through agreement with its creditors as the first goal of the system. Yet – as opposed to the Polish one – it does not proclaim that ensuring maximal satisfaction of creditors' claims is also a goal. See the one-sentence preamble in the Hungarian Insolvency Act.

555 See §40(1)(a) of the Hungarian Insolvency Act.

undervalue transactions. The same principle applies to preferential treatment of a creditor.

1.2. The conditions for the application of the rules

361. First, only the creditors and the liquidator, acting on behalf of the debtor, have the right to file a claim for avoidance of a transaction with the competent court.[556] Additionally, the administrator, often being in a better position to track avoidable transactions, has the duty to inform the creditors committee, the creditors representative, or the creditors themselves (if no committee is formed) about the problematic transaction(s) without delay and he has to transfer the supporting evidence as well.[557]

362. Second, if a creditor or the administrator is attacking a contract only based on the Civil Code, the generally applicable rules on jurisdiction and statute of limitations apply. Alternatively, if a contract is sought to be avoided on the basis, at least partly, of the Insolvency Act, the claim has to be filed with the insolvency court.[558]

363. Third, the avoidance claims can be filed with the competent court within 90 days from learning about the transaction that the insolvency administrator or a creditor considers as voidable. However, under no circumstances can the claim be filed after the expiry of one year from the date of the publication of the court order opening the liquidation proceedings.[559]

364. Fourth, if the attack is successful and the transaction is avoided, the Civil Code's provisions on void contracts (*érvénytelenség*) are to be applied.[560] In particular, the creditor or administrator may request restitution and the deletion of avoided rights that have been entered on public registers.[561]

365. Finally, the assets of the debtor are to be disposed of by the administrator exclusively through public sales (normally through public bids or invitations for

---

556 See §40(1) of the Hungarian Insolvency Act. For the rules on jurisdiction see §6(1). For conducting main or ancillary cross-border insolvency proceedings as per Regulation 1346/2000 against a business enterprise not registered in Hungary the Metropolitan Court of Budapest – <http://fovarositorvenyszek.birosag.hu/english> accessed 23 May 2016 – has exclusive jurisdiction according to §6(2).

557 See §40(5) of the Hungarian Insolvency Act.

558 See L. Juhász, *The Hungarian Insolvency Handbook*, 551. See §6(1) for the jurisdictions of courts.

559 See §40(1) of the Hungarian Insolvency Act.

560 See §40(1a) of the Hungarian Insolvency Act. See §6:108 et seq. on the consequences of voidness in the new 2013 Civil Code.

561 See §40(1a) of the Hungarian Insolvency Act.

tender offers). The administrator is according to law, in other words, responsible for the proper sale of the debtor's assets. Moreover, the law imposes on the administrator concrete duties and standards. He is, for example, expected to start the sale no later than 100 days from the date of the public announcement on the opening of liquidation[562] as well as to achieve the highest possible price.[563] Being solely responsible for the disposal means as well, the administrator and the purchaser are jointly and separately liable vis-à-vis the insolvent debtor (enterprise) as if they were acting in collusion to sell an asset at an undervalue.[564]

1.3. The length of the 'suspect period'

366. The Insolvency Act makes a distinction between different suspect periods depending on the type of the avoidable transaction.

367. (a) In case of fraudulent transfers, the time is five years preceding the making of the request to the court for the opening of liquidation proceedings.[565]

368. (b) In the case of gratuitous and conspicuously undervalue bilateral transactions the suspect period is two years preceding the request to the court for opening of liquidation proceedings.[566]

369. (c) In the case of transactions providing a preference to a specific creditor the time is 90 days before the receipt of the request by the court for the opening of liquidation proceedings.

370. (d) Finally, if a creditor was provided with a preferential service (performance) or a service (performance) was out of the ordinary, the suspect period is 60 days before the receipt of the request for the opening of liquidation proceedings. In such a case, the liquidator may request, on behalf of the debtor, return of the services (performance, such as return of the prematurely paid debt.[567]

---

562 See §49(2) of the Hungarian Insolvency Act.

563 See §49(1) of the Hungarian Insolvency Act.

564 See the high court decision BH2011, 227, which proclaimed that court practice accepts as the highest possible price the one achieved via a public bid or tender unless there are some other data or circumstances that make that suspicious. In other words, the fact that the asset was sold at a public auction may not be sufficient but the price achieved and other circumstances of a case should also be taken into account when deciding on the possible liability of the liquidator.

565 See §40(1)(a) of the Hungarian Insolvency Act.

566 See §40(1)(b) of the Hungarian Insolvency Act.

567 See §40(2) of the Hungarian Insolvency Act.

1.4. *The applicability of the rules to transactions with a cross-border element*

371. As there are no territorial limitations on the operation of the avoidance provisions of the Insolvency Act, in principle, they apply also to transactions with a cross-border element.

1.5. *The applicability of the rules on debtor's insiders*

372. The Insolvency Act contains explicit rules applicable to transactions with insiders in the context of avoidance litigation. Transactions concluded with the following three categories of parties may qualify as insiders: first, business enterprises (*gazdálkodó szervezet*)[568] in which the debtor has a majority control; second, the member or chief officer of a business enterprise (*gazdálkodó szervezet tagja vagy vezető tisztségviselője*);[569] and third, business enterprises which, even though not linked directly or indirectly, are controlled by the same person or business enterprise.[570] These presume fraudulent intent where the transaction was made for no consideration or where the transaction is challenged as being a conspicuously undervalue bilateral transaction.[571]

1.6. *The defences available to defendants in avoidance actions*

373. The Insolvency Act explicitly excludes the application of the avoidance rules in two specific situations: (1) close-out netting (*pozíciólezáró nettósítás*), and (2) if the collateral is substituted by another asset of equal value or if an additional security is granted.[572] Otherwise, the generally applicable rules apply.

---

568 For the definition of business enterprise see §3(1)(a) of the Hungarian Insolvency Act, which includes a wide range of businesses, professional (e.g. law firm) and non-profit vehicles – with or without a juridical entity status – that have the centre of their main interest (COMI) in the European Union, from all Hungarian company forms, cooperatives, to sole proprietorships and associations and foundations.

569 For the definition of 'chief officer of a business enterprise' (*gazdálkodó szervezet vezetője*) see §3(1)(d), which limits this concept to the *registered* officers of an enterprise. In the case of foreign enterprises, this would be the person registered in Hungarian registers as the person being entitled to carry out legal acts on behalf of the entity. If there is no such designated person, then it is presumed that the person entitled to represent the entity before governmental bodies or to conclude contracts and other private legal acts will qualify.

570 See §40(3) of the Hungarian Insolvency Act.

571 See §40(3) of the Hungarian Insolvency Act.

572 See §40(5) of the Hungarian Insolvency Act.

2. Lithuania

2.1. *The rationale of the rules*

374. As far as the administrator's duty to review and avoid some transactions is concerned, this is a normal corollary of modern insolvency systems.[573] What is unusual in Lithuania is the broad, if not vague, criteria for determining what transactions should be avoided. In particular, the rationale of avoiding of all transactions that might prevent settlement with creditors is questionable.

375. The intention to sanction parties who have profited from fraudulent bankruptcies[574] is self-explanatory but the general (if not vague) nature of the criteria for avoidance somewhat obscures this rationale.

2.2. *The conditions for the application of the rules*

376. The provisions are as follows:

- first, the administrator has a statutory time limit of six months from the receipt of the underlying documents to review them, unless extended by the bankruptcy court for an additional six months;
- second, he has to review transactions entered into by the bankrupt within 36 months before the initiation of the bankruptcy proceedings;
- third, he is to start court proceedings for the invalidation of three classes of transactions: (1) those that are contrary to the debtor-enterprise's activities; (2) those that would prevent settlement with creditors; and finally (3) those that led to the fraudulent bankruptcy.

377. In case of fraudulent bankruptcies, the steps leading to invalidation of fraudulent transactions are the following:

- first, the bankruptcy court has to determine during the bankruptcy proceedings whether the debtor is intentionally bankrupted;
- second, the administrator must then review all transactions made within five years before the initiation of the bankruptcy proceedings; and
- third, the administrator has to review and initiate the invalidation of those transactions which are either contrary to the interests of the debtor and/or could lead to an inability to settle with creditors.[575]

---

573 See Article 11.5(8) of the Lithuanian Insolvency Act.

574 See Article 20 of the Lithuanian Insolvency Act.

575 See Article 20 of the Lithuanian Insolvency Act.

2.3. *The length of the 'suspect period'*

378. It is a general duty of the administrator to examine all transactions entered into by the bankrupt debtor within 36 months before the date of the initiation of bankruptcy proceedings. What makes the Lithuanian system peculiar is that the suspect period is qualified by the addition of the phrase 'at least 36 months.' This, in other words, means that the administrator must check transactions for at least the previous 36 months but he also has the right to check and attack those concluded even earlier. The administrator is constrained in that respect by the rule that he has only six months available as a rule. As this limited period of time may be extended only once and only for another six months, in the case of large corporations it is questionable whether the time frame is sufficient.

379. As opposed to that, if the bankruptcy court finds the case to be one of fraudulent bankruptcy,[576] the administrator is obliged to review all transactions made within five years before the opening of insolvency proceedings.[577]

2.4. *The applicability of the rules to transactions with a cross-border element*

380. In the absence of specific rules on the applicability of these rules to transactions with cross-border elements, one has to draw the conclusion that EU Regulation 1346/2000 and Lithuanian conflicts of law rules would apply.

2.5. *Stringency of the rules towards parties connected to the debtor*

381. Although the Lithuanian Insolvency Act imposes quite meaningful obligations and even liability for damages for failure to participate in the proceedings, there are no explicit avoidance rules specifically targeting only parties connected to the debtor.

2.6. *Defences of the counterparty to the transaction*

382. The Lithuanian Insolvency Act does not specify any particular defence mechanism that would be available to counterparties to suspect transactions.

---

576 Fraudulent bankruptcy is defined by Article 2.1. (12) of the Lithuanian Insolvency Act as 'deliberate bringing of the enterprise to bankruptcy.'

577 See Article 20 of the Lithuanian Insolvency Act.

3. Poland

3.1. *The rationale of the rules*

383. Under the Insolvency Act (liquidation) the rationale of the avoidance rules is the satisfaction of the claims to the greatest possible extent.[578] Consequently, if a transaction is declared ineffective, all that has been received by the party to the transaction must be transferred or credited to the bankruptcy estate. Under the new 2015 Restructuring Act the avoidance rules, however, serve, besides this purpose, to restore the debtor's capacity to service its debts.[579] Note here, however, that the avoidance rules under the Restructuring Act apply only to rehabilitation proceedings and not to the other three new restructuring proceedings.

384. As pronounced by the Polish Supreme Court, a set-off declared by the bankrupt debtor within one year before declaration of the opening of liquidation proceedings is ineffective if the counter-party knew of the existence of grounds for declaration of bankruptcy.[580]

385. The avoidance rules do not apply to financial collateral.[581]

3.2. *The conditions for the application of the rules*

3.2.1. *Common rules*

386. Three commonalities exist for each type of avoidable transactions: (1) the legal effect of voidability is ineffectiveness (invalidity) vis-à-vis the bankruptcy estate; (2) in each of the cases the benchmark date for calculation of the suspect period is 'the day of submission of a petition for bankruptcy'; and (3) the petition to declare a transaction ineffective must be brought within two years of the declaration of insolvency unless the claim expired earlier based on the Civil Code or was null and void (ineffective).[582]

---

578 See Article 2 of the Polish Insolvency Act.

579 Statement of reasons attached to the Restructuring Law proposal (bill), page 58.

580 Resolution of the Supreme Court dated 4 September 2013 in case III CZP 26/13.

581 Article 135(2) of the Polish Insolvency Act and Article 309(2) of the Restructuring Act. The text of the Articles is identical.

582 Judgment of the Appeal Court in Gdańsk dated 29 April 2015 in case V ACa 859/14. The case concerned a donation of a flat made by a father to his daughter (Article 127(1) case). Although the donation was made on 22 March 2010, insolvency was declared on 21 June 2010. Action based on Article 127(1) was brought on 17 February 2014 (after two years). The court held that both Articles 127 and 128 provide for ineffectiveness of a legal transaction ex lege (no court decision is necessary).

3.2.2. *Specific rules*

3.2.2.1. *Gratuitous and grossly undervalue transactions*

387. The Insolvency Act's rules on gratuitous and grossly undervalue transactions are the following:

(a) a transaction is deemed to be grossly undervalue if 'the value of the benefit provided by the bankrupt grossly exceeds the value of the benefit received by the bankrupt or reserved for the bankrupt or a third person; and
(b) the rules do not extend to security established in association with forward financial transactions, lending of financial instruments or sale of financial instruments with repurchase obligation;[583]
(c) yet the rules extend also to court settlements, waiver of claims and acknowledgement of a claim.

388. Under the Restructuring Act 2015 different rules apply. These are as follows:

(a) only legal transactions executed by the debtor within one year before the day of submission of a petition for opening of the rehabilitation proceedings may be attacked;
(b) however, if they were performed gratuitously or non-gratuitously but the value of the benefit provided by the debtor significantly exceeds the value of the benefit received by the debtor or reserved for the debtor or a third person;[584]
(c) the same rule applies to gratuitous or undervalue court settlements, acknowledgement of a complaint or writing off a claim.[585]

3.2.2.2. *Non-gratuitous transactions with connected persons*

389. As under the Restructuring Act there are no avoidance rules involving connected persons, only the list from the Insolvency Act can be provided.

390. According to this, the list of connected persons includes:

(i) individual bankrupts: (a) a spouse, relative or relative by affinity in the direct line; (b) a relative or relative by affinity in the collateral line up to the second degree inclusive; (c) adoptee or adoptive parent; and (d) as added by the 2015 amended Insolvency Act, persons living in a common household (cohabitation) (see also Question 27 above);

---

583 See Article 127(4) of the Polish Insolvency Act.
584 Article 304(1) of the Polish Restructuring Act.
585 Article 304(2) of the Polish Restructuring Act.

(ii) companies or other legal persons as bankrupts: (a) partners, sole shareholders or representatives (officers), or their spouses; (b) affiliated entities, their partners or representatives, or their spouses; (c) transactions between parent and subsidiary; as well as (d) as added by the 2015 amended Insolvency Act, single shareholder companies (see also Question 27 above).

391. According to the pertaining case law neither employees,[586] nor shareholders[587] (unless in the shoes of directors or officers) qualify as connected persons. As far as the former is concerned, the exemption applies if made as part of regular employment.

392. Finally, the list of connected persons listed for individual bankrupts applies mutatis mutandis here as well.[588]

3.2.2.3. Excessive remuneration paid to an officer of the bankrupt corporate

393. Excessive remunerations paid to an officer of the bankruptcy company may be avoided under the following conditions foreseen by the Insolvency Act:

(a) remuneration is to be paid based on an employment or service contract or resolution of an organ of the bankrupt concluded before declaration of bankruptcy;
(b) the excessiveness of the remuneration is measured against two cumulatively applicable criteria: (i) the average remuneration payable for the same type of work or service, and (ii) the amount of work done;
(c) the proceedings may be started by the judge decide ex officio or at the request of the receiver;
(d) a court decision is passed in the matter: (i) after having heard the receiver and the bankrupt's representative, whereby (ii) a portion of the remuneration will be declared ineffective.[589]

394. The following terms and conditions apply under the Restructuring Act for avoiding excessive remuneration paid to an officer of the bankruptcy corporate:

(a) the persons to whom the terms and conditions apply should be the debtor's representatives (directors and officers) or employees performing managerial activities, persons providing services of management or supervision of the debtor's enterprise based, either on employment or service contracts, or resolution of debtor's board;

586 Judgment of the Supreme Court dated 4 September 2014 in case I PK 23/14.
587 Judgment of the Appeal Court in Gdańsk dated 28 June 2013 in case V ACa 330/13.
588 See Article 128(1)–(3) of the Polish Insolvency Act.
589 See Article 129 of the Polish Insolvency Act.

(b) the time span in the purview of the system is three months before the day of opening of rehabilitation proceedings;
(c) remuneration paid to these persons will be avoidable if excessively large compared to the average remuneration for the same type of work or services and not justified by the amount of labour; and
(d) the restructuring judge is to determine, ex officio or at the request of the administrator, that a certain portion of the remuneration due for a certain period before the day of opening of rehabilitation proceedings, is ineffective with respect to the restructuring estate, even if the remuneration has already been paid.[590]

3.2.2.4. Securing the debt of a third party at no or extremely low consideration (benefit) for the bankrupt

395. According to the Insolvency Act securing the debt of a third party at no or extremely low consideration for the bankrupt may be avoided if the following conditions are fulfilled:

(a) the related provision may be triggered only at the request of the receiver;
(b) only specific types of security transactions may be attacked (i.e. mortgage, pledge, registered pledge and maritime pledge);
(c) a court decision is to be passed; and
(d) the provisions apply if (i) the security was given by the bankrupt to a third party for which it did not receive any consideration (benefit), or (ii) a security was established for a consideration (benefit) 'that is excessively small compared to the value of the [collateral].'

396. As already hinted at above, if the security was given for the benefit of a connected person, the collateral value versus benefit for the bankrupt ratio is not of relevance as in such a case the system presumes that the transaction is ineffective.[591]

397. The preconditions under the Restructuring Act are stated in more general terms compared to the Insolvency Act. They provide that such no or low-consideration securities granted by the bankrupt may be avoided if, on the one hand, the security interest was granted by the debtor within one year before the day of submission of a petition for opening of the rehabilitation proceedings and, on the other hand, if the debtor is not receiving a commensurate benefit directly.[592]

---

590 Article 305 of the Polish Restructuring Law.
591 See Article 130 of the Polish Insolvency Act.
592 Article 304(3) of the Polish Restructuring Act.

3.3. *The length of the suspect period*

398. The length of the suspect period differs for each type of the avoidance rules under both, the Insolvency Act and the Restructuring Act.

3.3.1. *The suspect period under the Insolvency Act*

399. Under the Insolvency Act the suspect periods are the following:

(a) in case of gratuitous and grossly undervalue transactions (including court settlements, waiver of claims) the suspect period is one year before the day of submission of a petition for bankruptcy;[593]
(b) in case of granting of a security or payment of an immature debt the suspect period is six months before the day of submission of a petition for bankruptcy;[594]
(c) six months before the day of submission of a petition for bankruptcy is the period in the case of non-gratuitous transactions with connected parties;[595]
(d) the same six months applies also to excessive remuneration paid to a director or officer of the bankrupt corporate;[596]
(e) finally, securing the debt of a third party at no or an extremely small consideration (benefit) for the bankrupt will be ineffective vis-à-vis the bankruptcy estate if made one year before the filing for bankruptcy.[597]

3.3.2. *The suspect period under the Restructuring Act 2015*

400. According to the Restructuring Act different rules apply as far as the length of the avoidance suspect periods are concerned. These are the following:

(a) in the case of gratuitous and grossly undervalue transactions (including waivers and settlements) the suspect period is one year before the day of the submission of a petition for opening of rehabilitation proceedings;[598]
(b) one year before the day of submission of a petition for opening of rehabilitation proceedings is the period that applies in the case of granting of a security at no consideration or if the value of the collateral exceeds by more than half the secured claim;[599]

---

[593] See Article 127(1) of the Polish Insolvency Act.
[594] See Article 127(3) of the Polish Insolvency Act.
[595] See Article 128(1) of the Polish Insolvency Act.
[596] See Article 129(1) of the Polish Insolvency Act.
[597] See Article 130(1) of the Polish Insolvency Act.
[598] See Article 304(1)(2) of the Polish Restructuring Act.
[599] See Article 304(3)(4) of the Polish Restructuring Act.

(c) and finally three months applies also to excessive remuneration paid to a director or to an executive.[600]

3.4. *The applicability of the rules to transactions with a cross-border element*

401. The basic rule is that the Polish Insolvency Act (including therefore the avoidance rules) does not apply if it contradicts either an international treaty to which *Poland* is a party or EU legislation.[601] As the Polish Insolvency Act, in principle, cannot contradict EU law, Polish avoidance rules should be applied whenever Polish law is the applicable one. This applies primarily when the main proceedings are conducted in *Poland*. The same applies also to the Restructuring Act.

402. The Polish Insolvency Act, however, has some specific rules affecting the applicability of Polish avoidance rules even where the main proceedings are in another EU Member State. These are:

(a) The basic principle is that for assets and debts located in *Poland*, Polish law applies.[602] This basically means the application of Polish avoidance rules for assets located in *Poland*.[603]
(b) If a foreign insolvency proceeding was recognised as the main proceeding, the foreign representative may intervene in any proceedings to which the bankrupt is a party. Thus, he may also bring actions to declare ineffective transactions detrimental to creditors.[604] If a foreign representative was appointed in secondary bankruptcy proceedings, the right to intervene can be exercised solely in respect to the assets involved in those proceedings.[605]
(c) If secondary bankruptcy proceedings are instituted in *Poland* after recognition of foreign bankruptcy proceedings, the administration of the bankrupt's assets located in the *Republic of Poland*, previously performed by a foreign representative shall be continued by a receiver or administrator appointed in the secondary bankruptcy proceedings.[606]

600 See Article 305(1) of the Polish Restructuring Act.
601 See Article 378(1) of the Polish Insolvency Act.
602 See Article 403(1) of the Polish Insolvency Act.
603 See Article 403(2) of the Polish Insolvency Act.
604 See Article 400(2) of the Polish Insolvency Act.
605 See Article 400(3) of the Polish Insolvency Act.
606 See Article 410(1) of the Polish Insolvency Act.

3.5. *Stringency of the rules towards parties connected to the debtor*

403. The Restructuring Act introduced no avoidance rules for connected parties.

404. The Insolvency Act, however, not only has such rules but they are more stringent if connected parties are at involved. Two specific provisions are dedicated to these transactions: (1) non-gratuitous transactions with connected parties, and (2) disproportionately high remuneration paid to corporate officers (see Question 27 above). Additionally, the law presumes that the transaction is avoidable if security was granted to a connected party.[607]

3.6. *Defences of the counterparty to the transaction*

3.6.1. *Defences under the Insolvency Act*

405. The Insolvency Act provides the counterparty to voidable transactions with different types of defences as described in the next paragraphs.

406. The rule in case of gratuitous and grossly undervalue transactions is a non-rebuttable presumption of the system.[608] This means that if a transaction was performed 'gratuitously or non-gratuitously but the value of the benefit provided by the bankrupt grossly exceeds the value of the benefit received by the bankrupt or reserved for the bankrupt or a third person',[609] it is deemed that such transactions will be ineffective vis-à-vis the estate. The law foresees no right of objection or appeal.

407. A transaction whereby a security is granted, or an immature debt is paid, is also presumed to be voidable. The counter-party may, however, petition the bankruptcy court to declare the transaction valid if he could prove that he was not aware of the fact that the grounds for declaration of insolvency were present at the time when the security was granted or the payment made.[610] As opposed to the former rule, non-gratuitous transactions with connected parties are non-rebuttable presumptions of the system.[611]

408. The decision of the court voiding the transactions whereby excessive remuneration was paid to an officer (representative) of the bankrupt corporate may only be appealed.[612]

---

607 See Article 130(3) of the Polish Insolvency Act.
608 See Article 127(1) of the Polish Insolvency Act.
609 See Article 127(1) of the Polish Insolvency Act.
610 See Article 127(2) of the Polish Insolvency Act.
611 See Article 128(1) of the Polish Insolvency Act.
612 See Article 129(4) of the Polish Insolvency Act.

409. Securing the debt of a third party at no or extremely low consideration (benefit) for the bankrupt: the decision of the bankruptcy judge may be appealed.[613]

3.6.2. Defences under the Restructuring Act 2015

410. To reiterate what has already been said above: avoidance rules apply only in the context of rehabilitation proceedings from the four distinct types of proceedings introduced by the 2015 Restructuring Act. Hence, note that the next few sections will apply only to them.

411. Gratuitous and grossly undervalue transactions (including waivers and settlements) are non-rebuttable presumptions of the system.[614] Such transactions will be ineffective vis-à-vis the rehabilitation estate by operation of law and the law foresees no right of objection or appeal.

412. The treatment of transactions that grant a security at no consideration or if the value of the collateral exceeds by more than half the secured claim is the same as for gratuitous and grossly undervalue transactions: there is a non-rebuttable presumption that these transactions are voidable and the law foresees no right of objection or appeal.[615]

413. In case of excessive remuneration paid to a director or to an executive, however, the decision of the court declaring the transaction void is appealable.[616]

H. CONCLUSIONS

414. Admittedly, the above analysis of only three CEE jurisdictions does not yield a complete picture of the entire region. Nevertheless, since similar in-depth reforms have taken place in most of the other countries in this part of Europe – moreover more often than not in the same direction as well – conclusions may legitimately be drawn not only in respect of the three jurisdictions under consideration, but more generally in respect of other countries in the region as well.

415. In order to answer our central query whether European harmonisation of insolvency (substantive) and the law relating to security rights is appropriate and desirable from the perspective of CEE – in particular from the perspective of Hungary, Lithuania and Poland – the focus should be on the following main

613 See Article 130(4) of the Polish Insolvency Act.
614 See Article 304(1) of the Polish Restructuring Law.
615 See Article 304(3)(4) of the Polish Restructuring Law.
616 See Article 305(5) of the Polish Restructuring Law.

issues: (1) the quality and nature of the legal framework; (2) the efficency of the system (the operation of the registry system and of the enforcement system); (3) the technical and technological bases of the registration system(s); and (4) the prevailing social, polical and economic circumstances (in particular, the importance of credit, security and access to finance, reform fatigue, and willingness to learn from the experiences of others).

1. The legal environment (the quality of security and insolvency laws)

416. As far as security laws are concerned – especially reform of personal property security laws (i.e. security interests on movables, rights and claims) – it is common that in all systems the reform and upgrading of the system is the centre of interest in the post-1990 period. This includes in particular the matters set out in the following paragraphs.

417. A major mindshift occurred over 25 years. In this process a mindset in which credit and security were considered inherently (and ideologically) bad was gradually replaced with another one whereby credit is the alpha and omega of economic activities and the token of economic well-being. This claim stands notwithstanding that problems with overindebtedness have surfaced as well.

418. As part of this process, these systems have embraced the philosophy that in rem securities should be publicised (i.e. public notice must be provided to the outside world or a legally sanctioned substitute method must be employed). This is in stark contrast with, for example, German and Austrian laws.

419. Moreover, such often neglected yet important changes have occurred as: (a) the possibility of encumbering virtually all kinds of transferable assets has become a reality; (b) the domestication of floating types of enterprise (global) securities has also been concluded; and (c) to a great extent due to the introduction of global securities, these systems have in the meantime been transformed from an era of 'single-security per asset' to systems where encumbering of the same assets with more securities is normal.

420. Next to security laws, insolvency laws were also the focus of post-1990 reforms in each of the targeted countries. Perhaps the achievements are less conspicuous compared to secured transactions law yet the task of insolvency lawyers was tougher because they were given multiple tasks. The expectation was not only to draft modern Insolvency Acts – after four-and-a-half decades of legal vacuum – but also to reconcile the new system with the newly introduced common-law inspired secured transactions laws as well as to catch up with new challenges. The forging of a legal framework that would incentivise the rescue of enterprises instead of driving them out of the market through compulsory liquidation was obviously the toughest one, the results of which are modest at most.

2. The efficiency of the systems

421. Each of the countries has taken steps to increase the efficiency of the operation of their newly introduced secured transactions (movables, rights and claims as collateral only) systems. These efforts were intended, first, to make the process of the creation of security rights as easy, cheap and fast as possible and, second, to increase efficiencies in the enforcement of security interests. Both required rethinking and giving up some parts of inherited venerable legal principles or doctrines. In the case of mortgages on immovables, these efforts were directed only at improving the work of the registers.

422. Each of the systems has, through subsequent amendments, sought either to bypass or at least to minimise the involvement of courts in the process of creation of security rights. While in *Poland* we can talk only of the reduction of the involvement of courts, in *Hungary* and *Lithuania* responsibility was given exclusively to public notaries. The new 2013 Hungarian Civil Code went a step further by introducing the system of notice-filing, thereby reducing the role of notaries.

423. After the initial reluctance to give way to various methods of out-of-court enforcement of security rights, each of the systems has opened the door to some forms of self-help or private enforcement.[617] While self-help repossession is still illegal, sale of the collateral by the parties (without involvement of the court) and strict foreclosure (i.e. acquiring of the collateral upon default by the secured creditor) has become tolerated in some form. The most far-reaching change is the possibility of private enforcement of Polish global (enterprise) securities, which seemed to have remained a rarely exploited possibility in *Hungary* so far. Thus, while in the *UK* enforcement of floating charges privately through receivers has been radically reduced, the same practice has developed in some parts of CEE. All this was driven by the realisation that efficient enforcement is a measure of the success of the new secured transactions systems.

424. The evidence in respect of the new insolvency systems is less promising. While typically empirical research is lacking in the region and thus one may not be in the position to point to publicly available quality data, the

617 For an overview of related developments in some European jurisdictions, see C. Stanescu, *Self-Help, Private Debt Collection and the Concomitant Risks.*

large number of amendments to the new Insolvency Acts[618] and the growing number of insolvency-related high court decisions are appropriate yet indirect indicators of the gravity of problems these systems have witnessed in the post-1990 period.

425. It is common to the region as well that there is a considerable stigma attached to bankruptcy. This external factor is undoubtedly the most significant obstacle to introduction of a rescue culture, a problem well known to western systems as well.

426. Although avoidance litigation is intesifying in the countries observed in this report, it is still plagued with uncertainities and inefficiencies and is one of those specific aspects of insolvency law that would require much more attention in the future.

3. The technical and technological bases of the new systems

427. Each of the countries under consideration has introduced new registries, typically initially only for securities on movables. Later, these were extended to rights and claims (receivables), although in respect of these types of assets used as collateral the divergences are still significant. Most of the registries have by now become computerised and accessible by the Internet, although they are not necessarily open to the wider public and searchable free of charge. Moreover, in some jurisdictions of the region, the registries have become interlinked and entries have been synchronised. This may not necessarily be the case even in the most developed western countries.

428. Selected data related to *insolvency* have become registrable in publicly accessible computerised systems also linked to the Internet.[619] This is still in progress and one should not be completely satisfied with the achievements.

---

618 The new (post-1990) Hungarian Insolvency Act (enacted in 1991, entered into force on 1 January 1992) has been amended in the meantime 16 times by five major and 11 minor amendments. See L. Juhász, *The Hungarian Insolvency Handbook*, 38–40.

619 In Hungary, insolvency-related information is available through the website providing information on companies operated by an office under auspices of the Ministry of Justice at <http://www.e-cegjegyzek.hu/index.html> accessed 23 May 2016 (only Hungarian-language pages available).

In Lithuania the register for juridical persons contains such information at <http://www.jar.lt> accessed 23 May 2016.

Insolvency-related information is obtainable in Poland through the National Court Register at <http://bip.ms.gov.pl/pl/rejestry-i-ewidencje/> accessed 23 May 2016. It should be added, however, that a new Central Insolvency and Restructuring Registry (*Centralny Rejestr Restrukturyzacji i Upadłości*) has been introduced by the 2015 Restructuring Act with its operations foreseen to start on 1 February 2018. Like the other online registers, it will be operated by the Ministry of Justice and made available free of charge. It will make

429. Access to data on cross-border insolvencies is still problematic and problems persist on a domestic level as well. For example, in *Poland*, while the Land and Mortgage Register became searchable online and free of charge from 1 July 2014, this is still not the case with the Register of Pledges that was introduced by a law often considered to be very progressive. Nevertheless, one may validly claim that these countries possess solid foundations as far as the technical and technological bases are concerned to link their insolvency registered with the common European platform envisaged by the Recast Regulation 2015/848.

4. The social, political and economic climate

430. It is far from being irrelevant what the attitude of various stake-holders is and generally whether a society is open to learn from the good or bad experiences of others. As is well known from the many publications on legal reforms, transplantation and modernisation (no matter how labelled), many factors come into play during those processes. The issue is not only about the fear from the risks (known and unknown) corollary to novelties law reforms generate but also how to find the right balance between the tested venerable foundations of the old system and the new, foreign and thus unpredictable. What matters is that the reformed CEE countries have gained much experience of handling such problems, experience which is potentially to be taken advantage of by countries that have or are about to embark on reform of their systems – as is the tendency nowadays in Africa (e.g. Malawi, Nigeria,[620] Sierra Leone and Kenya).

431. From an economic point of view it matters also that due to the reforms, stakeholders, business persons and a significant part of the citizenry have realised the key role that credit and credit securities play. If one considers what an economics or law graduate at the end of the 1980s knew about these topics in CEE and compares this with the knowledge of current graduates, the difference would be considerable and indicate the changes that have occurred in the meantime.

---

provision for: (a) publication of decisions and other documents related to insolvency and restructuring proceedings; (b) making publicly available data included in the said decisions; (c) filing of applications and other documents; (d) service of process (delivery of documents in proceedings); (e) making available official forms of applications; and (f) containing list and addresses of relevant insolvency courts and insolvency practitioners. It will also include information on the main and secondary proceedings referred to in the Insolvency Regulation.

The Croatian website is also maintained by the Ministry of Justice at <https://sudreg.pravosudje.hr/registar> accessed 23 May 2016. In Romania insolvency-related information is available at <http://www.buletinulinsolventei.ro> accessed 23 May 2016.

620 C. Williams Iheme, *Towards Reforming the Legal Framework for Secured Transactions in Nigeria*.

5. The final verdict

432. On the basis of the above, one should not deny that the new systems do work quite well in the CEE jurisdictions that have been analysed, notwithstanding the gaps, dilemmas and occasional backpedalling. In many respects, these systems come closer to the unitary model and Book IX of the DCFR than that of some of the more economically developed systems of the EU.

433. In brief, should European harmonisation occur, for example, along the model enshrined in Book IX of the DCFR, *Hungary*, *Lithuania* and *Poland* would be in a pretty good position to relatively easily align themselves with it. If another model was pursued (e.g. the existing German system of latent security interests) this might cause serious problems in these countries as that would require discarding all the achievements made as part of the secured transactions reforms in the post-1990 period. This claim stands irrespective of the fact that each of these laws contains a number of idiosyncratic solutions.

434. Overall, the achievements of the CEE countries is fruitful soil not only for comparative lawyers but also for those looking for a common model for Europe.

INDEX

W

LIST OF AUTHORS

Reinhard Bork
Professor of Law, University of Hamburg, Germany

Marta Carballo Fidalgo
Associate Professor, University of Santiago de Compostela, Spain

Laura Carballo Piñeiro
Associate Professor, University of Santiago de Compostela, Spain

Renato Mangano
Professor of Law, University of Palermo, Italy

Gerard McCormack
Professor of Law, University of Leeds, United Kingdom

Tibor Tajti
Professor of Law, Central European University, Budapest, Hungary